Unraveling the Nagoya Protocol

Legal Studies on Access and Benefit-sharing

Series Editors

Elisa Morgera
Matthias Buck
Elsa Tsioumani

VOLUME 2

The titles published in this series are listed at *brill.com/labs*

Unraveling the Nagoya Protocol

*A Commentary on the Nagoya Protocol on Access
and Benefit-sharing to the Convention
on Biological Diversity*

By

Elisa Morgera, Elsa Tsioumani and Matthias Buck

BRILL

LEIDEN | BOSTON

Elisa Morgera, author.
   Unraveling the Nagoya Protocol : a commentary on the Nagoya Protocol on access and benefit-sharing to
the Convention on Biological Diversity/ by Elisa Morgera, Elsa Tsioumani and Matthias Buck.
      pages cm. — (Legal studies on access and benefit-sharing, ISSN 2213-493X ; v. 2)
   Includes bibliographical references and index.
   ISBN 978-90-04-21717-1 (pbk. : alk. paper) — ISBN 978-90-04-21718-8 (e-book) 1. Convention
on Biological Diversity (1992). Protocols, etc., 2010 October 29. 2. Biodiversity conservation—Law and
legislation. 3. Nature conservation—Law and legislation. 4. Renewable natural resources—Law and
legislation. 5. Sustainable development—Law and legislation. 6. Environmental law, International.
I. Morgera, Elisa, author. II. Tsioumani, Elsa, author. III. Title.

   K3488.B83 2014
   344.04'6—dc23

                                                                                    2014021779

This publication has been typeset in the multilingual 'Brill' typeface. With over 5,100 characters covering
Latin, IPA, Greek, and Cyrillic, this typeface is especially suitable for use in the humanities.
For more information, please see brill.com/brill-typeface.

ISSN 2213-493X
ISBN 978 90 04 21717 1 (paperback)
ISBN 978 90 04 21718 8 (e-book)

This book is printed on acid-free paper.

Printed by Printforce, the Netherlands

Contents

Foreword

Twenty-two years have passed since the adoption in May 1992 of the Convention on Biological Diversity. The Convention broke new ground in the progressive development of international law. It introduced the principle that biodiversity is a "common concern of humankind"; it restated the concept of "sustainable development" of biological resources, which a month later was to be proclaimed in general terms by Principle 1 of the Rio Declaration. It provided a legal framework for the protection and sustainable use of biodiversity as a global common good to be tapped in the general interest of humanity. In other respects the Convention on Biological Diversity remained attached to the traditional "Westphalian" model of international law as a legal order created by States and meant to govern relations between sovereign States. It explicitly embraced the principle that States have the sovereign right over their natural resources (Preamble, Articles 3 and 15), thus endorsing the entrenched idea that States are allowed to "privatize" parts of the physical space of the planet under the mantle of "territorial sovereignty." This idea runs counter to the cosmopolitan model of "common heritage" of biological resources, which was earlier foreshadowed in the Food and Agriculture Organization (FAO) 1983 Undertaking on Plant Genetic Resources. This "realistic" solution respectful of State sovereignty has been the key to the success of the Convention and to its almost universal support, as witnessed by its 194 contracting Parties at the time of this writing. At the same time, the State-oriented approach adopted by the Convention is counterbalanced by the introduction of two innovative principles: that of "facilitated access" to bio-genetic resources for environmentally sustainable development, and that of "fair and equitable sharing of benefits" arising from research and commercial exploitation of such resources. These two principles have a potential for progressive development of international law. First, State sovereignty is recast in a "modern" perspective – not any longer as absolute territorial power and *jus excludendi alios*, but as a form of public authority to be exercised in a manner that is functional to the goals of sustainable utilization of the common good of biodiversity. Second, the introduction of fair and equitable sharing of benefits entails the recognition of an entitlement under international law to an equitable remuneration of the providers of bio-genetic resources, thus departing from the previous regime of freedom for everyone to access and exploit genetic material with no obligation whatsoever to return some of the benefits accruing from its exploitation.

Facilitated access and benefit-sharing have important implications in terms of economic incentives to invest in the identification and sustainable use of bio-genetic resources and in terms of growing expectations of financial reward for source countries rich in biodiversity. At the same time, the concrete implementation of the two principles raises complex issues. An appropriate legislative and institutional setting is needed in order to operationalize the two principles at the national level so as to avoid not only the risk of free riding, but also the opposite risk of the "anti-common", that is the presence of so many layers of decision – national, regional, local, communal – as to make access to and management of biological resources unreasonably cumbersome and uneconomical. This presents a real challenge when we consider that the Convention on Biological Diversity has included indigenous and local communities among the title-holders of traditional knowledge which is relevant to the identification and utilization of genetic resources and which makes them indispensable participants in the decision-making process. At the same time, the principle of equity underlying the strategic concept of benefit-sharing needs to be clarified in terms of international standards, rather than left to the pure private-law bargaining between business actors and local titleholders.

It is in view of addressing these complex issues that the Parties to the Convention on Biological Diversity embarked in the negotiation of the Nagoya Protocol on Access and Benefit-sharing. The Protocol was adopted in October 2010 at the tenth meeting of the Parties to the Convention and will enter into force ninety days after the date of deposit of the 50th instrument of ratification or accession. With 29 ratifications so far, almost entirely by developing countries, the Protocol has still some way to go to meet its goal of providing a widely internationally accepted legal framework for governing access and benefit-sharing in the field of biodiversity resources.

With this publication, Elisa Morgera, Elsa Tsioumani and Matthias Buck have produced an outstanding contribution to the elucidation of the issues that will dominate, and in fact are already dominating, the agenda for the implementation of the Protocol. Their earlier work *The 2010 Nagoya Protocol on Access and Benefit-Sharing in Perspective*, published by the same team of authors as editors in 2013, was the first bold attempt at bringing together academics and policy-makers to enhance the collective understanding of the far-reaching implications of the Protocol in the many areas of international law, including environmental law, human rights, international economic law and the law of the sea. With this Commentary, which appears just a year after the earlier work, the authors have made two central contributions to the field of biodiversity law. They have provided an invaluable contribution to the understanding of the innovative provisions of the Protocol and of the challenges they pose for their effective implementation. At the same time, they have placed their textual analysis in the broader context of international law and of its dynamic evolution with regard to the development of solidarity obligations, the environmental dimension of human rights, the role of equity, and the emerging status of indigenous peoples and local traditional communities as title-holders of biodiversity-related knowledge. It is to be hoped that this book will contribute not only to operationalize the principle of access and benefit-sharing in national law and commercial practices, but also to place the sometimes competing concepts of intellectual property rights and sovereign rights in the modern perspective of biodiversity as a "common concern of humanity" and of the common good of sustainable development.

Francesco Francioni
European University Institute
Florence

Acknowledgements

This commentary is the result of three years of work, which started in preparation for an international workshop organized on 2–3 December 2011 by the University of Edinburgh School of Law, its Centre for Studies in Intellectual Property and Technology Law, the Scottish Centre for International Law and the Jean Monnet Centre for Excellence of the Europa Institute of the University of Edinburgh. The workshop aimed to create a synergetic dialogue between academics specialized in international law, legal officers in relevant bodies of the United Nations System, a regionally balanced selection of the negotiators of the Nagoya Protocol on Access and Benefit-sharing to the Convention on Biological Diversity, and stakeholders that participated in the Protocol negotiations and were pioneering its implementation. The authors of this commentary learnt significantly from all the contributions to the edited collection that resulted from the workshop: *The 2010 Nagoya Protocol on Access and Benefit-Sharing in Perspective: Implications for International Law and National Implementation* (Martinus Nijhoff, 2013).

In addition, the authors have greatly benefited from an exchange of ideas on a very preliminary draft of this commentary, as well as from specific comments and suggestions that were extremely generously offered by the workshop participants: Marco d'Alessandro (Federal Office for the Environment, Switzerland), Abbe Brown (University of Aberdeen), Geoff Burton (United Nations University Institute of Advanced Studies), Jorge Cabrera Medaglia (University of Costa Rica), Evanson Chege Kamau (University of Bremen), Claudio Chiarolla (Institute for Sustainable Development and International Relations), Alessandro Fodella (University of Trento), Lyle Glowka (at the time, Secretariat of the Convention on Biological Diversity), James Harrison (University of Edinburgh), Harry Jonas (Natural Justice), Stefan Jungcurt (Council of Canadian Academies), Vassilis Koutsiouris (European Commission), Alejandro Lago (Rey Juan Carlos University of Madrid), Sélim Louafi (Centre International de Recherche Agronomique pour le Développement), Ruth McKenzie (University of Westminster), Valérie Normand (Secretariat of the Convention on Biological Diversity), Paul Oldham (Lancaster University), Maria Julia Oliva (Union for Ethical BioTrade), Riccardo Pavoni (University of Siena), Charlotte Salpin (Division for Ocean Affairs and the Law of the Sea, Office of Legal Affairs of the United Nations), Annalisa Savaresi (University of Edinburgh), Francesco Sindico (University of Strathclyde), Gurdial Singh (University of Malaysia), Krystyna Swiderska (International Institute for Environment and Development), Marie Wilke (international consultant) and Tomme Young (international consultant).

A significantly revised draft of this commentary greatly benefited from another round of peer review by Geoff Burton, Claudio Chiarolla, Evanson Chege Kamau, Sélim

Louafi, Riccardo Pavoni, Tomme Young, as well as Federico Lenzerini (University of Siena), Nicole Schabus (Thompson Rivers University), Adriana Bessa (European University Intitute), Federica Cittadino (University of Trento) and an anonymous reviewer selected by Martinus Nijhoff.

The authors are further indebted to: Tomme Young for sharing her insights throughout the development of this commentary and going well beyond "the extra mile" in supporting this project; Annalisa Savaresi for her research assistance and a fruitful exchange of views on the human rights questions raised in this commentary; Francesca Morgera and Andrea D'Ambrogio (University College London) for sharing their scientific knowledge and checking the accuracy of the discussion on Article 2 of the Protocol; and Chloë Kennedy (University of Edinburgh) for her research assistance. The authors of course remain solely responsible for any errors and omissions in this book.

The authors are, in addition, very grateful to Marie Sheldon and Lisa Hanson and their team at Brill for their continued support throughout this project.

     Elisa Morgera
     Elsa Tsioumani
     Matthias Buck

List of Abbreviations

ABS	Access and Benefit-sharing
CAO	Compliance Advisor Ombudsman of the International Finance Corporation
CBD	Convention on Biological Diversity
CGRFA	Commission on Genetic Resources for Food and Agriculture
CITES	Convention on International Trade in Endangered Species
COP	Conference of the Parties
COP/MOP	Conference of the Parties Serving as the Meeting of the Parties to the Nagoya Protocol
DNA	Deoxyribonucleic Acid
ENB	Earth Negotiations Bulletin
EU	European Union
FAO	Food and Agriculture Organization of the United Nations
GEF	Global Environment Facility
ICCPR	International Covenant on Civil and Political Rights
ICESCR	International Covenant on Economic, Social and Cultural Rights
ICJ	International Court of Justice
ICNP	Open-Ended Ad Hoc Intergovernmental Committee for the Nagoya Protocol on Access to Genetic Resources and the Fair and Equitable Sharing of Benefits Arising from their Utilization
IFC	International Finance Corporation
IGC	Intergovernmental Committee on Intellectual Property and Genetic Resources, Traditional Knowledge and Folklore of the World Intellectual Property Organization
ILO	International Labour Organization
IPRS	Intellectual Property Rights
ITLOS	International Tribunal for the Law of the Sea
ITPGRFA	International Treaty on Plant Genetic Resources for Food and Agriculture
IUCN	International Union for Conservation of Nature
JUSCANZ	Japan, the United States, Canada, Australia and New Zealand
LMOS	Living Modified Organisms
MAT	Mutually Agreed Terms
MEAS	Multilateral Environmental Agreements
MLS	Multilateral System of Access and Benefit-Sharing of the International Treaty on Plant Genetic Resources for Food and Agriculture
NGO	Non-Governmental Organization
OECD	Organization for Economic Co-operation and Development

PIC	Prior Informed Consent
PIP	Pandemic Influenza Preparedness
RNA	Ribonucleic Acid
SMTA	Standard Material Transfer Agreement
TEEB	The Economics of Ecosystems and Biodiversity
TRIPS	Trade-Related Aspects of Intellectual Property Rights
UN	United Nations
UNCLOS	United Nations Convention on the Law of the Sea
UNCTAD	United Nations Conference on Trade and Development
UNDRIP	United Nations Declaration on the Rights of Indigenous Peoples
UNEP	United Nations Environment Programme
UNESCO	United Nations Educational, Scientific, and Cultural Organization
UNFCCC	United Nations Framework Convention on Climate Change
UNGA	United Nations General Assembly
UNPFII	United Nations Permanent Forum on Indigenous Issues
UNU	United Nations University
VCLT	Vienna Convention on the Law of Treaties
WHO	World Health Organization
WIPO	World Intellectual Property Organization
WSSD	World Summit on Sustainable Development
WTO	World Trade Organization

Table of Legal Materials Cited

International Treaties

European Convention for the Protection of Human Rights and Fundamental Freedoms (Strasbourg, 4 November 1950, in force 3 September 1953)

International Plant Protection Convention (Rome, 6 December 1951, in force 3 April 1952)

Convention on Civil Procedure (The Hague, 1 March 1954, in force 12 April 1957)

Convention on the Jurisdiction of the Selected Forum in the Case of International Sales of Goods (The Hague, 15 April 1958, not yet in force)

Convention on Recognition and Enforcement of Foreign Arbitral Awards (New York, 10 June 1958, in force 7 June 1959)

Convention on Abolishing the Requirement of Legalization for Foreign Public Documents (The Hague, 5 October 1961, in force 24 January 1965)

Convention on the Service Abroad of Judicial and Extrajudicial Documents in Civil or Commercial Matters (The Hague, 15 November 1965, in force 10 February 1969)

Convention on the Choice of Court (The Hague, 25 November 1965, not yet in force)

International Covenant on Civil and Political Rights (New York, 16 December 1966, in force 23 March 1976)

International Covenant on Economic, Social and Cultural Rights (New York, 16 December 1966, in force 3 January 1976)

Vienna Convention on the Law of Treaties (Vienna, 23 May 1969, in force 27 January 1980)

American Convention on Human Rights (San José, 22 November 1969, in force 18 July 1978)

Convention on the Taking of Evidence Abroad in Civil or Commercial Matters (The Hague, 18 March 1970, in force 7 October 1972)

Convention on the Recognition and Enforcement of Foreign Judgments in Civil and Commercial Matters (The Hague, 1 February 1971, in force 20 August 1977)

Supplementary Protocol to the Hague Convention on the Recognition and Enforcement of Foreign Judgments in Civil and Commercial Matters (The Hague, 1 February 1971, in force 20 August 1979)

Convention on International Trade in Endangered Species of Wild Fauna and Flora (Washington, 3 March 1973, in force 1 July 1975)

Convention on International Access to Justice (The Hague, 25 October 1980, in force 1 May 1988)

African Charter on Human and Peoples' Rights (Banjul, 27 June 1981, in force 21 October 1986)

UN Convention on the Law of the Sea (Montego Bay, 10 December 1982, in force 16 November 1994)

Montreal Protocol on Substances that Deplete the Ozone Layer (Montreal, 16 September 1987, in force 1 January 1989)

Basel Convention on the Control of Transboundary Movements of Hazardous Wastes and their Disposal (Basel, 22 March 1989, in force 5 May 1992)

International Labour Organisation Convention 169 Concerning Indigenous and Tribal Peoples in Independent Countries (Geneva, 27 June 1989, in force 5 September 1991)

Convention on the Protection and Use of Transboundary Watercourses and International Lakes (Helsinki, 17 March 1992, in force 6 October 1996)

UN Framework Convention on Climate Change (New York, 9 May 1992, in force 21 March 1994)

Convention on Biological Diversity (Rio de Janeiro, 5 June 1992, in force 29 December 1993)

WTO Agreement Establishing the World Trade Organization (Marrakesh, 15 April 1994, in force 1 January 1995), Annex 1C in WTO Secretariat, *The Legal Texts: The Results of the Uruguay Round of Multilateral Trade Negotiations* (Cambridge, Cambridge University Press, 1999)

Agreement relating to the Implementation of Part XI of the United Nations Convention on the Law of the Sea (New York, 28 July 1994, in force 28 July 1996)

UN Convention to Combat Desertification in Countries Experiencing Serious Drought and/or Desertification, Particularly in Africa (Paris, 14 October 1994, in force 26 December 1996)

Agreement for the Implementation of the Provisions of the United Nations Convention on the Law of the Sea of 10 December 1982 relating to the Conservation and Management of Straddling Fish Stocks and Highly Migratory Fish Stocks (New York, 4 August 1995, in force 11 December 2001)

Kyoto Protocol to the United Nations Framework Convention on Climate Change (Kyoto, 11 December 1997, in force 16 February 2005)

Convention on Access to Information, Public Participation in Decision-making and Access to Justice in Environmental Matters (Aarhus, 25 June 1998, in force 30 October 2001)

Rotterdam Convention on the Prior Informed Consent Procedure for Certain Hazardous Chemicals and Pesticides in International Trade (Rotterdam, 10 September 1998, in force 24 February 2004)

Protocol on Water and Health to the 1992 Convention on the Protection and Use of Transboundary Watercourses and International Lakes (London, 17 June 1999, in force 4 August 2005)

Cartagena Protocol on Biosafety (Montreal, 29 January 2000, in force 11 September 2003)

Stockholm Convention on Persistent Organic Pollutants (Stockholm, 22 May 2001, in force 17 May 2004)

International Treaty on Plant Genetic Resources for Food and Agriculture (Rome, 3 November 2001, in force 29 June 2004)

Protocol on Pollutant Release and Transfer Registers to the Convention on Access to Information, Public Participation in Decision-Making and Access to Justice in Environmental Matters (Kiev, 21 May 2003, in force 8 October 2009)

UNESCO Convention for the Safeguarding of the Intangible Cultural Heritage (Paris, 17 October 2003, in force 20 April 2006)

Convention on the Choice of Court Agreements (The Hague, 30 June 2005, not yet in force)

United States-Peru Trade Promotion Agreement (Washington DC, 12 April 2006, in force 1 February 2009)

Nagoya Protocol on Access to Genetic Resources and the Fair and Equitable Sharing of Benefits Arising from Their Utilization to the Convention on Biological Diversity (Nagoya, 29 October 2010, not yet in force), in CBD Decision 10/1, "Access to genetic resources and the fair and equitable sharing of benefits arising from their utilization" (20 January 2011) UN Doc UNEP/CBD/COP/10/27

Free Trade Agreement between the EU and Its Member States, of the One Part, and Colombia and Peru, of the Other Part (26 July 2012, provisionally applied since March 2013 with regard to Peru and since August 2013 with regard to Colombia)

Negotiating Texts of the Nagoya Protocol

Cali Draft – "Revised Draft Protocol on Access to Genetic Resources and the Fair and Equitable Sharing of Benefits Arising from their Utilization to the Convention on Biological Diversity" in "Report of the first part of the ninth meeting of the Ad Hoc Open-ended Working Group on Access and Benefit-sharing" (26 April 2010) UN Doc UNEP/CBD/WG-ABS/9/3, Annex.

Montreal I Draft – "Draft Protocol on Access to Genetic Resources and the Fair and Equitable Sharing of Benefits Arising from their Utilization to the Convention on Biological Diversity" in "Report of the second part of the ninth meeting of the Ad Hoc Open-ended Working Group on Access and Benefit-sharing" (28 July 2010) UN Doc UNEP/CBD/COP/10/5/Add.4, Annex.

Montreal II draft – "Draft Protocol on Access to Genetic Resources and the Fair and Equitable Sharing of Benefits Arising from their Utilization to the Convention on Biological Diversity" in "Report of the meeting of the Interregional Negotiating Group," (21 September 2010) UN Doc UNEP/CBD/WG-ABS/9/ING/1, Annex.

Nagoya Draft – "Draft Protocol on Access to Genetic Resources and the Fair and Equitable Sharing of Benefits Arising from their Utilization to the Convention on Biological Diversity" in "Report of the third part of the ninth meeting of the Ad Hoc Open-Ended Working Group on Access and Benefit-sharing" (17 October 2010) UN Doc UNEP/CBD/COP/10/5/Add.5, Annex.

Cases

African Commission on Human and Peoples' Rights
Social and Economic Rights Action Centre and Centre for Economic and Social Rights v. Nigeria, Communication no. 155/96 (27 October 2001)

Centre for Minority Rights Development (Kenya) and Minority Rights Group International on behalf of Endorois Welfare Council v. Kenya, Communication no. 276/2003 (25 November 2009)

European Court of Human Rights
The Countryside Alliance and Others v. The United Kingdom, Applications no. 16072/06 and no. 27809/08 (24 November 2009)

European Court of Justice (Court of Justice of the European Union)
Case C–377/98 *Biotech Patents* [2001] ECR I–7079

Human Rights Committee
Sandra Lovelace v. Canada, Communication no. 24/1977 (30 July 1981) UN Doc CCPR/C/13/D/24/1977

Kitok v. Sweden, Communication no. 197/1985 (27 July 1988) UN Doc CCPR/C/33/D/197/1985

Lubicon Lake Band v. Canada, Communication no. 167/1984 (26 March 1990) UN Doc CCPR/C/38/D/167/1984

Mahuika et al. v. New Zealand, Communication no. 547/1993 (27 October 2000) UN Doc CCPR/C/70/D/547/1993

Ángela Poma Poma v. Peru, Communication no. 1457/2006 (27 March 2009) UN Doc CCPR/C/95/D/1457/2006

Inter-American Court of Human Rights
Case of the Mayagna (Sumo) Awas Tingni Community v Nicaragua, Merits, Reparations and Costs, Judgement, Case no. 11,577 (31 August 2001)

Case of the Moiwana Community v. Suriname, Preliminary Objections, Merits, Reparations and Costs, Judgment, Case no. 11,821 (15 June 2005)

Case of the Yakye Axa Indigenous Community v. Paraguay, Merits, Reparations and Costs, Judgment, Case no. 12,313 (17 June 2005)

Case of the Saramaka People v. Suriname, Preliminary Objections, Merits, Reparations, and Costs, Judgment, Case no. 12,338 (28 November 2007)

Case of the Saramaka People v. Suriname, Interpretation of the Judgment of Preliminary Objections, Merits, Reparations, and Costs, Judgment, Case no. 12,338 (12 August 2008).

Case of the Kichwa Indigenous People of Sarayaku v. Ecuador, Merits and Reparations, Judgment, Case no. 12,465 (27 June 2012)

International Centre for Settlement of Investment Disputes
Biwater Gauff (Tanzania) Ltd v Tanzania, Case no. ARB/05/22, Award (24 July 2008)

International Court of Justice
Delimitation of the Maritime Boundary in the Gulf of Maine Area (Canada v. United States of America), Judgement (12 October 1984)

Elettronica Sicula S.p.A. (ELSI) (United States of America v. Italy), Judgement (20 July 1989)

Territorial Dispute (Libyan Arab Jamahiriya v. Chad), Judgment (3 February 1994)

Case concerning East Timor (Portugal v. Australia), Judgment (30 June 2005)

Case concerning Pulp Mills on the River Uruguay (Argentina v. Uruguay), Judgement (20 April 2010)

International Tribunal on the Law of the Sea

Southern Bluefin Tuna (New Zealand v. Japan; Australia v. Japan), Order (27 August 1999)

Responsibilities and obligations of States sponsoring persons and entities with respect to activities in the Area (Request for Advisory Opinion submitted to the Seabed Disputes Chamber), Advisory Opinion (1 February 2011)

Permanent Court of International Justice

Railway Traffic between Lithuania and Poland, Advisory Opinion (15 October 1931)

Introduction

The Nagoya Protocol on Access and Benefit-Sharing[1] (ABS) is an international agreement that concerns environmental sustainability,[2] other sustainable development issues[3] and justice.[4] It aims at sharing the benefits arising from the utilization of genetic resources and of the traditional knowledge associated with genetic resources held by indigenous and local communities in a fair and equitable way, including by appropriate access to genetic resources and by appropriate transfer of relevant technologies. By doing so, the Protocol aims at contributing to the conservation of biological diversity and the sustainable use of its components.

1　Nagoya Protocol on Access to Genetic Resources and the Fair and Equitable Sharing of Benefits Arising from Their Utilization to the Convention on Biological Diversity (Nagoya, 29 October 2010, not yet in force), in CBD Decision 10/1, "Access to genetic resources and the fair and equitable sharing of benefits arising from their utilization" (20 January 2011) UN Doc UNEP/CBD/COP/10/27 (hereinafter, Nagoya Protocol or the Protocol).

2　E.g., Nagoya Protocol 7th preambular paragraph (which reads: 'Acknowledging the potential role of access and benefit-sharing to contribute to the conservation and sustainable use of biological diversity ... and *environmental sustainability*", emphasis added) and 14th preambular paragraph (which reads: 'Recognizing the importance of genetic resources to ... biodiversity conservation and the mitigation of and adaptation to climate change'). See discussion in this commentary on Article 1, section 4.

3　E.g., Nagoya Protocol 5th preambular paragraph (which reads: 'Recognizing the important contribution to *sustainable development* made by technology transfer and cooperation to build research and innovation capacities for adding value to genetic resources in developing countries') and 7th preambular paragraph (which reads: 'Acknowledging the potential role of access and benefit-sharing to contribute to ... *poverty eradication* ... thereby contributing to achieving the *Millennium Development Goals*') (emphasis added). For a discussion, see Conclusions to this commentary, section 2.

4　For a discussion predating the adoption of the Nagoya Protocol, Bram De Jonge, "What Is Fair and Equitable Benefit-Sharing?," *Journal of Agricultural and Environmental Ethics* 24 (2011): 127; Philippe Cullet, "Environmental Justice in the Use, Knowledge and Exploitation of Genetic Resources," in *Environmental Law and Justice in Context*, ed. Jonas Ebbesson and Phoebe N. Okowa (Cambridge: Cambridge University Press, 2009), 371; and Peter-Tobias Stoll, "Access to Genetic Resources and Benefit-Sharing: Underlying Concepts and the Idea of Justice," in *Genetic Resources, Traditional Knowledge and the Law: Solutions for Access and Benefit Sharing*, ed. Evanson C. Kamau and Gerd Winter (London: Earthscan, 2009), 3. For a discussion after the conclusion of the negotiations of the Nagoya Protocol, see also Peter-Tobias Stoll, "ABS, Justice, Pools and the Nagoya Protocol," in *Common Pools of Genetic Resources Equity and Innovation in International Biodiversity Law*, ed. Evanson C. Kamau and Gerd Winter (Cheltenham: Edward Elgar, 2013), 305.

The Nagoya Protocol was adopted under the Convention on Biological Diversity (CBD).[5] Similarly to the CBD, it provides a flexible framework for accommodating developed and developing countries' concerns and capacities[6] and for encouraging partnerships between national and local authorities, indigenous and local communities, and the private sector.[7] The Protocol expands upon the text of the Convention by detailing obligations in relation to benefit-sharing and access to genetic resources[8] and traditional knowledge associated with such resources.[9] It contributes to developing significantly the concept of benefit-sharing[10] under international law. In addition, the Protocol seeks to strike an innovative balance between the economic and non-economic values

---

5   Convention on Biological Diversity (Rio de Janeiro, 5 June 1992, in force 29 December 1993) 1760 UNTS 79 (CBD).

6   Désirée McGraw, "The CBD – Key Characteristics and Implications for Development," *Review of European Community and International Environmental Law* 11 (2002): 17.

7   Lee Kimball, "Institutional Linkages between the Convention on Biological Diversity and Other International Conventions," *Review of European Community and International Environmental Law* 6 (1997): 239.

8   The literature on the CBD provisions on genetic resources is extensive: Daniel Robinson, *Confronting Biopiracy: Challenges, Cases and International Debates* (London: Earthscan, 2010); Suneetha M. Subramanian and Balakrishna Pisupati, *Learning from the Practitioners: Benefit Sharing Perspectives from Enterprising Communities* (Nairobi: UN Environment Programme (UNEP)/United Nations University (UNU), 2009); Charles McManis, *Biodiversity and the Law* (London: Earthscan, 2007); Morten W. Tvedt and Tomme Young, *Beyond Access: Exploring Implementation of the Fair and Equitable Sharing Commitment in the* CBD (Gland: IUCN, 2007); Natalie Stoianoff, ed, *Accessing Biological Resources: Complying with the Convention on Biological Diversity* (The Hague: Kluwer Law International, 2004); and Walter V. Reid et al., *Biodiversity Prospecting: Using Genetic Resources for Sustainable Development* (Washington DC: World Resources Institute, 1993).

9   Anja Meyer, "International Environmental Law and Human Rights: Towards the Explicit Recognition of Traditional Knowledge," *Review of European Community and International Environmental Law* 10 (2001): 37; Kamau and Winter, eds., *Genetic Resources, Traditional Knowledge and the Law*, op. cit.; Rachel Wynberg, Doris Schroeder and Roger Chennells, eds, *Indigenous Peoples, Consent and Benefit Sharing: Lessons from the San-Hoodia Case* (New York: Springer, 2009); Sarah A. Laird, ed, *Biodiversity and Traditional Knowledge: Equitable Partnerships in Practice* (London: Earthscan, 2002); Suneetha M. Subramanian and Balakrishna Pisupati, *Traditional Knowledge in Policy and Practice: Approaches to Development and Human Well-Being* (Tokyo: UNU, 2010); and Manuel Ruiz and Ronnie Vernooy, eds, *The Custodians of Biodiversity: Sharing Access to and Benefits of Genetic Resources* (London: Earthscan, 2012).

10   This concept has indeed been subject to evolving interpretation by the CBD Parties as a tool for inter-State cooperation as well as for partnership between States, indigenous and local communities, and the private sector: Elisa Morgera and Elsa Tsioumani,

of biodiversity, more tightly linking the third objective of the CBD (benefit-sharing) with its first and second objectives – conservation and sustainable use.[11] It thus contains provisions related to environmental management, international cooperation and human rights, while addressing a fairly complex subject matter that affects a range of research and commercial activities.

By way of introduction, the following sections will first trace the origins of the international debate on access and benefit-sharing (ABS) related to genetic resources, highlighting the evolution of the concept of fair and equitable benefit-sharing in inter-State relations under the international biodiversity regime. The key features of the negotiations of the Nagoya Protocol that have a bearing on its interpretation will then be outlined. Attention will then turn to the novelty of including traditional knowledge in an international regime on ABS, which highlights the intra-State dimension of benefit-sharing. This leads to a preliminary identification of legal questions arising from the inclusion of indigenous peoples and local communities among the beneficiaries of the Nagoya Protocol. On this basis, the introduction will then explain the objective, approach and methods of the present commentary, as well as its limitations.

1   The International Debate on Access and Benefit-sharing

Modern bio-sciences have led to the rapid growth of scientific research on the genetic base of life, on the relevance of genes for the biological and chemical make-up of cells and organisms, and on interactions between the genetic and bio-chemical make-up of organisms and their natural environment. Genes and naturally occurring bio-chemicals play significant and growing roles in different economic sectors and are considered as the basis for meeting important societal challenges in diverse areas such as agricultural research and food security, the development of medicines, cosmetics or bio-based sources of renewable energy, or adaptation to climate change, to name but a few.[12] Although the

---

"The Evolution of Benefit-Sharing: Linking Biodiversity and Communities' Livelihoods," *Review of European Community and International Environmental Law* 19 (2010): 150.

11   See commentary on Article 1, section 4, Article 5, section 6, Article 8, section 2, Article 9, section 2, Article 10, section 4, Article 12, section 5, Article 21, section 3, Article 22, section 3, and Article 23, section 3, discussing the promotion of coherent interpretation and integrative implementation of the CBD objectives under the Nagoya Protocol.

12   TEEB, *The Economics of Ecosystems and Biodiversity: Mainstreaming the Economics of Nature: A Synthesis of the Approach, Conclusions and Recommendations of TEEB* (Nairobi: UNEP, 2010), accessed 30 November 2013, <www.teebweb.org/>.

commercial value of genetic resources is still the object of dispute,[13] the value of products derived from genetic resources worldwide was estimated in 1999 between USD 500–800 billion.[14] According to more recent estimates, companies relying on genetic resources for their research and development include pharmaceutical and food companies earning more than USD 50 billion annually, with combined industry and government expenditures in research and development in the pharmaceutical sector totaling USD 68 billion in 2010.[15] In the field of medicine alone, terrestrial plants and microorganisms have been important natural sources used in the development of new medicines: approximately 75 percent of the top 20 hospital drugs and approximately 20 percent of the top 100 most widely prescribed drugs are derived from natural sources.[16]

Bioprospecting[17] is often a transnational activity:[18] it involves situations where genetic resources are acquired in one State but are used in another State. The role of international law is thus that of addressing the trans-jurisdictional aspects of regulating in one country access to genetic resources by users based in other countries, and rewarding States holding genetic resources for their contribution to the development of products that are eventually commercialized

---

13   Sebastian Oberthür and Kristin Rosendal, "Global Governance of Genetic Resources: Background and Analytical Framework," in *Global Governance of Genetic Resources: Access and Benefit Sharing After the Nagoya Protocol*, ed. Sebastian Oberthür and Kristin Rosendal (London: Routledge, 2013), 1, 3.

14   Kerry Ten Kate and Sarah A. Laird, *The Commercial Use of Biodiversity: Access to Genetic Resources and Benefit-Sharing* (London: Earthscan, 1999), cited by Oberthür and Rosendal, "Global Governance of Genetic Resources: Background and Analytical Framework," op. cit., 3.

15   Sarah A. Laird and Rachel P. Wynberg, "Bioscience at a Crossroads: Implementing the Nagoya Protocol in a Time of Scientific, Technological and Industry Change," CBD Factsheet (2012), accessed 1 February 2014, <www.cbd.int/abs/policy-brief/default. shtml/>.

16   Amy E. Wright, "Biological Diversity Equals Chemical Diversity – The Search for Better Medicines" US National Oceanic and Atmospheric Administration *Ocean Explorer*, accessed 13 December 2013, <http://oceanexplorer.noaa.gov/explorations/02sab/back ground/biodiversity/biodiversity.html>. See also Daniel A. Dias, Sylvia Urban and Ute Roessner, "A Historical Overview of Natural Products in Drug Discovery," *Metabolites* 2 (2012): 313.

17   'Bioprospecting' is understood as 'the search for plant and animal species from which medicinal drugs and other commercially valuable compounds can be obtained.' See Oxford Dictionary, accessed 6 March 2014, <www.oxforddictionaries.com/definition/ english/bioprospecting>.

18   Christine Godt, "Enforcement of Benefit-Sharing Duties in User Countries," in Kamau and Winter, *Genetic Resources, Traditional Knowledge and the Law*, op. cit., 419, 420–421.

by actors in other countries.[19] The debate on international law and ABS has thus not been concerned with the purely domestic uses of genetic resources. Rather, international law has been considered necessary to foster international cooperation for the protection of the sovereign entitlement of one State to derive benefits from the use of its genetic resources once these resources are brought outside of its jurisdiction.[20] In addition, international law is needed to ensure the realization of the international community's objective of ensuring fairness in transnational ABS transactions 'in recognition of the need to reduce enormous global asymmetries' among developed and developing States,[21] as explained below. As often ABS transactions concern private individuals/entities, international law is also needed to guide the development of domestic legislation and interaction of different countries' domestic legal frameworks creating rights and duties for individuals/entities within their jurisdiction in sharing and receiving benefits from access to genetic resources. This should ultimately ensure the implementation of fair and equitable private-law contractual arrangements that are to be negotiated between the individuals, private entities, indigenous and local communities, institutions or governments in each individual ABS transaction.[22] To that end, the role of international law in relation to ABS is that of setting a multilateral framework coordinating domestic measures governing contractual ABS transactions,[23] and fostering international cooperation, thereby operating "across the public-private divide."[24]

The CBD was pioneering in introducing the concepts of ABS for genetic resources in international environmental law in early recognition of the above-described scientific and technological developments and legal challenges. Until its negotiation and entry into force, an arguable[25] application

---

19   Cullet, "Environmental Justice in the Use, Knowledge and Exploitation of Genetic Resources," op. cit., 372.

20   Stoll, "ABS, Justice, Pools," op. cit., 309.

21   Braulio Dias, "Preface," in Morgera, Buck and Tsioumani, *2010 Nagoya Protocol on Access and Benefit-Sharing in Perspective*, op. cit., 1.

22   Tomme Young, "An International Cooperation Perspective," in *The 2010 Nagoya Protocol on Access and Benefit-Sharing in Perspective: Implications for International Law and Implementation Challenges*, ed. Elisa Morgera, Matthias Buck and Elsa Tsioumani (Leiden: Martinus Nijhoff, 2013) 451, 457.

23   Sebastian Oberthür and Kristin Rosendal, "Conclusions," in Oberthür and Rosendal, *Global Governance of Genetic Resources*, op. cit., 231, 237–239.

24   Ibid.

25   This understanding of common heritage should be compared with the common heritage regime, as provided for in the UN Convention on the Law of the Sea (Montego Bay,

of the concept of common heritage of mankind over biological resources had resulted in an almost free flow of genetic resources across boundaries.[26] Access to genetic resources in nature (in situ)[27] was considered free and unconditional, and the results of research on such resources were expected to benefit future generations. The CBD marked a paradigm shift vis-à-vis bioprospecting by recognizing national sovereignty over genetic resources.[28] In other words, the CBD subjected access to genetic resources to the prior informed consent (PIC) of the State providing the resource.[29] Furthermore, the CBD made it an objective for the international community

> the fair and equitable sharing of the benefits arising out of the utilization of genetic resources, including by appropriate access to genetic resources and by appropriate transfer of relevant technologies, taking into account all rights over those resources and to technologies, and by appropriate funding.[30]

This fundamental shift in principles can be explained in the light of the asymmetries between States providing and using genetic resources, exacerbated by the intellectual property system, as well as by growing expectations concerning the commercial value of biodiversity. These moral and economic reasons will be discussed below in turn.

---

10 December 1982, in force 16 November 1994) 1833 UNTS 3 (UNCLOS), Article 140(2) which subjects resources that cannot be appropriated to the exclusive sovereignty of States to an international managing and regulating institution with a view to providing benefits arising from the utilization of such resources to all States even if they are unable to participate in the actual process of extraction: see Patricia Birnie, Alan Boyle and Catherine Redgwell, *International Law and the Environment*, 3rd ed. (Oxford: Oxford University Press, 2009), 128–130 and 197.

26   Tvedt and Young, *Beyond Access*, op. cit., 1.

27   CBD Article 2 defines 'in situ conditions' as 'conditions where genetic resources exist within ecosystems and natural habitats, and in the case of domesticated or cultivated species, in the surroundings where they have developed their distinctive properties.'

28   See Lyle Glowka, Francoise Burhenne-Guilmin and Hugh Synge. *A Guide to the Convention on Biological Diversity* (Gland: IUCN, 1994), 76; and Elsa Tsioumani, "International Treaty on Plant Genetic Resources for Food and Agriculture: Legal and Policy Questions from Adoption to Implementation," *Yearbook of International Environmental Law* 15 (2004): 119, 122–124.

29   CBD Article 15(5). See commentary on Article 6, Section 3.

30   CBD Article 1.

1.1   *Asymmetries and the Ethical Rationale for ABS*

There are several asymmetries among States in relation to genetic resources. First of all, genetic variability is not distributed equally among States. Australia, Brazil, China, Colombia, the Democratic Republic of the Congo, Ecuador, India, Indonesia, Madagascar, Malaysia, Mexico, Papua New Guinea, Peru, the Philippines, South Africa, the United States of America and Venezuela host more than 70% of the world's biodiversity and are therefore considered mega-diverse.[31] Among these mega-diverse countries, tropical developing countries have formed a political grouping, the Like-minded Mega-diverse Countries, as their impressive richness in terrestrial genetic resources is not matched by the technological capacities to research and develop genetic resources held by them.[32] This asymmetry in technological capacities also implies unequal access to information on the scientific and technological value, and the commercial potential of genetic resources among developed and developing countries,[33] as well as unequal access to resources and knowledge (including legal knowledge and legal assistance) needed to negotiate ABS transactions.[34] All these elements translate into unequal bargaining powers between States.[35]

Against this background, a historical asymmetry should be highlighted. Colonialism fostered the collection and appropriation of cultural and natural heritage into museums, zoological and botanical gardens and other ex situ

---

31 The UNEP World Conservation Monitoring Centre identified these countries as mega-diverse in 2000; and megadiversity is determined on the basis of the 'total number of species in a country and the degree of endemism at the species level and at higher taxonomic levels:' see "State of the Environment Report (Biodiversity Theme Report)," Australia, 2001, accessed 30 November 2013, <www.environment.gov.au/node/21579>.

32 Oberthür and Rosendal, "Global Governance of Genetic Resources: Background and Analytical Framework," op. cit., 1.

33 Stoll, "ABS, Justice, Pools," op. cit., 309; and Stoll, "Access to Genetic Resources and Benefit-Sharing," op. cit., 12.

34 Joji Cariño et al., *Nagoya Protocol on Access to Genetic Resources and the Fair and Equitable Sharing of Benefits Arising from Their Utilization: Background and Analysis* (The Berne Declaration, Bread for the World, Ecoropa, Tebtebba and Third World Network, 2013), accessed 30 November 2013, <www.evb.ch/cm_data/Nagoya_Protocol_complete_final.pdf>, 5. On the North-South asymmetries and other conflicting objectives behind the ABS provisions of the CBD, see generally De Jonge, "What Is Fair and Equitable Benefit-Sharing?", op. cit.; and Bram De Jonge and Niels Louwaars, "The Diversity of Principles Underlying the Concept of Benefit Sharing," in Kamau and Winter, *Genetic Resources, Traditional Knowledge and the Law*, op. cit., 38.

35 Stoll, "ABS, Justice, Pools", op. cit., 309; and Stoll, "Access to Genetic Resources and Benefit-sharing," op. cit., 12.

collections in colonizing countries.[36] This asymmetry has more recently been compounded by the application of intellectual property rights (IPRs) to improved germplasm.[37] On the basis of the concept of the common heritage of mankind, developing countries provided their genetic resources freely, while the products incorporating them were protected by IPRs and their use was therefore restricted. Even after adoption of the CBD, which established the principle of national sovereignty over genetic resources, IPR holders are able to enforce their rights through private law in developed countries, whereas developing countries' claims based on their national sovereignty encounter significant barriers in foreign jurisdictions where the IPR holders are based. This asymmetry is likely to worsen in the face of the growth and increasing dominance of multinational corporations in the biotech sector.[38]

The latter asymmetry is complicated by a well-studied and still unresolved tension between international law on IPRs and on biodiversity.[39] While patenting based on the use of genetic resources is allowed under the World Trade Organization (WTO) Agreement on Trade-related Aspects of Intellectual Property Rights (TRIPS),[40] subject to meeting patentability criteria, these do not require evidence of PIC from the country providing genetic resources or of benefit-sharing.[41] There is thus nothing in the TRIPS Agreement to provide support for the CBD principle of national sovereignty over genetic resources. Although it can be argued that access to resources in violation of the CBD principles of PIC and benefit-sharing may not be legitimate, in the absence of national legislation implementing such principles particularly in user countries, private companies may obtain private rights on products derived from genetic resources from other countries without having to adhere to the CBD principles. It has thus been argued, in very broad terms, that unless the TRIPS Agreement is amended and the patent system ensures respect for the CBD

---

36 Cariño et al., *Nagoya Protocol*, op. cit., 2. CBD Article 2 defines 'ex situ conservation' as 'the conservation of components of biological diversity outside of their natural habitats.'

37 Michel Petit et al., *Why Governments Can't Make Policy: The Case of Plant Genetic Resources in the International Arena* (Lima: International Potato Center, 2001), 10 and 19.

38 Oberthür and Rosendal, "Conclusions," op. cit., 241.

39 Paul Oldham, Stephen Hall and Oscar Forero, "Biological Diversity in the Patent System," *PLoS ONE* 8 (2013): e78737.

40 Agreement Establishing the World Trade Organization (Marrakesh, 15 April 1994, in force 1 January 1995), Annex 1C in WTO Secretariat, *The Legal Texts: The Results of the Uruguay Round of Multilateral Trade Negotiations* (Cambridge: Cambridge University Press, 1999), 321.

41 See UK Commission on Intellectual Property Rights, *Integrating Intellectual Property Rights and Development* (London: Commission on Intellectual Property Rights, 2002), 84.

principles also in the intellectual property field, implementation and enforceability of such principles will be lacking.[42] The situation is further complicated
by the (mis)application of intellectual property rights over natural compounds,
which can hardly be considered inventions.[43]

An amendment of the TRIPS Agreement[44] incorporating a requirement
to disclose in IPR applications the origin of the genetic resources used in an
invention, as well as evidence of PIC and benefit-sharing[45] would arguably
make the IPR system a mechanism to enforce the ABS provisions of the CBD
by linking to the WTO binding dispute settlement system.[46] Such proposals,
however, have been very controversial, and it remains to be seen whether
negotiations under the WTO will achieve any progress in that regard.[47] As the
impasse on this issue at the WTO continues at the time of writing,[48] it should

---

42   Ibid. Detailed analysis of the technically complex linkages between the intellectual prop-
      erty system and the CBD falls beyond the scope of this commentary. See, e.g., Martha
      Chouchena-Rojas et al., *Disclosure Requirements: Ensuring Mutual Supportiveness between
      the WTO TRIPS Agreement and the CBD* (Gland and Geneva: Center for International
      Environmental Law et al., 2005), accessed 30 November 2013, <https://portals.iucn.org/
      library/node/8766>.

43   We are grateful to Geoff Burton for drawing our attention to this point.

44   The original proposal, submitted by a group of developing countries led by India and
      Brazil, was eventually supported by a coalition of 110 WTO members by 2008, when a
      strategic alliance was made with the EU and Switzerland calling for a procedural decision
      to negotiate in parallel the biodiversity amendment and an extension of protected geo-
      graphical indications, another issue under discussion in the TRIPS Council: "Article 27.3b,
      Traditional Knowledge, Biodiversity," WTO, accessed on 30 October 2013, <www.wto.org/
      english/tratop_e/trips_e/art27_3b_e.htm>.

45   In the policy and academic debates, this is referred to as 'disclosure requirement.'
      Chouchena-Rojas et al., *Disclosure Requirements*, op. cit.; and Evanson C. Kamau,
      "Disclosure Requirements – A Critical Appraisal," in Kamau and Winter, *Genetic Resources,
      Traditional Knowledge and the Law*, op. cit., 399.

46   For a technical discussion of proposals to enhance the relationship between the intel-
      lectual property system and the CBD, including disclosure requirements, as well as the
      legal and policy issues such proposals raise for the patent system, see "Technical Study on
      Disclosure Requirements in Patent Systems Related to Genetic Resources and Traditional
      Knowledge submitted by the WIPO Secretariat" (15 December 2013) UN Doc UNEP/CBD/
      COP/7/INF/17.

47   Morgera and Tsioumani, "Evolution of Benefit-Sharing", op. cit., 168–169.

48   See the post-Nagoya Protocol version of the proposal: WTO Trade Negotiations Committee,
      "Draft Decision to Enhance Mutual Supportiveness between the TRIPS Agreement and
      the Convention on Biological Diversity" (19 April 2011) WTO DOC TN/C/W/59; and dis-
      cussion in Riccardo Pavoni, "The Nagoya Protocol and WTO Law," in Morgera, Buck and
      Tsioumani, *2010 Nagoya Protocol on Access and Benefit-Sharing in Perspective*, op. cit., 185,

be noted that many countries have also been calling for disclosure requirements and mechanisms[49] to be addressed in the framework of negotiations held under the World Intellectual Property Organization (WIPO) on IPRs and genetic resources.[50] Discussions on IPRs in both the WIPO and WTO context provided a critical background to the negotiations of the Protocol.

1.2   *An Incentive-based Approach to Biodiversity Conservation and the Economic Rationale for ABS*

ABS is expected to generate *economic* benefits for biodiversity conservation in States that share the genetic resources over which they hold sovereign rights with other CBD Parties. To a significant extent, it has been argued that ABS is 'assumed' to create strong incentives for biodiversity conservation 'quasi-automatically'.[51] In parallel, ABS seeks to enhance access for researchers and companies to quality samples of genetic resources, based on predictable access decisions at reasonably low transaction costs. This is expected to create new opportunities for nature-based research and development and the creation of innovative goods and services that help to meet societal challenges.

208–212. The TRIPS/CBD relationship was not on the agenda of the ninth WTO ministerial conference in Bali, 3–7 December 2013. See Bali Ministerial Declaration (11 December 2013) WTO Doc WT/MIN(13)/DEC. According to the report of the TRIPS Council, consultations continued 'on the earlier suggestion that the Secretariat of the Convention on Biological Diversity (CBD) be invited to brief the Council on the outcome of the tenth meeting of the Conference of the Parties to the CBD ...' See Annual Report (2013) of the Council for TRIPS (23 October 2013) WTO DOC IP/C/67.

49   For a recent study on national practice on disclosure requirements, see Paul Oldham and Geoff Burton, "Defusing Disclosure in Patent Applications: A Positive Strategy to Strengthen Legal Certainty in the Nagoya Protocol on Access to Genetic Resources and the Fair and Equitable Sharing of Benefits Arising from their Utilization to the Convention on Biological Diversity and Support WIPO's Intergovernmental Committee on Intellectual Property and Genetic Resources, Traditional Knowledge and Folklore" (2010), accessed 1 March 2014, <http://ssrn.com/abstract=1694899>.

50   The WIPO General Assembly established an Intergovernmental Committee on Intellectual Property and Genetic Resources, Traditional Knowledge and Folklore at its twenty-sixth session: WIPO General Assembly, "Matters concerning intellectual property and genetic resources, traditional knowledge and folklore" (3 October 2000) WIPO Doc WO/GA/26/6. The mandate of the Committee was subsequently renewed, most recently in October 2013, see WIPO General Assembly, "Matters concerning the Intergovernmental Committee on Intellectual Property and Genetic Resources, Traditional Knowledge and Folklore (IGC)" (14 August 2013) WIPO Doc WO/GA/43/14. See discussion in commentary on Article 4, section 3.1.

51   Oberthür and Rosendal, "Conclusions," op. cit., 244–5.

More broadly, ABS is expected to strengthen the political and economic interest in, and public awareness of the importance of, preserving genetic diversity in situ and in collections ex situ. As recognized in the preamble of the Nagoya Protocol,

> public awareness about the economic value of ecosystems and biodiversity and the fair and equitable sharing of this economic value with the custodians of biodiversity are key incentives for the conservation of biological diversity and the sustainable use of its components.[52]

The primary contribution of ABS to conservation thus arguably rests with the idea that the utilization of genetic resources leads to the development of new products, and in doing so provides both an incentive and additional economic benefits to support conservation efforts.[53] These linkages should thus be understood[54] against the background of increased international attention to the concepts of ecosystem services[55] and the green economy,[56] and the emerging importance of bio-based economies.[57] The report 'The Economics of Ecosystems and Biodiversity' (TEEB), launched in 2010, argued that successful environmental protection needs to be grounded in the explicit recognition,

---

52   Nagoya Protocol 6th preambular recital.

53   We are grateful to Geoff Burton for suggesting this point.

54   The linkages between ABS and the complex (and often controversial) concepts mentioned in this section would deserve further academic analysis, which, however, falls beyond the scope of this commentary.

55   Ecosystem services are the benefits that people obtain from ecosystems: Millennium Ecosystem Assessment, *Ecosystem and Human Well-Being: Biodiversity Synthesis* (Washington DC: World Resources Institute, 2005), accessed 30 November 2013, <www.unep.org/maweb/documents/document.354.aspx.pdf>; and intergovernmental endorsement of the concept of ecosystem services in UN General Assembly, "World Summit Outcome" (24 October 2005) UN Doc A/RES/60/1, paragraph 12. See discussion in Elisa Morgera, "The 2005 UN World Summit and the Environment: The Proverbial Half-Full Glass," *Italian Yearbook of International Law* 15 (2006): 53, 61.

56   Elisa Morgera and Annalisa Savaresi, "A Conceptual and Legal Perspective on the Green Economy," *Review of European, Comparative and International Environmental Law* 22 (2013): 14.

57   Organization for Economic Co-operation and Development (OECD), "The Application of Biotechnology to Industrial Sustainability" (Paris: OECD, 2001), accessed 30 November 2013, <www.oecd-ilibrary.org/environment/the-application-of-biotechnology-to-industrial-sustainability_9789264195639-en>; and OECD, "Towards the Development of OECD Best Practices for Assessing the Sustainability of Bio-based Products" (Paris: OECD, 2010), accessed 30 November 2013, <www.oecd.org/sti/biotech/45598236.pdf>.

efficient allocation, and fair distribution of the costs and benefits of conservation and sustainable use of natural resources,[58] which is seen as an essential approach to ensure the mainstreaming of biodiversity concerns in all relevant policy- and decision-making processes.[59] In that sense ABS for genetic resources may arguably be seen as one of the front-runners for linking economic activities more clearly to the services provided by healthy ecosystems.[60]

A few words of caution should be added on the economic rationale for ABS as a tool for conservation and sustainable use. First, conservation and sustainable use in principle are a precondition for the preservation of genetic resources until the time research and development can be conducted upon them. Second, directing benefits from research and development of genetic resources to biodiversity conservation and sustainable use is to a large extent in the discretion of the provider country, so it remains to be seen whether specific ABS deals will effectively contribute to the other two objectives of the CBD.[61] Third, difficulties in enforcing implementing measures may also have a great bearing on the actual functioning of ABS as an incentive for conservation and sustainable use.[62] Fourth, biodiversity-related economic instruments have so far produced 'modest effects at best'[63] and demand for genetic resources is

---

58   TEEB, *Economics of Ecosystems and Biodiversity*, op. cit., 6. See discussion in Elisa Morgera and Elsa Tsioumani, "Yesterday, Today and Tomorrow: Looking Afresh at the Convention on Biological Diversity," *Yearbook of International Environmental Law* 21 (2011): 3, 9–11.

59   CBD Decision 10/4, "Third edition of the Global Biodiversity Outlook: implications for the future implementation of the Convention" (20 January 2011) UN Doc UNEP/CBD/COP/10/27, paragraph 5(a) and (e). Morgera and Tsioumani, "Yesterday, Today and Tomorrow," op. cit., 9–11.

60   CBD Secretariat, "Access and Benefit-sharing in Practice: Trends in Partnerships Across Sectors" CBD Technical Series No. 38. (Montreal: CBD Secretariat, 2008), 37.

61   We are grateful to Tomme Young for making this point. See discussion in this commentary on Article 1, section 4.

62   We are grateful to Tomme Young for making this point. See CBD Decision 10/44, "Incentive measures" (20 January 2011) UN Doc UNEP/CBD/COP/10/27, paragraph 14.

63   Franziska Wolff, "The Nagoya Protocol and the Diffusion of Economic Instruments for Ecosystem Services in International Environmental Governance," in Oberthür and Rosendal, *Global Governance of Genetic Resources*, op. cit., 134, 135–139, 151 and 153 as part of a broader trend in incentive-based governance of biodiversity. See also Riccardo Pavoni, "Channeling Investment into Biodiversity Conservation: ABS and PES Schemes," in *Harnessing Foreign Investment to Promote Environmental Protection Incentives and Safeguards*, ed. Pierre-Marie Dupuy and Jorge E. Viñuales (Cambridge: Cambridge University Press, 2013), 206; and CBD and UNEP-World Conservation Monitoring Centre (WCMC), "Global Biodiversity Outlook (Montreal and Cambridge: 2010 CBD and UNEP-WCMC), accessed 30 November 2013, <http://gbo3.cbd.int/> 19, where it is stated that

affected by free availability of pre-CBD (and arguably pre-Protocol)[64] material ex situ.[65]

More fundamentally, the commodification of biodiversity arguably underlying the discourse on ecosystem services has not gone unchallenged. Increasing attention is being paid to addressing ethical questions raised by market-based approaches to biodiversity conservation and sustainable use.[66] This principled debate is reflected in multilateral policy-making, as the concept of ecosystem services as developed within the CBD framework has arguably attempted to reconcile an economic approach[67] with an increased focus on its contribution to poverty eradication[68] and on the need for broader stakeholder engagement, particularly the vulnerable.[69] These tensions clearly emerge also in the context

---

'There are few examples of the benefit arising from the commercial and other utilization of genetic resources being shared with the countries providing such resources.'

64   On pre-Protocol material, see this commentary on Article 3, Section 3.1.

65   Wolff, "Nagoya Protocol and the Diffusion," op. cit., 151. Along the same lines, Stoll, "Access to Genetic Resources and Benefit-Sharing," op. cit., 4. Laird and Wynberg, "Bioscience at a Crossroads", op. cit., at 2, note that 'In higher tech industries like pharmaceuticals, agriculture and biotech, the need to access genetic resources is less than in previous years, through large-scale field collections, but interest persists; in lower tech industries consumer demand for novel, and natural ingredients is often a central part of product identity and marketing.'

66   For example, see papers collected in the special issue of *Transnational Environmental Law* published in October 2013, in particular the contribution by Colin T. Reid, "Between Priceless and Worthless: Challenges in Using Market Mechanisms for Conserving Biodiversity," *Transnational Environmental Law* 2 (2013): 217, where the author draws attention to the challenges of 'defining the units that can be the subject of the economic or market devices,' 'ensuring that such mechanisms do deliver conservation gains and establishing appropriate governance arrangements', as well as to 'ethical concerns' associated with the commodification of nature. Ibid., 218.

67   CBD Decision 5/6, "Ecosystem approach" (22 June 2000) UN Doc UNEP/CBD/COP/5/23; and CBD Decision 7/11, "Ecosystem approach" (13 April 2004) UN Doc UNEP/CBD/COP/7/21.

68   CBD COP Decision 10/6, "Integration of biodiversity into poverty eradication and development" (20 January 2011) UN Doc UNEP/CBD/COP/10/27; and CBD Decision 11/22, "Biodiversity for poverty eradication and development" (5 December 2012) UN Doc UNEP/CBD/COP/11/35.

69   For instance, CBD Decision 10/4, "Third edition of the Global Biodiversity Outlook: Implications for the Future Implementation of the Convention" (20 January 2011) UN Doc UNEP/CBD/COP/10/27, paragraphs 5(d) and (f), points to: enhancing the benefits from biodiversity to contribute to local livelihoods; empowering indigenous and local community; and ensuring their participation in decision-making processes to protect and encourage their customary sustainable use of biological resources.

of the Nagoya Protocol, as evidence of a positive interaction between benefit-sharing and biodiversity conservation remains meager.[70]

1.3   *The ABS Provisions of the CBD*

Against this background, fair and equitable benefit-sharing was at the heart of the political agreement at the time of adoption of the Convention: it was conceived both as an economic incentive for the developing world to conserve biodiversity, as well as a means to correct injustices.[71] Benefit-sharing, as enshrined in the CBD, thus embodies an inter-State approach to achieve sustainable development and equity.[72] In particular, it points to a bilateral relation between a country providing genetic resources and a country using them.

The legally binding language of CBD Article 15(7) points to an inter-State benefit-sharing obligation, that is not expressly linked to specific access activities and that is to be implemented through the adoption of domestic measures on benefit-sharing. Fair and equitable benefit-sharing, however, is not defined in the CBD other than by reference to the means for its realization. The language of the third CBD objective seems to point to three such means, each underpinned by specific provisions in the Convention: appropriate access to genetic resources;[73] appropriate transfer of relevant technologies,[74] including biotechnology;[75] and appropriate funding.[76] For each ABS transaction, the articulation and implementation of specific benefit-sharing obligations rest on the conclusion of mutually agreed terms (MAT), i.e. a private law contract between individual providers and users upon access to specific genetic resources.[77] Benefits to be shared on the basis of MAT are not only research and development results, but also the commercial or other benefits derived from the utilization of the genetic resources provided.[78]

---

70   Oberthür and Rosendal, "Conclusions," op. cit., 244–245, where it is argued that the assumption that ABS will 'quasi-automatically' create strong incentives for biodiversity conservation may be unrealistic.

71   Morgera and Tsioumani, "Evolution of Benefit-Sharing," op. cit., 153.

72   Ibid., 151–159.

73   Addressed in CBD Article 15.

74   CBD Article 16.

75   CBD Article 19.

76   CBD Articles 20 and 21.

77   CBD Article 15(4) and (7).

78   CBD Article 15(6) reads: 'Each Contracting Party shall endeavor to develop and carry out scientific research based on genetic resources provided by other Contracting Parties with the full participation of, and where possible in, such Contracting Parties.'

Accordingly, the CBD calls upon Parties to legislate (or adopt other domestic measures) on ABS to develop a domestic system for requiring and granting PIC, coupled with the requirement to establish MAT, with a view to sharing benefits.[79] PIC may be embodied in a public act (an authorization/permit issued by the national competent authority), while the details of the ABS transaction will then be worked out in MAT.[80] The contract embodying MAT will set out any conditions for access and specific benefit-sharing obligations, in order to achieve the overarching benefit-sharing objective of the Convention in the context of specific ABS transactions.[81] There may be instances, however, in which PIC may be issued as a private-law act (possibly, part and parcel of MAT), for instance when the power to grant access to genetic resources is delegated to non-State actors (such as research centers). In addition, there may be also instances in which MAT may be incorporated into PIC, if, for example, the latter includes standard contractual clauses as part of the conditions for granting a permit.[82] It could also be the case that the establishment of MAT may precede the granting of PIC (i.e., national authorities may condition the granting of PIC to the successful conclusions of negotiations on MAT).[83]

The country providing genetic resources would normally be the 'country of origin', which is defined by the CBD as the country which possesses those

---

79   CBD Article 15(4–5) and (7).

80   Claudio Chiarolla, "The Role of Private International Law under the Nagoya Protocol," in Morgera, Buck and Tsioumani, *2010 Nagoya Protocol on Access and Benefit-Sharing in Perspective*, op. cit., 423, 428, fn. 13, who explains that consequently, even where MAT will involve a private party/user and a national authority/State actor, when the latter concludes MAT it will act in its capacity as a private law party to the contract. See also Morten W. Tvedt, "Beyond Nagoya: Towards a Legally Functional System of Access and Benefit-Sharing," in Oberthür and Rosendal, *Global Governance of Genetic Resources*, op. cit., 158, 172.

81   On the objective of the Nagoya Protocol, see commentary on Article 1 (where there is no reference to MAT). For a discussion on MAT, see this commentary on Articles 5, section 5, Article 6, section 7, and Article 18, as well as Conclusions to this commentary, section 3. See also CBD Article 15(7), second sentence. As noted in this commentary on Article 5, there may also be two separate sets of MATs: one on access and one on benefit-sharing to be established at a later stage when the value of the genetic resources is better understood (or there may be a re-opener clause in the MAT established at the time of access, calling for renegotiations of benefit-sharing obligations if at a later stage when the value of the genetic resources is better understood).

82   Tvedt, "Beyond Nagoya," op. cit., 172.

83   Tvedt and Young, *Beyond Access*, op. cit., 71; and Tvedt, "Beyond Nagoya," op. cit., 172.

genetic resources in 'in situ conditions.'[84] So a Party is considered 'country of origin' wherever a specific genetic resource exists in ecosystems[85] or natural habitats[86] within its territory. This may appear fairly straightforward. However, practical challenges may arise in specific ABS transactions in the case two or more countries share the same genetic resources. Particular difficulty may also arise in relation to 'domesticated or cultivated species' – a term which includes genetic resources for food and agriculture (agricultural biodiversity). In such cases, continuous exchanges of genetic resources over long periods of time and interactions between the organisms and the environment leading to adaptation of varieties result in a situation where determining a country of origin is impractical.[87] To address this situation, the CBD also defines as 'country providing genetic resources' the countries supplying genetic resources collected from in situ or ex situ sources that may not have originated from that country.[88] In this regard, the CBD further specifies that only provider countries that 'acquired the genetic resources in accordance with the Convention' (that is, in accordance with CBD requirements on PIC and MAT) have a right to receive a share in the benefits arising from their utilization.[89] On the other side of ABS transactions, there are 'user countries.' This term is not defined in the Convention, but has become a common expression used by CBD Parties and in ABS literature. Although it is generally understood that all countries can be both users and providers of genetic resources,[90] during the negotiations of the Protocol certain (developed) countries saw themselves as predominantly user

---

84   CBD Article 2, which also defines 'in situ conditions' as 'conditions where genetic resources exist within ecosystems and natural habitats, and, in the case of domesticated or cultivated species, in the surroundings where they have developed their distinctive properties.'

85   A dynamic complex of plant, animal and micro-organism communities and their non-living environment interacting as functional unit: CBD Article 2.

86   The place where an organism or population naturally occurs: CBD Article 2.

87   Claudio Chiarolla, Sélim Louafi and Marie Schloen, "An Analysis of the Relationship between the Nagoya Protocol and Instruments Related to Genetic Resources for Food and Agriculture and Farmers' Rights," in Morgera, Buck and Tsioumani, *2010 Nagoya Protocol on Access and Benefit-Sharing in Perspective*, op. cit., 83, 84.

88   CBD Article 2.

89   CBD Article 15(3). Tvedt and Young, *Beyond Access*, op. cit., 14. See this commentary on Article 15, section 3.1.

90   CBD Decision 7/19, "Access and benefit-sharing as related to genetic resources (Article 15)" (13 April 2004) UN Doc UNEP/CBD/COP/7/21, 16th preambular recital, which reads: 'Parties that are countries of origin of genetic resources may be both users and providers and…Parties that have acquired these genetic resources in accordance with the Convention on Biological Diversity may also be both users and providers.'

countries, because of their highly developed research sector and biotechnology industry and therefore high economic stakes in having access to genetic resources in other countries. The Like-Minded Mega-diverse Countries, on the other hand, together with other developing countries, saw themselves as predominantly provider countries. These terms remain relevant also in the context of specific ABS transactions, where a Party will act as provider country and another as a user country in the bilateral exchange envisaged under the CBD.

2   From the CBD to the Nagoya Protocol via the Bonn Guidelines

CBD Parties were given significant leeway in devising their domestic ABS frameworks. Nevertheless, few have translated the relevant CBD provisions into national ABS legislation.[91] In addition, most industrialized country Parties have been very hesitant to adopt measures supporting effective benefit-sharing by their researchers and companies towards provider countries.[92] As a reaction, conditions for access to genetic resources in some countries have become very restrictive.[93] At the same time, researchers and companies have repeatedly been exposed to allegations of 'biopiracy.' Such allegations cover a diversity of circumstances, ranging from the lack of steps to ensure PIC is granted or benefits are shared, to the violation of domestic ABS requirements and of contractual obligations under MAT,[94] the granting of erroneous patents on inventions not fulfilling patentability criteria or the granting of patents on

---

91   As of 2007, 39 countries had enacted legislation referring to ABS: CBD Secretariat, "Overview of recent developments at national and regional levels relating to access and benefit-sharing" (30 August 2007) UN Doc UNEP/CBD/WG-ABS/5/4. By 2013, 57 CBD Parties have adopted measures to implement ABS provisions in the Convention: "ABS measures database," CBD, accessed 30 November 2013, <www.cbd.int/abs/measures/>.

92   'Deficiencies in implementation of user country measures have equally or even more undermined effective governance of genetic resources:' Oberthür and Rosendal, "Conclusions," op. cit., 238. See also comments by Susette Biber-Klemm et al., "Governance Options for Ex Situ Collections in Academic Research," in Oberthür and Rosendal, *Global Governance of Genetic Resources*, op. cit., 213, 216.

93   The national ABS legislation of the Philippines has often been cited in this regard. See Aphrodite Smagadi, "National Measures on Access to Genetic Resources and Benefit Sharing – The Case of the Philippines", *Law Environment and Development Journal* 1 (2005): 50, at 68.

94   Chiarolla, "Role of Private International Law," op. cit., 427–8.

inventions developed on the basis of genetic resources accessed in violation of provider countries' sovereign rights.[95]

Difficulties in developing national ABS frameworks have been due to the complexity of the subject matter and limited international guidance. The CBD in fact provides a set of basic principles on ABS, but gives very little guidance on how to address non-ideal ABS situations. In a hypothetical scenario of an ABS arrangement, a European research team working for the food industry, wishes to conduct research on a wild African plant with high nutritional value to further advance the development of a functional food. In this ideal case, both the African (provider country) and the European country in question (user country) have national legislation in place clearly setting out, among others, conditions for access, including the authority to grant PIC, modalities for the negotiation of specific benefit-sharing arrangements through the establishment of MAT, and a framework that supports the reporting and tracking of ABS-related obligations. The European research team contacts the provider country's national authority in order to request a research permit (embodying PIC). Following negotiations, where both sides are equally aware of their rights and obligations, MAT for fair and equitable benefit-sharing are established, including for instance the participation of African researchers in the research team (non-monetary benefit-sharing) and a percentage of royalties in case of commercialization of a product based on the use of the plant provided (monetary benefit-sharing). The European team conducts its research, develops a highly successful functional food with immune system-boosting properties and acts in full compliance with MAT. Benefits flow back to the African country and are consistently used for the conservation and sustainable use of the plant in question, as well as to improve the livelihoods of local communities that have for many centuries used the said plant for its recovery properties and whose traditional knowledge provided useful leads to the research team.[96]

Very rarely, however, are real ABS cases that straightforward. In the example above, it could well be that none of the countries involved had national legislation in place; or that the provider country had not established the authority competent to grant PIC. Or that the users decided to proceed without requesting PIC or entering into MAT for benefit-sharing. Or that the access proceeded

---

95   Tomme Young, "An Analysis of Claims of Unauthorised Access and Misappropriation of Genetic Resources and Associated Traditional Knowledge," in *Covering ABS: Addressing the Need for Sectoral, Geographical, Legal, and International Integration in the ABS Regime: Papers and Studies of the ABS Project*, ed. Tomme Young (Gland: IUCN, 2009), 97.

96   For an introduction to the role of traditional knowledge in the ABS discourse, see section 3 below.

as required by the national legislation of the African country, but later, one member of the research team breached the MAT and continued doing research on the plant in another company without sharing benefits. To complicate matters further, we can picture a university researcher who requests PIC and enters into MAT for academic, non-commercial research on the African plant. He publishes the results of his research in a scientific journal without mentioning the country of origin of the samples, the limitations on the use, or the existence of a benefit-sharing agreement. Two years later, another scientist undertaking applied research in the food industry reads the article and acquires a sample of the African plant from a botanical garden in his country: the research on the plant sample leads to a highly successful (and maybe patented) product. Yet another complexity would arise if the researchers were only interested in the resin produced by a certain plant (a 'derivative')[97] rather than its genetic resources. A whole additional level of complication arises then if the plant in question could be found in situ only in indigenous territories in a provider country, and had been traditionally used by an indigenous group that enjoys a high degree of autonomy from the State. The situation could, once again, be complicated by the fact that the same genetic resource could be found in various indigenous territories located in different countries, and researchers' interest in these genetic resources has been sparked by the traditional knowledge of indigenous or local communities that have been customarily using the plant.

The first effort by the international community to provide more detailed guidance on ABS to support countries in addressing non-ideal ABS scenarios led to the development of the non-legally binding Bonn Guidelines[98] in April 2002. The Guidelines aim to guide governments in establishing legislative, administrative or policy measures on ABS. In particular, the Bonn Guidelines provide some guidance with regard to the types, timing and distribution of benefits, and mechanisms for benefit-sharing, in order to assist Parties and stakeholders in the development of MAT. Notably, the Bonn Guidelines provide a list of examples of *monetary and non-monetary* benefits,[99] which is

---

97 See this commentary on Article 2, section 2.2.1.

98 "Bonn Guidelines on Access to Genetic Resources and Fair and Equitable Sharing of the Benefits Arising out of their Utilization" in CBD Decision 6/24, "Access and benefit-sharing as related to genetic resources" (27 May 2002) UN Doc UNEP/CBD/COP/6/20, Annex (hereinafter, Bonn Guidelines).

99 See Bonn Guidelines, paragraphs 45–50, and Appendix II. See Lyle Glowka and Valérie Normand, "The Nagoya Protocol on Access and Benefit-Sharing: Innovations in International Environmental Law," in Morgera, Buck and Tsioumani, *2010 Nagoya Protocol on Access and Benefit-Sharing in Perspective*, op. cit., 21, 25.

reproduced almost *verbatim* in the Annex to the Nagoya Protocol. The Bonn Guidelines further acknowledge that specific benefit-sharing arrangements may vary depending upon the type of benefits, the specific conditions in the country and the stakeholders involved, and should thus be determined by the partners involved on a case-by-case basis.[100]

All CBD Parties were expected to adopt measures related to both the provider and the user side of ABS transactions, including provisions clarifying each country's sovereign rights over genetic resources, and the identification of access procedures and requirements; and addressing the responsibility of users under their jurisdiction who are utilizing genetic resources from other countries.[101] Nevertheless, only a limited number of countries developed domestic ABS legislation after adoption of the Bonn Guidelines.[102]

Only four months after the adoption of the Bonn Guidelines, in August 2002, heads of State and government attending the World Summit on Sustainable Development (WSSD) agreed to launch negotiations on an international regime on benefit-sharing.[103] The WSSD mandate triggered the negotiations that eventually led to the adoption of the Nagoya Protocol.

The Nagoya Protocol is the result of six years of intergovernmental negotiations,[104] which mostly occurred in the context of an Ad Hoc Open-Ended Working Group on ABS already established under the Convention, with input from the CBD Working Grup on Article 8(j) and Related Provisions.[105] The Working Group on ABS was assisted by expert, informal and regional consultations[106] and, in the final phases of the negotiations convened as an inter-

---

100   Bonn Guidelines, paragraph 49.

101   Ibid., 3.

102   See note 91 above.

103   "Plan of Implementation of the World Summit on Sustainable Development" (September 2002) UN Doc A/CONF.199/20, Resolution 2 (hereinafter, Johannsburg Plan of Implemenation), paragraph 44(o). For a discussion of the mandate, see commentary on Article 1, section 2.

104   For a more detailed discussion of the negotiating process, see Thomas Greiber et al., *An Explanatory Guide to the Nagoya Protocol on Access and Benefit-Sharing* (Gland: IUCN, 2012), 18–24; Gurdial Singh Nijar and Gai Pei Fern, *The Nagoya ABS Protocol: A Record of the Negotiations* (Kuala Lumpur: CEBLAW, 2012), 3–29; and Cariño et al., *Nagoya Protocol*, op. cit., 11–23. For an academic analysis of the negotiations, see Oberthür and Rosendal, *Global Governance of Genetic Resources*, op. cit., particularly chapters 3–7.

105   CBD Decision 7/19, Section D: 'International Regime on Access to Genetic Resources and Benefit-Sharing'.

106   "Relevant Documentation from the Negotiations of the Nagoya Protocol," CBD, accessed 30 November 2013, <www.cbd.int/abs/pre-protocol/documentation/default.shtml>.

regional negotiating group.[107] The negotiations also benefited from inputs by non-governmental actors. In particular, representatives of indigenous peoples and local communities had been recognized specific opportunities to contribute to the negotiations since March 2006.[108] Opportunities for multi-stakeholder participation were extended in the final phases of the negotiations: the interregional negotiating group comprised, in addition to government delegates, two representatives for indigenous and local communities, civil society, industry and public research, respectively.[109]

CBD Parties had set as a deadline for completing the negotiations 'the earliest possible time before' the tenth meeting of the CBD Conference of the Parties (COP) scheduled in October 2010,[110] but in autumn 2010 several key aspects of the Protocol remained outstanding. To increase political momentum CBD Parties treated as a package the adoption of the Protocol together with the adoption of the CBD Strategic Plan,[111] and specific funding commitments,

---

107   The Inter-governmental Group setting entailed a roundtable format, inspired by the 'Vienna setting' used during the biosafety negotiations. It included five representatives for each UN region, and two representatives for indigenous and local communities, civil society, industry and public research, respectively. In what was termed a 'Vienna plus' setting, spokespersons and representatives could change freely, and discussions were open to the attendance of all Working Group participants: CBD Working Group on ABS, "Report of the first part of the ninth meeting of the Ad Hoc Open-ended Working Group on Access and Benefit-sharing" (26 April 2010) UN Doc UNEP/CBD/WG-ABS/9/3, paragraphs 87–89.

108   CBD Decision 8/5 "Article 8(j) and related provisions", section C "International regime on access and benefit-sharing: collaboration with the Ad Hoc Working Group on Access and Benefit-sharing and participation of indigenous and local communities" (15 June 2006) UN Doc UNEP/CBD/COP/8/31, paragraph 7 invited chairpersons of negotiating meetings on the international ABS regime 'to facilitate the effective participation of representatives of indigenous and local communities and to consult them, as appropriate, on issues related to traditional knowledge, innovations and practices and associated genetic resources.'

109   See fn. 107 above.

110   CBD Decision 8/4 "Access and benefit-sharing" (15 June 2006) UNEP/CBD/COP/8/31, paragraph 8.

111   See G77/China proposal at the sixty-fifth session of the UN General Assembly, high-level meeting of the General Assembly as a contribution to the International Year of Biodiversity, 22 September 2010: "Secretary-General, at High-Level Meeting, Stresses Urgent Need to Reverse Alarming Rate of Biodiversity Loss," UN General Assembly (22 September 2010), accessed 30 November 2013, <www.un.org/News/Press/docs/2010/ga10992.doc.htm>; and "Press Conference on Biodiversity by Minister for Environment of Brazil," UN (22 September 2010), accessed 30 November 2013, <www.un.org/News/briefings/docs//2010/100922_Brazil.doc.htm>. In the last phases of the CBD COP 10, the

including a decision on the implementation of the Convention's Strategy for Resource Mobilization. Two days before the end of the meeting of the CBD COP 10, however, the most contentious issues in the ABS negotiations remained still unresolved. The Japanese environment minister, as president of the COP and thus with political responsibility for the overall success of the Conference, took the initiative to convene a closed meeting in conjunction with the COP ministerial segment, including (allegedly some) key negotiating groups.[112] As a result, the COP Presidency tabled a comprehensive compromise proposal on a take-it-or-leave-it basis, which was found to be sufficiently representative of all of the groups' priorities and was accompanied by substantive finance pledges for ABS by the Japanese government.[113] The Nagoya Protocol was thus adopted by consensus on the basis of the Japanese compromise text, as part of a political package that also included adoption of a global strategic plan for biodiversity policy until 2020 and of guidance on the implementation of the CBD global strategy for resource mobilization.[114]

Two implications of significance for any legal analysis of the Protocol should be drawn from the specific circumstances of its adoption. First, from a practical perspective, the Japanese COP Presidency's politically successful strategy did not leave time for the rigorous language and legal consistency checks that normally take place at the end of a treaty negotiation, thereby inevitably creating several interpretative questions. Second, from a principled perspective, CBD Parties did not have a possibility to negotiate and reach agreement on all

---

European Union proposed to also include the CBD budget in the package and, indeed, this is how these key outcomes of the COP were eventually adopted. See Earth Negotiations Bulletin (ENB), "Summary of the Tenth Conference of the Parties to the Convention on Biological Diversity: 18–29 October 2010," Vol. 9 No. 544, 1 November 2010, 25.

112   Ibid., 26. See also Gurdial Singh Nijar, *The Nagoya Protocol on ABS: An Analysis* (Kuala Lumpur: CEBLAW, 2011), 248–249 and fn. 9.

113   See ENB, "CBD COP 10 Highlights: Wednesday, 27 October 2010," Vol. 9 No. 542, (2010), 28 October 2010. See also the guidance circulated for the ministerial consultation [on file with authors]. The Japanese contribution for ABS has been included, together with funds from France, Norway, and Switzerland, in the Nagoya Implementation Fund, which is managed by the Global Environment Facility (GEF) and operated by the CBD Secretariat: "GEF Establishes the Nagoya Protocol Implementation Fund," CBD (3 June 2011), accessed 30 November 2013, <www.cbd.int/doc/press/2011/pr-2011-06-03-GEF-ImpFund-en. pdf>. For a discussion of this approach to conclude the negotiations, see Morgera and Tsioumani, "Yesterday, Today, and Tomorrow," op. cit., 12–13.

114   CBD Decision 10/2, "The Strategic Plan for Biodiversity 2011–2020 and the Aichi Biodiversity Targets" (20 January 2011) UN Doc UNEP/CBD/COP/10/27; and CBD Decision 10/3, "Strategy for resource mobilisation in support of the achievement of the Convention's three objectives" (20 January 2011) UN Doc UNEP/CBD/COP/10/27.

the details of the final text of the Protocol before adopting it as a whole by consensus. In that regard, it should be emphasized that normally adoption by consensus has a 'powerful law-making effect.'[115] As Boyle and Chinkin underscore, this way of securing widespread support for a legal text *per se* legitimizes and promotes consistent State practice even before the treaty enters into force.[116] The actual extent of law-making in the context of the adoption of the Protocol, however, may not be so clearly identified. Due to the unusual conclusion of its negotiations, some of its innovative provisions, for example Article 10 on a Global Multilateral Benefit-sharing Mechanism, were not actually negotiated by CBD Parties, but resulted from the Japanese compromise proposal. This fact possibly qualifies the law-making effect of the consensus, package-deal adoption of the Nagoya Protocol.[117] And in effect, some regional groups declared that the Protocol is 'far from perfect.'[118]

It should be finally noted here that upon adopting the Nagoya Protocol, CBD Parties asserted that the ABS provisions of the CBD and the Bonn Guidelines remain pillars of the 'international ABS regime.'[119] The CBD provisions will of course remain the only legally binding obligations for CBD Parties that do

---

115   Alan Boyle and Christine Chinkin, *The Making of International Law* (Oxford: Oxford University Press, 2007), 160.

116   That is, 'there is a marked tendency to legitimise implementation in practice of treaties adopted by consensus without waiting for widespread ratification or entry into force': ibid., 260.

117   We are grateful to Tomme Young for drawing our attention to this point.

118   During the closing plenary, a number of delegations including the African Group, the Central and Eastern European Group, Venezuela, and Bolivia made statements for the record to underscore their doubts about the new instrument's quality: CBD COP, "Report of the tenth meeting of the Conference of the Parties to the Convention on Biological Diversity" (20 January 2011) UN Doc UNEP/CBD/COP/10/27, paragraphs 98–102. Boyle and Chinkin caution that even consensus adoption will not be as significant as it may at first appear if accompanied by statements which 'seriously qualify what has been agreed,' or if consensus 'simply papers over an agreement to disagree': Boyle and Chinkin, *Making of International Law*, op. cit., 226.

119   CBD COP Decision 10/1, "Access to genetic resources and the fair and equitable sharing of benefits arising from their utilization" (20 January 2011) UN Doc UNEP/CBD/COP/10/27, 6th preambular paragraph, which reads: '*Recognizing* that the International Regime is constituted of the Convention on Biological Diversity, the Nagoya Protocol on Access to Genetic Resources and the Fair and Equitable Sharing of Benefits Arising from their Utilization to the Convention on Biological Diversity, as well as complementary instruments, including the International Treaty on Plant Genetic Resources for Food and Agriculture and the Bonn Guidelines on Access to Genetic Resources and Fair and Equitable Sharing of the Benefits Arising out of their Utilization.'

not become Parties to the Nagoya Protocol, and for those CBD Parties that become Parties to the Nagoya Protocol before the latter enters into force. As to the Bonn Guidelines, it can be argued that they play a complementary role vis-à-vis the Nagoya Protocol: while the latter sets the procedural framework for ABS, the Guidelines can continue to provide guidance to Parties in relation, for instance, to the substantive criteria for the establishment of MAT.[120] Further legal analysis, however, is warranted to fully understand the extent and implications of the relationship between the Convention provisions on ABS, the Bonn Guidelines and the Nagoya Protocol, which is beyond the scope of this commentary.[121]

Nonetheless, as opposed to its predecessors, the Nagoya Protocol provides for the first time legally binding rules on *compliance* in the context of ABS transactions, with a view to operationalizing the third objective of the CBD more effectively. Basically, the Protocol creates innovative international obligations that *link* the performance of provider and user countries. Establishing such a link entails a dynamic web of diverse legal relationships: administrative decisions on access are set out in domestic permits (PIC), linking to contractual benefit-sharing agreements (MAT) with private parties, which are backed by an enabling framework of national laws in provider and user countries, as well as by international cooperation at the bilateral and multilateral level. The effective implementation of the Nagoya Protocol will thus ultimately rely on a plurality of legal orders[122] in a particularly challenging – and in many respects unprecedented – way.

3   Traditional Knowledge and ABS

The Nagoya Protocol has spelt out, for the first time in legally binding provisions, the benefit-sharing obligation arising from the use of the traditional knowledge of indigenous and local communities in research and development.[123]

---

120   Ulrich Beyerlin and Thilo Marauhn, *International Environmental Law* (Oxford: Hart Publishing, 2011), 198. This is discussed this commentary on Article 13, section 3, and Article 18, section 2.

121   We are grateful to Tomme Young for drawing our attention to this point.

122   Elisa Morgera, "Bilateralism at the Service of Community Interests? Non-Judicial Enforcement of Global Public Goods in the Context of Global Environmental Law," *European Journal of International Law* 23 (2012): 743.

123   Nagoya Protocol Articles 5(5) and 7. For a discussion prior to the conclusions of the negotiations of the Protocol, see Gurdial Singh Nijar, "Incorporating Traditional Knowledge in an International Regime on Access to Genetic Resources and Benefit Sharing: Problems

In that regard, the Nagoya Protocol makes reference to a qualitatively different concept of benefit-sharing – namely, *intra*-State benefit-sharing as opposed to *inter*-State benefit-sharing discussed above. In other words, in the case of traditional knowledge, benefit-sharing makes reference to an internal, State-to-community contribution to sustainable development, social justice and equity.[124]

An intra-State notion of benefit-sharing was already present in the CBD, but the Convention only linked it to its first and second objectives (conservation and sustainable use), not to research and development in the context of ABS. CBD Article 8(j) in effect envisages the establishment of a relationship between the State and the local or indigenous community whose traditional knowledge is utilized for the conservation and sustainable use of biodiversity.[125] Traditional knowledge is not defined in there, although it can be understood as the knowledge, innovations and practices of indigenous and local communities embodying traditional lifestyles relevant for the conservation and sustainable use of biodiversity. And on the basis of CBD Article 10(c), traditional knowledge also refers to the customary use of biological resources in accordance with traditional cultural practices that are compatible with conservation or sustainable use requirements. The reference to 'traditional lifestyles' has been interpreted by some commentators as excluding the knowledge of groups that descended from indigenous and local communities but have 'assimilated into mainstream, non-traditional economy and society.'[126] A preferable reading, however, would rather be a more inclusive one, that is based on international human rights caselaw[127] and takes into account the

---

and Prospects," *European Journal of International Law* 21 (2010): 457. For a discussion following the conclusions of the negotiations of the Protocol, see Gurdial Singh Nijar, "Traditional Knowledge Systems, International Law and National Challenges: Marginalization or Emancipation?," *European Journal of International Law* 24 (2013): 1205.

124   Morgera and Tsioumani, "Evolution of Benefit-Sharing", op. cit., 150–151.

125   Ibid., 159–168.

126   See Glowka, Burhenne-Guilmin and Synge, *Guide to the Convention on Biological Diversity*, op. cit., 11; and Gregory F. Maggio, "Recognizing the Vital Role of Local Communities in International Legal Instruments for Conserving Biodiversity," UCLA *Journal of Environmental Law and Policy* 16 (1998): 179, 210.

127   Cf. Inter-American Court of Human Rights, *Case of the Saramaka People v. Suriname*, Preliminary Objections, Merits, Reparations, and Costs, Judgment, Case no. 12,338 (28 November 2007) (hereinafter, *Saramaka People v. Suriname* 2007); and African Commission on Human and Peoples' Rights, *Centre for Minority Rights Development (Kenya) and Minority Rights Group International on behalf of Endorois Welfare Council v.*

placement of the provision on traditional knowledge in the context of in situ conservation under the CBD. Accordingly, the essential elements for understanding traditional knowledge are the link between indigenous and local communities and the land and biological resources that they traditionally occupy or use[128] for livelihood purposes or for ensuring their distinctive cultural practices, and the existence of customary rules about the preservation and protection of such traditional knowledge.

Indeed, recent research has shown that biological and cultural diversity are deeply linked: in 35 regional biodiversity hotspots, which contain more than half of the world's vascular plants and 43 percent of terrestrial vertebrate species, are found 3,202 languages, nearly half of all languages spoken on Earth. Although the researchers cannot conclude why areas of endangered species concentration and endangered languages coexist, a possible explanation is that indigenous cultures, supported by their languages, create the conditions to maintain species and keep the ecosystems working.[129] At the same time, the asymmetries already highlighted in the context of genetic resources are exacerbated in the case of traditional knowledge. Historically, colonization, mandatory assimilation, relocation policies, and globalization forces have resulted in the marginalization of indigenous peoples and local communities and the erosion of their cultures, governance and traditional knowledge systems.[130] Furthermore, (ab)use of the IPR system has resulted in a series of famous biopiracy cases involving misappropriation of traditional knowledge.[131]

Kenya, Communication no. 276/2003 (25 November 2009) (hereinafter, *Endorois Welfare Council v. Kenya*). Cf. also International Law Association, *The Hague Conference Report, Rights of Indigenous Peoples* (International Law Association, 2010), accessed 30 November 2013, <www.ila-hq.org/en/committees/index.cfm/cid/1024>, 7–8.

128 The latter term aims to cover nomadic communities, see for example *Endorois Welfare Council v. Kenya*, 206–210, where the African Commission found that the Endorois nomadic pastoralists were granted the recognition of their rights of ownership and restitution of their ancestral land, as well as unrestricted access to sites they traditionally 'used' for religious and cultural rites and for grazing their cattle.

129 See Larry J. Gorenflo et al., "Co-Occurrence of Linguistic and Biological Diversity in Biodiversity Hotspots and High Biodiversity Wilderness Areas," *Proceedings of the National Academy of Sciences* 19 (2012): 8032.

130 For a comprehensive account of the threats and challenges that indigenous peoples face and the response of the international community, see UN Permanent Forum on Indigenous Issues (UNPFII), *State of the World's Indigenous Peoples* (New York: United Nations, 2009), accessed 6 March 2014, <www.un.org/esa/socdev/unpfii/documents/SOWIP_web.pdf>.

131 Controversial patent cases involving traditional knowledge and genetic resources include the cases of turmeric, neem, ayahuasca and hoodia. Among the rich bibliography, see UK

CBD Article 8(j) requires Parties to 'respect, preserve and maintain' traditional knowledge, promote its wider application with the approval and involvement of the holders of such knowledge, and 'encourage the equitable sharing of the benefits arising from its utilization of such knowledge, innovations and practices.'[132] CBD Article 8(j) further calls for benefit-sharing related to traditional knowledge as a recognition of and reward for the contribution of indigenous and local communities to the conservation of biodiversity[133] and – based on a combined reading with CBD Article 10(c)[134] – to the sustainable use of biodiversity components. This is in consideration of the fact that traditional knowledge contributing to the conservation of biodiversity derives from the customary sustainable use of biodiversity components.[135] Numerous decisions adopted by the CBD COP have detailed how benefit-sharing from traditional knowledge related to conservation and sustainable use should be operationalized, including through the use of environmental and sociocultural impact assessments, the integration of traditional knowledge and community concerns in management plans and the legal recognition and active support of community-based management arrangements.[136] In addition, CBD

Commission on Intellectual Property Rights, op. cit., 73. The discussion on the tensions between IPRs and traditional knowledge is very complex, and basically rests on the fact that traditional knowledge does not satisfy easily the general requirements of new and innovative creation for patentability and copyright, and its protection cannot be limited to a specific time period, as is the case for IPRs: see e.g. Cullet, "Environmental Justice in the Use, Knowledge and Exploitation of Genetic Resources," op. cit.

132   The CBD preamble only stresses the 'desirability' of sharing equitably benefits arising from the use of traditional knowledge relevant to the conservation of biodiversity and the sustainable use of its components: CBD 12th preambular recital.

133   Doris Schroeder, "Justice and Benefit Sharing," in Wynberg, Schroeder and Chennells, *Indigenous Peoples, Consent and Benefit Sharing*, op. cit., 11 where benefit-sharing is considered a reward for the custodians of biodiversity.

134   CBD Article 10 reads as follows: 'Each Contracting Party shall, as far as possible and as appropriate: [...](c) Protect and encourage customary use of biological resources in accordance with traditional cultural practices that are compatible with conservation or sustainable use requirements.'

135   See Glowka, Burhenne-Guilmin and Synge, *Guide to the Convention on Biological Diversity*, op. cit., 60.

136   Other mechanisms include the setting-up of benefit-sharing mechanisms when revenue generated through conservation and sustainable use activities is accrued by the State or outside investors, the provision of livelihood-based mitigation and compensatory measures, the use of other incentives such as payments for ecosystem services, as well as the re-investment of benefits in the protection of traditional knowledge and traditional sustainable practices.

COP decisions have indicated additional/alternative functions of benefit-sharing as a broader incentive to ensure the full and effective participation of indigenous and local communities in decision-making and adaptive management of biodiversity, and as compensation[137] for the costs and negative impacts of biodiversity conservation or sustainable management activities on indigenous and local communities.[138]

Notwithstanding the fact that the CBD did not expressly link the concepts of ABS and traditional knowledge,[139] Article 8(j) has been significantly discussed in the context of ABS negotiations,[140] on the basis of a combined reading of CBD Articles 15 and 8(j). This interpretation beyond the letter of the Convention may be explained by the fact that on many occasions, genetic resources attract the interest of bioprospectors and gain value because of the traditional knowledge associated with them.[141] In other words, it is traditional knowledge that sparks the utilization process or provides the lead to the potentially useful properties of a genetic resource.[142] For instance in the case of the pharmaceutical sector, traditional knowledge was 'found to increase the success ratio of bioprospecting by 400 percent.'[143] It can thus be understood

---

137   Benefit-sharing may also be linked to food security. See Bram De Jonge and Michiel Korthals, "Vicissitudes of Benefit Sharing of Crop Genetic Resources: Downstream and Upstream," *Developing World Bioethics* 6 (2006): 144.

138   See primary legal materials cited in Morgera and Tsioumani, "Evolution of Benefit-Sharing," op. cit., 159–168.

139   Ibid., 155–156. See also Geoff Burton, "Implementation of the Nagoya Protocol in JUSCANZ Countries: The Unlikely Lot," in Morgera, Buck and Tsioumani, *2010 Nagoya Protocol on Access and Benefit-Sharing in Perspective*, op. cit., 295, 316

140   Since the launch of the negotiations for an international ABS regime, the CBD Article 8(j) Working Group has been addressing ABS as a permanent issue on its agenda. E.g., "Report of the fifth meeting of the Ad Hoc Open-ended Working Group on Article 8(j) and related provisions of the Convention on Biological Diversity" (13 November 2007) UN Doc UNEP/CBD/COP/9/7; and "Report of the sixth meeting of the Ad Hoc Open-ended Inter-Sessional Working Group on Article 8(j) and related provisions of the Convention on Biological Diversity" (21 November 2009) UN Doc UNEP/CBD/COP/10/2, Annex II.

141   The evolving interpretation of the CBD in relation to traditional knowledge is discussed in Morgera and Tsioumani, "Evolution of Benefit-Sharing," op. cit.; and Morgera and Tsioumani, "Yesterday, Today, and Tomorrow," op. cit.

142   See CBD Working Group on Article 8(j), "Report of the sixth meeting," UNEP/CBD/COP/10/2, 36.

143   Oberthür and Rosendal, "Global Governance of Genetic Resources: Background and Analytical Framework," op. cit., 3. Laird and Wynberg, "Bioscience at a Crossroads", op. cit., at 1, note that 'The cosmetic, botanicals, and food and beverage industries use traditional

that in these cases, genetic resources and traditional knowledge are seen as inseparable.[144]

The Bonn Guidelines contributed to cement the link between traditional knowledge and ABS by noting that benefits should be shared fairly and equitably with all those, including indigenous and local communities, who have been identified as having contributed to the management of the resource used in a scientific and/or commercial process.[145] The express reference to indigenous and local communities as potential beneficiaries in the ABS process can be arguably read in conjunction with references, in the objectives of the Guidelines to poverty alleviation and realization of food security, health and cultural integrity.[146]

The Nagoya Protocol definitely crystallizes this understanding and breaks new ground by establishing a clear international obligation to share benefits arising from the utilization of 'traditional knowledge associated with genetic resources'.[147] As opposed to genetic resources that are subject to national sovereignty,[148] traditional knowledge belongs to the community/ies:

---

knowledge associated with genetic resources in product development (as a guide towards finding useful species or to help determine safety and efficacy) and in marketing, but there appears to be a trend towards decreased use of traditional knowledge for higher pharmaceuticals and biotech industries increasingly focused on microorganisms.'

144 Nagoya Protocol 22nd preambular recital. See also this commentary on Article 8, Section 4.

145 Bonn Guidelines, paragraph 48.

146 Bonn Guidelines, paragraph 11.

147 The Bonn Guidelines use two expressions in relation to traditional knowledge: 'associated traditional knowledge' (paragraphs 9 and 37) and 'traditional knowledge associated with genetic resources' (paragraph 31). Both terms were considered during the negotiations of the Protocol, see: CBD Working Group on ABS, "Report of the meeting of the Group of Technical and Legal Experts on Traditional Knowledge Associated with Genetic Resources in the Context of the International Regime on Access and Benefit-sharing" (15 July 2009) UN Doc UNEP/CBD/WG-ABS/8/2; and "Revised draft Protocol on Access to Genetic Resources and the Fair and Equitable Sharing of Benefits Arising from their Utilization to the Convention on Biological Diversity" (hereinafter, Cali Draft) in CBD Working Group on ABS, "Report of the first part of the ninth meeting" UNEP/CBD/WG-ABS/9/3, Annex I, draft articles 3(1) and 14(1). Negotiators eventually decided to use consistently the latter out of concern that the former could have led to broader interpretations. It should be noted that the negotiations under WIPO are also considering both expressions, as discussed below in this commentary on Article 4, section 3.1.

148 Leaving aside for the moment the question of 'genetic resources held by indigenous and local communities': see this commentary on Article 5, section 3, and on Article 6, section 4.

it is created in a cultural context, is local in nature and evolves continually.[149] Against this background, the regulation of traditional knowledge associated with genetic resources under the Protocol brings in a whole new dimension to the ABS context – that is, an internal dimension within the provider State. Questions related to who negotiates, receives or (re)distributes benefits on a sub-national level will have to be clarified between the provider State and the communities,[150] taking into account relevant international law.[151] As the vast majority of CBD Parties have not legislated on traditional knowledge associated with genetic resources, the relevant provisions of the Protocol will be particularly challenging to implement.[152]

It should be stressed that traditional knowledge in the Protocol is only that 'associated with genetic resources' – so a narrow, undefined notion that leaves several other aspects of traditional knowledge outside of the scope of the Protocol[153] (such as knowledge related to traditional healthcare and building techniques, for instance). The notion of traditional knowledge under the Protocol is therefore narrower than that under the Convention on Biological Diversity, where traditional knowledge refers more broadly to biological diversity at the ecosystem, species and genetic levels. The notion of traditional knowledge is even broader in the context of ongoing negotiations under WIPO on intellectual property and genetic resources, traditional knowledge and traditional cultural expressions,[154] where traditional knowledge is generally seen as the

---

149   Gurdial Singh Nijar, "An Asian Developing Country's View on the Challenges of the Nagoya Protocol," in Morgera, Buck and Tsioumani, *2010 Nagoya Protocol on Access and Benefit-Sharing in Perspective*, op. cit., 247, 258; CBD Working Group on ABS, "Report of the expert meeting on Traditional Knowledge" UNEP/CBD/WG-ABS/8/2, paragraph 33; and Jack K. Githae, "Potential of TK for Conventional Therapy – Prospects and Limits," in Kamau and Winter, *Genetic Resources, Traditional Knowledge and the Law*, op. cit., 77, 77–82.

150   We are grateful to Tomme Young for highlighting this point.

151   See discussion in section 4 below.

152   Elisa Morgera, Matthias Buck and Elsa Tsioumani, "Conclusions," in Morgera, Buck and Tsioumani, *2010 Nagoya Protocol on Access and Benefit-Sharing in Perspective*, op. cit., 507.

153   We are grateful to Tomme Young for highlighting this point.

154   The WIPO Intergovernmental Committee on Intellectual Property and Genetic Resources, Traditional Knowledge and Folklore: see fn. 50 above and commentary on Article 4, section 3.1.

accumulated knowledge which at the same time provides indigenous peoples and local communities with a sense of identity. It is evolving and dynamic, holistic in its conception and is a strong component of the cultural heritage of indigenous peoples and their communities.[155]

That being said, the WIPO negotiations are also attempting to define 'traditional knowledge associated with genetic resources' or 'associated traditional knowledge', as the substantive knowledge of the properties and uses of genetic resources and their derivatives held by indigenous peoples and local communities.[156] As will be discussed below, it remains to be seen whether the WIPO negotiations will conclude with an understanding of traditional knowledge associated with genetic resources that is mutually supportive with that of the Protocol.[157]

4   Indigenous Peoples and Local Communities as Beneficiaries of the CBD and the Nagoya Protocol

The Nagoya Protocol not only makes indigenous and local communities beneficiaries when traditional knowledge is concerned, but also when genetic resources are held by these communities.[158] Complex questions thus arise related to national sovereignty over genetic resources and the control that

---

155   "TK Documentation Toolkit. A Consultation Draft," WIPO (2012), accessed 30 November 2013, <www.wipo.int/export/sites/www/tk/en/resources/pdf/tk_toolkit_draft.pdf>, 21. Specific elements that are being considered for a definition of traditional knowledge in the textual negotiations under WIPO include: knowledge that is the 'unique product' or 'distinctively associated with' indigenous peoples and local communities; knowledge that is developed within a traditional context and/or is passed on from generation to generation; knowledge that is part of the collective, ancestral, territorial, cultural, intellectual and material heritage of indigenous peoples and local communities; and that is collectively generated, shared and preserved and is integrally linked with the cultural identities of indigenous peoples and local communities: WIPO General Assembly, "Matters concerning the Intergovernmental Committee on Intellectual Property and Genetic Resources, Traditional Knowledge and Folklore (IGC)" (12 August 2011) WIPO Doc WO/GA/40/7.

156   WIPO General Assembly, "Matters concerning the IGC," WO/GA/40/7.

157   "Draft Articles on the Protection of Traditional Knowledge" in WO/GA/40/7, Annex B, draft article 10: 'consistency with general legal framework.'

158   Nagoya Protocol Articles 5(2) and 6(2). See commentary on Article 5, section 3, Article 6, section 4 and Article 7.

indigenous peoples[159] and local communities exercise over these resources located in their territories, which in their understanding are inextricably linked with their traditional knowledge.[160]

While the Protocol does not provide a clear answer to these questions, it still represents the culmination of a normative process under the CBD that has gradually explored the human rights-based dimensions[161] of the international concern over biodiversity conservation.[162] The text of the CBD carefully avoids the use of the term 'right' or cross-references to human rights instruments.[163] Nevertheless, the CBD has progressively emerged as the preferred international environmental forum for indigenous peoples and local communities to express their interests and demands for the protection of their nature-related interests.[164]

These developments, however, have not occurred without continued opposition from certain CBD Parties, and the relevant provisions of the Nagoya Protocol are, as a result, heavily qualified. One notable instance is the use of the expression 'indigenous and local communities,' which is also used under the CBD, rather than the term 'indigenous peoples,' which refers to the subjects specifically protected by international human rights instruments.[165] In this

---

159   See Federico Lenzerini, "Sovereignty Revisited: International Law and Parallel Sovereignty of Indigenous Peoples," *Texas International Law Journal* 42 (2006): 155, where the author argues that the scope of States' sovereignty is subject to the influence of other competing values, which represent the foundations for asserting the existence of a 'degree' of indigenous sovereignty 'parallel' to that held by the State. Ibid., 156 and 186–187. Also see UNPFII, "Contribution to the International Expert Meeting on the Convention on Biological Diversity's International Regime on Access and Benefit-sharing and Indigenous Peoples' Human Rights" (17–19 January 2007) UN Doc PFII/2007/ws.4/7, accessed 4 February 2014, <www.un.org/esa/socdev/unpfii/documents/workshop_CBDABS_mahren_en.doc>.

160   Nagoya Protocol 22nd preambular recital.

161   Notably, the CBD programmes of work on Article 8(j) in CBD Decision 5/16, "Article 8(j) and related provisions" (22 June 2000) UN Doc UNEP/CBD/COP/5/23, Annex; on protected areas, in CBD Decision 7/28, "Protected areas" (13 April 2004) UN Doc UNEP/CBD/COP/7/21, Annex; and on forest biodiversity, in CBD Decision 6/22, "Forest biological diversity" (27 May 2002) UN Doc UNEP/CBD/COP/6/20.

162   Elisa Morgera, "Against All Odds: The Contribution of the Convention on Biological Diversity to International Human Rights Law," in *Unity and Diversity of International Law: Essays in Honour of Professor Pierre-Marie Dupuy*, ed. Dennis Alland et al. (Leiden: Martinus Nijhoff, 2014), 983.

163   Birnie, Boyle and Redgwell, *International Law and the Environment*, op. cit., 626–28.

164   Meyer, "International Environmental Law and Human Rights," op. cit., 41–42; Benjamin J. Richardson, "Indigenous Peoples, International Law and Sustainability," *Review of European Community and International Environmental Law* 10 (2001): 1, 8.

165   Meyer, "International Environmental Law and Human Rights," op. cit., 38.

respect, it should be noted that since 2010 the United Nations Permanent Forum on Indigenous Issues (UNPFII) has been calling on CBD Parties to adopt the more human rights-cognizant terminology 'indigenous peoples and local communities.'[166] This would have been in line with the terminology already adopted by the UN General Assembly,[167] the UN Forum on Forests,[168] and under the international climate change regime.[169] The question was discussed most recently in 2012, but CBD Parties could not yet find consensus.[170]

For the purposes of interpreting the several provisions of the Protocol that concern 'indigenous and local communities', the lack of a definition of both terms and their combined use raise questions as to the actual identification of the beneficiaries (and, arguably, of right-holders)[171] under the Protocol. While there is no agreed definition of indigenous peoples in international law, the distinctive nature of their rights has been recognized.[172] And the lack of an

---

166   UNPFII, "Report on the ninth session" (19–30 April 2010) UN Doc E/2010/43–E/C.19/2010/15; and "Report on the tenth session" (16–27 May 2011) UN Doc E/2011/43–E/C.19/2011/14, paragraphs 26–27.

167   UN General Assembly, "Agriculture development and food security" (24 March 2011) UN Doc A/RES/65/178.

168   Economic and Social Council (ECOSOC) Resolution 2006/49, "Outcome of the sixth session of the United Nations Forum on Forests" (28 July 2006) UN Doc E/2006/INF/2/Add.1, paragraph 3.

169   In the context of safeguards for REDD+ (Reducing emissions from deforestation and forest degradation and the role of conservation, sustainable management of forests and enhancement of forest carbon stocks), see UN Framework Convention on Climate Change (New York, 9 May 1992, in force 21 March 1994) 1771 UNTS 107 (hereinafter, UNFCCC) Decision 1/CP.16, "Outcome of the Work of the Ad Hoc Working Group on Long-Term Cooperative Action under the Convention" (15 March 2011) UN Doc FCCC/CP/2010/7/Add.1, Appendix I.

170   CBD Parties postponed the issue for consideration until October 2014, following consideration of 'all its implications for the Convention on Biological Diversity and its Parties': CBD Decision 11/14, "Article 8(j) and related provisions" (5 December 2012) UN Doc UNEP/CBD/COP/11/35, Annex I, paragraph 2; and CBD Article 8(j) Working Group, "Recommendations from the United Nations Permanent Forum on Indigenous Issues" in "Report of the eighth meeting of the Ad Hoc Open-Ended Inter-Sessional Working Group on Article 8(j) and Related Provisions of the Convention on Biological Diversity" (11 November 2013) UN Doc UNEP/CBD/COP/12/5, Annex, section 8/6.

171   Annalisa Savaresi, "The International Human Rights Law Implications of the Nagoya Protocol," in Morgera, Buck and Tsioumani, *2010 Nagoya Protocol on Access and Benefit-Sharing in Perspective*, op. cit., 53, 73–79.

172   See Human Rights Council, "Promotion and protection of all human rights, civil, political, economic, social and cultural rights, including the right to development. Report of the Special Rapporteur on the situation of human rights and fundamental freedoms of indigenous people, S. James Anaya" (5 August 2008) UN Doc A/HRC/9/9, paragraph 40,

international definition also corresponds to the right of indigenous peoples to self-identify in light of their broader right to self-determination.[173] On the other hand, an international definition could act as a 'limit to States' discretion' in identifying (and thereby possibly excluding certain groups from) relevant right holders. That is, States could enact a restrictive definition that would result in excluding certain groups from relevant international protection as implemented domestically.[174] Relevant sections of this commentary will aim to draw the implications of the interpretation of the Nagoya Protocol in the light of the international law on human rights,[175] as required by general international law.[176]

which reads: 'The Declaration does not affirm or create special rights separate from the fundamental human rights that are deemed of universal application, but rather elaborates upon these fundamental rights in the specific cultural, historical, social and economic circumstances of indigenous peoples. These include the basic norms of equality and non-discrimination, as well as other generally applicable human rights in areas such as culture, health or property, which are recognized in other international instruments and are universally applicable.'

173   See UN Commission on Human Rights, "Discrimination against indigenous peoples. Report of the Working Group on Indigenous Populations on its fourteenth session" (16 August 1996) UN Doc E/CN.4/Sub.2/1996/21, paragraphs 28–30.

174   International Law Association, *The Hague Conference Report*, op. cit., 6.

175   The rights of indigenous peoples have been considered 'essential principles of international law': ICJ, *Case Concerning East Timor (Portugal v. Australia)*, Judgment (30 June 2005), (hereinafter, *Case Concerning East Timor*), paragraph 29. See more generally on indigenous peoples' rights: Elvira Pulitano, ed, *Indigenous Rights in the Age of the UN Declaration* (Cambridge: Cambridge University Press, 2012); James S. Anaya, *Indigenous Peoples in International Law* (Oxford: Oxford University Press, 2004); and Benjamin J. Richardson, Shin Imai and Kent McNeil, eds, *Indigenous Peoples and the Law: Comparative and Critical Perspectives* (Oxford: Hart Publishing, 2009).

176   Namely, the general principle of *pacta sunt servanda* would require specific Parties to the Protocol to read the Protocol provisions with human rights implications in light of their specific obligations under applicable human rights treaties. Vienna Convention on the Law of Treaties (Vienna, 23 May 1969, in force 27 January 1980) 115 UNTS 331 (VCLT), Article 31(3)(c). Mark E. Villiger, "1969 Vienna Convention on the Law of Treaties: Forty Years After," *Recueil des Cours* 344 (2009): 1, 122–124. Note that the 'case law of the International Court of Justice suggests that where possible it prefers an integrated conception of international law to a fragmented one:' Boyle and Chinkin, *Making of International Law*, op. cit., 210–211.

4.1   *Internationally Recognized Human Rights of Indigenous Peoples*

With regards to the human rights of indigenous peoples, a legally binding treaty (the International Labour Organization (ILO) Convention No. 169)[177] and the UN Declaration on the Rights of Indigenous Peoples (UNDRIP)[178] provide an obvious frame of reference. Perhaps due to the limited membership of the ILO Convention,[179] however, the Nagoya Protocol only refers explicitly (in its preamble) to UNDRIP.[180] In that regard, it should be noted that while formally UNDRIP is a non-legally binding instrument, several arguments can be put forward with regard to its actual legal force. It has been contended that the Declaration 'reflects an important level of consensus at the global level about the content of indigenous peoples' rights, [which] informs the general obligation that States have under the UN Charter to respect and promote human rights.'[181] It has also been underscored that some rights recognized in the Declaration, such as non-discrimination,[182] cultural integrity and property 'constitute, or are becoming, part of customary international law or are general principles of international law.'[183] Furthermore, in as far as the Declaration

---

177   International Labour Organisation Convention 169 Concerning Indigenous and Tribal Peoples in Independent Countries (Geneva, 27 June 1989, in force 5 September 1991) ILO/C169 (hereinafter, ILO Convention No. 169).

178   UN General Assembly, "United Nations Declaration on the Rights of Indigenous Peoples" (13 September 2007) UN Doc A/RES/61/295 (UNDRIP).

179   Note that the ILO Convention No. 169 counts only 22 Parties, namely: Argentina, Bolivia, Brazil, Central African Republic, Chile, Colombia, Costa Rica, Denmark, Dominica, Ecuador, Fiji, Guatemala, Honduras, Mexico, Nepal, the Netherlands, Nicaragua, Norway, Paraguay, Peru, Spain, and Venezuela: "Ratifications of C/169," ILO, accessed 30 November 2013, <www.ilo.org/dyn/normlex/en/f?p=NORMLEXPUB:11300:0::NO:1130 0:P11300_INSTRUMENT_ID:312314:NO>.

180   Nagoya Protocol 26th preambular recital.

181   UN General Assembly, "Report of the Special Rapporteur on the rights of indigenous peoples" (14 August 2013) UN Doc A/68/317, paragraph 60.

182   Non-discrimination is seen as a general principle of international law by the African Commission on Human Rights (*Endorois Welfare Council v. Kenya*, 196) and the ICJ (*Case Concerning East Timor*, 29), albeit the Court used the expression 'essential principle'); as customary international law by International Law Association, *The Hague Conference Report*, op. cit., 45 and is even seen as a *jus cogens* norm. See Alessandro Fodella, "Indigenous Peoples, the Environment and International Jurisprudence," in *International Courts and the Development of International Law – Essays in Honour of Tullio Treves*, ed. Nerina Boschiero et al. (The Hague: Asser Press, 2013), 349.

183   UN General Assembly, "Report of the Special Rapporteur on the rights of indigenous peoples" A/68/317, paragraph 64.

offers an interpretation of standards found in other, legally binding human rights treaties, it can be considered binding to the extent to which the States party to such treaties have agreed to such interpretation.[184] Ultimately, it is a question of good faith for the States that have adhered to UNDRIP[185] to live up to their commitments and the expectations they created, particularly as the Declaration is seen as incorporating 'norms that indigenous peoples themselves have advanced.'[186]

Beyond the significance of UNDRIP, several general, well-established international human rights have been recognized as specifically relevant for indigenous peoples, such as the right to non-discrimination, to the protection of their culture,[187] and to freely dispose of their natural resources.[188] Those supporting the existence of international customary law on the overarching right to self-determination[189] (in its internal dimension – that is, guaranteeing a certain degree of autonomy to the indigenous peoples concerned within States'

---

184   Ibid. On UNDRIP, see generally: Mauro Barelli, "The Role of Soft Law in the International Legal System: The Case of the United Nations Declaration on the Rights of Indigenous Peoples," *International and Comparative Law Quarterly* 58 (2009): 957; Siegfried Wiessner, "Indigenous Sovereignty: A Reassessment in Light of the UN Declaration on the Rights of Indigenous Peoples," *Vanderbilt Journal of Transnational Law* 41 (2008): 1141; and Siegfried Wiessner, "The Cultural Rights of Indigenous Peoples: Achievements and Continuing Challenges," *European Journal of International Law* 22 (2011): 121.

185   UNDRIP was adopted by a majority of 143 states in favour, 4 votes against (Australia, Canada, New Zealand and the United States) and 11 abstentions (Azerbaijan, Bangladesh, Bhutan, Burundi, Colombia, Georgia, Kenya, Nigeria, Russian Federation, Samoa and Ukraine). Australia, Canada, New Zealand and the United States have later endorsed the Declaration and expressed their own understanding on certain aspects of the text: "Indigenous Rights Declaration Endorsed by States," UN Office of the High Commissioner for Human Rights, accessed 30 November 2013, <www.ohchr.org/EN/NewsEvents/Pages/Indigenousrightsdeclarationendorsed.aspx>.

186   UN General Assembly, "Report of the Special Rapporteur on the rights of indigenous peoples" A/68/317, paragraph 66. See also Human Rights Council, "Report of the Special Rapporteur on the rights of indigenous peoples" A/HRC/9/9, paragraph 41.

187   International Covenant on Civil and Political Rights (New York, 16 December 1966, in force 23 March 1976), 999 UNTS 171 ('ICCPR'), Article 27.

188   ICCPR and International Covenant on Economic, Social and Cultural Rights (New York, 16 December 1966, in force 3 January 1976), 993 UNTS 3, ('ICESCR') common Article 1(2). See also ICESCR Article 25; and ICCPR Article 47.

189   Anaya, Indigenous Peoples in International Law, op. cit., 8–9. On continuous difficulties in fully understanding the right to self-determination of indigenous peoples, Malgosia Fitzmaurie, "The Question of Indigenous Peoples' Rights: a Time for Reappraisal?" in *Statehood and Self-Determination: Reconciling Tradition and Modernity in International Law*, ed. Duncan French (Cambridge: Cambridge University Press, 2013), 349.

constitutional structures)[190] argue in favor of an international obligation for every State to take into account the interests of indigenous peoples in maintaining and managing their distinct culture and unique relationship with their land and biological resources also in the context of ABS,[191] based on the effective participation[192] of these peoples in relevant decisions and on benefit-sharing.[193] For those contesting the existence of customary international law on human rights, instead, the argument put forward is rather that different Parties to the Nagoya Protocol are to interpret and apply the Protocol in the light of their respective international treaty-based human rights obligations, depending on which key international treaties relevant for indigenous peoples they are party to.[194] Based on either view, human rights are to work as a benchmark against which to measure the legitimacy of measures relating to the application of modern science on traditional knowledge, and as a tool for balancing the freedom of scientific research against the rights to non-discrimination and to the sharing of the benefits of scientific advancements.[195] The consideration that "benefit-sharing cannot be 'decontextualized' from the [human] rights

---

190   James Summers, "The Internal and External Aspects of Self-determination Reconsidered" in French, *Statehood and Self-Determination*, op. cit., 229.

191   Francesco Francioni, *Genetic Resources, Biotechnology and Human Rights: The International Legal Framework*, Working Paper (Florence: European University Institute, 2006), accessed 30 November 2013, <http://cadmus.eui.eu/handle/1814/6070> 1.

192   See generally Human Rights Council, "Report of the Special Rapporteur on the rights of indigenous peoples, James Anaya. Extractive industries and indigenous peoples" (1 July 2013) UN Doc A/HRC/24/41, paragraphs 19–25. Note that regardless of whether States have ratified specific international conventions, 'there is currently a clearly recognized right to consultation' based on developments within the Inter-American system on the property rights of indigenous peoples, other international instruments, and case-law of the highest domestic courts in the Americas.' See Inter-American Court of Human Rights, *Case of the Kichwa Indigenous People of Sarayaku v. Ecuador*, Merits and Reparations, Judgment, Case No. 12,465 (IACtHR, 27 June 2012) (hereinafter, *Sarayaku v. Ecuador*), paragraph 165.

193   Francioni, *Genetic Resources, Biotechnology and Human Rights*, op. cit., 20.

194   Savaresi, "International Human Rights Law Implications," op. cit., 58; Hugh Thirlway, "The Sources of International Law," in *International Law*, ed. Malcolm D. Evans, 3rd ed. (Oxford: Oxford University Press, 2010), 95, 104; International Law Association, *The Hague Conference Report*, op. cit., 43–52. In that regard, note that while the CBD has 193 Parties, the ICCPR has 167 and the ICESCR 161. Also note that there is no regional human rights instrument in Asia, although see: "ASEAN Human Rights Declaration," Association of Southeast Asian Nations (2012), accessed 30 November 2013, <www.asean.org/news/asean-statement-communiques/item/asean-human-rights-declaration>.

195   Ibid., 2.

that form its basis"[196] thus appears to apply to all provisions of the Nagoya Protocol that may concern indigenous peoples.

4.2   *Internationally Recognized Rights of Local Communities*

A related question that emerges in the context of the CBD and the Nagoya Protocol is that of the definition of local communities, and their conceptual and normative differentiation from indigenous peoples. Although CBD Parties have engaged in a discussion of the specific characteristics of local communities,[197] the exercise did not lead to a clear understanding of the distinction. Indeed many of the key characteristics of local communities are commonly attributed also to indigenous peoples: self-identification; lifestyles linked to traditions associated with natural cycles; occupation of a definable territory; and customary and/or collective rights.[198] The question is particularly relevant for those CBD Parties that claim that they do not have indigenous peoples in their territories.[199] There is no guidance, however, at present under the CBD as to whether the status and rights of local communities are to be understood as similar or even equivalent to those of indigenous peoples under international law.

---

196   Francioni, *Genetic Resources, Biotechnology and Human Rights*, op. cit., 20.

197   CBD Decision 10/43, "Multi-year programme of work on the implementation of Article 8(j) and related provisions of the Convention on Biological Diversity" (20 January 2011) UN Doc UNEP/CBD/COP/10/27, paragraph 21; and CBD Decision 11/14, paragraphs 17–21.

198   CBD Article 8(j) Working Group, "Participatory mechanisms for indigenous and local communities in the work of the Convention. Draft recommendation submitted by the Chair" (3 November 2011) UN Doc UNEP/CBD/WG8J/7COP/12/L.3, paragraph19.

199   That is the case of many European countries, see Alejandro Lago Candeira and Luciana Silvestri, "Challenges in the Implementation of the Nagoya Protocol from the Perspective of a Member State of the European Union: The Case of Spain," in Morgera, Buck and Tsioumani, *2010 Nagoya Protocol on Access and Benefit-Sharing in Perspective*, op. cit., 269, 291); certain Asian countries (Benedict Kingsbury, " 'Indigenous Peoples" in International Law; A Constructivist Approach to the Asian Controversy' *American Journal of International Law* 92 (1998): 414; and African countries (Singh Nijar, "An Asian Developing Country's View," op. cit., 258; and "African Model Legislation for the Protection of the Rights of Local Communities, Farmers and Breeders and for the Regulation of Access to Biological Resources" endorsed by the 68th Ordinary Session of the Council of Ministers in 1996, Organization of African Unity, accessed 30 November 2013, <www.cbd.int/doc/measures/abs/msr-abs-oau-en.pdf>, Article 1, where a local community is defined as: 'a human population in a distinct geographical area with ownership over its biological resources, innovations, practices, knowledge and technologies governed partially or completely by its own customs, traditions or laws').

Against this background, there are at least three arguments that can be made in relation to the status of local communities under the Protocol in the light of international human rights law. First of all, local communities may be recognized, on a case-by-case basis, some of the collective rights that are typically bestowed upon indigenous peoples – that is, 'when these communities share characteristics with indigenous peoples.'[200] To make such a determination, attention is drawn to the 'distinct social, cultural and economic group with a special relationship with its ancestral territory' that justify the adoption of special measures to guarantee the full exercise of their rights, particularly with regards to their enjoyment of property rights, in order to safeguard their physical and cultural survival.[201]

Second, local communities may in specific circumstances be regarded as minorities[202] and, because of that, enjoy specific human rights protection. To be recognized as minorities, local communities cannot be simply characterized by 'mere participation in a common social activity.'[203] Rather, their common social activities should amount to a 'particular lifestyle which is so inextricably linked to the identity of those who practice it that [to interfere with the exercise of such common activity] would be to jeopardize the very essence of their identity.'[204] The reference to 'particular lifestyles' does resonate quite distinctly with the CBD language in Article 8(j) on 'traditional lifestyles.' In particular, the development and maintenance of traditional knowledge by local communities

---

200 Tribal peoples are expressly included in the scope of ILO Convention No. 169. For an in-depth discussion of this argument, see Adriana Bessa, *Traditional Local Communities in International Law*, PhD thesis European University Institute, 2013, chapter 6.

201 *Saramaka People v. Suriname* 2007, 80–85. See also Inter-American Court of Human Rights, *Case of the Moiwana vs. Community v. Suriname*, Preliminary Objections, Merits, Reparations and Costs, Judgment, Case No. 11,821 (IACtHR, 15 June 2005) (hereinafter, *Moiwana Community v. Suriname*).

202 For an in-depth discussion of this argument, see Bessa, *Traditional Local Communities in International Law*, op. cit., chapter 6. On terminological questions related to indigenous peoples and minorities, see Federico Lenzerini, "Indigenous Peoples' Cultural Rights and the Controversy over Commercial Use of Their Traditional Knowledge," in *Cultural Human Rights*, ed. Francesco Francioni and Martin Schenin (Leiden: Martinus Nijhoff, 2008), 119, 135, fn. 73.

203 See *a contrario* European Court of Human Rights, *The Countryside Alliance and Others v. The United Kingdom*, Applications no. 16072/06 and no. 27809/08 (ECtHR, 24 November 2009), 44, where the Court rejected the argument that fox-hunters and communities that depended on foxhunting for their income may be regarded as a distinguished social group that deserves specific protection. Note, however, that this case was dismissed at the admissibility stage and was not considered by the Court on the merits.

204 Ibid.

is an 'essential element of the collective identity' of these communities, whose unlawful appropriation 'may actually result in a serious threat to the integrity of the idiosyncratic identity of the [community] concerned.'[205] Local communities holding traditional knowledge associated with genetic resources may therefore be considered 'cultural minorities' when their way of life is closely associated with their territory and the use of its resources,[206] community's customary laws regulate their relationship with the lands and resources,[207] and traditional knowledge safeguards a community value upon which the ability of the group to maintain its culture depends.[208]

Third, even where local communities may not be recognized as minorities, they may still be protected by international human rights law when an ABS activity may affect their substantive social, economic and cultural human rights, on a case-by-case basis.[209] In particular, the right to property can be interpreted in an extensive way to protect the rights of users of natural resources through customary tenure, including communal rights.[210]

As it has been argued that local communities are at present a category of right-holders of unclear status in international human rights law,[211] the question ultimately arises as to whether the Nagoya Protocol, in arguably applying

---

205   Lenzerini, "Indigenous Peoples' Cultural Rights," op. cit., 199 (although referring to 'indigenous groups').

206   Human Rights Committee, "General Comment No. 23: The rights of minorities (Art. 27)" (4 August 1994) UN Doc CCPR/C/21/Rev.1/Add.5 (hereinafter, General Comment No. 23), paragraph 3(2). See discussion in Lenzerini, "Indigenous Peoples' Cultural Rights," op. cit., 135.

207   Lenzerini, "Indigenous Peoples' Cultural Rights," op. cit., 137.

208   General Comment No. 23, paragraphs 6(2) and 9; Lenzerini, "Indigenous Peoples' Cultural Rights," op. cit., 125.

209   This argument draws, by analogy, on current international normative developments on the free PIC of 'forest-dependent communities' in the context of the "Guidelines on Free, Prior and Informed Consent," UN-REDD Programme (2013), accessed 30 November 2013, <www.unredd.net/index.php?option=com_docman&task=doc_download&gid= 8717&Itemid=5>, 11–12. We are grateful to Annalisa Savaresi for drawing our attention to this point and for an exchange of ideas on all the arguments outlined in this section.

210   Olivier De Schutter, "The Emerging Human Right to Land," *International Community Law Review* 12 (2010): 303, 324–325 and 319: 'There is no reason not to extend the recognition of communal rights beyond indigenous or traditional communities' particularly where the management of common pool resources at the local level proves effective. Along these lines, he also points to the role of the right to food to justify protection of local communities' special relationship with land and resources traditionally used.

211   This is the main conclusion of Bessa, *Traditional Local Communities in International Law*, op. cit.

by analogy concepts that are traditionally referred to indigenous peoples also
to local communities in the ABS context, entails an expansive interpretation of
extant international human rights law. The question goes beyond the purposes
of this study, but it is hoped that the findings of this commentary will provide
useful departure points for such an in-depth investigation from a human rights
viewpoint.

4.3 *Human Rights-related Risks and Opportunities, Limitations and Innovations under the Protocol*

As the Nagoya Protocol provides little indication as to how to address at the
national level complex questions related to indigenous peoples and local communities, it remains to be seen whether it will actually provide opportunities
or risks for the effective protection and progressive realization of their rights
related to traditional knowledge and genetic resources held by them. While
Parties to the Protocol are expected to interpret and apply relevant Protocol
obligations in good faith and in light of applicable international human rights
obligations, they will certainly face several challenges. In particular, the issue
of compliance with regard to access to, and use of traditional knowledge is
an uncharted field in international law as well as in domestic law in many
countries.[212]

It should be further emphasized that international human rights law also
sets limitations to indigenous peoples and local communities' own laws and
practices in the context of the Nagoya Protocol, and may thereby call for
some balancing of internationally protected, but possibly conflicting, human
rights. This could be the case of communities' rules and practices related to
traditional knowledge and genetic resources that are at variance with international norms against discrimination, such as discrimination based on gender.[213]
This complex[214] case seems particularly relevant as in the Protocol preamble

---

212 Notably in the Member States of the EU: see Lago Candeira and Silvestri, "Challenges in
the Implementation of the Nagoya Protocol," op. cit., 269, 290.

213 See also considerations related to a possible conflict between the protection of the rights
on traditional knowledge of indigenous and local communities and the protection of the
right to health of the population discussed in commentary on Article 8, section 3.

214 The case is quite complex as it creates the risk of 'disentrenching...longstanding
identity-shaping system'; see Benedict Kingsbury, "Indigenous Peoples," in *Max Planck
Encyclopedia of Public International Law* ed. Rüdiger Wolfrum (Oxford: Oxford University
Press, 2012, online edition), paragraph 61, referring to Human Rights Committee,
Sandra Lovelace v. Canada, Communication No. 24/1977 (30 July 1981) UN Doc CCPR/
C/13/D/24/1977 and US Supreme Court, *Santa Clara Pueblo v. Martinez*, (15 May 1978) 436
U.S. 49; and Human Rights Council, "Report of the Special Rapporteur on indigenous

Parties recognize the vital role that women play in the ABS context and affirm the need for women's full participation at all levels of policy-making and implementation.[215]

Overall, the Nagoya Protocol certainly provides abundant food for thought on possible tensions and synergies between international environment law and international human rights law. The present analysis will in particular focus on the extent to which the Nagoya Protocol may implicitly recognize procedural and substantive[216] *environmental rights*[217] of indigenous and local communities under the Protocol. Indigenous peoples and local communities' rights to PIC and benefit-sharing in the ABS context should in fact be seen as *intrinsically* aimed at the protection of traditional knowledge and customary ownership *contributing to* the conservation of indigenous cultures, biodiversity and the sustainable use of its components.[218]

---

peoples' rights," A/HRC/24/41, paragraph 70. We are grateful to Annalisa Savaresi for drawing our attention to this point.

215 Nagoya Protocol 11th preambular recital and Article 12(3)(b). Note, however, that this proposition is not free from challenges: '... subjecting pre-colonial societies to the social or gender equity critique tends to diminish the value of indigenous knowledge in general to the extent that in most cases such knowledge has evolved within the strictures of the patriarchal order. It would seem paradoxical even for ecofeminists to praise women's traditional ecological knowledge given that such knowledge has largely been acquired through the oppressive dictates of patriarchy. Consequently, even though feminists, critical theorists, and post-modernists might all advocate for the replacement of science with indigenous knowledge, it would be naive to assume they necessarily speak with one voice or from one perspective.' Bosire Maragia, "The Indigenous Sustainability Paradox and the Quest for Sustainability in Post-Colonial Societies: Is Indigenous Knowledge All That Is Needed?," *Georgetown International Environmental Law Review* 18 (2006): 197, 210.

216 John Merrils, "Environmental Protection and Human Rights: Conceptual Aspects," in *Human Rights Approaches to Environmental Protection*, ed. Alan Boyle and Michael R. Anderson (Oxford: Oxford University Press, 1998), 25; and Dinah Shelton, "Human Rights and the Environment: Substantive Rights," in *Research Handbook on International Environmental Law*, ed. Malgosia Fitzmaurice, David M. Ong and Panos Merkouris (Cheltenham: Edward Elgar, 2010), 265.

217 Environmental rights can be defined as 'rights understood to be related to environmental protection.' Human Rights Council, "Report of the Independent Expert on the issue of human rights obligations relating to the enjoyment of a safe, clean, healthy and sustainable environment, John H. Knox" (24 December 2012) UN Doc A/HRC/22/43, paragraph 7.

218 Or biocultural rights: see United Nations Educational, Scientific and Cultural Organisation (UNESCO) "Universal Declaration on Cultural Diversity" in UNESCO General Conference 31 C/Resolution 25 (2 November 2001), Annex, paragraph 14; Federico Lenzerini and Maurizio Fraboni, "Indigenous Peoples' Rights, Biogenetic Resources and Traditional Knowledge: The Case of the Sateré-Mawé People," in *Biotechnology and International Law*,

5 About This Commentary

This commentary explains each of the Protocol's Articles in accordance with the Vienna Convention on the Law of Treaties (VCLT) provisions on interpretation.[219] It focuses on a teleological and systematic interpretation[220] wherever a strict literal interpretation may prove problematic due to the peculiar way in which the final text of the Protocol had been arrived to.[221] For the same reason, this commentary pays particular attention to the principle of effectiveness – that is, it engages in interpretations that contribute to give coherent meaning and ensure full effect of the treaty[222] – and the principle of good faith. As to the latter, excessively strict literal interpretations will be avoided when they would allow a Party to obtain an unfair advantage, disregard legitimate expectations, or exercise rights in a way that would be damaging to another Party.[223]

---

ed. Francesco Francioni and Tullio Scovazzi (Oxford: Hart Publishing, 2006), 201, 207. Note, however, that this proposition needs to be ascertained on a case-by-case basis: 'The assumption that indigenous knowledge is essential to promoting sustainability tends to idolize pre-colonial societies which are credited for being good exemplars of sustainability.' See Maragia, "The Indigenous Sustainability Paradox," op. cit., 210. This concern is already balanced in the text of the CBD Article 10(c), where reference is made to the 'sustainable' customary use of biological resources by indigenous and local communities.

219 VCLT Articles 31–33. Although the VCLT is not close to universal ratification, it is generally regarded as an authoritative statement of customary law by States, as well as international and national courts: Anthony Aust, "Limping Treaties: Lessons from Multilateral Treaty-Making," *Netherlands International Law Review* 50 (2003): 243, 248–252. In particular, the VCLT provisions on treaty interpretation 'have been applied in the case law of nearly all international tribunals and many national courts.' See Boyle and Chinkin, *Making of International Law*, op. cit., 190–191. But see the cautionary commentary in Villiger, "1969 Vienna Convention on the Law of Treaties," op. cit., 133.

220 VCLT Article 31(1). See Villiger, "1969 Vienna Convention on the Law of Treaties," op. cit., 113–134. For this reason, the Protocol preambular provisions will be discussed in the context of the proposed interpretation of the operative provisions of the Protocol, and not in a separate section commenting on the preamble *per se*. An appendix to this commentary includes the full text of the Protocol's preamble, with numbering suggested by the authors (as the preambular paragraphs of the Nagoya Protocols are unnumbered in the original text) to facilitate references, the Annex to the Protocol will similarly be discussed in the context of Article 5 in which the Annex is referred to.

221 See section 2 above.

222 Malgosia Fitzmaurice, "The Law of Treaties," in *International Law*, ed. Malcolm N. Shaw, 6th edition (Oxford: Oxford University Press, 2008), 810, 832–838.

223 Villiger, "1969 Vienna Convention on the Law of Treaties," op. cit., 116–117.

That being said, the wording of each of the Protocol operative provisions will be carefully analyzed with a view to determining the legal implications of qualified, conditional, vague or general formulations that leave ample room for interpretation and elaboration.[224] This commentary will thus assess the relevance of open-textured provisions in creating 'expectations concerning matters which must be taken into account in good faith in the interpretation and implementation of the treaty,'[225] and in providing 'predictability regarding the parameters within which Parties are required to work towards the objectives of the [treaty]'[226] collectively and individually. Where necessary, it will also be recalled that even obligations framed in heavily qualified terms impose legally binding obligations, albeit they leave a margin of discretion in the choice of means of implementation to State Parties.[227]

The negotiating history of the Protocol[228] will only be referred to where it appears indispensible, also with a view to clarifying linkages with relevant academic and policy debates.[229] To that end, this commentary will in particular

---

224   See discussion on treaties as soft law in Boyle and Chinkin, *Making of International Law*, op. cit., 220–222.

225   Ibid., 222.

226   Ibid.

227   The High Court of Australia, in *Commonwealth v. Tasmania* [1983] HCA 21] held that notwithstanding qualified language of the World Heritage Convention Articles 4 and 5, these articles impose a legally binding obligation that is 'real' and 'substantive' and could not be read as a mere statement of intention: it was expressed in the form of a command requiring each Party to endeavor to bring about the matters dealt with - although there is an element of discretion and value judgment on the part of the State to decide what measures are necessary and appropriate, the discretion only concerns the manner of performance not the issue of performance or not. The case is discussed by Anna Huggins, "Protecting World Heritage Sites from the Adverse Impacts of Climate Change: Obligations for States Parties to the World Heritage Convention," *Australian International Law Journal* 14 (2007): 121, 131–132. Similar qualifiers to those used in the World Heritage Convention Articles 4 and 5 ('as appropriate' and 'as far as possible') can also be found frequently in the text of the Nagoya Protocol.

228   VCLT Article 32. The travaux préparatoires include 'all documents relevant to the forthcoming treaty and generated by the Parties during the treaty's preparation up to its conclusion': Villiger, "1969 Vienna Convention on the Law of Treaties," op. cit., 26. In addition, the VCLT also allows taking into account the 'political, social and cultural factors – *the milieu* – surrounding the treaty's conclusion. Ibid., 126. See also Jan Klabbers, "International Legal Histories: The Declining Importance of Travaux Préparatoires in Treaty Interpretation?," *Netherlands International Law Review* 50 (2003): 267.

229   Recourse to the preparatory work of a treaty and the circumstances of its conclusion is limited as a supplementary means of interpretation: VCLT Article 32.

rely on the official documents produced by the CBD Secretariat, such as the expert groups' meetings reports that explored some of the conceptual challenges arising from the Protocol negotiations,[230] to discuss whether and to what extent arising issues have been eventually tackled in the Protocol. As key stages of the negotiations were held in informal settings for which no official records are available,[231] this commentary will also rely on the reports of the *Earth Negotiations Bulletin* (ENB).[232]

Another key aspect of this commentary is its emphasis on placing the Protocol in the context of other relevant international legal instruments[233] given its far-reaching implications in other areas of international law beyond environmental protection, notably human rights but also food and agriculture, health, oceans, development cooperation, trade and investment.[234] Specific questions related to the relationship of the Protocol with other international agreements were in fact particularly significant during its negotiations.[235] Questions of systemic interpretation and mutual supportiveness will thus be raised throughout this commentary with a view to clarifying the Protocol's relevance for other areas of international law. That being said, it should be equally emphasized that this commentary has been mainly prepared from an international environmental law viewpoint and does, therefore, not seek to answer all questions related to other areas of international law.

---

230   Note that as in other modern multilateral negotiations, most of the Protocol's text did not rely on preparatory work laid down by legal experts before the intergovernmental negotiations, but rather was developed by the participants themselves in the course of the negotiations: Boyle and Chinkin, *Making of International Law*, op. cit., 148.

231   See "Relevant Documentation from the Negotiations of the Nagoya Protocol," CBD, accessed 30 November 2013, <www.cbd.int/abs/pre-protocol/documentation/>.

232   The *Earth Negotiations Bulletin* is an independent, authoritative summary and analysis of multilateral environmental negotiations that is produced by the international think-tank International Institute for Sustainable Development/Reporting Services and is often referred to in official UN websites. See Pamela S. Chasek and Lynn M. Wagner, "An Insider's Guide to Multilateral Environmental Negotiations since the Earth Summit," in *The Roads from Rio: Lessons Learned from Twenty Years of Multilateral Environmental Negotiations*, ed. Pamela S. Chasek and Lynn M. Wagner (New York: Routledge, 2012), 1, 10.

233   VCLT Article 31(3)(c). Villiger, "1969 Vienna Convention on the Law of Treaties," op. cit., 122–124, note that the 'case law of the International Court of Justice suggests that where possible it prefers an integrated conception of international law to a fragmented one': Boyle and Chinkin, *Making of International Law*, op. cit., 210–211.

234   In this respect, this commentary builds upon Morgera, Buck and Tsioumani, *2010 Nagoya Protocol on Access and Benefit-Sharing in Perspective*, op. cit., Part I.

235   See this commentary on Articles 3–4.

Furthermore, as the Nagoya Protocol "does not actually *create* an ABS regime, but *calls for its creation* through a myriad paths of 'implementation' and 'regime development'",[236] this commentary will also point to areas that will likely require further clarification through implementation-related decisions taken collectively by the Parties to the Nagoya Protocol at the international level.[237] Like other multilateral environmental agreements (MEAs), Parties will articulate their understanding of the Protocol obligations[238] through the progressive development of international guidance and measures supporting the realization of its objective, under the institutional structure created by the Protocol.[239] As such evidence of subsequent agreement between Parties regarding the interpretation of the Protocol or widespread practice in its application are not available at the time of writing, given that the Protocol has not entered into force,[240] this commentary will rather take into account the outcomes of intergovernmental negotiations (ongoing at the time of writing) among CBD Parties that are preparing for the entry into force of the Nagoya Protocol.[241] These negotiations have clearly confirmed that CBD Parties still need to find common understanding on some of the unprecedented or ambiguous provisions of the Protocol,[242] and may provide some indication of the likely interpretation of the Protocol and some guidance for incipient practice at the national level. That being said, these sources will be treated with caution as the recommendations resulting from the current intergovernmental negotiations among CBD Parties are still subject to approval by the Protocol's governing body following entry into force.[243] The role of domestic courts and other judicial mechanisms in the implementation of the Protocol in the context of specific ABS transactions is briefly addressed in the conclusions.

---

236   Young, "An International Cooperation Perspective," op. cit., 457 (emphasis in the original).

237   In this connection, occasionally this commentary identifies also open questions that could be addressed at the level of domestic ABS frameworks implementing the Nagoya Protocol: it does not, however, systematically seek to discuss all questions arising from national implementation.

238   Adapting from what Boyle and Chinkin, *Making of International Law*, op. cit., 155, observe in the human rights context.

239   Boyle and Chinkin, *Making of International Law*, op. cit., 151–154.

240   VCLT Article 31(3)(a–b): see Villiger, "1969 Vienna Convention on the Law of Treaties," op. cit., 120–122.

241   In the context of the Intergovernmental Committee for the Nagoya Protocol (ICNP) established by the CBD COP in CBD Decision 10/1, Section 2.

242   Elisa Morgera, "First Meeting of the Intergovernmental Committee for the Nagoya Protocol: All about Compliance," *Environmental Policy and Law* 41 (2011): 189.

243   See comments by Young, "An International Cooperation Perspective," op. cit., 486

Finally, this commentary has greatly benefitted from the views shared by certain negotiators of the Nagoya Protocol, experts from the United Nations bodies and non-governmental organizations that participated in the negotiations and/or are pioneering the implementation of the Protocol, and academics who kindly agreed to peer-review two drafts of this commentary.[244] As usual, the authors remain solely responsible for any error or omission. The law and policy developments discussed in this commentary are reflected as they were on 1 November 2013.

---

244 For a list of the peer reviewers, see Acknowledgements (supra). Specific acknowledgements of individual peer-reviewers' contribution to this commentary are also provided in footnotes in subsequent sections.

Article 1. Objective

> The objective of this Protocol is the fair and equitable sharing of the benefits arising from the utilization of genetic resources, including by appropriate access to genetic resources and by appropriate transfer of relevant technologies, taking into account all rights over those resources and to technologies, and by appropriate funding, thereby contributing to the conservation of biological diversity and the sustainable use of its components

1 Overview

The opening provision of the Nagoya Protocol clarifies that fair and equitable sharing of benefits arising from the utilization of genetic resources is the objective – the 'essential goal'[1] – of the Protocol. It further indicates three means for its realization – *in primis*, access to genetic resources, but also technology transfer and funding.

Two notable features of Article 1 are the explicit link established between benefit-sharing and the other two objectives of the CBD – conservation and sustainable use; and the absence of any reference to traditional knowledge, which, however, is a key component of the regime created by the Protocol. The following sections will first introduce the reader to the relation between benefit-sharing and access to genetic resources, highlighting key tensions between CBD Parties underlying the whole text of the Protocol. Second, the missing reference to traditional knowledge will be addressed. Then we will turn to the relevance of the connection between the Protocol's objective and the first and second objectives of the CBD. Finally, the practical and legal functions of Article 1 will be illustrated, to equip the reader to understand references to the objective in other provisions of the Protocol.

---

1   David Jonas and Thomas Saunders, "The Object and Purpose of a Treaty: Three Interpretative Methods." *Vanderbilt Journal of Transnational Law* 43 (2010): 565, 567.

2   Objective and Means

The objective replicates *verbatim* the third objective of the CBD, which refers prominently to fair and equitable benefit-sharing in its Article 1 (Objectives)[2] and points to three *means* of sharing benefits, each underpinned by specific provisions of the Convention: appropriate access to genetic resources;[3] appropriate transfer of relevant technologies,[4] including biotechnology;[5] and appropriate funding.[6] Among these three means, the Nagoya Protocol emphasizes access, by referring to 'access *and* benefit-sharing' in its title and devoting two central provisions to it.[7] Technology transfer and finance are addressed in successive provisions of the Protocol.[8]

The preamble confirms that the Protocol aims to implement the third objective of the CBD,[9] by spelling out the steps for the operationalization of CBD Article 15 on access to genetic resources,[10] with a view to further supporting the effective implementation of the ABS provisions of the Convention.[11]

---

2   CBD Article 1 reads: 'The objectives of this Convention, to be pursued in accordance with its relevant provisions, are the conservation of biological diversity, the sustainable use of its components and *the fair and equitable sharing of the benefits arising out of the utilization of genetic resources, including by appropriate access to genetic resources and by appropriate transfer of relevant technologies, taking into account all rights over those resources and to technologies, and by appropriate funding*,' emphasis added. Tvedt and Young, *Beyond Access*, op. cit., 5.

3   CBD Article 15.

4   CBD Article 16.

5   CBD Article 19.

6   Addressed in CBD Articles 20 and 21. See generally, Glowka, Burhenne-Guilmin and Synge, *Guide to the Convention on Biological Diversity*, op. cit., 15. It should be noted that the text of Nagoya Protocol Article 1 does not include cross-references to these specific CBD Articles.

7   See this commentary on Articles 6 (Access to Genetic Resources) and 7 (Access to Traditional Knowledge).

8   See this commentary on Articles 23 and 25 respectively. The reference to 'taking into account all rights . . . to technologies' in Article 1 foreshadows legal issues related to intellectual property rights on relevant technologies and their bearing on Parties' ability to facilitate technology transfer. This question will be discussed more in detail in this commentary on Article 23.

9   Nagoya Protocol 2nd preambular recital, which reiterates the relevant wording of CBD Article 1.

10   The latter is specifically recalled in Nagoya Protocol 4th preambular recital.

11   Nagoya Protocol 12th preambular recital.

The preamble also points to providing legal certainty and promoting equity and fairness in negotiations between users and providers of genetic resources.[12]

Fairness and equity are indeed two critical features of benefit-sharing in international biodiversity law, and part and parcel of the objective of the Protocol. Fairness can be understood as encapsulating both the need for legitimacy (the degree to which rules are made and applied in accordance with what the participants perceive as right process) and for equity or justice (the degree to which the rules satisfy the participants' expectations of justifiable distribution of costs and benefits).[13] In the latter sense, it introduces notions of reasonableness and a common ethic of the international community through consideration of a broader array of socio-economic factors and a committment in principle to a notion of fair allocation that aims to 'narrow the gap between the haves and have-nots'.[14]

The preamble also serves to clarify that the Protocol is expected more broadly to contribute through fair and equitable benefit-sharing to the achievement of sustainable development.[15] CBD Parties acknowledge the potential role of ABS to contribute not only to the other objectives of the CBD (conservation and sustainable use), but also to poverty eradication and environmental sustainability more generally, thereby contributing to achieving the Millennium Development Goals.[16] In addition, reference is made to technology transfer and cooperation, as means of benefit-sharing, that can build research and

---

12   Nagoya Protocol 9–10th preambular recitals.

13   Thomas Franck, *Fairness in International Law and Institutions* (Oxford: Oxford University Press, 1995), 7.

14   Ibid, 12–13 and 47–80.

15   Braulio Dias, "Preface," op. cit., 1; and discussion in the Conclusions to this commentary, section 2.

16   Nagoya Protocol 7th preambular recital. The Millennium Development Goals were developed by the UN, following consultations among international agencies, as a set of interconnected and mutually reinforcing development goals, accompanied by targets and benchmarks based on the time-bound commitments contained in UN General Assembly, "United Nations Millennium Declaration" (8 September 2000) UN Doc A/RES/55/2. The Millennium Development Goals were then intergovernmentally approved at the 2005 UN Summit, "World Summit Outcome," paragraph 17. The eight Millennium Development Goals are to: eradicate extreme poverty and hunger; achieve universal primary education; promote gender equality and empower women; reduce the mortality rate of children; improve maternal health; combat HIV/AIDS, malaria and other diseases; ensure environmental sustainability; and develop a global partnership for development. See: "Millennium Development Goals and Beyond 2015," UN, accessed 30 November 2013, <www.un.org/millenniumgoals/>.

innovation capacity for adding value to genetic resources in developing countries, as an important contribution to sustainable development.[17]

Against this background, the relation between benefit-sharing as the objective of the Protocol and access to genetic resources is not as straightforward as the wording of Article 1 may imply. The preamble in a sibylline formulation simply 'acknowledges the linkage' between the two without any further elaboration.[18] While it may be intuitive that without access to genetic resources there could be no benefits to share, it has been argued that the obligations to ensure benefit-sharing and to facilitate access to genetic resources under the Convention do not have the same legal force.[19] In fact, Article 1 represents the compromise[20] between CBD Parties emphasizing benefit-sharing as the main objective of the Protocol[21] and those Parties emphasizing access to genetic resources as an additional objective that should have been placed in the Nagoya Protocol on the same footing as benefit-sharing.[22] Tensions over the

---

17   Nagoya Protocol 5th preambular recital.

18   Nagoya Protocol 8th preambular recital.

19   See CBD Article 15(2), which requires Parties to 'endeavor to create conditions to facilitate access ... for environmentally sound uses'access' and 15(7), which requires Parties to 'take legislative, administrative or policy measures ... with the aim of sharing in a fair and equitable way the ... benefits arising from the commercial use and other utilization of genetic resources.' See comments by Morgera and Tsioumani, "Evolution of Benefit-Sharing," op. cit., 154.

20   ENB, "Summary of Resumed Ninth Meeting of the Ad Hoc Open-ended Working Group on Access and Benefit-sharing: 10–16 July 2010," Vol. 9 No. 527, 19 July 2010.

21   The current formulation emerged from the resumed ninth meeting of the CBD Working Group on ABS: "Draft Protocol on Access to Genetic Resources and the Fair and Equitable Sharing of Benefits Arising from their Utilization to the Convention on Biological Diversity" in "Report of the second part of the ninth meeting of the Ad Hoc Open-ended Working Group on Access and Benefit-sharing" (28 July 2010) UN Doc UNEP/CBD/COP/10/5/Add.4, Annex (hereinafter, Montreal I Draft), on the basis of an initial formulation in the Cali Draft, which was limited to declaring benefit-sharing the objective of the Protocol and making a link with the other two objectives of the CBD. In the Cali Draft, draft article 1 read: 'The objective of this Protocol is to ensure the fair and equitable sharing of the benefits arising from the utilization of genetic resources, contributing to the conservation of biological diversity and the sustainable use of its components.'

22   Note the EU proposal to this end in CBD Working Group on ABS, "Report of the first part of the ninth meeting," UNEP/CBD/WG-ABS/9/3, 19 'the facilitation of access to genetic resources and the fair and equitable sharing of the benefits arising from the utilization of genetic resources that were obtained after the entry into force of this Protocol, also contributing to the conservation of biological diversity and the sustainable use of its components.'

appropriate framing of the objective of the Protocol had in fact emerged from the inception of its negotiating mandate. On the one hand, without mentioning access, the Johannesburg Plan of Implementation called for:

> negotiat[ing] within the framework of the Convention on Biological Diversity, bearing in mind the Bonn Guidelines, an international regime to promote and safeguard the fair and equitable sharing of benefits arising out of the utilization of genetic resources.[23]

On the other hand, the mandate agreed upon by the CBD COP clearly mentioned both:

> *The COP ... Decides* to mandate the Ad Hoc Open-ended Working Group on Access and Benefit- sharing with the collaboration of the Ad Hoc Open ended Inter-Sessional Working Group on Article 8(j) and Related Provisions, ensuring the participation of indigenous and local communities, non-governmental organizations, industry and scientific and academic institutions, as well as intergovernmental organizations, to elaborate and negotiate an international regime *on access to genetic resources and benefit-sharing* with the aim of adopting an instrument/instruments to effectively implement the provisions in Article 15 and Article 8(j) of the Convention and the three objectives of the Convention.[24]

Overall, Article 1 confirms that fair and equitable benefit-sharing is the ultimate objective of the implementing measures to be adopted by the Protocol Parties. However, the underlying tension in the relationship between the 'access' and 'benefit-sharing' pillars of the Protocol is reflected in the various compromises reached between those CBD Parties mostly characterizing themselves as user countries and those characterizing themselves as provider countries.[25] It should be preliminarily noted that access, benefit-sharing and compliance are the three constitutive elements of the political deal behind the Protocol adoption – the so-called 'ABC of ABS.'[26] Ultimately, the actual balance struck between access and benefit-sharing is to be determined on the basis of

---

23   Johannesburg Plan of Implementation, paragraph 44(o).

24   CBD Decision 7/19, section D, paragraph 1, emphasis added.

25   CBD Decision 7/19, section D, 16th preambular recital. See Introduction to this commentary, section 1.3.

26   CBD Friends of the Co-Chairs Meeting on access and benefit-sharing, "Paper on selected key issues submitted by the Co-Chairs" (26–29 January 2010), accessed 30 November

the more specific provisions contained in the Nagoya Protocol,[27] which are to be interpreted in the light of the objective of realizing fairness and equity in benefit-sharing.

3   Traditional Knowledge

Article 1 does not mention benefit-sharing in relation to *traditional knowledge*, in line with the Protocol's own title ('Access to Genetic Resources and the Fair and Equitable Sharing of Benefits from Their Utilization'). Nevertheless, as the CBD COP mandate for the Protocol negotiations clearly indicated, CBD Parties had come to an understanding that access and benefit-sharing would also apply to traditional knowledge *associated with genetic resources*, based on a combined reading of CBD Articles 15 and 8(j),[28] notwithstanding the fact that the former does not mention traditional knowledge and the latter does not mention genetic resources.[29] As the object and purpose of a treaty are also to be deduced from its preamble and other programmatic articles,[30] attention should be drawn to several substantive provisions of the Protocol that are wholly or significantly devoted to traditional knowledge associated with genetic resources.[31] It can therefore be asserted that benefit-sharing related to the use of traditional knowledge associated with genetic resources[32] is part and parcel of the objective of the Protocol. This interpretation appears confirmed by the express provision on the Protocol scope, which extends to

---

      2013, \<www.cbd.int/doc/?meeting=ABS-FOCC-01\>, paragraph 3. See also: ENB 9/527, "Summary of the Resumed Ninth Meeting of the Working Group on ABS," 14.

27   See in particular this commentary on Articles 5–6, 15 and 17–18.

28   As confirmed in Nagoya Protocol 21st preambular recital, which recalls the 'relevance' of CBD Article 8(j) '*as it relates to* traditional knowledge *associated with* genetic resources,' emphasis added. The Bonn Guidelines already foreshadowed this development, by stating: 'These Guidelines may serve as inputs when developing and drafting legislative, administrative or policy measures on access and benefit-sharing with particular reference to provisions under *Articles 8(j)*, 10(c), 15, 16 and 19 [of the CBD]; and contracts and other arrangements under mutually agreed terms for access and benefit-sharing': Bonn Guidelines, paragraph 1, emphasis added.

29   As discussed in the Introduction to this commentary, sections 1.3 and 3. See also this commentary on Article 7.

30   E.g. Richard Gardiner, *Treaty Interpretation* (Oxford: Oxford University Press, 2008), 196.

31   See commentary on Article 5, section 4 and Articles 7, 12 and 16.

32   Unless otherwise specified, the rest of the commentary will always refer to 'traditional knowledge' as 'associated with genetic resources.'

traditional knowledge.[33] The objective of sharing in a fair and equitable manner benefits arising from the use of traditional knowledge with indigenous and local communities needs thus to be taken into account in the interpretation of the whole Protocol. In this connection, the reference to 'taking into account all rights over those resources' points to the question of the indigenous peoples' and local communities' rights over genetic resources[34] and also their rights related to traditional technologies.[35]

4   Links with Conservation and Sustainable Use

The third objective of the CBD as the objective of the Protocol is not to be pursued in isolation from the broader framework established by the CBD. Notably, the objective of the Nagoya Protocol is clearly and expressly linked to the other two objectives of the CBD, as it specifies that benefit-sharing is seen as a 'contribution' to the conservation of biological diversity and the sustainable use of its components.[36] This seeks to ensure a coherent interpretation and integrative implementation of the CBD three objectives in the context of the Nagoya Protocol.[37] It encapsulates the idea that ABS can function as a source of funding or incentive for, or otherwise contribute to, the achievement of the other two objectives of the Convention.[38] This idea is more concretely pursued in several operational provisions.[39]

'Sustainable use' is defined by the CBD as 'the use of components of biological diversity in a way and at a rate that does not lead to the long-term decline

---

33   See commentary on Article 3, sections 1–2.

34   Nagoya Protocol Articles 5(2) and 6(2). We are grateful to Krystyna Swiderska for drawing our attention to this point, which will be discussed in detail in the commentary on Articles 5, section 3 and 6, section 4.

35   See commentary on Article 23. See also Ajit Bhalla, Dilmus James and Yvette Stevens, eds., *Blending of New and Traditional Technologies: Case Studies* (Geneva: ILO, 1984).

36   As already highlighted in the Bonn Guidelines, paragraph 48.

37   Morgera and Tsioumani, "Evolution of Benefit-Sharing," op. cit., 173.

38   Nagoya Protocol 7th preambular recital. See also the "Strategy for resource mobilisation in support of the achievement of the Convention's three objectives for the period 2008–2015" in CBD Decision 9/11, "Review of implementation of Articles 20 and 21" (9 October 2008) UN Doc UNEP/CBD/COP/9/29, Annex, which includes a goal on enhancing implementation of ABS initiatives, considering them a tool for generating financial returns to support conservation and sustainable use initiatives in provider countries, Goal 7.

39   See commentary on Article 5, section 6, Article 8, section 2, Article 9, section 2, Article 10, section 4, Article 12, section 4, Article 21, section 3, Article 22, and Article 23, section 3.

of biological diversity, thereby maintaining its potential to meet the needs and aspirations of present and future generations.'[40] There is, however, no definition of 'conservation' as such in the Convention but rather a clarification of the distinction between ex situ and in situ conservation as respectively 'outside natural habitats' and in genetic resources' 'natural surroundings' or 'in the surroundings where they have developed their distinctive properties.'[41] Thus, to better understand how the Nagoya Protocol is expected to contribute to conservation and sustainable use it is necessary to make reference to relevant provisions in the CBD, namely its Articles 8–10. On that basis, benefit-sharing under the Protocol can be expected to contribute to, *inter alia*, the selection and management of protected areas and species, the restoration of degraded ecosystems and the recovery of threatened species, the protection and promotion of traditional knowledge, the creation of measures and/or facilities for ex situ conservation, the support towards sustainable customary use and remedial action by local communities.[42] Notably, both CBD Articles 8 and 10 also contain references to the central role of indigenous and local communities in contributing to conservation and sustainable use.[43] A combined reading of Article 8(j) and 10(c) in particular leads to connecting the aim of fair and equitable benefit-sharing with the use of traditional knowledge contributing to in situ conservation and also with communities' sustainable traditional use of biological resources.[44]

It should also be noted that the Nagoya Protocol seeks to contribute to the first and second objectives of the CBD by calling upon Parties to promote and encourage research activities contributing to conservation and sustainable usd of biodiversity, particularly in developing countries.[45] Furthermore, the

---

40 CBD Article 2.

41 CBD Article 2.

42 But also: control of living modified organisms (LMOS) and invasive alien species, and cooperation between authorities and the private sector on sustainable use. For a discussion on how inter-State benefit-sharing can reach indigenous and local communities, see Morgera and Tsioumani, "Evolution of Benefit-Sharing," op. cit., 155–158. For a discussion of the potential contribution of ABS to development, see Reid et al., *Biodiversity Prospecting*, op. cit.; and Rachel Wynberg and Sarah A. Laird, "Bioprospecting, Access and Benefit Sharing: Revisiting the 'Grand Bargain,'" in Wynberg, Schroeder and Chennells, *Indigenous Peoples, Consent and Benefit Sharing*, op. cit., 69.

43 CBD Articles 8(j) and 10(c). We are grateful to Krystina Swiderska for drawing our attention to this point.

44 Morgera and Tsioumani, "Evolution of Benefit-Sharing", op. cit., 159.

45 Nagoya Protocol Article 8(a), which expands on CBD Article 12: see this commentary on Article 8, section 2.

Protocol foresees not only a contribution of ABS to biodiversity conservation, but also to environmental protection more broadly conceived. In fact, its preamble notes the importance of genetic resources also for the mitigation of and adaptation to climate change.[46]

The importance of the Protocol's support for a coherent implementation of the three CBD objectives[47] should not be underestimated. With two new protocols and an ever-growing range of decisions adopted by the CBD COP, States' obligations and commitments have expanded considerably under the Convention at the risk of substantive and procedural fragmentation. This has become particularly visible in the context of the Cartagena Protocol:[48] in many respects, the biosafety regime has developed into an independent sub-process that has little, if any, link with the CBD. This development can be explained and arguably justified on the basis of the very specific and technical nature of the Cartagena Protocol's subject matter.[49] On the other hand, the negotiators of the Nagoya Protocol have specifically arranged for keeping the Protocol in close relation with the CBD, through substantive provisions that expressly link benefit-sharing to the conservation of biological diversity and the sustainable use of its components,[50] as well as the institutional arrangement to hold meetings of its Parties in conjunction with the meetings of CBD Parties.[51]

5   Legal and Practical Functions

According to general international law, Article 1 seeks to clarify the 'object and purpose' of the Protocol as the chief criterion for the interpretation of the whole treaty.[52] As explained above, a correct understanding of the scope of the

---

46   Nagoya Protocol 14th preambular recital. On the links between genetic resources and climate change, see e.g. FAO Commission on Genetic Resources for Food and Agriculture (CGRFA), "Roadmap on climate change and genetic resources for food and agriculture" FAO Doc CGRFA-14/13/5 (2013); and "Selected processes and initiatives on climate change of relevance to genetic resources for food and agriculture" FAO Doc CGRFA-14/13/Inf.10 (2013).

47   See this commentary on Articles 1, section 4; 5, section 6; 9, section 2 and 10, section 4.

48   Cartagena Protocol on Biosafety (Montreal, 29 January 2000, in force 11 September 2003) 2226 UNTS 208.

49   Morgera and Tsioumani, "Yesterday, Today, and Tomorrow," op. cit., 38.

50   See fn. 39 above.

51   Nagoya Protocol Article 26(6): see this commentary on Article 26, section 3.

52   VCLT Article 31(1). See Jonas and Saunders, "The Object and Purpose of a Treaty," op. cit., 577–582.

Protocol necessarily requires reading Article 1 together with the Protocol's pre-amble and other programmatic provisions.

Where the meaning imparted by the text of a treaty itself is equivocal or inconclusive or where confirmation of the correctness of the reading of the text is desired, the object and purpose of the treaty as a whole may shed some light.[53] While the object and purpose cannot override the ordinary meaning of the text of a treaty, they can be interpreted as 'modifiers' of the ordinary meaning.[54] Thus, the object and purpose of a treaty can facilitate its evolutive interpretation.[55] In addition, the object and purpose of a treaty can be used as a means to reconcile divergences in the text of the Protocol in two or more of its authenticated languages, when no text has been agreed to prevail in case of divergence and the difference in meaning cannot be resolved by applying the other general rules on treaty interpretation, as long as the chosen meaning is that which best reconciles the texts.[56]

The interpretative relevance of the object and purpose of the treaty is particularly significant in the context of the often open-ended or heavily qualified language used in the Nagoya Protocol. In that regard, it is of the utmost importance that its object and purpose (i.e. ensuring the fair and equitable sharing of benefits arising from genetic resources and/or traditional knowledge among and within States, with a view to contributing to conservation and sustainable use) guide Parties in unilaterally implementing the Protocol where they are allowed a wide margin of discretion, and collectively[57] in further developing certain provisions of the Protocol that require further negotiations.[58] In both regards, the object and purpose of a treaty can serve to 'maintain the balance of rights and obligations created by the treaty.'[59] This is particularly – but not exclusively – the case in Protocol operative provisions that specifically refer to the 'objective' of the Protocol. For instance, the objective serves as a substantive limit to the Parties' negotiating and legislative discretion in the development and implementation of future 'specialized ABS instruments,' as well as a substantive limit to the interpretative discretion of Parties in achieving

---

53   VCLT Article 33. See ICJ, *Territorial Dispute* (*Libyan Arab Jamahiriya v. Chad*), Judgment (3 February 1994), paragraph 41.

54   Gardiner, *Treaty Interpretation*, op. cit., 190 and 192.

55   Boyle and Chinkin, *Making of International Law*, op. cit., 246.

56   VCLT Article 33(4). See Gardiner, *Treaty Interpretation*, op. cit., 193.

57   Nagoya Protocol Article 26(4)(a): see this commentary on Article 26, section 2.

58   See for example this commentary on Articles 10 and 30.

59   Villiger, "1969 Vienna Convention on the Law of Treaties," op. cit., 118.

mutual supportiveness between the Protocol and other relevant international instruments.[60] In addition, it serves as an aim for transboundary cooperation.[61]

Furthermore, this Article is relevant in relation to the international obligations of States signatories to the Protocol. Signatories of an international treaty are obliged not to defeat the object and purpose of a treaty prior to its entry into force, unless these States afterwards explicitly express their intention not to ratify it.[62] This general rule appears particularly significant at the time of writing, as the Protocol is not yet in force,[63] but a significant number of signatories are developing domestic ABS frameworks and undertaking other activities, such as providing capacity building[64] on ABS on the ground.[65]

---

60   See this commentary on Article 4, section 3.

61   See this commentary on Article 11. Interpretative questions arise however from the fact that the provision on transboundary cooperation in relation to genetic resources just refers to 'with a view to implementing the Protocol' – Nagoya Protocol Article 11(1) – whereas the provision on transboundary cooperation in relation to traditional knowledge specifically refers to 'implementing the objective of this Protocol' – Nagoya Protocol Article 11(2), emphasis added – even if Nagoya Protocol Article 1 does not mention 'traditional knowledge.' For completeness' sake, Nagoya Protocol Article 1 is also the object, among others, of awareness-raising obligations: Article 21(a). See this commentary on Article 21.

62   VCLT Article 18 reads: 'A State is obliged to refrain from acts which would defeat the object and purpose of a treaty when: (*a*) it has signed the treaty or has exchanged instruments constituting the treaty subject to ratification, acceptance or approval, until it shall have made its intention clear not to become a Party to the treaty; or (*b*) it has expressed its consent to be bound by the treaty, pending the entry into force of the treaty and provided that such entry into force is not unduly delayed.' It should be noted, however, that 'the extent of [such an] interim obligation has never been conclusively defined': Jonas and Saunders, "The Object and Purpose of a Treaty," op. cit., 572–572 and more generally 594–608.

63   At the time of writing the Protocol had 26 ratifications and 92 signatures: see "Status of Signature, and Ratification, Accession, Approval and Acceptance," CBD, accessed 30 November 2013, <www.cbd.int/abs/nagoya-protocol/signatories/default.shtml>.

64   See this commentary on Article 22.

65   CBD Executive Secretary, "Progress report on the Nagoya Protocol on Access to Genetic Resources and the Fair and Equitable Sharing of Benefits Arising from their Utilization and related developments" (7 September 2012) UN Doc UNEP/CBD/COP/11/11 and ADD.1.

Article 2. Use of Terms

The terms defined in Article 2 of the Convention shall apply to this Protocol. In addition, for the purposes of this Protocol:

(a) "Conference of the Parties" means the Conference of the Parties to the Convention;

(b) "Convention" means the Convention on Biological Diversity;

(c) "Utilization of genetic resources" means to conduct research and development on the genetic and/or biochemical composition of genetic resources, including through the application of biotechnology as defined in Article 2 of the Convention.

(d) "Biotechnology" as defined in Article 2 of the Convention means any technological application that uses biological systems, living organisms, or derivatives thereof, to make or modify products or processes for specific use.

(e) "Derivative" means a naturally occurring biochemical compound resulting from the genetic expression or metabolism of biological or genetic resources, even if it does not contain functional units of heredity.

1   Overview

The most notable function of Article 2 is to introduce in international biodiversity law new definitions,[1] some of which seek to delimit the scope of the Protocol[2] and were negotiated as a package.[3] The first key definition is 'utilization of genetic resources,' and has implications for the subject-matter scope of the Protocol and several of its operative provisions.[4] This is particularly

---

1   VCLT Article 31(4); and comments by Villiger, "1969 Vienna Convention on the Law of Treaties," op. cit., 125. Among the additional definitions, the terms established in Article 2(a) and (b) simply allow using short references to the 'Conference of the Parties' and to the 'Convention' rather than their full official name.

2   Nagoya Protocol Article 2(c–e).

3   ENB, "Summary of the Interregional Negotiating Group on Access and Benefit-Sharing: 18–21 September 2010," unnumbered, 2–3, accessed 30 November 2013, <http://www.iisd.ca/biodiv/absing/brief/absing_briefe.html>.

4   It informs the potential scope of domestic access frameworks (Nagoya Protocol Article 6) as well as the scope of 'user measures' (see this commentary on Article 15, section 3.1) and related monitoring obligations of Parties (see this commentary on Article 17, section 2).

significant in the absence of consistent State practice in defining/understanding the concept of genetic resources domestically or internationally.[5] The term 'utilization of genetic resources,' also appears in the ABS provisions of the CBD[6] to delimit the scope of potential benefits falling under the provisions of the Convention, but was left undefined. As defined in the Protocol, the term expands the interpretation of 'genetic resources,' which was defined in the CBD as 'genetic material' of actual or potential value ('any material of plant, animal or other origin *containing functional units of heredity*').[7] The Protocol, instead, includes not only the genetic composition, but also the 'biochemical composition' of genetic resources,[8] with the aim of including 'derivatives' – another key definition introduced by the Protocol. These two new definitions, therefore, aim to include in the Protocol's scope not only genetic resources, but also material that *does not* contain 'functional units of heredity' (i.e. DNA),[9] such as snake venoms, resins or alkaloids found in plants, or proteins. Inclusion of these definitions aimed to address one of the most challenging issues in the Protocol negotiations. But as will be discussed below, the way in which the terms are used (or not) in the Protocol raises interpretative doubts.

In addition, Article 2 clarifies that the terms defined in the CBD are to apply also to the Nagoya Protocol.[10] As a result, the definitions of CBD Article 2 constitute an integral part of the Nagoya Protocol.[11] Among these, the ones that are clearly relevant for the interpretation of the Protocol include:

---

5   Morten W. Tvedt and Peter J. Schei, "The Term 'Genetic Resources': Flexible and Dynamic While Providing Legal Certainty?," in Oberthür and Rosendal, *Global Governance of Genetic Resources*, op. cit., 18 and 25–27.

6   CBD Articles 1 and 15(7).

7   CBD Article 2, emphasis added.

8   Glowka and Normand, "The Nagoya Protocol on Access and Benefit-sharing," op. cit., 28. It should be noted that the term 'biochemical composition of genetic resources' is vague from a scientific viewpoint, and could either refer to the biochemical composition of the gene – i.e., which can be subject to human manipulation by using biotechnology (for instance, introducing synthetic gene segments to improve gene expression) or it could refer to the biochemical composition of the organism (i.e., derivatives as products of cellular metabolism). For a scientific background, see Bruce Alberts et al., *Molecular Biology of the Cell*, 5th ed. (New York: Garland Science, 2012).

9   Biologically speaking, only DNA contains functional units of heredity (meaning genes), not RNA. RNA is thus included among derivatives in Figure 1, as it retains the *information from* functional units of heredity. We are extremely thankful to Francesca Morgera and Andrea D'Ambrogio for their inputs on scientific terminology addressed in this chapter. Any remaining errors are the authors' sole responsibility.

10   As clarified in the first sentence of the chapeau to Nagoya Protocol Article 2.

11   This is significant because CBD Article 2 (Use of terms) only applies 'for the purpose of [the] Convention.'

biodiversity,[12] biological resources,[13] biotechnology,[14] country of origin,[15] country providing genetic recourses,[16] genetic resources,[17] in situ conditions,[18] sustainable use[19] and technology.[20]

---

12 CBD Article 2 defines 'biological diversity' as 'the variability among living organisms from all sources including, *inter alia*, terrestrial, marine and other aquatic ecosystems and the ecological complexes of which they are part: this includes diversity within species, between species and of ecosystems.' The term appears in the Nagoya Protocol in the 1st, 6th, 7th, 11th, 14th, 22nd and 25th preambular recitals; as well as in Articles 1, 2(b), 4(1), 8(a), 9, 10 and 22(5)(h); and in the Annex, 2(f) and (k). The term 'biodiversity' is used in the 6th and 11th preambular recitals; and in the Annex, 1(f).

13 CBD Article 2 defines 'biological resources' as including genetic resources, organisms or parts thereof, populations, or any other biotic component of ecosystems with actual or potential use or value for humanity. The term appears in Article 2(e) of the Nagoya Protocol.

14 CBD Article 2 defines 'biotechnology' as 'any technological application that uses biological systems, living organisms, or derivatives thereof, to make or modify products or processes for specific use.' The term appears in the Nagoya Protocol in Articles 2(c–d) and in the Annex, 2(f). The adjective 'biotechnological' appears in Article 23 and in the Annex, 2(b).

15 CBD Article 2 defines 'country of origin of genetic resources' as 'the country which possesses those genetic resources in in situ conditions.' The term appears in Articles 5(1), 6(1) and 23 of the Nagoya Protocol.

16 CBD Article 2 defines 'country providing genetic resources' as 'the country supplying genetic resources collected from in situ sources, including populations of both wild and domesticated species, or taken from ex situ sources, which may or may not have originated in that country.' The term appears in the Nagoya Protocol Articles 5(1), 6(1), 23 and in the Annex, 2(b), (j) and (m). Note also that CBD Article 2 defines 'genetic material' as 'any material of plant, animal, microbial or other origin containing functional units of heredity.' The latter expression, however, is not used in the Protocol as such.

17 CBD Article 2 defines 'genetic resources' as 'genetic material of actual or potential value.' The term appears in the Nagoya Protocol 2nd, 5th, 8th, 9th, 10th, 13th, 14th, 16th, 19th, and 21st through 25th preambular recitals; in Articles 1, 2(c) and (e), 3, 4(4), 5(1–2) and (5), 6(1–2) and (3)(b) and (f), 7, 8(b–c), 9, 10, 11(1–2), 12(1–2 and 4) and 12(3)(a) and (c); 13(1) (a–b) and 13(4), 14(3)(c), 15(1), 16(1), 17(1)(a–b), (3) and (4)(f), 18(1), 21, 22(4)(d) and (5) (j), 23 and in the Annex, (2)(b), (e), (f), (j) and (m).

18 CBD Article 2 defines 'in situ conditions' as 'conditions where genetic resources exist within ecosystems and natural habitats, and in the case of domesticated or cultivated species, in the surroundings where they have developed their distinctive properties.' The term appears in Article 11(1) of the Nagoya Protocol.

19 CBD Article 2 defines 'sustainable use' as 'the use of components of biological diversity in a way and at a rate that does not lead to the long-term decline of biological diversity, thereby maintaining its potential to meet the needs and aspirations of present and future generations.' The term appears in the Nagoya Protocol in the 6th, 7th, 22nd and 25th preambular recitals; in Articles 1, 8(a), 9, 10, 22(5)(h) and in the Annex, 1(f) and 2(k).

20 CBD Article 2 defines 'technology' as including biotechnology. The term appears in the Nagoya Protocol in the 5th preambular recital; in Articles 2(c–d), 22(5)(g) and 23, and in the Annex, at 2(f) and (g).

It should be further noted that the Nagoya Protocol does not define 'utilization of traditional knowledge associated with genetic resources,' although the expression is used in its operative provisions.[21] This gap is particularly noteworthy as no other international treaty has referred to this concept or more generally to 'traditional knowledge associated with genetic resources.'[22]

The following sections will focus on explaining the definition of utilization of genetic resources, by breaking it down into its components, and linking it to the definition of derivatives. The implicit exclusion of biological resources[23] (as opposed to genetic resources) used as commodities in trade from the scope of the Protocol, and the lack of definition of utilization of traditional knowledge will be also briefly discussed.

2 Utilization of Genetic Resources

The term first appeared, without being defined, in the CBD, both in its objectives and in its provision devoted to access to genetic resources, when referring to benefit-sharing arising from the 'utilization of genetic resources.'[24] To fill this gap, the Nagoya Protocol negotiators initially considered a list of activities falling under the term 'utilization',[25] but eventually decided in favor of a general definition that could allow for covering rapidly developing technologies and uses, potentially unknown at the time of negotiation.[26] In particular, the

---

21 E.g. Nagoya Protocol Articles 3, 5(5), 10, 12 (2–4), 16(1) and 18(1). The term appears also in the preamble and in the Annex to the Protocol.

22 Tvedt and Schei, "The Term 'Genetic Resources,'" op. cit., 24–25. See also Introduction to this commentary, section 3.

23 CBD Article 2.

24 CBD Articles 1 and 15(7).

25 See non-exhaustive list of activities in the CBD Working Group on ABS, "Report of the meeting of the Group of Legal and Technical Experts on Concepts, Terms, Working Definitions and Sectoral Approaches" (12 December 2008) UN Doc UNEP/CBD/WG-ABS/7/2, paragraphs 7–8, including: genetic modification, biosynthesis, breeding and selection, propagation and cultivation of genetic resources in the form received, conservation, characterisation and evaluation, and production of compounds naturally occurring in genetic material. The final text of Article 2 includes only one specific activity, namely the application of biotechnology.

26 See Peter J. Schei and Morten W. Tvedt, *The Concept of "Genetic Resources" in the Convention on Biological Diversity and How It Relates to a Functional International Regime on Access and Benefit-Sharing* (Lysaker: Fridthof Nansen Institute, 2010), circulated in the ABS negotiations as UNEP/CBD/WG-ABS/9/INF/1.

Protocol hinges the definition on the *intent*[27] underlying 'utilization of genetic resources' (by reference to 'research and development'), as well as the *material* on which the conduct focuses ('on the genetic and/or biochemical composition of genetic resources').

2.1   *The Intent*

The terms 'research' and 'development' are not defined in the Nagoya Protocol or in the CBD.[28] Based on their ordinary meaning,[29] 'research' means the investigation or experimentation *aimed at* the discovery and interpretation of facts.[30] In the context of the Protocol and when it is used in combination with 'development,' it refers to the two closely related processes *intended to* create new products and new forms of old products through technological innovation.[31] This may include all types of systematic work on the genetic or biochemical composition of genetic resources aimed to discover potentially interesting properties and to devise practical applications of such discoveries.

In practice, different sectors (e.g., agriculture, cosmetics and pharmaceuticals) have different approaches to research and development.[32] For the purposes of the Protocol, however, it does not matter where research and development take place – in the provider country or in another jurisdiction – and by whom it is carried out – by a public or private individual or entity. Arguably, while the Protocol applies to all types of research, whether it is characterized as

27   Based on legislative experience in Australia: see Burton, "Implementation of the Nagoya Protocol in JUSCANZ Countries," op. cit., 301–302.

28   CBD Articles 17(7) and 25(2).

29   VCLT Article 31(1) states that 'the ordinary meaning [is] to be given to the terms of the treaty in their context and in the light of its object and purpose.'

30   'Research' in *Oxford Dictionaries Online*, accessed 10 October 2013, <http://oxforddictio naries.com/definition/english/research>: 'A search or investigation undertaken to discover facts and reach new conclusions by the critical study of a subject or by a course of scientific inquiry.'

31   'Research and Development' in *Encyclopædia Britannica Online*, accessed 10 October 2013, <www.britannica.com/EBchecked/topic/499010/research-and-development>: 'two intimately related processes by which new products and new forms of old products are brought into being through technological innovation.'

32   CBD Working Group on ABS, "Report of the expert meeting on definitions," UNEP/CBD/ WG-ABS/7/2, paragraph 17; CBD Secretariat, "Access and Benefit-Sharing in Practice: Trends in Partnerships Across Sectors," CBD Technical Series No. 38 (Montreal: CBD Secretariat, 2008); Institute for European Environmental Policy, "Study to analyse legal and economic aspects of implementing the Nagoya Protocol on ABS in the European Union" (2010), accessed 30 October 2013, <http://ec.europa.eu/environment/biodiver sity/international/abs/pdf/ABS%20FINAL%20REPORT.pdf>, Annex 3

'fundamental' research without commercial objective or whether it explicitly aims at developing commercial products,[33] it draws a distinction between research carried out for commercial purposes and research for non-commercial purposes to which special considerations apply.[34] The Protocol itself acknowledges, however, that difficulties arise in practice in determining the presence of the commercial intent in specific research activities at a specific point in time,[35] particularly when a commercial purpose may arise at successive stages of research, either because the original researcher changed his/her intent[36] or where another researcher with commercial purposes uses the results of non-commercial research.[37]

2.2   *The Material*
Utilization relates to 'the genetic and/or biochemical composition of genetic resources'. This formulation was the result of a long-standing debate among CBD Parties and ABS stakeholders on the exact understanding of the term 'genetic resources' under the Convention. This debate revolved around whether

---

33   Ibid., paragraphs 17 and 43–45. See also CBD Group of Legal and Technical Experts on Concepts, Terms, Working Definitions and Sectoral Approaches, "Concepts, terms, working definitions and sectoral approaches relating to the international regime on access and benefit-sharing, Submission from the International Workshop on the topic of 'access and benefit-sharing in non-commercial biodiversity research'" (29 November 2008) UN Doc UNEP/CBD/ABS/GTLE/1/INF/2, paragraph 5.

34   Nagoya Protocol Article 8(a). See this commentary on Article 8, section 2.

35   Nagoya Protocol Article 8(a) underscores the need to address a change of intent in the context of non-commercial research.

36   This could be the case where access to a plant was sought for non-commercial purposes by a university team of researchers from a user country in accordance with the national legislation of the provider country, but later one member of the research team continues doing research on the plant in another company leading to a highly successful (and maybe patented) product: Elisa Morgera, Matthias Buck and Elsa Tsioumani, "Introduction," in Morgera, Buck and Tsioumani, *2010 Nagoya Protocol on Access and Benefit-Sharing in Perspective*, op. cit., 1, 5.

37   This could be the following case: a university researcher requests prior informed consent and enters into mutually agreed terms for academic, non-commercial research on a plant. He publishes the results of his research in a scientific journal without mentioning the country of origin of the samples, the limitations on the use, or the existence of a benefit-sharing agreement. Two years later, another scientist undertaking applied research in the food industry reads the article and acquires a sample of the African plant from a botanical garden in his country: the research on the plant sample leads to a highly successful (and maybe patented) product. Morgera, Buck and Tsioumani, "Introduction," op. cit., 6.

the term referred only to material containing functional units of heredity (i.e. DNA) or more broadly gene expressions such as RNA, proteins and enzymes (which do not contain functional units of heredity *per se*, but retain information from them) and any naturally occurring biochemical compounds resulting from cellular metabolism (i.e., resins, essential oils, and fragrances).[38] The latter does not contain functional units of heredity or information from them,[39] and therefore can only be synthesized if the compounds are extracted directly from the organism.

While the reference to 'biochemical composition of genetic resources' in Article 2(c) does not clarify the material that is the object of utilization self-evidently, the combined reading of this provision with the other new definitions provided in the Protocol, in particular that of derivatives (explained below), leads to the conclusion that all of the above is covered by the Protocol.[40]

2.2.1   Derivatives

Derivative is a term used in the CBD in relation to the definition of 'biotechnology'[41] and in the Bonn Guidelines as an item to be potentially addressed in relation to benefit-sharing as part of the information required for obtaining PIC[42] and when establishing MAT.[43] Neither instrument, however, define the term. During the negotiations of the Protocol, there was no common understanding of what the term 'derivative' (i.e., material not containing functional units of heredity) may include. It could refer to the results of cellular metabolism.[44] It could further be understood as information on genetic resources. But it could also refer to any result of human activity utilizing a genetic resource, such as a chemical compound extracted from an organism and purified by human activity, gene segments isolated by human manipulation of genetic material, synthetic gene segments produced by human manipulation or a synthetic

---

38   See Singh Nijar and Pei Fern, *Nagoya ABS Protocol*, op. cit., 113–114.

39   See Figure 1.

40   This is the only interpretation that would give effect to the entirety of Article 2 (on the effectiveness principle for treaty interpretation, see Introduction to this commentary, section 5). See also Burton, "Implementation of the Nagoya Protocol in JUSCANZ Countries," op. cit., 302–303.

41   CBD Article 2.

42   Bonn Guidelines, paragraph 36(1).

43   Bonn Guidelines, paragraph 44(i).

44   CBD Working Group on ABS, "Report of the expert meeting on definitions," UNEP/CBD/WG-ABS/7/2, paragraphs 9–10, refers to 'organism's metabolism' in that regard.

analogue of a gene segment inspired by a natural gene.[45] Developing countries sought to include specific reference to derivatives within the Protocol general provisions, arguing that this is where the actual or potential value of genetic resources lies primarily as the main interest of modern biosciences.[46] Accordingly, failure to specifically mention derivatives in the Protocol would have significantly narrowed the scope for benefit-sharing and would not have served the ultimate fulfillment of neither the Protocol's nor the CBD objectives. Some industrialized countries, in contrast, argued that the CBD only refers to 'genetic resources' (genetic material containing functional units of heredity).[47] Behind this argument were concerns about legal and economic costs arising from an international ABS instrument that would introduce the need for PIC and benefit-sharing requirements to a broad spectrum of industrial activities. These countries thus rather preferred to leave it to MAT to clarify how derivatives are understood on a case-by-case basis by the individual parties to a specific ABS transaction and set out specific benefit-sharing modalities in that contractual context.[48]

As this divergence of views continued, the compromise reached was to eliminate all references to the term 'derivative' in the operational provisions of the Protocol with the understanding that the term 'utilization of genetic resources' (or its alternative forms – e.g., 'utilized', 'use', 'used') would include the notion of derivatives.[49] This led to the puzzling inclusion of the term 'derivatives' only in

---

45   Drawing from CBD Working Group on ABS, "Report of the expert meeting on definitions," UNEP/CBD/WG-ABS/7/2, paragraphs 9–10.

46   Matthias Buck and Claire Hamilton, "The Nagoya Protocol on Access to Genetic Resources and Benefit-sharing Arising from Their Utilization to the Convention on Biological Diversity," Review of European Community and International Environmental Law 20 (2011): 47, 56.

47   Making reference to CBD Article 15. Note however that not all developed countries shared this view. The 2005 Australian legislation, for instance, defined access as the taking of a biological resource for the purpose of research and development on its genetic and biochemical compounds. See EPBC Regulations 2000 Part 8A.03, accessed 14 February 2014, <www.comlaw.gov.au/Details/F2005L03473>. We are grateful to Geoff Burton for drawing our attention to this.

48   ENB 9/527, "Summary of the Resumed Ninth Meeting of the Working Group on ABS," 6.

49   Ibid., 16. See also Ryo Kohsaka, The Negotiating History of the Nagoya Protocol on ABS: Perspective from Japan (2012), accessed 30 November 2013, <www.ipaj.org/english_jour nal/pdf/9-1_Kohsaka.pdf>, 61. The compromise was developed at the meeting of the Interregional Negotiating Group on Access and Benefit-sharing in September 2010 and then again by the Japanese COP Presidency during CBD COP 10. See CBD Working Group on ABS, "Draft Protocol on Access to Genetic Resources and the Fair and Equitable Sharing of Benefits Arising from their Utilization to the Convention on Biological Diversity" in

the Protocol provision on 'definitions', although the term as such is not referred to anywhere else in the Protocol. Its relevance, however, to the interpretation of 'utilization of genetic resources' (or its alternative forms) throughout the Protocol operative text can be argued on two grounds. First, there is an indirect link between 'utilization' and 'derivatives' via an explicit reference to 'including through the application of biotechnology' in the definition of 'utilization.' That is, the definition of 'biotechnology' in the Protocol – which uses the wording of the CBD[50] – refers to 'any technological application that uses ... derivatives [of living organisms] to make or modify products or processes for specific use.' Therefore, utilization implicitly refers also to research and development through the application of biotechnology on derivatives. In this connection, it should be emphasized that the CBD notion of biotechnology is broader than 'modern biotechnology' that is exclusively understood as genetic engineering,[51] and therefore allows the Protocol to cover a series of biological technologies involving materials not containing functional units of heredity.[52] Second, the definition of 'utilization' makes reference to the 'biochemical composition of

---

"Report of the meeting of the Interregional Negotiating Group," (21 September 2010) UN Doc UNEP/CBD/WG-ABS/9/ING/1, Annex (hereinafter, Montreal II draft), draft article 2(c); and ENB, "Summary of the Interregional Negotiating Group on Access and Benefit-Sharing: 18–21 September 2010", 2–3. This terminology is deployed in Nagoya Protocol Article 5(1): benefits arising from the 'utilization of genetic resources;' Article 6(1): access to genetic resources 'for their utilization;' Article 15(1): 'genetic resources utilized;' and Article 17(1): 'utilization of genetic resources'. The compromise also included: referring to 'subsequent applications and commercialization' not in the definition of 'utilization' but in Article 5; and providing for the issuance of a permit 'at the time of access' (Nagoya Protocol Article 6.3(e)). See Buck and Hamilton, "The Nagoya Protocol," op. cit., 56.

50   The definition of 'biotechnology' in Nagoya Protocol Article 2(d) is a *verbatim* reproduction of the definition of the term in CBD Article 2. Thus, its inclusion in the Nagoya Protocol is not strictly necessary, since CBD definitions also apply to the Nagoya Protocol. Its inclusion in Article 2 can only be explained by the fact that it creates an explicit, albeit indirect, link between 'derivatives' and 'utilization of genetic resources.' Beyond its implicit relevance whenever 'utilization of genetic resources' appears in other operational provisions of the Protocol, the term 'biotechnology' appears only once in the Protocol text, in the Annex listing examples of monetary and non-monetary benefits which Parties may consider for inclusion in MAT (see Nagoya Protocol Article 5(4) and this commentary on Article 5, section 6).

51   That is, as opposed to the restrictive understanding of biotechnology under the Biosafety Protocol. We are thankful to Riccardo Pavoni for drawing our attention to this point.

52   See CBD Working Group on ABS, "Report of the expert meeting on definitions," UNEP/CBD/WG-ABS/7/2, paragraph 19.

genetic resources'[53] which arguably relates to the reference to 'biochemical compounds' in the definition of 'derivatives', as it is only the latter that provides the necessary elements to circumscribe this otherwise vague concept.[54] The operational value of the definition of 'derivatives' for the Protocol, therefore, is to further clarify the definition of 'utilization of genetic resources': it serves to articulate that *naturally occurring* biochemical compounds *resulting from genetic expression or cellular metabolism, and not containing DNA*, can be the focus of utilization for the purposes of research and development.

While this interpretation of the role of the definition of derivatives in the Protocol appears as the only one to give effect to the entirety of Article 2, the unfortunate drafting may raise doubts in interpreters and as a consequence lead to variations in national legislation implementing the Protocol.[55] When developing domestic ABS frameworks, national legislators would be well advised to establish that they apply not only to genetic resources collected in situ in their territory but also to compounds extracted or resulting from such resources. Guidance from the Protocol's governing body[56] would be beneficial in that regard.

International guidance could also address the case of 'isolated derivatives' – i.e. derivatives acquired and utilized without physical access to genetic resources, such as those already extracted and isolated from their natural environment and available ex situ – which are arguably covered by the definition of 'utilization of genetic resources' and thus by the Protocol.[57] For example:

---

53   Singh Nijar, "An Asian Developing Country's View," op. cit., 250.

54   See fn. 8 above on the vagueness of the notion from a scientific perspective. Note also that the WIPO negotiating text includes a bracketed definition of derivatives that reiterates the wording of Nagoya Protocol Article 2(e): WIPO General Assembly, "Matters concerning the IGC" WO/GA/43/14, Annex A, paragraph 2.

55   See divergence of views between the European Parliament and the Council of the European Union (EU) as to the need for explicit inclusion of derivatives in proposed EU regulation implementing the Nagoya Protocol in the EU in "Amendments adopted by the European Parliament on 12 September 2013 on the proposal for a regulation of the European Parliament and of the Council on Access to Genetic Resources and the Fair and Equitable Sharing of Benefits Arising from their Utilization in the Union (COM(2012)0576 – C7-0322/2012 – 2012/0278(COD))," accessed 30 November 2013, <www.europarl.europa.eu/sides/getDoc.do?type=TA&reference=P7-TA-2013-0373&language=EN&ring=A7-2013-0263>, amendments 38, 39 and 43.

56   Nagoya Protocol Article 26(4): see this commentary on Article 26, section 2.

57   Singh Nijar "An Asian Developing Country's View," op. cit., 250; see also Greiber et al., *Explanatory Guide*, op. cit., 67. This implies that the definition of 'utilization' may lead to situations where there can be benefit-sharing without access in situ (see this commentary on Article 5, section 2). Indeed, at least in the case of the EU, it appears that most commercial users of genetic resources source new material from ex situ collections, including

a plant produces a resin. Such resin is collected, its biochemical compounds are extracted and isolated in the laboratory of the local university. A foreign researcher obtains access only to the isolated biochemical compounds but not to the resin, nor to the plant that produced the resin. As domestic ABS frameworks may cover isolated derivatives differently in provider and user countries, such discrepancy may eventually play out in the cooperation between specific provider and user countries in the context of the compliance provisions of the Protocol.[58]

Finally, an issue that is not explicitly addressed by the Protocol and remains to be clarified relates to bioinformatics, i.e. the application of computer science and information technology to the field of biology, molecular biology in particular. By applying information technology, mankind can further expand and develop the understanding of biological processes. In practice, bioinformatics is a way of realizing the value in the genetic material without the need for access to the biological sources where it was originally found.[59] Thus, it remains unclear whether the definition of 'utilization' covers, and thus the Protocol may apply to, exchanges of *information* concerning derivatives (but no longer exchanges of derivatives as such). However, on the basis of the definition of 'derivative,' it has been observed that 'functional' could refer both to the genetic structure *per se* and to the information encapsulated in the DNA sequence that can be screened and transferred electronically and become

<hr>

from collections in countries of origin. See European Commission, Impact Assessment (Part I) accompanying the Commission proposal for an EU regulation on access to genetic resources and benefit-sharing, SWD(2012) 292 final (4 October 2012), 15. In addition, Schei and Tvedt argue that the interpretation of the definition of 'genetic resources' and their uses needs to be dynamic as regards new technologies, in order to meet the overall objectives of the benefit-sharing objective and obligation in the CBD. See Schei and Tvedt, *Concept of Genetic Resources*, op. cit., 17.

58 See this commentary on Article 15. Practical questions related to ensuring benefit-sharing and enforceability are expected to be addressed on a case-by-case basis, see Singh Nijar "An Asian Developing Country's View," op. cit., 254. In particular, triggering of the Protocol's compliance provisions would be facilitated by national legislation in both user and provider countries providing for documentation requirements or standards to identify the source or origin of the isolated derivative in question, and thus a clear chain of information connecting the genetic resource to the compound used in research and development and requiring due diligence by researchers in that regard. See Buck and Hamilton, "The Nagoya Protocol," op. cit., 53. Impossibility to trace the country of origin and obtain PIC would lead to a situation specifically foreseen by the Protocol as a consideration for the possible creation of a multilateral benefit-sharing mechanism: see this commentary on Article 10, section 2.2.

59 See Schei and Tvedt, *Concept of Genetic Resources*, op. cit., 15.

functional in a new, digital form."[60] In that light, it has been argued that 'the biological *origin* rather than the biological *form* [of the information] matters' for falling under the definition of utilization of genetic resources.[61] Another argument could be made on the basis of the definition of 'utilization of genetic resources,' as research and development on the genetic and/or biochemical 'composition' could be interpreted to include the information this composition is transcribed to. In effect, the definitions of the Protocol appear capable to be interpreted dynamically in the light of relevant technological developments,[62] with a view to including any new technique that 'in fact realizes the value of functional units of heredity'[63] and avoiding that the Protocol become obsolete in a few years' time. That being said, such broad interpretation may create challenges for the architecture of the Protocol, which has been conceived without specific consideration of bioinformatics.

While guidance by the Protocol's governing body on this issue will be needed, the issue has already arisen in the context of the International Treaty on Plant Genetic Resources for Food and Agriculture (ITPGRFA):[64] in 2013, Secretary Shakeel Bhatti highlighted the 'increasing trend for the information and knowledge content of genetic material to be extracted, processed and exchanged in its own right, detached from the physical exchange of the plant genetic material' and called on Parties to widen the focus of the ITPGRFA provisions with the potential to address the non-material values of genetic resources.[65]

---

60   Tvedt and Schei, "The Term 'Genetic Resources,'" op. cit., 20–21.

61   Ibid.

62   Ibid., 21.

63   Ibid., 29. On the question, see also Joseph Henry Vogel et al., "The Economics of Information, Studiously Ignored in the Nagoya Protocol on Access to Genetic Resources and Benefit Sharing," *Law, Environment and Development Journal* 7 (2011): 52.

64   International Treaty on Plant Genetic Resources for Food and Agriculture (Rome, 3 November 2001, in force 29 June 2004) 2400 UNTS 303.

65   See Report of the Secretary of the International Treaty on Plant Genetic Resources on Food and Agriculture, Appendix I in the Report of the Fifth Session of the Governing Body of the International Treaty on Plant Genetic Resources on Food and Agriculture, (2013) FAO Doc IT/GB-5/13/Report, 4–5.

Gene expression

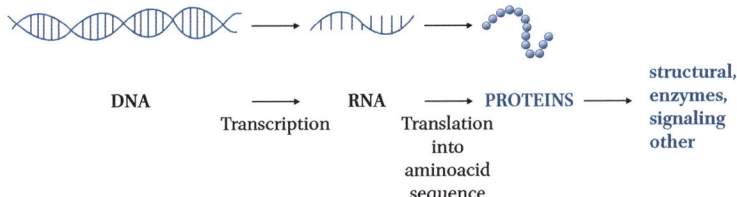

DNA ⟶ RNA ⟶ PROTEINS ⟶ structural, enzymes, signaling other

Transcription   Translation into aminoacid sequence

Genetics resources

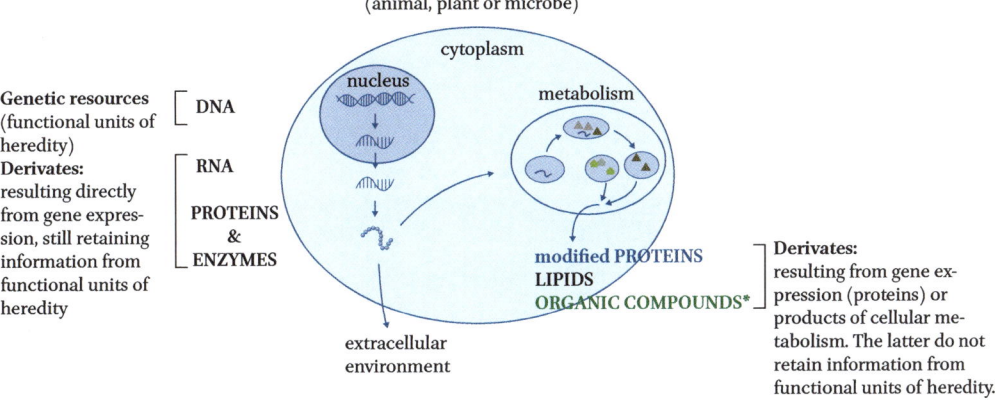

Biological organism (animal, plant or microbe)

cytoplasm

nucleus

metabolism

Genetic resources (functional units of heredity)   DNA

Derivates: resulting directly from gene expression, still retaining information from functional units of heredity   RNA

PROTEINS & ENZYMES

modified PROTEINS
LIPIDS
ORGANIC COMPOUNDS*

extracellular environment

Derivates: resulting from gene expression (proteins) or products of cellular metabolism. The latter do not retain information from functional units of heredity.

ORGANIC COMPOUNDS*

flavonoids, essential oils from plants, resins from plants, and others.

FIGURE 1   *Figure developed by Francesca Morgera on the basis of Bruce Alberts et al.,* Molecular Biology of the Cell, *4th ed (New York: Garland Science; 2002).*

2.2.2   Commodities in Trade

Since the beginning of the negotiations of the Nagoya Protocol, questions have arisen about whether it would affect international trade in commodities (agricultural and forest products, cut flowers, herbal teas, etc.).[66] This was based on some CBD Parties' understanding that ABS could also apply to *biological* resources (as opposed to *genetic* resources), an understanding which was reflected in certain pieces of national legislation.[67] The rationale behind this expansive approach is to prevent a loophole: that access to biological resources for consumptive uses can lead to the use of their genetic or biochemical composition for research and development purposes, without respecting the Protocol requirements on PIC and benefit-sharing at the time of access to the resources (i.e., when they entered international trade).[68] Other CBD Parties, particularly from the industrialized world, were concerned about an excessively broad approach subjecting international trade in commodities to ABS rules and its potential (ab)use by some Parties with a view to establishing non-tariff barriers to trade.[69]

As emerged shortly after the conclusion of the Nagoya Protocol, the use of imported commodities for research and development purposes is not just a matter of academic speculation. In May 2010, Nestlé, the world's largest food company, faced allegations of biopiracy after it applied for five patents involving medicinal uses of two plants found and commonly used in South Africa, rooibos and honeybush, and commonly traded internationally as herbal teas,

---

66   In response, some Parties submitted proposals of operational text at the seventh meeting of the Working Group on ABS that explicitly excluded 'commodities in trade' from the scope of the regime: see CBD, "Compilation of submissions by Parties, governments, international organisations, indigenous and local communities and relevant stakeholders in respect of the main components of the international regime on access and benefit-sharing listed in Decision IX/12, Annex I" (2 February 2009) UN Doc UNEP/CBD/WG-ABS/7/INF/1, paragraphs 24 and 43.

67   See for example Costa Rica's Biodiversity Law No. 7788, 1998, analysed in Jorge Cabrera Medaglia, "The Implementation of the Nagoya Protocol in Latin America and the Caribbean: Challenges and Opportunities," in Morgera, Buck and Tsioumani, *2010 Nagoya Protocol on Access and Benefit-Sharing in Perspective*, op. cit., 331, 343–347. See also Australia, Environment Protection and Biodiversity Conservation Regulations, No. 181, 2000, where 'access to biological resources' means 'the taking of biological resources of native species for research and development on any genetic resources, or biochemical compounds, comprising or contained in the biological resources...'

68   CBD Working Group on ABS, "Report of the expert meeting on definitions," UNEP/CBD/WG-ABS/7/2, paragraph 6.

69   Pavoni, "Nagoya Protocol and WTO Law," op. cit., 197–199.

without having negotiated the relevant permit with the South African government. Two non-governmental organizations (NGOs) alleged that the patent applications were in violation of the South African Biodiversity Act, which implements the CBD provisions on ABS in South Africa. According to it, a company needs a permit from the South African government to do research with commercial intent on, or patent the use of, genetic resources occurring in South Africa. Such a permit can only be obtained if a benefit-sharing agreement has been negotiated.[70] Nestlé maintained that any biopiracy claims are baseless since it neither sourced the plants in South Africa nor did research on them there. Rooibos and honeybush extracts and material were provided by South African suppliers to two Nestlé research facilities in Switzerland and France, which used them for basic research on active ingredients.[71] The company added that the patents were filed to protect research results, but there was no plan for their commercial use. The controversy illustrates the need for additional clarity with regard to the use for research of plants exported as commodities, to address the change of intent and the time when the benefit-sharing obligation arises.[72]

While the final text of the Protocol does not include any explicit reference to commodities,[73] Parties are nonetheless broadly required to take measures, under the compliance provisions of the Protocol, to avoid the circumvention of the general provisions on PIC and benefit-sharing that could potentially arise in the context of the international commodity trade. In view of the Protocol's objective and based on an effectiveness-driven interpretation, these provisions[74] should be interpreted as implying that Parties prevent genetic material and biochemical compounds originated from biological resources imported as commodities from being subjected to research and development without

---

70   "Rooibos robbery: Nestlé accused of biopirating South African genetic resources," Berne Declaration (27 May 2010), accessed 30 November 2013 <www.evb.ch/en/f25001910.html>.

71   "Lessons from the 'rooibos robbery,'" International Centre for Trade and Sustainable Development, *Bridges* vol. 14 no. 4 (10 December 2010), accessed 30 November 2013, <http://ictsd.org/i/news/bridges/98765/>.

72   Ibid.

73   An explicit exclusion was considered during the negotiations but was eventually abandoned: CBD Working Group on ABS, "Draft Protocol on Access to Genetic Resources and the Fair and Equitable Sharing of Benefits Arising from their Utilization to the Convention on Biological Diversity" in "Report of the Third Part of the Ninth Meeting of the Ad Hoc Open-Ended Working Group on Access and Benefit-sharing" (17 October 2010) UN Doc UNEP/CBD/COP/10/5/Add.5, Annex (hereinafter, Nagoya Draft), draft article 3(d).

74   See this commentary on Article 15.

seeking PIC and establishing MAT according to the domestic ABS framework
of the Party where the 'commodity' was acquired.

3   Utilization of Traditional Knowledge

In the absence of an explicit definition, utilization of traditional knowledge
needs to be understood by combining different elements of the Protocol. It
can be interpreted along similar lines to the definition of 'utilization of genetic
resources.' In other words, as traditional knowledge under the Protocol would
serve as lead information for the utilization of genetic resources,[75] it can be
understood as hinging on the same intent (research and development) as in
the case of genetic resources. In addition, this lacuna in the Protocol should be
seen as part of a general approach to avoiding definitions or specifications for
several other expressions used in relation to traditional knowledge. Therefore,
the interpretation of utilization of traditional knowledge needs to allow for
flexibility at the national and sub-national level, given the wide range of contexts within which any traditional knowledge-related concepts and provisions
apply in practice.[76] Furthermore, as any other traditional knowledge-related
term or provision in the Protocol 'utilization of traditional knowledge' needs to
be understood in light of relevant international human rights law,[77] as well as
taking into account indigenous and local communities' customary laws, protocols and procedures.[78]

---

75   CBD Working Group on Article 8(j), "Report of the sixth meeting," UNEP/CBD/COP/10/2,
      36. See discussion in the Introduction to this commentary, section 3.
76   See CBD Working Group on ABS, "Report of the expert meeting on traditional knowledge,"
      UNEP/CBD/WG-ABS/8/2, paragraph 10.
77   See discussion in Introduction to this commentary, section 4.
78   In light of the cross-cutting provision of Nagoya Protocol Article 12(1): see this commen-
      tary on Article 12, section 2.

Article 3. Scope

This Protocol shall apply to genetic resources within the scope of Article 15 of the Convention and to the benefits arising from the utilization of such resources. This Protocol shall also apply to traditional knowledge associated with genetic resources within the scope of the Convention and to the benefits arising from the utilization of such knowledge.

1   Overview

This short provision[1] aims to clarify the ambit of application of the Protocol: it, however, only addresses its subject-matter scope and it does so in a rather obscure manner. Several other scope-related issues, notably the temporal and spatial scope of the Protocol, were heavily debated during the negotiations but were eventually not explicitly addressed in its final text.

Article 3 at least implicitly clarifies that[2] the Protocol applies not only to access to and benefit-sharing from the utilization of genetic resources, but also to traditional knowledge associated with genetic resources. And the Article appears to draw a distinction between the scope of application related to genetic resources and to traditional knowledge.

The following sections will discuss the ambiguity in the delineation of the subject-matter scope of the Protocol and analyze outstanding questions related to its temporal and spatial scope. It should also be noted that other Articles in the Protocol contribute to defining its scope.[3]

---

1   The text reproduces the final compromise proposal of the Japanese COP10 Presidency, which closely follows the text of draft article 3 in the Cali Draft. The only modification was the insertion of an explicit reference to the 'scope of Article 15' of the Convention in relation to genetic resources.

2   As opposed to what can be inferred from the title of the Protocol and its Article 1: see this commentary on Article 1, section 3.

3   See, e.g., this commentary on Articles 2, 4 and 8.

2   Subject-matter Scope

Article 3 appears to distinguish between the scope of the Protocol in relation to genetic resources, which is delimited by a specific reference to Article 15 of the Convention, and the scope in relation to traditional knowledge, which refers to the general scope of Convention.

With regards to traditional knowledge, however, it is difficult to understand what the Nagoya Protocol intends by making a general reference to the Convention, as its text is silent on 'traditional knowledge associated with genetic resources'.[4] With regards to genetic resources, the specific reference to CBD Article 15 is equally puzzling, as that Article does not address questions related to subject-matter scope, but simply reaffirms Parties' rights to regulate access to genetic resources under their national jurisdiction through national law.[5] The only possible explanation for the obscure drafting of Article 3 can be traced back to the negotiators' intention to de-link the spatial scope of the Nagoya Protocol in relation to genetic resources from the CBD provision on jurisdictional scope. The latter states that the Convention applies to processes and activities under Parties' jurisdiction or control also in areas beyond the limits of national jurisdiction.[6] Basically, the Protocol drafters' main concern was to implicitly exclude bioprospecting activities on marine genetic resources in areas beyond national jurisdiction from the scope of the Protocol, as discussed below.

As the overall usefulness of Article 3 of the Protocol is questionable, it will fall on the Protocol's governing body[7] to clarify any questions on subject-matter scope that may arise in the future.

2.1   *Human Genetic Resources*

Although the text of the Convention is silent about human genetic resources, CBD Parties adopted Decision 2/11 stating that human genetic resources are not included within the framework of the Convention.[8] Negotiators debated

---

4 As explained in the Introduction in this commentary, section 3, there is no explicit link between traditional knowledge and genetic resources in the text of the Convention.

5 CBD Article 15(1) reads: 'Recognizing the sovereign rights of States over their natural resources, the authority to determine access to genetic resources rests with the national governments and is subject to national legislation.'

6 CBD Article 4(b). See also Buck and Hamilton, "Nagoya Protocol," op. cit., 57.

7 Nagoya Protocol Article 26(4)(a). See this commentary on Article 26, section 2.

8 See CBD Decision 2/11, "Access to genetic resources" (30 November 1995) UN Doc UNEP/CBD/COP/2/19, paragraph 2.

whether to explicitly exclude human genetic resources from the Protocol's scope,[9] but eventually decided against such an explicit reference. However, CBD Parties, when adopting the Protocol, recalled Decision 2/11 and restated that human genetic resources are not included within the framework of the Protocol, noting that this decision was without prejudice to further consideration of the issue by its governing body.[10]

3   Outstanding Questions

The Protocol is silent on questions related to temporal and spatial scope, although these were heavily debated in the negotiations. Other questions addressed in that context related to the relationship between the Protocol and other international treaties and processes,[11] that will be discussed in the sections of this commentary concerning Articles 4 (Relationship with International Agreements and Instruments) and 8 (Special Circumstances). The following sub-sections will focus on outstanding questions related to the temporal and spatial scope.

3.1   *Temporal Scope*
As regards temporal scope,[12] the Protocol clearly applies to genetic resources and traditional knowledge associated with such resources utilized after the entry into force of the Protocol for a Party. Negotiators, however, had discussed whether the Protocol should address more complex questions related to genetic resources and traditional knowledge acquired after the entry into force of the Convention but before the entry into force of the Protocol. The argument was put forward by developing countries. They argued that the international obligation to share benefits and obtain informed consent prior to access pre-existed the Protocol, as it was already included under the Convention.[13]

---

9   See Montreal I Draft, draft article 3.

10   CBD Decision 10/1, paragraph 5.

11   See references to the ITPGRFA and to human pathogens in Montreal I Draft, draft article 3.

12   Tvedt and Young, *Beyond Access*, op. cit., 14, note some of the uncertainties that already existed regarding the temporal coverage of CBD Article 15.

13   See submissions by Namibia on behalf of the African Group to the CBD Working Group on ABS, "Collation of operative text submitted by Parties, governments, international organisations, indigenous and local communities and relevant stakeholders in respect of the main components of the international regime on access and benefit-sharing listed in Decision IX/12, Annex I" (28 January 2009) UN Doc UNEP/CBD/WG-ABS/7/4, paragraphs 11–12.

They further argued that the benefit-sharing obligation in CBD Article 15(7) is independent from the creation of national ABS frameworks and the establishment of MAT.[14] They thus proposed that the benefit-sharing obligation of the Protocol apply to new and continuing uses of genetic resources and traditional knowledge acquired after the entry into force of the Convention (but before the Protocol's entry into force), under 'modified procedures for benefit-sharing' to be developed by the Protocol's governing body.[15] This, it was argued, would not constitute a retroactive application of the Protocol since the focus would be on new facts.[16] The underlying rationale of the proposal was to expand the range of situations in which the benefit-sharing obligations of the Protocol would apply, and to address possible loopholes related to ex situ collections already existing in developed countries' genebanks. The proposal encountered firm opposition from most developed countries, who wished instead to explicitly exclude 'genetic resources and traditional knowledge associated with genetic resources acquired prior to the entry into force of the Protocol.'[17] A compromise proposal was then put forward by Norway and the African Group to at least create an obligation for States to encourage individual users to take all

---

14   ENB 9/527, "Summary of the Resumed Ninth Meeting of the Working Group on ABS," 5. An argument can be made that, because Article 15(7) is clearly worded, unconditional and framed in unequivocally legally binding terms, it could be self-executing. This point remains contentious: see Tvedt and Young, *Beyond Access*, op. cit., 2 and fn. 9.

15   CBD Working Group on ABS, "Report of the first part of the ninth meeting," UNEP/CBD/ WG-ABS/9/3, paragraph 119; and Montreal I Draft, draft article 3.

16   See Singh Nijar and Pei Fern, *Nagoya ABS Protocol*, op. cit., 26; and Evanson C. Kamau, Bevis Fedder and Gerd Winter, "The Nagoya Protocol on Access to Genetic Resources and Benefit Sharing: What Is New and What Are the Implications for Provider and User Countries and the Scientific Community?," *Law, Environment and Development Journal* 6 (2010): 246, 255, where the authors argue that 'Clearly, this means that any genetic resource or traditional knowledge accessed before [entry into force of the Protocol] cannot retroactively be made subject to PIC requirements. Likewise, any benefits obtained before that date cannot retroactively be subjected to a benefit-sharing obligation. However, it can be argued that the generation of benefits after that date is a new act in terms of Article 28 of the Vienna Convention, or that the holding of the genetic resource or traditional knowledge is a situation which has not ceased to exist.' See also Berne Declaration and Natural Justice, *Access or Utilization – What Triggers User Obligations? A Comment on the Draft Proposal of the European Commission on the Implementation of the Nagoya Protocol on Access and Benefit Sharing* (Cape Town and Zurich: Berne Declaration and Natural Justice, 2013), accessed 1 November 2013, <http://naturaljustice.org/wp-content/uploads/pdf/Submission-EU-ABS-Regulation.pdf>, 6–8.

17   CBD Working Group on ABS, "Report of the second part of the ninth meeting," UNEP/ CBD/COP/10/5/ADD.4, paragraph 133; and Montreal I Draft, draft article 3.

reasonable measures to enter into benefit-sharing arrangements with a country of origin for new and continuous utilization of genetic resources acquired before the entry into force of the Protocol.[18] None of these proposals, however, made it in the final text of the Nagoya Protocol.

As a result, issues related to temporal scope are not specifically addressed by the text of the Protocol.[19] Nevertheless, some commentators have argued that while the Protocol does not apply to genetic resources acquired prior to the entry into force of the CBD, it does not prevent Parties from requiring, in their domestic ABS frameworks, benefit-sharing arising from new and continuing uses of genetic resources acquired after the entry into force of the Convention but before the entry into force of the Protocol.[20] Equally, the text of the Protocol does not exclude that Parties may require benefit-sharing arising from new and continuing uses of traditional knowledge acquired prior to the entry into force of the Protocol.[21] Others, instead, exclude both possibilities, arguing that the main operational provisions of the Protocol refer to genetic resources provided by a *Party to the Protocol* on the basis of its domestic ABS framework.[22]

It may be tentatively concluded that the Protocol does not apply to genetic resources acquired prior to the entry into force of the Convention,[23] but it remains debatable whether benefit-sharing obligations arise under the Protocol for new or continuing uses of genetic resources acquired in the interim period between the entry into force of the CBD and that of the Protocol. As the Protocol is silent on these complex questions, it appears that an interpretative decision or guidance reached by the Protocol Parties collectively through

---

18 See Montreal I Draft, draft article 3, second last paragraph. A similar proposal on traditional knowledge in draft article 9(5) of the Cali Draft was also deleted in the final compromise proposal. CBD Working Group on ABS, "Report of the second part of the ninth meeting," UNEP/CBD/COP/10/5/ADD.4, paragraph 133.

19 VCLT Article 28 reads: 'Unless a different intention appears from the treaty or is otherwise established, its provisions do not bind a Party in relation to any act or fact which took place or any situation which ceased to exist before the date of the entry into force of the treaty with respect to that Party.'

20 Greiber et al, *Explanatory Guide*, op. cit., 72–73.

21 Ibid., 90.

22 Buck and Hamilton, "Nagoya Protocol," op. cit., 57, making reference to Nagoya Protocol Articles 5–6 and 15.

23 The Protocol reference to 'genetic resources within the scope of Article 15 of the Convention' presupposes the existence of a Party to the Convention, i.e., that the Convention has entered into force. That being said, the possibility cannot be excluded that this discussion may be reopened in the context of Nagoya Protocol Article 10: see below in this section.

the Protocol's governing body[24] on how to address new and continuing uses would be desirable. This is particularly critical as practical and legal problems could arise if different Parties were to base their domestic ABS frameworks on different understandings of the temporal scope.[25] To name but a few of such problems, pre-Nagoya Protocol decisions on PIC and MAT may not conform with the Protocol requirements; no internationally recognized certificate of compliance would exist; or users may have already obtained intellectual property rights on material and innovations developed on the basis of genetic resources acquired in good faith before the entry into force of the Protocol. The status of ex situ collections pre-dating the entry into force of the Protocol may be also addressed by the Protocol's governing body in this context. These discussions could also be (and actually have already been)[26] entertained in relation to a possible global benefit-sharing mechanism under the Protocol.[27] The absence of a collective solution on the temporal scope could possibly lead to a situation in which the Protocol's compliance procedures and mechanisms[28] would be used to consider whether lack of implementing measures in a user Party taking a restrictive approach to the question of the temporal scope, that does not support the benefit-sharing claims of a provider Party taking a broader approach to the temporal scope with regard to new uses of material accessed before the Protocol's entry into force, would constitute non-compliance.

---

24   Nagoya Protocol Article 26(4)(a).

25   For example, the draft EU regulation for implementing the Nagoya Protocol in the EU would explicitly apply to genetic resources accessed after the entry into force of the Nagoya Protocol for the Union, with the term 'access' defined as 'the acquisition of genetic resources or traditional knowledge associated with genetic resources *in a Party to the Nagoya Protocol*' (emphasis added): European Commission, Proposal for a Regulation of the European Parliament and of the Council on Access to Genetic Resources and the Fair and Equitable Sharing of Benefits Arising from their Utilization in the Union, COM(2012) 576 final, (hereinafter, EU draft regulation), draft article 2.1.

26   "Draft decision for the consideration of the first meeting of the Conference of the Parties Serving as the Meeting of the Parties to the Nagoya Protocol," in ICNP, "Report of the second meeting of the Open-ended Ad Hoc Intergovernmental Committee for the Nagoya Protocol on Access to Genetic Resources and the Fair and Equitable Sharing of Benefits Arising from Their Utilization," (26 July 2012), UN Doc UNEP/CBD/COP/11/6, Annex, section 2/3, where specific reference is made to issues related to ex situ conservation. See also ENB, "Summary of the Second Meeting of the Intergovernmental Committee for the Nagoya Protocol on Access and Benefit-sharing to the Convention on Biological Diversity: 2–6 July 2012," Vol. 9 No. 579, 9 July 2012, 10.

27   See this commentary on Article 10, section 2.2.

28   See this commentary on Article 30.

3.2   *Spatial Scope*

The negotiators also considered whether the Protocol should only apply to genetic resources over which Parties exercise sovereign rights, and thus whether to include or exclude explicitly from its scope genetic resources from beyond areas of national jurisdiction. The latter include genetic resources located in marine areas beyond the limits of national jurisdiction (the high seas[29] and the Area)[30] or the Antarctic Treaty Area.[31]

With regard to marine genetic resources located beyond national jurisdiction, the reference to CBD Article 15 in the Protocol arguably serves to emphasize genetic resources over which States exercise sovereign rights and implicitly indicate the negotiators' intention to de-link the spatial scope of the Nagoya Protocol from CBD Article 4(b). This would suggest that bioprospecting for genetic resources in areas beyond national jurisdiction does not fall under the scope of the Nagoya Protocol.[32] Whether this is indeed the case,

---

29   UNCLOS Part VII.

30   The Area is 'the sea-bed and ocean floor and subsoil thereof, beyond the limits of national jurisdiction' (UNCLOS Article 1(1)(1)). UNCLOS Part XI and Agreement relating to the Implementation of Part XI of the United Nations Convention on the Law of the Sea (New York, 28 July 1994, in force 28 July 1996) 1836 UNTS 3.

31   See references to excluding or specifically inducing in the scope 'genetic resources located in the Antarctic Treaty Area, which is the area south of latitude 60° South,' 'genetic resources beyond national jurisdictions' and 'genetic resources from marine areas beyond national jurisdiction' in Montreal I Draft, draft article 3, which foresaw (in case of inclusion in the scope) a mandate for the Protocol's governing body to adopt modified procedures for benefit-sharing for genetic resources. For a discussion of this specific issue, see CBD Working Group on ABS, "Study on the relationship between an international regime on access and benefit-sharing and other international instruments and forums that govern the use of genetic resources. The Antarctic Treaty System (ATS) and the United Nations Convention on the Law of the Sea (UNCLOS). Note by the Executive Secretary" (3 March 2009) UN Doc UNEP/CBD/WG-ABS/7/INF/3/Part3; Patrizia Vigni, "Antarctic Bioprospecting: Is It Compatible with the Value of Antarctica as a Natural Reserve?," in Francioni and Scovazzi, *Biotechnology and International Law*, op. cit., 111; Morten W. Tvedt, "Patent Law and Bioprospecting in Antarctica," *Polar Record* 47 (2011): 46; and Dagmar Lohan and Sam Johnston, *The International Regime for Bioprospecting. Existing Policies and Emerging Issues for Antarctica* (Tokyo: United Nations University Institute of Advanced Studies, 2003).

32   In favour of this interpretation: Buck and Hamilton, "Nagoya Protocol," op. cit., 57; Veit Koester, *The Nagoya Protocol on ABS: Ratification by the EU and Its Member States and Implementation Challenges* (Paris, France: IDDRI, 2012), accessed 30 November 2013, <www.iddri.org/Publications/Collections/Analyses/STUDY0312_VK_nagoya%20abs.pdf>, 16–17; Charlotte Salpin, "The Law of the Sea: A before and an after Nagoya?" in

however, remains debatable,[33] as ultimately the Protocol (and the CBD provision referred to in this context) are silent on this complex question and a clear determination on this issue is needed at the multilateral level. It cannot thus be excluded that the Nagoya Protocol's governing body may consider the matter explicitly in the future. This may well be the case depending on progress or lack thereof in ongoing discussions[34] on marine biodiversity in areas beyond national jurisdiction under the UN General Assembly.[35] It should in fact be emphasized that at the time of writing, discussions under the General Assembly have not reached the stage of formal intergovernmental negotiations on that matter.[36] An interpretative decision or guidance by the Protocol's

Morgera, Buck and Tsioumani, *2010 Nagoya Protocol on Access and Benefit-Sharing in Perspective*, op. cit., 149, 177; and Greiber et al., *Explanatory Guide*, op. cit., 73.

33   Sebastian Oberthür and Justyna Pozarowska, "The Impact of the Nagoya Protocol on the Evolving Institutional Complex of ABS Governance," in Oberthür and Rosendal, *Global Governance of Genetic Resources*, op. cit., 178, 188, conclude that the 'the situation of the geographical scope of the Nagoya Protocol remains ambiguous and it should in any event be difficult to oppose the notion of mutual supportiveness.' On mutual supportiveness between the Protocol and a future instrument on marine genetic resources in areas beyond national jurisdiction, see this commentary on Article 4, section 3.3.

34   UN General Assembly, "Oceans and the Law of the Sea" (2005) UN Doc A/RES/59/24, paragraph 73.

35   For a discussion of the possible interactions between the UN General Assembly and the Nagoya Protocol, see Salpin, "Law of the Sea," op. cit., 179–182.

36   In the context of the Ad Hoc Open-ended Informal Working Group to study issues relating to the conservation and sustainable use of marine biological diversity beyond areas of national jurisdiction, under the authority of the UN General Assembly. At its fourth meeting in 2011 the Working Group concluded that 'A process be initiated, by the General Assembly, with a view to ensuring that the legal framework for the conservation and sustainable use of marine biodiversity in areas beyond national jurisdiction effectively addresses those issues by identifying gaps and ways forward, including through the implementation of existing instruments and the possible development of a multilateral agreement under the United Nations Convention on the Law of the Sea': UN General Assembly, "Letter dated 30 June 2011 from the Co-Chairs of the Ad Hoc Open-ended Informal Working Group to the President of the General Assembly" (30 June 2011) UN Doc A/66/119, Annex, paragraph 1(a). At its sixth meeting in 2013, the Working Group decided 'to establish a process within the Working Group to prepare for a decision by the General Assembly before the end of its sixty-ninth session on marine biodiversity in areas beyond national jurisdiction, including by taking a decision on the development of an international instrument under UNCLOS.' UN General Assembly, "Letter dated 23 September 2013 from the Co-Chairs of the Ad Hoc Open-ended Informal Working Group to the President of the General Assembly," (23 September 2013) UN Doc A/68/399, Annex, paragraph 9.

governing body[37] may thus become necessary, particularly if the discussions under the General Assembly do not make significant progress by the time the Nagoya Protocol comes into force. In that regard, it may also be possible that Parties may decide to address some of this and the other above-mentioned questions in the context of the possible multilateral benefit-sharing mechanism under Article 10.[38]

---

37   Nagoya Protocol Article 26(4)(a): see this commentary on Article 26, section 2.

38   As a situation where it is not possible to grant or obtain PIC for the use of genetic resources: see this commentary on Article 10, section 2.2. Note that for those arguing that marine genetic resources beyond national jurisdiction fall outside the scope of the Nagoya Protocol, consideration of marine genetic resources in areas beyond national jurisdiction in the context of a possible multilateral benefit-sharing mechanism would require renegotiating the scope of the Protocol: Salpin, "Law of the Sea," op. cit., 177–179. The question has been put on the agenda of the first meeting of the Parties to the Protocol: see "Draft Decision for the consideration of the first meeting of the Conference of the Parties Serving as the Meeting of the Parties to the Nagoya Protocol," in ICNP, "Report of the second meeting of the Open-ended Ad Hoc Intergovernmental Committee for the Nagoya Protocol on Access to Genetic Resources and the Fair and Equitable Sharing of Benefits Arising from Their Utilisation," (26 July 2012) UN Doc UNEP/CBD/COP/11/6, Annex, Recommendation 2/3.

Article 4. Relationship with International Agreements and Instruments

1. The provisions of this Protocol shall not affect the rights and obligations of any Party deriving from any existing international agreement, except where the exercise of those rights and obligations would cause a serious damage or threat to biological diversity. This paragraph is not intended to create a hierarchy between this Protocol and other international instruments.

2. Nothing in this Protocol shall prevent the Parties from developing and implementing other relevant international agreements, including other specialized access and benefit-sharing agreements, provided that they are supportive of and do not run counter to the objectives of the Convention and this Protocol.

3. This Protocol shall be implemented in a mutually supportive manner with other international instruments relevant to this Protocol. Due regard should be paid to useful and relevant ongoing work or practices under such international instruments and relevant international organizations, provided that they are supportive of and do not run counter to the objectives of the Convention and this Protocol.

4. This Protocol is the instrument for the implementation of the access and benefit-sharing provisions of the Convention. Where a specialized international access and benefit-sharing instrument applies that is consistent with, and does not run counter to the objectives of the Convention and this Protocol, this Protocol does not apply for the Party or Parties to the specialized instrument in respect of the specific genetic resource covered by and for the purpose of the specialized instrument.

1 Overview

Article 4 is a complex provision seeking to clarify the relationship of the Protocol with existing *and* future international agreements.[1] First, it encapsu-

---

1   From a political science perspective, this has been seen as 'an attempt to reinforce the central position of the international biodiversity regime in global ABS governance' by seeking

lates the implied compromise reached by CBD Parties that the Nagoya Protocol will not serve as a *comprehensive* framework,[2] in the global governance of ABS transactions. As it will be argued below, it indicates (although not very clearly) that the Protocol will address ABS issues when and to the extent to which these are not addressed by other international ABS instruments. It will not subsume previous ABS agreements or subordinate to the Protocol rules future ABS agreements.[3] Vis-à-vis these instruments, the Protocol thus establishes a residual regime.

Nonetheless, this provision aims to limit the discretion of Protocol Parties in negotiating new international instruments, by reference to mutual support-iveness with the objective of the CBD and the Protocol.[4] In that connection, it is significant that the question of the relationship of the Protocol with other international instruments is addressed in the operative part of the Protocol, rather than in its preamble. This placement would make Article 4 a 'substan-tive standard of conduct incumbent upon State Parties,' rather than just an aid to contextual interpretation.[5] The provision's convoluted language, however, complicates interpretation and may well prevent the Article from realizing

---

to clarify the division of labour among different international processes and providing guid-ance for future developments in other institutions, and has been considered to have had some success in that direction (in the context of the General Assembly Working Group on Marine Biodiversity, the Antarctic Treaty System, the World Health Organization (WHO) and WIPO): Oberthür and Pozarowska, "Impact of the Nagoya Protocol," op. cit., 179, 187–189, 231, 240 and 243.

2   Note the proposed preambular language that did not make it into the final text of the Protocol *'noting* that this Protocol will be the *comprehensive* protocol on access and benefit-sharing and that WIPO should use this Protocol as a basis for its ongoing work', emphasis added, CBD Working Group on ABS, "Report of the third part of the ninth meeting of the Ad Hoc Open-ended Working Group on Access and Benefit-Sharing" (17 October 2010) UN Doc UNEP/CBD/COP/10/5/Add.5, 8.

3   This is also reflected in the CBD COP decision adopting the final text of the Nagoya Protocol (CBD Decision 10/1, 6th preambular recital, where CBD Parties recognized 'that the International Regime is constituted of the Convention on Biological Diversity, the Nagoya Protocol..., *as well as complementary* instruments, including the International Treaty on Plant Genetic Resources for Food and Agriculture and the Bonn Guidelines...,' emphasis added).

4   The role of the Protocol as a regime that applies by default (when and to the extent to which other international ABS instruments do not apply) also explains the provisions on 'special considerations' in Article 8. See this commentary on Article 8.

5   Riccardo Pavoni, "Mutual Supportiveness as a Principle of Interpretation and Law-Making: A Watershed for the 'WTO-and-Competing-Regimes' Debate?," *European Journal of International Law* 21 (2010): 649, 658.

its aim. Article 4 in part combines language from the CBD,[6] with language on mutual supportiveness that was borrowed (in a slightly different formulation) from other multilateral environmental agreements.[7]

The sections below aim to suggest a coherent and effective interpretation of this Article by differentiating between its bearing on the relationship between the Protocol and other *existing* agreements, *future* international agreements, and more specifically other (existing and future) international agreements or instruments *specialized* in ABS. The negotiating history is particularly significant to understand which existing and future international instruments were identified by the Protocol negotiators as directly relevant for the interpretation or implementation of the Nagoya Protocol.[8]

2   Relationship with *Existing* Agreements

Article 4(1) focuses on the relationship of the Protocol with existing international agreements. The provision attempts to clarify the relationship between the Protocol and other international treaties (not necessarily environmental ones)[9] in existence at the time of its adoption (or possibly at the time of its entry into force). In doing so, Article 4 relies on the text of CBD Article 22(1) *verbatim*.[10] Furthermore, it adds that the provision is 'not intended to create a hierarchy between this Protocol and other international instruments'.[11]

---

6   CBD Article 22(1), which reads 'The provisions of this Convention shall not affect the rights and obligations of any Contracting Party deriving from any existing international agreement, except where the exercise of those rights and obligations would cause a serious damage or threat to biological diversity.' This accords with VCLT Article 30(2), which reads: 'When a treaty specifies that is subject to, or that it is not to be considered incompatible with, an earlier or later treaty, the provisions of that other treaty prevail.'

7   Pavoni, "Mutual Supportiveness," op. cit., 205–206.

8   See CBD Working Group on ABS, "Study on the relationship between an international regime on access and benefit-sharing and other international instruments and forums that govern the use of genetic resources" (3 March 2009) UN Doc UNEP/CBD/WG-ABS/7/INF/3/Part.1.

9   Glowka, Burhenne-Guilmin and Synge, *Guide to the Convention on Biological Diversity*, op. cit., 109.

10   See fn. 6 above.

11   The same language can be found in the preamble of the Rotterdam Convention on the Prior Informed Consent Procedure for Certain Hazardous Chemicals and Pesticides in International Trade (Rotterdam, 10 September 1998, in force 24 February 2004) 2244 UNTS 337 ('Rotterdam PIC Convention') and ITPGRFA. Note that instead the Cartagena Protocol preamble refers to 'not [being] intended to *subordinate* this Protocol to

The overall meaning of Article 4(1) is, however, quite unclear. The wording borrowed from the CBD is that of a *reverse conflict clause*. It has been interpreted as giving 'conditional priority' to CBD Parties' obligations arising from other treaties existing at the time of the conclusion of the CBD over their obligations arising from the Convention, but only in the absence of a 'serious damage or threat' to biodiversity.[12] In the presence of such damage or threat, conversely, the CBD would oblige its Parties to give their obligations under the Convention precedence over their obligations from other international agreements. But the Protocol Article 4(1) then adds that the reverse conflict clause is not intended to create a hierarchy among international instruments. The additional wording presumably limits to a case-by-case application the conditional priority assigned to the Protocol by the beginning of Article 4(1). Since priority – rather than 'hierarchical' superiority – should be assigned to other international agreements, in the absence of a serious damage or threat to biodiversity, Article 4(1) expresses the intention to preclude an interpretation of the Protocol that would lead to a modification of Protocol Parties' obligations under other existing international agreements[13] relevant for ABS.

In doing so, Article 4(1) seems to reflect the wide margin of discretion also afforded by the CBD reverse conflict clause to CBD Parties. It equally implies a duty for Parties (collectively) to be constantly alert to, and promptly identify, any 'serious damage or threat' to biodiversity that may materialize from other international regimes.[14] In that connection, the normative activity of the CBD governing body is highly significant in periodically crystallizing consensus in the identification of serious threats to biodiversity, thereby triggering the prevalence of the CBD over other obligations arising from existing international agreements.[15] A similar approach in the context of the Nagoya Protocol could thus be adopted, although it is difficult to identify *in abstracto* specific

---

other international agreements' (emphasis added) and discussion by Pavoni, "Mutual Supportiveness," op. cit., 654. Note also proposals to include language on non-subordination in the Protocol that were not included in the final text: CBD Working Group on ABS, "Report of the first part of the ninth meeting," UNEP/CBD/WG-ABS/9/3, 108 and ENB 9/527, "Summary of the Resumed Ninth Meeting of the Working Group on ABS," 4.

12   Pavoni, "Mutual Supportiveness," op. cit., 655.

13   Similarly to what was suggested in interpreting comparable language in the Biosafety Protocol by Ruth Mackenzie et al., *An Explanatory Guide to the Cartagena Protocol on Biosafety* (Gland: IUCN, 2003), 29.

14   Based on a similar interpretation of CBD Article 22, see discussion in Elisa Morgera, "Faraway, So Close: A Legal Analysis of the Increasing Interactions between the Convention on Biological Diversity and Climate Change Law," *Climate Law* 2 (2011): 85, 88.

15   Ibid., 91.

ABS-related activities that could cause a serious damage or threat to biodiversity. Ultimately, the most effective interpretation of Article 4(1) is thus that Parties should avoid any 'principled' or *a priori* approach in assessing and addressing the relationship of the Nagoya Protocol with other existing international agreements, but rather focus on a pragmatic, case-by-case approach to mutual supportiveness – as confirmed by the first sentence in Article 4(3).

The concept of 'mutual supportiveness' – that is key to the whole of Article 4 – has a two-fold implication for the conduct of States.[16] First, it requires, at the *interpretative* level, that States 'disqualify' solutions to tensions between competing regimes involving the subordination of one regime to the other. Second, at the *law-making* level, it requires that States exert good-faith efforts to negotiate and conclude instruments that clarify the relationship between competing regimes, particularly when interpretative reconciliation efforts have been exhausted.[17] Article 4(1) thus seems to relate to the first dimension of mutual supportiveness. This is further clarified by the Protocol preamble, where Parties 'recogniz[e] that international instruments related to [ABS] should be mutually supportive with a view to achieving the objectives of the Convention'.[18]

In addition, Article 4(3) mandates Parties to implement the Protocol in a mutually supportive manner with other 'relevant' international instruments. It implicitly expects Parties to identify, monitor and take into account international instruments that may not necessarily focus on ABS, but directly or indirectly relate to it. It provides, however, no specific guidance as to how to resolve any conflict that may arise between the Protocol and other international agreements, but rather reflects Parties' 'awareness of the potential for conflict and their aspiration that any such conflict be resolved in a manner that respects both instruments.'[19]

Article 4(3) further encourages[20] 'due regard . . . to useful and relevant ongoing work or practices under such international instruments and relevant international organizations, provided that they are supportive of and do not run counter to the objectives of the Convention and this Protocol' in implementing

---

16   Pavoni, "Mutual Supportiveness," op. cit., 650–651.

17   Ibid., particularly 661–669.

18   Nagoya Protocol 20th preambular recital.

19   As was noted in the context of the Biosafety Protocol: see Mackenzie et al., *Explanatory Guide to the Cartagena Protocol*, op. cit., 27.

20   Note the non-legally binding language of the second sentence of Nagoya Protocol Article 4(3): 'should.'

the Protocol. The drafting is quite unusual and highly unclear.[21] The imprecise expression 'ongoing work and practices'[22] could arguably include not only negotiations of treaties but also of soft-law instruments. It may also refer to negotiations of other (technical) documents or to the conduct of activities on the ground undertaken in the context of international agreements or under the auspices, or with the technical support, of intergovernmental institutions. It remains to be seen which specific 'work and practices' will be deemed 'useful and relevant' to trigger this provision. At the time of the Protocol negotiations, relevant international instrument(s) were being negotiated under the World Health Organization (WHO)[23] and under WIPO,[24] and relevant discussions were held under the FAO's Commission on Genetic Resources for Food and Agriculture (CGRFA).[25] As these developments are inherently subject to evolution and other relevant work may be initiated in other intergovernmental contexts, a collective determination of ongoing work and practices for the purposes of Article 4(3) by the Parties may be necessary at regular intervals. The Protocol's governing body is consequently to monitor ongoing *intergovernmental*[26] developments on matters related to ABS, as long as they are 'supportive of, and do not run counter to the objectives' of the CBD and the Nagoya Protocol. The Protocol's governing body may then provide consensus guidance in this regard, if necessary, including in the context of its provision on assessment and review.[27]

---

21   Singh Nijar "An Asian Developing Country's View," op. cit., 263; Singh Nijar and Pei Fern, *Nagoya ABS Protocol*, op. cit., 26; and Greiber et al., *Explanatory Guide*, op. cit., 78–80.

22   The expression 'ongoing work in other international forums relating to access and benefit-sharing' can also be found in the Nagoya Protocol 18th preambular paragraph, which does not shed further light on the matter.

23   See Marie Wilke, "A Healthy Look at the Nagoya Protocol – Implications for Global Health Governance," in Morgera, Buck and Tsioumani, *2010 Nagoya Protocol on Access and Benefit-Sharing in Perspective*, op. cit., 123, 142–143; and section 4.2 below.

24   See section 3.1 below.

25   Chiarolla, Louafi and Schloen, "Analysis of the Relationship", op. cit., 114–115.

26   Ongoing work and practices that involve State *and* non-State actors, or *only* non-State actors (i.e., *transnational* work and practices on ABS as opposed to intergovernmental ones) is not addressed by Nagoya Protocol Article 4(3), since this provision is limited to work or practices 'under [international] instruments and relevant international organizations.' Transnational work and practices may rather be considered as 'codes of conduct, guidelines and best practices and/or standards: see this commentary on Article 20.

27   See this commentary on Article 31, as CBD Decision 10/1, paragraph 6 suggests with specific regard to the WIPO negotiations.

2.1   *Examples of Existing Agreements*

While existing international instruments specializing on ABS will be discussed below, at least five sets of existing international norms may be considered relevant for the purposes of Article 4(1) and (3). Parties, in their implementation of the Protocol at the domestic level, as well as in the context of the Protocol's governing body or in other concerned multilateral fora, will have to ensure mutual supportiveness between the Protocol and: i) international law on human rights, ii) the UNESCO Convention on Intangible Cultural Heritage,[28] iii) the law of the sea, iv) the law of the World Trade Organization (WTO) and v) international investment law.

With regards to *international human rights law*, the Protocol preamble notes the relevance of the UN Declaration on the Rights of Indigenous Peoples.[29] While it may be debatable whether, as a formally non-legally binding instrument, UNDRIP may be considered an 'existing international agreement' for the purposes of Article 4, it is certainly true that the Nagoya Protocol will have to be interpreted so as not to derogate from the obligations of Parties under their applicable international human rights agreements, many of which are reflected in UNDRIP.[30] This relationship may be particularly relevant with regard to indigenous peoples and local communities.[31] But international human rights law also applies to individuals as users and providers in relation to the notions of participation, access to information and access to justice under the Protocol.[32] Specific instances where the relationship between the Protocol and international human rights law is particularly relevant will be discussed more specifically in this commentary in relation to the relevant operative provisions of the Protocol.[33]

The scope of the *UNESCO Convention on Intangible Cultural Heritage* extends to 'knowledge and practices concerning nature',[34] so also traditional knowledge associated with genetic resources.[35] To that extent, the UNESCO

---

28   UNESCO Convention for the Safeguarding of the Intangible Cultural Heritage (Paris, 17 October 2003, in force 20 April 2006) 2368 UNTS 35 (hereinafter, UNESCO Convention on Intangible Cultural Heritage).

29   Nagoya Protocol 26th preambular recital.

30   See Introduction to this commentary, section 4.1.

31   On the relevance of indigenous peoples' human rights for local communities, see Introduction to this commentary, section 4.2.

32   Savaresi, "International Human Rights Law Implications," op. cit., 74.

33   See this commentary on Articles 5, 6, 7, 12, 14, 13, 17, 18 and 21.

34   UNESCO Convention on Intangible Cultural Heritage, Article 2(2)(d).

35   Lenzerini, "Indigenous Peoples' Cultural Rights," op. cit., 129. The relevance of the UNESCO Convention for traditional knowledge associated with biodiversity more generally

Convention appears to qualify as a relevant existing agreement for the purposes of Article 4 of the Protocol. The Convention creates several obligations for its Parties that are of relevance to traditional knowledge associated with genetic resources, such as the obligation to develop inventories of traditional knowledge present in its Parties' territory with the 'participation of communities,'[36] and a best-endeavor obligation to adopt domestic measures aimed at 'ensuring *access* to the intangible cultural heritage while respecting customary practices governing access to specific aspects of such heritage.'[37] Parties both to the Protocol and to the UNESCO Convention will thus have to interpret and implement their respective obligations related to traditional knowledge associated with genetic resources in a mutually supportive manner. In particular, Parties to the Nagoya Protocol will have to raise the bar significantly compared to the UNESCO Convention by ensuring PIC (or approval and involvement) is obtained from indigenous and local communities before access to traditional knowledge associated with genetic resources is granted and by ensuring fair and equitable benefit-sharing, in light of the more specific standards included in the Protocol in that regard.[38]

With regard to the *law of the sea*,[39] the Protocol will have to be implemented in relation to ABS-related activities in marine areas 'consistently with' the rights and obligations arising from the UN Convention on the Law of the Sea (UNCLOS) or relevant customary law for those Parties to the Protocol that are not Parties to UNCLOS.[40] In other words, the application of the Nagoya

---

is currently discussed under the CBD Working Group on Article 8(j) pursuant to the mandate on misappropriation of traditional knowledge in CBD Decision 11/14, section C, paragraph 2. See CBD Article 8(j) Working Group, "How Tasks 7, 10 and 12 could best contribute to work under the Convention and to the Nagoya Protocol. Revised note by the Executive Secretary" (23 September 2013) UN Doc UNEP/CBD/WG8J/8/4/Rev.2, paragraphs 3 and 55; and "Study on How Tasks 7, 10 And 12 of the Revised Programme of Work on Article 8(j) and Related Provisions Could Best Contribute to Work under the Convention and the Nagoya Protocol" (12 September 2013) UN Doc UNEP/CBD/WG8J/8/INF/5, paragraphs 13–14.

36   UNESCO Convention on Intangible Cultural Heritage Articles 11(b) and 12(1).

37   UNESCO Convention on Intangible Cultural Heritage Article 13(d)(ii), emphasis added. Article 13(d)(iii) also foresees the development of domestic measures aimed at establishing documentation institutions for the intangible cultural heritage and facilitating access to them.

38   We are grateful to Federico Lenzerini for a very useful preliminary exchange of ideas on this question.

39   See CBD Working Group on ABS, "Study on the relationship between an international ABS regime, the Antarctic Treaty System and UNCLOS," UNEP/CBD/WG-ABS/7/INF/3/PART3.

40   While the CBD has 193 Parties, UNCLOS has 166.

Protocol will have to respect the general jurisdictional framework applicable to the oceans established by the law of the sea, which distinguishes between different areas within and beyond national jurisdiction. In doing so, however, Protocol Parties may face several uncertainties and challenges in implementing the two instruments in a mutually supportive manner, as the law of the sea does not address explicitly questions related to genetic resources.[41] In areas within national jurisdiction, even when it can be argued that existing provisions under the law of the sea and the Protocol may be interpreted in a mutually supportive way, challenges may arise from the proceduralization and contractualization of ABS transactions required by the Protocol and the UNCLOS consent regime for marine scientific research for commercial purposes,[42] or from the application of the Protocol provisions concerning indigenous and local communities, on whose rights and traditional knowledge UNCLOS is silent.[43] Much more uncertainty and controversy surrounds the status and regime applicable to marine genetic resources in areas beyond national jurisdiction, as discussed below.[44]

With regard to *WTO law*, while possible conflicts were very prominent in the negotiations of the Protocol, in particular in relation to IPRs,[45] the final compromise text carefully avoids any reference to this specific relationship.[46] In that respect, it has been noted that the Nagoya Protocol was a 'golden opportunity [that] has been lost' for shielding environmental measures taken in the common interest of humanity against essentially reciprocal trade obligations under the WTO.[47] In fact, it is argued that while the Nagoya Protocol does not impose WTO-inconsistent obligations on its Parties, its neutral[48] provisions vis-à-vis trade-related measures may allow Parties to pass national ABS legis-

---

41   An exhaustive analysis of these challenges exceeds the scope of this commentary. A preliminary, but systematic analysis can be found in Salpin, "Law of the Sea", op. cit.

42   Ibid., 161–163.

43   Ibid., 169. Although note that Articles 5(i) and 24(2)(b) of the Agreement for the Implementation of the Provisions of the United Nations Convention on the Law of the Sea of 10 December 1982 relating to the Conservation and Management of Straddling Fish Stocks and Highly Migratory Fish Stocks (New York, 4 August 1995, in force 11 December 2001) 2167 UNTS 3, may be relevant in relation to indigenous peoples and local communities. We are grateful to Adriana Bessa for drawing our attention to this point.

44   See section 4.3 below.

45   See Introduction to this commentary, section 1.1.

46   For this reason, this commentary will address questions related to IPRs only to the extent necessary to better understand the sparse references in the Protocol.

47   Pavoni, "Nagoya Protocol and WTO Law," op. cit., 212.

48   Ibid.

lation that may be considered at variance with WTO rules and possibly put those Parties on the losing side in a WTO law dispute, because they are unable to justify these measures on the basis of an authoritative mandate from the Protocol.[49]

Finally, *international investment law* may also be relevant. Although there have been no international decisions on a conflict between ABS norms and investment disciplines, it remains a possibility that an investment dispute-resolution mechanism may be seized by users who can claim to act as foreign investors against provider-country Parties when domestic ABS provisions implementing the Nagoya Protocol in relation to access[50] or benefit-sharing[51] may be alleged to conflict with the terms of bilateral investment treaties.[52] Each Party has thus to ensure that the Nagoya Protocol and applicable invest-ment treaties are implemented in a mutually supportive way. Provider coun-tries may be well advised to explicitly justify domestic ABS frameworks on the basis of the Protocol, as well as of applicable international human rights law in as far as indigenous and local communities are concerned,[53] to reduce their investment-related litigation risk.[54] On the other hand, it has been noted that the existence of 'broad permissive commitments' in the Protocol suffices to alert international investors to include risks arising from ABS regulation in their due diligence assessments.[55]

3   Relationships with *Future* Agreements

Article 4(2) acknowledges the possibility that Protocol Parties may negoti-ate new international agreements that may 'relate' to the Protocol, including

---

49   Ibid., 204. Note that bilateral trade agreements could also address WTO law-related issues: see section 3 below.

50   See this commentary on Article 6.

51   Such as joint ventures: Nagoya Protocol Annex, 1(i). See this commentary on Article 5, section 6.

52   Jorge E. Viñuales, *Foreign Investment and the Environment in International Law* (Cambridge: Cambridge University Press, 2012), 205.

53   As investment tribunals are generally more reluctant to fully consider the implications of international environmental law for the disputes they are tasked to decide: Ibid., 215.

54   Ibid., 206.

55   As a highly specialized bioprospecting investor would find it difficult to argue that it was not (and could not have been) aware of relevant international environmental rules when arguing before an investment dispute settlement tribunal: ibid., 213. See discussion in this commentary on Article 6, Section 3.1.

specialized ABS agreements but also other international instruments that only indirectly or partly concern ABS. But such possibility is conditioned upon ensuring that future international agreements 'are supportive of and do not run counter to the objectives of the Convention and of the Protocol'. The second (law-making) dimension of mutual supportiveness, therefore, comes into play when Article 4 refers to *future* international agreements. In light of the understanding of the principle of mutual supportiveness outlined above, it can be argued that Article 4(2) limits Parties' international law-making discretion by requiring that they exert good-faith efforts to negotiate and conclude new instruments with a view to clarifying the relationship with the Protocol and ensuring that the objectives of the CBD and the Protocol on achieving fair and equitable benefit-sharing among and within States[56] are respected. That is, at the very least, Protocol Parties should seek to ensure not only that these objectives are not undermined, but also that their realization is contributed to, by future international agreements.[57]

Besides its relevance for future specialized ABS agreements (discussed below), the provision is of particular relevance for the ongoing negotiations under WIPO, also discussed below. It may also become particularly relevant for *bilateral* agreements to be concluded between a provider and user country to address either ABS issues in general or the implementation of the Protocol in particular.

Bilateral agreements may be particularly relevant in situations specifically foreseen by the Protocol, such as where transboundary cooperation may be necessary,[58] but also focus on[59] or deal with ABS in the context of broader bilateral trade and/or cooperation agreements.[60] These agreements could certainly raise issues related to their mutual supportiveness with the Protocol, and Parties are therefore to exercise their negotiating discretion to ensure that

---

56   See this commentary on Article 1.

57   Indeed, Nagoya Protocol Article 4(2) explicitly points the negative and positive side – 'supportive of and do not run counter to the objectives of the Convention and [the] Protocol'. See Pavoni, "Nagoya Protocol and WTO Law," op. cit., 207.

58   See this commentary on Article 11. Young, "An International Cooperation Perspective," op. cit., 496.

59   Ibid., 496–8. Young refers in particular to bilateral negotiations initiated by traditionally user countries, such as the US and Japan.

60   E.g., United States-Peru Trade Promotion Agreement (Washington, DC, 12 April 2006; in force 1 February 2009), Article 18(1) and "US-Peru TPA, Understanding Regarding Biodiversity and Traditional Knowledge," US Government (2006), accessed 30 November 2013, <www.ustr.gov/sites/default/files/uploads/agreements/fta/peru/asset_upload_file 719_9535.pdf>; Free Trade Agreement between the EU and Its Member States, of the One Part, and Colombia and Peru, of the Other Part, [2012] OJ L354/3, Articles 272(2)–272(5).

these agreements do not run counter to the CBD and Protocol objectives. This may prove particularly difficult in the case of free trade and/or investment agreements, whose lengthy text may include several non-ABS related clauses that may promote biodiversity-damaging activities.[61] This also applies when bilateral agreements involve non-Parties to the Protocol, and can indeed provide a specific opportunity in which Parties can comply with their obligation to encourage non-Parties to adhere to the Protocol.[62] In addition, international human rights law may also apply to these bilateral negotiations. Thus States are expected to ensure that they maintain adequate policy space to meet their international obligations relating to indigenous peoples,[63] including when negotiating bilateral trade and investment agreements that may affect human rights applicable to ABS transactions.[64]

3.1   *WIPO Negotiations*

Established in 2001, the WIPO Intergovernmental Committee on Intellectual Property and Genetic Resources, Traditional Knowledge and Folklore (IGC) is a result of the influence of the CBD principles, as well as of developing countries' concerns regarding the consequences of patents over genetic resources and traditional knowledge, and injustices enshrined in the intellectual property system.[65] The IGC has been undertaking text-based negotiations towards an international legal instrument or instruments to ensure the effective protection of genetic resources, traditional knowledge and traditional cultural expressions through intellectual property rights 'without prejudice to the work pursued in other fora.'[66] Such fora include in particular the TRIPS Council, other WIPO committees and bodies such as the Working Group on the Patent

---

61   Both the EU and the US have put in place environmental assessments of their bilateral trade negotiations with a view to identify possible negative impacts on the environment, but these and similar practices may require further refinement to better assess impacts on biodiversity and ABS-related issues. For a non-ABS related discussion, see Sikina Jinnah and Elisa Morgera, "Environmental Provisions in US and EU Free Trade Agreements: A Preliminary Comparison and Research Agenda," *Review of European, Comparative and International Environmental Law* 22 (2013): 324.

62   See this commentary on Article 24.

63   See Introduction to this commentary, section 4.

64   UN General Assembly, "Human rights and transnational corporations and other business enterprises: note by the Secretary General" (6 August 2013) UN Doc A/68/279 (advanced version), paragraph 55(e).

65   WIPO General Assembly, "Matters concerning the IGC," WO/GA/26/6.

66   In accordance with the IGC mandate as most recently renewed by the 2013 WIPO General Assembly. See Decision on agenda item 35 of WIPO Assemblies 43rd (21st ordinary) session, 23 September–2 October 2013, "Matters concerning the IGC" WO/GA/43/14.

Cooperation Treaty,[67] but also the CBD regarding the Nagoya Protocol negotiations and now the deliberations preparing for the Protocol's entry into force.[68] While the WIPO negotiations go well beyond the scope of the Protocol,[69] as they also concern traditional cultural expressions and are not linked to the conservation and sustainable use of biodiversity and the utilization of genetic resources, any future international instrument(s) on genetic resources and on traditional knowledge associated with genetic resources in the context of intellectual property will be implemented at a certain stage of the research and development chain (i.e. commercialization or pre-commercialization), that is also regulated by the Nagoya Protocol.

At the time of writing, the negotiations under WIPO are still ongoing.[70] The Protocol's negotiating history appears to include the WIPO IGC negotiations among the 'ongoing work' expected to be kept under review under Article 4(3).[71] Should the WIPO negotiations be completed successfully, the resulting international instrument(s) will be 'relevant' to the Protocol pursuant to Article 4(3). This would be particularly true with regard to the intersection between ABS and intellectual property rights, especially in view of the fact that the Nagoya Protocol shies away from imposing IPR-related benefit-sharing [72] or a requirement of mandatory disclosure of the origin or source of genetic resources used in a product at the time of filing a patent application[73] – issues which are currently under negotiation in the WIPO IGC framework. The scope and

---

67 See for instance the Swiss proposal for amending the WIPO International Patent Cooperation Union Working Group on reform of the Patent Cooperation Treaty, "Declaration of the source of genetic resources and traditional knowledge in patent applications. Proposals submitted by Switzerland," (7 March 2007) WIPO Doc PCT/R/WG/9/5.

68 See for instance inclusion of references to the Nagoya Protocol in the WIPO IGC draft negotiating texts regarding the definitions, disclosure requirement and defensive protection of traditional knowledge: WIPO General Assembly, "Matters concerning the IGC," WO/GA/43/14, Annex A, 2.

69 See Introduction to this commentary, section 3. See also CBD Working Group on ABS, "Study on the relationship between an international regime on access and benefit-sharing and other international instruments and forums that govern the use of genetic resources. The World Trade Organization (WTO); the World Intellectual Property Organization (WIPO); and the International Union for the Protection of New Varieties of Plants (UPOV)" (3 March 2009) UN Doc UNEP/CBD/WG-ABS/7/INF/3/PART2.

70 See WIPO General Assembly, "Matters concerning the IGC," WO/GA/43/14.

71 CBD Decision X/1, paragraph 6.

72 Pavoni, "The Nagoya Protocol and WTO," op. cit., 202.

73 Which had been considered through a combination of provisions during the negotiations: Cali Draft, draft article 13(1)(a), 13(1)(a)(iv) and 13(3) – see comments by Pavoni, "Nagoya Protocol and WTO Law," op. cit., 203–204, and this commentary on Article 17.

specific provisions of a future WIPO instrument may thus result in strengthening (or weakening, depending on the outcome of the negotiations) the linkages between the two instruments, as well as the Protocol's objective. Overall, the effect of Article 4(2) and 4(4) for the Parties that are involved in the WIPO negotiations is that they 'are bound *not* to develop and implement agreements that would be at variance with the CBD and Protocol objectives,'[74] notably achieving fair and equitable benefit-sharing between and within States, with a view to contributing to biodiversity conservation and sustainable use.

4 Relationship with *Specialized* ABS Instruments

As indicated above, Article 4(2) specifically foresees the conclusion of future *specialized* ABS agreements. The provision thereby implies that CBD Parties expect that more specific international instruments will be developed to deal with certain sectors of genetic resources.[75] It thus clarifies that the Protocol is not expected to be a comprehensive instrument, but rather applies by default where more specific international agreements have not been adopted to ensure the implementation of the ABS provisions of the Convention. Interpreting Article 4(2) in the light of the principle of mutual supportiveness,[76] Parties are subject to an international obligation to negotiate such specialized ABS instruments in a manner that proactively supports the realization of the objectives of the Convention and the Protocol, or at least avoids running counter to these objectives.

The adoption of instruments in compliance with Article 4(2) is then characterized by Article 4(4) as a *condition* for specialized ABS instruments to prevail as *lex specialis* over the Protocol for those Parties that are Party to both instruments, as well as in respect of the specific genetic resources covered by and for the purpose of the specialized instrument. Thus, if a specialized ABS

---

74   Pavoni, "The Nagoya Protocol and WTO," op. cit., 207.

75   CBD Working Group on ABS, "Access and benefit-sharing arrangements existing in specific sectors" (11 January 2008) UN Doc UNEP/CBD/WG-ABS/6/INF/4/REV1.

76   Laurence Boisson de Chazournes and Makane M. Mbengue, "A Propos du Principe Soutien Mutuel: les Relations entre le Protocol de Cartagena et les Accords de l'OMC," *Revue Générale de Droit International Public* 4 (2007): 829; Laurence Boisson de Chazournes and Makane M. Mbengue, "A 'Footnote as a Principle.' Mutual Supportiveness and Its Relevance in an Era of Fragmentation," in *Coexistence, Cooperation and Solidarity: Liber Amicorum Rüdiger Wolfrum*, ed. Holger P. Hestermeyer et al. (Leiden: Martinus Nijhoff, 2011), 1615; and Pavoni, "Mutual Supportiveness," op. cit.

agreement is deemed inconsistent with the objectives of the CBD and the Protocol, Parties should not apply it.[77]

As to *existing* specialized ABS agreements that would come into play in implementing Article 4(4), the Protocol preamble points to the International Treaty on Plant Genetic Resources for Food and Agriculture,[78] and the WHO International Health Regulations (2005),[79] suggesting that, as of 2010, these meet the criteria of Article 4(4). As to the latter, it should be emphasized that shortly after the conclusion of the negotiations of the Protocol, the WHO completed the negotiations of a Pandemic Influenza Preparedness Framework (PIP Framework), which can also be seen as a specialized ABS instrument.[80] In addition, the negotiating history of Article 4 points to possible future specialized ABS instruments,[81] such as a new international instrument or provisions on marine genetic resources in areas beyond national jurisdiction; and possible new sectoral instruments to be developed under the FAO Commission on Genetic Resources for Food and Agriculture (CGRFA). The following subsections will discuss each of the existing and potential future specialized ABS agreements in turn.

4.1   *Genetic Resources Covered by the ITPGRFA*
The preamble to the Protocol acknowledges the 'fundamental role' of the ITPGRFA in relation to the interdependence of all countries with regard to plant genetic resources for food and agriculture, their special nature, and

---

77   Chiarolla, Louafi and Schloen, "Analysis of the Relationship," op. cit., 102.

78   Nagoya Protocol 16th and 19th preambular recitals.

79   Nagoya Protocol 17th preambular recital. Revision of the WHO International Health Regulations (Geneva, 23 May 2005, in force 15 June 2007).

80   Note that the Nagoya Protocol refers to specialized ABS 'agreements' in Article 4(2), but 'instruments' in Article 4(4). The WHO Pandemic Influenza Preparedness Framework for the sharing of influenza viruses and access to vaccines and other benefits (effective 24 May 2011) WHO DOC WHA64.5, is a soft-law instrument and not a legally-binding treaty, although arguably its effects on the conduct of WHO Member States go well beyond those traditionally ascribed to soft-law instruments, as discussed below (see section 4.2 below).

81   CBD COP, "Report of the Ad Hoc Open-ended Working Group on Access and Benefit-Sharing on the work of its sixth meeting" (31 January 2008) UN Doc UNEP/CBD/COP/9/6, 14–16; and Montreal I Draft draft article 3(c), which reads: 'Genetic resources [contained in Annex I of the International Treaty on Plant Genetic Resources for Food and Agriculture provided they are used for the purposes of the International Treaty on Plant Genetic Resources for Food and Agriculture][under the Multilateral System of the International Treaty on Plant Genetic Resources for Food and Agriculture, both current and as may be amended by the Governing Body of the International Treaty on Plant Genetic Resources for Food and Agriculture].' (brackets in the original).

importance for achieving food security worldwide and sustainable development of agriculture in the context of poverty alleviation and climate change.[82]
The preamble further recalls the Multilateral System of ABS established under
the ITPGRFA 'in harmony with the Convention.'[83] For its part, the ITPGRFA
was specifically negotiated to ensure harmony with the CBD,[84] and its stated
objective refers to 'harmony with the CBD and its objectives.'[85] It can thus be
asserted that the ITPGRFA is an existing specialized international ABS instrument 'that has the same legal status of, and is consistent with, the CBD and
its Nagoya Protocol.'[86] Accordingly, Article 4(4) can be interpreted as a legal
presumption of compatibility between the International Treaty, the CBD and
the Nagoya Protocol, that may not be rebutted.[87]

In view of the distinctive features of agricultural biodiversity,[88] the International Treaty takes a markedly different approach to ABS than the Protocol,

---

82   Nagoya Protocol 16th preambular recital.
83   Nagoya Protocol 19th preambular recital.
84   FAO Conference Resolution 7/93 "Revision of the international undertaking on plant
      genetic resources," (1993) requested intergovernmental negotiations on: the revision of
      the International Undertaking on Plant Genetic Resources for Food and Agriculture to be
      in harmony with the CBD; the issue of access, on mutually agreed terms, to plant genetic
      resources, including ex situ collections not addressed by the CBD; and the realization of
      farmers' rights.
85   ITPGRFA Article 1 reads: '1 The objectives of this Treaty are the conservation and sus-
      tainable use of plant genetic resources for food and agriculture and the fair and equita-
      ble sharing of the benefits arising out of their use, in harmony with the Convention on
      Biological Diversity, for sustainable agriculture and food security. 2 These objectives will
      be attained by closely linking this Treaty to the Food and Agriculture Organization of the
      United Nations and to the Convention on Biological Diversity.'
86   Chiarolla, Louafi and Schloen, "Analysis of the Relationship," op. cit., 105. See also CBD
      Working Group on ABS, "Study on the relationship between an international regime on
      access and benefit-sharing and other international instruments and forums that govern
      the use of genetic resources. The International Treaty on Plant Genetic Resources for Food
      and Agriculture and the Commission on Genetic Resources for Food and Agriculture of
      the Food and Agriculture Organization of the United Nations" (3 March 2009) UN DOC
      UNEP/CBD/WG-ABS/7/INF/3/Part.1.
87   Ibid., 103. Note, however, that the ITPGRFA will have to be interpreted and applied in a
      mutually supportive manner with regard to the Nagoya Protocol provisions on indigenous
      and local communities' PIC and benefit-sharing concerning traditional knowledge and
      genetic resources held by them, which may pose specific challenges as the International
      Treaty provisions on farmers' rights are markedly different in approach and in level of
      detail than the relevant provisions of the Nagoya Protocol. For a discussion, Chiarolla,
      Louafi and Schloen, "Analysis of the Relationship," op. cit., 110–114.
88   See also this commentary on Article 8, section 4.

namely it is built on a *multilateral* – rather than prevalently bilateral – approach.[89] The rationale is to some degree described in the preamble to the Treaty. First, agriculture in all countries depends largely on plant genetic resources that have originated elsewhere. Continued and unrestricted access to plant genetic resources, therefore, is indispensable for the crop improvements that are necessary for sustainable agriculture and food security, in the face of genetic erosion, environmental changes, and future human needs. Furthermore, given the millennia of agricultural history, the geographical origins of plant genetic resources are often impossible to locate, and thus, identification of the country of origin is very difficult. Genebanks all over the world now have collections of all major crops, making the search for genetic resources in situ unnecessary.[90]

Against this background, the International Treaty has created a multilateral system aimed at facilitating access to, and exchange of, a specified list of crops[91] considered vital for food security and agricultural research, and at institutionalizing the sharing of benefits arising from the utilization of these resources.[92] Benefits include non-monetary ones, such as exchange of information, access to and transfer of technology, capacity building and facilitated access to crops, recognized as a benefit in itself. Sharing of benefits arising from commercialization is done through standard payments by the users of material accessed from the multilateral system, according to the provisions of the standard Material Transfer Agreement (SMTA), adopted by the ITPGRFA Governing Body.[93]

---

89   UN General Assembly, "Interim report of the Special Rapporteur on the right to food: Seed policies and the right to food: enhancing agrobiodiversity and encouraging innovation" (23 July 2009) UN Doc A/64/170, paragraphs 10 and 21–22. See also Michael Halewood et al., "Implementing 'Mutually Supportive' Access and Benefit Sharing Mechanisms under the Plant Treaty, Convention on Biological Diversity, and Nagoya Protocol," *Law Environment and Development Journal* 9 (2013): 68, 71.

90   See David H. Cooper, "The International Treaty on Plant Genetic Resources for Food and Agriculture," *Review of European Community and International Environmental Law* 11 (2002): 1, 4; Gerald K. Moore and Witold Tymowski, *Explanatory Guide to the International Treaty on Plant Genetic Resources for Food and Agriculture* (Gland: IUCN, 2005), 2–6.

91   ITPGRFA Annex I.

92   ITPGRFA Articles 10–13. See Tsioumani, "International Treaty on Plant Genetic Resources for Food and Agriculture," op. cit., 128.

93   ITPGRFA Governing Body Resolution 2/2006, "On the Standard Material Transfer Agreement" (16 June 2006). Users of material accessed from the Multilateral System must choose between two mandatory monetary benefit-sharing options: a default benefit-sharing scheme, according to which the recipient will pay 1.1 percent of gross sales to the Treaty's benefit-sharing fund in case of commercialization of new products incorporating material accessed from the MLS and if its availability to others is restricted; and

Such payments, together with voluntary donations, are directed to the Treaty's benefit-sharing fund, which allocates funds under the direction of the ITPGRFA Governing Body, to particular activities designed to support farmers in developing countries in conserving crop diversity in their fields, and assist farmers and breeders globally in adapting crops to changing needs and demands. The benefit-sharing fund is thus mandated to prioritize projects that support not only the conservation and sustainable use of agricultural biodiversity, but also the livelihoods of farmers and rural communities.[94]

In this connection, the Protocol negotiators debated whether to specifically exclude the ITPGRFA Annex I resources from the scope of the Protocol,[95] but eventually opted for a more general provision in the form of Article 4. As a specialized ABS agreement consistent with the objectives of the CBD and the Protocol as per Article 4(4), the provisions of the Treaty 'will prevail over those of the Protocol with respect to [plant genetic resources for food and agriculture] that are covered by the MLS and that are accessed for the purpose of research, breeding and training for food and agriculture.'[96] In cases where the resources under the Treaty are used for other purposes (such as for chemical, pharmaceutical and/or non-food and non-feed industrial uses), the Nagoya Protocol will apply.[97] With regard to agricultural research, however, and on the basis of the recognition of the specific features of agricultural biodiversity and the role and scope of the International Treaty in that regard, the Nagoya Protocol arguably does not preclude making available non-Annex I plant genetic resources under the same conditions provided for under the Multilateral

---

an alternative formula whereby recipients pay 0.5 percent of gross sales on all PGRFA products of the species they accessed from the MLS, regardless of whether the products incorporate the material accessed and regardless of whether or not the new products are available without restriction. See "Standard Material Transfer Agreement," ITPGRFA (16 June 2006), accessed 30 November 2013, <ftp://ftp.fao.org/ag/agp/planttreaty/agree ments/smta/SMTAe.pdf> (SMTA) Articles 6(7) and 6(11).

94   See Tvedt and Young, *Beyond Access*, op. cit., 124.

95   Montreal II Draft, draft article 3(c).

96   Chiarolla, Louafi and Schloen, "Analysis of the Relationship," op. cit., 103. See also Michael Halewood, Isabel Lopez Noriega and Sélim Louafi, "The Global Crop Commons and Access and Benefit-Sharing Laws: Examining the Limits of International Policy Support for the Collective Pooling and Management of Plant Genetic Resources," in *Crop Genetic Resources as a Global Commons. Challenges in International Law and Governance*, ed. Michael Halewood, Isabel Lopez Noriega and Sélim Louafi (London: Routledge, 2013), 1, 7.

97   Chiarolla, Louafi and Schloen, "Analysis of the Relationship," op. cit., 109.

System (MLS), i.e. using the SMTA,[98] as long as this is specifically decided upon by the ITPGRFA Governing Body, which would take into consideration also the Nagoya Protocol's provisions and requirements. This may be the case of plant genetic resources covered by the agreements between the international agricultural research centers of the Consultantive Group on International Agricultural Research (CGIAR Consortium) and the ITPGRFA Governing Body.[99] This may also be the case of materials voluntarily made available by ITPGRFA Parties under the conditions of the SMTA,[100] as long as they are the countries of origin or have acquired the material in accordance with the CBD. Therefore, on the basis of a combined reading of Articles 4 and 8, the Protocol seems to allow for differentiated treatment of plant genetic resources for food and agriculture purposes both at the international level, using the multilateral ABS framework of the ITPGRFA, and at the national level, on the basis of national legislation.[101]

4.2   *Genetic Resources with Pathogenic Properties*
Some genetic resources have pathogenic properties, i.e. they may cause disease to other organisms. The same genetic resources are used for medical research

---

98   Ibid., 106–9. See also CBD Working Group on ABS, "Study on the relationship with the ITPGRFA," UN Doc UNEP/CBD/ABS/7/INF.3/Part I, paragraphs 2.2.2–3 and 3.3.15.

99   The issue of the use of the SMTA for exchanges of non-Annex I plant genetic resources for food and agriculture collected before the Treaty's entry into force (ITPGRFA Article 15(1)(b)) was addressed at the second session of the ITPGRFA Governing Body, which endorsed including an interpretative footnote or series of footnotes to relevant provisions of the SMTA, to indicate that the provisions should not be interpreted as precluding the use of the SMTA for transfers of non-Annex I material collected before the entry into force of the Treaty. See ITPGRFA, "Report of the Second Session of the Governing Body of the ITPGRFA" (2007) FAO Doc IT/GB-2/07/Report, 11; and ITPGRFA Secretariat "Consideration of the Material Transfer Agreement to be used by international agricultural research centres for plant genetic resources for food and agriculture not included in Annex 1 of the Treaty" (2007) FAO Doc IT/GB-2/07/13. Accordingly, the international agricultural research centres have been using the SMTA, including interpretative footnotes, for transfer of non-Annex I material. The Governing Body reviewed this use of the SMTA at all its subsequent sessions, without amending its decision. At its fourth session, it noted the continued successful use of the SMTA by the centres, and at the latest fifth session, it commended the centres for their continued use of the SMTA for the transfer of non-Annex I plant genetic resources. See ITPGRFA, "Report of the Fourth Session of the Governing Body to the ITPGRFA" (2011) FAO Doc IT/GB-4/11/Report, Appendix A, 28; and "Report of the Fifth Session of the Governing Body to the ITPGRFA (2013) FAO Doc IT/GB-5/13/Report, Appendix A, 5.

100   Chiarolla, Louafi and Schloen, "Analysis of the Relationship," op. cit., 106–7

101   See Nagoya Protocol Article 8(c) and this commentary on Article 8, section 4.

purposes and production of vaccines. Pathogens were not considered as an issue in the negotiation of the CBD, or later by CBD Parties when deliberating on the implementation of the Convention. The issue surfaced for the first time in the negotiation of the Nagoya Protocol in 2009.[102] This followed developments in the context of WHO negotiations to increase equitable access to vaccines for highly pathogenic avian influenza A and pandemic influenza A.[103] Concerns that developing country populations may not have access to influenza vaccines due to insufficient global production, and the lack of any mechanism to ensure equitable access to other benefits from research on influenza viruses, prompted Indonesia to refuse to share its H5N1 virus samples with the WHO, on the basis of CBD Article 15(7).[104] Concretely, Indonesia sought preferential access to vaccines and transfer of related patents developed from its virus sample to enable its own pharmaceutical companies to produce vaccines at low cost.[105] This move was explicitly supported by most developing countries

---

102 Nagoya Draft, draft article 3(f). See CBD Working Group on ABS, "Report of the Seventh Meeting" (5 May 2009) UN Doc UNEP/CBD/WG-ABS/7/8, paragraphs 58, 115–116. See also ENB, "Summary of the Seventh Meeting of the Working Group on Access and Benefit-Sharing of the Convention on Biological Diversity: 2–8 April 2009," Vol 9 No 465, 10 April 2009.

103 David P. Fidler, "Negotiating Equitable Access to Influenza Vaccines: Global Health Diplomacy and the Controversies Surrounding Avian Influenza H5N1 and Pandemic Influenza H1N1, *PLoS Medicine* 7 (2010): 1.

104 Indonesia's refusal to share its virus samples was based on CBD principles: it was argued that it had the right to refuse to share the samples because it controlled access on samples collected in its territory. Other Parties could not use them without their prior informed consent, and their use should result in benefits for Indonesia. See Morgera and Tsioumani, "Evolution of Benefit-Sharing," op. cit., 170; David P. Fidler, "Influenza Virus Samples, International and Global Health Diplomacy," *Emerging Infectious Diseases* 14 (2008): 88, cited in Regine Andersen et al., *International Agreements and Processes Affecting an International Regime on Access and Benefit Sharing Under the Convention on Biological Diversity: Implications for Its Scope and Possibilities of a Sectoral Approach*, Fridtjof Nansen Institute Report No. 3/2010 (Lysaker: Fridtjof Nansen Institute, 2010), 40.

105 See Marie Wilke, "A Healthy Look," op. cit., 123. For an overview of the WHO negotiations see also South Centre and Centre for International Environmental Law, *Intellectual Property Quarterly Update, Third Quarter* (South Centre and Centre for International Environmental Law, 2009), accessed 30 November 2013, <www.ciel.org/Publications/IP_Update_3Q09.pdf>, 10; WHO Secretariat, "Pandemic Influenza Preparedness: Sharing of Influenza Viruses and Access to Vaccines and Other Benefits" (27 November 2008) WHO Doc EB124/4; and WHO Secretariat, "Pandemic Influenza Preparedness: Sharing of Influenza Viruses and Access to Vaccines and Other Benefits: Outcome of the Process to Finalize Remaining Elements under the Pandemic Influenza Preparedness Framework for

and initiated a fully-fledged negotiation in the WHO to reform the system for the rapid sharing of virus samples and access to vaccines. This resulted in the adoption of the PIP Framework only months after adoption of the Nagoya Protocol.

During the Protocol negotiations, the issue was addressed under deliberations on scope, when developed countries sought an explicit exclusion of genetic resources with pathogenic properties from the Protocol's scope, and developing countries sought to explicitly include viruses and other pathogenic material within the Protocol's scope. [106] Negotiators finally decided against a specific inclusion or exclusion of pathogens in the Protocol, in favor of the general provisions under Articles 3–4 and the special considerations under Article 8(b). The WHO framework and the importance of ensuring access to human pathogens for public health purposes are also reflected in the preamble.[107]

While it is acknowledged that pathogens used to develop vaccines and medicines are economic resources covered by the commercial dimension of ABS, strict ABS rules based on the principle of national sovereignty in the case of pathogens are generally not regarded as conducive to facilitating timely sharing of virus samples required to improve global health governance.[108] In recognition of this, the PIP Framework is considered 'the first ABS mechanism in the area of public health.'[109] Its scope is, however, limited: the PIP Framework applies only to influenza viruses with pandemic potential. All other pathogens remain under the scope of the Protocol.[110] This is in particular the case of seasonal influenza viruses, and other non-influenza pathogens or biological substances that may be contained in clinical specimens shared through the Framework, which, even when accidentally shared, remain outside the scope of the WHO Global Influenza Surveillance and Response System, and thus within the scope of the Nagoya Protocol.[111]

In addition, it has been argued that, as the Framework was adopted through a formally non-binding WHO Assembly resolution, it only functions as a

---

the Sharing of Influenza Viruses and Access to Vaccines and other Benefits" (10 December 2009) WHO Doc EB126/4.

106   See ENB 9/465, "Summary of the Seventh Meeting of the Working Group on ABS." For a broader discussion on the negotiations on scope, see this commentary on Article 3.

107   Nagoya Protocol 17th preambular recital.

108   Andersen et al., *International Agreements and Processes*, op. cit., 37.

109   Wilke, "A Healthy Look," op. cit., 137. For a discussion of the framework, see ibid., 138.

110   Ibid., 126.

111   PIP Framework Article 3(2). See Wilke, "A Healthy Look," op. cit., 146; and this commentary on Article 8, section 3.

specialized ABS agreement for transfer of influenza viruses that are covered by the Framework's binding contractual clauses that are stipulated in standard material transfer agreements (WHO-SMTAS).[112] The WHO-SMTAS, which regulate the exchange of samples and introduce binding benefit-sharing obligations, automatically apply to any actor that makes use of the WHO system, whether it is a submitting National Influenza Centre, a WHO laboratory or an outside institution that seeks to receive processes material for commercial or non-commercial utilization. Thus, while the Framework agreement is non-binding for Member States, use of the system is governed by binding WHO-SMTAS in the form of contract clauses. WHO-SMTA1 applies automatically to institutions within the Global Influenza Surveillance and Response System (i.e., the National Influenza Centres and the WHO laboratories) in accordance with standard terms of reference attached to the Framework.[113] WHO-SMTA2 applies to recipients of material outside the system and needs to be negotiated by WHO and any outside institution requesting material, prior to the transfer.[114]

The discussion above indicates that the PIP Framework establishes a *specialized* ABS framework covering influenza viruses with pandemic potential, that combines a multilateral system and a bilateral one, which however is governed internationally. The PIP Framework negotiations were finalized following conclusion of the Nagoya Protocol negotiations and were informed by those.[115] In addition, the Framework's objective is to establish a fair, transparent, equitable, efficient, effective system for, on an equal footing, the sharing of viruses, and access to vaccines and sharing of other benefits. Therefore, in line with the Nagoya Protocol, the PIP Framework seeks to ensure *both* access *and* benefit-sharing, and this objective is strengthened through the provisions of the Framework and the WHO-SMTAS. It can thus be concluded that the PIP Framework is consistent with, and does not run counter to the objectives of the Convention and the Nagoya Protocol, and can therefore be considered a specialized instrument in the context of Article 4(4).[116]

---

112   Included in an Annex to the Framework. Wilke, "A Healthy Look," op. cit., 126.

113   PIP Framework Annexes 4–8. Note that SMTA1 includes no benefit-sharing obligations but a statement prohibiting the granting of intellectual property rights on the material. See Wilke, "A Healthy Look," op. cit., 140.

114   PIP Framework Annex 2, Article 4(4). Note that SMTA2 allows for intellectual property rights, but combines them with at least two different benefit-sharing activities. See Wilke, "A Healthy Look," op. cit., 140.

115   See Wilke, "A Healthy Look," op. cit., 146.

116   Ibid., 144. With regard to the CBD objectives of biodiversity conservation and sustainable use, Wilke further argues that the fight against highly aggressive zoonotic viruses supports these objectives, along with public health efforts.

4.3   Marine Genetic Resources in Areas Beyond National Jurisdiction

A specialized ABS regime concerning marine genetic resources in areas beyond national jurisdiction may emerge from ongoing discussions[117] that have been entertained since 2006 under the UN General Assembly's Ad Hoc Open-ended Informal Working Group to study issues relating to the conservation and sustainable use of marine biological diversity beyond areas of national jurisdiction.[118] Such an instrument could cover ABS in relation to genetic resources from the seabed beyond national jurisdiction (the Area), and genetic resources from the water column beyond national jurisdiction (the high seas).[119]

At the time of writing, these discussions, while not having yet reached the stage of formal intergovernmental negotiations, have identified a package of issues that could be addressed in a new implementing agreement under the UN Convention on the Law of the Sea, namely: *marine genetic resources, including questions on benefits-sharing*; but also measures such as area-based management tools, including marine protected areas and environmental impact assessments; capacity building and the transfer of marine technology.[120] It is

---

117   UN General Assembly, "Oceans and the Law of the Sea," (17 November 2004) UN Doc A/
       RES/59/24 establishing the original mandate of the Working Group. See generally, Tullio
       Scovazzi, "Bioprospecting on the Deep Seabed: A Legal Gap Requiring to Be Filled," in
       Francioni and Scovazzi, *Biotechnology and International Law*, op. cit., 81; Lyle Glowka,
       "Evolving Perspectives on the International Seabed Area's Genetic Resources Fifteen Years
       after the 'Deepest of Ironies,'" in *Law, Technology and Science for Oceans in Globalisation*,
       ed. Davor Vidas (Leiden: Martinus Nijhoff, 2010) 397; Tullio Scovazzi, "The Exploitation
       of Genetic Resources in Areas Beyond National Jurisdiction," in *Confronting Ecological
       and Economic Collapse: Ecological Integrity for Law, Policy and Human Rights*, ed. Laura
       Westra, Prue Taylor and Agnès Michelot (London: Routledge, 2013), 47; Louise A. de la
       Fayette, "A New Regime for the Conservation and Sustainable Use of Marine Biodiversity
       and Genetic Resources Beyond the Limits of National Jurisdiction," *The International
       Journal of Marine and Coastal Law* 24 (2009): 221; Thomas Greiber, "Common Pools for
       Marine Genetic Resources: A Possible Instrument for a Future Multilateral Agreement
       Addressing Marine Biodiversity in Areas Beyond National Jurisdiction," in Kamau and
       Winter, *Common Pools of Genetic Resources Equity and Innovation in International
       Biodiversity Law*, op. cit., 399; Morten W. Tvedt and Ane E. Jørem, "Bioprospecting in
       the High Seas: Regulatory Options for Benefit Sharing," *The Journal of World Intellectual
       Property* 16 (2013): 150; and Bevis Fedder, *Marine Genetic Resources, Access and Benefit-
       Sharing* (London: Routledge, 2013).
118   For a discussion of the possible interactions between the Working Group and the Nagoya
       Protocol, see Salpin, "Law of the Sea," op. cit., 179–182.
119   Ibid., 174.
120   UN General Assembly, "Oceans and the Law of the Sea," (5 April 2012) UN Doc A/
       RES/66/231, paragraph 14.

expected that the Working Group will reach a conclusion on the feasibility, scope and parameters of a new international instrument on marine biodiversity under UNCLOS towards the end of 2015, with a view to preparing for a decision by the General Assembly before the end of its sixty-ninth session.[121]

Should a formal negotiating process be launched under the General Assembly, Parties to the Protocol will be bound by Article 4(2) to ensure that specialized ABS arrangements in the context of a new implementing agreement under UNCLOS do not run counter to the objectives of the Convention and the Protocol in achieving fair and equitable benefit-sharing among and within States, and biodiversity conservation and sustainable use. Even from the viewpoint of those arguing that areas beyond natural jurisdiction are outside the scope of the Protocol,[122] a similar obligation would still exist on the basis of a general principle of mutual supportiveness.[123]

In all events, the concepts of 'biodiversity' and 'genetic resource' are not mentioned in UNCLOS, therefore a certain reliance on the CBD and the Nagoya Protocol will be inevitable in the context of negotiations under the authority of the UN General Assembly. There is certainly scope for a mutually supportive interpretation of the law of the sea and the international biodiversity regime that can build on the open-textured environmental provisions of UNCLOS and take advantage of the several textual hooks for an evolving, biodiversity-cognizant interpretation.[124] On the other hand, however, the fundamental difference between the two sets of international rules is that while the CBD and the Nagoya Protocol are mainly premised on genetic resources within national jurisdiction and appear to favor a bilateral approach to ABS, a future specialized ABS agreement on marine genetic resources in areas beyond national jurisdiction[125] will inevitably deal with genetic resources that are open to appropriation by any State in the high seas and possibly subject to the common heritage regime of mankind if found in the Area.[126] It therefore appears

---

121   UN General Assembly, "Oceans and the Law of the Sea," (9 December 2013) UN Doc A/
       RES/68/70, paragraphs 197–198.
122   See this commentary on Article 3, section 3.2.
123   See generally Pavoni, "Mutual Supportiveness," op. cit.
124   Boyle and Chinkin, *Making of International Law*, op. cit., 256–259; and Birnie, Boyle and
       Redgwell, *International Law and the Environment*, op. cit., 746–751.
125   Salpin, "Law of the Sea," op. cit., 174.
126   States participating in the UN General Assembly's Working Group have put forward two
       different legal interpretations about the legal status of marine genetic resources in the
       Area: they may be subject to the general regime of the freedom of the high seas, as a
       residual regime (UNCLOS Article 86) because the common heritage regime applicable to
       the Area only concerns mineral resources in light of UNCLOS Article 133(a); or they may

more likely that a multilateral system of benefit-sharing may be conceived in that context.[127]

4.4   *CGRFA*

Since 2007 the FAO Commission on Genetic Resources for Food and Agriculture has reviewed arrangements and policies on uses and exchanges of genetic resources in different subsectors of food and agriculture. These subsectors include animal, aquatic, forest and microbial genetic resources.[128] Following the adoption of the Nagoya Protocol, the Commission engaged in assessing

---

be subject to the common heritage regime under the understanding that the Area and its resources include biological resources, as part of customary international law. See ENB, "Summary of the Sixth Meeting of the Working Group on Marine Biodiversity beyond Areas of National Jurisdiction: 19–23 August 2013," unnumbered, accessed 30 November 2013, <www.iisd.ca/oceans/marinebiodiv6/brief/brief_marinebiodiv6e.html>) or a contextual interpretation of UNCLOS according to which the relevant rights and obligations are not determined by the nature (mineral or genetic) of the resource, but by the relevant maritime area in which resources are found: see Elisa Morgera, "Impressions on the UN General Assembly Working Group on Marine Biodiversity," *Environmental Policy and Law* 40 (2010): 67.

127   The EU has in effect suggested drawing inspiration from the ITPGRFA approach in that context: ENB, "Summary of the Working Group on Marine Biodiversity Beyond Areas of National Jurisdiction: 1–5 February 2010," unnumbered, accessed 30 November 2013, <www.iisd.ca/oceans/marinebiodiv3/brief/brief_marinebiodiv3.pdf>, 5; and ENB, "Summary of the Second Meeting of the Working Group on Marine Biodiversity Beyond Areas of National Jurisdiction: 28 April–2 May 2008," Vol. 25 No. 49, 5 May 2008, 7.

128   Chiarolla, Louafi and Schloen, "Analysis of the Relationship," op. cit., 116. See FAO, *The Use and Exchange of Animal Genetic Resources for Food and Agriculture* (FAO, 2009), accessed 30 November 2013, <ftp://ftp.fao.org/docrep/fao/meeting/017/ak222e.pdf>; FAO, *The Use and Exchange of Aquatic Genetic Resources for Food and Agriculture* (FAO, 2009), ftp://ftp.fao.org/docrep/fao/meeting/017/ak527e.pdf.; FAO, *The Use and Exchange of Forest Genetic Resources for Food and Agriculture* (FAO, 2009), accessed 30 November 2013, <ftp://ftp.fao.org/docrep/fao/meeting/017/ak565e.pdf>; and FAO, *The Use and Exchange of Microbial Genetic Resources for Food and Agriculture* (FAO, 2009), accessed 30 November 2013, <ftp://ftp.fao.org/docrep/fao/meeting/017/ak566e.pdf>. See also, pre-Nagoya Protocol: CBD Working Group on ABS, "The use and exchange of animal genetic resources for food and agriculture - Submission by the Food and Agriculture Organization of the United Nations (FAO)" (9 March 2010) UN Doc UNEP/CBD/WG-ABS/9/INF/10; "The use and exchange of forest genetic resources for food and agriculture - Submission by the Food and Agriculture Organization of the United Nations (FAO)" (9 March 2010) UN Doc UNEP/CBD/WG-ABS/9/INF/11; and "The use and exchange of aquatic genetic resources for food and agriculture - Submission by the Food and Agriculture Organization of the United Nations (FAO)" (9 March 2010) UN Doc UNEP/CBD/WG-ABS/9/INF/12.

whether distinctive features of the different sectors and sub-sectors of genetic resources for food and agriculture may require distinctive solution and in particular specific ABS modalities 'taking into account the full range of options, including those presented in the Nagoya Protocol.'[129]

In 2013, the Commission considered it premature to negotiate an international agreement or agreements on ABS for genetic resources for food and agriculture. It rather proposed to engage in further work towards the development of a voluntary tool to facilitate domestic implementation of ABS for different sub-sectors of genetic resources for food and agriculture, taking into account relevant international instruments on ABS, and considering stakeholder groups' voluntary codes of conduct, guidelines and best practices in relation to ABS for all sub-sectors of genetic resources for food and agriculture.[130] So, while this work does not yet seem relevant for the purposes of the Protocol Article 4(4), it will certainly be relevant for the review of ongoing intergovernmental work and practices under Article 4(3). Depending on its focus (i.e., if addressed to stakeholder groups directly), it could also potentially feed into the review of codes of conduct and other voluntary instruments by the Protocol's governing body.[131]

---

129   CGRFA, "Report of the thirteenth regular session of the Commission on Genetic Resources for Food and Agriculture" (18–22 July 2011) FAO DOC CGRFA-13/11/Report, paragraph 60 and Appendix D(1).

130   CGRFA, "Report of the fourteenth regular session of the Commission on Genetic Resources for Food and Agriculture" (15–19 April 2013) FAO DOC CGRFA-14/13/DR, paragraph 40(xv).

131   Nagoya Protocol Article 20(2). See also this commentary on Article 20, section 3.

Article 5. Fair and Equitable Benefit-sharing

1. In accordance with Article 15, paragraphs 3 and 7 of the Convention, benefits arising from the utilization of genetic resources as well as subsequent applications and commercialization shall be shared in a fair and equitable way with the Party providing such resources that is the country of origin of such resources or a Party that has acquired the genetic resources in accordance with the Convention. Such sharing shall be upon mutually agreed terms.

2. Each Party shall take legislative, administrative or policy measures, as appropriate, with the aim of ensuring that benefits arising from the utilization of genetic resources that are held by indigenous and local communities, in accordance with domestic legislation regarding the established rights of these indigenous and local communities over these genetic resources, are shared in a fair and equitable way with the communities concerned, based on mutually agreed terms.

3. To implement paragraph 1 above, each Party shall take legislative, administrative or policy measures, as appropriate.

4. Benefits may include monetary and non-monetary benefits, including but not limited to those listed in the Annex.

5. Each Party shall take legislative, administrative or policy measures as appropriate, in order that the benefits arising from the utilization of traditional knowledge associated with genetic resources are shared in a fair and equitable way with indigenous and local communities holding such knowledge. Such sharing shall be upon mutually agreed terms.

Annex. Monetary and Non-monetary Benefits

1. Monetary benefits may include, but not be limited to:
    (a) Access fees/fee per sample collected or otherwise acquired;
    (b) Up-front payments;
    (c) Milestone payments;
    (d) Payment of royalties;
    (e) Licence fees in case of commercialization;
    (f) Special fees to be paid to trust funds supporting conservation and sustainable use of biodiversity;
    (g) Salaries and preferential terms where mutually agreed;

© KONINKLIJKE BRILL NV, LEIDEN, 2014 | DOI 10.1163/9789004217188_007

    (h)   Research funding;

    (i)   Joint ventures;

    (j)   Joint ownership of relevant intellectual property rights.

2.   Non-monetary benefits may include, but not be limited to:

    (a)   Sharing of research and development results;

    (b)   Collaboration, cooperation and contribution in scientific research and development programmes, particularly biotechnological research activities, where possible in the Party providing genetic resources;

    (c)   Participation in product development;

    (d)   Collaboration, cooperation and contribution in education and training;

    (e)   Admittance to ex situ facilities of genetic resources and to databases;

    (f)   Transfer to the provider of the genetic resources of knowledge and technology under fair and most favourable terms, including on concessional and preferential terms where agreed, in particular, knowledge and technology that make use of genetic resources, including biotechnology, or that are relevant to the conservation and sustainable utilization of biological diversity;

    (g)   Strengthening capacities for technology transfer;

    (h)   Institutional capacity-building;

    (i)   Human and material resources to strengthen the capacities for the administration and enforcement of access regulations;

    (j)   Training related to genetic resources with the full participation of countries providing genetic resources, and where possible, in such countries;

    (k)   Access to scientific information relevant to conservation and sustainable use of biological diversity, including biological inventories and taxonomic studies;

    (l)   Contributions to the local economy;

    (m)   Research directed towards priority needs, such as health and food security, taking into account domestic uses of genetic resources in the Party providing genetic resources;

    (n)   Institutional and professional relationships that can arise from an access and benefit-sharing agreement and subsequent collaborative activities;

    (o)   Food and livelihood security benefits;

    (p)   Social recognition;

    (q)   Joint ownership of relevant intellectual property rights.

1 Overview

This Article includes three inter-related obligations for State Parties: 1) an inter-State obligation to share benefits;[1] 2) an obligation to share benefits with indigenous and local communities when benefits derive from genetic resources held by these communities;[2] and 3) an obligation to share benefits arising from the utilization of traditional knowledge with indigenous and local communities holding such knowledge.[3] All these obligations (with slightly different wording) are to be fulfilled by the enactment of national legislative, administrative or policy measures. In all these cases, benefits may be monetary and non-monetary, as exemplified in the Annex to the Protocol, which is also discussed here in conjunction with Article 5.

Article 5 largely[4] reproduces the content of CBD Articles 15(7) and 15(3). The indicative list of monetary and non-monetary benefits annexed[5] to the Protocol furthermore reproduces the list in Appendix II of the Bonn Guidelines almost *verbatim*.[6] However, the Protocol breaks new ground by: i) using more forceful language with respect to benefit-sharing from genetic resources;[7] ii) addressing for the first time questions related to benefit-sharing with indigenous and local communities when genetic resources are held by these communities; and iii) addressing benefit-sharing from the use of their traditional knowledge for the first time in as far as it is 'associated with genetic resources.'

---

1 Nagoya Protocol Article 5(1) and (3).

2 Nagoya Protocol Article 5(2).

3 Nagoya Protocol Article 5(5). See CBD Working Group on Article 8(j), "How Tasks 7, 10 and 12 could best contribute," UNEP/CBD/WG8J/8/4/Rev.2, paragraph 14 and CBD Working Group on ABS, "Vienna Workshop on Matters related to Traditional Knowledge Associated with Genetic Resources and the International Regime on Access and Benefit-sharing" (18 March 2009) UN Doc UNEP/CBD/WG-ABS/7/INF/7.

4 Particularly Nagoya Protocol Article 5(1) and 5(3).

5 Note that the Annex to the Protocol was not negotiated by CBD Parties, and was introduced as Co-Chairs' text following the Cali meeting: Cali Draft, draft annex I.

6 Besides minor editorial differences (the term 'provider Party/country'), the only substantive difference between the list of benefits in the Bonn Guidelines and the Nagoya Protocol is section 2(g) in relation to strengthening capacity for technology transfer. This divergence has also resulted in the deletion of a reference to indigenous and local communities.

7 The Nagoya Protocol decidedly indicates that benefits from genetic resources 'shall be shared,' whereas the CBD Article 15(7) used the more qualified expression 'Each Contracting Party shall take legislative, administrative or policy measures ... *with the aim of* sharing in a fair and equitable way the ... benefits arising from the commercial and other utilization of genetic resources ...' (emphasis added).

Albeit heavily qualified, the obligations contained in Articles 5(2) and 5(5) are major developments in international environmental law. First, while not phrased in human rights terms, they nevertheless address an internal situation between a State and its communities, which is usually the object of human rights treaties.[8] Second, the obligations appear underpinned not only by purely procedural environmental rights,[9] but also substantive environmental rights,[10] as will be discussed below.

The following sections will first identify the innovations of this provision vis-à-vis the text of the CBD, and then discuss in more detail the content of the three inter-related obligations established by Article 5, in turn. A reflection will then be offered on the role of mutually agreed terms in the architecture of the Protocol, and on the usefulness of contemplating both monetary and non-monetary benefits in ABS transactions.

---

8   On the debate on environmental human rights, see Human Rights Council, "Human rights and the environment" (12 April 2011) UN Doc A/HRC/RES/16/11; Human Rights Council, "Report of the Independent Expert John H. Knox," A/HRC/22/43; F. Francioni, 'International Human Rights in an Environmental Horizon', *European Journal of International Law* 21 (2010): 41; Alan Boyle, "Human Rights or Environmental Rights? A Reassessment," *Fordham Environmental Law Review* 18 (2007): 471; and Alan Boyle, "Human Rights and the Environment: Where Next?," *European Journal of International Law* 23 (2012): 1.

9   See Introduction to this commentary, section 4.3. Human Rights Council, "Report of the Independent Expert John H. Knox," A/HRC/22/43, paragraph 7, also discusses the distinction between procedural and substantive rights, paragraphs 40–43.

10 Compare with recognition of certain substantive environmental rights in few regional human rights treaties and human rights case law as discussed in Shelton, "Human Rights and the Environment," op. cit. Compare also with the international obligations related to purely procedural environmental rights that can be found in the Convention on Access to Information, Public Participation in Decision-making and Access to Justice in Environmental Matters (Aarhus, 25 June 1998, in force 30 October 2001) 2161 UNTS 447 (hereinafter, Aarhus Convention). Although the Aarhus Convention makes reference to a substantive right to a healthy environment in an operative provision (Article 1), such a right is only referred to as a rationale for guaranteeing procedural environmental rights, which constitute the core of the Convention. E.g., Declaration of the United Kingdom of Great Britain and Northern Ireland, in "Convention on Access to Information, Public Participation in Decision-making and Access to Justice in Environmental Matters," UN Treaty System, accessed 30 November 2013, <http://treaties.un.org/Pages/ViewDetails.aspx?src=TREATY&mtdsg_no=XXVII-13&chapter=27&lang=en>.

2   Inter-State Benefit-sharing from the Utilization of Genetic
       Resources

Article 5(1) establishes an inter-State obligation to share benefits arising
from the utilization of genetic resources but also from 'subsequent applications and commercialization' with the Party providing such resources. It thus
strengthens the legal obligation already existing under CBD Article 15, which is
expressly recalled, and confirms that benefit-sharing can arise both from 'commercial' and other utilization of genetic resources. The reference to 'subsequent applications and commercialization' – an expression that is not defined
in the Protocol – attempts to address practical difficulties in separating different phases of the research and development chain. The reference thus underlines that inter-State benefit-sharing is to be understood broadly, based on the
expectation that benefits that must be shared might arise during all the phases
after a genetic resource was accessed. Necessary details about benefit-sharing
arising from subsequent applications and commercialization will likely be provided in domestic ABS frameworks and possibly guidance may be provided by
the Protocol's governing body in the future.[11]

      In a *regular* scenario, the general, inter-State benefit-sharing obligation is
specified at the time of access, when PIC is obtained and MAT are established.[12]
In this scenario, the Protocol envisages that the permit, which is the basis for
the internationally recognized certificate of compliance,[13] is to be issued 'at
the time of access.' Frequently, however, it is during the utilisation of a genetic
resource, rather than at the time of access, that its actual or potential value
becomes evident and more easily verifiable.[14] So the time of access will often be
too early to conclusively determine what is fair and equitable benefit-sharing.[15]
For this reason, CBD Article 15 has been interpreted as prescribing two MAT-
related obligations: the establishment of MAT at the time of access, and the
re-establishment or reopening of MAT with regard to benefit-sharing at a later
stage, in which further or different information on utilization becomes available. As a result, although MAT are normally established upon access (and can
possibly be (re)negotiated at a later stage),[16] there may be situations in which

---

11   Nagoya Protocol Article 26(4)(a). See this commentary on Article 26, section 2.
12   In accordance with Nagoya Protocol Articles 6–7: see this commentary on Article 6, sec-
       tions 3–4, and on Article 7, section 2.
13   Nagoya Protocol Articles 6(3)(e) and 17(2). See this commentary on Article 17, section 3.
14   Tvedt, "Beyond Nagoya," op. cit., 160.
15   Ibid., 163.
16   See Introduction to this commentary, Section 1.3.

negotiations and establishment of MAT on access and on benefit-sharing can occur at different points in time.[17] This is why the PIC decision and the initial MAT would oblige users to renegotiate the terms of utilisation and benefit-sharing in case for instance of changes in the understanding of the resource's value, change of the user's intent (e.g., from non-commercial to commercial), or change of the agreed type of utilization.[18]

In all events, access to genetic resources without PIC and/or MAT in the logic of the Convention and the Protocol should not deprive States and/or indigenous and local communities of their right to benefit-sharing. Article 5(1) links the benefit-sharing obligation to the definition of 'utilization of genetic resources,' which is provided by the Protocol,[19] and which does not mention 'access' to the resources. On that basis, an argument can be made that benefit-sharing requirements may not necessarily be connected with access procedures, as utilization can take place long after the acquisition of genetic resources and involve other countries or private parties.[20] An alternative interpretation would point to Article 6(1), which refers to 'access to genetic resources for their utilization,' thereby arguably suggesting a sequence and direct temporal link between access for, and benefit-sharing from, utilisation. Such interpretation would tend to emphasize that the realization of the benefit-sharing obligation rests on the Protocol provisions on compliance, which in turn rely on the existence of a domestic ABS framework.

As anticipated, the benefit-sharing obligation presupposes a bilateral relationship between States, with benefits flowing to a 'Party providing such resources that is the country of origin of such resources or the Party that has acquired genetic resources in accordance with the Convention.' This mirrors language found in CBD Article 15(3). The reference to 'genetic resources acquired in accordance with the Convention' points to a country that, with the consent of the country of origin, facilitated access to those resources and is entitled to receive a share of benefits arising from their utilization.[21] The opposite situation (i.e., genetic resources acquired *not* in accordance with the Convention) may point to two distinct cases: resources acquired prior to the Convention's entry into force, and resources acquired from the country

---

17   Tvedt and Young, *Beyond Access*, op. cit., 71; and Tvedt, "Beyond Nagoya," op. cit., 172. See Introduction to this commentary, section 1.3.

18   As anticipated in Nagoya Protocol Articles 6(3)(g) and 8(a).

19   Nagoya Protocol Article 2(c). See this commentary on Article 2, section 2.

20   Greiber et al., *Explanatory Guide*, op. cit., 84–85.

21   Tvedt and Young, *Beyond Access*, op. cit., 14.

of origin without PIC and MAT after the Convention's entry into force.[22] The first case is linked to the question of temporal scope, which has already been discussed.[23] In the second case, those countries that have acquired resources without PIC and MAT from the country of origin after the Convention's entry into force will have no rights under the Protocol. In other words, they are in violation of the Convention and are not entitled to benefit-sharing in case of further transfer of the resources originally acquired without PIC and MAT.[24]

The benefit-sharing obligation in Article 5(1) does not identify specific addressees (it uses an indeterminate passive form 'benefit-sharing...shall be shared'). This can be explained by the understanding that in practice benefits will be most likely obtained from private parties, such as research institutions and biotech companies, who utilize genetic resources. For this reason, the Protocol establishes that benefit-sharing shall be upon MAT,[25] as MAT is likely the most effective way to guide the implementation of Article 5(1). In the light of this, the related obligation for States as spelt out in Article 5(3) is to take legislative, administrative or policy measures, as appropriate, to create obligations for private users under their jurisdiction to share benefits, so as to implement the corresponding international benefit-sharing obligations.[26]

Article 5(1) leaves a broad range of implementing measures (by reference to 'legislative, administrative or policy measures') to the discretion of its Parties, and does not attempt to establish any guidance on how to address questions of fairness and equity in domestic ABS frameworks.[27] Nevertheless, it can be argued that these measures should be able to contribute to legal certainty in ABS transactions, the importance of which is emphasized in the Protocol preamble.[28] In addition, it should be stressed that the qualifier 'as appropriate',

---

22   Glowka, Burhenne-Guilmin and Synge, *Guide to the Convention on Biological Diversity*, op. cit., 77.
23   See this commentary on Article 3, section 3.1.
24   Glowka, Burhenne-Guilmin and Synge, *Guide to the Convention on Biological Diversity*, op. cit., 79.
25   As is explicitly foreseen in the last sentence of Nagoya Protocol Article 5(1).
26   Greiber et al., *Explanatory Guide*, op. cit., 84.
27   Compare with Nagoya Protocol Article 6(3)(a–b); see this commentary on Article 6, section 5. In practical terms, such measures may be taken in the context of access in provider jurisdictions or in the context of utilisation activities in user jurisdictions. In the former case, Parties should consider whether to move beyond the minimum access requirements set out in Article 6. In the latter case, Parties must be mindful of their overarching benefit-sharing obligation when implementing their obligations related to compliance (Nagoya Protocol Articles 15, 16 and 18).
28   Nagoya Protocol 9th preambular recital.

while emphasizing the margin of appreciation of States in choosing *how* to implement this provision, does not call into question *whether* States are to perform their obligation at all.[29] Ultimately the good-faith implementation of this provision may be judged against the objective of the Protocol on realizing fair and equitable benefit-sharing among and within States.[30]

3   Intra-State Benefit-sharing from the Utilization of Genetic Resources Held by Indigenous and Local Communities

While the wording of Article 5(2) is largely similar to CBD Article 15(7), it is worth underlining the fundamental conceptual difference between the two provisions. Article 5(2) does not deal with 'inter-State' benefit-sharing, but with an *internal* situation: it creates an obligation for each Party to share benefits with indigenous and local communities (non-State actors) 'holding' genetic resources.

Article 5(2) arguably presupposes that each Party identifies indigenous and local communities (for the purposes of implementing the Protocol)[31] in its territory in order to clarify whether these (or some of these) communities 'hold' genetic resources. For these Parties the provision sets out an obligation to create measures to 'channel' resulting benefits to the communities concerned. Similarly to the general obligations to share benefits in Article 5(1), ultimately the terms of benefit-sharing for indigenous and local communities will be spelt out in MAT,[32] as most likely private parties will actually do the sharing of benefits.

The groundbreaking nature of Article 5(2) should be highlighted from the outset: for the first time in international environmental law, a treaty creates an obligation for States to establish measures to reward indigenous and local communities responsible for the stewardship of genetic resources and their resulting contribution to scientific progress for the benefit of the global community. Article 5(2) in fact goes significantly beyond the letter of the CBD,[33]

---

29   Introduction to this commentary, section 5, fn. 225.

30   See this commentary on Article 1.

31   As discussed in section 3.2 below, the identification of indigenous peoples and local communities may not be a straightforward matter, also in the absence of an international definition of either term or international consensus on the difference between the two terms: Savaresi, "International Human Rights Law Implications," op. cit., 73–74.

32   Final part of Nagoya Protocol Article 5(2).

33   CBD Articles 15 and 8(j).

and the Protocol's own negotiating mandate,[34] as neither mentions communities' rights over genetic resources, nor refers to indigenous and local communities as recipients of a share of the benefits arising from the utilization of genetic resources held by them.[35]

From a broader international law perspective, this provision can be possibly interpreted as implicitly underpinned by a substantive environmental right[36] of indigenous and local communities to their genetic resources.[37] It embodies an obligation *owed directly* to them,[38] deriving from established international human rights, in their collective dimension,[39] to indigenous peoples' self-determination, ownership and cultural identity.[40] In comparison, UNDRIP only includes genetic resources in a list of manifestations of indigenous

---

34   As set out in CBD Decision 7/19, section D.

35   CBD Working Group on Article 8(j), "How Tasks 7, 10 and 12 could best contribute," UNEP/CBD/WG8J/8/4/Rev.2, 14.

36   On the lack of substantive environmental rights in international law, except for the African context: Rhona K.M. Smith, *Textbook on International Human Rights*, 5th ed (Oxford: Oxford University Press, 2012), 390–1; Boyle, "Human Rights and the Environment," op. cit., 29–30; and Malgosia Fitzmaurice, "Environmental Degradation," in *International Human Rights Law*, ed. Daniel Moeckli, Sangeeta Shah and Sandesh Sivakumaran (Oxford: Oxford University Press, 2010), 622, 622.

37   Compare with ITPGRFA Article 9, that although titled 'farmers' rights', only contains a hortatory provision for States to enact supportive legislation; and the Aarhus Convention, that only focuses on procedural environmental rights.

38   International human rights can be identified in 'obligations [that] are owed directly to individuals (and not to the national government of an individual)': Rosalyn Higgins, *Problems and Process: International Law and How We Use It* (Oxford: Oxford University Press, 1994) 94.

39   On the 'communitarization' of indigenous peoples' rights, see Alessandro Fodella, "International Law and the Diversity of Indigenous Peoples," *Vermont Law Review* 30 (2001): 565; Wiessner, "The Cultural Rights of Indigenous Peoples," op. cit.; Human Rights Committee, "General Comment No. 31: Nature of the general legal obligations on State Parties to the Covenant" (26 May 2004) UN Doc CCPR/C/21/Rev.1/Add.13, paragraph 9, which reads: 'The beneficiaries of the rights recognized by the Covenant are individuals. Although, with the exception of article 1, the Covenant does not mention the rights of legal persons or similar entities or collectivities, many of the rights recognized by the Covenant ... may be enjoyed in community with others ... '

40   Human Rights Council, "Report of the Special Rapporteur on indigenous peoples' rights" A/HRC/9/9, paragraph 40. See also UNDRIP, Article 1, which reads: 'Indigenous peoples have the right to the full enjoyment, as a collective or as individuals, of all human rights and fundamental freedoms as recognized in the Charter of the United Nations, the Universal Declaration of Human Rights and international human rights law.' We are grateful to Annalisa Savaresi for drawing our attention to this point.

sciences, technologies and cultures,[41] and otherwise generally refers to indigenous peoples' right to manage their natural resources,[42] their right to maintain
and strengthen their distinctive spiritual relationship with their traditionally
owned resources,[43] and the right to own, use, develop and control the resources
that they possess by reason of traditional ownership or use.[44] In that respect,
the Nagoya Protocol implicitly confirms and clarifies that the above-cited
UNDRIP provisions apply to the specific case of genetic resources.[45]

In addition, UNDRIP generally calls upon States, in conjunction with indigenous peoples, to take effective measures to recognize and protect the exercise
of their right to maintain, control, protect and develop the manifestations of
their culture, including genetic resources,[46] and to create effective mechanisms of preventing and redressing dispossession of their resources.[47] UNDRIP
then only foresees a right of *redress* for indigenous peoples' *resources* that they
have traditionally owned or otherwise used, and which have been confiscated,
taken, used or damaged *without* their PIC.[48] The Nagoya Protocol, instead, goes
beyond UNDRIP by encapsulating, in a legally binding provision, a *benefit-
sharing* obligation owed directly to[49] indigenous and local communities. This

---

41   UNDRIP Article 31(1), which reads: 'Indigenous peoples have the right to maintain, con-
     trol, protect and develop their cultural heritage, traditional knowledge and traditional
     cultural expressions, as well as the manifestations of their sciences, technologies and cul-
     tures, including human and genetic resources, seeds, medicines, knowledge of the prop-
     erties of fauna and flora, oral traditions, literatures, designs, sports and traditional games
     and visual and performing arts. They also have the right to maintain, control, protect and
     develop their intellectual property over such cultural heritage, traditional knowledge,
     and traditional cultural expressions.'

42   UNDRIP Article 3.

43   UNDRIP Article 25.

44   UNDRIP Article 26(2).

45   The argument that indigenous peoples' rights over their resources also encompass their
     rights to their 'genetic' resources had been put forward by Lenzerini, "Indigenous Peoples'
     Cultural Rights," op. cit., 140, on the basis of UN Commission on Human Rights, "Final
     report of the Special Rapporteur on indigenous peoples' permanent sovereignty over
     natural resources" (12 July 2004) UN Doc E/CN.4/Sub.2/2004/30/Add.1, paragraph 11 and
     the inextricable link between genetic resources and traditional knowledge as 'two insepa-
     rable elements of a unique social (and legal) concept that expresses the spiritual rela-
     tionship of indigenous groups to their natural resources.' See also Nagoya Protocol 22nd
     preambular recital.

46   UNDRIP Article 31(2).

47   UNDRIP Article 8(2)(b).

48   UNDRIP 28(1).

49   Paraphrasing Higgins, *Problems and Process*, op. cit., 94 (see quote at fn. 38 above).

obligation arises specifically from the use of *genetic* resources held by them,[50] even in the absence of any *restriction or deprivation* of their right to use their genetic resources[51] that may result from an ABS transaction (that is, when they have exercised their right to PIC). The Nagoya Protocol also goes beyond existing human rights instruments by identifying as beneficiaries of such entitlement not only indigenous peoples, but also *local communities*.[52]

Nonetheless, Article 5(2) is heavily qualified. The following subsections will thus first offer an interpretation of the obligation in the light of relevant international human rights standards, and then discuss questions arising from the qualifications in Article 5(2), focusing on the lack of a definition of 'indigenous and local communities' as right-holders under the Protocol, and the references to 'accordance with domestic legislation regarding established rights.'

3.1   *States' Obligation*
Article 5(2) sets out an obligation for Parties to adopt (or, implicitly, to revise) domestic measures ensuring the fair and equitable sharing of benefits arising from the utilization of genetic resources held by indigenous and local communities. The modalities of such an internal mechanism will be dependent on the modalities of the exercise of these communities' rights over genetic resources in a given Party, which will likely vary from one domestic legal framework to another.

In light of international human rights standards, Parties are to discharge this obligation with the participation of the communities concerned. UNDRIP, for instance, calls upon States to consult and cooperate in good faith with the indigenous peoples concerned through their own representative institutions in order to obtain their PIC[53] before adopting legislative or administrative measures that may affect them:[54] clearly domestic measures on benefit-sharing fall

---

50   Note that the ILO Convention No. 169 Article 15(2) provides more timidly that indigenous peoples shall *wherever possible* participate in the benefits of exploration or exploitation of 'resources pertaining to lands' (emphasis added).

51   Compare with the understanding of benefit-sharing as 'compensation' in *Case of the Saramaka People v. Suriname*, Interpretation of the Judgment of Preliminary Objections, Merits, Reparations, and Costs, Judgment, Case No. 12,338 (IACtHR, 12 August 2008), paragraph 140 (hereinafter, *Saramaka People v. Suriname* 2008).

52   For a preliminary discussion on the possible legal arguments on the status of the human rights of local communities, see Introduction to this commentary, section 4.2.

53   See further discussion on community PIC in this commentary on Article 6, section 4.2 and on Article 7, section 2.

54   UNDRIP Articles 19 and 32(2); ILO Convention No. 169, Article 6(2). See also Human Rights Council, "Report of the Special Rapporteur on indigenous peoples' rights," A/HRC/24/41,

into this category. Consultations should be carried out through the establish-ment and implementation, in conjunction with indigenous peoples concerned, of a fair, independent, impartial, open and transparent process, recognizing the right of indigenous peoples to participate in such process and giving due recognition to indigenous peoples' laws,[55] traditions, customs and land tenure systems, in order to recognize and adjudicate the rights of indigenous peo-ples pertaining to their lands, territories and resources, including those which were traditionally owned or otherwise occupied or used.[56] Implementation of domestic ABS frameworks, then, should be based on States' obligation to consult and cooperate in good faith with the indigenous peoples concerned through their own representative institutions in order to obtain their PIC.[57]

In addition, national measures should not diminish or extinguish existing rights of indigenous peoples.[58] Taking note of relevant provisions of UNDRIP,[59] these rights include the right of indigenous peoples to maintain, control, pro-tect and develop manifestations of their sciences, technologies and cultures, including genetic resources, seeds, medicines, and knowledge of the proper-ties of fauna and flora.[60] This specifically includes the right to their traditional medicines and to maintain their health practices, including the conservation of their vital medicinal plants, animals and minerals.[61] UNDRIP also calls for just and fair redress if indigenous peoples are deprived of their means of subsistence and development,[62] which may well include genetic resources obtained without their PIC.

paragraphs 19–25; *Sarayaku v. Ecuador*, paragraph 165: 'there is currently a clearly rec-ognized right to consultation based on developments within the Inter-American sys-tem on the property rights of indigenous peoples, other international instruments, and case-law of the highest domestic courts in the Americas.'; and note that '[i]t appears that through the process evolved from the drafting and adoption of UNDRIP and the creation of UNPFII that there is now a principle backed by supporting State practice that rights of indigenous peoples cannot be determined without their participation and consent.' Boyle and Chinkin, *Making of International Law*, op. cit., 50.

55   Note that this is also reflected in Nagoya Protocol Article 12(1): see this commentary on Article 12, section 2.

56   UNDRIP Article 27. See section 3.3 below.

57   UNDRIP Article 32(2), which refers explicitly to 'particularly in connection with the development, utilization or exploitation of mineral, water or other resources.' We are grateful to Annalisa Savaresi for her inputs on this section.

58   Nagoya Protocol 27th preambular recital.

59   Nagoya Protocol 26th preambular recital.

60   UNDRIP Article 31(1).

61   UNDRIP Article 24(1).

62   UNDRIP Article 20.

In the light of international human rights standards, it will be necessary to ascertain who are the 'communities concerned' in a specific Party (considering questions of national and international law, as discussed below). UNDRIP recognizes the right to maintain and develop indigenous peoples' political, economic and social systems or institutions, which in the context of the Protocol raises a specific question as to the appropriate community authorities that should be engaged in ABS transactions.[63] This arguably implies that the Party must actively identify all relevant communities that are entitled to receive benefits, or at least carefully avoid excluding relevant communities rightfully claiming to have a right over the genetic resources at stake from receiving benefits.[64] The obligation to achieve 'fair and equitable' benefit-sharing not only refers to the relationship between users of genetic resources and the communities holding rights over these resources, but arguably also encompasses notions of inter- or intra-community fairness in distributing benefits.[65]

3.2   'Established Rights' and Other Qualifications
International human rights law also indicates how States should interpret the puzzling qualifications in Article 5(2) in good faith so as to protect and progressively realize indigenous and local communities' rights related to genetic resources in light of their applicable international human rights obligations.

This is particularly the case of the qualification that benefit-sharing from the use of genetic resources held by indigenous and local communities is to occur 'in accordance with domestic legislation regarding the *established rights* of indigenous and local communities' over these genetic resources.

---

63   UNDRIP Article 20. Note that the individuals holding the traditional knowledge within a certain community may not necessarily be those that are authorised according to the community's customary laws and practices to provide PIC: we are grateful to Nicole Schabus for a useful exchange of ideas on this matter. See this commentary on Article 7, section 3.

64   On the relevance of indigenous peoples' human rights for local communities, see Introduction to this commentary, section 3.2.

65   Rachel Wynberg, "Rhetoric, Realism and Benefit Sharing: Use of Traditional Knowledge of Hoodia Species in the Development of an Appetite Suppressant," *Journal of World Intellectual Property* 7 (2004): 851, 862; Singh Nijar "An Asian Developing Country's View," op. cit., 262. An example can be found in Peru's Law Introducing a Protection Regime for the Collective Knowledge of Indigenous Peoples Derived from Biological Resources, No. 27811, 2002 Article 10. The same law also makes provision for the sharing of profits arising from the commercialization of collective knowledge of indigenous peoples and local communities that has entered the public domain in the last 20 years. See Singh Nijar "An Asian Developing Country's View," op. cit., 261–262.

The formulation arguably illustrates concerns that benefit-sharing should follow recognition in domestic legislation of rights of indigenous and local communities over specific genetic resources,[66] or concerns that questions related to ownership of genetic resources should not be treated in isolation from general property laws that differ significantly from one jurisdiction to another.[67] In that regard, it should first be noted that in many countries no legal provisions exist determining ownership over genetic resources.[68] Second, there may be a discrepancy between the customary law of indigenous and local communities recognizing their rights over natural resources and national legislation. International human rights bodies, however, have indicated that indigenous peoples have rights over natural resources *even in the absence* of recognition in domestic frameworks.[69]

---

66   Greiber et al., *Explanatory Guide*, op. cit., 87. For a criticism of this approach, see "Nagoya Protocol on access and benefit sharing: Substantive and procedural injustices relating to indigenous peoples' human rights. Joint submission Grand Council of the Crees (Eeyou Istchee) et al. to the ICNP," CBD, (June 2011), accessed 30 November 2013, <www.cbd .int/abs/doc/protocol/icnp-1/joint-submission-grand-council-and-others-en.pdf>, paragraphs 68–75.

67   We are grateful to Tomme Young for drawing our attention to this point.

68   CBD, "Overview of recent developments at national and regional levels relating to access and benefit-sharing," UNEP/CBD/WG-ABS/5/4. See also CBD Working Group on ABS, "Analysis of existing national, regional and international legal instruments relating to access and benefit-sharing and experience gained in their implementation, including identification of gaps. Note by the Executive Secretary" (10 November 2004) UN Doc UNEP/CBD/WG-ABS/3/2; and Jorge Cabrera Medaglia, Frederic Perron-Welch and Olivier Rukundo, *Overview of National and Regional Measures on Access to Genetic Resources and Benefit-Sharing: Challenges and Opportunities in Implementing the Nagoya Protocol* (Ottawa: Centre for International Ssustainable Development Law, 2011), accessed 30 November 2013, <http://cisdl.org/biodiversity-biosafety/public/docs/Overview_of_ ABS_Measures_2011.doc>.

69   Human Rights Council, "Report of the Special Rapporteur of indigenous peoples' rights," A/HRC/24/41, paragraphs 9, 12 and 35. The latter paragraph reads: 'It should be recalled that under various sources of international law, indigenous peoples have property, cultural and other rights in relation to their traditional territories, *even if those rights are not held under a title deed or other form of official recognition*,' emphasis added. See Savaresi, "International Human Rights Law Implications," op. cit., 70; Lenzerini, "Indigenous Peoples' Cultural Rights," op. cit., 137, on the basis of *Case of the Mayagna (Sumo) Awas Tingni Community v Nicaragua*, Merits, Reparations and Costs, Judgement, Case No. 11,577 (IACtHR, 31 August 2001), (hereinafter, *Awas Tingni Community v Nicaragua*) 153: 'The Court believes that, in light of article 21 of the Convention, the State has violated the right of the members of the Mayagna Awas Tingni Community to the use and enjoyment of their property, and that it has granted concessions to third parties to utilize the property

Against this background, the reference to 'established rights,' which can be traced back to the Bonn Guidelines,[70] may be interpreted in a narrow or broad sense with significant implications for the rights of indigenous and local communities under the Protocol. According to a narrow interpretation, the term 'established' may only refer to situations where a particular community can demonstrate that its right to genetic resources is already affirmed by *domestic* legislation, agreement or judicial ruling. According to this interpretation, if such rights are not already proved within their national legal order, communities are not entitled to any right to PIC for access to genetic resources in their territories under the Protocol.[71] Accordingly, the reference to 'established rights' may possibly leave it to the absolute discretion of the Party concerned to determine whether such community rights exist and therefore whether or not to develop domestic measures on sharing benefits with relevant communities.[72]

This interpretation, however, appears overly restrictive and not in harmony with international human rights standards and the Protocol objective.[73] In that regard, 'established rights' can also include community *customary* rights. This alternative interpretation has been supported by the UN Permanent Forum on Indigenous Issues,[74] recalling that a government distinguishing between 'existing' rights as enshrined in domestic law and the customary rights of indigenous peoples was found to be discriminatory by the UN Committee on the

---

and resources located in an area which could correspond, fully or in part, to the lands which must be delimited, demarcated, and titled.' See further *Moiwana Community v. Suriname*, 101: 'the proven facts demonstrate that a N'djuka community's connection to its traditional land is of vital spiritual, cultural and material importance.'

70 Bonn Guidelines, paragraph 31 reads: '*Respecting established legal rights* of indigenous and local communities associated with the genetic resources being accessed or where traditional knowledge associated with these genetic resources is being accessed, the prior informed consent of indigenous and local communities and the approval and involvement of the holders of traditional knowledge, innovations and practices should be obtained, in accordance with their traditional practices, national access policies and subject to domestic laws,' emphasis added.

71 See expression of concern in that regard in "Joint submission Grand Council of the Crees (Eeyou Istchee) et al.," 12.

72 This possible interpretation was identified with concern by Gurdial Singh Nijar, *The Nagoya Protocol on Access and Benefit Sharing of Genetic Resources: Analysis and Implementation Options for Developing Countries* (South Centre and CEBLAW, 2011), accessed 30 November 2013, <www.southcentre.int/wp-content/uploads/2013/08/Ev_130201_GNjar1.pdf>, 25–26.

73 See this commentary on Article 1.

74 UNPFII, "Report on the tenth session," E/2011/43–E/C.19/2011/14, paragraph 6.

Elimination of Racial Discrimination.[75] The expression 'established rights' can also be interpreted to encompass relevant *internationally protected* human rights of indigenous and local communities to the lands and natural (including genetic) resources traditionally used by them,[76] as upheld in international human rights case law.[77] Interpreting 'established rights' on the basis of relevant international human rights law and in light of community customary laws would thus imply an obligation for Parties to map customary rights at the domestic level, in consultation with the concerned communities,[78] provide for their legal recognition, and enact domestic measures to ensure benefit-sharing with communities when their customary rights over genetic resources are so ascertained.[79] The inseparable nature of genetic resources and traditional knowledge for indigenous and local communities, recognized in the Protocol preamble[80] and largely underpinning the rationale behind this provision, further substantiates the need for a broader interpretation of Article 5(2). As noted below,[81] the obligation for Parties to enact domestic measures to ensure benefit-sharing for indigenous and local communities in relation to traditional knowledge associated with genetic resources is not conditioned on the existence

---

75   See CERD, "Concluding observations of the Committee on the Elimination of Racial Discrimination. Guyana" (4 April 2006) CERD/C/GUY/CO/14, 1; and *Awas Tingni Community v. Nicaragua*, parapgrah 140(d).

76   Lenzerini, "Indigenous Peoples' Cultural Rights," op. cit., 139–140; and this commentary on Article 5, section 3.

77   For instance, the Inter-American Commission on Human Rights has noted that there is a 'customary international law norm, which affirms the rights of indigenous peoples to their traditional lands': *Awas Tingni Community v. Nicaragua*, paragraphs 148–155. See also *Endorois Welfare Council v. Kenya*, paragraphs 140(d), 196 and 207. For a discussion on the existence of customary international law in this regard, see Fodella, "Indigenous Peoples, the Environment and International Jurisprudence," op. cit., 360 (fn. 73) and 354–356; Hendrick A. Strydom, "Environment and Indigenous Peoples," in Wolfrum, *Max Planck Encyclopedia*, op. cit., paragraphs 4–8 and 17–19; Wiessner, "Indigenous Sovereignty", op. cit.; and International Law Association, *The Hague Conference Report*, op. cit., 48.

78   See fn. 54 above.

79   On global jurisprudence on indigenous peoples' rights to land and natural resources, see sources analysed by Fodella, "Indigenous Peoples, the Environment and International Jurisprudence," op. cit., 349 (fn. 59), 351 and 353 (fn. 11 and 26). On the human right to land as a self-standing right that is part of indigenous peoples' right to property and as a component of the right to food, see also De Schutter, "The Emerging Human Right to Land," op. cit., particularly 310–314.

80   Nagoya Protocol 22nd preambular recital.

81   See section 4 below on Article 5(5).

of specific rights, but it is rather based on the right to cultural identity[82] of these communities.

According to the broad interpretation of 'established rights,' a human rights-cognizant interpretation of Article 5(2) seems to point to an underlying obligation for Parties to the Protocol to recognize the rights of communities in national legislation, in accordance with their international human rights obligations, taking into account the customary laws of indigenous and local communities[83] and as a result of good-faith consultation with these communities.[84] In light of these considerations, the right of communities extends to retaining possession of genetic resources that are decisive for the enjoyment of their rights to safeguard their cultural identity and integrity.[85] Should the State, however, claim ownership over genetic resources held by communities, specific procedures are to be put in place to ascertain to which degree indigenous peoples' rights are prejudiced, and still ensure benefit-sharing for the relevant communities in light of their right to PIC.[86] As a minimum, therefore, Parties are to ensure respect for indigenous peoples' right to participate in the decision-making and management of any kind of initiative taken by the government concerning their genetic resources, as well as to guarantee a certain degree of legal and administrative autonomy for these communities in the administration of these resources.[87]

Two other qualifications are worth briefly discussing here. First, it should be noted that Article 5(2) only refers to benefit-sharing for the *utilization* of genetic resources held by communities. Unlike Article 5(1), it does not refer

---

82   Fodella, "Indigenous Peoples," op. cit., 350, (fn. 4): Human Rights Committee, *Kitok v. Sweden*, Communication no. 197/1985 (27 July 1988), UN Doc CCPR/C/33/D/197/1985, paragraph 9(2); Human Rights Committee, *Lubicon Lake Band v. Canada*, Communication no. 167/1984 (26 March 1990), UN Doc CCPR/C/38/D/167/1984, paragraph 32(2); General Comment No. 23, paragraphs 3(2) and 7.

83   Nagoya Protocol Article 12(1).

84   See fn. 54 above.

85   Lenzerini, "Indigenous Peoples' Cultural Rights," op. cit., 137, based on *Awas Tingni Community v. Nicaragua*, paragraph 153; and *Moiwana Community v. Suriname*, paragraph 101.

86   Lenzerini, "Indigenous Peoples' Cultural Rights," op. cit., 139, based on ILO Convention No. 169 Article 15 and Inter-American Court of Human Rights, *Case of the Yakye Axa Indigenous Community v. Paraguay*, Merits, Reparations and Costs, Judgment, Case No. 12,313 (IACtHR, 17 June 2005), paragraphs 140–148.

87   Lenzerini, "Indigenous Peoples' Cultural Rights," op. cit., 135, based on Committee on the Elimination of Racial Discrimination, "General Recommendation No. 23: indigenous peoples" (18 August 1997) UN Doc A/52/18, paragraph 5.

explicitly to 'subsequent applications and commercialization'. A strictly literal interpretation that would result in depriving indigenous and local communities from benefit-sharing arising from the subsequent applications and commercialization related to genetic resources held by them should be rejected. Such restrictive reading would unfairly limit the scope of benefits flowing back to indigenous and local communities concerned, which would not serve the Protocol objective of realizing equitable and fair benefit-sharing vis-à-vis these communities.[88] Furthermore, as Article 5(2) addresses a sub-set of benefit-sharing under Article 5(1), a systemic interpretation would support an understanding of benefit-sharing from subsequent applications and commercialization both for genetic resources held by States and for those held by communities. In practice, it will be particularly significant for Parties to clearly address this point in their domestic ABS frameworks, and for indigenous and local communities representatives to be involved in the development of domestic measures on this point. Second, the qualifier 'as appropriate' leaves discretion as to the type of implementing measures that Parties have to adopt, but not as to whether to adopt measures at all or not.[89]

4   Benefit-sharing from the Utilization of Traditional Knowledge

In accordance with Article 5(5), Parties are required to take the appropriate legislative, administrative or policy measures, to ensure that benefits arising from the utilization of traditional knowledge associated with genetic resources are shared in a fair and equitable way with the indigenous and local communities holding such knowledge. In contrast to the obligation included in 5(2), Parties' obligation with regard to traditional knowledge is unencumbered by references to the need for accordance with national law.[90]

Article 5(5) is a new obligation that goes beyond the CBD text.[91] For the first time in international environmental law, a treaty creates a binding obligation for States to establish measures to reward communities for developing and preserving traditional knowledge associated with genetic resources and for thus contributing to scientific progress for the benefit of the global community. From

---

88   See this commentary on Article 1, section 2.

89   See Introduction to this commentary, section 5 and fn. 227.

90   As observed earlier, the qualifier 'as appropriate' leaves discretion in relation to the type of implementing measures that Parties have to adopt, not as to whether these measures should be adopted at all or not.

91   Compare with CBD Article 15(7).

a broader international law perspective, even if this provision does not employ human rights language, it can be interpreted as implicitly underpinned by a substantive environmental right[92] for indigenous and local communities to their traditional knowledge associated with genetic resources. This can be seen as an implication deriving from the established international human rights, in their collective dimension, concerning indigenous peoples' self-determination and cultural identity. The Nagoya Protocol, however, goes beyond the letter of international human rights instruments, by encapsulating, in a legally binding provision, a *benefit-sharing* obligation *owed directly* to communities that arises specifically from the use of *traditional knowledge associated with the genetic resources*. In comparison, UNDRIP recognizes more generally the right to maintain, control, protect and develop traditional knowledge, including intellectual property over such traditional knowledge.[93] In addition, the Protocol identifies not only indigenous peoples, but also *local communities*[94] as beneficiaries of such obligation.

As opposed to the rest of Article 5, the obligation is two-fold. On the one hand, it entails the development of national measures to ensure that a benefit-sharing obligation arises from the utilization of traditional knowledge at the inter-State level (hence, the provision on inter-State collaboration on compliance elsewhere in the Protocol).[95] On the other hand, it entails the development of a domestic mechanism for such benefits to be shared internally with the relevant indigenous and local communities.

As regards Parties where an indigenous or local community is located, Article 5(5) obliges governments to put in place conditions that enable indigenous and local communities to engage in ABS-related activities concerning their traditional knowledge associated with genetic resources. At a minimum – reading Article 5(5) in conjunction with Article 16(1) and 7 – Parties with indigenous and local communities in their territories must establish domestic ABS measures that articulate how to engage with these communities so as to obtain either their PIC or their prior approval and involvement for access to their traditional knowledge, and how to establish MAT. In this regard, Parties with such communities holding traditional knowledge must also be mindful of

---

92 See parallel discussion in section 3 above.

93 UNDRIP Article 31(1). Note that the ILO Convention No. 169 does not mention benefit-sharing in relation to traditional knowledge.

94 For a preliminary discussion on the possible legal arguments on the status of the human rights of local communities, see Introduction to this commentary, section 4.2.

95 See this commentary on Article 16.

their obligations to take into account communities' customary laws,[96] ensure communities' effective participation[97] and endeavor to support these communities in ABS transactions,[98] as well as take into account their capacity needs and priorities as identified by them.[99]

Difficulties may arise in practice in determining which indigenous and local communities are 'holding' traditional knowledge concerned in a specific ABS transaction and should therefore be the 'beneficiaries' of benefit-sharing.[100] Article 5(5) seems to apply only to situations where the traditional knowledge is actually held by one or more communities.[101] Read in light of the preamble, it is then up to these communities to identify the rightful holders in that connection,[102] in light of the diversity of circumstances in which traditional knowledge is held or owned by them.[103]

One particular situation arises in the case of traditional knowledge that has been documented or held in other form by a State entity,[104] such as in traditional knowledge registries or digital libraries.[105] Traditional knowledge in such registries could be publicly available or not, depending on who is authorized to

---

96 Nagoya Protocol Article 12(1). See this commentary on Article 12, section 2.

97 UNDRIP Article 19 and comments by Boyle and Chinkin, *Making of International Law*, op. cit., 50

98 Nagoya Protocol Article 12(3). See this commentary on Article 12, section 4.

99 Nagoya Protocol Article 22(3). See this commentary on Article 22, section 4.

100 The Inter-American Court of Human Rights found that 'the determination of those beneficiaries must be made in consultation with the Saramaka people, and not unilaterally by the State' and that 'these matters can be discussed and addressed during the consultations and process of reaching agreement on the legislative and administrative measures required to give effect to, *inter alia*, the benefit sharing requirement.' *Saramaka People v. Suriname* 2008, paragraphs 25–27.

101 Greiber et al., *Explanatory Guide*, op. cit., 88.

102 Nagoya Protocol 24th preambular recital. Although general international human rights law may call for States to engage in a complex balancing of competing international human rights in that regard, particularly in the case of variance with international norms against discrimination (based on gender, in light of the Protocol 11th preambular recital). See Introduction to this commentary, section 4.3.

103 Nagoya Protocol 23rd preambular recital.

104 Nagoya Protocol 25th preambular recital.

105 See, for example "Traditional Knowledge Digital Library," Indian Government, accessed 30 November 2013, <www.tkdl.res.in/tkdl/langdefault/common/Home.asp?GL=Eng>; "Traditional Chinese Medicine Patents Database," Chinese Government, accessed 30 November <http://chmp.cnipr.cn/englishversion/help/help.html>. See also discussion in this commentary on Article 7, section 3.

have access to the registries.[106] In this case, traditional knowledge may either have not been obtained directly by the relevant communities or may no longer be attributable to them.[107] While the Protocol negotiators discussed whether to address or not publicly available traditional knowledge,[108] the Protocol eventually remains silent on this issue. It thus remains to be clarified whether and how the benefit-sharing obligation applies to traditional knowledge that is publicly available.[109] This may be particularly complicated depending on whether such traditional knowledge is regarded as national heritage and/ or whether it can still be traced back to one or more particular community. Parties would be well advised to clarify in their domestic ABS frameworks this question,[110] or consider the development of guidance by the Protocol's governing body.[111]

Another difficulty may arise from traditional knowledge shared by different indigenous and local communities within the territory of the same Party, as only some of these communities may wish to grant access and enter into MAT and others may not. Parties are well advised, therefore, to articulate in their domestic ABS frameworks how to engage with indigenous and local communities so that all communities holding relevant knowledge do (or have at least a fair and reasonable opportunity to) receive benefits arising from the utiliza-

---

106   In India, for instance, the Traditional Knowledge Digital Library (TKDL) is only accessible
       to the patent offices that have signed a TKDL access agreement, including the European
       Patent Office, and the patent offices of Australia, Canada, Germany, the UK and the US.
       See V.K. Gupta "Protecting India's Traditional Knowledge," *WIPO Magazine* (June 2011),
       accessed 30 November 2013, <www.wipo.int/wipo_magazine/en/2011/03/article_0002.
       html>.

107   Singh Nijar, *The Nagoya Protocol on ABS: An Analysis*, op. cit., 28.

108   See draft article 9(5) in Nagoya Draft, which reads: '[5. Parties shall [encourage][require]
       the users of [publicly available] traditional knowledge associated with genetic resources
       [which has been lawfully obtained by that user from a source other than an indigenous
       and local community] to take reasonable measures to enter into fair and equitable ben-
       efit-sharing arrangements with the [rightful] holders of [such] knowledge.]' (brackets in
       the original).

109   Singh Nijar "An Asian Developing Country's View," op. cit., 259–263; Greiber et al.,
       Explanatory Guide, op. cit., 113.

110   Unless this case is further complicated by the presence of traditional knowledge occur-
       ring in transboundary situations, in which case Nagoya Protocol Article 11(2) and possibly
       Article 10 apply.

111   Nagoya Protocol Article 26(4)(d): see this commentary on Article 26, section 2. Note that
       the issue of 'publicly known' traditional knowledge is currently being negotiated under
       WIPO, with regard to issues including disclosure requirements, the creation of digital
       libraries and the prevention of erroneous patents. See WIPO General Assembly, "Matters
       concerning the IGC," WO/GA/43/14, Annex B, 5.

tion of their traditional knowledge associated with genetic resources.[112] A truly inclusive and transparent domestic process of consultation between the government and communities, taking in consideration of communities' customary laws, protocols and procedures,[113] seems to be a pre-requisite for effectively and fairly addressing these questions. Such process should also allow for consultations within and among communities, with a view to ensuring inter- and intra-community fairness in relation to benefit-sharing.[114]

5   The Role of Mutually Agreed Terms

Article 5 reiterates that benefit-sharing deriving from genetic resources (whether held by the State or indigenous or local communities) and from traditional knowledge is to be based on mutually agreed terms.[115] This is because, as noted above,[116] the international obligations enshrined in Article 5 will in practice most often lead to sharing benefits obtained from private parties, such as research institutions and biotech companies, utilizing genetic resources and traditional knowledge. MAT, a private-law contract,[117] is thus seen in the Protocol's architecture as an effective and easily enforceable way to realize benefit-sharing obligations.[118] A key element in a functioning ABS relationship based on mutual confidence, such a contract is expected to clarify individual parties' specific rights and obligations, restrictions in the use of specific material and/or traditional knowledge throughout the research and development chain, as well as information sharing and monitoring duties.

---

112   Nagoya Protocol Article 11(2).

113   See this commentary on Article 12, section 2.

114   The Inter-American Court observed that 'in the event that any internal conflict arises between members of the Saramaka community regarding [benefit-sharing], it 'must be resolved by the Saramaka people in accordance with their own traditional customs and norms, not by the State or this Court in this particular case.' *Saramaka People v. Suriname* 2008), paragraphs 25–27.

115   See final clause of Nagoya Protocol Article 5(1–2) and (5).

116   See section 2 above.

117   This is, to some extent, a simplification for the sake of clarity. As explained in the Introduction to this commentary, section 1.3, parties to and the form of MAT, as well as their relation with PIC, may vary significantly from one jurisdiction to another, and possibly also from one case to another. In some instances, the goverment or its designee negotiates MAT and there is at least one separate negotiation with the specific provider(s): we are grateful to Tomme Young for drawing our attention to this point.

118   As is explicitly foreseen in the last sentence of Nagoya Protocol Article 5(1).

Article 5(2) is silent on the question whether representatives of indigenous and local communities will be parties to MAT spelling out benefit-sharing arrangements for utilizing genetic resources held by these communities, and who will be the other parties (individual users, or the government who may have established a separate set of MAT with the users). The government could also be acting on behalf of relevant communities in establishing MAT with users. In all events, governments may be expected to strengthen the capacity of indigenous and local communities,[119] upon their request. Similar observations can be made with regard to MAT spelling out specific benefit-sharing modalities arising from the use of traditional knowledge under Article 5(5). One difference, however, is that States have also a best-endeavor obligation to support the development by indigenous and local communities of minimum requirements for MAT to secure fair and equitable benefit-sharing from the utilization of traditional knowledge.[120]

In any of the cases envisaged in Article 5, one should expect that concrete terms for the implementation of the benefit-sharing obligations of the Protocol will, on the basis of applicable national measures, be set out in MAT, such as the conditions, types, timing, and procedures/mechanisms for distribution of benefits.[121] Notably, however, the Protocol does not attempt to set any substantive or procedural criteria[122] for establishing MAT[123] so as to provide for *fair and equitable* benefit-sharing, but rather leaves any consideration of what is fair and equitable to contractual negotiations. Parties providing genetic resources may consider establishing some substantive rules on the contents of MAT in their domestic ABS frameworks. That being said, it may be difficult for provider countries to rely on their domestic ABS frameworks in a foreign court in that regard, if the determination of what is fair and equitable benefit-sharing is not reflected also under MAT.[124] Perhaps for this reason, the Protocol requires Parties individually and collectively through the Protocol's governing body to

---

119   Nagoya Protocol Article 22(1) and (5)(j).

120   See commentary on Article 12, section 4. Note, however, that the Protocol only establishes such as obligation in relation to MAT concerning the utilization of traditional knowledge in Article 12(3)(b), but not about MAT concerning genetic resources held by indigenous and local communities.

121   Greiber et al., *Explanatory Guide*, op. cit., 90.

122   Tvedt, "Beyond Nagoya," op. cit., 161 and 163.

123   Note the reference to 'benefit-sharing' (and the absence of reference to 'fair and equitable') in Nagoya Protocol Article 6(3)(g)(ii): see this commentary of Article 6, section 7.

124   Greiber et al., *Explanatory Guide*, op. cit., 160–161 and 163. See this commentary on Article 18.

explore model contractual clauses[125] and voluntary instruments[126] as a source of inspiration for fair and equitable benefit-sharing contracts. It also points to awareness-raising[127] and training activities[128] to that end. That being said, the Protocol preamble reflects Parties' recognition of the importance of promoting equity and fairness in the negotiations of MAT,[129] which appears crucial for Parties to effectively and in good faith contribute to the realization of the fair and equitable benefit-sharing objective of the Protocol.[130]

Other provisions of the Protocol, however, do not address this point, but rather contain a list of minimum requirements on the content of MAT to be included in domestic access measures;[131] envisage that Parties support indigenous and local communities in determining minimum requirements for MAT concerning traditional knowledge;[132] provide for legal recourse in user countries for ensuring users' compliance with MAT, which can rely on existing rules of private international law;[133] and encourage including in MAT requirements on information-sharing and reporting on implementation.[134]

6   Monetary and Non-monetary Benefits

According to Article 5(4), benefits arising from the utilization of genetic resources and from traditional knowledge concern monetary and non-monetary benefits, including but not limited to those in the Annex to the Protocol. Read together with the Annex, therefore, Article 5(4) provides guidance to Parties developing domestic ABS frameworks and engaging in the establishment of MAT in their consideration of a range of benefits to be shared. It will also guide private providers and users when negotiating MAT.

Non-monetary benefits may be more immediately identifiable and available, given the usually lengthy research and development process and uncertainty related to ultimate commercialization. Non-monetary benefits can also contribute to gradually building the capacity of provider countries in utilizing their

---

125   Nagoya Protocol Article 19.
126   Nagoya Protocol Article 20.
127   Nagoya Protocol Article 21.
128   Nagoya Protocol Article 22(4)(c) and 22(5)(b).
129   Nagoya Protocol 10th preambular recital.
130   See this commentary on Article 1, section 2 and Conclusions to this commentary, section 2.
131   Nagoya Protocol Article 6(3)(g). See this commentary on Article 6, section 6.
132   Nagoya Protocol Article 12(3)(b).
133   See this commentary on Article 18.
134   Nagoya Protocol Article 17(1)(b).

genetic resources.[135] In that connection, some non-monetary benefits may be seen as having 'high value to the provider and low marginal cost to the user.'[136] Certain types of non-monetary benefits may be targeted to support long-term cooperative relations among the parties to the ABS transaction, such as sharing of research and development results, collaboration in scientific research and development, participation in product development, and admittance to ex situ facilities and databases.[137] This is also the case of capacity building and training.[138] In addition, non-monetary benefits may be targeted to specifically contribute to conservation efforts,[139] and/or to the sustainable development at the national and local level,[140] such as food and livelihoods security benefits, and contributions to the local economy.[141] These types of benefits, however, may raise concerns about undue interferences of user countries and users into the exercise of provider countries' sovereignty in determining the domestic sharing of benefits.[142]

That being said, monetary benefits may also contribute to long-term collaboration among parties to ABS transactions through joint ventures and joint ownership of relevant IPRs.[143] It is worth emphasizing that the Annex to the Protocol includes, both in relation to monetary and non-monetary benefits, one of the very few references to IPRs that can be found in the whole Protocol text.[144] This may be surprising as IPR-related concerns were prominent throughout the negotiations of the operative text of the Protocol. Eventually, however, the relationship between ABS and IPRs was not addressed in the Protocol.[145]

In addition, monetary benefits may also contribute to conservation efforts (special fees to be paid to trust funds supporting conservation and sustainable use of biodiversity).[146] Most notably, they also include actual financial benefits

---

135   Glowka and Normand, "The Nagoya Protocol on Access and Benefit-Sharing," op. cit., 32.

136   We are thankful to Geoff Burton for making this point, which is also reflected in Greiber et al., *Explanatory Guide*, op. cit., 88.

137   E.g. Nagoya Protocol Annex, 2(a–c) and (e).

138   Nagoya Protocol Annex, 2(d), (g–i), (n) and (j).

139   Nagoya Protocol Annex, 2(k) and (m).

140   Greiber et al., *Explanatory Guide*, op. cit., 269.

141   Nagoya Protocol Annex, 2(o) and (l).

142   We are grateful to Tomme Young for drawing our attention to this point.

143   Nagoya Protocol Annex, 1(i) and (j).

144   Nagoya Protocol Annex, 1(j) and 2(q), both reading 'joint ownership of relevant intellectual property rights.' The other reference can be found in Article 6(3)(g)(ii) on possible elements of MAT.

145   On this issue, see Introduction to this commentary, section 1.1 and Pavoni, "The Nagoya Protocol and WTO," op. cit., 200–205.

146   Nagoya Protocol Annex, 1(f).

reaching the provider country and relevant communities in the form of access fees, up-front or milestone payments, royalties and license fees.[147]

Finally, it should be noted that while the Annex identifies types of benefits to be shared, it is silent on possible links between specific benefit types and specific ABS transactions. Parties to the Protocol, and subject to possible limitations in national legislation, individual parties to specific ABS transactions, therefore, retain quite some flexibility in tailoring benefit-sharing on a case-by-case basis. Nevertheless, the objective of the Protocol to achieve fairness and equity through benefit-sharing, and to contribute to biodiversity conservation and sustainable use,[148] should guide Parties in the exercise of their discretion when setting relevant domestic measures and directly participating in the establishment of MAT. When government entities are not directly involved in the establishment of MAT, their good-faith efforts in realizing the objective of the Protocol will rather take the form of proactive encouragement,[149] and possibly also control and monitoring,[150] of private parties. In the specific case of benefit-sharing reaching indigenous and local communities, relevant international human rights standards should also be taken into account: caution should be exercised in identifying benefits that are culturally appropriate and endogenously identified,[151] as certain benefit types or benefit-sharing arrangements can have disruptive effects on the communities' identities and internal governance structures.[152]

---

147 Nagoya Protocol Annex, 1(a–e).

148 See this commentary on Article 1.

149 As specifically mandated by Nagoya Protocol Article 9 in relation to directing benefits towards conservation and sustainable use: see this commentary on Article 9.

150 In the light of the general notion of due diligence in international law: see discussion in Conclusions to this commentary, section 3.

151 As a result of the interpretation of human rights instruments, such as ILO Convention No. 169, Article 15(2) and UNDRIP Article 32. See also American Convention on Human Rights (San Jose, 22 November 1969, in force 18 July 1978) 1144 UNTS 123, Articles 1(1) and 21.

152 For example, Munyi and Jonas report how the Hoodia benefit-sharing agreement represents 'a process that has arguably further undermined [communities'] traditional values and knowledge and resource governance system' and 'weakened the San's traditional form of authority,' increasing reliance on 'external expert opinion,' leading to 'largely misunderstood and, at times corrupt new forms of governance,' and exacerbating 'power and information asymmetries in and across San communities,' as well as fostering mistrust. Peter Munyi and Harry Jonas, "Implementing the Nagoya Protocol in Africa: Opportunities and Challenges for African Indigenous Peoples and Local Communities," in Morgera, Buck and Tsioumani, *2010 Nagoya Protocol on Access and Benefit-Sharing in Perspective*, op. cit., 217, 227.

Article 6. Access to Genetic Resources

1. In the exercise of sovereign rights over natural resources, and subject to domestic access and benefit-sharing legislation or regulatory requirements, access to genetic resources for their utilization shall be subject to the prior informed consent of the Party providing such resources that is the country of origin of such resources or a Party that has acquired the genetic resources in accordance with the Convention, unless otherwise determined by that Party.

2. In accordance with domestic law, each Party shall take measures, as appropriate, with the aim of ensuring that the prior informed consent or approval and involvement of indigenous and local communities is obtained for access to genetic resources where they have the established right to grant access to such resources.

3. Pursuant to paragraph 1 above, each Party requiring prior informed consent shall take the necessary legislative, administrative or policy measures, as appropriate, to:

    (a) Provide for legal certainty, clarity and transparency of their domestic access and benefit-sharing legislation or regulatory requirements;

    (b) Provide for fair and non-arbitrary rules and procedures on accessing genetic resources;

    (c) Provide information on how to apply for prior informed consent;

    (d) Provide for a clear and transparent written decision by a competent national authority, in a cost-effective manner and within a reasonable period of time;

    (e) Provide for the issuance at the time of access of a permit or its equivalent as evidence of the decision to grant prior informed consent and of the establishment of mutually agreed terms, and notify the Access and Benefit-sharing Clearing-House accordingly;

    (f) Where applicable, and subject to domestic legislation, set out criteria and/or processes for obtaining prior informed consent or approval and involvement of indigenous and local communities for access to genetic resources; and

    (g) Establish clear rules and procedures for requiring and establishing mutually agreed terms. Such terms shall be set out in writing and may include, *inter alia*:

© KONINKLIJKE BRILL NV, LEIDEN, 2014 | DOI 10.1163/9789004217188_008

> (i)   A dispute settlement clause;
> (ii) Terms on benefit-sharing, including in relation to intellectual property rights;
> (iii) Terms on subsequent third-party use, if any; and
> (iv) Terms on changes of intent, where applicable.

1   Overview

Access to genetic resources is one of the main pillars of the Nagoya Protocol and is considered to be one of the preconditions for the sharing of benefits arising from the utilization of genetic resources. This is recognized in the Protocol's preamble, which points to the 'linkage' between access to genetic resources and benefit-sharing.[1] Concluded following intense negotiations, the Protocol's provisions on access aim to build the foundation for the cooperation between provider and user countries that will lead to benefit-sharing. These provisions represent the compromise between developed countries that considered themselves as predominantly user countries, which prioritized efficiency in access-related decision-making and legal certainty, in order to avoid hampering research on genetic resources; and developing countries considering themselves as predominantly provider countries, which called for benefit-sharing as a self-standing obligation of result for user countries, irrespective of provider countries' regulatory requirements on access.[2]

The Protocol's provisions on access build on the foundational principle enshrined in the CBD[3] that sovereign rights over genetic resources are the basis for requiring PIC and establishing MAT. At the same time, Article 6 goes significantly beyond the CBD in three respects. First, it elaborates in greater detail the rights and obligations of Parties in regulating access to genetic resources, aiming to address the enforcement challenges resulting from the transnational component of the ABS transactions.[4] Second, it promotes best practice in contractual drafting, by providing for clauses that could be negotiated as part

---

1   Nagoya Protocol 8th preambular recital. See discussion in this commentary on Article 1, section 2.

2   Cariño et al., *Nagoya Protocol*, op. cit., 57–59.

3   CBD Article 15. Glowka and Normand, "The Nagoya Protocol on Access and Benefit-sharing," op. cit., 29; Greiber et al., *Explanatory Guide*, op. cit., 94.

4   Young, "An International Cooperation Perspective," op. cit., 453; see also Introduction to this commentary, section 1.

of MAT.[5] Third, it addresses, for the first time in a legally-binding international treaty,[6] the issue of access to genetic resources held by indigenous and local communities.

Following a brief discussion of the background to Article 6, with reference to the CBD provisions and the Bonn Guidelines, the following sections will focus on each of the components of Article 6, namely: the inter-State obligations related to access to genetic resources;[7] the obligations related to genetic resources held by indigenous and local communities;[8] the access standards that will inform the development of domestic ABS frameworks; the minimum procedural requirements for PIC; and the minimum requirements for MAT.[9]

2   Background

By clarifying that the principle of national sovereignty over natural resources also applies to genetic resources,[10] and by establishing the obligation for fair and equitable benefit-sharing, the CBD introduced key rules on access to genetic resources: the authority of national governments to authorize access to genetic resources under their jurisdiction as part of States' sovereign rights over their natural resources;[11] the general requirement of PIC for access, unless otherwise determined by the provider Party;[12] and establishment of MAT in cases access is granted.[13] These provisions are coupled by the CBD benefit-sharing obligation,[14] which applies only to genetic resources provided by Parties that are countries of origin or that have acquired them in accordance with the Convention.[15]

Early attempts to implement these CBD provisions and develop domestic ABS frameworks revealed lack of conceptual clarity about ABS transactions and corresponding legal challenges. These related, for instance, to the frequently

---

5   Glowka and Normand, "The Nagoya Protocol on Access and Benefit-sharing," op. cit., 30.
6   Ibid., 40.
7   Based on a combined reading of Nagoya Protocol Article 6(1) and the chapeau of Article 6(3).
8   Nagoya Protocol Article 6(2).
9   The latter three are covered by Nagoya Protocol Article 6(3).
10   See Introduction to this commentary, section 1.3.
11   CBD Article 15(1).
12   CBD Article 15(5).
13   CBD Article 15(4).
14   As set out in CBD Article 15(7). See this commentary on Article 5.
15   CBD Article 15(3). See discussion in Introduction to this commentary, section 1.3.

unclear status of the ownership over genetic resources at the domestic level, resulting in lack of clarity on who was responsible to grant PIC.[16] In addition, early ABS laws tended to focus mostly on the safeguarding of Parties' sovereign rights to genetic resources in order to secure benefit-sharing, including through permitting and oversight systems, rather than on the efficiency of access-related processes.[17] This resulted in practical challenges, stemming from the lack of standardized access procedures, as well as the lack of capacity to negotiate benefit-sharing agreements.[18]

Researchers and companies have frequently reported that they avoid jurisdictions with unclear ABS legal frameworks and prefer operating in provider countries where they managed to create predictable working relationships.[19] However, even countries with supposedly simple access systems have not been significantly more successful in attracting researchers and companies.[20] Overall what seemed to be lacking was confidence in functioning ABS frameworks as tools for the generation of benefits and support of biodiversity-based research. In addition, ex situ collections in non-CBD parties continued providing genetic material without having to adhere to the CBD requirements.[21]

This reality, which reflected the legal and practical challenges to develop and implement domestic ABS legislation, did not change significantly after the adoption of the Bonn Guidelines, which represented a first attempt to operationalize the provisions of CBD Article 15,[22] and constituted the background to the negotiations of Article 6 of the Nagoya Protocol.

---

16   E.g., Cabrera Medaglia, "The Implementation of the Nagoya Protocol," op. cit., 332 and 357.

17   Young, "An International Cooperation Perspective," op. cit., 453.

18   See CBD Secretariat, *Access and Benefit-Sharing in Practice: Trends in Partnerships Across Sectors. CBD Technical Series No. 38* (Montreal: CBD Secretariat, 2008); FAO, *Framework Study on Food Security and Access and Benefit-Sharing for Genetic Resources for Food and Agriculture* (FAO, 2009), accessed 30 November 2013, <ftp://ftp.fao.org/docrep/fao/meeting/017/ak526e.pdf>; and Jorge Cabrera Medaglia and Christian Silva López, *Addressing the Problems of Access: Protecting Sources, While Giving Users Certainty* (Gland: IUCN, 2007).

19   CBD Secretariat, *Access and Benefit-Sharing in Practice*, op. cit., 25.

20   Cabrera Medaglia and Silva López, *Addressing the Problems of Access*, op. cit., 1.

21   Notably collections in the US, which is not a Party to the CBD. See FAO *The Second Report on the State of the World Plant Genetic Resources for Food and Agriculture* (Rome: FAO, 2010), chapter 3.

22   See Introduction to this commentary, section 2.

3   Access to Genetic Resources: The Inter-State Dimension

The term 'access to genetic resources' is not defined in the CBD or the Nagoya Protocol.[23] Under the Protocol, it can be argued that in light of the definition of 'utilization of genetic resources' (which itself does not include reference to 'access'),[24] and considering the wording of Article 6(1) ('access for their utilization'), access may constitute the beginning of the conduct aimed at research and development in the jurisdiction of one Party on the genetic or biochemical composition of genetic resources that are provided by another Party. In addition, taking into account the CBD definition of 'country providing genetic resources,'[25] it can be inferred that genetic resources supplied by a Party to the Nagoya Protocol may originate from both in situ or ex situ sources. In practice, therefore, 'access' can be achieved through different activities in the jurisdiction of the Party providing genetic resources, including by: collecting biological material in the wild; obtaining samples of genetic resources or biochemicals from genebanks,[26] research institutions or the private sector; or, arguably, obtaining digitalized information about genetic resources and their genetic or biochemical composition.[27] Against all these possible scenarios, a definition or clarification of the term 'access' in domestic ABS frameworks, possibly following a decision by the Protocol's governing body,[28] would likely assist in promoting common understanding among Parties and thus legal certainty. It would also facilitate the issuance of domestic permits, which provide

---

23   For a discussion on this term in relation to Article 15 CBD see Glowka, Burhenne-Guilmin and Synge, *Guide to the Convention on Biological Diversity*, op. cit., 79.

24   See discussion of the relevance of utilization, rather than 'access', for the triggering of the benefit-sharing obligation in this commentary on Article 5, section 2.

25   CBD Article 2, defines the term as 'the country supplying genetic resources collected from in situ sources, including populations of both wild and domesticated species, or taken from ex situ sources, which may or may not have originated in that country.' In addition, according to CBD Article 15(3), in case the provider country is not the country of origin, the access-related provisions apply if that Party has acquired the genetic resources in accordance with the Convention. See Tvedt and Young, *Beyond Access*, op. cit., 14; Cariño et al., *Nagoya Protocol*, op. cit., 63. See also this commentary on Article 5, section 2.

26   Cariño et al., *Nagoya Protocol*, op. cit., 63.

27   See this commentary on Article 2, section 2.1.1. Margo A. Bagley and Arti K. Rai, *The Nagoya Protocol and Synthetic Biology Research: A Look at the Potential Impacts* (Washington DC: Wilson Centre, 2013), accessed 30 November 2013, <www.wilsoncenter.org/publication/the-nagoya-protocol-and-synthetic-biology-research-look-the-potential-impacts>.

28   Article 26(4)(a). See this commentary on Article 26, section 2.

the basis for the internationally recognized certificates of compliance,[29] that is to occur 'at the time of access.'

The following sub-sections will first discuss the notion of national sovereignty over genetic resources and the Protocol's obligation to develop domestic measures on access – based on a combined reading of Article 6(1) and 6(3), and then the concept of State PIC concerning access to genetic resources.

3.1   National Sovereignty over Genetic Resources and Domestic Measures on Access

Based on the reaffirmation of the principle of national sovereignty over natural resources,[30] Parties have the authority to regulate access to genetic resources and require PIC as the key precondition for access, unless they determine otherwise, subject to domestic ABS legislation or regulatory requirements.[31] The latter reference is elaborated upon in Article 6(3), which lists, *inter alia*, a series of standards and minimum requirements for the development of legislative, administrative or policy measures of the provider country regulating access to its genetic resources. The combined reading of the two provisions, however, may arguably give rise to differing interpretations.[32] Article 6(1) clearly indicates that access to genetic resources is subject to the provider Party's PIC, unless that Party *specifically* determines that it does not require PIC. Article 6(3) calls on Parties 'requiring PIC' to take the necessary legislative, administrative or policy measures satisfying a series of standards and minimum requirements. Article 6(3) may thus be interpreted so as to imply that the PIC requirement must be explicitly spelt out in domestic measures. Such an interpretation could lead to a practical problem when a Party is silent with regard to its access requirements – i.e., it has not (yet) regulated access in any way nor it has expressly waived its right to PIC – and a user accesses its genetic resources assuming that no PIC is required. In this case, giving priority to the wording of one provision of Article 6 over the other has significant consequences. Is it the user's responsibility to confirm whether PIC is required, in the absence

---

29   Nagoya Protocol Articles 6(3)(e) and 17(2). See this commentary on Article 17, section 3.

30   Nagoya Protocol Article 6(1).

31   In line with CBD Article 15(1), which reads: 'Recognizing the sovereign rights of States over their natural resources, the authority to determine access to genetic resources rests with the national governments and is *subject to national legislation*,' emphasis added; and CBD Article 15(5), which reads: 'Access to genetic resources shall be subject to prior informed consent of the Contracting Party providing such resources, unless otherwise determined by the Party.'

32   We are grateful to Tomme Young for drawing our attention to this point.

of any indication from the provider country, to respect Article 6(1)? Or is it the responsibility of the provider country to set up its regulatory framework, based on a reading of Article 6(3) creating an obligation for Parties to actively exercise their right to require PIC through the establishment of a domestic ABS framework?[33] The former interpretation seems to be supported by the fact that Article 6(3) is expressly subordinated to Article 6(1).[34] It is also supported by the wording of Article 6(1), which indicates that a Party should make an explicit decision against requiring PIC.[35] Furthermore, even if the mandatory wording of Article 6(3) indicates an obligation for countries requiring PIC to regulate access to genetic resources at the domestic level ('shall'), failure to do so could possibly qualify as an instance of non-compliance with the Protocol provisions,[36] rather than leading to the deprivation of the Party's right to PIC, which is protected in mandatory terms under Article 6(1) and is a fundamental expression of national sovereignty. That being said, lack of domestic measures on PIC could make it very difficult for the compliance provisions of the Protocol to apply.[37] Provider countries, therefore, are well advised to develop their domestic ABS frameworks to take full advantage of the Protocol provisions fostering international cooperation, particularly with regard to compliance.

Against this background, users will therefore be well advised to take a cautious approach in cases in which a Party's domestic framework is silent on access to genetic resources, and as a default position assume that PIC is required.[38] This is already reflected in what is currently considered best practice for user groups: users confirm this with the CBD national focal point of the provider country even in cases where PIC has been specifically waived.[39]

---

33   See Singh Nijar, *The Nagoya Protocol on ABS: An Analysis*, op. cit., 16; and Buck and Hamilton, "Nagoya Protocol," op. cit., 51.

34   Note that Nagoya Protocol Article 6(3) starts with the expression 'Pursuant to paragraph 1.'

35   As Nagoya Protocol Article 6(1) specifically states 'unless otherwise determined by that Party.' See Greiber et al., *Explanatory Guide*, op. cit., 96.

36   See this commentary on Article 30.

37   See this commentary on Articles 15–16. Similar concerns about enforceability arose in the context of the CBD: Glowka, Burhenne-Guilmin and Synge, *Guide to the Convention on Biological Diversity*, op. cit.

38   See also reference to foreign investors' due diligence in this regard in this commentary on Article 4, section 2.1.

39   Greiber et al., *Explanatory Guide*, op. cit., 96, citing "Access and Benefit-Sharing – ABS," Ornamental Aquatic Trade Association (2010), accessed 30 November 2013, <www.ornamental-fish-int.org/uploads/c2/c8/c2c896efd06e24d26710d8b90a40d478/ABS.pdf>.

Developing a comprehensive domestic ABS framework would protect first and foremost the rights of the provider country, as well as facilitate implementation of, and compliance with, other provisions of the Protocol.[40] To that end, Parties enjoy a wide margin of discretion in developing their regulatory approach to ABS under Article 6(3), and could in practice opt for a gradual approach to the setting up of their domestic ABS framework, first through interim policy and administrative measures,[41] and then legislative measures. This would allow Parties to comply with Article 6(3) in the context of time-consuming legislative processes and in dealing with unprecedented legal questions at the domestic level.[42] In these situations, users should ensure they consult with national authorities competent to implement the Nagoya Protocol in a given country, who could be mandated to advise on interim procedures and requirements for PIC and MAT.[43] Provider countries, in turn, would be well advised to promptly identify competent national authorities while the domestic ABS framework is being developed.[44] Overall, peer learning and developing guidance at the international level (to be agreed upon by the Protocol's governing body)[45] in this regard would certainly be welcome.

It should be further noted that a vast variety of situations could be possible, including Parties waiving their right to PIC and still regulating otherwise access to their genetic resources (for instance, by allowing free access to their genetic resources, but requiring users to establish MAT directly with private providers and provide information to relevant authorities for inclusion into a national register). In these cases, waiving PIC does not necessarily mean renouncing to benefit-sharing.[46]

---

40   In particular due to the linkages between Nagoya Protocol Article 6(3) and the compliance-related provisions under Articles 15–18.

41   On whether policy and administrative measures would qualify as 'domestic ABS legislation or regulatory requirements', for the purposes of triggering the compliance provisions of the Protocol (Articles 15–16), see this commentary on Article 15, section 3.1.

42   See discussion on law-making capacity issues raised by the Nagoya Protocol in this commentary on Article 22.

43   Nagoya Protocol Article 13(2): see this commentary on Article 13, section 3.

44   We are grateful to Geoff Burton for drawing our attention to this point.

45   Article 26(4)(a): see this commentary on Article 26, section 2.

46   See this commentary on Article 5, section 2.

3.2   *The Concept of State PIC*

PIC is a well-known tool in international law, used in and adapted to different contexts.[47] It has been used widely in international instruments in the fields of chemicals and hazardous waste.[48] In that context, it was based on the principle that prior to an activity involving risks, those affected and authorized to make a decision should be informed in detail about the potential risks, and was used to protect importing countries from environmental and health hazards. The concept has been used differently in the CBD context, as a tool to protect countries' sovereignty over natural, including genetic, resources.

Like the CBD, the Protocol's provisions on access are based on the concept of PIC, as an expression of the principle of national sovereignty over natural resources. In this case, therefore, PIC is meant to protect the Party *providing* genetic resources, rather than the one *acquiring* them.[49] This means that, to give its consent to a request for access to genetic resources, the provider country must be informed in advance and in detail about the envisioned research or bioprospecting activity from the applicant. On the basis of this information, the competent authority[50] of the provider country makes a decision regarding the access request,[51] and sets (or orders the negotiation of) the MAT that will apply to the transaction. According to the Protocol provisions, the country's national ABS framework must include a procedure by which the decision on PIC is documented at the time of access by the issuance of a permit or its equivalent.[52]

---

47   One example of its use in international environmental instruments is found in the FAO International Code of Conduct on the Distribution and Use of Pesticides: "International Code of Conduct on the Distribution and Use of Pesticides" in FAO Council Resolution 1/123 "Revised Version of the International Code of Conduct onthe Distribution and Use of Pesticides" (1 November 2002). See Greiber et al., *Explanatory Guide*, op. cit., 95.

48   Rotterdam PIC Convention; see generally Katharina Kummer Peiry, "Prior Informed Consent," in Wolfrum, *Max Planck Encyclopedia*, op. cit.

49   Note that in the context of the Biosafety Protocol, CBD Parties opted for using the Advance Informed Agreement, rather than PIC, as the central administrative procedure for regulating transboundary movements of living modified organisms. The Advance Informed Agreement procedure was loosely modelled along the PIC processes of the Rotterdam PIC Convention and Basel Convention on the Control of Transboundary Movements of Hazardous Wastes and their Disposal (Basel, 22 March 1989, in force 05 May 1992) 1673 UNTS 57, but allowing for a greater degree of flexibility. See Mackenzie et al., *Explanatory Guide to the Cartagena Protocol*, op. cit., 63.

50   See this commentary on Article 13, section 3.

51   Greiber et al., *Explanatory Guide*, op. cit., 95.

52   Nagoya Protocol Article 6(3)(e). On the internationally recognized certificate of compliance, see this commentary on Article 17, section 3.

Parties to the Nagoya Protocol have discretion to exercise their right to require PIC fully or partially, or fully exempt access from the PIC requirement. A Party may decide, for instance, to use as criteria for exemption from the PIC requirement the ownership (public or private), location (for example, within or outside protected areas), type (plant, animal, aquatic, forest, micro-organisms) of genetic resources or the intent of the research envisioned (non-commercial or commercial purpose, or aiming to address health emergencies, or agricultural research purposes).[53]

4   Access to Genetic Resources Held by Indigenous and Local Communities

State PIC, as enshrined in the CBD and the Protocol, should be differentiated from indigenous and local community PIC. Article 6(2) represents a notable development with respect to the Convention, as well as from an international human rights perspective.[54] It is the first international legally binding provision explicitly and specifically addressing the regulation of access to *genetic* resources 'held by' indigenous and local communities. The provision, however, is heavily qualified, both by reference to cases where communities have 'the established right' to grant access to such resources and by reference to 'in accordance with national legislation,' in parallel with Article 5(2).

Parties are required to take domestic measures to ensure that community PIC, or approval and involvement, is obtained. The Protocol does not, therefore, directly recognize rights for indigenous and local communities to grant access to genetic resources in their territories. Rather, it requires Parties to put legislation or other domestic measures in place on community PIC (or approval and involvement) in case communities' rights over genetic resources are already established or will be explicitly established in the future. The provision therefore embodies a 'community PIC requirement' that is separate from

---

53   See this commentary on Article 8.

54   Bavikatte and Robinson note: 'If we approach the law as a site of struggle, Article 6(2) of the Nagoya Protocol is a monumental achievement by communities. It is a testimony to six years of hard work and careful lobbying and has extended the scope of Article 8(j) in ways that were inconceivable in 1993. It had capitalised on the important victory ... that for indigenous peoples and local communities, there is an inseparable link between genetic resources and traditional knowledge.' See Kabir Bavikatte and Daniel F. Robinson, "Towards a People's History of the Law: Biocultural Jurisprudence and the Nagoya Protocol on Access and Benefit Sharing," *Law, Environment and Development* 7 (2011): 35, 47.

(and possibly additional to) State PIC for access to relevant genetic resources pursuant to Article 6(1). As discussed in relation to the corresponding Protocol provisions on benefit-sharing for indigenous and local communities,[55] these provisions may be considered an implicit recognition of an underlying substantive environmental right of these communities to their genetic resources. Article 6(2) specifies the UNDRIP standard on PIC concerning the use of indigenous peoples' natural resources in as far as it concerns genetic resources used for research and development.[56] The Nagoya Protocol also goes beyond existing international human rights standards by extending the community PIC requirement to local communities.

The following analysis of Article 6(2) and its implications will focus first on the *contours* of Parties' obligations with respect to genetic resources held by indigenous and local communities (that is, how Parties will comply with the Protocol's community PIC *requirement*); and then on the *concept* of 'community PIC' (or approval and involvement) concerning genetic resources.[57]

4.1   *Parties' Obligation*

With regard to the community PIC *requirement* established by the Protocol, the mandatory wording of Article 6(2) ('shall') leaves little doubt that Parties are under an obligation to enact domestic measures with the aim of ensuring PIC (or approval and involvement) for indigenous and local communities that hold genetic resources within their jurisdiction. This requirement therefore limits the discretion of those Parties considering not requiring PIC for access to genetic resources in accordance with Article 6(1). At the same time, the qualifications found in the text ('in accordance with domestic law' and 'as appropriate') leave a degree of discretion to Parties with regard to the types of measures to be taken for the implementation of the community PIC requirement. The term 'as appropriate', however, does not leave discretion with regard to whether to take any domestic measures at all on this matter, as long as indigenous or local communities are found in the territory[58] and have established

---

55   Nagoya Protocol Article 5(2). See this commentary on Article 5, section 3.

56   UNDRIP Article 32(2) reads: 'States shall consult and cooperate in good faith with the indigenous peoples concerned through their own representative institutions in order to obtain their free and informed consent prior to the approval of any project affecting their ... resources, particularly in connection with the development, utilization or exploitation of mineral, water or *other* resources' (emphasis added).

57   For a complementary discussion of community PIC in relation to traditional knowledge, see this commentary on Article 7, section 2.

58   On the identification of indigenous peoples and local communities, in the absence of an international definition, see Introduction to this commentary, section 4.

rights over genetic resources.[59] As for other provisions in the Protocol that relate to indigenous peoples and local communities, Article 6(2) is to be interpreted and implemented in the light of relevant international human rights standards,[60] and with due consideration of communities' customary laws, protocols and procedures.[61]

A difficulty, however, arises from the reference in Article 6(2) to 'the established right' for indigenous and local communities to grant access to genetic resources. Depending on its interpretation, this qualification could prove highly limiting for the involvement of indigenous and local communities in ABS transactions concerning genetic resources in their territories. The reference reflects language in Article 5 on benefit-sharing arising from the use of genetic resources held by communities, and the same considerations already discussed in that context apply here.[62] According to a narrow interpretation, the term 'established' may only refer to situations where a particular community can demonstrate that its right to genetic resources is already affirmed in the *domestic* legal order, possibly leaving it to the absolute discretion of the Party concerned to determine whether such community rights exist and therefore whether or not to develop domestic measures on community PIC on genetic resources.[63] This, however, appears overly restrictive and not in harmony with international human rights standards and the Protocol objective.[64] A broader interpretation of 'established rights' on the basis of relevant international human rights law and in light of community customary laws would instead imply an obligation for Parties to map customary rights at the domestic level, in consultation with the concerned communities,[65] provide for their legal recognition, and enact domestic measures to ensure community PIC in case communities' customary rights are ascertained. The inseparable nature of genetic resources and traditional knowledge for indigenous and local communities[66] further substantiates the need for a broader interpretation of Article 6(2): as

---

59   See Introduction to this commentary, section 5 and fn. 225.
60   See Introduction to this commentary, section 4.
61   Nagoya Protocol Article 12(1). See this commentary on Article 12, section 2.
62   See this commentary on Article 5, section 3.2.
63   This possible interpretation was identified with concern by Singh Nijar, *The Nagoya Protocol: Analysis and Implementation Options for Developing Countries*, op. cit., 25–26.
64   See this commentary on Article 1, section 3.
65   UNDRIP Articles 19 and 32(2); ILO Convention No. 169, Article 6(2). See also *Sarayaku v. Ecuador*, paragraph 165.
66   Nagoya Protocol 22nd preambular recital.

noted below,[67] the obligation for Parties to enact domestic measures to ensure community PIC to traditional knowledge associated with genetic resources is not conditioned on the existence of specific rights.

4.2   The Concept of Community PIC Concerning Genetic Resources

While State PIC is premised on the general principle of national sovereignty over natural resources, community PIC for access to genetic resources is based on international human rights law, namely indigenous peoples' rights to: manage their natural resources;[68] maintain and strengthen their distinctive spiritual relationship with their traditionally owned resources;[69] own, use, develop and control the resources that they possess by reason of traditional ownership or use;[70] be secure in the enjoyment of their own means of subsistence and development;[71] and obtain just and fair redress if deprived of their means of subsistence and development,[72] or dispossession of their resources.[73]

Community PIC is in fact a well-known tool in the human rights field, where it has been interpreted as integrating both 'positive' and 'defensive' protection sides.[74] As a positive tool, PIC is used to empower indigenous peoples by giving them the right to control and benefit from the use of their natural resources. As a defensive tool, for instance with regard to development projects affecting indigenous peoples' lands and resources, PIC focuses on the potential negative impacts of the proposed activity – this is a connotation that is more akin to the

---

67   See this commentary on Article 7, section 2.

68   UNDRIP Article 3. For the relevance of these and other sources on indigenous peoples' human rights with respect to local communities, see Introduction to this commentary, section 4.2.

69   UNDRIP Article 25.

70   UNDRIP Article 26(2). On the international judicial recognition of the right to 'dispose of their natural resources', see Fodella, "Indigenous Peoples," op. cit., 350–1 and fns. 5 and 15–16; Human Rights Committee, *Mahuika et al. v. New Zealand*, Communication no. 547/1993 Views (27 October 2000), UN Doc CCPR/C/70/D/547/1993, paragraph 9(2); Committee on the Elimination of Racial Discrimination (CERD), "General Recommendation No. 23," paragraph 5.

71   UNDRIP Article 20(1).

72   UNDRIP Article 20(2).

73   UNDRIP Article 8(2)(b).

74   CBD Working Group on Article 8(j), "How Tasks 7, 10 and 12 could best contribute," UNEP/CBD/WG8J/8/4/Rev.2, paragraph 43. On the international judicial recognition of the right to PIC, see sources analysed by Fodella, "Indigenous Peoples," op. cit., 350–352 and fns. 6, 13, 17 and 20.

use of PIC in multilateral chemicals conventions than in the CBD.[75] Given that CBD Parties have not yet elaborated consensus guidance on community PIC concerning their genetic resources, it appears useful to draw on international human rights standards on community PIC for access to natural resources or, *mutatis mutandis*, on community PIC to developments/extractive activities in their lands.

In the context of international human rights processes, community PIC has been interpreted as entailing that consent should be given freely, without coercion, intimidation or manipulation (hence, the emphatic use of 'free' before PIC in UNDRIP).[76] In addition, it should be sought sufficiently at all stages, from the inception to the final authorization and implementation of proposed activities ('prior'). It should be based on an understanding of the full range of issues and implications entailed by the activity or decision in question ('informed'), and given by the legitimate representatives of the indigenous peoples concerned.[77] With a view to providing indigenous peoples with 'full and objective information about all aspects of the project that will affect them, including the impact of the project on their lives and environment,' an environmental and socio-cultural impact study should be carried out and its outcome should be presented to indigenous communities concerned at an early stage of the consultations preceding the community's decision on PIC.[78]

---

75   See however "Akwé: Kon Guidelines for the Conduct of Cultural, Environmental and Social Impact Assessment regarding Developments Proposed to Take Place on, or which are Likely to Impact on, Sacred Sites and on Lands and Waters Traditionally Occupied or Used by Indigenous and Local Communities" in CBD Decision 7/16, "Article 8(j) and related provisions" (13 April 2004) UN Doc UNEP/CBD/COP/DEC/VII/16 (hereinafter, Akwé: Kon Guidelines). On the risks that knowledge exchanges may entail for indigenous peoples and local communities, see Terry Williams and Preston Hardison, "Culture, Law, Risk and Governance: Contexts of Traditional Knowledge in Climate Change Adaptation," *Climatic Change* (2013) 120: 531.

76   In strictly legal terms, 'consent' is always free as the notion inherently embodies the absence of any coercion. See Findlaw Legal Dictionary, accessed 30 November 2013, <http://dictionary.findlaw.com/definition/consent.html>: 'compliance in or approval of what is done or proposed by another; (...) the voluntary agreement or acquiescence by a person of age or with requisite mental capacity who is not under duress or coercion and usually who has knowledge or understanding. In fact, *coercion nullifies/invalidates any expression of consent.*' (emphasis added). Compare Greiber et al., *Explanatory Guide*, op. cit., 110–111.

77   UNPFII, "Report on the tenth session," E/2011/43-E/C.19/2011/14, paragraphs 34–38, particularly paragraph 34.

78   Human Rights Council, "Promotion and protection of all human rights, civil, political, economic, social and cultural rights, including the right to development. Report of the

Several challenges arise for States to ensure community PIC. International human rights bodies have confirmed that PIC 'does not necessarily require unanimity and may be achieved even when individuals or groups within the community explicitly disagree.'[79] Nonetheless, States are still responsible to ensure the genuine involvement of legitimate representatives of indigenous peoples and the true nature of 'consent' in the context of indigenous customary institutions, including applicable customary decision-making processes and taking into account that consent may be withdrawn at a later stage.[80] States are also expected to ensure that women and other potentially disenfranchised groups are included in the community PIC process.[81]

Overall, what emerges hitherto from relevant human rights processes is that PIC entails good-faith and culturally-appropriate consultation procedures, according to the communities' customs and traditions, where every effort is made to build consensus on the part of all concerned in reaching an agreement that is seen as legitimate by the community[82] and leads to benefit-sharing arrangements that must accord with indigenous peoples' own understanding of benefits.[83] Thus, assimilating PIC to a veto power for communities, referring to the possibility to reject a proposal without providing adequate justification, is an oversimplification.[84] Ultimately, the right to PIC is seen as a

Special Rapporteur on the situation of human rights and fundamental freedoms of indigenous people, James Anaya" (15 July 2009) UN Doc A/HRC/12/34, paragraph 53. See also: *Saramaka People v. Suriname* 2007, parapgraph 134; African Commission on Human and Peoples' Rights, *Social and Economic Rights Action Centre and Centre for Economic and Social v. Nigeria*, Communication no. 155/96 (27 October 2001), paragraph 53; and Fodella, "Indigenous Peoples," op. cit., 356 and 360.

79   UN General Assembly, "Human rights and transnational corporations and other business enterprises," paragraph 11.

80   Ibid.

81   Ibid. See also Nagoya Protocol 11th preambular recital and Article 12(3)(b), and brief discussion on the challenges in tackling discrimination based on gender in the Introduction to this commentary, section 4.3.

82   Human Rights Council, "Promotion and protection of all human rights," A/HRC/12/34, paragraphs 46–48.

83   Human Rights Council, "Follow-up report on indigenous peoples and the right to participate in decision-making, with a focus on extractive industries" (16 August 2012) UN Doc A/HRC/21/55, paragraph 43; also UN General Assembly, "Report of the Special Rapporteur on the rights of indigenous peoples" (13 August 2012) UN Doc A/67/301, paragraph 78.

84   Human Rights Council, "Promotion and protection of all human rights," A/HRC/12/34, paragraphs 46–48; and Human Rights Council, "Report of the Special Rapporteur on indigenous peoples' rights," A/HRC/24/41, paragraph 30, which reads '... But it must be

procedural safeguard for the exercise of indigenous peoples' substantive right to self-determination, including their rights to property, culture, religion and non-discrimination, as well as the right to set and pursue their own priorities for development.[85] Despite conceptual progress at the international level, however,[86] questions remain concerning the implementation of the right to community PIC.[87] In addition, the community PIC requirement may be particularly challenging to implement when two or more indigenous peoples or local communities share genetic resources.[88]

---

emphasized that the consent is not a free-standing device of legitimation. The principle of free, prior and informed consent, arising as it does within a human rights framework, does not contemplate consent as simply a yes to a predetermined decision, or as a means to validate a deal that disadvantages affected indigenous peoples. When consent is given, not just freely and on an informed basis, but also on just terms that are protective of indigenous peoples rights, it will fulfil its human rights safeguard role'.

85   Human Rights Council, "Report of the Special Rapporteur on the rights of indigenous peoples, James Anaya" (6 July 2012) UN Doc A/HRC/21/47, paragraph 50; and Human Rights Council, "Report of the Special Rapporteur on indigenous peoples' rights," A/HRC/24/41, paragraph 28.

86   E.g., UNPFII, "Report of the international workshop on methodologies regarding free, prior and informed consent and indigenous peoples" (17 February 2005) UN Doc E/C.19/2005/3; "Report of the international technical workshop on indigenous traditional knowledge" (15 December 2005) UN Doc E/C.19/2006/2); "Report on the fifth session" (13 June 2006) UN Doc. E/2006/43–E/C.19/2006/11; and "An overview of the principle of free, prior and informed consent and indigenous peoples in international and domestic law and practices. Contribution by Parshuram Tamang Paper prepared for the UNPFII workshop on free, prior and informed consent" (17–19 January 2005) UN Doc PFII/2004/ws.2/8.

87   The Permanent Forum has therefore indicated that it will explore the opportunity to develop guidelines on the implementation of free PIC, in collaboration with the UN Expert Mechanism on the Rights of Indigenous Peoples and the Special Rapporteur on the Rights of Indigenous Peoples: UNPFII, "Report on the tenth session," E/2011/43–E/C.19/2011/14, paragraph 37.

88   We are grateful to Geoff Burton for drawing our attention to this point. The Nagoya Protocol only addresses situations in which traditional knowledge is shared by different indigenous and local communities located in different States (Article 11(2); see this commentary on Article 11, section 4), although it can be argued that the provision on inter-State cooperation in relation to genetic resources found in situ within the territory of more than one Party can also include instances in which different indingeous and local communities in different Parties share genetic resources (Article 11(1);); see this commentary on Article 11, section 3).

4.2.1   Approval and Involvement

The reference to 'or approval and involvement' in Article 6(2) reiterates the wording of CBD Article 8(j) and reflects the reluctance by some CBD Parties to fully endorse in the Protocol the right to community PIC as developed in international human rights law and enshrined in UNDRIP. The expression 'approval and involvement' was introduced in the Protocol in order to allow for a greater degree of flexibility in implementation at the national level,[89] in the light of different domestic legal arrangements concerning the relations between governments and indigenous and local communities within their territories.[90] This reluctance is also illustrated by the timid preambular reference to UNDRIP,[91] and by references to 'PIC and approval and involvement' in previous CBD COP decisions.[92] The matter continues to remain very contentious in relevant discussions under the CBD at the time of writing,[93] although

---

89   Caution about using PIC in the Nagoya Protocol text was explained by the possible implication of 'creating/expanding "sovereign rights" for communities to control genetic resources that would run against constitutional provisions or domestic practices in certain countries': Burton, "Implementation of the Nagoya Protocol in JUSCANZ Countries," op. cit., 318–328, particularly 318–319. See also CBD Working Group on ABS, "Concerns relating to CBD process, revised draft Protocol and indigenous peoples' human rights" (22 September 2010) UN Doc UNEP/CBD/WG-ABS/9/INF/21. For an academic argument on 'parallel' sovereignty of States and indigenous peoples, see generally Lenzerini, "Sovereignty Revisited," op. cit.

90   "Joint submission Grand Council of the Crees (Eeyou Istchee)," 133–136, and comments by Savaresi, "International Human Rights Law Implications," op. cit., 70. The Special Rapporteur on the Rights of Indigenous Peoples reported on concerns raised in the submission above, in UN General Assembly, "Report of the Special Rapporteur on indigenous peoples' rights," A/67/301, paragraphs 58–59. Buck and Hamilton, "Nagoya Protocol," op. cit., 55.

91   Nagoya Protocol 26th preambular recital simply 'notes' UNDRIP.

92   E.g., Bonn Guidelines, paragraph 31; and CBD Decision 5/16, paragraph 5: 'access to traditional knowledge, innovations and practices of indigenous and local communities should be subject to prior informed consent or prior informed approval from the holders of such knowledge...' Note, however, the 2004 Akwé: Kon Voluntary Guidelines refer consistently only to 'prior informed consent' (Akwé: Kon Guidelines, paragraphs 29, 52–53 and 60).

93   For an indication of continued divergence of views on utilising UNDRIP language in the context of the CBD, see ENB, "Summary of the Seventh Meeting of the Working Group on Article 8(j) of the Convention on Biological Diversity: 31 October–4 November 2011," Vol. 9 No. 557, 7 November 2011, 5–6; and ENB, "Summary of the Eighth Meeting of the Working Group on Article 8(j) and 17th Meeting of the Subsidiary Body on Scientific, Technical and Technological Advice of the Convention on Biological Diversity: 7–18 October 2013," Vol. 9 No. 611, 21 October 2013, 4, 6–7 and 20.

commentators have suggested that CBD Parties can consider the two expressions as having essentially the same meaning in practice.[94]

Given that the right to PIC is considered to imply the right for indigenous and local communities to allow or refuse[95] access to their genetic resources, the crucial issue with regard to the alternative term 'approval and involvement' is whether it provides equal guarantees in the context of communities' own decision-making processes or communities' participation in government decision-making processes.[96] In the latter case, it may well be that community PIC is embodied in the same decision embodying State PIC. This may raise particular difficulties in situations where ownership over genetic resources is not clarified in domestic ABS frameworks or where the government also asserts its own sovereignty over genetic resources held by communities and consultations with communities in this regard are inconclusive.

In this connection, the UN Special Rapporteur on Indigenous Peoples' Rights has recommended interpreting and implementing relevant international environmental treaties in a way that is consistent with UNDRIP, whether or not the specific text of these instruments matches exactly the terms of the Declaration.[97] So, 'approval and involvement' should still provide

---

94   Singh Nijar, *The Nagoya Protocol on ABS: An Analysis*, op. cit., 26; Buck and Hamilton, "Nagoya Protocol," op. cit., 55; and Greiber et al., *Explanatory Guide*, op. cit., 110–111. Note that any community PIC process should be as far as possible determined and controlled by the particular indigenous community: Human Rights Council, "Promotion and protection of all human rights," A/HRC/12/34; Human Rights Council, "Report of the Special Rapporteur on indigenous peoples' rights," A/HRC/24/41 paragraphs 26–36; CERD, "General Recommendation No. 23;" and Human Rights Committee, *Ángela Poma Poma v. Peru*, Communication No. 1457/2006, (27 March 2009) UN Doc CCPR/C/95/D/1457/2006.

95   A definition recently discussed (but not intergovernmentally approved) in the CBD framework considers PIC as the procedure through which indigenous or local communities properly supplied with all the required information, *decide to allow or refuse* access to their traditional knowledge under mutually agreed conditions of equality, respect and fair compensation. See "Set of relevant definitions/glossary of terms for Article 8(j) and related provisions," in CBD Article 8(j) Working Group, "Development of elements of sui generis systems for the protection of traditional knowledge, innovations and practices. Note by the Executive Secretary" (24 November 2005) UN Doc UNEP/CBD/WG8J/4/7, Annex II, which refers to UNPFII, "Report of the international workshop on methodologies regarding free, prior and informed consent and indigenous peoples," E/C.19/2005/3, emphasis added.

96   E.g., the Sami People have set up Sami parliaments that constitute an integral part of the governmental structure in Sweden, Finland and Norway ("Politics," Sami People, accessed 6 February 2014, <www.eng.samer.se/servlet/GetDoc?meta_id=1009>).

97   UN General Assembly, "Report of the Special Rapporteur on indigenous peoples' rights," A/67/301, paragraphs 92 and 61, where the Special Rapporteur specifically expresses the

a genuine and effective guarantee to uphold indigenous peoples' right to self-determination and to protect their rights over genetic resources found in their territories, by empowering them to 'effectively determine the outcome of decision-making... not merely a right to be *involved* in such processes.'[98] Thus, when States claim ownership on, or otherwise assert the power to expropriate community property interests in, genetic resources in order to have or permit access to these resources, this amounts to a limitation of community rights, including their right to property and culture, even if those rights are not held under a title deed or other form of official recognition, and even if just compensation is provided. Such expropriation can only be considered valid from an international human rights perspective if it is pursuant to a valid public purpose, which cannot be a mere commercial interest, revenue-raising objective, or the conduct of activities that are primarily for private gain.[99] In addition, the limitation must comply with standards of strict necessity and proportionality, be determined by law and be non-discriminatory.[100]

Furthermore, even if it is an alternative standard to PIC, 'approval and involvement' should be interpreted and applied also in light of more general international human rights standards such as the right to access information, participation and transparency in decision-making and access to adequate remedies.[101] Ultimately, Parties to the Protocol will need to strike an equitable balance between the need to establish some formal processes to effectively engage indigenous and local communities in good faith when access to genetic resources in their territories is requested and the need to genuinely respect their rights as enshrined in international human rights law.[102]

'hopeful expectation' that the provisions of the Nagoya Protocol will be implemented 'in harmony with' UNDRIP.

98   Expert Mechanism on the Rights of Indigenous Peoples, "Advice No. 2, Indigenous peoples and the right to participate in decision-making," (2011), accessed 30 October 2012, <www.ohchr.org/Documents/Issues/IPeoples/EMRIP/Advice2_Oct2011.pdf>, paragraph 1, emphasis added.

99   Human Rights Council, "Report of the Special Rapporteur on indigenous peoples' rights," A/HRC/24/41, paragraph 35.

100   Ibid.; and UNDRIP Article 46(2).

101   Savaresi, "International Human Rights Law Implications," op. cit., 70. Compare with ICCPR Article 2(3), although the latter refers only to access to remedies.

102   See Human Rights Council, "Report of the Special Rapporteur on indigenous peoples' rights," A/HRC/24/41, paragraph 25. We are grateful to Annalisa Savaresi for a useful exchange of ideas on this matter.

4.2.2 Community PIC and Private-sector Users

International human rights processes have started to provide guidance on the role of States in legislating for, and supporting community PIC vis-à-vis private developers, and have also elaborated on private operators' own responsibility to respect community PIC.[103] These international developments, that are based on the recognition that community PIC and the substantive human rights tied to PIC requirements are often directly affected by business,[104] may have significant resonance in the context of community PIC and ABS transactions involving private parties.

In that connection, the duty of States to protect indigenous peoples' rights applies also when granting permits to private parties relating to indigenous peoples' resources,[105] and includes the obligation to provide business with clarity on the right of indigenous peoples in that regard, including when indigenous peoples do not have a State-recognized title to the lands and resources affected by extractive activities.[106] States are also called upon to establish mechanisms and procedures to verify that community PIC has been sought by private-sector operators, and to include indigenous peoples in the development of such mechanisms. Should these mechanism lead to the determination that community PIC has not been respected, the State may revoke any authorization given.[107] These indications can certainly apply to provider countries under the Protocol.

With regard to user countries, even if no indigenous peoples reside within their borders, other indications from human rights bodies appear relevant, particularly for home States of transnational corporations operating in territories

---

103   Elisa Morgera, "From Corporate Social Responsibility to Accountability Mechanisms," in *Harnessing Foreign Investment to Promote Environmental Protection Incentives and Safeguards*, ed. Pierre-Marie Dupuy and Jorge E. Viñuales (Cambridge: Cambridge University Press, 2013), 321.

104   UN General Assembly, "Human rights and transnational corporations," A/68/279, paragraph 10.

105   ILO Convention No. 169 Article 15(1); Inter-American Commission on Human Rights, *Maya Indigenous Community of the Toledo District v. Belize*, Merits, Judgment, Case no. 12.053 (12 October 2004), 194–195 (hereinafter, *Maya Indigenous Community v. Belize*); and, more generally, Inter-American Commission on Human Rights, "Indigenous and Tribal Peoples' Rights over Their Ancestral Lands and Natural Resources. Norms and Jurisprudence of the Inter-American Human Rights System," *American Indian Law Review* 35 (2010): 386.

106   Human Rights Council, "Follow-up report," A/HRC/21/47, paragraphs 32–35; and Human Rights Council, "Report of the Special Rapporteur on indigenous peoples' rights," A/HRC/24/41, paragraphs 26–40.

107   UN General Assembly, "Human rights and transnational corporations," A/68/279, paragraph 11.

used or inhabited by indigenous peoples.[108] In particular, user countries are to consider ways to ensure that indigenous peoples affected by the operations of their biotech multinationals abroad have access to effective remedy,[109] taking into account the specificities of indigenous peoples and ensuring that any barriers to their access to the mechanisms are addressed and removed.[110]

With regards to business enterprises' own responsibility to respect human rights,[111] companies' due diligence is increasingly expected to factor in risks related to the respect for indigenous peoples' rights, in particular respect for their collective rights to lands and resources in accordance with their own customary laws, traditions and practices.[112] Companies' policies are expected to include a commitment to seek to ensure respect for community PIC, based on international human rights law, including UNDRIP and ILO Convention 169.[113] This should be operationalized through the conduct of human rights impact assessment,[114] leverage in business relationships to prevent and address adverse impacts, and the exercise of regular and direct consultations with indigenous peoples when their human rights may be affected, taking into account language and other potential barriers to effective engagement. In addition, companies are expected to establish mediation-based and culturally appropriate operational-level grievance mechanisms that take into account traditional indigenous mechanisms.[115] Specific reference, in that context, is made to business' responsibility to respect PIC in relation to benefit-sharing arrangements that must accord with indigenous peoples' own understanding

---

108   Ibid., paragraph 55(a).

109   Ibid., paragraph 55(j). See also this commentary on Article 18.

110   Ibid., paragraph 37.

111   Human Rights Council, "Report of the Special Representative of the Secretary-General on the issue of Human Rights and Transnational Corporations and Other Business Enterprises: Protect, Respect and Remedy: A Framework for Business and Human Rights" (7 April 2008) UN Doc A/HRC/8/5; and "Guiding Principles on Business and Human Rights to implement the UN Protect, Respect and Remedy Framework" (21 March 2011) UN Doc A/HRC/17/31, paragraph 11.

112   UN General Assembly, "Human rights and transnational corporations," A/68/279, paragraph 24.

113   Ibid., paragraph 56.

114   Note that the relevance of the CBD Akwé: Kon Guidelines in this respect has already been highlighted by human rights bodies: see discussion in Morgera, "From Corporate Social Responsibility to Accountability Mechanisms," op. cit., 335–336 and 348–349.

115   UN General Assembly, "Human rights and transnational corporations," A/68/279, paragraph 56; Human Rights Council, "Follow-up report," A/HRC/21/47, paragraph 28(d); and Human Rights Council, "Report of the Special Rapporteur on indigenous peoples' rights," A/HRC/24/41, paragraph 78.

of benefits.[116] These indications are clearly relevant to private-sector users under the Protocol.

Consequently, in the absence of an adequate State-led process to ensure community PIC, private-sector users may need to consider carefully whether they can proceed with access to genetic resources without the risk of causing or contributing to adverse impacts on the rights of indigenous peoples.[117] This in effect provides an incentive for provider and user countries to establish appropriate measures on community PIC, with a view to attracting responsible users.

5   Access Standards

When a Party develops domestic measures on access to its genetic resources, it has discretion in choosing legislative, administrative or policy measures 'as appropriate.' Each Party will therefore have to determine what types (or what mix) of measures are necessary to regulate access to its genetic resources domestically. The choice will reflect the constitutional, legal and administrative context of a Party, and will also likely be based on an assessment of the capacities and resources to implement and enforce the proposed ABS framework (in the case of developing countries, the Protocol provisions on capacity and financial support are therefore relevant).[118]

In developing domestic access measures, Parties must respect a series of 'standards'[119] and include a series of minimum requirements that are detailed in Article 6(3)(a–g). The list of standards and requirements is cumulative. Parties therefore do not have discretion to implement only one or other standard/requirement from the list – with the exception of the criteria and

---

116   Human Rights Council, "Follow-up report," A/HRC/21/47, paragraph 43; and Human Rights Council, "Report of the Special Rapporteur on indigenous peoples' rights," A/HRC/21/47. On benefit-sharing and business' responsibility to respect human rights, see Elisa Morgera, "Environmental Accountability of Multinational Corporations: Benefit-Sharing as a Bridge between Human Rights and the Environment," in *The Environmental Dimension of Human Rights*, ed. Ben Boer (Oxford: Oxford University Press, forthcoming, 2014).

117   UN General Assembly, "Human rights and transnational corporations," paragraph 21.

118   See this commentary on Articles 22 and 25.

119   The Protocol negotiators referred to Article 6(3)(a–g) as 'international access standards' and this were among the most contentious issues in the negotiation of the Nagoya Protocol: Buck and Hamilton, "Nagoya Protocol," op. cit., 51. As the commentary will discuss below, however, only Article 6(a–b) can be technically considered legal 'standards.'

processes to obtain community PIC, because it is the only requirement qualified by 'where applicable.'[120] Parties may, however, go beyond the standards
and requirements set out in Article 6(3), which can be considered a minimum
necessary to support user countries in understanding the applicable rules of
the provider country, and therefore be put in an easier position when implementing their compliance-related obligations under the Protocol.[121]

Some commentators have criticized the standards contained in Article 6(3)
because they are framed in too general terms and do not appear amenable to
an objective assessment of whether domestic measures satisfy them or not.[122]
In general international law, legal provisions of a more general normative content than rules[123] can be considered 'legal standards'.[124] They imply the idea
of a 'level or model to which to conform and with reference to which one can
evaluate or critically appraise certain behavior.'[125] In other words, they provide a legal benchmark allowing an appreciation of whether a certain conduct[126] can be considered 'reasonable' or 'just'[127] in specific circumstances.[128]

---

120   Nagoya Protocol Article 6(3)(f).

121   See this commentary on Articles 15–18.

122   Gurdial Singh, *The Nagoya Protocol: An Analysis*, op. cit., 16. The concern may be
      understood in the light of a proposal to allow user countries to decide whether and to
      what extent users' non-compliance in their jurisdictions was partly due to deficiencies in
      the domestic ABS framework of a provider country. The EU maintained until September
      2010 bracketed text to this effect in draft article 12(2) in Montreal I Draft: 'Parties may
      refrain from taking such measures if the domestic access and benefit-sharing framework
      of another Party providing the misappropriated genetic resources at the time of
      misappropriation was not in conformity with Article 5(2).'

123   According to Hart, rules require human beings to do or abstain from certain actions,
      whether they wish to or not: Herbert L. A. Hart, *The Concept of Law* (Oxford: Oxford
      University Press, 1994), 81.

124   Jean Salmon, ed., *Dictionnaire de Droit International Public* (Bruxelles: Bruylant, 2001),
      1049; Abd Al-Razzâq Al-Sanhoury and Édouard Lambert, *Les Restrictions Contractuelles
      à la Liberté Individuelle de Travail dans la Jurisprudence Anglaise. Contribution à l'étude
      Comparative de la Règle de Droit et du Standard Juridique* (Paris: Marcel Giard, 1925).

125   These elements are suggested by Hart, *The Concept of Law*, op. cit., 32.

126   Jules Basdevant, ed., *Dictionnaire de la Terminologie du Droit International* (Paris: Sirey,
      1960), 581. Pound, along the same lines, defines standards as 'measures of conduct
      prescribed by law from which one departs at his peril of answering for resulting damage':
      Roscoe Pound, Social Contract through Law (New Haven: Yale University Press, 1942)
      44–49.

127   Ibid., 47–49.

128   Richard Dworkin, 'Is Law a System of Rules?' in *The Philosophy of Law*, ed. Richard
      Dworkin, (Oxford: Oxford University Press, 1977), 38, 43.

Legal standards therefore involve an idea of striking a reasonable balance between legal requirements and legitimate expectations based on experience or on moral sentiment.[129] It follows that legal standards are used when it would be 'unreasonable to attempt to formulate a definition of reasonable'[130] *ex ante*.

Against this background, the recourse to legal standards in Article 6(3)(a–b) seems suitable to give direction to domestic implementation efforts while allowing for case-by-case determinations of the appropriate, context-specific measure on access that appear apt to reach the objective of the Protocol of realizing fair and equitable benefit-sharing,[131] taking into account national legal and administrative traditions and constraints, as well as capacity needs particularly in the time period immediately following the entry into force of the Protocol. As the other provisions in Article 6(3)(c–g) clearly point to a specific conduct, rather than a legal standard, they will be discussed separately below, as minimum requirements.

The access standards and minimum requirements in Article 6(3) may contribute to a certain common approach to the development of domestic access rules that could facilitate the creation of an international functional ABS legal system (as applicants will better understand what is expected of them and enforcement in user countries may be easier). But it has been observed that the Protocol does not provide similar minimum standards and requirements also for benefit-sharing obligations.[132] Proposals to this effect were considered during the negotiations. As opposed to establishing international standards in the Protocol, however, the proposal was to insert an obligation for Parties to establish domestically minimum conditions and standards for sharing results of research, and benefits arising from every commercial and other forms of utilization of genetic resources, derivatives and traditional knowledge, upon MAT, building on the list of monetary and non-monetary benefits that is now included the Protocol Annex.[133] It can thus be argued that the Nagoya

---

129   Pound, *Social Control through Law*, op. cit., 80; Hart, *The Concept of Law*, op. cit., 132; and André-Jean Arnaud, ed., *Dictionnaire Encyclopédique de Théorie et de Sociologie du Droit* (Paris: Librairie Générale de Droit et de Jurisprudence, 1988), 581. For a more detailed discussion on standards, on which this section draws upon, see Elisa Morgera, *Corporate Accountability in International Environmental Law* (Oxford: Oxford University Press, 2009), 66–70.

130   Pound, *Social Control through Law*, op. cit., 48.

131   See this commentary on Article 1.

132   Under Nagoya Protocol Article 5. See Tvedt, "Beyond Nagoya," op. cit., 166.

133   Proposal by India in CBD Working Group on ABS, "Collation of operative text submitted," UNEP/CBD/WG-ABS/7/4, 13.

Protocol rather encourages indirectly the achievement of substantive fairness of benefit-sharing conditions set out in MAT, through lessons learnt by various stakeholders that participate in the elaboration of model contractual clauses and voluntary instruments,[134] and through training and capacity-building of relevant stakeholders.[135]

5.1   *Legal Certainty, Clarity and Transparency*

The first legal standard for domestic access measures is legal certainty,[136] clarity and transparency. These concepts reflect very concrete concerns that had emerged in the development and implementation of national ABS frameworks preceding the conclusion of the negotiations of the Nagoya Protocol. These concerns include difficulties encountered by users in trying to obtain PIC to access genetic resources and ensuring that such access was indeed lawful under the provider countries' legal system.[137] Legal certainty, clarity and transparency generally aim to promote the rule of law[138] and good governance[139] in the ABS context.

Based on a literal interpretation, legal certainty may refer to the role of law in providing those subject to it with an unambiguous basis on which to determine whether their actions are legal and thereby protecting them from arbitrary use of State power.[140] Clarity may refer to sufficiently precise content and internal coherence that allow foreseeing, to a reasonable degree, the consequences of a given action.[141] Transparency may refer to the provision of relevant information in a manner that is accessible and easily understandable to those affected, including information on how national authorities'

---

134   See this commentary on Articles 19–20.

135   See this commentary on Articles 21 and 12, section 4.

136   Nagoya Protocol Article 6(3)(a). See also Nagoya Protocol 9th preambular recital.

137   Tomme Young, "Summary Analysis: Legal Certainty for Users of Genetic Resources under Existing Access and Benefit-Sharing (ABS) Legislation and Policy," in Young, *Covering ABS*, op. cit., 77. See also Glowka and Normand, "The Nagoya Protocol on Access and Benefit-sharing," op. cit., 29; and Cabrera Medaglia, "The Implementation of the Nagoya Protocol," op. cit., 357.

138   Simon Chesterman, "Rule of Law," in Wolfrum, *Max Planck Encyclopedia* op. cit., specifically section C "Promotion of the Rule of Law Through International Forums."

139   Edith Brown Weiss and Ahila Sornarajah, "Good Governance," in Wolfrum, *Max Planck Encyclopedia*, op. cit.

140   Greiber et al., *Explanatory Guide*, op. cit., 102.

141   Ibid., 103.

decision-making on access, and implementation and enforcement of ABS decisions, comply with applicable rules and procedures.[142]

At the same time, however, these concepts have been elaborated in the context of other areas of international law, such as foreign investment and human rights. As to the latter, international case law has elaborated on the meaning of transparency in the context of procedural rights, such as the right of access to information and public participation in decision-making.[143] As to the former, international investment case law has elaborated on notions of certainty, consistency and transparency with a view to protecting the reasonable expectations of investors vis-à-vis the application of domestic laws or their reform in as far as these may affect the stability and predictability of the legal and business framework in which investors operate.[144] It remains to be seen whether and to what extent courts (or the Protocol's compliance mechanism)[145] will take these indications into account if requested to assess compliance by Parties with this access standard. Other applicable international treaties, such as regional human rights treaties (note, in particular the relevance of the Aarhus Convention) or bilateral agreements,[146] may also provide indications as to how this standard may be interpreted and expected to apply in specific countries.

---

142   Brown Weiss and Sornarajah, "Good Governance," op. cit. See also Greiber et al.,
       Explanatory Guide, op. cit., 103.

143   Savaresi, "International Human Rights Law Implications," op. cit., 70–71.

144   Christoph Schreuer, "Investments, International Protection," in Wolfrum, *Max Planck
       Encyclopedia*, op. cit., 4; and Matthias Herdegen, "International Economic Law," in
       Wolfrum, *Max Planck Encyclopedia*, op. cit., 37. See also Thomas W. Wälde and Abba
       Kolo, "Coverage of Taxation under Modern Investment Treaties," in *The Oxford Handbook
       of International Investment Law*, ed. Peter Muchlinski, Federico Ortino and Christoph
       Schreuer (Oxford: Oxford University Press, 2008), 305, 356. See also Akira Kotera,
       "Regulatory Transparency," in Muchlinski, Ortino, and Schreuer, *Oxford Handbook
       of International Investment Law*, op. cit., 617; Todd J. Grierson-Weiler and Ian I. Laird,
       "Standards of Treatment," in Muchlinski, Ortino and Schreuer, *Oxford Handbook of
       International Investment Law*, op. cit., 259; Wenhua Shan, "Towards a Balanced Liberal
       Investment Regime: General Report on the Protection of Foreign Investment," *ICSID
       Review* 25 (2010): 421; and Michele Potestà, "Legitimate Expectations in Investment
       Treaty Law: Understanding the Roots and the Limits of a Controversial Concept," *ICSID
       Review* 28 (2013): 88.

145   See this commentary on Article 30.

146   See this commentary on Article 4, section 3.

5.2   *Fair and Non-arbitrary Access Rules and Procedures*

The second standard for domestic access measures concerns fair and non-arbitrary rules and procedures. This expression appears to cover both substantive and procedural measures, and aims at providing guarantees against an unjustified or unreasonable exercise of discretion in the decision-making process[147] (that is, access decisions that are based on prejudice or personal preference).[148] It may also extend to guarantees against excessive delays,[149] or against corruption[150] in domestic decision-making on access.

This provision was intensely negotiated, as an alternative to a reference to 'non-discriminatory'[151] access measures, amidst developing countries' concerns that either expression would 'import' into the Protocol notions such as national treatment from international economic law.[152] Negotiators debated whether provider countries could differentiate among foreign users depending on the domestic ABS framework of the users' country (that is, as an incentive for user countries to develop and implement appropriate domestic ABS systems that can effectively ensure compliance with the provider country's domestic ABS framework) or depending on whether the user country has ratified the CBD or the Nagoya Protocol.[153] As the proposed reference to 'non-discriminatory' was dropped from the Protocol's text, it can be assumed that such distinctions are acceptable as long as they support the effective functioning of the Protocol. This is the case of domestic ABS measures requiring

---

147   Krista Nadakavukaren Schefer, *International Investment Law: Text, Cases and Materials* (Cheltenham: Edward Elgar, 2013), 275.

148   Schreuer, "Investments, International Protection," op. cit., 60–62, who provides a concise review of relevant international case law.

149   Viñuales, *Foreign Investment and the Environment*, op. cit., 356. See also Nagoya Protocol Article 6(3)(d) and section 4 below.

150   We are grateful to Geoff Burton for drawing our attention to this point. See generally Kenneth W. Abbott, "Corruption, Fight against," in Wolfrum, *Max Planck Encyclopedia*, op. cit.

151   See draft article 5(2)(a bis) in Nagoya Draft, which reads: "[[Provide for equal treatment in applications for access to genetic resources between similar domestic and foreign applicants and between similar foreign applicants of different Parties][Parties shall avoid application of discriminatory rules in processing access permits except where such rules aim at advancing local, non-commercial biodiversity and ecosystem research and education][Provide for fair and non-arbitrary rules and procedures on accessing genetic resources];]" (brackets in the original). On environmental measures and non-discriminatory standards, Viñuales, *Foreign Investment and the Environment*, op. cit., Ch. 13.

152   Singh Nijar "An Asian Developing Country's View," op. cit., 251–252.

153   Pavoni, "Nagoya Protocol and WTO Law," op. cit., 193.

foreign users to be affiliated or represented by a local person or entity,[154] with a view to encouraging capacity-building and non-monetary benefit-sharing;[155] or accord preference to local users engaged in non-commercial biodiversity research.[156] It may also be the case of users based in countries that have concluded a bilateral treaty with the provider country.[157]

Similarly to Article 6(3)(a), the access standard concerning fair and non-arbitrary rules and procedures in Article 6(3)(b) resonates with concepts that have been elaborated in the context of international investment law, but also international human rights law.[158] In international investment law, for instance, 'fair treatment' can be seen as a combination of the protection of legitimate expectations, good faith, transparency and consistency.[159] 'Non-arbitrary' may point to the avoidance of unreasonable treatment that affects certain investors.[160] In that context, it has also been emphasized that the concepts of 'non-arbitrariness' differs in international and national law: consequently, a national court's determination of arbitrariness based on national administrative law may be a useful indication, but not conclusive proof, of arbitrariness as it is understood at the international level.[161] In other words, a broader notion of arbitrariness may be drawn on the basis of international investment law.[162]

---

154 Some examples of the latter can be found in Latin America: see Cabrera Medaglia, "The Implementation of the Nagoya Protocol," op. cit., 357–8. For potential WTO law incompatibility issues, see Pavoni, "Nagoya Protocol and WTO Law," op. cit., 195.

155 See this commentary on Articles 22 and 5.

156 Greiber et al., *Explanatory Guide*, op. cit., 104. While a country may certainly differentiate among its own nationals and foreign users, the first instance will not need to be governed by the Nagoya Protocol rules, as it is a purely national situation.

157 See this commentary on Article 4, section 3.

158 Lorand Bartels, "Trade and Human Rights," in Wolfrum, *Max Planck Encyclopedia*, op. cit., 5.

159 E.g. International Centre for Settlement of Investment Disputes, *Biwater Gauff (Tanzania) Ltd v Tanzania*, Case no ARB/05/22, Award (24 July 2008), paragraph 591, as commented upon by James Harrison, "United Kingdom Report on the Protection of Foreign Investment" (presented at the International Congress of Comparative Law, Washington DC, 2010). See generally, Viñuales, *Foreign Investment and the Environment*, op. cit., Ch 14.

160 Schreuer, "Investments, International Protection," op. cit., 57–66. We are thankful to James Harrison for a useful preliminary exchange of ideas on this point.

161 ICJ, *Elettronica Sicula S.p.A. (ELSI) (United States of America v. Italy)*, Judgement (20 July 1989), paragraphs 124–125; as discussed in Nadakavukaren Schefer, *International Investment Law*, op. cit., 275.

162 For instance, procedural irregularities amounting to bad faith, wilful disregard of due process, or extreme insufficiency of action, measures inflicting damage on investor without serving any apparent legitimate purpose (reasonable and proportionate reaction

It remains to be seen whether and to what extent courts (or the Protocol's compliance mechanism) will take these indications into account if requested to assess compliance by Parties with this access standard.

Even if the terms of the Protocol were not going to be interpreted in the light of international investment law, however, it cannot be excluded that an investment dispute settlement mechanism may be seized to consider whether restrictive domestic access provisions may conflict with the terms of bilateral investment treaties concluded by the provider country,[163] including when the domestic access measures are specifically aimed at operationalizing the PIC requirement for access to genetic resources held by indigenous and local communities. In the latter case, provider countries may be well advised to justify their domestic access measures on the basis of relevant international human rights obligations, in addition to the relevant provisions of the Nagoya Protocol, as investment tribunals are generally reluctant to fully consider the implications of international environmental law for the disputes they are tasked to decide.[164]

6   Minimum Procedural Requirements for PIC

Article 6(3)(c–f) spells out minimum procedural requirements that must be included in domestic access frameworks of Parties requiring PIC. First of all, Parties are to specify in domestic access measures how to apply for PIC.[165] This includes clarifying which national authorities[166] are empowered to grant PIC, which specific requirements should be fulfilled to apply for PIC (such as details on the application format and content) and specific procedures to be followed.[167] These minimum requirements should be read in conjunction with other Protocol provisions requiring Parties to provide general and specific information, namely: the obligation to submit information about domestic ABS frameworks, national focal point and competent national authority or

---

to objectively verifiable circumstances); measures that are based on discretion, prejudice or personal preference, or measures based on pretext: Christoph Schreuer, "Protection against Arbitrary or Discriminatory Measures," in *The Future of Investment Arbitration*, ed. Catherine A. Rogers and Roger P. Alford (Oxford: Oxford University Press, 2009), 183, 188.

163   Viñuales, *Foreign Investment and the Environment*, op. cit., 205–206.

164   Ibid., 215.

165   Nagoya Protocol Article 6(3)(c).

166   See this commentary on Article 13, section 3.

167   Greiber et al., *Explanatory Guide*, op. cit., 104.

authorities to the ABS Clearinghouse;[168] the obligation for national ABS focal points to make information on procedures for obtaining PIC and establishing MAT available to applicants seeking access to genetic resources;[169] and the responsibility of competent national authorities to advise on applicable procedures and requirements for obtaining PIC.[170]

The second minimum requirement calls for providing a clear and transparent written[171] decision on PIC[172] by the competent national authority, in a cost effective manner and within a reasonable period of time.[173] Notably, the Protocol does not set itself specific time limits for domestic access decision-making,[174] but rather leaves discretion to Parties in striking a balance between the interests of users and providers, taking into account the specific circumstances and capacities of relevant authorities. What is considered 'reasonable' may also vary depending on the complexity of the access request, and should be understood in connection with the fair and transparent standards enshrined in Article 6(3)(a–b). There is therefore no expectation that the Protocol will lead to uniform national practices in this regard.[175] The provision basically seeks to prevent unreliable/unpredictable decision-making on access and to reduce transaction costs, with a view to reasonably meet users' expectations.[176]

The third requirement for domestic access measures is to provide for the issuance at the time of access of a permit or its equivalent,[177] as evidence of the decision to grant PIC and of the establishment of MAT, and notify[178] the ABS Clearinghouse accordingly.[179] This complements the previous requirement,

---

168 Nagoya Protocol Article 14(2)(a–b). See this commentary on Article 14, section 3.

169 Nagoya Protocol Article 13(1)(a). See this commentary on Article 13, section 2.

170 Nagoya Protocol Article 13(2). See this commentary on Article 13, section 3.

171 Note that the reference to the 'written decision' on access should be read in conjunction with the Protocol provision on national competent authorities 'issuing written evidence that access requirements have been met': Nagoya Protocol Article 13(2).

172 Based on a combined reading with Article 6(3)(c) and (e): Greiber et al., *Explanatory Guide*, op. cit., 104.

173 Nagoya Protocol Article 6(3)(d).

174 Compare with Biosafety Protocol Article 10.

175 Greiber et al., Explanatory Guide, op. cit., 104.

176 Ibid., 104.

177 Article 6(3)(3). On the meaning of 'its equivalent,' see this commentary on Article 14, section 4.

178 Note that this provision may create some interpretative difficulties when read in conjunction with the other Protocol provisions on the internationally recognized certificate of compliance. See this commentary on Article 17, section 3, and Young, "An International Cooperation Perspective," op. cit., 470.

179 Nagoya Protocol Article 6(3)(e).

which basically requires the creation in domestic ABS frameworks of a legal basis for domestic decision-making on granting PIC by competent national authorities. The third requirement instead addresses the necessary evidence of such decisions with a view to facilitating implementation of the Protocol's compliance obligations[180] and protecting the interests of those acquiring genetic resources and of subsequent users. The third requirement must therefore be read in conjunction with other Protocol provisions concerning the internationally recognized certificate of compliance,[181] as well as on the possibility for competent national authorities to issue either a permit or 'its equivalent.'[182]

An interpretative problem may arise with reference to 'the time of access', as there is no definition of 'access' in the Nagoya Protocol or the CBD. Nevertheless, as discussed above,[183] access can occur at the time of different activities in the jurisdiction of the Party providing genetic resources both from in situ or ex situ sources that led to their 'utilization'[184] in another Party's jurisdiction. From a practical perspective, it has also been noted that it is at the point of utilization, rather than at the time of access, that actual or potential value of genetic resources becomes evident and more easily verifiable.[185] So the time of access may be too early to decide what is fair and equitable benefit-sharing.[186] This may be particularly relevant as negotiations on MAT may precede the issuance of PIC. Ultimately, the uncertainty at the time of access about the actual or potential value of genetic resources may be addressed by a clause in MAT requiring parties to re-negotiate benefit-sharing at the time of utilization.[187]

The fourth requirement concerns the inclusion in domestic access measures of criteria and processes for obtaining PIC or approval and involvement of indigenous and local communities for access to genetic resources held by them,[188] for Parties on the territory of which these communities hold genetic resources ('where applicable'). In other words, Parties are under an obligation to provide potential users of genetic resources with information on how to apply for community PIC when indigenous and local communities have

---

180   See this commentary on Article 15.
181   Nagoya Protocol Article 17(2–4).
182   Nagoya Protocol Article 13(2).
183   See section 3 above.
184   Nagoya Protocol Article 2(c).
185   Tvedt, "Beyond Nagoya," op. cit., 160.
186   Ibid., 163.
187   See this commentary on Article 5, section 2.
188   Nagoya Protocol Article 6(3)(f).

established rights to grant access to their genetic resources.[189] This complements the obligation for Parties to establish domestic measures on community PIC for genetic resources held by indigenous and local communities.[190] The reference to 'accordance with domestic legislation' seems to indicate here that criteria and processes for obtaining community PIC will likely vary from one Party to another. As for other community-related provisions of the Protocol, this requirement should be implemented by taking into consideration the customary laws, protocols and procedures of indigenous and local communities,[191] and with their effective participation.[192] It should also be interpreted and implemented in the light of other relevant international human rights obligations and standards.[193]

7 Minimum Requirements for MAT

The final portion of Article 6(3)(g) sets out minimum requirements on establishing MAT, to be included in domestic access measures: it therefore requires Parties to specify at least some 'clear' rules and procedures for requiring and establishing MAT.[194] In effect, this is a critical provision, because besides requiring that MAT be established in writing, Article 6(3)(g) contains one of the very few sources of substantive guidance on the establishment of MAT under the Protocol.[195] That being said, Article 6(3)(g) only contains a non-exhaustive and non-prescriptive list of minimum requirements on the *content* of MAT.[196] Parties therefore have discretion to decide to what extent to determine the minimum content of MAT in their domestic ABS frameworks.

---

189 This complements the obligation under Nagoya Protocol Article 12(2) and in line with relevant international human rights law: see section 4.2.2 above. On established rights, see section 4.1 above.

190 Nagoya Protocol Article 6(2). See also Article 13(1)(b).

191 Nagoya Protocol Article 12(1). See this commentary on Article 12, section 2.

192 UNDRIP Article 19 and 32(2); ILO Convention No. 169, Article 6(2).

193 See Introduction to this commentary, section 4.

194 Nagoya Protocol Article 6(3)(g).

195 The only other provision of the Protocol detailing the establishment of MAT is Article 18(1), whereas the remaining provisions in Article 18 refer to ensuring compliance with MAT: see this commentary on Article 18. See also the obligation for Parties to encourage users and providers to include provisions facilitating monitoring of the utilization of genetic resources in MAT in Nagoya Protocol Article 17(1)(b) and this commentary on Article 17.

196 As appears evident from the use of the terms 'may include, inter alia'. Along the same lines, Greiber et al., *Explanatory Guide*, op. cit., 106.

In a light-touch manner, therefore, the Protocol 'promotes best practice in contractual drafting with the aim of protecting the provider of genetic resources.'[197] This minimalist approach, however, may be criticized in light of experience accrued in ABS transactions occurred prior to the negotiations of the Protocol, which demonstrated that MAT 'are the most complex and controversial elements of ABS practice.'[198] The same commentator also underscores that there are few, if any, national ABS measures that regulate the establishment of MAT in a manner that guarantees enforceability; and that therefore international guidance on this matter is necessary.[199]

Specifically, the Protocol limits itself to suggesting that the minimum content of MAT[200] be specified in domestic access measures to include, but not be limited to: a dispute settlement clause, the details of which are further elaborated elsewhere in the Protocol;[201] terms on benefit-sharing including IPRs; terms of subsequent third-party use; and terms on change of intent, which may be particularly relevant when access is sought to conduct non-commercial research.[202] As to the latter two instances, the Protocol acknowledges that ABS transactions often involve a chain of providers and users and underscores the need to address in contractual terms whether and which MAT are to apply to subsequent users. That can be the case of genetic resources utilized by the initial user for non-commercial purposes and then utilized by a subsequent user for commercial purposes, in which case 'MAT could include a requirement either for the initial user or the third-party user to first seek the PIC of the initial provider.'[203] It can also be the case of the same user changing his/her intent, in which case 'MAT could provide a requirement to seek [anew] the PIC of the provider country to use the same genetic resources for a new purpose.'[204] The reference to IPRs is particularly noteworthy. It has been argued that Article 6(3)(g) serves to recall that the sharing of benefits arising

---

197 Glowka and Normand, "The Nagoya Protocol on Access and Benefit-sharing," op. cit., 30.
198 Young, "An International Cooperation Perspective," op. cit., 500.
199 Ibid. Such guidance could arguably be provided by the Protocol's governing body at a future stage, in the context of its review of the effectiveness of the international obligations concerning compliance with MAT: Nagoya Protocol Article 18(3).
200 For an indication of possible specific items to be included in domestic access measures in this regard, see Greiber et al., *Explanatory Guide*, op. cit., 106–107.
201 Nagoya Protocol Article 18(1).
202 Nagoya Protocol Article 8(a). See this commentary on Article 8, section 2.
203 Glowka and Normand, "The Nagoya Protocol on Access and Benefit-sharing," op. cit., 31.
204 Ibid., 31.

from IPRs should explicitly be addressed through MAT,[205] because the Protocol itself 'does *not impose* IPRs-related benefit-sharing.'[206]

Based on domestic experience predating the Nagoya Protocol, it has been observed that the crucial matter is to ensure that domestic access frameworks create the right system of incentives for private and public entities to engage in legal ABS transactions and share benefits.[207] For this reason, the Protocol also foresees that inspiration may be drawn from pre-existing and ongoing practice, including through the use of model contractual clauses and voluntary instruments.[208] Furthermore, as the Protocol specifically provides for legal recourse in user countries for ensuring users' compliance with MAT (but not with PIC),[209] it has been argued that Parties would be well advised to set conditions for access in MAT as much as in the decision on PIC, so as to maximize the chance of enforcing any conditions set in PIC.[210] Finally, it should be anticipated that the Protocol envisages that Parties support indigenous and local communities in their determination of minimum requirements for MAT with specific regard to benefit-sharing from the use of traditional knowledge.[211]

---

205   Ibid., 30.
206   Pavoni, "The Nagoya Protocol and WTO," op. cit., 202, emphasis in the original, and his discussion on potential incompatibility with WTO law at 203.
207   Tvedt, "Beyond Nagoya," op. cit., 160–161.
208   See this commentary on Articles 19–20.
209   As compliance with MAT can rely on existing rules of private international law: see this commentary on Article 18.
210   Tvedt, "Beyond Nagoya," op. cit., 172–173.
211   Nagoya Protocol Article 12(3)(b).

Article 7. Access to Traditional Knowledge Associated with Genetic Resources

> In accordance with domestic law, each Party shall take measures, as appropriate, with the aim of ensuring that traditional knowledge associated with genetic resources that is held by indigenous and local communities is accessed with the prior and informed consent or approval and involvement of these indigenous and local communities, and that mutually agreed terms have been established.

1 Overview

Article 7 goes significantly beyond the text of the CBD by establishing an obligation for Parties to develop domestic measures on access to traditional knowledge. Such measures are aimed at ensuring that access to traditional knowledge can only proceed with the PIC or approval and involvement of indigenous and local communities. In line with the other access provisions of the Protocol,[1] such domestic measures are to provide for the establishment of MAT.

The conceptual difference between State PIC over genetic resources and community PIC over traditional knowledge will be examined below, followed by an interpretation of the qualified language of Article 7.

2 Community PIC in Relation to Traditional Knowledge

While the Protocol does not explicitly recognize 'the right' of indigenous and local communities to PIC for granting access to their traditional knowledge, it does so implicitly by requiring Parties to put legislation or other domestic measures in place on community PIC (or approval and involvement) in that regard. Conceptually, Article 7 embodies a 'community PIC requirement' that is separate from and possibly additional to State PIC for access to associated genetic resources,[2] and that is parallel to the 'community PIC requirement' for

---

1 Nagoya Protocol Article 6(3)(g). See this commentary on Article 6, section 7.
2 Nagoya Protocol Article 6(1): see this commentary on Article 6, section 3.

genetic resources 'held' by indigenous and local communities.[3] While State PIC is premised on the general principle of national sovereignty over natural resources, the requirement for community PIC concerning traditional knowledge is based on international human rights law, namely the right to cultural identity.[4] From an international environmental law perspective, the rationale for this provision can be found in the preamble to the Protocol, where Parties note

> the *interrelationship* between genetic resources and traditional knowledge, their *inseparable* nature for indigenous and local communities, and the importance of the traditional knowledge for the conservation of biological diversity and the sustainable use of its components and for the sustainable livelihoods of these communities.[5]

From a broader international law perspective, the Protocol further elaborates on UNDRIP's recognition of the right of indigenous peoples[6] to maintain, control, protect and develop indigenous peoples' traditional knowledge,[7] providing for more specific rules about traditional knowledge associated with genetic resources. As discussed in relation to the corresponding Protocol provisions on benefit-sharing arising from the use of traditional knowledge,[8] these provisions may be considered an implicit recognition of an underlying substantive

---

3   Nagoya Protocol Article 6(2): see this commentary on Article 6, section 4.2.
4   See ICCPR, Articles 1 and 27; ILO Convention No. 169, Article 2(b); and UNDRIP Articles 3–4. Note also that the Bonn Guidelines, paragraph 37, provide that 'Permission to access genetic resources does not necessarily imply permission to use associated knowledge and vice versa.'
5   Nagoya Protocol 22nd preambular recital, emphasis added.
6   On the rights of local communities under the Protocol and international human rights law, see Introduction to this commentary, section 4.2.
7   UNDRIP Article 31(1) reads: 'Indigenous peoples have the right to maintain, control, protect and develop their cultural heritage, traditional knowledge and traditional cultural expressions, as well as the manifestations of their sciences, technologies and cultures, including human and genetic resources, seeds, medicines, knowledge of the properties of fauna and flora, oral traditions, literatures, designs, sports and traditional games and visual and performing arts. They also have the right to maintain, control, protect and develop their intellectual property over such cultural heritage, traditional knowledge, and traditional cultural expressions.' The UN Special Rapporteur on the Rights of Indigenous Peoples considered the recognition of the right to PIC over traditional knowledge and the implicit recognition of indigenous peoples' ownership of traditional knowledge in the Protocol as 'positive aspects' of the adoption of the Protocol: Human Rights Council, "Follow-up report on indigenous peoples," A/HRC/C/21/55, paragraph 59.
8   Nagoya Protocol Article 5(2). See this commentary on Article 5, section 4.

environmental right of these communities to their traditional knowledge associated with genetic resources. The Protocol is also notable in extending this right to local communities.[9]

As opposed to community PIC over genetic resources held by indigenous and local communities,[10] the requirement for community PIC over traditional knowledge is put forward in stronger language in the Protocol and is not conditional upon the existence of 'established rights to grant access.' This can be explained by the fact that traditional knowledge is a product, as well as a part and parcel, of the identity and traditional way of life of a community, and therefore national sovereignty cannot be asserted over it.[11]

As traditional knowledge is therefore seen as 'owned' by the indigenous and local communities concerned and inextricably linked to its identity and way of life, it is essential that Parties to the Protocol develop the relevant implementing measures with the full and effective participation of these communities[12] and ensure due consideration of their customary laws, protocols and procedures.[13] How community PIC will be implemented in practice will likely vary from one country to another, or even within the same country, depending on the concerned communities' customary laws, protocols and procedures. As highlighted in the Protocol preamble, in fact, there is a 'diversity of circumstances under which traditional knowledge associated with genetic resources is held or owned by indigenous and local communities'[14] and there are 'unique circumstances where traditional knowledge associated with genetic resources is held in countries, which may be oral, documented or in other forms, reflecting a rich cultural heritage relevant for conservation and sustainable use.'[15]

No international process has yet spelt out the specific procedural and substantive requirements for community PIC over traditional knowledge associated with genetic resources,[16] although guidance developed by CBD Parties

---

9   See Introduction to this commentary, section 4.
10   Nagoya Protocol Article 6(2) and this commentary on Article 6, section 4 – although note the practical difficulty to regulate separately access to genetic resources held by indigenous and local communities and access to traditional knowledge associated with such genetic resources in light of their inseparable nature for indigenous and local communities.
11   See generally on traditional knowledge as part of the collective cultural rights of indigenous peoples: Lenzerini, "Indigenous Peoples' Cultural Rights," op. cit., and Lenzerini and Fraboni, "Indigenous Peoples' Rights, Biogenetic Resources, " op. cit., 201.
12   See fn. 54 in commentary on Article 5.
13   Nagoya Protocol Article 12(1). See this commentary on Article 12, section 2.
14   Nagoya Protocol, 23rd preambular recital.
15   Nagoya Protocol, 25th preambular recital.
16   In fact, CBD Parties have identified the need to develop guidelines in that respect: CBD Article 8(j) Working Group, Recommendation 8/4, "How tasks 7, 10 and 12 could best

provides consensus, soft-law determinations in that regard, in particular in the framework of the Working Group on Article 8(j).[17] First, the CBD Akwé: Kon Guidelines[18] provide specifications for community PIC, also touching upon issues related to traditional knowledge. According to the Guidelines, the requirement for community PIC implies: consideration of the rights, knowledge, innovations and practices of indigenous and local communities;[19] respect of customary laws governing ownership, access, control, use and dissemination of traditional knowledge;[20] the use of culturally appropriate languages and processes; and the allocation of sufficient time and the provision of accurate, factual and legally correct information.[21] Modifications to the initial proposal require additional PIC of the affected community.[22] Community PIC may be established through protocols,[23] consistent with relevant national legislation, on access to and use of traditional knowledge, and assistance by the government in establishing such protocols should be provided by the government *if so requested*.[24] Second, according to the CBD Tkarihwaié:ri Code of

---

contribute to work under the Convention and to the Nagoya Protocol," in "Report of the eighth meeting," Annex 1, paragraph 2(2).

17 These normative developments may be explained by the broad participation that indigenous and local community representatives enjoy in the proceedings of the Working Group on Article 8(j). The 'fullest possible participation' of indigenous and local communities is ensured in all meetings, including in contact groups, by inviting community representatives as Friends of the Co-Chairs, Friends of the Bureau and Co-Chairs of contact groups. However, text proposals by indigenous and local communities' representatives must be supported by at least one Party. See the CBD Article 8(j) Working Group, "Report of the seventh meeting," UNEP/CBD/COP/11/7, paragraph 20.

18 Akwé: Kon Guidelines, section F, paragraph 29 reads: 'In the conduct of cultural impact assessments, due consideration should be given to the holders of traditional knowledge, innovations and practices and the knowledge itself. Customary laws governing ownership, access, control, use and dissemination of traditional knowledge, innovations and practices should be observed. Protocols with regard to indigenous and local communities should be followed with regard to the disclosure of secret and or sacred knowledge, including those that may involve public hearings and judicial processes in the courts. In the event of the disclosure of secret and or sacred knowledge, prior informed consent and proper protection measures should be ensured.'

19 Akwé: Kon Guidelines, paragraph 53.

20 Akwé: Kon Guidelines, paragraph 29.

21 Akwé: Kon Guidelines, paragraph 53.

22 Akwé: Kon Guidelines, paragraph 53.

23 Note that the Nagoya Protocol includes the notion of community 'protocols' in Article 12 and 21(1): see discussion on community protocols in this commentary on Article 12, section 2.1.

24 Akwé: Kon Guidelines, paragraph 60, emphasis added.

Ethical Conduct to Ensure Respect for the Cultural and Intellectual Heritage of Indigenous and Local Communities,[25] consent should not be coerced, forced or manipulated.[26] In addition, where consent or authority of indigenous and local communities is required with respect to traditional knowledge, it is the right of indigenous and local communities, according to their customary law and procedures, to identify the relevant holders of their knowledge.[27]

Significant work on the concept of free PIC has been undertaken in the context of international human rights processes, although without specific regard to traditional knowledge. International guidance on indigenous peoples' right to free PIC for development projects impacting their land[28]

---

25   "The Tkarihwaié: Ri Code of Ethical Conduct to Ensure Respect for the Cultural and Intellectual Heritage of Indigenous and Local Communities relevant to the Conservation and Sustainable Use of Biological Diversity" in CBD Decision 10/42, "The Tkarihwaié:ri Code of Ethical Conduct to Ensure Respect for the Cultural and Intellectual Heritage of Indigenous and Local Communities" (20 January 2011) UN Doc UNEP/CBD/COP/10/27 (hereinafter, Tkarihwaié: Ri Code).

26   Tkarihwaié: Ri Code, paragraph 11 reads: 'Any activities/interactions related to traditional knowledge associated with the conservation and sustainable use of biological diversity, occurring on or likely to impact on sacred sites and on lands and waters traditionally occupied or used by indigenous and local communities and impacting upon specific groups, should be carried out with the prior informed consent and/or approval and involvement of indigenous and local communities. Such consent or approval should not be coerced, forced or manipulated.'

27   Tkarihwaié: Ri Code, paragraph 4.

28   In relation, for instance, to the relocation of a community from its traditional lands due to the storage or disposal of toxic waste, or when large-scale development or investment projects have a major impact on traditional territories of indigenous peoples: Human Rights Council, "Promotion and protection of all human rights," A/HRC/12/34, paragraph 47; "Report of the Special Rapporteur on indigenous peoples' rights," A/HRC/24/41, section B. See also work undertaken by the Expert Mechanism, "Final report of the study on indigenous peoples and the right to participate in decision-making. Report of the Expert Mechanism on the Rights of Indigenous Peoples" (17 August 2011) UN Doc A/HRC/18/42. Note further worky by CERD, "Consideration of reports submitted by States Parties under Article 9 of the Convention. Concluding observations of the Committee on the Elimination of Racial Discrimination. India" (5 May 2007) UN Doc CERD/C/IND/CO/19, paragraph 19; "Consideration of reports submitted by States Parties under Article 9 of the Convention. Argentina" (8 June 2009) UN Doc CERD/C/ARG/CO/19–20, paragraph 26; "Consideration of reports submitted by States Parties under Article 9 of the Convention. Concluding observations of the Committee on the Elimination of Racial Discrimination. Philippines" (28 August 2009) UN Doc CERD/C/PHL/CO/20, paragraphs 22 and 26; "Consideration of reports submitted by States Parties under Article 9 of the Convention. Concluding observations of the Committee on the Elimination of Racial Discrimination.

may thus be of some use as a source of inspiration in implementing Article 7.[29]

3   Qualifications

The language of Article 7 is qualified and attention must be paid to the specific terms used in it. First of all, the obligation to provide for procedures for community PIC and establishment of MAT is limited to traditional knowledge 'held' by indigenous and local communities. The Protocol does not arguably require community PIC for access to traditional knowledge ex situ, for example documented in databases, genebanks or libraries outside community control, if it is *no longer held* by the community. On the other hand, the Protocol is silent as to the situation in which the traditional knowledge is still held by indigenous and local communities, but also publicly available in other forms. In either case, the non-applicability of the community PIC requirement may not necessarily exclude benefit-sharing, as it can be envisaged that Parties holding traditional knowledge in databases may require benefits in exchange for allowing access to it.[30] It could also be argued that in cases where no community 'holding' traditional knowledge can be identified, the multilateral benefit-sharing mechanism envisaged by the Protocol[31] could come into play.

A related question is the actual identification of the relevant communities ('*these* indigenous and local communities' – emphasis added) that have the right to provide PIC and engage in the negotiation of MAT. This may be particularly problematic where the same traditional knowledge is shared by more than one community located in several Parties: cooperation among relevant Parties, with the involvement of concerned communities, will be needed.[32]

In addition, Article 7 (similarly to the Protocol provision on community PIC on genetic resources held by indigenous and local communities), does not clearly endorse the international human rights-based standard of community

---

Chile" (7 September 2009) CERD/C/CHL/CO/15–18, paragraph 22; and other reports cited in Human Rights Council, "Follow-up report on indigenous peoples," A/HRC/C/21/55, fn. 14.

29   See this commentary on Article 6, section 4.2.

30   For a discussion on publicly available traditional knowledge, see this commentary on Article 5, section 4.

31   See this commentary on Article 10.

32   Nagoya Protocol Article 11(2). See this commentary on Article 11, section 4.

PIC, but adds 'or approval and involvement.' As already discussed,[33] Parties to the Protocol will need to establish some formal processes to engage indigenous and local communities and respect their rights as enshrined in human rights law.[34] This will be particularly important when community PIC may be embodied in the same decision providing State PIC as a result of communities' participation in government decision-making processes on access. It may raise particular difficulties in situations where under national legislation States have claimed that traditional knowledge is 'the patrimony of the State,'[35] or when traditional knowledge is held in centralized registries or databases outside community control.[36]

Similarly in Article 6,[37] the reference to 'accordance with domestic law,'[38] would not justify an interpretation that the right of community PIC on traditional knowledge is dependent on its recognition in national legislation. It should rather be implemented as referring to the need for Parties to devise implementing measures that functionally fit with other relevant areas of national legislation, while ensuring the respect of relevant international human rights obligations and taking into account communities' customary laws. The reference may also be interpreted as pointing to a facilitative role of the State in situations where indigenous and local communities within their jurisdiction may request support in their interactions with third parties seeking utilization of traditional knowledge.[39]

The due diligence obligation to establish measures providing for community PIC and the establishment of MAT specifically aimed at benefit-sharing with indigenous and local communities is also qualified. It can be assumed that Parties can take any legal, administrative or policy measures, binding or not, 'in accordance with domestic law' and 'as appropriate.' In all events, domestic measures should detail the procedural requirements to obtain the

---

33   Nagoya Protocol Article 6(2). See this commentary on Article 6, section 4.2.1.

34   See Human Rights Council, "Report of the Special Rapporteur," A/HRC/24/41, paragraph 25; and this commentary on Article 6, section 4.2.

35   E.g., Brazil, Medida Provisória No. 2186-16, 2001, Article 8(2); see discussion in Singh Nijar, "Incorporating Traditional Knowledge," op. cit., 465.

36   See for instance the inventories of intangible cultural heritage created under the UNESCO Convention on Intangible Cultural Heritage, Article 12 (for a brief discussion of the interactions between the UNESCO Convention and the Protocol, see this commentary on Article 4, section 2.1).

37   See this commentary on Article 6, section 4.2.

38   Which should be contrasted with CBD Article 8(j) language ('*subject* to national legislation'): Bavikatte and Robinson, "Towards a People's History of the Law," op. cit., 45.

39   Ibid.

PIC or approval and involvement of the community concerned, and to establish MAT with them, prior to access to their traditional knowledge, taking into
consideration customary laws, protocols and procedures of indigenous and
local communities.[40] This is in line with UNDRIP, that expects States to take
'effective measures to recognize and protect the exercise of [traditional knowl-
edge-related] rights', *in conjunction with* indigenous peoples.'[41]

The qualifications found in the provision allow Parties to take measures to
fit their national circumstances and regulatory traditions, but does not support
a potential decision by a Party not to take any measures at all to regulate access
to traditional knowledge. This conclusion is supported by the fact that Article 7
does not include the clause found in Article 6 'unless otherwise determined
by that Party,' which allows States not to require PIC for access to their genetic
resources.[42] Therefore, it can be argued that even if a State opts for not requiring PIC for access to genetic resources or some categories of them, it is still
obliged to develop the procedures required for users to obtain community PIC
for access to traditional knowledge associated with such resources.

It should be finally recalled that the in-built flexibility of Article 7 can also
benefit indigenous and local communities in the light of the diverse and
unique circumstances under which traditional knowledge is held or owned by
these communities.[43] These circumstances inevitably require a variety of legal
and other approaches to implement in an effective and culturally appropriate manner Article 7 in different countries, particularly where indigenous and
local communities may have conceptual relations to the land that do not fit
with statutory concepts of property and use.[44]

---

40   Nagoya Protocol Article 12(1) and this commentary on Article 12, section 2.
41   UNDRIP Article 31(2), emphasis added.
42   See this commentary on Article 6.
43   Nagoya Protocol 23rd and 25th preambular recitals.
44   We are grateful to Geoff Burton for drawing our attention to this point.

Article 8. Special Considerations

In the development and implementation of its access and benefit-sharing legislation or regulatory requirements, each Party shall:

(a) Create conditions to promote and encourage research which contributes to the conservation and sustainable use of biological diversity, particularly in developing countries, including through simplified measures on access for non-commercial research purposes, taking into account the need to address a change of intent for such research;

(b) Pay due regard to cases of present or imminent emergencies that threaten or damage human, animal or plant health, as determined nationally or internationally. Parties may take into consideration the need for expeditious access to genetic resources and expeditious fair and equitable sharing of benefits arising out of the use of such genetic resources, including access to affordable treatments by those in need, especially in developing countries;

(c) Consider the importance of genetic resources for food and agriculture and their special role for food security.

1 Overview

Article 8 identifies three sets of international concerns with regard to which Parties are called upon, with decreasing stringency, to differentiate in their domestic ABS framework: a) research contributing to conservation and sustainable use of biodiversity b) health-related emergencies and c) genetic resources for food and agriculture.

The obligations set out in Article 8 apply both in the development and in the implementation of national ABS legislation or regulatory requirements. In other words, Parties are to take into account these special considerations both when developing general rules implementing the Nagoya Protocol in their domestic legal system, and also when applying their domestic ABS frameworks to specific cases, including when granting PIC and establishing MAT. In addition, national legislation could possibly address some of these issues in its provisions on minimum requirements for MAT.[1]

---

1 Nagoya Protocol Article 6(3)(g): see this commentary on Article 6, section 7. The authors are grateful to Tomme Young for drawing their attention to this point.

© KONINKLIJKE BRILL NV, LEIDEN, 2014 | DOI 10.1163/9789004217188_010

As the special considerations identified by Article 8 allow for departures from the general provisions of the Protocol, they have to be interpreted restrictively.[2] The following sections will discuss each of the special considerations in turn, analyzing how each has been framed so as to avoid creating potential loopholes in the international ABS regime.

2   Research Contributing to Conservation and Sustainable Use

The obligation related to research contributing to conservation and sustainable use is the most stringent among those included in Article 8. It specifically requires Parties to create favorable 'conditions' to promote and encourage research contributing to the conservation and sustainable use of biodiversity. This may be particularly important in the light of CBD Parties' obligation to identify and monitor biodiversity components, which requires 'major scientific effort in basic science such as taxonomy, ecology and conservation biology.'[3] The following subsections will first discuss the rationale of this provision, and then analyze its text against that backdrop.

2.1   *Rationale*

The provision aims at addressing concerns that ABS rules may unnecessarily and unintentionally hamper scientific research, particularly with no commercial intent. The underlying rationale is that the Protocol should also contribute to the realization of the other two objectives of the CBD.[4] The expectation thus is that successful implementation of the international ABS regime will not only provide innovative funding, but also give rise to scientific findings, that may contribute to more effective conservation and sustainable use.

The provision implicitly recognizes the scientific research community as a key ABS stakeholder, allowing flexibility for transnational collaborative research partnerships and practices that advance the science of biodiversity conservation and sustainable use.[5] At the same time, it takes stock of the practical difficulties reportedly encountered by researchers facing overly stringent or

---

2   Luigi Crema, "Disappearance and New Sightings of Restrictive Interpretation(s)," *European Journal of International Law* 21 (2010): 681, 692–693.

3   Biber-Klemm et al., "Governance Options," op. cit., 218.

4   See this commentary on Article 1, section 4.

5   Tom Dedeurwaerdere et al., "Governing Scientific Research Commons under the Nagoya Protocol," in Morgera, Buck and Tsioumani, *2010 Nagoya Protocol on Access and Benefit-Sharing in Perspective*, op. cit., 389.

uncertain access conditions before the negotiations of the Protocol,[6] including fears of excessive waiting time for approval of access applications and transaction costs.[7] Article 8(a) is linked to other provisions in the Protocol, which allow for learning from, and possibly building on, the research community's codes of conduct in the implementation of the Protocol;[8] aim to contribute to building capacity and transferring technology for scientific research across Parties;[9] and aim to increase scientific research cooperation, particularly with researchers in developing countries, as a form of non-monetary benefit-sharing.[10]

Research contributing to conservation and sustainable use includes distinct 'communities of practice' such as those involved in taxonomy, systematics and evolutionary biology, microbial systematics and ecology, ecosystem research, genomics and metagenomics. Such research may provide a series of non-economic benefits (contribution of data to public databases, deposition of specimens and samples in ex situ collections, public dissemination of new knowledge through peer-reviewed publications and academic conferences, etc.) that could not be generated without access to genetic resources.

There is, however, always the possibility that a project that begins with non-commercial intent can develop commercial intent at a later stage, either because the researchers themselves may uncover potential for commercial development; or individuals not associated with the research team may use the published results and/or the specimens obtained from that research as a starting point for commercial development.[11] If access with non-commercial intent is left unregulated, commercial users could gain access to genetic

---

6   Cabrera Medaglia, "The Implementation of the Nagoya Protocol," op. cit., 357–358.

7   Draft article 6(a) titled 'Considerations relevant to research and emergency situations' in Cali Draft reads: 'In the development and implementation of their national legislation on access and benefit-sharing, Parties shall pay due regard to: a) Avoiding or minimizing *impediments* to biodiversity-related research, important for the conservation of biological diversity and the sustainable use of its components,' emphasis added. See also Sikina Jinnah and Stefan Jungcurt, "Could Access Requirements Stifle Your Research?," *Science* 323 (2009): 464.

8   See this commentary on Article 20.

9   See this commentary on Articles 22(4)(d) and 23 (and note in particular the reference to 'development and strengthening of a sound and viable technological and scientific base.')

10   Nagoya Protocol Article 5(5) and Nagoya Protocol Annex, paragraphs 2(a–b), also discussed in this commentary on Article 5, section 6.

11   CBD Working Group on ABS, "Report of a Workshop on Access and Benefit-Sharing in Non-commercial Biodiversity Research," (9 March 2009) UN Doc UNEP/CBD/WG-ABS/7/INF/6, 9.

resources and traditional knowledge via academic channels and circumvent benefit-sharing obligations.[12]

Against this background, a balance has been struck between creating favorable conditions for access to genetic resources and traditional knowledge for the purposes of conducting research needed to achieve the Convention's and Protocol's objectives, and the need to prevent circumvention of the ABS general rules to ensure benefit-sharing resulting from commercial research and development.[13] To that end, all Parties (both user and provider countries) need to consider measures from both perspectives of the ABS relationship: both with regard to foreign researchers seeking to access genetic resources in their jurisdiction, and with regard to users based in their jurisdiction seeking access in another jurisdiction for research purposes – in the latter case addressing in particular the issue of change of intent.

In doing so, Parties will face the practical challenge to distinguish between research projects that do or do not contribute to conservation and sustainable use.[14] In addition, it is not always easy to distinguish non-commercial from commercial research.[15] In broad approximation, commercial research may limit benefit-sharing by restricting the release of research findings (e.g., through non-disclosure agreements or unwillingness to publish results); delaying the public release of data resulting from the research; or engaging in product development or testing of technology or products as part of a wider undisclosed project.[16] Commercial research also raises the concern of excessive fees for access to data, technology, or materials resulting from the research; of retention of monetary benefits from sale or lease for profit, patenting, or licensing of research results; or of reserved rights to file patents or maintain ownership of IPRs.[17] While there is some regulatory experience in distinguishing commercial and non-commercial research on genetic resources (as discussed below),[18] in many countries this remains a challenge. Experience preceding the Nagoya Protocol shows that most requests for access to genetic resources are to conduct non-commercial research.[19]

---

12   Tvedt, "Beyond Nagoya," op. cit., 167.

13   Ibid., 4.

14   We are thankful to Tomme Young for drawing our attention to this point.

15   See this commentary on Article 2, section 2.1.

16   CBD Working Group on ABS, "Report of a Workshop on ABS in Non-commercial Biodiversity Research," UNEP/CBD/WG-ABS/7/INF/6, 9.

17   Ibid.

18   Mostly from developed countries, such as Australia: see Burton, "Implementation of the Nagoya Protocol in JUSCANZ Countries," op. cit., 303.

19   Cabrera Medaglia, "The Implementation of the Nagoya Protocol," op. cit., 363–364.

2.2   *The Obligation*

Article 8(a) establishes a general obligation for Parties to 'create conditions' favorable to research contributing to conservation and sustainable use when developing and implementing their national ABS frameworks. It specifies that this should be implemented particularly when such research is carried out in developing countries. The provision appears to complement an often-forgotten CBD obligation for Parties to 'endeavor to develop and carry out scientific research based on genetic resources provided by other Parties with the full participation of, and where possible in, such Parties.'[20] Thus, while Article 8(a) does not mention explicitly provider countries and benefit-sharing, it could be inferred that national measures creating favorable conditions for research contributing to conservation and sustainable use are to ensure the sharing of benefits with provider developing countries. Such benefits could include the participation of provider-country researchers in research endeavors and the building of research capacity in developing countries.[21] The provision is to be implemented both by providing for favorable conditions for research contributing to conservation and sustainable use and support to developing countries in ABS legislation, as well as through MAT.[22] It could also impact on the regulation (or self-regulation) of research funders.

Article 8(a) does not specify what kinds of 'conditions' are expected to favor research contributing to conservation and sustainable use. Standardized terms and streamlined procedures for ABS agreements are an obvious option. The provision, however, provides one specific example ('including')[23] that relates in particular to non-commercial research – 'simplified measures for access.' The Australian legislation provides a useful illustration in this regard. Australia already introduced simplified procedures for non-commercial research in 2005, which provided for the grant of a succinct non-commercial access permit and an accompanying Statutory Declaration, without fees.[24] However, as in other open-ended provisions of the Protocol, Parties will have considerable

---

20   CBD Article 15(6): we are thankful to Tomme Young for drawing our attention to this point.

21   The obligation thus to create favourable conditions for research does not exclude the regulation of benefit-sharing from biodiversity-related research.

22   As inferred by the reference to 'the implementation' of ABS legislation.'

23   We are thankful to Tomme Young for drawing our attention to this point. See also Greiber et al., *Explanatory Guide*, op. cit., 121.

24   "Permits for non-commercial purposes," Australian Government Department of Sustainability, Environment, Water, Population and Communities, accessed 30 November 2013, <www.environment.gov.au/biodiversity/science/access/permits/non-commercial .html>. As discussed in Burton, "Implementation of the Nagoya Protocol in JUSCANZ

leeway in selecting and implementing favorable conditions for research contributing to conservation and sustainable use, and also in determining how
to 'simplify' access in the specific case of non-commercial research. Although
Article 8(a) does not make the creation of simplified measures on access for
non-commercial research mandatory, Parties will be well advised to specifically provide for those cases. Parties will also be well advised to couple simplified access with enforceable and simplified benefit-sharing obligations if any
monetary benefit occurs from non-commercial research, and detail rules on
change of intent.[25]

As anticipated above, it may be challenging in practice to distinguish
between research of commercial and non-commercial nature, and national
legislators may rely on the stated intention of a researcher at the time of
access. In addition, the importance of addressing possible changes in intent is
also addressed elsewhere in the Protocol, namely in the context of the minimum requirements for MAT.[26] National legislation should therefore address
this situation by including a clause on change of intent among the minimum
requirements for MAT,[27] whereby researchers are subjected to a contractual
obligation to inform the provider country authority of any change of intent
and to negotiate benefit-sharing arrangements,[28] or to obtain a new PIC and
establish new MAT before any IPRs can be retained or commercial research
can begin.[29]

It cannot be excluded that the favourable conditions mandated[30] by
Article 8(a) may apply also to commercial research. On the one hand, this could
be inferred from the implicit distinction that Nagoya Protocol Article 8(a)
draws when referring to 'including through simplified measures on access for
non-commercial research purposes' (emphasis added). Commercial research
such as that leading to the development of biodiversity-friendly technology

---

Countries," op. cit., 308. More examples are summarised in Greiber et al., *Explanatory
Guide*, op. cit., 121.

25   Tvedt, "Beyond Nagoya," op. cit., 168.

26   Nagoya Protocol Article 6(3)(g)(iv). See this commentary on Article 6.

27   Greiber et al., *Explanatory Guide*, op. cit., 119–120 and generally CBD Working Group on
      ABS, "Report of a Workshop on ABS in Non-commercial Biodiversity Research." UNEP/
      CBD/WG-ABS/7/INF/6.

28   This is the case of Australia: Burton, "Implementation of the Nagoya Protocol in JUSCANZ
      Countries," op. cit., 327–328.

29   CBD Working Group on ABS, "Report of a Workshop on ABS in Non-commercial
      Biodiversity Research," 10.UNEP/CBD/WG-ABS/7/INF/6, 10.

30   But not the simplified measures on access, which specifically refer to non-commercial
      research.

could thus be promoted and encouraged, as long as it can be demonstrated that it contributes to conservation and sustainable use. On the other hand, the beginning of Article 8(a) refers to 'research' (used on its own)[31] rather than to 'research and development', which characterizes research with commercial intent elsewhere in the Protocol.[32] A clarification by the Protocol's governing body[33] may become necessary in this regard, if divergent State practice emerges on the basis of different interpretation of this provision.

It should be finally noted that Article 8(a) refers specifically to neither genetic resources nor traditional knowledge with regard to access. While it can be assumed that the provision applies to both instances, particularly given the inextricable link between genetic resources and traditional knowledge,[34] the general community PIC requirement with regard to traditional knowledge, as well as genetic resources held by indigenous and local communities, continues to apply even in the context of favorable conditions for research contributing to conservation and sustainable use.[35] Therefore, a requirement for community PIC should be clearly articulated in Parties' regulation of research contributing to conservation and sustainable use under Article 8(a). As long as this fundamental obligation is observed, Article 8(a) as regards traditional knowledge reflects the importance of better understanding knowledge, innovations and practices of indigenous and local communities embodying traditional lifestyles for conserving and sustainably using biodiversity. It thus complements CBD Article 8(j) from the specific angle of the contribution of traditional knowledge associated with genetic resources to scientific research. In addition, it can be argued that the full and effective participation of indigenous and local communities,[36] taking into account their customary laws, procedures and

---

31   CBD Working Group on ABS, "Report of the expert meeting on definitions," UNEP/CBD/ WG-ABS/7/2, paragraph 10.

32   Ibid., paragraphs 17 and 43–45. See also CBD Group of Legal and Technical Experts on Concepts, Terms, Working Definitions and Sectoral Approaches, "Concepts, terms, working definitions and sectoral approaches relating to the international regime on access and benefit-sharing, Submission from the International Workshop on the topic of 'access and benefit-sharing in non-commercial biodiversity research' " (29 November 2008) UN Doc UNEP/CBD/ABS/ GTLE/1/INF/2, paragraph 5. We are grateful to Evanson Chege Kamau for an exchange of ideas on this question.

33   Nagoya Protocol Article 26(4): see this commentary on Article 26, section 2.

34   Nagoya Protocol 22nd preambular recital.

35   As in Nagoya Protocol Articles 7 and 6(2). See this commentary on Article 6, section 4.2 and on Article 7, section 2.

36   UNDRIP Article 19 and 32(2); ILO Convention No. 169, Article 6(2); and fn. 53 in this commentary on Article 5.

protocols,[37] should be ensured during the development of simplified access measures in the context of Article 8(a), in case such measures might affect these communities' rights over genetic resources and traditional knowledge.

3   Genetic Resources and Health-related Emergencies

Article 8(b)[38] creates the regulatory space for Parties to ensure that general ABS rules and procedures do not interfere with public health efforts, both in terms of development of needed pharmaceutical products and access to them.[39] While its inclusion in the Protocol was mainly motivated by parallel negotiations related to pathogens under the WHO,[40] the provision refers generally to situations of emergency that threaten or damage health.[41]

As opposed to Article 8(a), the provision does not establish an obligation to 'create conditions' – but rather to 'pay due regard' to health-related emergencies; and it does not make reference as an option to 'simplified' measures for access, but rather to 'expeditious' measures that may concern access, but also benefit-sharing. It therefore rather requires that Parties 'ensure that public health objectives can be met and are indeed supported by access as well as benefit-sharing rules.'[42]

Special ABS procedures can therefore be established under Article 8(b) upon the condition that a 'present or imminent emergency that threatens or damages human, animal or plant health' is determined nationally or internationally. The Protocol determines the 'subjects threatened by the emergency, the cause of the emergency and the regulatory status of the emergency.'[43] The wording is broad enough to include emergencies that threaten biodiversity

---

37   Nagoya Protocol Article 12(1). See this commentary on Article 12, section 2.

38   The authors are particularly grateful to Marie Wilke, as this section in great part draws upon her book chapter: Wilke, "A Healthy Look," op. cit.

39   Ibid., 125.

40   See this commentary on Article 4, section 3.2. See also draft article 3.H in Montreal I Draft; and ENB 9/465, "Summary of the Seventh Meeting of the Working Group on ABS," 5. See also Wilke, "A Healthy Look," op. cit., 127.

41   Tvedt, "Beyond Nagoya," op. cit., 169–170, criticizing International Chamber of Commerce, *Pathogens and the International Regime on Access and Benefit-Sharing in Non-Commercial Biodiversity Research* (Paris: International Chamber of Commerce, 2009), accessed 30 November 2013, <www.iccwbo.org/Data/Policies/2009/Pathogens-and-the-International-Regime-on-Access-and-Benefit-Sharing/>, 5–6.

42   Wilke, "A Healthy Look," op. cit., 126.

43   Ibid., 127.

and that are caused by non-natural pathogens or other instances (that is, not necessarily by genetic resources but rather by natural disasters, industrial accidents or contaminated food products).[44] In these situations, therefore, Article 8(b) applies to genetic resources that are 'relevant' either as a cause of the emergency or as an emergency response to it – in other words, both genetic material with pathogenic potential but also material with anti-pathogenic[45] or adaptive properties.[46]

Health emergencies that trigger Article 8(b) should either already be present ('existing'), therefore demanding immediate action, or be likely or about to occur ('imminent'), thereby calling for preparedness and prevention.[47] Article 8(b) refers to an international or national determination of a health emergency, as alternatives. An international determination of a health emergency can certainly be that provided by the WHO on the basis of its International Health Regulations,[48] that are referred to in the Protocol preamble in relation to the importance of ensuring access to human pathogens for public health preparedness and response purposes.[49] The broad formulation of Article 8(b), however, does not exclude that other international organizations working on pathogens, such as the International Plant Protection Convention,[50] or the World Organization for Animal Health, and potentially others may also be considered relevant for the purposes of determining an international health emergency. National determinations of health emergencies, instead, are left to the discretion of individual States, as there is no internationally agreed definition of local or national health emergency.[51] The latter instances raise more complicated scenarios for the application of Article 8(b): are only provider countries to determine whether a nationally determined health emergency exist in relation to ABS from their own genetic resources? And if user countries establish such an emergency, would this unilateral determination in and of itself facilitate access to genetic resources in third countries?[52] It can be expected that further clarification on these questions will be solicited from the Nagoya

---

44   Ibid., 128–130.
45   Ibid., 133.
46   We are grateful to Geoff Burton for drawing our attention to this point.
47   Greiber et al., *Explanatory Guide*, op. cit., 122.
48   Wilke, "A Healthy Look," op. cit., 130.
49   Nagoya Protocol 17th preambular recital.
50   International Plant Protection Convention (Rome, 6 December 1951, in force 3 April 1952) 2367 UNTS 223.
51   Wilke, "A Healthy Look," op. cit., 131.
52   We are grateful to Tomme Young for drawing out attention to these points.

Protocol's governing body, under its power to make recommendations on any matter necessary for the implementation of the Protocol.[53]

Article 8(b) enables Parties to take into consideration the need for 'expeditious' access to genetic resources and 'expeditious' benefit-sharing arising out of the use of such genetic resources, including access to affordable treatments by those in need, especially in developing countries. The expression 'expeditious' may not be understood as 'immediate',[54] but rather, on the basis of its ordinary meaning, as a fast-track procedure.[55] Overall, Parties are to consider ways to prevent delays that would otherwise arise from the application of their general ABS procedures,[56] so that effective access should be commensurate to the magnitude of the emergency situation. With specific regard to expeditious benefit-sharing, the provision does not exclude usual benefit-sharing arrangements with the provider country. But it creates an expectation for Parties to consider expeditious benefit-sharing towards those in 'need,' in particular developing countries, possibly through donations and development aid, including through multilateral channels.[57] In that regard, the provision refers to the specific example of access to affordable medical treatments. It remains within the purview of Parties to determine in their national ABS frameworks and their implementation who will be the recipient of benefit-sharing on the basis of 'need.' As there are no further specifications, Article 8(b) can cover all benefit-sharing obligations that are relevant to ensure appropriate public health responses in times of emergency, ranging from knowledge or technology transfer to in-kind contributions of pharmaceutical products, in accordance with established MAT.[58]

Finally, as traditional knowledge is not mentioned in this provision, whereas genetic resources are explicitly referred to (as opposed to Article 8(a)), it may be inferred that this provision does not apply to access to traditional knowledge, for which the general ABS provisions, including the community PIC

---

53   Nagoya Protocol Article 26(4)(a). See this commentary on Article 26, section 2.

54   Greiber et al., *Explanatory Guide*, op. cit., 122.

55   Wilke, "A Healthy Look," op. cit., 133.

56   Greiber et al., *Explanatory Guide*, op. cit., 122 and fn. 8.

57   Wilke, "A Healthy Look," op. cit., 134–5. This provision may therefore embody a departure from the general bilateral ABS approach of the Protocol towards multilateral solutions (we are thankful to Riccardo Pavoni for drawing our attention to this point). Note that the need to couple expeditious access and expeditious benefit-sharing should be reflected also in other multilateral processes, such as under the WHO: Tvedt, "Beyond Nagoya," op. cit., 170–171.

58   Wilke, "A Healthy Look," op. cit., 134–5.

requirement,[59] apply also in case of a present or imminent health emergency. That being said, there might be situations in which a conflict arises between international human rights, i.e. the rights of indigenous and local communities over their traditional knowledge and the right to health of the general population.[60] Such situations may potentially lead to a permissible exception to the community PIC requirement as long as it is strictly necessary, solely for the purpose of securing due recognition and respect for the rights and freedoms of others, and is proportionate, determined by law, and non-discriminatory.[61]

4   Genetic Resources for Food and Agriculture

Article 8(c)[62] addresses the concern that most domestic ABS frameworks currently in existence do not sufficiently factor in the special characteristics of genetic resources for food and agriculture that are important to world food security.[63] The Protocol preamble also recognizes the 'special nature of agricultural biodiversity,[64] its *distinctive* features and problems needing *distinctive*

---

59   See this commentary on Article 7, section 2.

60   In an apocalyptic scenario, a case might arise where a specific indigenous or local community survives an epidemic using its traditional knowledge. Whether it would have to share such knowledge or not is an issue of balancing human rights-related considerations that could be addressed either by the international community or by a Party in its national legislation. See Lenzerini, "Indigenous Peoples' Cultural Rights," op. cit., 146.

61   UNDRIP Article 46(2) and Human Rights Council, "Report of the Special Rapporteur on indigenous peoples' rights," A/HRC/24/41, 32. We are grateful to Annalisa Savaresi for having drawn our attention to this point.

62   Originally proposed in the negotiations in the non-paper by the co-chairs of the Working Group on ABS of 19 March 2010, "Draft Protocol on Access to Genetic Resources and the Fair and Equitable Sharing of Benefits Arising from their Utilization to the Convention on Biological Diversity" (on file with the authors).

63   Gurdial Singh Nijar et al., *Framework Study on Food Security and Access and Benefit-Sharing for Genetic Resources for Food and Agriculture* (Kuala Lumpur: CEBLAW, 2009), accessed 30 November 2013, <www.planttreaty.org/sites/default/files/framework.pdf>; and CBD Decision 9/12, "Access and benefit-sharing" (9 October 2008) UN Doc UNEP/CBD/COP/9/29.

64   See the CBD programme of work on agricultural biodiversity: CBD Decision 3/11, "Conservation and sustainable use of agricultural biological diversity" (11 February 1997) UN Doc UNEP/CBD/COP/3/38; and COP Decision 5/5, "Agricultural biological diversity: review of phase I of the programme of work and adoption of a multi-year work programme" (22 June 2000) UN Doc UNEP/CBD/COP/5/23, Annex. See also Greiber et al., *Explanatory Guide*, op. cit., 52.

solutions,'[65] and more generally the importance of genetic resources for food security and for climate change mitigation and adaptation.[66] The international community, however, is still seeking consensus on the exact determination of these distinctive features.[67] Nevertheless, for the purposes of understanding the rationale of this provision, it can be pointed out that some of the most important distinguishing characteristics include, first, that genetic resources for food and agriculture are to a large extent the result of human activity and intense transfrontier exchanges from time immemorial. As a result, no country is self-sufficient with regard to genetic resources for food and agriculture – in contrast, all countries depend on genetic resources originating from

---

65   Nagoya Protocol 15th preambular recital, emphasis added. This language was inspired by CGRFA Resolution 18/2009, "Policies and arrangements for access and benefit-sharing for genetic resources for food and agriculture," paragraph 3 (transmitted to the attention of the Protocol negotiations as "Extract from the report of the twelfth regular session of the Commission on Genetic Resources for Food and Agriculture, Rome, 19–23 October 2009" (11 November 2009) UN Doc UNEP/CBD/WG-ABS/8/INF/7): 'The CGRFA invites the Conference of the Parties of the Convention on Biological Diversity and its Ad Hoc Open-ended Working Group on Access and Benefit-sharing, to *take into account the special nature of agricultural biodiversity, in particular genetic resources for food and agriculture, their distinctive features, and problems needing distinctive solutions*; in developing policies they might consider sectoral approaches which allow for differential treatment of different sectors or subsectors of genetic resources, different genetic resources for food and agriculture, different activities or purposes for which they are carried out,' emphasis added.

66   Nagoya Protocol 16th preambular recital. On CGRFA and climate change, see CGRFA, "Roadmap on climate change and genetic resources for food and agriculture" (2013) CGRFA-14/13/5 and CGRFA, "Selected processes and initiatives on climate change of relevance to genetic resources for food and agriculture" (2013) CGRFA-14/13/Inf.10.

67   CGRFA, "Report of the fourteenth regular session," paragraph 40(x) and Appendix E, where the FAO Commission on Genetic Resources for Food and Agriculture requests the Secretary to develop explanatory notes to the distinctive features of CGRFA, taking into account the specificities of the different sub-sectors, for consideration by CGRFA 15, while acknowledging the need to further refine the list of distinctive features and to focus on the utilization of CGRFA; and an appended list of distinctive features of CGRFA requiring specific solutions for ABS, which focuses on: the role of CGRFA for food security; the role of human management; international exchange and independence; the nature of innovation processes; holders and users of CGRFA; CGRFA exchange practices; and benefits generated with the use of CGRFA. The list contains the indication that the features are distinctive, but not necessarily unique to CGRFA, although the specific combination of the listed features distinguishes CGRFA from most other genetic resources.

somewhere else.[68] It is therefore difficult to distinguish between provider and user countries when it comes to agricultural biodiversity. Furthermore, the genetic erosion in the food and agriculture sector comes as a result of under-utilization rather than over-exploitation.[69] The survival of genetic resources for food and agriculture depends on the active cooperation among all stake-holders involved in their conservation, breeding, sustainable utilization and benefit-sharing, which includes dynamic management by farmers, pastoral-ists, and indigenous and local communities.[70] Finally, it is important to note that most products derived from genetic resources for food and agriculture can themselves be used both as a biological resource (for production and trade) and as genetic resources (for research and development).[71]

Against this background, it should be recalled that the International Treaty on Plant Genetic Resources for Food and Agriculture is considered as a special-ized ABS instrument under the Protocol. Therefore, the plant genetic resources under the Treaty's Multilateral System are excluded from the Protocol's scope when they are used for food and feed purposes.[72] As a result, Article 8(c) could apply to the development and implementation of national ABS frame-works covering plant genetic resources for food and agriculture, not included in ITPGRFA Annex I,[73] and other genetic resources for food and agriculture, including animal, aquatic, forest and microbial genetic resources.[74] In addi-tion, Article 8(c) is particularly important for Protocol Parties that are not Parties to the ITPGRFA.[75] Arguably, ITPGRFA Annex I plant genetic resources *not* used for food and feed purposes, but used for instance for pharmaceutical and cosmetic research and development, would fall under the general Protocol

---

68   CGRFA Resolution 18/2009, 3rd preambular paragraph. See Tsioumani, "International Treaty on Plant Genetic Resources," op. cit., 122.

69   Chiarolla, Louafi and Schloen, "Analysis of the Relationship," op. cit., 84–86.

70   CGRFA Resolution 18/2009, 4th preambular paragraph.

71   See this commentary on Article 2, section 2.2.2.

72   See this commentary on Article 4, section 4.1. Similarly to Article 8(b), Article 8(c) may also embody a departure from the general bilateral ABS approach of the Protocol towards multilateral solutions. We are thankful to Riccardo Pavoni for drawing our attention to this point.

73   In cases of countries of origin or when the material was acquired in accordance with the CBD, this differentiated treatment could include the voluntary use of the ITPGRFA SMTA for transfer of non-Annex I material. See also this commentary on Article 4, fn. 99.

74   Greiber et al., *Explanatory Guide*, op. cit., 124.

75   The ITPGRFA has 131 Parties: "The International Treaty on Plant Genetic Resources for Food and Agriculture," ITPGRFA, accessed 30 November 2013, <www.planttreaty.org/list_of_countries>.

provisions and not Article 8(c), as in this case food security considerations are not relevant.

With a notably weak formulation, Parties are thereby required to 'consider the importance' of these resources and their 'special role for food security.' As opposed to the previous provisions in Article 8, therefore, the Protocol does not necessarily require the adoption of any specific measures in this regard or even the identification of possible ways to implement the provision. Nonetheless, it creates the regulatory space for Parties to differentiate ABS concerning genetic resources for food and agriculture from other genetic resources, with a view to striking a balance between fostering and preserving patterns of use, exchange and benefit-sharing adapted for the food and agricultural sectors, on the one hand, and preventing such specialized ABS measures from being abused to circumvent users' benefit-sharing obligations, on the other hand.[76] In that regard, it remains unclear whether Protocol Parties which are not countries of origin may allow for facilitated access to genetic resources for food and agriculture in their ex situ collections without the consent of the country of origin or the country that had acquired the material in accordance with the CBD.

Finally, it should be noted that traditional knowledge is not mentioned in this provision, whereas genetic resources are explicitly referred to. Although it could be inferred from a textual interpretation that the provision does not apply to traditional knowledge in the food and agriculture sector, it should be taken into account that traditional knowledge in this area is practically *embodied* in the genetic resources themselves, the landraces and varieties developed by farmers in the field and on the basis of continuous exchanges of genetic material and breeding techniques. Therefore, a preferable interpretation would allow for a differentiated treatment in national ABS frameworks of farmers' varieties, as genetic resources embody traditional knowledge, and the customary exchanges that allow for their development.[77]

---

76   Chiarolla, Louafi and Schloen, "Analysis of the Relationship," op. cit., 100–101.

77   See also Nagoya Protocol Article 12(4) and this commentary on Article 12, section 5.

Article 9. Contribution to Conservation and Sustainable Use

> The Parties shall encourage users and providers to direct benefits arising from the utilization of genetic resources towards the conservation of biological diversity and the sustainable use of its components.

1 Overview

This provision[1] aims to ensure a coherent interpretation and integrative implementation of the CBD three objectives in the context of the Nagoya Protocol, by placing an obligation on Parties to encourage individual users and providers to direct benefits arising from the utilization of genetic resources towards conservation and sustainable use.

The obligation may not appear very demanding, as Article 9 limits itself to require Parties to 'encourage', but not necessarily to 'ensure,' directing benefits to conservation and sustainable use, or adopt specific measures in this regard. Arguably, it may simply be interpreted as an obligation for Parties to create incentives to that end, but not necessarily enshrining such incentives in domestic law. Nonetheless, Parties could possibly be found in non-compliance with this obligation if, for instance, their domestic ABS frameworks (or other relevant legislation)[2] created obstacles or disincentives, or made it otherwise impossible, for private users and providers to direct benefits towards conservation and sustainable use. To that extent, it cannot be excluded that compliance

---

1 Note that this is one of the provisions that was not subject to textual negotiation: it was first incorporated in the Cali Draft, draft article 7 and remained unchanged until the very end of the negotiation in Nagoya, when the final words '... direct benefits arising from the utilization of genetic resources towards the conservation and sustainable use of *biological diversity in support of the objectives of the Convention*' were replaced by '*its components*' (emphasis added).

2 Young identifies a series of domestic laws that will affect the effective functioning of domestic ABS frameworks, such as general environmental law, social-welfare law, property law, administrative law, commercial law, contract law, etc.: Young, "An International Cooperation Perspective," op. cit., 462–463.

© KONINKLIJKE BRILL NV, LEIDEN, 2014 | DOI 10.1163/9789004217188_011

with this provision could be assessed under the Protocol's compliance mechanisms and procedures.[3]

The following sections will discuss the contribution of Article 9 to the coherent interpretation of the three CBD objectives, the means for this provision's implementation, and questions arising from Article 9 in relation to indigenous and local communities.

2 Contribution to a Coherent Interpretation of the Three CBD Objectives

Article 9 encapsulates the idea that ABS can function as a source of funding or non-monetary incentives for the achievement of the other two objectives of the Convention at the level of individual providers and users of genetic resources.[4] It has been suggested that Article 9 aims to address real-life situations in which users and providers may not have an interest in, or be aware of, conservation and sustainable use efforts in need of support.[5] That being said, Article 9 should be read in conjunction with Article 1, which makes the Convention's first and second objectives part and parcel of the Protocol's objective of fair and equitable benefit-sharing.[6] Parties should therefore take this obligation seriously with a view to effectively contributing to the realization of the Protocol's objective.

It can also be noted that Article 9 can be seen as a complement to the possible establishment of a global multilateral benefit-sharing mechanism, through which benefits arising in specific circumstances[7] will be directed to support conservation and sustainable use globally.[8] In comparison, Article 9 applies to a significantly wider range of circumstances (as it covers potentially any instance of ABS transaction related to genetic resources), and it focuses on the

---

3 See *contra* Wolff, "Nagoya Protocol and the Diffusion," op. cit., 136. See this commentary on Article 30.

4 The idea was already reflected in the Bonn Guidelines, paragraph 48, last sentence, which reads: 'Benefits should be directed in such a way as to promote conservation and sustainable use of biological diversity.' See comments on Article 9 in this regard by Wolff, "Nagoya Protocol and the Diffusion," op. cit., 134.

5 Greiber et al., *Explanatory Guide*, op. cit., 125.

6 See this commentary on Article 1, section 4.

7 Namely, benefits arising from the use of genetic resources and traditional knowledge that occur in transboundary situations (see also this commentary on Article 11), or for which it is not possible to grant or obtain PIC.

8 See this commentary on Article 10, section 4.

private relations between individual users and providers, rather than on the relations between Parties to the Protocol.

3   Means of Implementation

The wording of Article 9 leaves a wide margin of discretion to Parties in choosing the specific means through which to implement their obligation. This therefore opens the door for voluntary measures as well as regulatory approaches at the national level. On the one hand, therefore, individual Parties could limit themselves to implement Article 9 through the provision of capacity-building (as explicitly foreseen by the Protocol),[9] the deployment of awareness-raising activities,[10] the development of model contractual clauses,[11] or the encouragement of voluntary instruments.[12] On the other hand, national ABS legal frameworks could include a general obligation on users and providers to consider ways to contribute to conservation and sustainable use, more specific requirements or incentives in that regard, or specific mechanisms such as national funds.[13] National ABS laws could also implement this provision in the context of their rules on minimum requirements for MAT.[14] Bilaterally, Parties could also explore ways to encourage users and providers to contribute to conservation and sustainable use through technology transfer.[15] Finally, Parties could multilaterally engage in an exchange of ideas and experiences with regard to the implementation of Article 9 through the Protocol's governing body,[16] including on the basis of information that may be included in the future in the ABS Clearinghouse.[17] Implementation of Article 9 could also be discussed

---

9   Article 22(5)(h), See this commentary on Article 22.

10   See this commentary on Article 21: in particular, it could be argued that this is implicitly referred to in Article 21(a), which makes reference to Article 1 of the Protocol.

11   See this commentary on Article 19.

12   See this commentary on Article 20.

13   Singh Nijar "An Asian Developing Country's View," op. cit., 263; and Lago Candeira and Silvestri, "Challenges in the Implementation of the Nagoya Protocol," op. cit., 290.

14   Nagoya Protocol Article 6(3)(g). See this commentary on Article 6, section 7.

15   See this commentary on Article 23, where reference is made to enabling the development and strengthening of a sound and viable technological and scientific base for the attainment of the objectives of the CBD and the Nagoya Protocol.

16   Nagoya Protocol Article 26(4)(a). See this commentary on Article 26, section 2.

17   Greiber et al., *Explanatory Guide*, op. cit., 126. See this commentary on Article 14, sections 3–4.

by the Protocol's governing body in the context of its consideration of model contractual clauses and voluntary instruments.[18]

Article 9 does not specify whether preference should be accorded to monetary or non-monetary benefits, although elsewhere the Protocol specifically clarifies that both types of benefits are relevant in this regard. The Protocol's Annex, in fact, singles out special fees to be paid to a trust fund supporting conservation and sustainable use; and the transfer of technology, or access to scientific information, including biological inventories and taxonomic studies, that are relevant for conservation and sustainable use.[19]

4   Benefits for Indigenous and Local Communities

In case genetic resources are held by indigenous or local communities,[20] particular attention should be paid by Parties to encourage these communities as providers to direct benefits to conservation and sustainable use in a way that respects their entitlements under the Protocol in light of applicable international human rights law.[21] Thus, at a minimum, States should not unduly interfere with the terms of these communities' PIC, which may already express preference with regard to the channeling of benefits to specific uses that may be culturally appropriate in the specific instance and respect the objectives of the Protocol. In addition, States should implement Article 9 so as to actively contribute to channeling benefits towards indigenous or local communities' traditional practices that contribute to conservation and sustainable use, according to their preferences.[22]

It should be finally remarked that there is no reference to the sharing of benefits arising from the use of traditional knowledge in this provision. This may be motivated by the negotiators' desire to leave indigenous and local communities to decide on the direction of the benefits arising from the use of traditional knowledge without any State interference. It is worth recalling that numerous decisions adopted by the CBD COP have provided indications on how benefit-sharing from traditional knowledge should be operationalized,

---

18   Nagoya Protocol Articles 19(2) and 20(2).

19   Nagoya Protocol Annex, paragraphs 2(f) and (k). See this commentary on Article 5, section 6.

20   Nagoya Protocol Articles 5(2) and 6(2).

21   See Introduction to this commentary, section 4.

22   Human Rights Council, "Report of the Special Rapporteur on indigenous peoples' rights," A/HRC/24/41, paragraphs 75–77.

and some of them may be directly applicable in relations between individual providers and users.[23] This is the case of the integration of traditional knowledge and community concerns in management plans, the setting-up of benefit-sharing mechanisms when revenue is accrued by outside investors, the provision of livelihood-based mitigation and compensatory measures, payments for ecosystem services, as well as the re-investment of benefits in the protection of traditional knowledge and traditional sustainable practices.[24] These options seem to reflect the assumption that the maintenance of traditional knowledge, lifestyles and sustainable customary practices of indigenous and local communities already contribute to the conservation and sustainable use of biodiversity.

---

23   See Introduction to this commentary, section 3; and this commentary on Articles 5 and 7.
24   Morgera and Tsioumani, "Evolution of Benefit-Sharing," op. cit., 167–168 and sources cited therein.

Article 10. Global Multilateral Benefit-sharing Mechanism

Parties shall consider the need for and modalities of a global multilateral benefit-sharing mechanism to address the fair and equitable sharing of benefits derived from the utilization of genetic resources and traditional knowledge associated with genetic resources that occur in transboundary situations or for which it is not possible to grant or obtain prior informed consent. The benefits shared by users of genetic resources and traditional knowledge associated with genetic resources through this mechanism shall be used to support the conservation of biological diversity and the sustainable use of its components globally.

1   Overview

In the context of the mainly bilateral ABS system set up by the Nagoya Protocol, Article 10 refers to the possible creation of a *multilateral* benefit-sharing mechanism at the global level for two situations – transboundary situations or situations when it is not possible to grant or obtain PIC. To be considered as part of the exercise of national sovereignty over natural resources,[1] a multilateral benefit-sharing mechanism therefore would not be intended to replace the regulation of bilateral ABS transactions supported by the Protocol[2] but to supplement it. That is, it would be intended to address situations in which sovereignty is not clear[3] and thus the bilateral approach

---

1   CBD, "Report of the Expert Meeting on Article 10 of the Nagoya Protocol on Access and Benefit-Sharing," (19 September 2013) UN Doc UNEP/CBD/ABSEM-A10/1/3, paragraph 3. Compare with ITPGRFA Articles 10(1) and 10(2) which state that 'In the exercise of their sovereign rights [over plant genetic resources for food and agriculture], the Contracting Parties agree to establish a multilateral system, which is efficient, effective, and transparent, both to facilitate access to plant genetic resources for food and agriculture, and to share, in a fair and equitable way, the benefits arising from the utilization of these resources, on a complementary and mutually reinforcing basis.'

2   CBD, "Report of the Expert Meeting on Article 10," UNEP/CBD/ABSEM-A10/1/3, paragraph 4.

3   Dedeurwaerdere et al., "Governing Global Scientific Research Commons," op. cit., 418.

may not be feasible.[4] Potentially, the situations covered by Article 10 could apply to 'a very large percentage of the planet's genetic resources and traditional knowledge',[5] as a significant portion of genetic resources and traditional knowledge is shared by different countries.

It should be recalled from the outset that this provision was considered a compromise solution to the protracted debates during the negotiations on the scope of the Protocol.[6] The African Group had proposed the idea of a 'trust fund' for sharing the benefits arising from transactions that CBD Parties could not agree to include or exclude from the temporal and spatial scope of the Protocol – namely, acquisitions before the entry into force of the Protocol, notably in ex situ collections, and acquisitions from areas beyond national jurisdiction. The African proposal was argued on the rationale that users have a moral obligation to share benefits from new and continued uses of genetic resources and traditional knowledge accessed before the entry into force of the Protocol, and that benefits could be used to contribute to conservation and sustainable use efforts.[7] In the final hours of the negotiations of the Protocol, as part of its comprehensive compromise proposal, the Japanese COP Presidency introduced Article 10, which was never subject to formal negotiation.

It is noteworthy that the obligation created by Article 10 is of a purely procedural nature: it requires Parties to 'consider the need for and modalities' of a global multilateral benefit-sharing mechanism. It does not mandate Parties to establish such a mechanism and/or provide for a deadline to that end (as is the case, for instance, of the compliance procedures and mechanisms).[8] It could thus be argued that nothing in this Article prevents Parties from deciding against establishing such a mechanism, although the Protocol preamble stresses that 'an innovative solution *is required* to address the fair and equitable sharing of benefits derived from the utilization of genetic resources and traditional knowledge associated with genetic resources that occur in transboundary situations or for which it is not possible to grant or obtain prior informed consent.'[9] A decision against establishing a global benefit-sharing mechanism,

4   Ibid., 417; and Maria Julia Oliva, "The Implications of the Nagoya Protocol for the Ethical Sourcing of Biodiversity," in Morgera, Buck and Tsioumani, *2010 Nagoya Protocol on Access and Benefit-Sharing in Perspective*, op. cit., 381.

5   Young, "An International Cooperation Perspective," op. cit., 489.

6   Glowka and Normand, "The Nagoya Protocol on Access and Benefit-sharing," op. cit., 42–43; Elsa Tsioumani, "Access and Benefit Sharing: The Nagoya Protocol," *Environmental Policy and Law* 40 (2010): 288, 289. See this commentary on Article 3, section 3.

7   ENB 9/527, "Summary of the Resumed Ninth Meeting of the Working Group on ABS," 4–5.

8   See this commentary on Article 30.

9   Nagoya Protocol 13th preambular recital, emphasis added.

however, would be politically difficult to take, as it could be considered to undermine the trust between developed and developing country Parties under the Protocol.[10] In recognition of this situation, the CBD Conference of the Parties had decided to address Article 10 at the second meeting of the Intergovernmental Committee preparing for the entry into force of the Nagoya Protocol, which convened in April 2012.[11] Discussions in that forum highlighted the need for Parties to find common ground in interpreting the fairly open and laconic wording of Article 10 before making a decision on its establishment.[12] An intersessional process established to that end[13] attempted to explore questions raised by the provision and its linkages with other Protocol provisions in a non-negotiating setting.[14] It revealed, however, continued lack of common understanding on the scope of the provision, while participants acknowledged the need to 'build trust and enhance legal certainty and transparency for the situations covered in Article 10.'[15] In general terms, a narrow interpretation would point to genetic resources of unknown origin found in user countries' jurisdictions, for example in their ex situ collections; while a broader interpretation would also address genetic resources collected in areas beyond national jurisdiction or the Antarctic Treaty System area.[16]

---

10   ENB 9/579, "Summary of the Second Meeting of the Intergovernmental Committee for the Nagoya Protocol," 9, where the African Group is reported to have recalled the African Group's agreement to the Nagoya Protocol with the understanding that there would be future good-faith efforts to establish the mechanism. See also Elisa Morgera, "Second Meeting of the Intergovernmental Committee for the Nagoya Protocol on Access and Benefit-Sharing: Emerging Legal Questions," *Environmental Policy and Law* 42 (2012): 246.

11   CBD Decision 10/1, section B, paragraph 10.

12   ENB 9/579, "Summary of the Second Meeting of the Intergovernmental Committee for the Nagoya Protocol," 9 and 14, and Morgera, "Second Meeting of the ICNP," op. cit., 247.

13   See fn. 20 below.

14   For instance, if a Party decides to waive PIC under Article 6(1) or Article 8, could the relevant benefit-sharing obligations be met through a multilateral mechanism? And how would a multilateral mechanism be used in the case of genetic resources and traditional knowledge found in situ in transboundary areas, in view also of Article 11: see CBD, "Report of the Expert Meeting on Article 10," UNEP/CBD/ABSEM-A10/1/3, paragraph 4.

15   Ibid.

16   Dedeurwaerdere et al., "Governing Global Scientific Research Commons," op. cit., 418. See also ICNP, "A Report from the First Reflection Meeting on the Global Multilateral Benefit-Sharing Mechanism Submitted by the Fridtjof Nansen Institute," (10 January 2012) UN Doc UNEP/CBD/ICNP/2/INF/2, 7; and list of questions in CBD, "Report of the Expert Meeting," on Article 10," UNEP/CBD/ABSEM-A10/1/3, paragraph 5. As discussed in this commentary on Article 3, section 3.2 and fn. 32, for those arguing that genetic resources

2   The Need for a Multilateral Benefit-sharing Mechanism

Against this background, the following sub-sections will first discuss the two
situations in which a multilateral mechanism is envisaged to operate, which
inform current discussions on the *need* for its establishment. Attention will
then turn to the possible features of such a multilateral mechanism, as foreshadowed in Article 10, which will inform future discussion on the *modalities*
of the mechanism. A brief assessment of the possible contribution of Article 10
to the holistic implementation of the Convention in the context of ABS will
conclude this chapter.

2.1   *Transboundary Situations*
The first situation to which a potential multilateral benefit-sharing mechanism may apply is that of the utilization of genetic resources and of traditional
knowledge associated with genetic resources[17] that occur in 'transboundary
situations.' The latter expression could arguably cover two instances: 'an in situ
transboundary situation' in which genetic resources or traditional knowledge
have developed their special characteristics and are still found across borders
in natural circumstances; and 'an ex situ transboundary situation' in which
genetic resources or traditional knowledge are now found outside the habitats
where they developed their essential characteristics in more than one country.[18]
In the latter sense, it could be argued that Article 10 could cover situations in
which resources are accessed in situ but then 'become' transboundary because
of the need to share them among many researchers in different countries. In
microbial genetic resources, for instance, taxonomic type strains are deposited
in two different collections in two different countries.[19] In the former sense,
it remains to be clarified whether 'transboundary situations' would involve
countries sharing the same ecosystem, the same species (particularly in the
case of migratory species), or the same population of a species.[20] A future

---

in areas beyond national jurisdiction are outside the scope of the Protocol, this would
imply a decision to re-open the scope of the Protocol.

17   See this commentary on Article 2, section 3.

18   ICNP, "A Report from the First Reflection Meeting," UNEP/CBD/ICNP/2/INF/2, 6. Note,
however, that Article 11 only refers to in situ situations.

19   Dedeurwaerdere et al., "Governing Global Scientific Research Commons," op. cit., 418–419.

20   These questions have indeed been identified by CBD Parties as requiring further discussion
at the second meeting of the Intergovernmental Committee for the Nagoya Protocol,
which developed a roadmap for continuing discussions. The roadmap includes through
Secretariat-led consultations on the basis of an indicative list of questions prepared
by the Committee and the convening of an expert group to identify potential areas of

determination by the Protocol's governing body may be needed as to whether the mere occurrence of a species in two or more countries is sufficient for Article 10 to be triggered, and whether there is a need to distinguish situations in which only the genetic resources or only the traditional knowledge associated with those specific genetic resources is transboundary.[21]

A well-known case of traditional knowledge in a transboundary situation is that of the San peoples' knowledge of the hunger-suppressant properties of hoodia, which was shared by San communities in South Africa, Namibia, Angola and Botswana: eventually the San tribes formed a council to negotiate a benefit-sharing agreement among themselves.[22]

Another question that remains to be clarified is the relationship between Article 10 and Article 11 on 'transboundary cooperation,'[23] which covers situations where the same genetic resources are found in situ within the territory of more than one Party, and where the same traditional knowledge associated with genetic resources is shared by indigenous and local communities found in several Parties. When discussing the global multilateral benefit-sharing mechanism, Parties may clarify whether recourse to this mechanism is alternative, or a last resort, vis-à-vis transboundary cooperation called for under Article 11.[24]

2.2   Situations Where it is Not Possible to Grant or Obtain PIC

The second instance in which the potential multilateral benefit-sharing mechanism may come into play is that of the utilization of genetic resources and traditional knowledge associated with genetic resources 'for which it is not possible to grant or obtain PIC.' This laconic provision leaves the interpreter many options open. Arguably it could cover the following situations: genetic

---

common understanding and areas that could be further examined for consideration by a future meeting of the Committee or the Protocol governing body at its first meeting: Recommendation 2/3, "The need for and modalities of a global multilateral benefit-sharing mechanism (Article 10)," in ICNP, "Report of the second meeting," UNEP/CBD/COP/11/6, Annex, Part A, question 1 and Part B, questions 1–2.

21   ICNP, "A Report from the First Reflection Meeting," UNEP/CBD/COP/11/6, 10. As there may be significant genetic variety within species (as exemplified by the existence of subspecies, plant varieties and polymorphism), framing the discussion on species occurrence may be seen as inherently flawed: we are grateful to Geoff Burton for drawing our attention to this point.

22   Singh Nijar "An Asian Developing Country's View," op. cit., 261; and generally: Munyi and Jonas, "Implementing the Nagoya Protocol", op. cit.; and Wynberg, Schroeder and Chennells, Indigenous Peoples, Consent and Benefit Sharing, op. cit.

23   See this commentary on Article 11.

24   ICNP Recommendation 2/3, Annex, Part B, question 10.

resources accessed prior to the entry into force of the CBD and/or the Protocol; genetic resources of unknown origin held in ex situ collections; genetic resources accessed in areas beyond national jurisdiction; publicly available traditional knowledge of unknown origin;[25] or diffused traditional knowledge (traditional knowledge that is so widespread that it is no longer possible to attribute ownership to one or more indigenous and local communities).[26] Other issues under discussion relate to whether it could also cover benefit-sharing in cases PIC has been waived, or in the absence of a clear domestic framework on PIC.[27]

On the one hand, therefore, Parties will need to find agreement as to whether to interpret and operationalize Article 10 with a view to addressing certain questions related to its temporal and spatial scope that remain unclear under the Protocol,[28] notably questions related to ex situ collections holding material accessed before the entry into force of the Protocol,[29] materials in areas beyond national jurisdiction such as the high seas and the Area,[30] and publicly available traditional knowledge.[31]

In view of the mechanism's complementarity to the bilateral system established by the Protocol, several Parties have indicated their concern about the

---

25   ICNP, "A Report from the First Reflection Meeting," UNEP/CBD/ICNP/2/INF/2, 3.

26   Singh Nijar "An Asian Developing Country's View," op. cit., 261.

27   ICNP, "A Report from the First Reflection Meeting," UNEP/CBD/COP/11/6, 11; and CBD, "Report of the Expert Meeting on Article 10," UNEP/CBD/ABSEM-A10/1/3, paragraph 4. See this commentary on Article 6, section 2.

28   ICNP Recommendation 2/3, Annex, Part A, question 2 and Part B, questions 8–9. See this commentary on Article 3, section 3.2; and Dedeurwaerdere et al, "Governing Global Scientific Research Commons," op. cit., 418.

29   With regard to ex situ collections holding material acquired before the entry into force of the CBD (see this commentary on Article 3, Section 3.1), the multilateral benefit-sharing mechanism could prevent the 'chilling effect' that may derive from the exclusion of collections outside provider countries' jurisdictions from the Protocol's framework: that is, users may find it more convenient to use genetic resources in such collections rather than accessing them from a country of origin subject to the Protocol rules. Note that it has been suggested that in practice public-sector ex situ collections that do not differentiate between pre- and post-CBD/Nagoya Protocol accessions, have a 'moral duty for sharing benefits…via contributions to a funding system under Article 10': Biber-Klemm et al., "Governance options," op. cit., 225.

30   Salpin, "Law of the Sea," op. cit., 181–182, notes that 'Progress under the Protocol in regards of the global mechanism, or lack thereof, could sway discussions at the General Assembly [on marine biodiversity in areas beyond national jurisdiction, including on benefit-sharing form marine genetic resources] either way.'

31   See this commentary on Article 5, section 4.

need to ensure that any multilateral benefit-sharing mechanism does not undermine national sovereignty and would only be used when there is no *real* possibility to obtain PIC,[32] therefore implying a requirement for due diligence by users to actively seek PIC before resorting to the multilateral mechanism.[33] In addition, a question remains about how to ensure that a multilateral mechanism does not represent a disincentive for the implementation of the bilateral system of the Protocol.[34] Countries may be skeptical of the need to establish any multilateral mechanism, as users may find it easier to go to a global entity than to engage in bilateral negotiations. Such recourse would have the disadvantage for provider countries that the benefits to be shared, according to the letter of the provision, would be used to support biodiversity conservation and sustainable use *globally* rather than to their own advantage.[35]

That being said, in situations where resources are shared amongst several countries or where a clear distinction between provider and user countries is not so obvious, a bilateral approach to ABS would not reward all those who have contributed to the conservation of a specific genetic resource, particularly when these have greater needs and less capacity. In these cases, a multilateral approach (especially when associated to transnational cooperation) may be more efficient than a bilateral one and the main benefits are non-monetary: there is an overall gain for all concerned Parties in working jointly towards the conservation of the same resources and sharing information about it.[36]

3   Features of a Global Benefit-sharing Mechanism

Article 10 is quite laconic about the possible feature of the multilateral benefit-sharing mechanism, although the Protocol preamble indicates the need for an 'innovative' solution to the two situations identified under Article 10.[37] The choice of the term 'mechanism' may exclude the creation of a 'fund', so as to allow the sharing of not only monetary but also non-monetary benefits.[38] In that regard, the mechanism could serve as a platform for the

---

32   ICNP Recommendation 2/3, Annex, Part B, question 7.

33   See also this commentary on Article 6, section 3.

34   ICNP Recommendation 2/3, Annex, Part B, question 11.

35   See Dedeurwaerdere et al., "Governing Global Scientific Research Commons," op. cit., 418.

36   We are grateful to Sélim Louafi for drawing our attention to this point.

37   Nagoya Protocol 13th preambular recital.

38   ICNP, "A Report from the First Reflection Meeting," UNEP/CBD/ICNP/2/INF/2, 3.

exchange of information and technology transfer, as well as for the sharing of monetary benefits.[39]

It is also noteworthy that Article 10 focuses on 'benefits shared by *users* through the mechanism,' rather than by Parties or 'user countries.' It can therefore provide a specific way to operationalize the Protocol's general clause encouraging users and providers to direct benefits arising from the utilization of genetic resources towards conservation and sustainable use.[40] From the perspective of the private sector, Article 10 can therefore be seen as an acknowledgement of the need for further discussion on specific, proactive tools to facilitate the operationalization of benefit-sharing in the face of complex or unclear international obligations.[41] The multilateral mechanism could also create an opportunity for private companies to voluntarily apply ABS *principles* derived from the Protocol *beyond its legal obligations*. In other words, private users may decide to share benefits even if no international or domestic requirements are in place to that end, such as in the case of publicly available traditional knowledge or pre-CBD accessions,[42] because of ethical, corporate accountability or marketing reasons.[43]

Article 10 is, on the whole, silent on the governance of the multilateral mechanism: who would be managing the mechanism and decide about the allocation of benefits? It may be expected that the Protocol's governing body would be in charge of the mechanism, but the text of the Protocol leaves it open to Parties to decide otherwise. A related question is whether contributions to the mechanism would be mandatory or voluntary.[44] It has been argued that if the mechanism is established through a (formally non-binding) decision of the Protocol's governing body, the provision of benefits to the mechanism

---

39   Oliva, "Implications of the Nagoya Protocol," op. cit., 382. Compare with the platform for the co-development and transfer of technologies, an initiative developed in the framework of the Funding Strategy of the ITPGRFA by a group of institutions with expertise of various relevant types of technologies, for the benefit of small-scale farmers in developing countries. See ITPGRFA Governing Body, "Reports of meetings on the establishment of a platform for the co-development and transfer of technology," (24–28 September 2013) FAO Doc IT/GB-5/13/Inf.16.

40   See this commentary on Article 9, sections 1 and 3.

41   Oliva, "Implications of the Nagoya Protocol," op. cit., 381.

42   See this commentary on Article 6.

43   Oliva, "Implications of the Nagoya Protocol," op. cit., 381. This is indeed a question that will be considered by CBD Parties: see ICNP Recommendation 2/3, Annex, Part B, question 18.

44   ICNP Recommendation 2/3, Annex, Part B, question 17.

would also be of a voluntary nature.[45] The Protocol's governing body could, however, decide to amend the Protocol with a view to establishing a global benefit-sharing mechanism with legally binding features. Entry into force of such amendment would then require ratification by a sufficient number of Parties to the Protocol.[46]

In deciding the features of the multilateral benefit-sharing mechanism, Parties may likely consider other relevant existing international processes and instruments,[47] such as the benefit-sharing regime for the mineral resources in the Area, under the UN Convention on the Law of the Sea,[48] or the Global Mechanism established under the UN Convention to Combat Desertification.[49] The most prominent source of inspiration, however, would likely be the Multilateral System of Access and Benefit-sharing established under the ITPGRFA.[50]

Benefits shared under the Multilateral System include non-monetary ones, such as exchange of information, access to and transfer of technology, capacity building, as well as monetary benefits arising from commercialization. The latter is done through standard payments by the users of material accessed from the Multilateral System, according to the provisions of the standard Material Transfer Agreement, adopted by the ITPGRFA Governing Body.[51] Such payments, together with voluntary donations, are directed to the Treaty's benefit-sharing fund, which allocates funds under the direction of the ITPGRFA Governing Body, to particular activities designed to support farmers in developing countries conserve crop diversity in their fields, and assist farmers and

---

45   See Buck and Hamilton, "Nagoya Protocol," op. cit., 59; and Dedeurwaerdere et al., "Governing Global Scientific Research Commons," op. cit., 418.

46   In accordance with CBD Article 29.

47   ICNP Recommendation 2/3, Annex, Part A, question 7.

48   UNCLOS Part XI and 1994 Agreement: Salpin, "Law of the Sea," op. cit., 182; and Young, "An International Cooperation Perspective," op. cit., 490. See also David Kenneth Leary, *International Law and the Genetic Resources of the Deep Sea* (Leiden: Martinus Nijhoff, 2007), 179.

49   UN Convention to Combat Desertification in Countries Experiencing Serious Drought and/or Desertification, Particularly in Africa (Paris, 14 October 1994, in force 26 December 1996) 1954 UNTS 3, Article 21(4). Young, "An International Cooperation Perspective," op. cit., 490.

50   ITPGRFA Article 10. See Tsioumani, "International Treaty on Plant Genetic Resources," op. cit., 121; and Cooper, "The International Treaty on Plant Genetic Resources for Food and Agriculture," op. cit., 4. See also this commentary on Article 4, section 3.1.

51   ITPGRFA Governing Body Resolution 2/2006; SMTA Articles 6(7) and 6(11); and this commentary on Article 4, fn. 93.

breeders globally adapt crops to changing needs and demands. Mandatory payments, however, seem to be taking even longer than initially expected to materialize.[52] Despite two project cycles funded under the benefit-sharing fund, benefit-sharing seems to be lagging behind as a whole in comparison to facilitated access under the Multilateral System. As a result, Parties to the Treaty have recently decided to establish an intersessional process tasked to develop a range of measures that will increase user-based payments and contributions to the benefit-sharing fund in a sustainable and predictable long-term manner, as well as enhance the functioning of the Treaty's Multilateral System by additional measures.[53]

This recognized shortcoming in a system already operational for several years indicates that operationalization of Article 10 would be a challenging task. In addition, there are fundamental differences between the Nagoya Protocol and the International Treaty that will limit the opportunities for Parties to draw on the Multilateral System for inspiration. First of all, the ITPGRFA Multilateral System is a comprehensive system for ABS, of which the Benefit-sharing Fund is only a part, and addresses one specific sector only of genetic resources. Second, the Multilateral System in effect largely consolidated the operation of a pre-existing network of research centers under the Consultative Group on International Agricultural Research (CGIAR),[54] whereas the Nagoya Protocol would start from scratch.[55] Third, benefits under the Multilateral System should be directed to farmers in all countries, albeit *especially in developing countries and countries with economies in transition*,[56] whereas under the Nagoya Protocol mechanism, benefits would be directed to the conservation and sustainable use of biodiversity *globally*.[57]

---

52   See Nina I. Moeller and Clive Stannard, *Identifying Benefit Flows, Studies on the Potential Monetary and Nonmonetary Benefits Arising from the International Treaty on Plant Genetic Resources for Food and Agriculture* (Rome: FAO, 2013), accessed 30 November 2013, <www.planttreaty.org/content/identifying-benefit-flows>.

53   ITPGRFA Governing Body Resolution 2/2013 Implementation of the Funding Strategy of the International Treaty (2013). Part IV: Terms of Reference for the Ad Hoc Open-Ended Working Group to Enhance the Functioning of the Multilateral System of Access and Benefit-Sharing.

54   Young, "An International Cooperation Perspective," op. cit., 490.

55   Ibid.

56   See ITPGRFA Article 13(3).

57   Greiber et al., *Explanatory Guide*, op. cit., 130. See further discussion in this regard in section 4 below.

4   Promoting a Coherent Interpretation of the Three CBD Objectives

As already discussed,[58] the Nagoya Protocol promotes a coherent interpretation and integrative implementation of the three CBD objectives in the context of ABS. Article 10 further contributes to this end, by clearly making the objective of the global multilateral benefit-sharing mechanism that of supporting the conservation of biodiversity and the sustainable use of its components globally. If established, the multilateral fund might therefore be another source of funding and non-monetary benefits, together with the voluntary efforts of users and providers under Article 9, for the conservation and sustainable use of biodiversity.[59]

It should be emphasized, however, that by making reference to 'globally,' Article 10 refrains from directing benefits to countries of origin, exclusively or specifically, which could have a 'life-changing impact' on ABS under the Protocol.[60] In that regard, Parties will be well advised to ensure that the procedure for the allocation of benefits aims to recognize local contributions to conservation and sustainable use, reaching those countries and indigenous and local communities that made it possible for genetic resources and/or traditional knowledge to be used.[61] In devising the allocation method, lessons learnt in the context of the ITPGRFA Multilateral System could be taken into account, including the eligibility criteria for applying for funding, and identified priorities such as the focus on smallholder farmers and climate change adaptation

---

58   See this commentary on Article 1, section 4; Article 5, section 5; Article 8, section 2; and Article 9, section 2.

59   This may possibly contribute to make the Protocol, to some extent, a type of an 'innovative financial mechanism.' Note, however, that discussion of 'innovative financial mechanisms' for biodiversity conservation and sustainable use have been very controversial in the CBD processes: for instance, CBD COP 10 considered the creation of a 'green development fund' modelled after the Clean Development Mechanism to reward trade-certified 'land areas managed in compliance with the CBD,' in accordance with the requirements for offsets and restoration for the private sector. The proposal, however, encountered the opposition of developing countries, which wished to ensure that innovative financial mechanisms would supplement, and not replace, public funding under the CBD's financial mechanism. The other draft text on innovative financial mechanisms was withdrawn altogether during the final plenary: see ENB 9/544, "Summary of the Tenth Conference of the Parties to the Convention on Biological Diversity," 13. See comments in Morgera and Tsioumani, "Yesterday, Today, and Tomorrow," op. cit., 26–29. In the absence of a definition, it can be argued that the expression 'innovative financial mechanism' only applies to market-based mechanisms.

60   Young, "An International Cooperation Perspective," op. cit., 489–90.

61   Oliva, "Implications of the Nagoya Protocol," op. cit., 382.

needs.[62] That being said, there appears to be limitations to the project-based approach currently followed by the Treaty, which may be seen as introducing a competitive logic into a global cooperative framework and which may not be necessarily effective in fulfilling benefit-sharing expectations at national and local levels.[63] Attention would therefore be drawn on devising a global mechanism that is inclusive and does not disadvantage stakeholders who are less equipped to obtain the benefits generated at the global level.[64]

---

62   ICNP, "A Report from the First Reflection Meeting," UNEP/CBD/ICNP/2/INF/2, 14. For information on the ITPGRFA benefit-sharing fund, see "The Benefit-Sharing Fund," ITPGRFA, accessed 30 November 2013, <www.planttreaty.org/content/benefit-sharing-fund>. The list of projects approved under the first project cycle, see: "Projects under the Benefit-Sharing Fund (2009–2011) – 1st Call," ITPGRFA, accessed 30 November 2013, <www.planttreaty.org/content/projects-2009-2011>; and under the second one: "Call for Proposals 2010–2011," ITPGRFA, accessed 30 November 2013, <www.planttreaty.org/content/call-proposals-2010-2011>.

63   Sélim Louafi, "Reflections on the Resource Allocation Strategy of the Benefit Sharing Fund" (paper for the fifth meeting of the Governing Body of the International Treaty on Plant Genetic Resources for Food and Agriculture; Bern: Swiss Federal Office for Agriculture, 2013).

64   We are grateful to Sélim Louafi for drawing our attention to this point.

Article 11. Transboundary Cooperation

1. In instances where the same genetic resources are found *in situ* within the territory of more than one Party, those Parties shall endeavor to cooperate, as appropriate, with the involvement of indigenous and local communities concerned, where applicable, with a view to implementing this Protocol.

2. Where the same traditional knowledge associated with genetic resources is shared by one or more indigenous and local communities in several Parties, those Parties shall endeavor to cooperate, as appropriate, with the involvement of the indigenous and local communities concerned, with a view to implementing the objective of this Protocol.

1   Overview

Article 11 identifies two instances in which transboundary cooperation is required, at least as a best-endeavor effort: when the same genetic resources are found in the territory of more than one country; and when the same traditional knowledge is shared by indigenous and local communities located in several Parties. This is an acknowledgment of the complexities that will be faced in implementing the mainly bilateral ABS approach embodied in the Nagoya Protocol, in particular in consideration of the fact that several genetic resources and traditional knowledge are shared among different Parties. One of the best-known ABS transactions, in fact, involved the San peoples' knowledge of the hunger-suppressant properties of hoodia, which was shared by San communities in South Africa, Namibia, Angola and Botswana.[1]

Although similarly worded, the two provisions contained in Article 11 are based on different legal concepts. Transboundary cooperation related to genetic resources is based on the notion of sovereign rights of States over genetic resources and establishes a duty to endeavor to cooperate in instances where the same genetic resources are found in situ under the jurisdiction of more than one Party. It also foresees a role for indigenous and local communities

---

1   Singh Nijar "An Asian Developing Country's View," op. cit., 261; and generally: Munyi and Jonas, "Implementing the Nagoya Protocol," op. cit.; and Wyndberg, Schroeder and Chennels, *Indigenous Peoples, Consent and Benefit-sharing*, op. cit.

in case the genetic resources at stake are 'held' by these communities.[2] Article 11(1) thus specifically concerns countries of origin of genetic resources. Transboundary cooperation related to traditional knowledge, on the other hand, reflects the obligation of States under international law to protect the rights of indigenous and local communities over their traditional knowledge, which extends to inter-State cooperation with the involvement of the communities concerned.

Both obligations aim to address the concern about a possible competition for benefits in the development and implementation of national ABS frameworks to attract potential users interested in obtaining access to the same genetic resource or the same traditional knowledge that are present in different Parties.[3] The two obligations will be analyzed in turn below, after having commented on their common features in terms of the obligation to cooperate.

2   Obligation to Cooperate

The duty of international cooperation has never been defined internationally, but is understood as the obligation for States to *enter into coordinated action* under a legal regime so as to achieve its specific goal.[4] As opposed to an obligation of solidarity,[5] each State is expected to benefit from the cooperative relationship in a direct and concrete manner.[6] In both cases addressed by Article 11, the obligation to cooperate is qualified: it requires States to 'endeavor to cooperate, as appropriate.' The Protocol, therefore, does not require Parties to reach agreement on joint PIC and MAT.[7] It rather requires Parties to exert

---

2   Nagoya Protocol Articles 5(2) and 6(2). See this commentary on Articles 5, section 3, and 6, section 4.

3   See proposal of operational text on benefit-sharing by Namibia on behalf of the African Group in CBD Working Group on ABS, "Collation of Operative Text submitted," UNEP/CBD/ WG-ABS/7/4, 15, paragraphs 5–6. Greiber et al., *Explanatory Guide*, op. cit., 133.

4   Rüdiger Wolfrum, "Cooperation, International Law of," in Wolfrum, *Max Planck Encyclopedia*, op. cit., paragraph 2; and particularly in the case of international environmental law, paragraphs 28–31.

5   Discussed in this commentary on Articles 22–25.

6   Danilo Campanelli, "Solidarity, Principle of," in Wolfrum, *Max Planck Encyclopedia*, op. cit., paragraph 12.

7   The Permanent Court of International Justice has stated that 'an obligation to negotiate does not imply an obligation to reach agreement': Permanent Court of International Justice, *Railway Traffic between Lithuania and Poland*, Advisory Opinion (15 October 1931), 116. We are grateful to James Harrison for a useful exchange of ideas on this matter.

good-faith efforts to identify potentially concerned Parties and engage them with a view to reaching agreement on coordinated action.[8] The choice of the *means* to identify and engage other concerned States is left to each Party ('as appropriate'). But lack of *any reasonable* effort to identify and engage potentially concerned States would be in violation of this due diligence obligation. If agreement cannot be reached, Article 11 does not impede States from making unilateral decisions, but it creates the expectation that such decisions will be made taking in consideration other States' and, where relevant, indigenous and local communities' interests, in realizing the objective of the Protocol.[9] Article 11 may also entail the obligation for Parties to address persistent or recurring difficulties in implementing this provision by progressively developing the legal regime established by the Nagoya Protocol,[10] through its governing body.[11]

Article 11 does not specify which types of measures Parties should consider in transboundary cooperation. The purpose of such measures is, however, 'implementing this Protocol',[12] so transboundary cooperation arguably extends to access, benefit-sharing and compliance.[13] This could include collaboration to document existing genetic resources within the jurisdiction of cooperating Parties; establish joint facilities for deciding on access requests; engage in

---

8   International Tribunal on the Law of the Sea (ITLOS), *Southern Bluefin Tuna* (*New Zealand v. Japan; Australia v. Japan*), Order (27 August 1999), 280, paragraph 90(1)(e).

9   See this commentary on Article 1.

10   Wolfrum, "Cooperation," op. cit., paragraph 28.

11   Nagoya Protocol Article 16(4)(a). See this commentary on Article 26, section 2.

12   It remains unclear why Article 11 seems to establish two slightly different aims for transboundary cooperation: in the case of cooperation over shared genetic resources, cooperation is aimed to implement the Protocol in its entirety, whereas in the case of shared traditional knowledge, cooperation is specifically targeting the objective of the Protocol (Article 1). In particular, the aim of the cooperation effort under Article 11(2) is not to implement the Protocol *tout court*, but only to implement its objective. Given the close relationship between Article 11(2) and the obligation of Parties under Articles 7 and 12, this seems illogical; not least, since traditional knowledge is not referred to in Article 1 of the Nagoya Protocol. The limiting reference to 'implementing the objective of this Protocol' rather than to 'implementing this Protocol' thus appears as a drafting oversight, that might be explained by the fact that Parties closed negotiations on Article 11(2) already in July 2010, when all the main substantive issues and related draft articles under negotiation, in particular those on traditional knowledge, were still unresolved. Compare draft article 8 in Cali Draft and in Montreal I draft.

13   Transboundary cooperation is in the latter sense a sub-set of the cooperation obligation in relation to alleged violations of domestic ABS frameworks under Article 15(3). See this commentary on Article 15, section 5.

capacity building in neighboring Parties; establish common benefit-sharing mechanisms; and undertake joint compliance and enforcement initiatives. To provide an example, the 1996 Andean Community regime on genetic resources created a committee tasked with promoting management, monitoring, and control of access authorizations relating to genetic resources and their derivatives that exist in two or more member countries.[14] The conclusion of bilateral and regional agreements can also be envisaged to implement Article 11,[15] and could result in the establishment of future specialized ABS agreements.[16]

As already discussed,[17] the relationship between Article 11 and the 'transboundary situations' that may fall under a future multilateral benefit-sharing system under Article 10 is still to be clarified by Parties. So it may be expected that the interpretation of Article 11, and particularly the role of transboundary cooperation and its limitations vis-à-vis a possible multilateral benefit-sharing mechanism, will be clarified by the Protocol's governing body[18] in the context of negotiations under Article 10. In that connection, it may be worth noting that Article 11 does not provide guidance as to benefit-sharing specifically, whereas Article 10 requires allocating benefits to conservation and sustainable use globally: this difference may contribute to create an incentive for Parties to exhaust all possible means for transboundary cooperation with a view to obtaining arising benefits.[19]

It can also be expected that certain institutions established at the international level under the Nagoya Protocol can support Parties in implementing Article 11. Information on the ABS Clearinghouse[20] and instances of alleged non-compliance arising in the context of the Protocol's compliance procedures and mechanisms[21] may facilitate the identification of situations requiring transboundary cooperation.

---

14   Andean Community, Common Regime on Access to Genetic Resources (Decision 391, 2 July 1996, in force 17 July 1996), Article 51; cited in Greiber et al., *Explanatory Guide*, op. cit., 134.

15   Young, "An International Cooperation Perspective," op. cit., 496.

16   See this commentary on Article 4, section 3.

17   See this commentary on Article 10, section 3.

18   Nagoya Protocol Article 26(4)(a). See this commentary on Article 26, section 2.

19   Dedeurwaerdere et al., "Governing Global Scientific Research Commons," op. cit., 419.

20   See this commentary on Article 14, sections 3–4.

21   See this commentary on Article 30.

3   Transboundary Cooperation Concerning Genetic Resources

Parties are obliged to make a best-endeavor effort to cooperate in the Protocol's implementation in instances where more than one Party is the country of origin of genetic resources. The provision is, however, silent on how to establish that such situations exist. It remains to be seen how a Party can determine that the 'same genetic resource' is at stake. When are two or more Parties to be considered countries of origin of the same genetic resource?[22] Does the gene sequence need to be identical? Or mainly identical? Or only identical as regards genes that have expressed themselves in the organism under consideration? It seems to be excluded that Article 11 would bind all Parties within the geographical range of the 'species' whose genetic resources are utilized. Rather, as the 'genetic resources' utilized in research and development are frequently not present in all populations within a species, Article 11(1) may apply only when the *populations* of a species in these territories share the specific genetic or biochemical characteristics utilized.[23] It has been noted that, from a scientific perspective, only plant genetic resources can be found in more than one country, because they can be characterized by great genetic stability, whereas microbial strains within the same species are not the same, and animal genetic resources may present differences from one individual to another within the same breed.[24] As these questions were not discussed during the negotiation of the Protocol, some clarification by the Protocol's governing body would seem essential for operationalizing Article 11.

One possible challenge for the effective implementation of Article 11(1) could be situations where one Party that is a country of origin requires PIC and MAT for access to certain genetic resources, whereas another Party having the same genetic resources in its territory operates a free-access regime.[25] Parties operating a free-access regime might also be less interested in documenting their genetic resources in situ so as to identify situations within the scope of Article 11(1). It appears difficult for a Party allowing free access to cooperate with neighboring Parties harboring the same genetic resources so as not to undermine the effectiveness and integrity of the latter's access framework. A balance between the obligation to cooperate and the right of a Party to decide in favor of a free-access regime will have to be struck in practice.

---

22   Dedeurwaerdere et al., "Governing Global Scientific Research Commons," op. cit., 419.

23   Greiber et al., *Explanatory Guide*, op. cit., 134.

24   Dedeurwaerdere et al., "Governing Global Scientific Research Commons," op. cit., 419.

25   That could be the case if a Party waives its right to require PIC: see this commentary on Article 6, section 3.1.

When genetic resources are held by indigenous and local communities[26] ('where applicable'), transboundary collaboration must occur with the involvement of the communities concerned. In this respect, the obligation should be understood and implemented in conjunction with other relevant Protocol provisions on benefit-sharing and relevant procedural guarantees, read in the light of relevant international human rights standards.[27] Challenges may arise, in this respect, when indigenous and local communities have rights over genetic resources in one/some, but not, all relevant States. Still, all concerned States will be expected to exert best-endeavor efforts to effectively involve these communities in transboundary cooperation.

4   Transboundary Cooperation Concerning Traditional Knowledge

Article 11(2) calls for transboundary cooperation in the case of transboundary situations related to traditional knowledge, with a view to ensuring the effective involvement of all relevant communities in taking decisions on PIC and MAT. The provision may apply where members of the same indigenous or local communities live in more than one Party and where different indigenous or local communities in several Parties share the same traditional knowledge.[28] As opposed to Article 11(1), this provision does not include the term 'where applicable,' as the Protocol recognizes that access to traditional knowledge can only occur with community PIC, or approval and involvement.[29] As recalled above, the provision should be read in conjunction with other relevant Protocol provisions on benefit-sharing and relevant procedural guarantees, including relevant international human rights standards.[30]

It is not self-evident what 'same' traditional knowledge means, however. It could point to traditional knowledge linked to the same biochemical composition or to similar properties or applications[31] that is held by indigenous and local communities living across national boundaries. The determination of the

---

26   Nagoya Protocol Article 6(2). See this commentary on Article 6, section 4.
27   See Introduction to this commentary, section 4 and this commentary on Article 6, section 3, and Article 12.
28   On issues related to shared traditional knowledge, see Manuel Ruiz Muller, *Protecting Shared Traditional Knowledge: Issues, Challenges and Options* (Geneva: International Centre for Trade and Sustainable Development, 2013).
29   See this commentary on Article 7.
30   See fn. 27 above.
31   Greiber et al., *Explanatory Guide*, op. cit., 135.

existence of a situation falling under the scope of Article 11(2) could be left to indigenous peoples and local communities as the holders of the knowledge in question, in accordance with their customary laws and procedures,[32] and possibly through the development of community protocols.[33] The role of Parties is therefore to facilitate communities' identification of such situations and their effective involvement in transboundary cooperation. Challenges may arise, however, if different Parties in the territories of which the concerned communities are located regulate differently ABS in relation to traditional knowledge. There may also arise practical difficulties if the relevant traditional knowledge is considered a secret by some of the concerned communities, but not by others. Once again, peer learning and development of international guidance by the Nagoya Protocol's governing body would be useful,[34] particularly in the context of its consideration of model contractual clauses and voluntary instruments.[35]

---

32   Nagoya Protocol Article 12(1). See this commentary on Article 12, section 2.

33   See this commentary on Article 12, section 2.1.

34   Nagoya Protocol Article 26(4)(a). See this commentary on Article 26, section 2.

35   See this commentary on Articles 19–20.

Article 12. Traditional Knowledge Associated with Genetic Resources

1. In implementing their obligations under this Protocol, Parties shall in accordance with domestic law take into consideration indigenous and local communities' customary laws, community protocols and procedures, as applicable, with respect to traditional knowledge associated with genetic resources.

2. Parties, with the effective participation of the indigenous and local communities concerned, shall establish mechanisms to inform potential users of traditional knowledge associated with genetic resources about their obligations, including measures as made available through the Access and Benefit-sharing Clearing-House for access to and fair and equitable sharing of benefits arising from the utilization of such knowledge.

3. Parties shall endeavor to support, as appropriate, the development by indigenous and local communities, including women within these communities, of:

   (a) Community protocols in relation to access to traditional knowledge associated with genetic resources and the fair and equitable sharing of benefits arising out of the utilization of such knowledge;

   (b) Minimum requirements for mutually agreed terms to secure the fair and equitable sharing of benefits arising from the utilization of traditional knowledge associated with genetic resources; and

   (c) Model contractual clauses for benefit-sharing arising from the utilization of traditional knowledge associated with genetic resources.

4. Parties, in their implementation of this Protocol, shall, as far as possible, not restrict the customary use and exchange of genetic resources and associated traditional knowledge within and amongst indigenous and local communities in accordance with the objectives of the Convention.

© KONINKLIJKE BRILL NV, LEIDEN, 2014 | DOI 10.1163/9789004217188_014

1   Overview

Although generally recognized as a cross-cutting issue during the negotiations,[1] traditional knowledge associated with genetic resources has eventually been addressed in various, occasionally stand-alone, provisions in the Protocol.[2] Article 12 serves as an overarching and wide-reaching provision enshrining: a general clause concerning indigenous and local communities' customary laws, that is applicable in the implementation of all other obligations under the Protocol;[3] two broadly framed obligations for Parties to support understanding and fairness in ABS transactions involving traditional knowledge;[4] and a prohibition for Parties to restrict communities' customary use and exchange of genetic resources and traditional knowledge that are in accordance with the CBD.[5] The following sections will analyze these provisions in turn.

2   General Clause

Article 12(1) requires Parties to 'take into consideration' customary laws, community protocols and procedures of indigenous and local communities in their implementation of the Protocol with respect to traditional knowledge 'as applicable' and 'in accordance with domestic law.'[6] The provision therefore leaves a considerable degree of discretion to Parties: it does not go as far as to require Parties to *recognize* or *apply* customary law, community protocols and procedures. However, it does oblige Parties *at a minimum* to factor in the development and application of domestic ABS measures the existence and relevance of indigenous and local communities' customary laws, even if such consideration may not necessarily determine the content of the final legal act or administrative decision. This requires that national authorities *identify* and *understand* relevant communities' customary laws, protocols and procedures, which would be practically impossible to achieve without the full and effective involvement of indigenous and local communities in the development

---

1   See generally, Singh Nijar, "Incorporating Traditional Knowledge," op. cit.; and Singh Nijar, "Traditional Knowledge Systems," op. cit.
2   See this commentary on Article 5, section 4, Article 7 and Article 16.
3   Nagoya Protocol Article 12(1).
4   Nagoya Protocol Article 12(2–3).
5   Nagoya Protocol Article 12(4).
6   For a commentary on the term, see this commentary on Article 7, section 3.

and implementation of these measures.[7] In this context, national authorities will then have to determine whether legal recognition or other mechanisms to support the understanding and respect of customary laws, protocols and procedures are needed with a view to ensuring the implementation of the Protocol's provisions on community PIC and benefit-sharing.[8] That is, the consideration of customary laws, protocols and procedures needs to be *functional to the actual realization* of PIC and benefit-sharing for indigenous and local communities. And, as previously argued,[9] in applying Article 12(1), Parties will have to respect their relevant international human rights obligations.

The relevance of customary laws, protocols and procedures of indigenous and local communities in the implementation of the traditional knowledge-related provisions of the Protocol is an important development in international law. It has been considered an unprecedented recognition of legal pluralism in international treaty law.[10] The study of the role of indigenous peoples' and local communities' customary laws in contributing to sustainability is still in its infancy, but there are indications that customary laws may inspire innovation in administering living resources and adapting to changing circumstances.[11] The Protocol, therefore, opens the door for Parties individually and collectively (most likely in the course of the review of implementation by the Protocol's governing body[12] and possibly its compliance procedures and mechanisms)[13] to explore the interactions of indigenous and local communities' customary laws with international and national law on ABS, while ensuring a certain measure of inter-operability[14] among Parties' domestic ABS frameworks.[15] That

---

7   UNDRIP Article 19 and 32(2); ILO Convention No. 169, Article 6(2).

8   Nagoya Protocol Articles 5(2), 6(2) and 7.

9   See Introduction to this commentary, section 4 and this commentary on Article 5, sections 3–4, Article 6, section 4 and Article 7.

10   Bavikatte and Robinson, "Towards a People's History of the Law," op. cit., 45–46.

11   See generally Peter Orebech et al., *The Role of Customary Law in Sustainable Development* (Cambridge: Cambridge University Press, 2006). See also Brendan Tobin, "Setting Protection of TK to Rights – Placing Human Rights and Customary Law at the Heart of TK Governance," in Kamau and Winter, *Genetic Resources, Traditional Knowledge and the Law*, op. cit., 102.

12   Nagoya Protocol Article 26(4)(a). See this commentary on Article 26, section 2.

13   See this commentary on Article 30; and Morgera, "Bilateralism at the Service," op. cit., 760–763.

14   This concept is discussed in Young, "International Cooperation Perspective," op. cit., 491–492.

15   The Nagoya Protocol may therefore provide a laboratory for the understanding of 'global environmental law' – a concept that is emerging from the promotion of environmental

being said, principled and practical difficulties in understanding and providing due consideration for indigenous and local communities' customary laws in a 'transcultural context' should not be underestimated.[16]

Article 12(1) is a general clause applying to the implementation of *all* Protocol provisions. It applies in particular to those provisions expressly related to traditional knowledge associated with genetic resources, namely on benefit-sharing, access, the multilateral benefit-sharing mechanism, transboundary cooperation, compliance with domestic ABS frameworks and MAT, awareness-raising and capacity,[17] as well as the other provisions contained in Article 12 itself. It may also be argued, in light of the interrelationship between genetic resources and traditional knowledge,[18] that Article 12(1) also applies to the Protocol provisions on genetic resources held by indigenous and local communities.[19] It should be further noted that Article 12(1) does not exclude any provision of the Protocol from its applicability, so other Articles may be implemented in light of Article 12(1), when these turn out to be, on a case-by-case basis, relevant to traditional knowledge.[20]

2.1   *Community Protocols*

The reference to 'community protocols' in Article 12(1) is also particularly noteworthy in facilitating the understanding and due consideration of the laws and procedures of indigenous and local communities. A community protocol is a written document developed by a community following a consultative process, to outline the core ecological, cultural and spiritual values and customary laws relating to the community's traditional knowledge and resources, based on which the community provides clear terms and conditions to regulate access to and benefit-sharing from their knowledge and resources.[21] It typically

---

protection as a global public good through a plurality of legal mechanisms relying on a plurality of legal orders. Morgera, "Bilateralism at the Service Community Interests?," op. cit., 760–763.

16   Saskia Vermeylen, "The Nagoya Protocol and Customary Law: The Paradox of Narratives in the Law," *Law Environment and Development Journal* 9 (2013): 185.

17   Nagoya Protocol Articles 5(5), 7, 10, 11(2), 16, 18, 21 and 22. See this commentary on Articles 10–11, 16, 18 and 21–22.

18   Nagoya Protocol 22nd preambular recital; and Lenzerini, "Indigenous Peoples' Cultural Rights," op. cit., 140.

19   Nagoya Protocol Articles 5(2) and 6(2).

20   See, for example, this commentary on Article 18.

21   At the time of writing, existing literature is written by practitioners involved in the promotion of community protocols in the field and their recognition at the international level. See Kristina Swiderska et al., *Biodiversity and Culture: Exploring Community*

sets out the community's customary rights and responsibilities for resource management and access, and the provisions in national and international law that recognize their rights and responsibilities to those resources.[22] It may thus serve as a tool to promote recognition and application of customary laws and procedures concerning traditional knowledge and genetic resources through a bottom-up approach, by articulating them in a way that can be easily understood by national authorities and users. This may potentially make their recognition or integration in domestic law easier, as well as facilitate ABS transactions with potential users. At the same time, community protocols offer an articulation of the holistic approach of communities to the regulation and management of natural resources and the environment, which may challenge the sectoral approach to environmental regulation in statutory law.[23]

The process of developing a community protocol is believed to have a value *per se*: it may serve to bring the entire community together, as an opportunity to collectively map and evaluate customary laws, governance systems, traditional resource uses and community development plans.[24] A holistic community

---

Protocols, Rights and Consent, Participatory Learning and Action Series no. 65 (London: International Institute for Environment and Development, 2012), accessed 30 November 2013, <http://pubs.iied.org/14618IIED.html>, 28; Kabir Bavikatte and Harry Jonas, *Bio-Cultural Community Protocols: A Community Approach to Ensuring the Integrity of Environmental Law and Policy* (Nairobi: UNEP, 2009), accessed 30 November 2013, <www.unep.org/communityprotocols/PDF/communityprotocols.pdf>; Harry Jonas, Holly Shrumm and Kabir Bavikatte, *Biocultural Community Protocols and Conservation Pluralism* (Cape Town: Natural Justice, 2010), accessed 30 November 2013, <http://naturaljustice.org/wp-content/uploads/pdf/BCPs_and_conservation_pluralism_jonas_et_al2010.pdf>; Holly Shrumm and Harry Jonas, *Biocultural Community Protocols: A Toolkit for Community Facilitators* (Cape Town: Natural Justice, 2012), accessed 30 November 2013, <www.community-protocols.org/toolkit>; and Munyi and Jonas, "Implementing the Nagoya Protocol," op. cit., 238–244.

22   From this perspective, community protocols can be considered an essential tool for the understanding and development of global environmental law (Morgera, "Bilateralism at the Service of Community Interests?," op. cit., 762) and for facilitating the integrated implementation of different multilateral environmental agreements on the ground (Elisa Morgera, "No Need to Reinvent the Wheel for a Human Rights-Based Approach to Tackling Climate Change: The Contribution of International Biodiversity Law," in *Climate Change and the Law*, ed. Erkki Hollo, Kati Kulovesi and Michael Mehling (Springer, 2013), 350).

23   Jonas, Shrumm and Bavikatte, *Biocultural Community Protocols and Conservation Pluralism*, op. cit., at 104, refer to 'laws compartmentaliz[ing] the otherwise interdependent aspects of biocultural diversity by drawing legislative borders around them and addressing them as distinct segments.'

24   Bavikatte and Jonas, *Bio-Cultural Community Protocols*, op. cit., 20.

protocol usually involves a community's reflection about the interconnectedness of the elements of their way of life, as well as an increased understanding within the community of the international and national legal ABS frameworks and of the extent to which they impact on their customary practices, values and norms.[25] It can also lead to establishing internal community rules for the sustainable management of natural resources, equitable sharing of benefits and conflict resolution.[26]

The inter-community agreement established among the six communities managing communally Peru's Potato Park provides an illustration in that regard. The agreement aims to conserve the hundreds of potato varieties cultivated in the area and share equitably the financial benefits arising from a number of initiatives in the park. Following a three-year long participatory process, the agreement established new inter-community governance structures and a framework for equitably sharing the benefits from economic collectives in the park, including gastronomy and ecotourism initiatives, and the production and selling of medicinal plants, potatoes and crafts. The agreement is rooted in conservation and equity values enshrined in customary laws, and is regulated by community and inter-community authorities. It has minimized the risk of conflicts over resources and of elites unfairly benefiting from revenues. A percentage of the revenues is reinvested into a communal fund that is used to sustain and manage the park's agro-ecosystem, and provide a safety net for the poorest people in the park communities. At the same time, the agreement has acted as a community protocol in the sense of the Nagoya Protocol, as it sets out the rules for access by outsiders to the park's genetic resources and traditional knowledge and for equitable benefit-sharing by outsiders.[27]

Overall, community protocols appear to have two advantages for indigenous and local communities.[28] From an *outward* perspective, they provide a specific framework for defining in a participatory manner the types of benefits indigenous and local communities may wish to secure, to support their culture and

---

25   Ibid.

26   On questions related to intra-community equity and fairness in sharing benefits, see this commentary on Article 5, sections 3.1 and 4.

27   See Alejandro Argumedo, *Community Biocultural Protocols: Building Mechanisms for Access and Benefit-Sharing among the Communities of the Potato Park Based on Quechua Customary Norms* (London: International Institute for Environment and Development, 2011), accessed 30 November 2013, <http://pubs.iied.org/G03168.html>. See also Tobin, "Setting Protection of TK to Rights," op. cit., 101.

28   Elsa Tsioumani, "Community Protocols: An Emerging Tool for Managing the Commons" (presented at the Against Crisis, For the Commons: Towards a New Mediterranean, Mataroa, 2013), accessed 30 November 2013, <http://mataroanetwork.org/2013-conference-proceedings/public-events-2013/returning-to-the-commons/>.

livelihoods, prior to being required for PIC and having to engage in the establishment of MAT. As such, the process leading to the development of a community protocol allows a community to prepare in advance for negotiations
with outsiders of an ABS arrangement, rather than enter into such negotiations
in an *ad hoc* manner, contributing thus to a more level-playing field among the
parties. In addition, a community protocol can serve as a guide for outsiders
(whether it is the State, a company or a research institution) to begin interacting with an indigenous or local community. From an *inward* perspective, the
development of a community protocol may allow an indigenous or local community to identify any question related to the authority to provide PIC and
the governance of future benefit-sharing, thus preventing internal conflicts.[29]
Where in-depth participatory processes are followed, such process can also
strengthen communities' organizational capacity, and collective identity and
goals, and develop a sense of self-empowerment.[30]

Compliance with the provisions of community protocols, however, remains
voluntary, unless it is secured through national legislation or through contracts.
In addition, development of community protocols would generally require
capacity-building and legal assistance, so that community members can better
understand the relevant international and national legal regimes, the interests
involved and the consequences of their choices.[31] The development of community protocols is in fact often supported by international and transnational
networks of experts comprising State and non-State entities: community protocols have been developed before the conclusion of the negotiations of the
Nagoya Protocol through the involvement of networks of NGOs, intergovernmental organizations, and bilateral donors, as well as the private sector.[32]

In a broader perspective, community protocols attempt to bridge inter-State
obligations established at the international level vis-à-vis traditional knowledge and genetic resources held by indigenous and local communities with
specific communities' needs, aspirations and livelihoods at the local level.
Community protocols can therefore be seen as an instrument to link the local
and the international legal levels, according to standards set out in customary, national and international law, with a view to mobilizing communities to

---

29   Morgera and Tsioumani, "Evolution of Benefit-sharing," op. cit., 157–158.
30   Elsa Tsioumani, "Community Protocols," op. cit.
31   Morgera and Tsioumani, "Evolution of Benefit-sharing," op. cit., 157–158.
32   See the website of a coalition of different actors supporting community protocols:
     "Community Protocols," UNEP et al., accessed 30 November 2013,.

use international and national law to support the local manifestations of their right to self-determination.[33]

The importance of the development of community protocols for the implementation of traditional knowledge-related provisions of the Protocol is further highlighted elsewhere in the Protocol, which provides a best-endeavor obligation for Parties to 'support, as appropriate,' the development by indigenous and local communities of these protocols.[34] Community protocols are also to be supported through capacity-building,[35] awareness-raising measures,[36] and international funding.[37] It should be finally noted that further guidance for Parties' consideration and support of community protocols may be developed in the context of other work carried out under CBD Article 8(j), such as the *sui generis* system of protection of traditional knowledge[38] and customary sustainable use in protected areas.[39]

3   Obligation to Inform Potential Users

According to Article 12(2), Parties are under an unqualified obligation to establish mechanisms to inform potential users of traditional knowledge about their obligations towards indigenous and local communities, including through the ABS Clearinghouse.[40] Basically, this provision implicitly recognizes that it is the responsibility of State Parties to inform potential users of the rights of indigenous and local communities under the Protocol and to create ways to support the respect of such rights by private operators. This is particularly relevant in light of the 'right of indigenous and local communities to identify the rightful holders of their traditional knowledge associated with genetic resources

---

33   Harry Jonas, Kabir Bavikatte and Holly Shrumm, "Community Protocols and Access and Benefit-Sharing," *Asian Biotechnology and Development Review* 12 (2010): 49, 62.

34   Nagoya Protocol Article 12(3).

35   See this commentary on Article 22.

36   Nagoya Protocol Article 21(i). See this commentary on Article 21.

37   CBD Decision 11/14, paragraph 8 and as part of guidance to the GEF in CBD Decision 11/15, "Review of the programme of work on island biodiversity," (5 December 2012) UN Doc UNEP/CBD/COP/11/35, Appendix I, paragraph 1(d)(ii).

38   CBD Decision 11/14, section E, paragraphs 2 and 9.

39   Ibid., section F, paragraph 10(c)(iii) and Annex, section A, Tasks 3 and 14(c).

40   See this commentary on Article 14, sections 3–4, in particular on legal questions arising from the inclusion of information relevant to traditional knowledge and to indigenous and local communities through that mechanism.

within their communities,'[41] and supports also the consideration of applicable customary laws, procedures and protocols.[42] The rationale of Article 12(2) is to facilitate users' compliance with domestic ABS requirements related to traditional knowledge.[43] This provision is therefore complementary to Parties' international responsibility vis-à-vis users' violations of domestic ABS requirements related to traditional knowledge, which is spelt out elsewhere in the Protocol.[44]

In implementing this obligation, Parties must proceed with the effective participation of the indigenous and local communities concerned. This language should be read in light of the *principle* of full and effective participation of indigenous peoples in decision making,[45] which can be seen as an important aspect of indigenous peoples' right to self-determination[46] and is also considered a principle in the guidelines developed by CBD Parties by consensus, notably the Tkarihwaié:ri Code of Ethical Conduct.[47] As for other provisions of the Protocol, relevant international human rights obligations and standards should guide the interpretation and implementation of this obligation.[48]

4 Obligation to Support

Article 12(3) establishes a best-endeavor obligation for Parties to support indigenous and local communities in the development of a series of tools

---

41   Nagoya Protocol 24th preambular recital.

42   When read in conjunction with Nagoya Protocol Article 12(1).

43   Greiber et al., *Explanatory Guide*, op. cit., 140.

44   See this commentary on Article 16.

45   UNDRIP Article 19 and 32(2); ILO Convention No 169, Article 6(2).

46   "Joint submission Grand Council of the Crees (Eeyou Istchee)," 25–26. On the relevance of the internationally human rights of indigenous peoples for local communities, see Introduction to this commentary, section 4.

47   Tkarihwaié:Ri Code, paragraph 30, which reads: 'Full and effective participation/ participatory approach. This *principle* recognizes the crucial importance of indigenous and local communities fully and effectively participating in activities/interactions related to biological diversity and conservation that may impact on them, and of respecting their decision-making processes and time frames for such decision-making. Ethical conduct should acknowledge that there are some legitimate circumstances for indigenous and local communities to restrict access to their traditional knowledge,' emphasis added. Full and effective participation is also called for in the Akwé: Kon Voluntary Guidelines, paragraphs 3(a) and 15.

48   See Introduction to this commentary, section 4. Savaresi, "International Human Rights Law Implications," op. cit., 53.

aimed at ensuring fair and equitable ABS transactions concerning traditional knowledge. The tools include: community protocols,[49] minimum requirements for MAT,[50] and model contractual clauses.[51] These are not only tools supporting transparent and equitable internal governance within communities in relation to ABS, but also their capacity to negotiate with outsiders/users.[52] As to the latter, it has been observed that community protocols can be used as a basis for dialogue between communities and private companies.[53] In that regard, support from national authorities to the development of community protocols may lead to 'concrete tools [that] business needs to put ABS in practice.'[54] On the other hand, it has been cautioned that minimum requirements for MAT and model contractual clauses are among the 'most complex and controversial elements of ABS practice,' therefore mutual learning should be encouraged and possibly international guidance should be developed on this matter by the Protocol's governing body.[55]

Implementation of Article 12(3) will be supported by indigenous and local communities' own identification of their priority capacity-building needs.[56] As a result, it remains the prerogative of indigenous and local communities to develop the tools required for their traditional knowledge-related ABS arrangements. Support to this end can be expected from the State, particularly in light of its own obligations vis-à-vis an indigenous or local community under the Protocol, on the basis of good-faith and reasonable efforts. The provision, however, also implicitly points – when read in light of relevant international human rights obligations and standards – to a certain responsibility of Parties in ensuring some guarantees for the substantive equity of MAT concerning traditional knowledge.[57]

The best-endeavor obligation to support indigenous and local communities is qualified by the term 'as appropriate.' In this specific case, this qualifier may be understood as 'upon request from the relevant communities' or

---

49   Nagoya Protocol Article 12(1) See section 2 above.

50   Nagoya Protocol Article 6(3)(g). See this commentary on Article 6, section 7.

51   See this commentary on Article 19.

52   We are grateful to Tomme Young for drawing our attention to this point. See also Munyi and Jonas, "Implementing the Nagoya Protocol," op. cit., 222 and 234, who consider this provision as contributing to the legal empowerment of indigenous and local communities.

53   Oliva, "Implications of the Nagoya Protocol," op. cit., 379.

54   Ibid.

55   Young, "An International Cooperation Perspective," op. cit., 500.

56   Nagoya Protocol Article 22(3) and (5)(j).

57   Savaresi, "International Human Rights Law Implications," op. cit., 73.

'where these tools are not already in existence,'[58] with a view to preventing States from exercising undue control over communities' internal processes of governance in relation to ABS[59] in exercising their discretion in selecting the means to implement this provision. Specific emphasis is placed, in the context of the obligation to support, on the participation of women in community procedures for the development of the tools listed in Article 12(3),[60] while consideration should be given to communities' customary laws and procedures, as well as human rights obligations.[61]

Pragmatically, national authorities would be well advised to, first of all, determine whether community laws and protocols on traditional knowledge associated with genetic resources exist, and if so, support their respect. If these procedures do not exist, encourage and, where so required by these communities, support the development of community procedures in this regard. And only as a last resort and until such community procedures are in place, act on behalf of these communities in a facilitating role.[62] It can be argued that development of tools provided for under Article 12(3) has the potential to relieve Parties (at least partially) from developing from scratch processes for obtaining community PIC, which would be a 'formidable task.'[63] This is particularly true when taking into account the diversity of circumstances in which traditional knowledge is held by indigenous and local communities, the right of these communities to identify their rightful holders of traditional knowledge

---

58   Singh Nijar "An Asian Developing Country's View," op. cit., 256.

59   Greiber et al., *Explanatory Guide*, op. cit., 141, along similar lines, suggests that 'as appropriate' makes reference to the fact that 'not all communities may need or desire such assistance.'

60   See also Nagoya Protocol 11th preambular recital and this commentary on Article 5, section 3, and Introduction to this commentary, section 4. See also Akwé: Kon Voluntary Guidelines, paragraph 54, which reads: 'The vital role that women and youth play, in particular women and youth within indigenous and local communities, in the conservation and sustainable use of biological diversity and the need for the full and effective participation of women in policy-making and implementation for biological diversity conservation should be fully taken into consideration.'

61   Nagoya Protocol Article 12(1). On relevant international human rights law, see Introduction to this commentary, section 4.

62   These options have been identified and prioritized by Singh Nijar "An Asian Developing Country's View," op. cit., 257–8.

63   Ibid., 257. This perception is confirmed by Cabrera Medaglia, "Implementation of the Nagoya Protocol," op. cit., 360–361 and 364, where the author notes that even if certain Latin American countries have already legislated on ABS in relation to traditional knowledge, very few had developed detailed procedures for obtaining community PIC or model contractual clauses targeting traditional knowledge.

and the unique circumstances in which traditional knowledge is held in different countries.[64]

5 Prohibition to Restrict Customary Use and Exchange

According to Article 12(4), Parties are subject to a qualified obligation ('as far as possible') not to restrict the customary use and exchange of genetic resources and associated traditional knowledge within and amongst indigenous and local communities in accordance with the objectives of the Convention. This provision therefore envisages that States avoid placing restrictions on traditional use and exchanges within communities within their territory and also located in other States,[65] particularly as long as such traditional use and exchange contribute to the conservation and sustainable use of biodiversity. This provision confirms once again the holistic approach of the Protocol to the three objectives of the Convention,[66] in light of the importance of traditional knowledge for biodiversity conservation and sustainable use, as well as for indigenous and local communities' rich cultural heritage that is relevant for biodiversity conservation and sustainable use.[67] The rationale is to recognize, due to the inseparable nature of genetic resources and traditional knowledge for indigenous and local communities,[68] that traditional use and exchanges of genetic resources are essential for the preservation and continued evolution of traditional knowledge, and for its role in the preservation of communities' cultural identity. Tensions however may arise between certain customary practices and conservation objectives, which Parties would need to resolve in the light of this holistic interpretation of the CBD objectives and international human rights norms.[69]

---

64   Nagoya Protocol 23rd–25th preambular recitals.

65   Nagoya Protocol Article 11(2). See this commentary on Article 11, section 4.

66   See this commentary on Articles 1, section 4; 8, section 2; 9, section 2, and 10, section 4.

67   Nagoya Protocol 22nd and 25th preambular recitals. See also Konstantia Koutouki and Katharina von Bieberstein, "The Nagoya Protocol: Sustainable Access and Benefits-Sharing for Indigenous and Local Communities," *Vermont Journal of Environmental Law* 13 (2011): 513, 534.

68   Nagoya Protocol 22nd preambular recital.

69   Also from a human rights perspective, it can be argued that the right to own and use traditional resources implies an 'obligation of stewardship toward the resource, for the benefit of future generations of the community and for the planet': Wiessner, "The Cultural Rights of Indigenous Peoples," op. cit., 240.

Article 12(4) thus represents an elaboration of the more general obligation under the CBD to 'protect and encourage customary use of biological resources in accordance with traditional cultural practices that are compatible with conservation or sustainable use requirements.'[70] The provision can be compared with, and used to reinforce at the national level, farmers' rights currently addressed under the International Treaty on Plant Genetic Resources for Food and Agriculture.[71] When compared with the ITPGRFA provision, Article 12(4) of the Nagoya Protocol not only has a much wider scope (it applies to all genetic resources, encompassing – but not limited to – plant genetic resources for food and agriculture). It is also framed as a positive (albeit qualified) obligation for Parties, thereby providing an additional legal basis for national legislation on farmers' rights.

---

70   CBD Article 10(c). See Glowka and Normand, "The Nagoya Protocol on Access and Benefit-sharing," op. cit., 40.

71   ITPGRFA Article 9(3), whereby, using a formulation in the negative 'Nothing in this Article [on farmers' rights] shall be interpreted to limit any rights that farmers have to save, use, exchange and sell farm-saved seed/propagating material, subject to national law and as appropriate.' On the interactions between the Nagoya Protocol and the International Treaty provisions on farmers rights, see Chiarolla, Louafi and Schloen, "Analysis of the Relationship," op. cit., 93–100 and 110. See also Munyi and Jonas, "Implementing the Nagoya Protocol," op. cit., 222 and 234.

Article 13. National Focal Points and Competent National Authorities

1. Each Party shall designate a national focal point on access and benefit-sharing. The national focal point shall make information available as follows:
    (a) For applicants seeking access to genetic resources, information on procedures for obtaining prior informed consent and establishing mutually agreed terms, including benefit-sharing;
    (b) For applicants seeking access to traditional knowledge associated with genetic resources, where possible, information on procedures for obtaining prior informed consent or approval and involvement, as appropriate, of indigenous and local communities and establishing mutually agreed terms including benefit-sharing; and
    (c) Information on competent national authorities, relevant indigenous and local communities and relevant stakeholders.

    The national focal point shall be responsible for liaison with the Secretariat.

2. Each Party shall designate one or more competent national authorities on access and benefit-sharing. Competent national authorities shall, in accordance with applicable national legislative, administrative or policy measures, be responsible for granting access or, as applicable, issuing written evidence that access requirements have been met and be responsible for advising on applicable procedures and requirements for obtaining prior informed consent and entering into mutually agreed terms.
3. A Party may designate a single entity to fulfil the functions of both focal point and competent national authority.
4. Each Party shall, no later than the date of entry into force of this Protocol for it, notify the Secretariat of the contact information of its national focal point and its competent national authority or authorities. Where a Party designates more than one competent national authority, it shall convey to the Secretariat, with its notification thereof, relevant information on the respective responsibilities of those authorities. Where applicable, such information shall, at a minimum, specify which

© KONINKLIJKE BRILL NV, LEIDEN, 2014 | DOI 10.1163/9789004217188_015

competent authority is responsible for the genetic resources sought. Each Party shall forthwith notify the Secretariat of any changes in the designation of its national focal point or in the contact information or responsibilities of its competent national authority or authorities.

5.   The Secretariat shall make information received pursuant to paragraph 4 above available through the Access and Benefit-sharing Clearing-House.

1   Overview

Article 13 outlines the necessary institutional arrangements to be taken at the domestic level to implement the Protocol. It follows the model adopted in the Bonn Guidelines[1] and in the Biosafety Protocol[2] of relying on a combination of a national focal point and one or more competent national authorities. Accordingly, the former is the primary *external* contact point between a Party and the Secretariat of the Protocol or for users inquiring about access procedures, and the latter is responsible for granting access or issuing written evidence about PIC according to domestic requirements. The Nagoya Protocol, however, is much more detailed than the Bonn Guidelines and the Biosafety Protocol with respect to the tasks of the national focal points as key points of reference for users in understanding domestic ABS frameworks. This level of additional detail arguably seeks to address concerns expressed by both governments of developed countries and the research community, about difficulties in obtaining correct information on requirements for obtaining PIC and MAT.[3]

Article 13 refers to 'each Party' with a view to underlining that although the tasks for national focal points and competent national authorities are predominantly focused on access (and therefore of great importance to provider countries), the obligation applies also to Parties that see themselves as user countries. That being said, Article 13 leaves broad discretion to Parties as to the specific institutional arrangements to be put in place, which will ultimately depend on national and sub-national legal and institutional legal frameworks and practices. Accordingly, Article 13(3) explicitly provides that a Party may

---

1   Bonn Guidelines, paragraphs 13–14.
2   Biosafety Protocol, Article 19. For a commentary, Mackenzie et al., *Explanatory Guide to the Cartagena Protocol*, op. cit., 129.
3   We are grateful to Geoff Burton for drawing our attention to this point.

designate a single entity to fulfil the functions of both focal point and competent national authority.[4]

Information on national focal points and competent national authorities will be included in the ABS Clearinghouse,[5] possibly including information on relevant competent authorities of indigenous and local communities.[6] Parties are responsible for communicating any changes to these designations to the Secretariat, so that these can be promptly reflected in the ABS Clearinghouse and that relevant stakeholders may easily find out about the key officers for the national implementation of the Protocol.[7]

2   National Focal Points

The national focal point will have a dual external function. On the one hand, it will ensure direct communication with the Secretariat of the Protocol. In that capacity, the national officer serving as focal point will receive, for example, notifications of meetings relating to the Protocol and invitations to submit views on matters on the agenda of these meetings.[8] On the other hand, the national focal point is mandated to familiarize prospective users (applicants seeking access to genetic resources and traditional knowledge) with the domestic ABS framework, by providing information on procedures for obtaining PIC and establishing MAT,[9] including with indigenous and local communities.[10] In the latter sense, the national focal point will basically serve as a 'helpdesk' or 'information hub', whose practical role will be to enable potential users to avoid, and possibly prevent,[11] unintended breaches of domestic ABS frameworks and

---

4   Greiber et al., *Explanatory Guide*, op. cit., 144.

5   Nagoya Protocol Article 14(2)(b). See this commentary on Article 14.

6   Nagoya Protocol Article 14(3)(a).

7   Nagoya Protocol Article 13(4).

8   As suggested in relation to the corresponding provision in the Biosafety Protocol by Mackenzie et al., *Explanatory Guide to the Cartagena Protocol*, op. cit., 129.

9   See this commentary on Article 6.

10   Nagoya Protocol Articles 6(2) and 7. See this commentary on Article 6, section 4, and Article 7.

11   If the national focal point is so empowered at the national level (since nothing in the Protocol requires this, but nothing in the Protocol prevents this domestic implementation choice either): we are grateful to Tomme Young for drawing out attention to this point.

minimize users' costs and efforts in understanding provider countries' domestic ABS frameworks.[12]

The task of providing information on applicable rules and procedures or prospective users seeking access to traditional knowledge is qualified by the phrase 'where possible.' This may imply that in the case of countries with various, geographically remote or voluntarily isolated indigenous and local communities, the national focal point may not be aware of, and therefore be unable to share, relevant information. It remains to each Party, therefore, to clarify the extent of the role of national focal points with regard to these communities' requirements for access to traditional knowledge. This determination is to be made with the effective participation of the indigenous and local communities concerned,[13] in light of Parties' obligation to raise awareness and support the development of community protocols and procedures[14] and to take into consideration their customary laws, protocols and procedures.[15] These provisions are to be interpreted and applied in a manner consistent with relevant international human rights norms and standards.[16]

The task of providing information on competent national authorities, as well as on relevant indigenous and local communities and stakeholders[17] does not make reference to access. Consequently, Article 13(1) only provides an explicit indication of the role of national focal points in user countries, in addition to being the liaison with the Protocol Secretariat. It is left to the broad discretion of Parties to determine the role of national focal points when a State acts as the user country in a specific ABS transaction.

3   Competent National Authorities

Competent national authorities must be authorized by a Party to act on its behalf[18] in relation to two implementation functions: first, granting access or issuing written evidence that access requirements have been met; and second,

---

12   Greiber et al., *Explanatory Guide*, op. cit., 144; see also discussion of information to be
       provided: ibid., 145–146.
13   UNDRIP Articles 19 and 32(2); ILO Convention No. 169, Article 6(2).
14   Nagoya Protocol Articles 21(i) and 12(3)(a). See this commentary on Article 21.
15   Nagoya Protocol Article 12(1). See this commentary on Article 12, section 2.
16   See Introduction to this commentary, section 4.
17   Nagoya Protocol Article 13(1)(c).
18   As suggested in relation to the corresponding provision in the Biosafety Protocol by
       Mackenzie et al., *Explanatory Guide to the Cartagena Protocol*, op. cit., 129–130.

advising on procedures and requirements for PIC and MAT. As a consequence, although Article 13(2) clearly indicates that 'each Party' should designate competent national authorities, it remains unclear what tasks will be performed by relevant officers in user countries.[19]

As to the advisory role of competent national authorities, this is a complementary function to that of the national focal point. In that regard, the Protocol provides significantly less details than the Bonn Guidelines. The latter specify that competent national authorities should be responsible for advising on: the negotiating process and the requirements for obtaining PIC and establishing MAT; monitoring and evaluation of ABS agreements; implementation/enforcement of ABS agreements; processing of applications and approval of agreements; conservation and sustainable use of the genetic resources accessed; mechanisms for the effective participation of different stakeholders, as appropriate for the different steps in the process of ABS, in particular indigenous and local communities; and mechanisms for the effective participation of communities, while promoting the objective of having decisions and processes available in a language understandable to relevant communities.[20] A Party may opt for introducing such guidance in its national legislation in that regard.[21]

As to its role regarding access, the Protocol envisages that the national competent authority will be necessarily tasked with issuing *written evidence* that access requirements have been met.[22] The Protocol also indicates that the same authority may be mandated under the domestic ABS framework to *grant* access (i.e., provide PIC and engage in MAT negotiations). Notably, the provision is silent on whether national competent authorities are responsible for submitting permits to the ABS Clearinghouse,[23] thereby elevating them to an internationally recognized certificate of compliance.[24] It can be argued that to enhance legal certainty and predictability at the international level, domestic ABS legislation could specify that competent national authorities are the only authorized to submitting permits to the ABS Clearinghouse. In addition, through a combined reading of several Protocol provisions, it could be argued that national competent authorities in user countries will be responsible for

---

19   We are grateful to Tomme Young for a useful exchange of ideas on this provision.

20   Bonn Guidelines, paragraph 14(1). We are grateful to Geoff Burton for drawing our attention to this point.

21   See Introduction to this commentary, section 2.

22   Nagoya Protocol Article 13(2). This complements the obligation under Article 6(3)(d).

23   Nagoya Protocol Article 14(2)(c). This is also the case of Nagoya Protocol Article 6(3)(e): we are grateful to Evanson Chege Kamau for drawing our attention to this point.

24   Nagoya Protocol Article 17(2). See this commentary on Article 17, section 3.

managing the information received by checkpoints[25] and posting this and other required information to the ABS Clearinghouse, as appropriate.[26] In combination with the requirement that Parties notify the Secretariat of the contact information of their national focal point and competent authorities,[27] this would further enhance legal certainty and assist in maintaining the integrity and accuracy of the information in the ABS Clearinghouse.[28]

As revealed by the expression 'as applicable,' however, the Protocol does not prevent Parties (or their national competent authority in that regard)[29] from delegating the power to grant access to other individuals or entities.[30] That may be the case of Parties deciding to use a decentralized system of granting access due to the federal or devolved nature of government,[31] or Parties preferring to delegate such power to non-State entities, such as genebanks or research centers. In addition, in the case of genetic resources held by indigenous and local communities[32] and/or traditional knowledge, the authority to grant PIC or approval and involvement will be found within the relevant communities. This determination is to be made with the effective participation of the indigenous and local communities concerned,[33] taking into consideration these communities' customary laws, protocols and procedures.[34] Once again, Parties' obligation under the Protocol to support the development

---

25   See Nagoya Protocol Article 17(1)(a)(iii), which requires information from checkpoints to be provided to 'relevant national authorities.' See also this commentary on Article 17, section 2.

26   Nagoya Protocol Article 14(2).

27   Nagoya Protocol Article 13(4).

28   This would result in avoiding the posting of drafts by organizations or individuals – a problem experienced with the Biosafety Clearinghouse. See Tomme Young, "Use of the Biosafety Clearing-house in Practise," in *Legal Aspects of Implementing the Cartagena Protocol on Biosafety*, ed. Marie-Claire Cordonier Segger, Frederic Perron-Welch and Christine Frison (Cambridge: Cambridge University Press, 2013), 137.

29   As also foreseen in the Bonn Guidelines, paragraph 14(2).

30   Young, "An International Cooperation Perspective," op. cit., 459 fn. 22.

31   For a more general discussion of questions of multi-level governance of ABS arising from the implementation of the Protocol in context of federal or highly decentralised States, see Singh Nijar, "An Asian Developing Country's View," op. cit., 264–266; and Lago Candeira and Silvestri, "Challenges in the Implementation of the Nagoya Protocol," op. cit., 277 and 287–292.

32   Nagoya Protocol Article 6(2).

33   See fn. 13 above.

34   Nagoya Protocol Article 12(1).

of community protocols and procedures[35] is relevant to this end, as are international human rights norms and standards.[36] As noted above, for reasons of legal certainty and predictability at the international level, the designated competent authorities notified to the Secretariat would be the ones issuing written evidence that access requirements have been met.

The Protocol explicitly allows Parties to designate more than one competent national authority, and to specify the nature of their ABS-related (decisional or administrative) authority in detail, so each of these authorities could be responsible to grant access on genetic resources of different nature or for different intended uses.[37] The Protocol thus specifically requires Parties choosing to designate more than one competent national authority, to inform the Secretariat about which authority is responsible for dealing with which type of genetic resources.[38] As a result, specific institutional arrangements for granting access may vary significantly from one Party to another, and Parties will be well advised to set out in detail in their domestic ABS frameworks the specific arrangements for granting PIC.[39] In that respect, a distinction will likely be drawn between access in situ and ex situ. As regards the former, the decision-making process for reaching a decision on access is likely to involve a wide range of national authorities, including those involved in the implementation of other relevant international obligations, such as under the Convention on International Trade in Endangered Species and on animal and plant health,[40] or under the law of the sea,[41] as well as stakeholders. Parties thus will be well advised to spell out in their national ABS frameworks the specific domestic procedures for consultations to be carried out prior to granting access,[42] or to devise a 'one-stop-shop' system to streamline procedures.[43] The latter may

---

35   Nagoya Protocol Article 12(3)(a).

36   See Introduction to this commentary, section 4.

37   Greiber et al., *Explanatory Guide*, op. cit., 146.

38   Nagoya Protocol Article 13(4).

39   Particularly in view of the Protocol requirement for a clear and transparent written decision on access, in a cost-effective manner and within a reasonable period of time: Nagoya Protocol Article 6(3)(d).

40   We are grateful to Tomme Young for drawing our attention to this point.

41   Salpin, "Law of the Sea," op. cit., 168.

42   As suggested in relation to the corresponding provision in the Biosafety Protocol by Mackenzie et al., *Explanatory Guide to the Cartagena Protocol*, op. cit., 130.

43   E.g., Institute for European Environmental Policy, "Study to analyse legal and economic aspects of implementing the Nagoya Protocol on ABS in the European Union," (undated) accessed 1 November 2013, <http://ec.europa.eu/environment/biodiversity/

also be useful in situations where access to one or more samples is sought from a collection in a provider country.[44]

international/abs/pdf/ABS%20FINAL%20REPORT%20-%20Annexes.pdf>, 28; Martin Brink, "Implementation of Access and Benefit Sharing Policies in Sub-Sahara Africa: Inventory, Analysis and Proposals" (June 2013), accessed 11 November 2013, <http:// edepot.wur.nl/280508>, 13 and 19. See also discussion in Evanson C. Kamau and Gerd Winter, "Streamlining Access Procedures and Standards," in Kamau and Winter, *Genetic Resources, Traditional Knowledge and the Law*, op. cit., 38.

44   At least in the case of the EU, it appears that it is mostly university-based researchers and scientists affiliated with ex situ collections that engage in bioprospecting activities, usually with an explicitly non-commercial purpose. Commercial users of genetic resources, in contrast, rarely collect genetic resources in the wild but source new material from collections, except in some particular niches of innovation, such as the biocontrol industry, parts of industrial biotechnology, and some small pharmaceutical biotechnology companies. See European Commission, Impact Assessment (Part 1), SWD(2012) 292 final, 15.

Article 14. The Access and Benefit-sharing Clearing-House and Information Sharing

1. An Access and Benefit-sharing Clearing-House is hereby established as part of the clearing-house mechanism under Article 18, paragraph 3, of the Convention. It shall serve as a means for sharing of information related to access and benefit-sharing. In particular, it shall provide access to information made available by each Party relevant to the implementation of this Protocol.

2. Without prejudice to the protection of confidential information, each Party shall make available to the Access and Benefit-sharing Clearing-House any information required by this Protocol, as well as information required pursuant to the decisions taken by the Conference of the Parties serving as the meeting of the Parties to this Protocol. The information shall include:

    (a) Legislative, administrative and policy measures on access and benefit-sharing;

    (b) Information on the national focal point and competent national authority or authorities; and

    (c) Permits or their equivalent issued at the time of access as evidence of the decision to grant prior informed consent and of the establishment of mutually agreed terms.

3. Additional information, if available and as appropriate, may include:

    (a) Relevant competent authorities of indigenous and local communities, and information as so decided;

    (b) Model contractual clauses;

    (c) Methods and tools developed to monitor genetic resources; and

    (d) Codes of conduct and best practices.

4. The modalities of the operation of the Access and Benefit-sharing Clearing-House, including reports on its activities, shall be considered and decided upon by the Conference of the Parties serving as the meeting of the Parties to this Protocol at its first meeting, and kept under review thereafter.

© KONINKLIJKE BRILL NV, LEIDEN, 2014 | DOI 10.1163/9789004217188_016

1   Overview

Article 14 is a key provision for the effective and transparent implementation of the Protocol. It establishes an international clearinghouse (the ABS
Clearinghouse) to share information on ABS, that is linked to the pre-existing
CBD Clearinghouse Mechanism. It further places an obligation on Parties to
provide information to the ABS Clearinghouse, distinguishing between information to be provided on a mandatory and a voluntary basis. Notably, Article 14
also raises the issue of confidentiality concerns in ABS transactions.

The implementation of Article 14, however, poses a number of legal questions. In the following sections, the link between the ABS Clearinghouse and
the CBD Clearinghouse Mechanism will be discussed. Attention will then be
turned to the functions of the ABS Clearinghouse, the type of information to
be included in it, and outstanding legal issues.

2   **Link with the CBD Clearinghouse Mechanism**

The ABS Clearinghouse will be 'part' of the CBD Clearinghouse Mechanism.[1]
The latter aims to promote 'international technical and scientific cooperation in the field of the conservation and sustainable use of biodiversity' and
consists of the CBD website, including its Information Centre, the network of
national clearinghouse mechanisms and various partner institutions.[2]

It can be expected that the ABS Clearinghouse will be created along the lines
of the CBD Clearinghouse Mechanism. This implies taking into account the
CBD COP decisions that have gradually spelt out the latter's characteristics and
procedures, such as: compatibility with national capacities; need-driven and
decentralized functioning; access to metadata; support to decision-making;
and involvement of the private sector to the extent possible.[3] Similarly to the
Biosafety Protocol, Article 14 puts the Protocol's governing body in charge of

---

1   Established under CBD Article 18(3). For an introduction, see box 35 in Mackenzie et al.,
     Explanatory Guide to the Cartagena Protocol, op. cit., 132–133.
2   CBD Expert Meeting on the Modalities of Operation of the Access and Benefit-Sharing
     Clearing-house, "Issues for consideration in the Establishment of the Access and Benefit-
     Sharing Clearing-house" (22 March 2011) UN Doc UNEP/CBD/ABS/EM-CH/1/2, paragraph 9.
     Note that this is a study commissioned by the CBD Secretariat to support intergovernmental
     discussions.
3   Ibid., paragraph 10.

determining how the ABS Clearinghouse will operate and of keeping its functioning under review.[4]

That being said, both the CBD Clearinghouse Mechanism and Biosafety
Clearinghouse have been, according to critics, 'underutilized' and 'developed
rather haphazardly.'[5] It has thus been observed that the shortcomings of the
existing mechanisms under the international biodiversity regime should be
taken in serious consideration in designing the ABS Clearinghouse.[6] The intergovernmental negotiations preparing for the entry into force of the Protocol
have in effect identified the need to implement the ABS Clearinghouse in a
phased manner,[7] with a pilot phase being put in place at the time of writing with a view to refining the draft modalities of operation of the ABS
Clearinghouse on the basis of preliminary experience in the implementation
of the pilot phase.[8]

The experience gained in the framework of the ITPGRFA could also be useful to that end. At the time of writing, the Informal Advisory Committee to
the pilot phase of the ABS Clearinghouse has already considered the relevance
of an information technology system developed in support of users of the
ITPGRFA Multilateral System – the 'Easy-SMTA.' The Easy-SMTA supports users
in generating standard material transfer agreements and reporting on these
agreements to the ITPGRFA Governing Body.[9]

---

4   Biosafety Protocol Article 20(4). For a commentary, see Mackenzie et al., *Explanatory Guide
    to the Cartagena Protocol*, op. cit., 132.

5   Young, "An International Cooperation Perspective," op. cit., 473.

6   We are grateful to Tomme Young for sharing her views on some of the shortcomings of the
    CBD and Biosafety Clearinghouses. On the Biosafety Clearinghouse, see generally Young,
    "Use of the Biosafety Clearing-house in Practise," op. cit.

7   ICNP Recommendation 1/1, "The modalities of operation of the Access and Benefit-
    sharing Clearing-house" in ICNP, "Report of the first meeting of the Open-Ended Ad Hoc
    Intergovernmental Committee for the Nagoya Protocol on Access to Genetic Resources and
    the Fair and Equitable Sharing of Benefits Arising from their Utilization" (21 July 2011) UN
    Doc UNEP/CBD/ICNP/1/8.

8   CBD Decision 11/1, "Status of the Nagoya Protocol on Access to Genetic Resources and the
    Fair and Equitable Sharing of Benefits Arising from their Utilization and related develop-
    ments" (5 December 2012) UN Doc UNEP/CBD/COP/11/35, section C, paragraph 2. See also
    "ABS Clearinghouse," CBD, accessed 30 November 2013, <http://absch.cbd.int/>.

9   See CBD, "Summary of outcomes of the meeting of the Informal Advisory Committee to
    the Pilot Phase of the Access and Benefit-sharing Clearing-house" (2–4 October 2013) UN
    Doc UNEP/CBD/ABS/IAC-CH/1/3. Easy-SMTA combines the SMTA generating and report-
    ing functions, which enable data to flow into a secure Data Store, with two additional tools:
    the Online SMTA Generating and Reporting, which supports the full SMTA workflow with

3   The Functions of the ABS Clearinghouse

Article 14(1) quite succinctly indicates that the overall function of the ABS Clearinghouse will be 'sharing of information' related to ABS and, in particular, 'providing *access to information* made available by each Party relevant to the implementation of this Protocol.'[10] The provision does not indicate whether access to all or part of the information will be open to the general public, although practice under the CBD indicates that this will likely be the case for a great part of the information to be provided in the ABS Clearinghouse. It should also be noted that access to information is a well-established principle in international human rights law insofar as it is necessary to give effect to other human rights such as the rights to life, private life, or access to justice.[11] Given the relevance of the Nagoya Protocol for the internationally recognized human rights of indigenous peoples,[12] more general standards related to access to information under human rights law may be relevant in the context of Article 14.[13] In addition, access to information is a well-established principle in international environmental law,[14] which is relevant for individual providers and users, but also the public at large or NGOs interested in following up on the implementation of the Protocol.

To a significant extent, the ABS Clearinghouse is intended to function as an 'information hub' for both providers and users and may possibly also assist to ascertain their rights and obligations before entering into an ABS transaction in a specific country,[15] based on the information provided on domestic ABS

---

functions for the generation, revision and acceptable of new SMTAS, as well as for the reporting to the ITPGRFA Governing Body on concluded SMTAS; and the Online Reporting Form, which addresses exclusively the reporting to the Governing Body on concluded SMTAS. See ITPGRFA Secretariat, "Vision paper on the further development of Article 17, Global Information System" (24–28 September 2013) FAO Doc IT/GB-5/13/17.

10   Emphasis added.
11   Alan Boyle, "Environment and Human Rights," in Wolfrum, *Max Planck Encyclopedia*, op. cit., paragraph 28.
12   See Introduction to this commentary, section 4.
13   Savaresi, "International Human Rights Law Implications," op. cit., 74 and 72.
14   Rio Declaration on Environment and Development, in "Report of the UN Conference on Environment and Development" (14 June 1992) UN Doc A/CONF.151/26/Rev.1 (Vol I), Annex (hereinafter, Rio Declaration), Principle 10; Jonas Ebbesson, "Access to Information on Environmental Matters," in Wolfrum, *Max Planck Encyclopedia*, op. cit.
15   Greiber et al., *Explanatory Guide*, op. cit., 150–151. But note that absence of information posted on the ABS Clearinghouse does not provide a defense for an alleged failure to

frameworks.[16] As indicated elsewhere in the Protocol, the ABS Clearinghouse will also provide information for potential users of traditional knowledge about their obligations.[17] Overall, it can be expected to have a 'major impact on commercial aspects of ABS transactions.'[18] Checking information on the ABS Clearinghouse may thus likely become a step in the due diligence procedures carried out by users.[19]

In addition, the ABS Clearinghouse may help keeping tabs of progress in national implementation of the Protocol; as well as cross-checking information provided by checkpoints on PIC, source of genetic resources, establishment of MAT and/or utilization of genetic resources.[20] The ABS Clearinghouse may also contribute to capacity building[21] and awareness raising.[22] It will store information on capacity-building initiatives, with a view to promoting synergy and coordination on capacity-building on ABS,[23] and by sharing information it will itself build capacity and raise awareness. Finally, the ABS Clearinghouse may also provide an opportunity for national authorities of various countries to network with one another, as well as with providers, users and experts in other jurisdictions. It may also possibly facilitate communication between one country's ABS national focal point, competent national authorities and other national authorities under other international environmental agreements.[24]

4   Types of Information

Article 14 leaves quite some discretion as to the type of information that should be included in the ABS Clearinghouse, by making reference to information that is 'relevant for the implementation of the Protocol' and is to be

---

comply with the domestic ABS frameworks: we are grateful to Tomme Young for drawing our attention to this point.

16   Nagoya Protocol Article 14(2)(a).

17   Nagoya Protocol Article 12(2). See this commentary on Article 12, section 3.

18   Young, "An International Cooperation Perspective," op. cit., 469.

19   We are grateful to Geoff Burton for drawing our attention to this point. On users' due diligence (as opposed to States' due diligence under the Protocol), see Conclusion to this commentary, section 3.

20   Nagoya Protocol Article 17(1)(a)(iii). See this commentary on Article 17, section 2.

21   See this commentary on Article 22.

22   See this commentary on Article 21.

23   Nagoya Protocol Article 22(6). CBD, "Issues for consideration in the Establishment of the ABS Clearing-house," UNEP/CBD/ABS/EM-CH/1/2, paragraph 4.

24   Young, "An International Cooperation Perspective," op. cit., 473–475.

provided, updated and processed through national focal points and/or competent national authorities.[25]

Article 14(2) indicates information that should be mandatorily provided to the ABS Clearinghouse, notably information relating to domestic ABS frameworks[26] that will be the basis of the cooperation between provider and user countries and will determine the conditions for ABS among users and providers. In addition, Parties are to provide information on the national focal point and competent national authorities, which in case of multiple authorities[27] must be accompanied by information on the respective responsibilities and specifications as to which authorities are responsible for specific genetic resources.[28]

The third type of mandatory information is 'permits or their equivalent issued at the time of access as evidence of the decision to grant PIC and of the establishment of MAT.'[29] This is linked to the obligation for Parties to *notify* the ABS Clearinghouse of the issuance of a permit granting PIC,[30] and the related indication that permits made available on the ABS Clearinghouse 'shall constitute an internationally recognized certificate of compliance.'[31] The Protocol, however, does not clarify specifically *how* information about domestic permits will be made available to the ABS Clearinghouse. A decision of the Protocol's governing body is therefore necessary to choose either to place an electronic copy of each permit into the Clearinghouse, although these would have differing formats and possibly be submitted in different languages; or place the information contained in the domestic permit into a common format,[32] as was the case for the Biosafety Clearinghouse.[33] At the time of writing, it appears from the intergovernmental negotiations preparing for the entry into force of

---

25   See this commentary on Article 13.

26   See discussion on difference in terminology in Nagoya Protocol Articles 5–7 and 15–16 in this commentary on Article 15, section 3.1.

27   In accordance with Nagoya Protocol Article 13(4).

28   CBD, "Issues for consideration in the establishment of the ABS Clearing-house," UNEP/CBD/ABS/EM-CH/1/2, paragraph 3.

29   Nagoya Protocol Article 14(2)(c).

30   Which is 'alluded to' in Nagoya Protocol Article 6(3)(e), as underlined by Young, "An International Cooperation Perspective," op. cit., 470.

31   Nagoya Protocol Article 17(2).

32   Young, "An International Cooperation Perspective," op. cit., 470–471.

33   ICNP, "Report of the Expert Meeting on the Modalities of Operation of the Access and Benefit-Sharing Clearing-house" (2 May 2011) UN Doc UNEP/CBD/ICNP/1/2, paragraph 7.

the Protocol that a common format will likely be used for all information being included in the ABS Clearinghouse.[34]

In addition, it has been considered 'not entirely clear' if some verification of the permits (or information on permits) will be carried out at the international level, particularly if they are posted by individuals that do not appear to be the national competent authority issuing the permit.[35] That may be the case of national competent authorities of user countries[36] that are expected to receive information on permits provided by their users to their checkpoints and to provide such information to the ABS Clearinghouse.[37] In addition, as Article 14 does not exclude that information may be provided to the ABS Clearinghouse by entities other than national authorities, intergovernmental organizations and other stakeholders may also provide information to the ABS Clearinghouse. While such information may be useful for the Protocol's implementation, managing possible conflicts or uncertainty that may arise vis-à-vis the information provided by Parties may become necessary.[38] At the time of writing, there are indications that metadata about the record, including status and who published a record, is likely to be made publicly available, and that a clear distinction is likely to be made between records that have been validated by governments and records that have been made available by others.[39] In addition, discussions on the advantages and disadvantages of having one single person responsible for authorizing the publication of national records

---

34   CBD, "Summary of outcomes of the meeting of the Informal Advisory Committee to the Pilot Phase of the ABS Clearing-house," UNEP/CBD/ABS/IAC-CH/1/3.

35   Young, "An International Cooperation Perspective," op. cit., 470.

36   See this commentary on Article 13, section 3, noting that the Protocol is silent on the duties of user-country Parties' competent national authorities.

37   Nagoya Protocol Article 17(1)(a)(iii), where it is not clear whether the checkpoints themselves will submit such information to the ABS Clearinghouse ('such information ... will ... be provided'). It can be argued, however, that for reasons of legal certainty and practicality at the international level, the national competent authorities should be the only ones submitting information to the ABS Clearinghouse (this would indeed allow for easier receipt at the international level, as Parties are obliged to notify who these authorities are to the CBD Secretariat: Nagoya Protocol Article 13(4)). Indeed, at the time of writing, intergovernmental negotiations preparing for the Protocol's entry into force have concluded that the information being provided to the ABS Clearinghouse under Article 17(1)(a)(iii) would be published by the national publishing authority: see CBD, "Summary of outcomes of the meeting of the Informal Advisory Committee to the Pilot Phase of the ABS Clearing-house," UNEP/CBD/ABS/IAC-CH/1/3.

38   We are grateful to Tomme Young for drawing our attention to this point.

39   Ibid.

in the ABS Clearinghouse have resulted in the proposal for a 'national publishing authority' validating records entered by authorized national users.[40]

The provisions on mandatory information to be included in the ABS Clearinghouse should be read in conjunction with the minimum information required for the internationally recognized certificate of compliance spelt out elsewhere in the Protocol, namely: issuing authority, date of issuance, provider, unique identifier of the certificate, person or entity to whom PIC was granted, subject-matter or genetic resource covered by the certificate; confirmation that MAT were established; confirmation that PIC was obtained; and commercial or non-commercial use.[41] The reference to permits or 'their equivalent' includes the voluntary use of the ITPGR standard Material Transfer Agreement for transfers of plant genetic resources falling outside ITPGR Annex I,[42] leaving flexibility to Parties to include information on the SMTA in the ABS Clearinghouse rather than issuing an additional permit. Statutory collection permissions or reliance on long-standing agreements between institutions and governments may also be covered by the term 'their equivilent'.[43]

The accuracy of information provided in permits, and the need for updating or amending a certificate,[44] represent a specific concern. In effect, over the twenty years of experience in ABS transactions accrued before the conclusion of the Protocol negotiations, users have noted problems in understanding whether an ABS permit is 'final' – in other words, no longer subject to appeal, alteration or withdrawal.[45] Intergovernmental negotiations preparing for the entry into force of the Protocol have likely clarified that the ABS Clearinghouse should allow Parties to amend or update submitted information in a way that preserves legal certainty, clarity and transparency in accordance with the Protocol, particularly in the case of a permit or its equivalent, if necessary and if mutually agreed, to reflect new circumstances relating to the utilization of the genetic resource.[46] In such instances, the original permit or its equivalent

---

40   Ibid. It can be argued that such a body could likely be the national focal point or the national competent authority: we are grateful to Geoff Burton for drawing our attention to this point.

41   Nagoya Protocol Article 17(4). CBD, "Issues for consideration in the Establishment of the ABS Clearing-house," UNEP/CBD/ABS/EM-CH/1/2, paragraph 4.

42   Chiarolla, Louafi and Schloen, "Analysis of the Relationship," op. cit., 104.

43   We are grateful to Geoff Burton for drawing our attention to this point.

44   CBD, "Issues for consideration in the Establishment of the ABS Clearing-house," UNEP/CBD/ABS/EM-CH/1/2, paragraph 6.

45   Young, "An International Cooperation Perspective," op. cit., 472.

46   See this commentary on Article 2, section 2.

should be retained in archived form.[47] According to the expert group on the ABS Clearinghouse, 'circumstances warranting updating a permit may include the subsequent taxonomic identification of new species collected under the permit or the inclusion of information that would enhance legal certainty, such as evidence of compliance with permit conditions and/or with [MAT].'[48]

Article 14(3) lists types of information that may be provided on a voluntary basis, including methods and tools developed to monitor genetic resources,[49] model contractual clauses[50] and codes of conduct and best practices.[51] In this connection, the ABS Clearinghouse can contribute to peer learning and bottom-up development of the international ABS regime. Significantly, Article 14(3) also points to the need to include information on relevant competent authorities of indigenous and local communities and information on genetic resources held by them and traditional knowledge as so decided, in light of the Protocol provisions related to these communities. Parties are expected to involve these communities in making available through the ABS Clearinghouse measures related to ABS for the utilization of traditional knowledge.[52] Community protocols and procedures[53] could also be made available through the ABS Clearinghouse with a view to raising awareness.[54] Another key legal question relates to the submission and management of information from indigenous and local communities, and particularly the extent to which these communities could retain control over information submitted by them. The intergovernmental negotiations preparing for the entry into force of the Nagoya Protocol resulted in a recommendation that in the context of the guidance on the pilot phase, Parties 'could consider' the establishment of 'community contact points' for the ABS Clearinghouse to facilitate effective participation of indigenous and local communities.[55]

---

47   ICNP Recommendation 1/1, paragraph 11.
48   ICNP, "Report of the Expert Meeting on the Modalities of Operation of the ABS Clearing-house," UNEP/CBD/ICNP/1/2, paragraph 7.
49   Nagoya Protocol Article 17.
50   See this commentary on Article 19.
51   See this commentary on Article 20.
52   Nagoya Protocol Article 12(2). This was suggested in CBD, "Issues for consideration in the Establishment of the ABS Clearing-house," UNEP/CBD/ABS/EM-CH/1/2, paragraph 4.
53   In light of Article 12(1). On community protocols, see commentary on Article 12 section 2.1.
54   Nagoya Protocol Article 21(i). This is discussed in CBD, "Issues for consideration in the Establishment of the ABS Clearing-house," UNEP/CBD/ABS/EM-CH/1/2, paragraph 22.
55   ICNP Recommendation 1/1, paragraph 10.

Overall, nothing in the Protocol prevents the inclusion of additional information beyond what is required or specifically suggested. For instance, it would be interesting to provide information on bilateral, regional and multilateral ABS and ABS-related agreements and arrangements,[56] as is specifically required under the Biosafety Protocol.[57] This type of information, as well as further information on domestic ABS frameworks, would be particularly important when implementing Parties' obligation under the Protocol to encourage non-Parties to submit information to the ABS Clearinghouse.[58]

5   Outstanding Legal Issues

The intergovernmental negotiations preparing for the entry into force of the Protocol have identified the need for Parties to reach common understanding on a series of legal questions that arise from the Protocol provisions on the ABS Clearinghouse.[59]

First, Article 14(2) points to the need to address situations of confidentiality,[60] which is also recalled elsewhere in relation to checkpoints collecting information on PIC.[61] The Protocol, however, does not provide any indication as to the kind of information that could be regarded as confidential or how such information should be protected.[62] The Protocol leaves this determination to national law, which varies greatly from one country to another in the matter of confidentiality.[63] As a result, uncertainty arises as to whether the domestic law of the user country, provider country or other country may apply,[64] although it may be argued that the applicable law would be that of the country

---

56   See this commentary on Article 4, section 3.

57   Biosafety Protocol, Article 20(3)(b).

58   See this commentary on Article 24. See discussion on the US in Burton, "Implementation of the Nagoya Protocol in JUSCANZ Countries," op. cit., 323.

59   ICNP Recommendation 2/4, "Modalities of operation of the Access and Benefit-sharing Clearing house" (26 July 2012) UN Doc UNEP/CBD/ICNP/REC/2/4, paragraph 6; and ICNP Recommendation 1/1, paragraph 1.

60   See also reference to confidentiality in Nagoya Protocol Article 17(4).

61   Nagoya Protocol Article 17(1)(a)(iii).

62   Greiber et al., *Explanatory Guide*, op. cit., 153, where a comparison is drawn with the stand-alone article on confidential information in the Biosafety Protocol Article 21 and comments by Mackenzie et al., *Explanatory Guide to the Cartagena Protocol*, op. cit., 137 ff.

63   Young, "An International Cooperation Perspective," op. cit., 471–472.

64   Ibid.

providing information to the ABS Clearinghouse.[65] It would be particularly useful for the Protocol's governing body to clarify the matter.[66] Indeed, intergovernmental negotiations preparing for the entry into force of the Protocol have considered whether no confidential information should be made available to the ABS Clearinghouse; whether the ABS Clearinghouse could receive confidential information and keep it confidential until confidentiality is no longer required;[67] or whether only partial information could be posted, with the explicit clarification that portions of information are left out for reasons of confidentiality.[68] Reasons for confidentiality may vary, ranging from commercial confidentiality to protect the economic interests of users, matters affecting national security, secret knowledge of indigenous and local communities, and the need to protect biodiversity from possible damage (with regard, for instance, to the location of rare and fragile species or ecosystems).[69] At the time of writing, intergovernmental negotiations preparing for the entry into force of the Protocol appear oriented to conclude that confidential information should not be submitted to the ABS Clearinghouse, as all information published there is likely going to be publicly available.[70]

Second, questions arising from the combined reading of Articles 14 and 17 that may require further intergovernmental negotiations include third-party transfers,[71] which could be disclosed together with other information on the internationally recognized certificate to enhance legal certainty, although there is no provision to that end in the Protocol. Questions also concern the tracking of the utilization of genetic resources;[72] and the identification of genetic

---

65   We are grateful to Geoff Burton for drawing our attention to this point.

66   Joji Cariño et al., *Nagoya Protocol*, op. cit., 103.

67   ICNP, "Report of the Expert Meeting on the Modalities of Operation of the ABS Clearing-house," UNEP/CBD/ICNP/1/2, paragraph 7.

68   CBD, "Issues for consideration in the Establishment of the ABS Clearing-house," UNEP/CBD/ABS/EM-CH/1/2, paragraph 5.

69   We are grateful to Geoff Burton for drawing our attention to this point.

70   CBD, "Summary of outcomes of the meeting of the Informal Advisory Committee to the Pilot Phase of the ABS Clearing-house," UNEP/CBD/ABS/IAC-CH/1/3.

71   Nagoya Protocol Article 17(3). See ICNP, "Report of the Expert Meeting on the Modalities of Operation of the ABS Clearing-house," UNEP/CBD/ICNP/1/2, paragraph 17(c). It should be recalled that Article 6(3)(g)(iii) does not create an obligation to include as a minimum requirement for MAT in domestic ABS frameworks clauses on third party transfers ('may include'): see this commentary on Article 6, section 7.

72   ICNP, "Report of the Expert Meeting on the Modalities of Operation of the ABS Clearing-house," UNEP/CBD/ICNP/1/2, paragraph 7. Note discussion on 'tracking' in this commentary on Article 17, section 2.1.

resources covered by a certificate,[73] in case of changes in taxonomic nomenclature resulting from scientific research, or following changes in identification.[74]

---

73   Nagoya Protocol Article 17(4)(f).
74   ICNP, "Report of the Expert Meeting on the Modalities of Operation of the ABS Clearing-house," UNEP/CBD/ICNP/1/2, paragraph 7.

Article 15. Compliance with Domestic Legislation or Regulatory Requirements on Access and Benefit-sharing

1. Each Party shall take appropriate, effective and proportionate legislative, administrative or policy measures to provide that genetic resources utilized within its jurisdiction have been accessed in accordance with prior informed consent and that mutually agreed terms have been established, as required by the domestic access and benefit-sharing legislation or regulatory requirements of the other Party.
2. Parties shall take appropriate, effective and proportionate measures to address situations of non-compliance with measures adopted in accordance with paragraph 1 above.
3. Parties shall, as far as possible and as appropriate, cooperate in cases of alleged violation of domestic access and benefit-sharing legislation or regulatory requirements referred to in paragraph 1 above.

1 Overview

Article 15 is the first of a series of provisions on compliance, that as a whole address both the development of domestic measures in provider and user countries and forms of international cooperation.[1] These can be considered the 'most far-reaching innovations of the Protocol...with a view to ensuring PIC and benefit-sharing.'[2] Together with the creation of an international compliance committee under the Protocol,[3] Articles 15–18 form the *compliance pillar* of the Protocol.[4] They are aimed to address long-standing concerns about the difficulty for provider countries alone to prevent, detect or obtain

---

1 See also Nagoya Protocol Articles 16–18.
2 Glowka and Normand, "The Nagoya Protocol on Access and Benefit-sharing," op. cit., 3.
3 See this commentary on Article 30.
4 CBD Access and Benefit-sharing Friends of the Co-Chairs Meeting, "Paper on selected key issues submitted by the Co-Chairs" (26–29 January 2010), paragraphs 10–14.

© KONINKLIJKE BRILL NV, LEIDEN, 2014 | DOI 10.1163/9789004217188_017

remedy from breaches of their domestic ABS measures related to their genetic resources when they are utilized in another country.[5]

Article 15 focuses on compliance with domestic ABS frameworks on genetic resources, whereas compliance with domestic ABS frameworks on traditional knowledge is addressed in a separate, similarly worded provision.[6] Both are aimed at achieving the Protocol's objective, i.e. ensuring fair and equitable benefit-sharing,[7] by creating obligations for Parties with users in their jurisdiction to take measures to support compliance with PIC and MAT established in the provider country.[8] Specifically, Article 15 creates three sets of obligations for State Parties (be they predominantly user or provider countries) with respect to compliance by individual users: 1) an obligation to *adopt* domestic measures to 'provide' for the respect of provider countries' national ABS measures related to PIC and MAT; 2) an obligation to *enforce* the user countries' domestic measures providing for the respect of provider countries' national ABS measures related to PIC and MAT; and 3) an obligation to *cooperate* with other States in addressing the violation of provider countries' national ABS measures.

The following sections will first clarify which specific instance of 'compliance' is addressed by Articles 15 and 16, and then address each obligation under Article 15 in turn, discussing key interpretative questions. These include the details of the obligation to enact domestic measures; the practical implications of the obligation to enforce these measures; and the situations in which international cooperation may be needed.

---

5   Glowka and Normand, "The Nagoya Protocol on Access and Benefit-sharing," op. cit., 34. See also on national measures to support compliance with PIC, CBD Working Group on ABS, "Measures to support compliance with prior informed consent of the contracting party providing genetic resources and mutually agreed terms on which access was granted, in contracting parties with users of such resources under their jurisdiction" (2 December 2005) UN Doc UNEP/CBD/WG-ABS/4/INF/1; and on claims of misappropriations, CBD Working Group on ABS, "Analysis of claims of unauthorised access and misappropriation of genetic resources and associated traditional knowledge" (22 December 2005) UN Doc UNEP/CBD/WG-ABS/4/INF/6.

6   See this commentary on Article 16.

7   See this commentary on Article 1, section 2.

8   Glowka and Normand, "Nagoya Protocol on Access and Benefit-sharing," op. cit., 35.

2   'Compliance' under Articles 15 and 16: Context and Responses to Conceptual Challenges

It should be preliminarily emphasized that the Nagoya Protocol refers to 'compliance' not only in the traditional sense under international environmental law of *State Parties'* respect for their *international* obligations,[9] but also to address the case of *users'* compliance with *domestic* ABS requirements and private-law contractual arrangements (MAT) – where users will most likely be private individuals or entities.[10] Therefore, as opposed to the Protocol provision on a *multilateral* system to address cases of non-compliance with *international* ABS obligations by State Parties under Article 30, Articles 15–18 extend the *bilateral* approach to ABS transactions to issues of *compliance with domestic* ABS requirements and contractual arrangements.[11] In other words, the Protocol promotes the creation of 'direct lines of communication between a Party providing genetic resources and a Party with users in its jurisdiction that may have violated the former's ABS requirements,'[12] rather than requiring a harmonized approach to compliance among all Parties.[13] Against this background, under Articles 15 and 16, the Protocol focuses on a specific case of lack of compliance with domestic ABS frameworks and MAT, namely, *misappropriation*[14] – the

---

9   The term has been used to avoid the diplomatically more 'explosive' term 'violation' of international environmental law: Jan Klabbers, "Compliance Procedures," in *The Oxford Handbook of International Environmental Law*, ed. Daniel Bodansky, Jutta Brunnée and Ellen Hey (Oxford: Oxford University Press, 2008), 997, 1007.

10   See ENB, "Summary of the First Meeting of the Intergovernmental Committee for the Nagoya Protocol to the Convention on Biological Diversity: 5–10 June 2011," vol. 9 no. 551, 13 June 2011, 12; and discussion in Elisa Morgera, "First Meeting of the Intergovernmental Committee for the Nagoya Protocol," op. cit., 247; and Young, "An International Cooperation Perspective," op. cit., 459.

11   Lago Candeira and Silvestri, "Challenges in the Implementation of the Nagoya Protocol," op. cit., 292.

12   Glowka and Normand, "Nagoya Protocol on Access and Benefit-sharing," op. cit., 35.

13   Lago Candeira and Silvestri, "Challenges in the Implementation of the Nagoya Protocol," op. cit., 292.

14   Chiarolla, "Role of Private International Law," op. cit., 424. The terms 'misappropriation' and 'misuse' were referred to in the negotiations of the Protocol CBD, "Report of the eighth meeting of the Ad Hoc Open-ended Working Group on Access and Benefit-sharing" (20 November 2009) UN Doc UNEP/CBD/COP/10/5/Add.2, paragraphs 84–86; and draft article 1 in the Cali Draft. While these two terms were not included in the final text of the Protocol, they continue to be used in ABS literature: see Glowka and Normand, "Nagoya Protocol on Access and Benefit-sharing," op. cit.; Chiarolla, "Role of Private International Law," op. cit., and Young, "International Cooperation Perspective," op. cit.

violation by a user of the requirements of a provider country for obtaining and respecting PIC at the time of access[15] and establishing contractual arrangements in accordance with domestic ABS frameworks.

Articles 15 and 16, therefore, seek to address a series of conceptual difficulties arising in the context of ABS under the CBD. The first conceptual difficulty concerns the fact that while benefit-sharing according to the CBD rests on an inter-State approach, in practice it is mostly private actors that manage transactions of genetic resources and produce benefits to be shared.[16] The second, consequent difficulty is that PIC is normally issued as an administrative decision governed by domestic public and/or administrative law, whereas MAT are normally set out in contracts under private law that are governed, to differing extents, by contractual freedom and by, in situations involving more than one jurisdiction, private international law.[17] Matters may be further complicated when the authority to grant PIC is attributed to non-State entities such as research institutes, in which case PIC is embodied in a private-law act and possibly combined with MAT; and when public authorities may include in their PIC certain standard contractual clauses, so that MAT are to some extent embodied in the administrative decision issuing PIC. The CBD reflects these conceptual challenges by providing for an obligation of means for all States to take measures 'with the aim of' benefit-sharing,[18] while clarifying that concrete benefit-sharing arrangements must be set out in MAT.[19] Beyond this, however, the CBD is silent on the specific measures or the mix of specific measures that

---

15   Note that the reference to 'accessed in accordance with prior informed consent' in Nagoya Protocol Article 15(1) can be interpreted as an obligation to carry out a substantive check of whether the content of PIC has been complied with at the time of access. On the other hand, there seems to be no requirement under the Protocol for a substantive check of compliance with the content of PIC after the time of access.

16   Glowka, Burhenne-Guilmin and Synge, *Guide to the Convention on Biological Diversity*, op. cit., 82; and Buck and Hamilton, "Nagoya Protocol," op. cit., 48.

17   See generally Chiarolla, "Role of Private International Law," op. cit.; and also Tvedt, "Beyond Nagoya," op. cit., 172.

18   CBD Article 15(7).

19   Concrete benefit-sharing arrangements in MAT are thus linked to decision-making on access by Parties providing genetic resources: see CBD Articles 15(4–5). As discussed in the Introduction to this commentary, section 1.3 and fn. 81 and this commentary on Articles 5, section 5, and 6, section 2, however, MAT may entail two contractual negotiations (at the time of access and possibly at a later stage, if the benefit-sharing clauses need to be adjusted because the value of the genetic resources has become clearer as a result of research).

must be taken by Parties to ensure compliance with domestic requirements and contractual clauses on benefit-sharing.

Such specific measures have, however, been identified by the Bonn Guidelines in a non-exhaustive manner:

- mechanisms to provide information to potential users on their obligations regarding access to genetic resources;
- measures encouraging the disclosure of the country of origin of the genetic resources and of the origin of traditional knowledge in applications for IPRS;
- measures aimed at preventing the use of genetic resources obtained without the PIC of the Party providing such resources;
- cooperation between Parties to address alleged infringements of ABS agreements;
- voluntary certification schemes for institutions abiding by ABS rules;
- measures discouraging unfair trade practices; and
- measures encouraging users to comply with their contractual obligations set out in MAT.[20]

As 'virtually none of the user-side legislative requirements set out in the Bonn Guidelines have been adopted in any country,'[21] there was little relevant experience at the time of the negotiations of the Protocol.[22] As a result, the Protocol leaves considerable flexibility to Parties in deciding which domestic measures will be necessary to implement Articles 15 and 16.[23] Nonetheless, in practice there is an underlying need to achieve *inter-operability* among Parties' respective domestic ABS frameworks with a view to ensuring that 'individually tailored national measures' work together to support a coherent and functioning international ABS framework.[24] Thus, although nothing in the Protocol requires coordination among Parties in the development of domestic ABS measures, exchange of information and consideration of other countries'

---

20   Bonn Guidelines, paragraph 16(d).

21   Tvedt and Young, *Beyond* Access, op. cit., 129; and CBD Secretariat, "Overview of recent developments at national and regional levels relating to access and benefit-sharing" (30 August 2007) UN Doc UNEP/ CBD/WG-ABS/5/4, paragraph 3.

22   CBD Working Group on ABS, "Report of the meeting of the group of legal and technical experts on compliance in the context of the international regime on access and benefit-sharing" (10 February 2009) UN Doc UNEP/CBD/WG-ABS/7/3.

23   Greiber et al., *Explanatory Guide*, op. cit., 163.

24   Glowka and Normand, "Nagoya Protocol on Access and Benefit-sharing," op. cit., 37.

domestic ABS frameworks will likely occur.[25] These exchanges may be facilitated by the Protocol's governing body,[26] but may also arise in the context of bilateral negotiations among Parties,[27] including in the context of capacity-building activities.[28]

3   Obligation to Adopt Domestic User-side Measures

Article 15(1) obliges Parties to the Protocol to take domestic user-side measures. The reference to 'each Party' in that regard serves to underline that all countries should take such measures in recognition of the fact that no Party is uniquely a provider or user country.[29] In addition, this reference also indicates that a Party that waives its right to PIC remains subject to this obligation, in order to support the measures adopted in another Party.[30]

Under Article 15(1), user countries' obligations relate only *indirectly* to the breach of the provider countries' domestic ABS frameworks. That is, the obligation is to adopt domestic *user*-side measures that will relate to a breach of domestic *provider*-side measures on PIC and MAT. In practice, however, the breach of the domestic user-side measures is inherently linked to the 'original' breach of provider-side measures – that is, the misappropriation of genetic resources in violation of the PIC requirement and the requirement to establish MAT in accordance with provider countries' domestic ABS frameworks. The following sub-sections will first discuss the meaning of the obligation to 'provide' for the respect for provider-side domestic ABS frameworks, including interpretative difficulties arising from the text of Article 15(1), and then discuss means of implementation.

3.1   *The Obligation to 'Provide'*

Article 15(1) establishes a procedural obligation to 'provide for' the respect of provider countries' domestic ABS frameworks. Instead of requiring Parties to

---

25   We are grateful to Tomme Young for drawing our attention to this point.

26   Article 26(4)(a). See this commentary on Article 26, section 2.

27   Young, "An International Cooperation Perspective," op. cit., 496–498. See this commentary on Article 4, section 3.

28   The Protocol provision on capacity-building specifically mentions the need for assistance in developing domestic ABS measures, Nagoya Protocol Article 22(5)(a). See this commentary on Article 22.

29   See Introduction to this commentary, section 1.3.

30   Greiber et al., *Explanatory Guide*, op. cit., 160. On State PIC, see Nagoya Protocol Article 6(1) and this commentary on Article 6, section 3.1.

ensure users' compliance with provider countries' measures,[31] the obligation to *provide* can be interpreted as a procedural duty to *confirm* that users have complied with PIC at the time of access[32] and established MAT in accordance with the provider countries' ABS framework. It does not create an obligation for each Party to recognize and apply in its jurisdiction the ABS laws of another Party where genetic resources had been acquired, and sanction breaches of domestic legislation of other Parties by users in its jurisdiction.[33] Although such an approach is not excluded by the letter of the Protocol, it would in practice be quite difficult for Parties to enforce a variety of different approaches to ABS transactions regulated by different provider countries making use of the flexibility for national implementation built into the Protocol.[34] Against this background, the Protocol arguably requires at a minimum the adoption of domestic user-side measures that would task user countries to check the *formal* issuance of PIC and the *formal* establishment of MAT in another Party.[35] This would, as a first step, entail that user countries check the existence of the internationally recognized certificate of compliance in the ABS Clearinghouse.[36] This could also possibly entail more than simply requiring users to provide a declaration to that end without any form of verification by the provider country, particularly as Article 15(1) refers to 'accordance with' PIC (whereas it refers only to the existence, i.e. the establishment, of MAT). Rather, Parties to the Protocol need to exercise due diligence[37] in order to confirm that

---

31 Negotiators considered and eventually decided against using the term 'ensure:' Cali Draft, draft Article 12(1), paragraph 98. Agreement on the final wording 'to provide' was reached in July 2010: see Montreal I Draft, draft article 12(1), 27. Note, however, that the French and Spanish versions of the Protocol (that are equally authentic: Nagoya Protocol Article 36) use the terms *'garantir'* and *'asegurar'*, both of which can be translated as 'to guarantee' in English. We are grateful to an anonymous reviewer for drawing our attention to this point.

32 See fn. 15 above.

33 See CBD Working Group on ABS, "Report of the eighth meeting of the Ad Hoc Open-ended Working Group on Access and Benefit-Sharing" (20 November 2009) UN Doc UNEP/CBD/WG-ABS/8/8, Annex, paragraphs 60–61; Tvedt, "Beyond Nagoya," op. cit., 173, noting that the Protocol does not make the law of a provider country 'directly enforceable' under the jurisdiction of the user country.

34 CBD Working Group on ABS, "Report of the expert meeting on compliance", UNEP/CBD/WG-ABS/7/3, paragraphs 16 ff.; ENB 9/527, "Summary of the Resumed Ninth Meeting of the Working Group on ABS", 9–10.

35 Greiber et al., *Explanatory Guide*, op. cit., 163.

36 See this commentary on Article 14, section 3, and on Article 17, section 3.

37 See Conclusions to this commentary, section 3.

the users under their jurisdiction respected the applicable domestic framework of the provider country.

That being said, although the Protocol does not require user-side measures for the direct extraterritorial enforcement of domestic ABS frameworks of other Parties, these could still be given some extraterritorial application. It has in fact been argued that in as far as instances of non-compliance with PIC and MAT requirements have to be determined in the user-country jurisdiction, provider-country Parties' domestic ABS frameworks would need to be applied in user-country courts to qualify the disputed facts on the merit.[38]

Three other interpretative questions arise in the context of Article 15(1). One interpretative difficulty arises from the difference in wording between the provider country's domestic ABS measures mentioned in Article 15(1) ('legislation or regulatory requirements'), which reflects the expression used in Article 6(1), and those that are to be adopted under Article 6(3) ('legislative, administrative or policy measures').[39] While in principle these two sets of provisions speak to the same set of domestic measures that require PIC and MAT in the provider country prior to access to genetic resources, Article 6(3) allows Parties to adopt not only legislative, but also administrative or policy measures. Articles 6(1) and 15(1) in turn appear to refer only to ABS legal requirements established by parliament or the administration. A literal interpretation could lead one to understand that only in the case in which the provider country has adopted legislation, will it be able to benefit from the user compliance measures under Article 15(1).[40] In other words, policy or administrative measures on ABS would not trigger user countries' international obligations concerning their individual users' compliance under Article 15. A systematic and effectiveness-oriented interpretation, however, leads to consider that administrative or policy measures adopted under Article 6(3) could amount to 'regulatory requirements' for the purposes of Article 15(1) as long as they are properly publicized, understandable, internally coherent and containing clear indications about the need to obtain PIC and establish MAT (both in writing), and on benefit-sharing.[41] In that regard, even if a Party encounters difficulty in passing legislation on ABS immediately following the entry into force of the Protocol, it would be

---

38   Chiarolla, "Role of Private International Law," op. cit., 440.

39   The same terminological discrepancy can be found when comparing Nagoya Protocol Articles 16 and 7 on PIC and MAT for access to traditional knowledge: see this commentary on Article 16, section 2.

40   Greiber et al., *Explanatory Guide*, op. cit., 169.

41   In that regard, the ABS Clearinghouse could be used to publicize the measures, according to Nagoya Protocol Article 14(2)(a).

well advised to establish policy or administrative measures that are publicized, clear and comprehensive, with a view to benefitting from the compliance provisions of the Protocol.[42] A good-faith interpretation of Articles 6 and 15 also leads to this conclusion, in particular in consideration of the explicitly acknowledged capacity issues of developing countries in developing domestic ABS measures.[43] The absence of *any* domestic measure amounting to domestic 'regulatory requirements' on ABS would deprive provider countries of their possibility to trigger user countries' international obligations on their users' compliance under Article 15.[44]

Another element of Article 15(1) in need of clarification is the reference to 'the other Party', as opposed to the expression used elsewhere in the Protocol 'the Party providing [genetic] resources that is the country of origin or a Party that acquired genetic resources in accordance with the Convention'.[45] It has been argued that the expression 'the other Party' refers 'the Party that factually provided the material and issued PIC.'[46] This would suggest that Parties where genetic resources are utilized must accept PIC decisions of other Parties and internationally recognized certificates of compliance at their face value. In other words, unless there are indications to the contrary, user countries would not be expected to check whether sovereign claims of provider countries over the genetic resources at stake are well founded.[47] The potential for this interpretation to lead to contradictory results has, however, been highlighted. It may allow a Party to be in compliance with the Protocol even if it only takes measures to ensure compliance with domestic ABS requirements of intermediary countries regardless of whether the genetic resources have been legally acquired by such countries.[48] The provision may further be interpreted so that possible disputes about sovereignty claims over genetic resources would

---

42   Singh Nijar, "An Asian Developing Country's View," op. cit., 254.

43   The Nagoya Protocol specifically acknowledges these challenges in Article 22(4)(c).

44   Tvedt, "Beyond Nagoya," op. cit., 164, who notes that 'the main regulatory burden is left with the provider country.'

45   See this commentary on Article 5, section 2. The same expression also appears in Nagoya Protocol Articles 6(1) and 23, while 'the other Party' only appears in Article 16(1): Greiber et al., *Explanatory Guide*, op. cit., 163. Note that a reference to 'country of origin' appeared in draft article 12 in the Nagoya Draft. The reference was deleted in the final negotiation of the Protocol.

46   As reported by Chiarolla, "Role of Private International Law," op. cit., 442; see also reference in Nagoya Protocol Article 17(3) to 'the Party providing' PIC.

47   Greiber et al., *Explanatory Guide*, op. cit., 163–164. See this commentary on Article 6, section 3.

48   Chiarolla, "Role of Private International Law," op. cit., 443.

need to be settled between the States claiming sovereign rights over the same genetic resource.

Third, Article 15(1) focuses on genetic resources 'utilized' within user countries' jurisdiction, based on the definition of 'utilization of genetic resources' in the Protocol.[49] It can be argued that the flexibility inherent in the definition of utilization may lead Parties to adjust or possibly expand measures taken under Article 15(1) in response to new forms of research and development on gene sequences and naturally occurring biochemicals. In addition, Article 15(1) applies to the 'utilization' of genetic resources – i.e., on research and development. Article 15(1) in effect does not mention 'subsequent applications and commercialization' of genetic resources, although these are explicitly covered by the general, inter-State benefit-sharing obligation in Article 5(1). A combined reading of Article 15(1) and Article 5 would support the argument that obligations related to providing for users' compliance with provider countries' domestic ABS frameworks should be extended so as to correspond to the obligation to ensure benefit-sharing also from subsequent application and commercialization. This argument may be backed up by practical considerations: regulating only activities intended for research and development, which mostly occur as internal processes within private companies that are often covered by confidentiality, and distinguishing them clearly from further utilization and commercialization is very difficult in practice.[50] On the other hand, it can be contended that Protocol negotiators discussed, and eventually decided against, referring to 'subsequent application and commercialization' in Article 15,[51] because of practical enforcement challenges and concerns about possible implications for international trade. This may suggest that non-compliance issues related to the final phase of the genetic resource value chain should be addressed on the basis of contractual claims in the context of the Protocol's provision on compliance with MAT.[52] Ultimately, in the absence of an explicit exclusion of subsequent application and commercialization from the definition of 'utilization' in Article 2 and from Article 15(1), Parties have discretion to extend their implementing measures under Article 15(1) also to subsequent application and commercialization of genetic resources, particularly where – in their respective domestic context – this seems necessary to

---

49   See this commentary on Article 2, section 2.

50   We are grateful to Tomme Young for drawing our attention to this point.

51   ENB, "Summary of the Interregional Negotiating Group on Access and Benefit-sharing: 18–21 September 2010", 2–3.

52   Greiber et al., *Explanatory Guide*, op. cit., 162. See this commentary on Article 18.

effectively implement their obligation to ensure benefit-sharing also from subsequent application and commercialization.[53]

3.2   *Means of Implementation*

The reference in Article 15(1) to 'appropriate, effective and proportionate' measures implies that user-side measures should be fit for the purpose of contributing to compliance with provider countries' measures and of ensuring the realization of the Protocol's objective of fairly and equitably sharing benefits. That being said, such measures could also be understood as being reasonable, workable and not excessively burdensome,[54] taking into account the actual implementation and enforcement capacities of different countries. The reference to 'appropriate, effective and proportionate' user-side measures has also been interpreted in a more expansive way, so as to argue that domestic user-side measures would 'fall short of meeting [these requirements] unless the concerned Parties provide that an opportunity to seek recourse is available under their legal system in case of disputes arising from non-compliance with such user measures.'[55]

It should be emphasized, however, that there is a scarcity of examples of user-side measures.[56] Possible measures could include requiring users to prove that the genetic resources were accessed legally according to the provider country's domestic ABS framework at the time of import of the genetic resources, or at the time of seeking an authorization to develop and/or place on the market products based on genetic resources.[57] Some countries have interpreted this as obliging all users of genetic resources to exercise due diligence so that applicable ABS requirements in provider countries have been respected.[58]

---

53   Nagoya Protocol Article 5(1). See this commentary on Article 5, section 2.

54   Greiber et al., *Explanatory Guide*, op. cit., 161.

55   Chiarolla, "Role of Private International Law," op. cit., 434 and 439.

56   Tvedt, "Beyond Nagoya," op. cit., 164; one exception is Norwegian law, discussed by Morten W. Tvedt and Ole K. Fauchald, "Implementing the Nagoya Protocol on ABS: A Hypothetical Case Study on Enforcing Benefit Sharing in Norway," *The Journal of World Intellectual Property* 14 (2011): 383, 392–398.

57   Tvedt, "Beyond Nagoya," op. cit., 164.

58   EU draft regulation, draft article 4(1), which reads: 'Users shall exercise due diligence to ascertain that genetic resources and traditional knowledge associated with genetic resources used were accessed in accordance with applicable access and benefit-sharing legislation or regulatory requirements and that, where relevant, benefits are fairly and equitably shared upon mutually agreed terms.'

It is also noteworthy that, as opposed to the access standards outlined else-where in the Protocol with a view to guiding provider countries,[59] Article 15(1) does not provide any standard for user-side measures.[60] In particular, it does not address whether user countries should also assess the *content* of MAT and the extent to which benefit-sharing requirements contained in MAT correspond to the notions of *fairness and equity*.[61]

4   Obligation to Enforce

Article 15(2) creates an obligation for Parties to establish domestically how breaches of domestic *user*-side measures on their users' compliance with *provider* countries' domestic ABS frameworks will be identified and sanctioned. Put differently, the remedies and sanctions provided for in the law of the *user* country will be enforced against the user, for breaching *user*-side measures on compliance with PIC and MAT requirements of the provider country. Conversely, Article 15(2) does not imply that the remedies and sanctions provided for in the law of the *provider* country will be applied in user countries.[62]

Appropriate, effective and proportionate enforcement measures will vary from case to case depending on the type of domestic measure violated, the gravity of the breach, and also on whether measures are applied by the public administration or by domestic courts of a Party. As the Protocol leaves an ample margin of discretion to Parties, sanctions may include: revocation of IPRs and market approvals;[63] obligation on the user to seek PIC and establish MAT from the legitimate provider as a precondition for continuing utilization; in case economic benefits have already been accrued, obligation to negotiate benefit-sharing arrangement with the legitimate provider; obligation to pay a fixed amount to the legitimate provider, irrespective of MAT; monetary fines or the criminalization of certain acts and the prohibition of using genetic resources when obligations have been violated.[64] It has been suggested that

---

59   Nagoya Protocol Article 6(3)(a–b) See this commentary on Article 6, section 6.

60   Tvedt, "Beyond Nagoya," op. cit., 165.

61   Ibid. See also Nagoya Protocol Articles 6(3)(g) and 18; and this commentary on Article 6, section 7 and on Article 18, section 1; and Conclusions to this commentary, section 3.

62   Chiarolla, "Role of Private International Law," op. cit., 440, note 53.

63   These and other ideas were proposed in the negotiation: see, on disclosure requirement and tools to enforce compliance, CBD Working Group on ABS "Report of the seventh meeting," UNEP/CBD/WG-ABS/7/8, Annex, 51–53.

64   Greiber et al., *Explanatory Guide*, op. cit., 164.

sanctions should be at least as serious and costly as the implications arising from MAT, to avoid creating a disincentive for users to adhere to the rules of the providing country.[65] Against this backdrop, the Protocol's governing body may initiate a process to consider best practices in implementing Article 15(2) and possibly provide some guidance on this matter in the future.[66]

Article 15(2) in effect presupposes that Parties will actively detect instances where users within their jurisdiction are in a situation of non-compliance, in particular through the information gathered by checkpoints[67] and internationally recognized certificates of compliance in the ABS Clearinghouse, particularly if (some) Parties determine that issuance of the certificate is mandatory.[68] Additional information may be provided by users themselves, either on the basis of voluntary due diligence or mandatory reporting and auditing procedures. Factual, administrative and judicial findings by responsible authorities of provider countries may also serve as a useful source of evidence for relevant authorities in user countries. Although findings from provider countries will not be the only determinant factor in triggering user countries' enforcement measures, complete disregard for these determinations in the provider country may be considered as proof of lack of good faith in implementing Article 15(2).[69] Particularly in the case of third-party transfers – i.e., in cases when the person/entity misappropriating the material is not the one utilizing it, information from the provider country may be especially useful. Other sources that may contribute to detecting instances of users' non-compliance include media reports or communications from other Parties to the Protocol.

5   Obligation to Cooperate

The third obligation under Article 15 concerns an obligation to cooperate in cases of alleged violation of the 'other' countries' domestic ABS framework. Thus, as opposed to Article 15(1)–(2), the obligation is triggered in a broader set of instances, namely violation of the provider country's ABS legislation

---

65   Tvedt, "Beyond Nagoya," op. cit., 165.

66   See this commentary on Article 26.

67   Nagoya Protocol Article 17(2–4). See this commentary on Article 17, section 2.

68   Nagoya Protocol Article 17(1). See this commentary on Article 17, section 3.

69   It should be noted that questions related to the legal recognition and enforcement of foreign administrative or judicial decisions in the jurisdiction of Parties where genetic resources are utilized are addressed under Nagoya Protocol Article 18(2)(b). See this commentary on Article 18, section 3.

in general, and not necessarily limited to specific requirements on PIC and MAT. Clearly, violations of domestic ABS frameworks may occur even if PIC was granted and MAT were established. So the scope of application of Parties' obligation to cooperate could cover other instances, such as disregard for minimum requirements for MAT in provider country's legislation or failure to provide required information on bioprospecting activities to be included in national registries in provider countries.

Article 15(3) obliges all Parties (whether provider and user countries) to cooperate on specific cases of alleged violations of domestic ABS frameworks. According to general international law, the obligation to cooperate requires States to *enter into coordinated action* under a legal regime so as to achieve its specific goal.[70] In this specific case, the obligation entails that Parties exert good-faith efforts to identify potentially concerned Parties and engage them with a view to reaching agreement on coordinated action in the investigation of and/or follow up on alleged non-compliance by users.[71] Such cooperation can either involve the provision of information from user countries to provider countries trying to ascertain whether a violation of their own domestic ABS frameworks has occurred, or from provider countries to user countries trying to ascertain whether a violation of other Parties' domestic ABS frameworks has occurred. As Article 15(3) is broadly framed, cooperation with other Parties that were not involved in the potential situation of non-compliance[72] and on a multilateral (rather than merely bilateral) basis is also possible.

The choice of the *means* to identify and engage other concerned States is left to each Party ('as far as possible and as appropriate'), but the qualified language of this provision does not leave discretion for a Party to decide *against* cooperation.[73] Therefore, lack of *any reasonable* effort to identify and engage potentially concerned States would be in violation of this due diligence obligation. If agreement cannot be reached, the Protocol does not impede States from making unilateral decisions, but it creates the expectation that such decisions will be made taking into consideration other States' and, where relevant, indigenous and local communities' interests, in realizing the objective of the Protocol in relation to fair and equitable benefit-sharing.[74] It may also entail the obligation for Parties to address persistent or recurring difficulties in

---

70   For a discussion, see this commentary on Article 11, section 2.
71   Greiber et al., *Explanatory Guide*, op. cit., 164.
72   Greiber et al., *Explanatory Guide*, op. cit., 165.
73   See Introduction to this commentary, section 5 and fn. 227. See contra Greiber et al., *Explanatory Guide*, op. cit., 164.
74   See this commentary on Article 1, section 2.

implementing Article 15(3) by progressively developing the legal regime established by the Nagoya Protocol.[75] The reference to 'alleged' violations implies that there is no requirement to prove that there has been an actual violation in order for Parties to seek collaboration with each other.[76]

The obligation, as is customary in international treaties, also leaves Parties discretion in determining which administrative entity will be responsible for such cooperation. The point of first contact in this regard is likely to be the national ABS focal point,[77] which could then also support the channeling of cooperation requests to the political, administrative or judicial authority responsible for appropriate follow-up. This, however, is more likely to function as an initial, informal contact between Parties. Diplomatic processes must likely be followed to formalize the cooperation.[78] Depending on the designated authority, powers in carrying out such cooperation may vary.

---

75   This argument is developed in this commentary on Article 11, section 2.

76   Greiber et al., *Explanatory Guide*, op. cit., 164.

77   Nagoya Protocol Article 13(1); see this commentary on Article 13, section 2.

78   We are grateful to Tomme Young for drawing our attention to this point.

Article 16. Compliance with Domestic Legislation or Regulatory Requirements on Access and Benefit-sharing for Traditional Knowledge Associated with Genetic Resources

1. Each Party shall take appropriate, effective and proportionate legislative, administrative or policy measures, as appropriate, to provide that traditional knowledge associated with genetic resources utilized within their jurisdiction has been accessed in accordance with prior informed consent or approval and involvement of indigenous and local communities and that mutually agreed terms have been established, as required by domestic access and benefit-sharing legislation or regulatory requirements of the other Party where such indigenous and local communities are located.
2. Each Party shall take appropriate, effective and proportionate measures to address situations of non-compliance with measures adopted in accordance with paragraph 1 above.
3. Parties shall, as far as possible and as appropriate, cooperate in cases of alleged violation of domestic access and benefit-sharing legislation or regulatory requirements referred to in paragraph 1 above.

1   Overview

Article 16 creates a set of novel international obligations, going much beyond the CBD, which was silent on ABS related to traditional knowledge and therefore also on questions related to compliance in that connection. Article 16 was subject to arduous negotiations, due to a divergence of views as to whether other international processes such as negotiations under WIPO should provide for the protection of traditional knowledge[1] or whether the Protocol should

---

1 It was opposed in particular by the EU, who preferred that the issue be dealt with in the framework of the WIPO Intergovernmental Committee on Intellectual Property and Genetic Resources, Traditional Knowledge and Folklore: Lago Candeira and Silvestri, "Challenges in the Implementation of the Nagoya Protocol," op. cit., 292.

create a comprehensive compliance system that would apply both to the utilization of genetic resources and to the utilization of traditional knowledge.[2]

Specifically, Article 16 creates a series of obligations for Parties with respect to compliance by traditional knowledge users: 1) an obligation to *adopt* user-side domestic measures to 'provide' for the respect by users of domestic ABS requirements of 'other Parties where indigenous and local communities [providing PIC on traditional knowledge] are located'[3] regarding community PIC and MAT concerning traditional knowledge utilization;[4] 2) an obligation to *enforce* domestic user-side measures in relation to users' non-compliance with domestic ABS requirements of other Parties related to community PIC and MAT on access to traditional knowledge; and 3) an obligation to *cooperate* in addressing the violation of domestic ABS measures on traditional knowledge.

The following sections will briefly recapitulate the findings related to the interpretation of Article 15, which (given similarity in structure and wording) are of relevance for the interpretation of Article 16, and then discuss key asymmetries in the provisions of the Protocol on users' compliance in relation to traditional knowledge as opposed to users' compliance in relation to genetic resources.

2   Similarities and Differences vis-à-vis Article 15

Article 16 mirrors the structure and wording of Article 15. The general observations made with regard to the latter's rationale also apply here.[5] Some of the more specific arguments made in relation to the interpretation of the text of Article 15 are summarized below for ease of reference.

The obligation under Article 16(1) to adopt user-side measures on compliance with traditional knowledge applies to 'each Party,' in order to underline that all countries should take such measures in recognition of the fact that no Party is uniquely a provider or user country. It also indicates that countries where traditional knowledge is not present should enact user measures in relation to ABS from the utilization of traditional knowledge located in

---

2 Greiber et al., *Explanatory Guide*, op. cit., 168. On the lack of definition of utilization of traditional knowledge, see this commentary on Article 2, section 3.

3 This expression is considered more specific than the reference to 'other Party' in Nagoya Protocol Article 15: Chiarolla, "Role of Private International Law," op. cit., 441; and this commentary on Article 15, section 3.1.

4 I.e., measures adopted under Nagoya Protocol Article 7. See this commentary on Article 7.

5 See this commentary on Article 15, section 2.

other countries. The obligation to 'provide' respect for other Parties' national ABS frameworks entails at the very least confirming that users have complied with the PIC requirement and established MAT in accordance with the other Parties' domestic ABS framework. In other words, Parties are to exercise due diligence[6] in order to confirm that the users under their jurisdiction respected the applicable domestic framework of the provider country on PIC and MAT. While therefore the Protocol does not require user-side measures for the direct extraterritorial enforcement of domestic ABS frameworks of other Parties in relation to traditional knowledge, these could still be given some extraterritorial application. It has in fact been argued that in as far as instances of non-compliance with PIC and MAT have to be determined in the user-country jurisdiction, provider-country Parties' domestic ABS frameworks would need to be relied upon in user-country courts to qualify the disputed facts on the merit.[7]

The obligation in Article 16(1), however, contains the qualification 'as appropriate,' which is not present in Article 15(1), thereby indicating that while Parties are still obliged to fulfill this obligation, they have a larger margin of discretion in choosing the means of implementation.[8] In that regard, it may also be useful to recall that the reference to 'appropriate, effective and proportionate' user-side measures can be interpreted as implying the need to also provide an opportunity for recourse under the provider country's legal system in case of disputes arising from non-compliance with user-side measures related to traditional knowledge.[9] This qualification may also point to the challenge that might be encountered by a user country becoming aware of misappropriation of traditional knowledge from a provider country where no domestic ABS framework related to traditional knowledge is in place. In such a hypothetical scenario, the user country may find itself in the impossibility to apply its user-side compliance measures, as these would not be triggered by a violation of the provider country's domestic ABS framework. It can be speculated that in this case the concerned Parties, and possibly also representatives of indigenous and local communities,[10] may bring the case to the Protocol's compliance mechanism.[11]

---

6   See Conclusions to this commentary, section 3.
7   Chiarolla, "Role of Private International Law, " op. cit., 440.
8   See Introduction to this commentary, section 5 and fn. 227.
9   Chiarolla, "Role of Private International Law, " op. cit., 434 and 439.
10   See this commentary on Article 30, section 3.2.
11   This commentary on Article 30, section 3. It may also be observed that this could be a case in which the establishment of an international ombudsman (discussed in this commentary on Article 30, section 3.2) may be particularly useful.

The interpretative difficulty arising from the difference in wording between the provider country's domestic ABS measures on traditional knowledge mentioned in Article 16(1) and those that are to be adopted under Article 7,[12] should be addressed through systemic and effectiveness-oriented interpretation. Accordingly, administrative or policy measures adopted under Article 7 could amount to 'regulatory requirements' for the purposes of Article 16(1), as long as they are properly publicized, capable of comprehension, prospective, internally coherent and containing clear indications on issuing PIC and establishing MAT in writing, and on benefit-sharing. The absence of *any* domestic measure amounting to domestic 'regulatory requirements' on ABS from traditional knowledge would deprive provider countries of the possibility to trigger user countries' international obligations concerning users' compliance under Article 16.

Article 16(2) creates an obligation for Parties to establish domestically how breaches of domestic user-side measures on compliance with other Parties' domestic ABS requirements related to traditional knowledge will be identified and sanctioned. Non-compliance by users under Article 16(2) is constituted by a breach of the measures taken by the Party where traditional knowledge is utilized, and not directly by a breach of other Parties' domestic ABS frameworks provisions on access to traditional knowledge (i.e., violation of PIC and MAT requirements). Nonetheless, in practice, the breach of the user country's measures on compliance is inextricably linked to the breach of the other Party's domestic framework on PIC and MAT. Similarly to Article 15(2), this obligation presupposes that Parties will actively detect instances where users in their jurisdiction are in a situation of non-compliance vis-à-vis other Parties' domestic ABS frameworks on traditional knowledge.

Article 16(3) creates an obligation for all Parties to cooperate in following up on specific cases of alleged violations of Parties' domestic ABS frameworks in as far as they concern traditional knowledge, even where there is no proof of actual violation of the provider country's ABS legislation and not necessarily with regard only to possible violations of specific requirements on PIC and MAT.

Given the novelty of Article 16, this provision appears as one of the most challenging to implement at the national level, as it will present unprecedented legal questions, particularly with regard to the cross-cutting obligation under the Protocol to take due regard to indigenous and local communities'

---

12   Article 7 simply refers to the adoption of 'measures' (and not more specifically 'legislative, administrative or policy measures' on benefit-sharing arising from the utilization of traditional knowledge called for in Article 6(5)).

customary laws[13] and the duty under general international law to interpret and apply this provision in the light of relevant international human rights standards.[14] In the light of the open-ended drafting of Article 16, the Protocol's governing body may initiate a process to consider best practices in implementing Article 16 and possibly provide some guidance on this matter in the future.[15] This may also become necessary in case of subsequent developments in other relevant international processes. For this reason, the first review of the Protocol[16] is expected to assess in particular the implementation of Article 16 in light of developments in other relevant international organizations, including, *inter alia*, WIPO,[17] provided that they do not run counter to the CBD and the Protocol objectives.[18] It should be finally noted that the implementation of Article 16 may be facilitated by, and fuel, efforts to make indigenous and local communities' customary laws and procedures better understood by governments and users.[19]

3   **Lack of Parallel Provisions on Compliance Concerning ABS Related to Genetic Resources and ABS Related to Traditional Knowledge**

International obligations related to users' compliance with domestic ABS frameworks related to traditional knowledge, similarly to those related to genetic resources, may be expected to be triggered by monitoring activities,[20] which are addressed in Article 17. That provision, however, only focuses on monitoring utilization of genetic resources, and makes no reference to traditional knowledge. Therefore, the Protocol establishes no obligation for Parties' checkpoints to collect information on PIC and MAT relating to traditional knowledge utilization. Similarly, the internationally recognized certificate of compliance does not seem to relate to traditional knowledge associated

---

13   Nagoya Protocol Article 12(1) and this commentary on Article 12, section 2. See also CBD Working Group on ABS, "Study on compliance in relation to the customary law of indigenous and local communities, national law, across jurisdictions, and international law" (6 March 2009) UN Doc UNEP/CBD/WG-ABS/7/INF/5.

14   See Introduction to this commentary, section 4.

15   Nagoya Protocol Article 26(4)(a). See this commentary on Article 26, section 2.

16   See this commentary on Article 25.

17   See this commentary on Article 4, section 3.1.

18   CBD Decision 10/1, paragraph 6.

19   Nagoya Protocol Article 12: see this commentary on Article 12, section 2.

20   See this commentary on Article 15, section 4.

with genetic resources: its minimum information requirements make no reference to it.[21]

This arguably reflects the fact that the Protocol negotiators were unclear whether it would be feasible to include traditional knowledge in the internationally recognized certificate of compliance.[22] The effect of this omission seems to be a serious loophole in the Protocol with regard to implementation of Article 16, particularly since most biopiracy cases to date have related to IPRs with regard to traditional knowledge associated with genetic resources. In turn, it could be argued that the requirement for checkpoints to collect or receive, as appropriate, 'relevant information' related to PIC and the establishment of MAT[23] implies also PIC and MAT requirements concerning traditional knowledge, and if provided for in domestic ABS frameworks, such information would need to be supplied by the user.[24] This extensive interpretation would be based on the preambular reference to the interrelationship between genetic resources and traditional knowledge, and their inseparable nature for indigenous and local communities.[25] This interpretation could also possibly be supported by the reference to 'subject-matter' as information to be mandatorily included in the internationally recognized certificate.[26]

Conversely, it has been argued that the omission of traditional knowledge from this provision was intentional, as negotiators had specifically considered and then decided against including it in Article 17,[27] with a view to leaving regulatory space for the WIPO negotiations to address compliance with ABS on traditional knowledge.[28] In order to ensure the effective implementation

---

21   As laid out in Nagoya Protocol Article 17(4). See this commentary on Article 17, section 3.

22   Buck and Hamilton, "Nagoya Protocol," op. cit., 56. These concerns had already been raised in CBD Working Group on ABS, "Report of the Meeting of the Group of Technical Experts on an Internationally Recognized Certificate of Origin/Source/Legal Provenance" (20 February 2007) UN Doc UNEP/CBD/WG-ABS/5/7, paragraph 19.

23   Nagoya Protocol Article 17(1)(a)(i).

24   In accordance with Nagoya Protocol Article 17(1)(a)(ii): see Gurdial Nijar Singh, *The Nagoya Protocol: Analysis and Implementation Options for Developing Countries*, op. cit., 11.

25   Nagoya Protocol Preamble, 22nd paragraph.

26   Nagoya Protocol Article 17(4)(f).

27   Greiber et al., *Explanatory Guide*, op. cit., 174. This may be based also on the requirement, discussed above, to include in the review of the effectiveness of the Protocol a specific discussion on Article 16 and progress in WIPO negotiations: CBD Decision 10/1, paragraph 6.

28   Lago Candeira and Silvestri, "Challenges in the Implementation of the Nagoya Protocol," op. cit., 292. However, it remains to be clarified why the same solution was not adopted for genetic resources, as the WIPO negotiations cover both genetic resources and traditional

of the traditional knowledge-related provisions of the Protocol, in particular in the absence of progress under WIPO, the Protocol's governing body should consider developing guidance[29] on how Parties may include traditional knowledge in the internationally recognized certificate of compliance, since the Protocol only sets out the minimum information that must be contained in the certificate,[30] and does not exclude expanding its content to other issues. The Protocol's governing body could address this issue when considering whether the WIPO negotiations outcome is in support of and does not run counter to the objectives of the CBD and Protocol in this regard.[31] In alternative, Parties to the Protocol may consider (collectively or individually) whether to take into consideration future guidance to be developed under the Convention on the unlawful appropriation of traditional knowledge[32] and other relevant work,[33] under the CBD Work Programme on Article 8(j) and related provisions.

In the absence of international rules or guidance on this matter, provider countries would be well advised to include requirements related to the monitoring of traditional knowledge in their national ABS frameworks, including requiring inclusion of monitoring obligations in national permits, as well as in MAT.[34]

---

knowledge. In addition, at the time of writing, WIPO negotiators could not agree whether to include or not disclosure requirements and the draft text on traditional knowledge contains several options in brackets, see WIPO General Assembly, "Matters concerning the Intergovernmental Committee on Intellectual Property and Genetic Resources, Traditional Knowledge and Folklore (IGC)" (14 August 2013) WIPO Doc WO/GA/43/14, Annex B, draft articles Rev. 2 (26 April 2013).

29   Nagoya Protocol Article 26(4)(a). See this commentary on Article 26, section 2.

30   Nagoya Protocol Article 17(4).

31   See this commentary on Article 4, section 3.1.

32   CBD Working Group on Article 8(j), Recommendation 8/4 in "Report of the eighth meeting of the Article 8(j) Working Group" UNEP/CBD/COP/12/5, Annex.

33   CBD Working Group on Article 8(j), Recommendation 8/5 on sui generis systems for the protection of traditional knowledge in "Report of the eighth meeting of the Article 8(j) Working Group" UNEP/CBD/COP/12/5, Annex.

34   We are grateful to Ruth Mackenzie for drawing our attention to this point. See this commentary on Article 18, section 5, about easier enforceability in a transnational context of MAT than of PIC.

Article 17. Monitoring the Utilization of Genetic Resources

1. To support compliance, each Party shall take measures, as appropriate, to monitor and to enhance transparency about the utilization of genetic resources. Such measures shall include:

    (a) The designation of one or more checkpoints, as follows:

        (i) Designated checkpoints would collect or receive, as appropriate, relevant information related to prior informed consent, to the source of the genetic resource, to the establishment of mutually agreed terms, and/or to the utilization of genetic resources, as appropriate;

        (ii) Each Party shall, as appropriate and depending on the particular characteristics of a designated checkpoint, require users of genetic resources to provide the information specified in the above paragraph at a designated checkpoint. Each Party shall take appropriate, effective and proportionate measures to address situations of non-compliance;

        (iii) Such information, including from internationally recognized certificates of compliance where they are available, will, without prejudice to the protection of confidential information, be provided to relevant national authorities, to the Party providing prior informed consent and to the Access and Benefit-sharing Clearing-House, as appropriate;

        (iv) Checkpoints must be effective and should have functions relevant to implementation of this sub-paragraph (a). They should be relevant to the utilization of genetic resources, or to the collection of relevant information at, *inter alia*, any stage of research, development, innovation, pre-commercialization or commercialization.

    (b) Encouraging users and providers of genetic resources to include provisions in mutually agreed terms to share information on the implementation of such terms, including through reporting requirements; and

    (c) Encouraging the use of cost-effective communication tools and systems.

© KONINKLIJKE BRILL NV, LEIDEN, 2014 | DOI 10.1163/9789004217188_019

2.   A permit or its equivalent issued in accordance with Article 6, paragraph 3(e) and made available to the Access and Benefit-sharing Clearing-House, shall constitute an internationally recognized certificate of compliance.

3.   An internationally recognized certificate of compliance shall serve as evidence that the genetic resource which it covers has been accessed in accordance with prior informed consent and that mutually agreed terms have been established, as required by the domestic access and benefit-sharing legislation or regulatory requirements of the Party providing prior informed consent.

4.   The internationally recognized certificate of compliance shall contain the following minimum information when it is not confidential:
     (a)   Issuing authority;
     (b)   Date of issuance;
     (c)   The provider;
     (d)   Unique identifier of the certificate;
     (e)   The person or entity to whom prior informed consent was granted;
     (f)   Subject-matter or genetic resources covered by the certificate;
     (g)   Confirmation that mutually agreed terms were established;
     (h)   Confirmation that prior informed consent was obtained; and
     (i)   Commercial and/or non-commercial use.

1   Overview

Article 17 creates an obligation for each Party, particularly Parties with users in their jurisdiction, to take domestic measures to monitor and enhance transparency regarding the utilization of genetic resources,[1] as a way to support other provisions related to compliance in the Protocol.[2] The obligation mainly singles out two means of implementation: the establishment of checkpoints and the issuance of internationally recognized certificates of compliance. Checkpoints were one of the most contentious items in the negotiations of the Protocol, which may explain the unfortunate and convoluted drafting of Article 17(1), mainly due to political sensitivities concerning the linkages to the

---

1   Nagoya Protocol Article 17(1).
2   Nagoya Protocol Articles 14–16 and 18.

IPR system.[3] Article 17(2–4) focuses on the internationally recognized certificate of compliance:[4] a conceptually complex tool that serves as *evidence* in a transnational context of the granting of PIC and establishment of MAT.

To fully appreciate the relevance of Article 17 in the international ABS regime created by the Protocol, it should be recalled that the CBD is silent on specific measures to monitor the utilization of genetic resources and the implementation of related benefit-sharing obligations. Some commentators have argued that the CBD[5] contains an obligation of result to share benefits arising from research and development in a fair and equitable way, and the need for monitoring measures is a logical consequence of functional ABS frameworks.[6] The Bonn Guidelines paid little attention to monitoring measures, although they included some reference to national monitoring and reporting,[7] as well as to means for verification.[8] State practice so far has been limited in implementing user measures in general, let alone in providing for systematic monitoring for the purpose of ABS.[9] Against this background, the role of Article 17 is to complement the general obligations for Parties to provide for users' compliance with domestic ABS frameworks[10] and facilitate compliance with MAT.[11] To that end, Article 17 contains more detailed obligations focusing on 'concrete tools'[12] for monitoring uses and/or users of genetic resources to *detect* possible instances of users' violations of domestic ABS measures.

---

3   Pavoni, "Nagoya Protocol and WTO Law," op. cit., 200–205, particularly 203–204, and 213.

4   Brendan Tobin, Geoff Burton and José C. Fernandez-Ugalde, *Certificates of Clarity or Confusion: The Search for a Practical, Feasible and Cost Effective System for Certifying Compliance with PIC and MAT* (Yokohama: UNU-IAS, 2008), accessed 30 November 2013, <http://collection.unu-mc.org/view/UNU:3123>.

5   CBD Article 15(7) first sentence.

6   E.g., Tvedt and Young, *Beyond Access*, op. cit., 40.

7   Bonn Guidelines, paragraphs 55–56.

8   Bonn Guidelines, paragraphs 57–58.

9   Brendan Tobin, Sam Johnston and Charles V. Barber, *Options for Developing Measures in User Countries to Implement the Access and Benefit-Sharing Provisions of the Convention on Biological Diversity* (Yokohama: UNU-IAS, 2003), accessed 30 November 2013, <http://unu.edu/publications/policy-briefs/options-for-developing-measures-in-user-countries-to-implement-the-access-and-benefit-sharing-provisions-of-the-convention-on-biological-diversity-2nd-edition.html>; Morgera, Buck and Tsioumani, "Conclusions," op. cit., 515; Tvedt and Fauchald, "Implementing the Nagoya Protocol on ABS," op. cit., 383–402.

10   Nagoya Protocol Articles 15–16.

11   Nagoya Protocol Article 18.

12   Glowka and Normand, "Nagoya Protocol on Access and Benefit-sharing," op. cit., 37.

Article 17 also includes other mandatory means of implementation (as part of a non-exhaustive list), such as an obligation to 'encourage' (i.e. at least to remove barriers to, and/or create incentives for)[13] users and providers to include in MAT provisions on reporting and information-sharing,[14] and all ABS stakeholders to use cost-effective communication tools.[15] As to the latter, Parties may consider encouraging users to participate in existing initiatives,[16] such as IT-based communication tools for exchanging information on genetic resources.[17] The following sections will focus on the more complex interpretative questions raised by the provisions on checkpoints and the internationally recognized certificate of compliance, in turn.

2   Checkpoints

Checkpoints under the Protocol have the responsibility to monitor the utilization[18] of genetic resources, in order to support the possible detection of user's violations of domestic ABS frameworks in other countries. It remains to be seen whether Parties may empower checkpoints to also check breaches of MAT, although the Protocol does not require checking their content but only their formal establishment.[19] On the other hand, domestic ABS frameworks may provide for specific requirements on the substantive content of MAT[20]

---

13   On the obligation to encourage, see this commentary on Article 9, section 1.

14   Nagoya Protocol Article 17(1)(b). See also Article 6(3)(g) and this commentary on Article 6, section 7. It may be usefully recalled that Parties will be well advised to effectively encourage such inclusion in MAT, which are more easily enforced than PIC in a transnational context, as discussed in this commentary on Article 18, section 5.

15   Nagoya Protocol Article 17(1)(c).

16   For example, the EU draft regulation would encourage users' associations to seek recognition of a combination of procedures, tools or mechanisms (e.g., on the deployment of data-sharing tools for tracking) developed for the purpose of implementing their obligations under the regulation as 'best practice', by subjecting users implementing such recognized best practice to less intense compliance checks (see draft articles 8–9).

17   One example can be found in the microbial sector, where efforts are undertaken to integrate all known equivalent strain numbers and corresponding information into a single strain passport page: "StrainInfo," University of Gent et al., accessed on 7 February 2014, <www.straininfo.net/>.

18   Nagoya Protocol Article 2(c). See this commentary on Article 2, section 2.

19   Article 17(1)(a)(i).

20   As the list of minimum requirements for MAT to be established in domestic ABS frameworks at Article 6(3)(g) is non-exhaustive: see this commentary on Article 6, section 7.

and Parties can therefore require their checkpoints to carry out monitoring tasks also in that regard, particularly if these requirements are well publicized. The designation of checkpoints needs to be backed up by domestic measures to obtain from users relevant information.[21] This is coupled with an obligation for each Party to take measures to address situations of non-compliance by users with requirements to provide relevant information.[22]

During the negotiations, developing countries argued for the obligatory establishment of predetermined checkpoints, particularly at patent offices, so that users seeking IPRs on inventions using genetic resources would be obliged to disclose information on PIC and MAT. This was based on the understanding that IPRs are usually sought at an early stage of the research and development, and/or commercialization, process with a view to securing monetary benefits from the utilization of genetic resources. Industrialized countries, on the other hand, argued against creating unduly burdensome procedures at the national level in relation to IPRs,[23] and expressed concerns about flexibility and cost-effectiveness.[24] Certain developed countries explicitly opposed any mandatory requirement for disclosure of ABS-related information in IPR applications and an obligation to designate patent offices as checkpoints, in line with their position in the WTO TRIPS negotiations.[25] The question of how to establish mechanisms or obligations that can capture genetic resources-related benefits from the IPR systems and channel them back to the country providing genetic resources and/or traditional knowledge[26] remains open in various fora.[27]

---

21 Nagoya Protocol Article 17(1)(a)(ii), first sentence.

22 Nagoya Protocol Article 17(1)(a)(ii), second sentence. This provision can be read together with Parties' obligations to establish appropriate, effective and proportionate measures to address situations of non-compliance, which is provided for in Nagoya Protocol Article 15.

23 Singh Nijar, "An Asian Developing Country's View," op. cit., 252–254.

24 Buck and Hamilton, "Nagoya Protocol," op. cit., 53. These concerns were related to the expectation that Parties with users within their jurisdiction would need to carry out inspections of private research facilities and laboratories in their territory and determine the source of 'all biological material involved in such utilization' in order to effectively monitor users within their jurisdiction: Young, "An International Cooperation Perspective," op. cit., 476.

25 A number of developed countries oppose amendment of Article 27(3)(b) of the TRIPS Agreement to introduce a mandatory disclosure requirement: see Morgera and Tsioumani, "Evolution of Benefit-Sharing", op. cit., 168–169; and Pavoni, "Nagoya Protocol and WTO Law," op. cit., 208–212.

26 The omission of traditional knowledge from Nagoya Protocol Article 17 is discussed in this commentary on Article 16, section 3.

27 See Introduction to this commentary, section I.1. Andersen et al., *International Agreements and Processes*, op. cit., 34. Note also Oldham and Burton, "Defusing Disclosure in Patent

As a result, Article 17(1) places an obligation on each Party (whether it characterizes itself mainly as provider or as user of genetic resources) to designate one or more checkpoints to gather/receive information on the utilization of genetic resources. In other words, the Protocol requires Parties to designate at least one checkpoint, but leaves them flexibility in deciding which national entity will play that role. So, nothing in the Protocol prevents Parties from designating patent offices as checkpoints. It has been argued however that, in the absence of a 'clear mandate and authoritative guidance from the Protocol' in that regard, Parties' domestic rules designating patent offices as checkpoints may arguably be considered in tension with WTO law.[28]

Parties may as well decide to designate other entities as checkpoints, including competent national authorities,[29] other authorities providing regulatory or marketing approval of products, customs officers,[30] and/or research funding institutions.[31] The flexibility left by Article 17 is such that Parties may also decide to provide government incentives for user self-monitoring and for otherwise creating transparency in the chain of users (for instance, through independent third-party monitoring such as certification),[32] and also designate

---

Applications," op. cit., who argue that as a result of unilateral action on disclosure in patent applications in major national product markets, no significant genetic resource-based product can be launched internationally without disclosure having taken place in several key markets.

28   Pavoni, "Nagoya Protocol and WTO Law," op. cit., 204. Note also conceptual and practical difficulties in utilising the patent system for enforcement of ABS laws discussed by Young, "An International Cooperation Perspective," op. cit., 478–479. Such difficulties include the imposition of significant costs on providers challenging a patent and the fact that the patent offices are 'strongly skewed in favour of patent issuance' because they are funded by patent application fees (ibid., 479).

29   See lack of Protocol indications on role of competent national authorities in user countries: this commentary on Article 13, section 3. See also EU draft regulation, draft article 7(2).

30   This could arguably include also the Convention on International Trade in Endangered Species of Wild Fauna and Flora (Washington DC, 3 March 1973, in force 1 July 1975) 993 UNTS 243 (CITES) enforcement officers: on the difficulties in combining systems of enforcement under the two multilateral environmental treaties, see Young, "An International Cooperation Perspective," op. cit., 479–481.

31   Some of these options were outlined in the Nagoya Draft, draft article 13(1)(a). For a brief discussion in the European region and in Latin America, see Lago Candeira and Silvestri, "Challenges in the Implementation of the Nagoya Protocol," op. cit., 279–280 and 291; and Cabrera Medaglia, "Implementation of the Nagoya Protocol," op. cit., 362–363.

32   Note that certification was one of the means to support compliance suggested in the Bonn Guidelines, paragraph 16(d)(v). On the likely shortfalls of certification in the ABS context, see Young, "An International Cooperation Perspective," op. cit., 481–482.

non-government entities as checkpoints, such as researchers in receipt of pub-lic funding and genebanks.[33] It remains to be seen, however, whether these non-government checkpoints would ensure monitoring of the entirety of ABS transactions in a given country, and could be considered 'effective' to perform all the functions foreseen in Article 17 and ultimately contribute to the realiza-tion of the objectives of the Protocol on fair and equitable benefit-sharing.[34]

2.1   *Characteristics and Functions*

Designated checkpoints must meet all of the cumulative criteria concerning their characteristics and functions set out in Article 17(1)(a). First of all, desig-nated checkpoints must either actively gather ('collect') or at least be the recip-ients ('receive') of information on PIC, the source[35] of the genetic resource, the establishment of MAT, and/or the utilization of genetic resources.[36] It may be argued that tasking checkpoints with active duties in this regard may facili-tate the detection of cases of misappropriation. Article 17(1)(a) leaves Parties discretion as to whether to task checkpoint(s) to take *both* an active and a pas-sive role, and whether to extend their duties to utilization. The qualification 'as appropriate' points to different tasks depending on the different types of checkpoints that will be designated. The reference to 'and/or' at the end of the list of types of information to be collected/received, read together with the qualification 'as appropriate', suggests that designated checkpoints will need to collect one, more or all of the types of information listed.

Second, checkpoints are mandated[37] to provide relevant information to relevant national authorities (including competent national authorities),[38] the Party providing PIC, and to the ABS Clearinghouse,[39] as appropriate. Information to be channeled by checkpoints may also include information from the internationally recognized certificates of compliance 'where they are available.' The latter expression points to instances in which the genetic

---

33   Glowka and Normand, "Nagoya Protocol on Access and Benefit-sharing," op. cit., 39.

34   See this commentary on Article 1.

35   This was inserted to achieve consistency with some pending proposal on the disclosure of origin or source in the WTO/TRIPS negotiation. Reference to 'source' might be quite useful in case in which users obtained genetic resources from a country that is not the country of origin: Tobin, Johnston and Barber, *Options for Developing Measures*, op. cit.

36   Nagoya Protocol Article 17(1)(a)(i). See Article 2(c) and this commentary on Article 2, section 2.

37   Nagoya Protocol Article 17(1)(a) (iii), although the wording relies on a passive formulation that may engender some uncertainty in that regard.

38   Nagoya Protocol Article 13(2). See this commentary on Article 13, section 3.

39   Nagoya Protocol Article 14.

resources utilized are considered outside the scope of the Nagoya Protocol,[40] countries do not require PIC[41] or do not require issuance of certificates of compliance,[42] or may have taken into account in different ways the 'special considerations' identified in the Protocol.[43] The qualification of the mandate for checkpoints to channel relevant information 'without prejudice to the protection of confidential information' points to unresolved legal questions regarding confidentiality that still need to be clarified under the Protocol.[44]

Third, designated checkpoints must be 'effective.'[45] Such effectiveness refers to the actual capabilities of designated checkpoints to ensure monitoring and enhanced transparency in the utilization of genetic resources, and ultimately contribute to realizing the objective of the Protocol.[46] Effectiveness is therefore the yardstick to evaluate whether Parties comply with Article 17, including by the compliance procedures and mechanisms to be established under the Protocol.[47] Effectiveness of designated checkpoints in a user country may also be used as a criterion for evaluating individual applications for access to genetic resources, if so determined by provider countries' national access measures.[48]

Fourth, checkpoints' functions as spelt out in domestic measures should effectively contribute to gathering or at least receiving relevant information, as well as channeling it appropriately (domestically or externally). The provision, however, leaves discretion to Parties in determining whether designated checkpoints will monitor the whole of the research-development value chain, or just some of its stages ('at, *inter alia*, any stage').[49] So, it remains to be determined on a case-by-case basis whether in countries where checkpoints(s) collect information only at the very early stages of the research and development process, such checkpoints can be considered effective in achieving the objective of Article 17 and ultimately the objective of the Protocol.

Finally, it remains to be seen whether countries implementing Article 17 will empower checkpoints to *track* genetic resources from the stage of research to the stage of commercialization. The Protocol negotiators considered, and

---

40   See this commentary on Article 3, section 3.
41   Nagoya Protocol Article 6(1). See this commentary on Article 6, section 3.
42   See section 3 below.
43   Nagoya Protocol Article 8.
44   Nagoya Protocol Article 14(2). These questions are discussed in this commentary on Article 14, section 5.
45   Beginning of Nagoya Protocol Article 17(1)(a)(iv).
46   See this commentary on Article 1.
47   See this commentary on Article 30.
48   Nagoya Protocol Article 6(3)(b) and this commentary on Article 6, section 5.2.
49   Nagoya Protocol Article 17(1)(a)(iv).

eventually decided against, a substantive obligation for Parties to 'track' genetic resources at all stages of the user chain through a range of specific measures, including a unique identifier for genetic resources, for gathering the information needed to establish whether a user is in compliance or not.[50] In the absence of such a provision, there is no basis in the Protocol for setting up a multilateral framework supporting coordinated efforts to track the flow of genetic resources across jurisdictions.[51] The Protocol, however, does not prevent Parties to mandate their checkpoints to track genetic resources from the stage of research to the stage of commercialization through measures that do not require collaboration from other Parties, or possibly by joining efforts with other willing Parties through bilateral or regional agreements.[52]

3   The Internationally Recognized Certificate of Compliance

Article 17(2–4) concerns the internationally recognized certificate of compliance as a tool to facilitate acceptance of evidence of compliance with the provider countries' domestic ABS frameworks in a transnational context.[53] Article 17(2) establishes that certificates are created by making available permits

---

50   A proposal by the African Group, for example, would have obliged Parties to 'facilitate an efficient, easy to use certification process through the use of new technology which may include: (i) Cost efficient publicly searchable certificate databases providing evidence of PIC and MAT, (ii) Recording of progressive compliance on such databases as conditions of PIC and MAT are met, (iii) Searchable patent application and registration databases, (iv) Integration of genomic and morphological taxonomy to create species certainty, (v) Low cost, portable, gene based bar-coding technology to create rapid attack taxonomy, (vi) Linking unique identifiers to gene based bar-coding.' CBD Working Group on ABS, "Collation of operative text submitted," UNEP/CBD/WG-ABS/7/4, 28–29. See also draft article 13 in the Nagoya Draft, which was titled 'MONITORING[, TRACKING] AND REPORTING THE [UTILIZATION] OF GENETIC RESOURCES [AND ASSOCIATED TRADITIONAL KNOWLEDGE]' (brackets in the original).

51   The technical challenges and opportunities related to monitoring and tracking the flow of genetic resources are succinctly described by George M. Garrity et al., "Studies on Monitoring and Tracking Genetic Resources" (2 March 2009) UN Doc UNEP/CBD/WG-ABS/7/INF/2.

52   See this commentary on Article 4, section 3.

53   Nagoya Protocol Article 17(3). On possible WTO law implications of the internationally recognized certificate of compliance, see Tobin, Johnston and Barber, *Options for Developing Measures*, op. cit., 197–199.

or their equivalent[54] to the ABS Clearinghouse.[55] The wording of Article 17(2) does not specify who has the responsibility to make available a domestic permit to the international ABS Clearinghouse (as it is formulated in the passive form), although elsewhere in the Protocol this appears to be the responsibility of provider countries.[56] This is compounded by the Protocol's silence as to whether national competent authorities are the ones obliged to make the permits available to the ABS Clearinghouse.[57] More importantly, Article 17(2) does not specify whether all permits (as it mentions 'a permit') should be made available, with a view to elevating them to the status of internationally recognized certificate of compliance. This interpretative uncertainty also arises from a combined reading of the other Protocol provision requiring 'notify[ing]'[58] the ABS Clearinghouse of the issuance of a permit (rather than 'submitting' the permit), and the fact that the explicit requirement to submit the permit to the ABS Clearinghouse is expressed in the passive form elsewhere in the Protocol.[59] Because of these textual inconsistencies, some commentators have argued that the certificate is not mandatory.[60] However, Parties would be well advised to clarify (either multilaterally through the Protocol's governing body[61] or unilaterally through their domestic ABS frameworks) whether there is a mandatory requirement for permits to be elevated to internationally recognized certificates of compliance, with a view to promoting legal certainty.[62] A mandatory certificate could in particular minimize room for uncertainty for user countries implementing their obligations to monitor and provide for compliance under the Protocol.

Article 17(3) clarifies that the legal effect of the certificate is to oblige Parties to consider it acceptable evidence under their national legal systems that the genetic resource covered has been accessed in accordance with PIC and that

---

54   Issued under Nagoya Protocol Article 6(3)(e). The meaning of the term 'its equivalent' is explained in this commentary on Article 14, section 4.

55   Nagoya Protocol Article 14.

56   Nagoya Protocol Article 6(3) refers to 'each Party requiring PIC'.

57   Nagoya Protocol Article 13(2).

58   Nagoya Protocol Article 6(3)(e).

59   Nagoya Protocol Article 14(2)(c).

60   Glowka and Normand, "Nagoya Protocol on Access and Benefit-sharing," op. cit., 37 (who refer to the '*possibility* to elevate a permit ... to the status of an internationally recognized certificate of compliance' – emphasis added). See also countries arguing for voluntary certification during the Protocol negotiations: Singh Nijar and Pei Fern, *Nagoya ABS Protocol*, op. cit., 279–350.

61   Nagoya Protocol Article 26(4)(a); see this commentary on Article 26, section 2.

62   Nagoya Protocol 9th preambular paragraph.

MAT were established according to another country's domestic ABS framework. Ultimately, therefore, the certificate may assist users in fending off allegations of misappropriation.

Article 17(4) lists minimum information (of a procedural nature) that must be contained in the certificate.[63] If a permit is made available to the ABS Clearinghouse without containing all the required information, it may arguably not be considered an internationally recognized certificate of compliance,[64] although it remains unclear who will verify that all required information has been submitted.[65] The Protocol allows Parties to add to the list of mandatory information in their domestic ABS frameworks. Article 17(4) once again draws attention to issues of confidentiality, which however still need to be clarified under the Protocol.[66]

The 'unique identifier of the certificate' is intended to minimize efforts by users and public administrators carrying out computer-based searches of certificates;[67] it would basically allow for searches based on a 'registration number' allocated to each certificate. It may be particularly useful to identify permits that have been modified or updated,[68] as their successive iterations should have the same identifier in common. It should thus not be confused with the proposed *unique identifier of genetic resources* as part of a multilateral tracking system that was not included in the Protocol.[69] Parties could still decide to explore opportunities resulting from advances in identifying a

---

63   Nagoya Protocol Article 17(4) also determines the information that needs to be made available on a permit to the ABS Clearinghouse. Contingent on the interpretation of Nagoya Protocol Article 17(2), this list will either result in a minimum harmonization of domestic permits and their equivalents, or it could be implemented by providing a common format for registering information on domestic permits or equivalents in the ABS Clearinghouse. See this commentary on Article 14, section 4.

64   Glowka and Normand, "Nagoya Protocol on Access and Benefit-sharing," op. cit., 37.

65   See this commentary on Article 14, section 4.

66   Nagoya Protocol Article 14(2). See this commentary on Article 14, section 5.

67   Greiber et al, *Explanatory Guide*, op. cit., 181.

68   As discussed in this commentary on Article 14, section 4.

69   See section 2 above. Note that unique identifiers of living modified organisms are used to satisfy the documentation requirements of the Cartagena Protocol on Biosafety: the OECD Unique Identifiers of Transgenic Plants are alphanumeric codes given to each living modified organism approved for commercial use, a registry of which is maintained on the Biosafety Clearinghouse: "LMO Registry," CBD, accessed 19 February 2014, <http://bch .cbd.int/database/lmo-registry>. This registry provides summary information on all living modified organisms registered in the Biosafety Clearinghouse including transformation events and genetic modifications, as well as links to all relevant decisions and risk assessment reports.

genetic resource[70] to further develop the internationally recognized certificate
of compliance, by including in the information contained in certificates available unique identifiers for genetic resources in the future.

On a final, substantive note, the purely procedural reference to the 'confirmation that MAT were established' in Article 17(4) confirms that the Protocol
does not provide for any mechanism to check compliance vis-à-vis the *content*
of MAT.[71] This also means that the Protocol does not contain any international
mechanism for assessing the fairness and equity of benefit-sharing requirements in specific ABS transactions.[72]

---

70   Garrity et al., "Studies on Monitoring and Tracking", op. cit., 29–85.

71   See also section 2 above.

72   See this commentary on Article 6, section 2 and conclusions to this commentary, section
      2, where the critical relevance of MAT for ensuring fairness and equity of benefit-sharing
      is discussed.

Article 18. Compliance with Mutually Agreed Terms

1. In the implementation of Article 6, paragraph 3(g)(i) and Article 7, each Party shall encourage providers and users of genetic resources and/or traditional knowledge associated with genetic resources to include provisions in mutually agreed terms to cover, where appropriate, dispute resolution including:
    (a) The jurisdiction to which they will subject any dispute resolution processes;
    (b) The applicable law; and/or
    (c) Options for alternative dispute resolution, such as mediation or arbitration.
2. Each Party shall ensure that an opportunity to seek recourse is available under their legal systems, consistent with applicable jurisdictional requirements, in cases of disputes arising from mutually agreed terms.
3. Each Party shall take effective measures, as appropriate, regarding:
    (a) Access to justice; and
    (b) The utilization of mechanisms regarding recognition and enforcement of foreign judgments and arbitral awards.
4. The effectiveness of this article shall be reviewed by the Conference of the Parties serving as the meeting of the Parties to this Protocol in accordance with Article 31 of this Protocol.

1   Overview

Specific conditions for the utilization of genetic resources[1] or the utilization of traditional knowledge must be set out in MAT, which are normally contracts governed by private law.[2] As already discussed,[3] MAT are normally established upon access (and can possibly be (re)negotiated at a later stage)[4] and must

---

1   See this commentary on Article 2, section 2.
2   See Introduction to this commentary, section 1.3; and Greiber et al., *Explanatory Guide*, op. cit., 184.
3   Nagoya Protocol Articles 5(1–2) and (5) and 6(3)(g). See this commentary on Article 5, section 5, and Article 6, section 7.
4   See Introduction to this commentary, Section 1.3 and fn. 81.

primarily include conditions for benefit-sharing, as well as address dispute settlement, third-party use and change of intent. Against this background, Article 18 aims to create the legislative preconditions at the domestic level in order to address procedural challenges for individual providers and users that are located in different countries[5] arising from situations of non-compliance with MAT – that is, violations of contractual obligations.[6] This may be critical, for instance, for situations in which the user's intent changes,[7] particularly if the MAT allowed only non-commercial research.[8] In these instances, the MAT may create a contractual obligation for users to re-negotiate MAT as soon as commercial research starts,[9] in the absence of which the provider is entitled to obtain contractual penalties or damages.[10]

Article 18 addresses two issues related to compliance with MAT through three obligations. First, it complements Parties' obligation to detail the minimum content of MAT in domestic ABS frameworks,[11] by establishing a qualified obligation for Parties to 'encourage' (i.e., at least to remove barriers to, and/or create incentives for)[12] the inclusion in MAT of provisions on dispute resolution. Second, it aims to support users' compliance with MAT by establishing an obligation for Parties to 'ensure' an opportunity to seek recourse for disputes on MAT; and a qualified obligation to take domestic measures on access to justice and on the recognition of foreign judgments and arbitral awards. The Protocol, however, does not provide any guidance on how national courts

---

5   Glowka and Normand, "Nagoya Protocol on Access and Benefit-sharing," op. cit., 36. CBD Working Group on ABS, "Comparative study of the real and transactional costs involved in the process of access to justice across jurisdictions" (26 February 2009) UN Doc UNEP/CBD/WG-ABS/7/INF/4; "Analytical study on administrative and judicial remedies available in countries with users under their jurisdiction and in international agreements" (20 July 2007) UN Doc UNEP/CBD/WG-ABS/5/INF/3; and "Analysis of claims of unauthorised access and misappropriation of genetic resources and associated traditional knowledge" (22 December 2005) UN Doc UNEP/CBD/WG-ABS/4/INF/6.

6   The breach of MAT has been termed 'misuse,' in contrast to 'misappropriation' which generally refers to the appropriation of genetic resources and traditional knowledge in violation of the applicable domestic requirements, i.e., generally without PIC and MAT. See Chiarolla, "Role of Private International Law," op. cit., 427–428; and fn. 14 in this commentary on Article 15.

7   Nagoya Protocol Article 6(g)(iv). See this commentary on Article 6, section 7.

8   Nagoya Protocol Article 8(a). See this commentary on Article 8, section 2.

9   That is, 'research and development' for the purposes of the Protocol definition of 'utilization': see Article 2(c) and this commentary on Article 2, section 2.

10   Godt, "Enforcement of Benefit-Sharing Duties," op. cit., 423–424.

11   Nagoya Protocol Article 6(3)(g).

12   On the obligation to encourage, see this commentary on Article 9, section 1.

should interpret ABS contracts,[13] regarding for instance the interpretation of the contractual terms on benefit-sharing and the assessment as to whether they are *fair* and *equitable* pursuant to the Protocol's objective. Article 18 also calls for a review of its effectiveness by the Protocol's governing body, as part of its general assessment and review process.[14]

The following sections will discuss the three obligations enshrined in Article 18 in turn. The final section will explore the relevance of Article 18 for cases of misappropriation – that is, violation of domestic ABS frameworks (addressed in Articles 15–16).

2 Dispute Resolution Provisions in MAT

Article 18(1) aims to 'promote best practice in drafting more easily enforceable ABS contracts.'[15] It obliges each Party to encourage providers and users of genetic resources and/or traditional knowledge to specifically address in MAT how to resolve disputes among them. The implementation of this provision is explicitly linked (and is, in effect, complementary to) Parties' obligation to establish 'clear [domestic] rules and procedures' for requiring and establishing MAT, including a clause on dispute settlement,[16] and to take appropriate domestic measures to ensure that MAT have been established for access to traditional knowledge associated with genetic resources.[17]

Even where foreigners could enjoy equal access to domestic courts in a certain jurisdiction, there is broad understanding that further measures are needed for foreign users or providers wishing to bring legal action before a court of a State other than that in which they are based.[18] This may be particularly the case of providers that lack the resources and knowledge of the relevant legal system to bring a case, probably of a long duration, in another country, in order to obtain redress from a user that has allegedly violated the ABS contract. In order to cope with these obstacles, the Bonn Guidelines already elaborated on suggested elements for MAT, such as change of use, dispute settlement and choice of law, as well as permitted uses, IPRs, commitment to share monetary

---

13   Tvedt, "Beyond Nagoya," op. cit., 163.

14   Nagoya Protocol Article 18(4). See this commentary on Article 31.

15   Glowka and Normand, "Nagoya Protocol on Access and Benefit-sharing," op. cit., 36.

16   Nagoya Protocol Article 6(3)(g)(i).

17   Nagoya Protocol Article 7.

18   Hiroji Isozaki, "Enforcement of ABS Agreements in User States," in Kamau and Winter, *Genetic Resources, Traditional Knowledge, and the Law*, op. cit., 442.

and non-monetary benefits, and termination of the agreement.[19] The aim was for detailed guidance to increase the chances for a court to come to an unambiguous decision thanks to the fact that the contract under dispute is sufficiently clear and specific.[20] In that regard, the Bonn Guidelines appear more detailed than the Nagoya Protocol. In addition, it should be borne in mind that the Hague Conference on Private International Law, the UN Commission on International Trade Law and the International Institute for the Unification of Private Law[21] have been working on judicial cooperation among countries in facilitating the judicial process for foreign applicants,[22] including towards the harmonization of legal systems on civil and commercial law.

Article 18(1) sets out three legal issues related to transboundary contractual dispute resolution. First, it underlines the importance for parties to MAT to identify the jurisdiction to which they will subject any dispute resolution process (that is, MAT should explicitly clarify in which jurisdiction a MAT-related dispute will be brought).[23] It has been noted that providers may prefer to bring an action for breach of MAT in the jurisdiction of the user, with a view to obtaining a judgment that can be directly enforced against the user in his/her own jurisdiction.[24] Absent such identification, legal uncertainty will arise as to whether a national court in a given country where legal action has been

---

19   Bonn Guidelines, Appendix I.

20   Isozaki, "Enforcement of ABS Agreements in User States," op. cit., 442.

21   Ibid. See Convention on Abolishing the Requirement of Legalization for Foreign Public Documents (The Hague, 5 October 1961, in force 24 January 1965) 20 ILM 1405; Convention on the Service Abroad of Judicial and Extrajudicial Documents in Civil or Commercial Matters (The Hague, 15 November 1965, in force 10 February 1969); Convention on the Taking of Evidence Abroad in Civil or Commercial Matters (The Hague, 18 March 1970, in force 7 October 1972) 8 ILM 37; Convention on International Access to Justice (The Hague, 25 October 1980, in force 1 May 1988) 19 ILM 1505; Convention on Civil Procedure (The Hague, 1 March 1954, in force 12 April 1957); Convention on the Jurisdiction of the Selected Forum in the Case of International Sales of Goods (The Hague, 15 April 1958, not yet in force); Convention on the Choice of Court (The Hague, 25 November 1965, not yet in force); Convention on the Recognition and Enforcement of Foreign Judgments in Civil and Commercial Matters (The Hague, 1 February 1971, in force 20 August 1977) 5 ILM 636; Supplementary Protocol of to the Hague Convention on the Recognition and Enforcement of Foreign Judgments in Civil and Commercial Matters (The Hague, 1 February 1971, in force 20 August 1979) 6 ILM 1083; Convention on the Choice of Court Agreements (The Hague, 30 June 2005, not yet in force).

22   Isozaki, "Enforcement of ABS Agreements," op. cit., 442.

23   Chiarolla, "Role of Private International Law," op. cit., 430.

24   Singh Nijar, *The Nagoya Protocol on Access and Benefit Sharing of Genetic Resources*, op. cit., 12.

brought will deem to have competence to consider a dispute concerning MAT. Provided that the jurisdiction to which dispute resolution processes will be subjected is clarified in MAT, the decision on which court will have competence will be made on the basis of domestic norms applicable in the given country, unless an international or regional instrument for judicial cooperation is applicable.[25]

Second, Article 18(1) underscores the importance for parties to MAT to identify in their contract the substantive law to be applied to resolve any dispute among them. Absent such a clause, legal uncertainty will arise as the determination of the law that will govern the dispute, which would be left to the domestic court where legal action has been brought, on the basis of the domestic norms on private international law in its jurisdiction. The question of applicable law is particularly complex in the context of private-law contracts. The domestic court may have to make a choice, on the basis of private international law norms and taking into consideration the interest of the parties, between two different sets of law, such as for instance its own domestic law or the law of another country, or it may decide that different questions in a given case may be governed by different countries' law.[26]

Third, Article 18(1) highlights the important possibility for parties to MAT to agree up-front to settle disputes through alternative dispute resolution mechanisms rather than domestic courts.[27] This may be useful when such non-judicial means entail higher flexibility, simpler procedures and lower costs than judicial mechanism.[28] The provision explicitly mentions mediation or arbitration, but does not exclude that parties to MAT may also agree to have recourse to other mechanisms, including community-based dispute resolution systems or an international institution that may facilitate the resolution of the dispute. With regard to the latter, it is noteworthy that during the negotiations of the Protocol the creation of an international ombudsman had been proposed in relation to this provision.[29] As discussed below in more detail,[30] this proposal has been revived in the context of negotiations on the Protocol's

---

25   Greiber et al., *Explanatory Guide*, op. cit., 185.

26   Godt, "Enforcement of Benefit-Sharing Duties," op. cit., 423.

27   See for instance Article 8 of the ITPGRFA SMTA which provides for the following steps on dispute resolution: amicable dispute settlement, mediation and arbitration.

28   Isozaki, "Enforcement of ABS Agreements in User States," op. cit., 446.

29   We are grateful to Geoff Burton for drawing our attention to this point. See also Greiber et al., *Explanatory Guide*, op. cit., 190–191; Chiarolla, "Role of Private International Law," op. cit., 433 and note 29; and CBD Working Group on ABS, "Collation of operative text submitted," UNEP/CBD/WG-ABS/7/5, 27–28.

30   See this commentary on Article 30, section 3.2.

compliance procedures and mechanisms that are ongoing at the time of writing. With regard to the former, Parties' obligation to encourage parties establishing MAT to include alternative dispute resolution mechanisms as options should be interpreted and implemented taking in due consideration indigenous and local communities' customary laws and procedures, when these communities are concerned by the ABS transaction.[31]

Finally, it has been noted that the Protocol glosses over the complexity of utilizing alternative dispute resolution mechanisms generally used in commercial law disputes for the purposes of achieving fair and equitable benefit-sharing, and that in that connection development of guidance by the Protocol's governing body would be useful.[32]

3   Opportunity to Seek Recourse

Article 18(2) aims to ensure opportunities to seek recourse in any Party's legal systems in case of cross-border dispute arising from MAT.[33] This may be particularly complicated as domestic rules may vary on (and possibly prevent) standing for foreign government entities or for non-incorporated collective entities such as an indigenous or local community that is party to MAT.[34]

Language from the ITPGRFA[35] was relied upon in the drafting of Article 18(2), thereby obliging Parties to provide in their domestic legal systems for existing or new mechanism for parties to MAT to settle their contractual disputes. Article 18(2) arguably aims to ensure that some remedies against breaches of MAT will be made available in all jurisdictions independently of the nationality of the claimant,[36] taking into account *de facto* barriers such as costs and differing requirements about the entitlement to bring legal actions before foreign courts.

---

31   Nagoya Protocol Article 12(1): see this commentary on Article 12, section 2.
32   Young, "An International Cooperation Perspective," op. cit., 488. See this commentary on Article 26, section 2.
33   Glowka and Normand, "Nagoya Protocol on Access and Benefit-sharing," op. cit., 36.
34   Godt, "Enforcement of Benefit-Sharing Duties," op. cit., 422.
35   ITPGRFA Article 12(5), which reads: '*Contracting Parties shall ensure that an opportunity to seek recourse is available, consistent with applicable jurisdictional requirements, under their legal systems, in case of contractual disputes arising under such MTAS,* recognizing that obligations arising under such MTAS rest exclusively with the parties to those MTAS' (emphasis added). On the interpretation of this provision, see Moore and Tymowski, *Explanatory Guide to the International Treaty,* op. cit., 100–101.
36   Greiber et al., *Explanatory Guide,* op. cit., 186.

The Protocol, however, does not provide guidance on how the courts should decide whether they have jurisdiction over MAT-related disputes.[37] The expression 'consistent with applicable jurisdictional requirements' of the Party concerned has been interpreted as an acknowledgement or a safeguard clause that the availability of recourse to courts will depend on applicable rules on the choice of jurisdiction, as established in contracts and accepted by the named court, or in their absence by [the] private international law of the seized forum.'[38] Fundamentally, Article 18(2) places a duty on Parties to provide to individual parties to MAT opportunities to seek recourse in other Parties and arguably to ensure that when such recourse is provided, the seized forum 'should assert jurisdiction unless the complaint is apparently based on dubious grounds (e.g., where none of the parties to the MAT have real connection with the forum).'[39]

4   Access to Justice and Recognition of Foreign Judgments

Article 18(3) requires the development of domestic measures on access to justice and utilization of mechanisms of mutual recognition and enforcement of foreign judgments and arbitral awards,[40] with a view to supporting providers that usually do not have easy access to courts in third countries.[41]

It has been noted that in the context of Article 18 the reference to 'each Party' indicates that the requirement targets the *unilateral* development of domestic measures, rather than the *multilateral* development of harmonized requirements.[42] It may also serve to underline that both Parties that see themselves as mostly user countries or provider countries have to develop such domestic measures.

Article 18(3)(a) obliges Parties to take effective measures, as appropriate, regarding access to justice. While the term 'access to justice' is not defined in the Protocol, it has particular resonance in international environmental law. In the latter context, it is generally seen as a necessary tool for the enforcement of environmental law and as a means for reviewing the decisions, acts, and

---

37   Chiarolla, "Role of Private International Law," op. cit., 431.

38   Ibid., 432. See also Greiber et al., *Explanatory Guide*, op. cit., 186.

39   Chiarolla, "Role of Private International Law," op. cit., 432.

40   Glowka and Normand, "Nagoya Protocol on Access and Benefit-sharing," op. cit., 36.

41   We are grateful to Geoff Burton for drawing our attention to this point.

42   Greiber et al., *Explanatory Guide*, op. cit., 187.

omissions of public authorities with regard to environmental matters.[43] Access to justice is well-established in international human rights law[44] in relation to the independence and impartiality of a court with a view to ensuring a fair trial, and 'truly effective' remedies in determining that a violation has occurred and in providing redress.[45] It has thus been argued that human rights standards may be used as a yardstick to ensure that access to justice has been provided in a specific case under the Protocol.[46]

Under Article 18(3)(b), Parties have an obligation to adopt effective measures addressing the *utilization* of mechanisms for the recognition and enforcement of foreign judgments and arbitral decisions. In other words, they are to support participation in existing mechanisms or establish new ones if they do not exist.[47] Recognition of foreign judgments remains a complex matter,[48] whereas the recognition of foreign arbitral awards may be considered 'generally easier' as a high number of countries are Parties to the 1958 New York Convention on

---

43   See Rio Declaration Principle 10; and Guidelines for the development of national legislation on access to information, public participation and access to justice in environmental matters, adopted by UNEP Governing Council in decision SS.XI/5, part A, 26 February 2010, accessed 30 November 2013, <www.unep.org/civil-society/Portals/24105/documents/Guidelines/GUIDELINES_TO_ACCESS_TO_ENV_INFO_2.pdf>. See also Ebbesson, "Access to Information on Environmental Matters," op. cit., particularly paragraphs 31–33, who concludes that 'Despite the close link to the notions of access to information and public participation in decision-making on environmental matters, access to justice remains a *less established concept* than the latter two in international environmental law,' emphasis added, paragraph 33.

44   E.g. Article 14 ICCPR; Francesco Francioni, ed. *Access to Justice as a Human Right* (Oxford: Oxford University Press, 2007); and Louise Doswald-Beck, "Fair Trial, Right To, International Protection," in Wolfrum, *Max Planck Encyclopedia*, op. cit.

45   *Maya Indigenous Community of the Toledo District v. Belize*, paragraph 184; Ebbesson, "Access to Information on Environmental Matters," op. cit., paragraph 31.

46   Savaresi, "International Human Rights Law Implications," op. cit., 72. It has also been noted that the use of this term in the Protocol was inspired by the Aarhus Convention (Koester, *Nagoya Protocol on ABS*, op. cit., section 5), which can in effect provide a standard for the interpretation and implementation of the Protocol in as far as Parties to that Convention are Parties to the Protocol (Chiarolla, "Role of Private International Law," op. cit., 432–233).

47   Chiarolla, "Role of Private International Law," op. cit., 445.

48   CBD Working Group on ABS, "Report of the expert meeting on compliance," UNEP/CBD/WG-ABS/7/3. For a discussion based on the case of Japan, see Isozaki, "Enforcement of ABS Agreements in User States," op. cit., 443–444.

the Recognition and Enforcement of Foreign Arbitral Awards.[49] There is also the possibility for Parties to conclude an ex post arbitration arrangement.[50]

Article 18(3) does not specify which measures must be taken by Parties, but qualifies the obligation by reference to 'as appropriate,' thereby leaving flexibility to Parties in its implementation. Parties can thus choose among various ways to facilitate access to courts or alternative dispute resolution mechanisms for foreign users or providers. Insofar as indigenous and local communities are parties to MAT, consideration must be given to their customary laws and procedures,[51] in accordance with relevant international human rights norms and standards.[52] In that regard, it has been recommended that States ensure the best means to attain access to justice in line with indigenous peoples' self-determination and related rights to participate in decision-making affecting them.[53] States are also expected to work with indigenous peoples to address the underlying issues that prevent them from having access to justice on an equal basis with others, and facilitate their access to legal remedies including by supporting their capacity development in making use of legal systems.[54]

5   Jurisdiction and Access to Justice in Cases of Violation of Provider Country ABS Frameworks

It is noteworthy that the Protocol does not contain a provision on jurisdiction and access to justice specifically devoted to compliance with the requirement for PIC and establishment of MAT,[55] corresponding to Article 18 for the content of already established MAT. In other words, the Protocol does not

---

49   Chiarolla, "Role of Private International Law," op. cit., 444.

50   Ibid.

51   Nagoya Protocol Article 12(1). See this commentary on Article 12, section 2.

52   See Introduction to this commentary, section 4.

53   Human Rights Council, "Expert Mechanism Advice No. 5 Access to justice in the promotion and protection of the rights of indigenous peoples," (2013), accessed 30 November 2013, <www.ohchr.org/Documents/Issues/IPeoples/EMRIP/Session6/A-HRC-EMRIP-2013-2_en.pdf>, Annex, paragraph 4.

54   Ibid., paragraphs 8 and 10.

55   Note that 'With regard to illegal bioprospecting, both the applicability of the provider country's law and the user country's law can be argued. In essence, the law cannot be determined in the abstract in advance': Godt, "Enforcement of Benefit-Sharing Duties," op. cit., 431 and previous discussion at 424–431. The author concludes that 'it is possible to litigate a (meaningful) benefit-sharing claim for biopiracy in a user country's court. Prospects for success are better with regard to immaterial property than to material

contain provisions on jurisdiction and access to justice in cases of violation of provider countries' domestic ABS frameworks under Articles 15–16.[56] This may be explained by the fact that contractual arrangements can be more easily enforced in other jurisdictions thanks to the operation of private international law. Conversely legal recourse in user countries on the basis of an administrative decision embodying PIC (or lack thereof) may be difficult, as foreign courts may be hesitant to decide on the validity of foreign administrative decisions because of different administrative systems and principles of interpretation of administrative decisions.[57] These cases may rather be addressed under the Protocol' compliance procedures and mechanisms.[58]

It has been argued, however, that the reference to 'appropriate, effective and proportionate' measures under Articles 15 and 16 may support an expansive systemic interpretation of Article 18, whereby the same jurisdictional principles and access to justice standards that apply to contractual disputes arising from MAT under Article 18(2)–(3) should be applied, *mutatis mutandis*, to cases of misappropriation under Articles 15–16.[59] Consequently, Parties would be expected to provide opportunities to seek recourse within their jurisdiction for foreigners alleging violations by users of domestic ABS measures or for foreigners alleging inaction by a competent national authority[60] of a user country in enforcing domestic user-side measures.[61] The same commentator has also argued that Parties' duty to take measures to use mechanisms regarding the recognition and enforcement of foreign judgments and arbitral awards may extend to cases of misappropriation.[62]

---

property. Against common wisdom, it is not the applicable law that forms an obstacle' (ibid., 432).

56   Chiarolla, "Role of Private International Law," op. cit., 432–434. See this commentary on Articles 15–16.

57   Tvedt, "Beyond Nagoya," op. cit., 165, 172–172 and 174.

58   See this commentary on Article 30, section 3, and on Article 15, section 2.

59   Chiarolla, "Role of Private International Law," op. cit., 435.

60   See this commentary on Article 13, section 3.

61   Chiarolla, "Role of Private International Law," op. cit., 434–435.

62   Nagoya Protocol Articles 15(3) and 16(3). See Chiarolla, "Role of Private International Law," op. cit., 444.

Article 19. Model Contractual Clauses

1. Each Party shall encourage, as appropriate, the development, update and use of sectoral and cross-sectoral model contractual clauses for mutually agreed terms.
2. The Conference of the Parties serving as the meeting of the Parties to this Protocol shall periodically take stock of the use of sectoral and cross-sectoral model contractual clauses.

1   Overview

Article 19 identifies Parties' responsibility to encourage the development and use of model clauses for MAT, namely the private ABS contract to be negotiated between an individual provider and an individual user.[1] As discussed above, the Protocol contains little guidance on the content of MAT,[2] although this is the only tool that explicitly aims to operationalize the Protocol's objective to achieve fairness and equity in sharing benefits[3] and is expected to be enforceable across jurisdictions.[4] Article 19, therefore, opens the door to the future development of further international guidance on the content of MAT by tapping into user-led practices and other ABS stakeholders' experience in developing and operationalizing standard contractual clauses.[5]

The rationale of Article 19 is the need to create legally enforceable and inter-operable ABS contracts in different jurisdictions that may have different national ABS frameworks and whose national courts may have different standards in recognizing as valid and enforcing contracts.[6] This was in fact one of the main concerns related to legal certainty[7] that arose from the early implementation of ABS laws and motivated the negotiations of the Nagoya Protocol.

---

1   Generally on MAT, see this commentary on Article 5, section 5.
2   Nagoya Protocol Article 6.3(g) and this commentary on Article 6, section 7.
3   See this commentary on Article 1 and Conclusions to this commentary, section 2.
4   See this commentary on Article 18.
5   Chiarolla, Louafi and Schloen, "Analysis of the Relationship," op. cit., 118.
6   Young, "An International Cooperation Perspective," op. cit., 490–494; and Tomme Young, "Applying Contract Law to ABS," in *Contracting for ABS: The Legal and Scientific Implications of Bioprospecting Contracts*, ed. Shakeel Bhatti et al., (Gland: IUCN, 2009), 39.
7   Nagoya Protocol 9th preambular recital.

© KONINKLIJKE BRILL NV, LEIDEN, 2014 | DOI 10.1163/9789004217188_021

The importance of standardized contractual clauses[8] therefore lies in their potential contribution to the predictability and consistency of ABS transactions, thereby reducing burdens and transaction costs in establishing MAT[9] and monitoring compliance.[10] It should be stressed, however, that model contractual clauses cannot replace the need for Parties to develop their national ABS frameworks supporting and regulating the negotiations of MAT.[11]

Notably, Article 19 emphasizes the importance of developing model contractual clauses for specific sectors of ABS transactions, as well as cross-sectoral ones. This reflects the understanding that each sector is part of a unique research network or market, with distinct practices of accessing and using genetic resources and undertaking research and development.[12] Article 19 may thus possibly serve to further understand how the Protocol operates in different sectors. In addition, implementation of Article 19 may arguably also contribute to promoting best practices and building the capacity of concerned sectors in countries in which such sectors are less developed.[13]

The following sections will analyze the obligation of Parties, and the mandate for the Protocol's governing body contained in Article 19, in turn.

2   Obligation for Parties

Article 19(1) creates a best-endeavor obligation for all Parties to support the development, update and use of model contractual clauses for MAT. This

---

8   See "Database of Model Contractual Clauses," CBD, accessed 30 November 2013, <www.cbd.int/abs/resources/contracts.shtml>; and WIPO online searchable database of biodiversity-related ABS agreements, with a particular emphasis on the intellectual property aspects of such agreements: "Biodiversity-Related Access and Benefit-Sharing Agreements," WIPO, accessed 30 November 2013, <www.wipo.int/tk/en/databases/contracts/index.html>.

9   See Nagoya Protocol Article 6(3)(g) and this commentary on Article 6, section 7.

10   See this commentary on Article 18.

11   We are grateful to Tomme Young for having drawn our attention to this point. The Protocol negotiators reflected this understanding when they placed draft operational text on model clauses in a section on tools to *support* compliance, rather than in a section on tools for *enforcing* compliance. See ENB 9/465, "Summary of the Seventh Meeting of the Working Group on ABS," 6–7; and ENB, "Summary of the Eighth Meeting of the Working Group on Access and Benefit-Sharing of the Convention on Biological Diversity: 9–15 November 2009," Vol. 9 No. 489, 18 November 2009, 7–9.

12   CBD Secretariat, "Access and Benefit-sharing in Practice," op. cit., 8.

13   Ibid. Note that the Protocol provision on capacity building explicitly points also to the needs of ABS 'stakeholders': Nagoya Protocol Article 22(5)(i) and this commentary on Article 22, section 4.

obligation can be undertaken unilaterally by Parties establishing 'default' or 'standard' MAT for specific categories of genetic resources under their jurisdiction or for specific cases.[14] Such default MAT would likely have to be accepted by a user upon applying for access to genetic resources and/or traditional knowledge, or could apply automatically unless different MAT are negotiated.[15] Parties could also implement this obligation collectively in the context of bilateral or regional ABS frameworks,[16] and at the multilateral level. One precedent of multilateral nature is the standard Material Transfer Agreement adopted by the ITPGRFA Governing Body for exchanges of material within its Multilateral System.[17] In addition, States have initiated work on model clauses for other sectors of genetic resources for food and agriculture, which could include for instance animal genetic resources and microorganisms, under the FAO Commission on Genetic Resources for Food and Agriculture.[18]

It should be further noted that model contractual clauses are included among the information that can be voluntarily submitted by Parties to the ABS Clearinghouse.[19] In addition, Article 19 should be read in conjunction with the obligation for Parties to endeavor to support, as appropriate, the development by indigenous and local communities of model contractual clauses for benefit-sharing arising from the utilization of traditional knowledge associated with genetic resources.[20] Article 19 is further related to the obligation to encourage individual users and providers to include provisions in MAT on information-sharing and contractual reporting aimed at monitoring the

---

14 See this commentary on Article 6, section 3.2.

15 See for instance the standard conditions that apply to bioprospecting activities with non-commercial purpose on Commonwealth territories in Australia: "Permits for Non-Commercial Purposes," Government of Australia, accessed 30 November 2013, <www.environment.gov.au/node/14465>.

16 See this commentary on Article 4, section 3.

17 In practice, the SMTA of the ITPGRFA is also used for transactions of plant genetic resources outside the Treaty's Multilateral System acquired before the Treaty's entry into force, in particular between the international agricultural research centres of the Consultative Group on International Agricultural Research. See this commentary on Article 4, fn. 99; and Chiarolla, Louafi and Schloen, "Analysis of the Relationship," op. cit., 108–109.

18 The CGRFA, "Report of the fourteenth regular session," paragraph 40 (viii), requested its Secretary to compile the information obtained by Parties for consideration by the Commission's intergovernmental technical working groups, to enable the Commission to take a decision on the collection of model contractual clauses for subsectors of genetic resources other than plant genetic resources for food and agriculture at its fifteenth Regular Session.

19 Nagoya Protocol Article 14(3)(b). See this commentary on Article 14, section 4.

20 Nagoya Protocol Article 12(3)(c). See this commentary on Article 12.

utilization of genetic resources once they have left the jurisdiction of the country providing PIC.[21]

3   Mandate for the Protocol's Governing Body

Article 19(2) tasks the Protocol's governing body to periodically 'take stock' of the use of standardized contractual clauses. At a minimum, in accordance with CBD practice, the governing body will likely invite Parties on a periodic basis to submit reports of sectoral reviews and examples of model contractual clauses, synthesize this information and make it available through the ABS Clearinghouse.[22] The wording of Article 19(2) does not exclude the possibility[23] that the governing body could also endorse certain model contractual clauses, whether generally or as a 'predetermination of enforceability' that would enable Parties to ensure their automatic recognition in domestic courts.[24] As endorsed by the Protocol's governing body, certain model contractual clauses could come to represent 'subsequent practice in the application of the treaty which establishes the agreement of the [P]arties regarding its interpretation.'[25] It remains to be seen, however, whether such an assessment would be conducted by the Protocol's governing body, could require the establishment of an *ad hoc* process given the high number of standard contractual clauses to be examined, or even be a function that might be subsumed under the Protocol's compliance procedures and mechanisms.[26]

The Protocol, overall, seeks to tap into normative activities undertaken by various ABS stakeholders such as the research community, the private sector, indigenous peoples and local communities, and NGOs at the national (but also sub-national and transnational) levels as a bottom-up source of inspiration for multilateral discussions on ways to facilitate implementation of and compliance with the Protocol.[27]

---

21   Nagoya Protocol Article 17(1)(b). See this commentary on Article 17. The availability of relevant model contractual clauses could also support the effective implementation of Nagoya Protocol Articles 6(3)(g), 7 and 18(1).

22   Greiber et al., *Explanatory Guide*, op. cit., 194.

23   Although it does not mandate the Protocol's governing body to do so. Compare Nagoya Protocol Article 20(2). See also this commentary on Article 20.

24   Young, "An International Cooperation Perspective," op. cit., 493. Such endorsement could be provided on the basis of Nagoya Protocol Article 26(4)(f).

25   VCLT, Article 31(3)(b).

26   We are grateful to Geoff Burton for a useful exchange of ideas on this point.

27   Morgera, Buck and Tsioumani, "Introduction," op. cit., 10.

Article 20. Codes of Conduct, Guidelines and Best Practices and/or Standards

1. Each Party shall encourage, as appropriate, the development, update and use of voluntary codes of conduct, guidelines and best practices and/or standards in relation to access and benefit-sharing.
2. The Conference of the Parties serving as the meeting of the Parties to this Protocol shall periodically take stock of the use of voluntary codes of conduct, guidelines and best practices and/or standards and consider the adoption of specific codes of conduct, guidelines and best practices and/or standards.

1   Overview

ABS transactions involve a multitude of relationships between governmental, non-governmental and private-sector actors at different levels of governance and across jurisdictions. Albeit exemplary in the context of modern environmental law,[1] this multitude of relationships also points to the limitations of a purely inter-governmental approach to ABS regulation and to the relevance of more informal, complementary tools for shaping common expectations and behavior of all stakeholders involved in ABS transactions.

In this context, Article 20 calls attention to the role of voluntary instruments in the implementation of the Protocol. The terms 'codes of conduct, guidelines and best practices and/or standards' may include self-regulation instruments adopted by research entities/associations, funders, users' groups, private enterprises and business associations, as well as good-practice advice elaborated by indigenous and local communities, NGOs, donors and others. These voluntary instruments will be particularly relevant for stakeholders interested in pioneering its implementation on the ground, including before the entry into force of the Protocol, and also to provide ideas for national ABS legislation and procedures. Several such voluntary instruments on ABS already exist.[2]

---

1   Morgera, Buck and Tsioumani, "Conclusions," op. cit., 515–516.
2   Greiber et al., *Explanatory Guide*, op. cit., 196 make reference to the International Plant Exchange Network's codes of conduct: "The International Plant Exchange Network (IPEN): An Instrument of botanic gardens to fulfil the ABS Provisions," University of Bonn, accessed

© KONINKLIJKE BRILL NV, LEIDEN, 2014 | DOI 10.1163/9789004217188_022

After the development of domestic ABS frameworks, voluntary instruments may contribute to establish/maintain excellence in the conduct of institutions involved in ABS transactions, or serve to support compliance with national ABS frameworks, providing tools and guidelines to ensure respect of legally binding rules.[3] They may also provide standards targeted to ABS in specific sectors.[4] Furthermore, voluntary instruments may be useful to address certain genetic resources that are outside the scope of the Protocol[5] or to go otherwise beyond existing legal requirements.[6] Best practice standards may also become relevant in ABS relationships between Parties and non-Parties to the Nagoya Protocol.[7]

The following sections will analyze the obligation for Parties, and the mandate for the Protocol's governing body contained in Article 20, in turn.

2   Obligation for Parties

Article 20(1) creates, similarly to Article 19(1), a best-endeavor obligation for all Parties to support the development, update and use of voluntary ABS instruments unilaterally or collectively (in the context of bilateral or regional ABS frameworks,[8] and at the multilateral level).[9] This obligation entails removing obstacles to the development of such voluntary instruments and arguably providing incentives in that regard. Parties may have recourse to awareness-raising and capacity-building activities to this end.[10] Adherence to voluntary instruments may be taken into account by Parties' national authorities at the stage of authorizing access to genetic resources[11] and possibly by indigenous and local communities authorizing access to traditional knowledge,[12] particu-

---

    30 November 2013, <www.botgart.uni-bonn.de/ipen/criteria.html>; "ABS Management Tool," International Institute for Sustainable Development and Swiss Government, accessed 30 November 2013, <www.sib.admin.ch/en/nagoya-protocol/abs-management-tool/index.html>; and the Ethical BioTrade standard, managed by the Union for Ethical BioTrade. As to the latter, see Oliva, "Implications of the Nagoya Protocol," op. cit., 373.

3   Ibid., 195.

4   Chiarolla, Louafi and Schloen, "Analysis of the Relationship," op. cit., 119.

5   See this commentary on Article 3.

6   Oliva, "Implications of the Nagoya Protocol," op. cit., 383.

7   See this commentary on Article 24.

8   See this commentary on Article 4, section 3.

9   See this commentary on Article 26, section 2.

10   Nagoya Protocol Article 21(e). See this commentary on Articles 21–22.

11   See this commentary on Article 6, section 3.2.

12   See this commentary on Article 6, section 4, and Article 7.

larly when these voluntary agreements constitute the basis for independent verification of compliance.[13] Parties may also decide to submit information on voluntary instruments to the ABS Clearinghouse.[14]

In as far as voluntary instruments developed by users concern traditional knowledge and genetic resources held by indigenous and local communities,[15] Parties are to act under Article 20(1) with the effective participation of the communities concerned,[16] taking into consideration their customary laws, protocols and procedures.[17] And as part of the obligation to carry out awareness-raising activities, Parties are to promote voluntary instruments in consultation with these communities.[18] From a provider community's perspective, a community protocol,[19] code of conduct or inter-community agreement (in case of shared traditional knowledge) could also serve as a voluntary instrument for the purposes of Article 20. In the case of long-standing ABS relationships, such voluntary instruments could also be developed in cooperation with private-sector users.[20]

3 Mandate for the Protocol's Governing Body

Like Article 19, the Protocol's governing body is tasked with the periodic stock-taking of voluntary initiatives. In line with CBD practice, the governing body will likely invite Parties on a periodic basis to submit reports of sectoral reviews and examples of voluntary instruments, synthesize this information and make it available through the ABS Clearinghouse.

As opposed to Article 19, the Protocol's governing body is also explicitly tasked to consider the adoption of specific voluntary instruments. Adoption of these instruments by the Protocol's governing body would increase their legitimacy[21] due to the underlying intergovernmental consensus, in serving as official guidance for the interpretation and application of the Protocol. As endorsed by the Protocol's governing body, voluntary instruments could thus

---

13   Oliva, "Implications of the Nagoya Protocol," op. cit., 384.
14   Nagoya Protocol Article 14(3)(d). See this commentary on Article 14, section 4.
15   Nagoya Protocol Articles 5(2), 6(2) and 7.
16   UNDRIP Articles 19 and 32(2); ILO Convention No 169, Article 6(2); and fn. 54 in this
      commentary on Article 5.
17   Nagoya Protocol Article 12(1). See this commentary on Article 12, section 2.
18   Nagoya Protocol Article 21(e).
19   See this commentary on Article 12, section 2.1.
20   Oliva, "Implications of the Nagoya Protocol," op. cit., 384–385.
21   Oliva, "Implications of the Nagoya Protocol," op. cit., 385.

come to represent 'subsequent practice in the application of the treaty which establishes the agreement of the [P]arties regarding its interpretation.'[22] It may also be possible for the governing body to recognize or endorse pre-existing and future domestic, transnational and multilateral ABS frameworks.[23] That being said, the Protocol does not clarify whether such an assessment would be conducted by the Protocol's governing body, could require the establishment of an *ad hoc* process given the high number of standard contractual clauses to be examined, or even be a function that might be subsumed under the Protocol's compliance procedures and mechanisms. It also remains to be seen whether the Protocol's governing body would engage in ascertaining the compliance with the Protocol of voluntary instruments that have been intergovernmentally approved in other fora,[24] and what would be the fate of those instruments that are considered non-compliant.[25]

Overall, similarly to Article 19, this provision seeks to tap into normative activities undertaken by various ABS stakeholders such as indigenous and local communities, the research community, the private sector and NGOs at the national (but also sub-national and transnational) level(s) as a bottom-up source of inspiration for discussions on ways to facilitate implementation of the Protocol at the multilateral level.[26] In particular, voluntary instruments may arguably prove to be a useful basis to find agreement on difficult issues arising from the implementation of the Protocol, such as the distinction between commercial and non-commercial research,[27] by taking into account actual experiences in scientific research collaborations, including those working in public domain-like conditions (i.e., without any ownership claims that would restrict access and use of the research results and basic research materials).[28]

---

22 VCLT, Article 31(3)(b).

23 Chiarolla, Louafi and Schloen, "Analysis of the Relationship," op. cit., 118.

24 This may be the case of intergovernmentally approved guidelines targeting non-State actors: see discussion in the context of the CGRFA in this commentary on Article 4, section 4.4.

25 We are grateful to Geoff Burton for a useful exchange of ideas on this point.

26 Morgera, Buck and Tsioumani, "Introduction," op. cit., 10.

27 Pursuant to Nagoya Protocol Article 8(a). See this commentary on Article 8, section 2.

28 Dedeurwaerdere et al., "Governing Global Scientific Research," op. cit., 419–420.

Article 21. Awareness-Raising

Each Party shall take measures to raise awareness of the importance of genetic resources and traditional knowledge associated with genetic resources, and related access and benefit-sharing issues. Such measures may include, *inter alia*:

(a) Promotion of this Protocol, including its objective;
(b) Organization of meetings of indigenous and local communities and relevant stakeholders;
(c) Establishment and maintenance of a help desk for indigenous and local communities and relevant stakeholders;
(d) Information dissemination through a national clearing-house;
(e) Promotion of voluntary codes of conduct, guidelines and best practices and/or standards in consultation with indigenous and local communities and relevant stakeholders;
(f) Promotion of, as appropriate, domestic, regional and international exchanges of experience;
(g) Education and training of users and providers of genetic resources and traditional knowledge associated with genetic resources about their access and benefit-sharing obligations;
(h) Involvement of indigenous and local communities and relevant stakeholders in the implementation of this Protocol; and
(i) Awareness-raising of community protocols and procedures of indigenous and local communities.

1 Overview

Article 21 includes a clear and unconditional obligation for Parties to raise awareness about the Protocol and ABS issues, providing an indicative list of activities[1] that can be undertaken to fulfill this obligation. The importance of awareness-raising in the ABS context and its contribution to the functioning of the Protocol should not be underestimated. ABS is still a little-known issue to the general public, as well as to the numerous government and stakeholder

---

1 Tsioumani, "Access and Benefit Sharing: The Nagoya Protocol," op. cit., 293.

sectors that will be affected by the Protocol. Thus, the preamble indicates that Parties

> recogniz[e] that public awareness of the economic value of ecosystems and biodiversity and the fair and equitable sharing of this economic value with the custodians of biodiversity are key incentives for the conservation of biological diversity and the sustainable use of its components.[2]

Article 21 builds upon the obligations found in the CBD on communication, education and public awareness[3] and exchange of information.[4] In the light of the importance of awareness-raising activities for the effective implementation of the Protocol, the Intergovernmental Committee preparing the ground for the Protocol's entry into force has already discussed the need to develop an awareness-raising strategy.[5]

As Article 21 does no raise particular interpretative difficulties, the following sections will first discuss the specific relevance of this provision for the implementation of the Protocol provisions related to indigenous and local communities, and then offer final observations on the linkages between Article 21 and other provisions of the Protocol.

2   Specific Relevance for Indigenous and Local Communities

It should be emphasized that the non-exhaustive list of awareness-raising activities pays particular attention to the implementation challenges raised

---

2 Nagoya Protocol 6th preambular recital.

3 CBD Article 13. See Glowka, Burhenne-Guilmin and Synge, *Guide to the Convention on Biological Diversity*, op. cit., 68–70; and "Programme of Work for the Global Initiative on Communication, Education and Public Awareness (CEPA)" in CBD Decision 6/19, "Communication, education and public awareness" (22 May 2002) UN DOC UNEP/CBD/COP/6/20, Annex.

4 CBD Article 17. See Glowka, Burhenne-Guilmin and Synge, *Guide to the Convention on Biological Diversity*, op. cit., 92–93; and Greiber et al., *Explanatory Guide*, op. cit., 200.

5 ICNP Recommendation 1/3, "Measures to raise awareness of the importance of genetic resources and associated traditional knowledge and access and benefit-sharing related issues" in "Report of the first meeting of the Open-Ended Ad Hoc Intergovernmental Committee for the Nagoya Protocol on Access to Genetic Resources and the Fair and Equitable Sharing of Benefits Arising from their Utilization" (21 July 2011) UN Doc UNEP/CBD/ICNP/1/8, Annex; and Recommendation 2/6, "Measures to raise awareness of the importance of the genetic resources and associated traditional knowledge, and related access and benefit-sharing issues" in ICNP, "Report of the second meeting," UNEP/CBD/COP/11/6, Annex.

by the Protocol with regards to the role of indigenous and local communities. That is, several of the activities listed under Article 21 concern raising these communities' awareness about their rights under the Protocol and their role in its implementation, and aim at addressing information asymmetries between users and community representatives negotiating MAT.[6] Ultimately, Article 21 may contribute to legal empowerment of indigenous and local communities,[7] by enhancing their ability to use legal tools to tackle power asymmetries and exercise greater control over decisions and processes that affect their lives and rights.[8]

In addition, several of the activities listed under Article 21 aim to raise the awareness of relevant government actors and other stakeholders as to their obligations vis-à-vis indigenous and local communities under the Protocol, such as through the organization of meetings of these communities and other stakeholders and the creation of a help desk. These awareness-raising activities can be part of the mechanisms required by the Nagoya Protocol to inform potential users of traditional knowledge associated with genetic resources about their obligations.[9] These activities may also contribute to Parties' efforts in supporting indigenous and local communities' development of community protocols, minimum requirements for MAT and model contractual clauses.[10] In all these cases, Parties are to act with the effective participation of the indigenous and local communities concerned,[11] taking into consideration their customary laws, protocols and procedures[12] and being mindful of relevant international human rights norms.[13]

3   Linkages with Other Provisions

Article 21 is linked explicitly and implicitly to other provisions in the Protocol. The inclusion among the list of awareness-raising activities of the promotion

---

6   Greiber et al., *Explanatory Guide*, op. cit., 202.

7   Munyi and Jonas, "Implementing the Nagoya Protocol," op. cit., 234–235.

8   Lorenzo Cotula and Paul Mathieu, eds., *Legal Empowerment in Practice, Using Legal Tools to Secure Land Rights in Africa* (London: International Institute for Environment and Development, 2008).

9   Nagoya Protocol Article 12(2). See Greiber et al., *Explanatory Guide*, op. cit., 201. See this commentary on Article 12, section 3.

10   Nagoya Protocol Article 12(3). See this commentary on Article 12, section 4.

11   UNDRIP Articles 19 and 32(2); ILO Convention No. 169, Article 6(2); and fn. 54 in this commentary on Article 5.

12   Nagoya Protocol Article 12(1). See this commentary on Article 12, section 2.

13   See Introduction to this commentary, section 4.

of the 'objective' of the Protocol implies the need to raise awareness about how ABS transactions contribute to fairness and equity between and within States,[14] as well as to biodiversity conservation and sustainable use.[15]

Article 21 is also linked to the promotion of voluntary instruments in consultation with indigenous and local communities and relevant ABS stakeholders,[16] and its implementation will be influenced by the implementation of capacity-building activities.[17] Finally, the ABS Clearinghouse can help in promoting domestic, regional and international exchanges of awareness-raising experiences and in delivering education and training of users and providers.[18]

---

14   See this commentary on Article 1, sections 1–2.
15   See this commentary on Article 1, section 4; Article 5, section 4; Article 8, section 2; Article 9, section 2; Article 10, section 4; and Article 12, section 5.
16   See this commentary on Article 20.
17   See this commentary on Article 22.
18   Young, "An International Cooperation Perspective," op. cit., 472–473. See this commentary on Article 14, section 3.

Article 22. Capacity

1. The Parties shall cooperate in the capacity-building, capacity develop-
    ment and strengthening of human resources and institutional capaci-
    ties to effectively implement this Protocol in developing country
    Parties, in particular the least developed countries and small island
    developing States among them, and Parties with economies in tran-
    sition, including through existing global, regional, subregional and
    national institutions and organisations. In this context, Parties should
    facilitate the involvement of indigenous and local communities and
    relevant stakeholders, including non-governmental organisations and
    the private sector.
2. The need of developing country Parties, in particular the least devel-
    oped countries and small island developing States among them, and
    Parties with economies in transition for financial resources in accor-
    dance with the relevant provisions of the Convention shall be taken
    fully into account for capacity-building and development to imple-
    ment this Protocol.
3. As a basis for appropriate measures in relation to the implementa-
    tion of this Protocol, developing country Parties, in particular the
    least developed countries and small island developing States among
    them, and Parties with economies in transition should identify their
    national capacity needs and priorities through national capacity self-
    assessments. In doing so, such Parties should support the capacity
    needs and priorities of indigenous and local communities and rel-
    evant stakeholders, as identified by them, emphasising the capacity
    needs and priorities of women.
4. In support of the implementation of this Protocol, capacity-building
    and development may address, *inter alia*, the following key areas:
    (a) Capacity to implement, and to comply with the obligations of,
        this Protocol;
    (b) Capacity to negotiate mutually agreed terms;
    (c) Capacity to develop, implement and enforce domestic legisla-
        tive, administrative or policy measures on access and benefit-
        sharing; and
    (d) Capacity of countries to develop their endogenous research
        capabilities to add value to their own genetic resources.

5.   Measures in accordance with paragraphs 1 to 4 above may include,
     inter alia:
     (a)   Legal and institutional development;
     (b)   Promotion of equity and fairness in negotiations, such as train-
           ing to negotiate mutually agreed terms;
     (c)   The monitoring and enforcement of compliance;
     (d)   Employment of best available communication tools and
           Internet-based systems for access and benefit-sharing activities;
     (e)   Development and use of valuation methods;
     (f)   Bioprospecting, associated research and taxonomic studies;
     (g)   Technology transfer, and infrastructure and technical capacity to
           make such technology transfer sustainable;
     (h)   Enhancement of the contribution of access and benefit-sharing
           activities to the conservation of biological diversity and the sus-
           tainable use of its components;
     (i)   Special measures to increase the capacity of relevant stakehold-
           ers in relation to access and benefit-sharing; and
     (j)   Special measures to increase the capacity of indigenous and
           local communities with emphasis on enhancing the capacity of
           women within those communities in relation to access to genetic
           resources and/or traditional knowledge associated with genetic
           resources.
6.   Information on capacity-building and development initiatives at
     national, regional and international levels, undertaken in accordance
     with paragraphs 1 to 5 above, should be provided to the Access and
     Benefit-sharing clearing-house with a view to promoting synergy
     and coordination on capacity-building and development for access
     and benefit-sharing.

1   Overview

The length of this provision signals at the outset the paramount importance
of capacity building for the successful implementation of the Protocol and
for sensuring compliance with it. The Protocol addresses capacity building
in detail, linking it to implementation and compliance, negotiation of MAT,
development and enforcement of domestic ABS frameworks, and development of endogenous research capabilities.[1] The following sections will analyze

---

1   Nagoya Protocol Article 22(4).

the obligation to cooperate in this context, the emphasis on country-driven capacity building, and provisions specifically targeting indigenous and local communities. The final section will offer an assessment of possible challenges in development cooperation for ABS capacity building.

2 The Obligation to Cooperate

Article 22 creates an unconditional obligation for all Parties to cooperate in building capacity[2] for the implementation of the Protocol. The obligation is underpinned by concerns about optimal utilization of resources and avoidance of duplicative activities. As per standard CBD terminology, the provision singles out two groups of countries that will benefit from capacity-building support: developing-country Parties, in particular the least developed countries and small island developing States among them, and Parties with economies in transition.[3]

Article 22, therefore, embodies an obligation of solidarity – that is, an intensified form of international cooperation, whereby individual States are to take into consideration in their own policy the interests of other States and the common interests of the global community, and be ready to accept to bear certain costs and burdens of cooperation.[4] This is based on the understanding that costs and burdens have been distributed fairly 'in accordance with basic principles of equity and social justice' to address global challenges.[5] Obligations of solidarity are to be fulfilled *without expectations of reciprocity*, and can be

---

2　On the different meanings of the expressions 'capacity-building,' 'capacity development' and 'strengthening of human resources and institutional capacities,' see Greiber et al., *Explanatory Guide*, op. cit., 207–208, relying on: "UN Public Administration Glossary," UN, accessed 30 November 2013, <www.unpan.org>.

3　The first two paragraphs of Nagoya Protocol Article 22 are modelled after Biosafety Protocol Article 22.

4　Wolfrum, "Cooperation," op. cit., paragraph 3.

5　UN General Assembly, "Promotion of a Democratic and Equitable International Order" (8 February 2002) UN Doc A/RES/56/151, paragraph 3(f), and "Promotion of a Democratic and Equitable International Order" (25 February 2003) UN Doc A/RES/57/213, paragraph 4(f), which (both) read: 'Solidarity, as a fundamental value, by virtue of which global challenges must be managed in a way that distributes costs and burdens fairly, in accordance with basic principles of equity and social justice, and ensures that those who suffer or benefit the least receive help from those who benefit the most.' See also UN Millennium Declaration, paragraph 6; and Campanelli, "Solidarity," op. cit., paragraph 17.

considered inherent to specific areas of international law such as sustainable development and human rights.[6]

Article 22(1) can be interpreted as requiring Parties to enter into negotiations with a view to engaging in the coordinated or joint determination and allocation of capacity-building support. However, if agreement cannot be reached, the obligation does not impede Parties from making unilateral determinations, but in doing so they are expected to take in consideration other Parties' initiatives and concerns.[7] While Article 22 does not provide specific indications as to how such cooperation should be carried out, it suggests recourse to existing global, regional, subregional and national institutions and organizations. These institutions may include the Global Environment Facility (GEF),[8] the ITPGRFA and the multi-donor ABS Capacity Development Initiative,[9] as well as the CBD itself through its Action Plan on Capacity-building for Access to Genetic Resources and Benefit-sharing.[10]

In addition, Article 22 does not prevent cooperation among Parties to be carried out on an *ad hoc* basis, including through bilateral agreements (specifically related to ABS or having a broader scope).[11] The usefulness and cost-effectiveness of subregional and regional approaches to capacity-building and development, in particular where countries have similar biological resources and common capacity-building and development needs, have also been underscored in intergovernmental discussions preparing for the entry into force of the Protocol.[12] Based on these intergovernmental discussions, it can also be expected that the Protocol's governing body will facilitate coordination on capacity-building, through reporting, creating a specific coordination

---

6   Ibid., paragraphs 5–6 and 9–10, and 16–20 specifically on sustainable development.

7   See discussion on the general duty of cooperation in this commentary on Article 11, section 2.

8   Note that the GEF is also the financial mechanism for the implementation of the CBD and the Nagoya Protocol: see this commentary on Article 25, section 2.

9   ICNP Recommendation 1/2, "Measures to assist in capacity-building, capacity development and strengthening of human resources and institutional capacities in developing countries and Parties with economies in transition" in ICNP, "Report of the first meeting," UNEP/CBD/ICNP/1/8, Annex, 2nd preambular recital.

10   CBD Decision 7/19, "Access and benefit-sharing as related to genetic resources (Article 15)" Annex (13 April 2004) UN Doc UNEP/CBD/COP/7/21. See also "Database of ABS Capacity-Building Activities," CBD, accessed 30 November 2013, <www.cbd.int/abs/projects.shtml>; and Greiber et al., *Explanatory Guide*, op. cit., 206–207.

11   See discussion of bilateral agreements in this commentary on Article 4, section 3.

12   ICNP Recommendation 1/2, 5th preambular recital.

mechanism, and monitoring and reviewing of activities undertaken.[13] This will build upon information (that 'should' be provided) on capacity-building activities to the ABS Clearinghouse.[14] By storing and sharing information on capacity-building materials, the ABS Clearinghouse is itself expected to contribute to capacity building.[15]

In cooperating on capacity building, Parties are to operate in the framework of relevant provisions of the CBD on technical cooperation and financial solidarity. Article 22(1) implicitly refers back to the CBD requirement for Parties to undertake technical and scientific cooperation, especially with respect to the development and strengthening of national capabilities in human resources development and institution building.[16] According to Article 22(2), the financial needs of developing countries shall be taken into full account for capacity building to implement the Protocol. Explicit reference, in that context, to 'accordance with relevant provisions of the Convention' may thus be interpreted as a reference to CBD requirement for developed countries to provide 'new and additional financial resources' to developing countries to enable them to meet the costs of implementing their obligations under the CBD.[17] It may also refer to the CBD text on taking into account that the implementation by developing countries of their international obligations will depend on the degree to which developed country Parties provide financial resources to the former.[18]

---

13   ICNP Recommendation 1/2, paragraph 1 and Annex, where reference is made to a coordination mechanism and its possible elements, including the reporting of capacity-building and development initiatives to the ABS Clearinghouse; and monitoring and review, including developing a set of indicators to facilitate the monitoring and review of the implementation of the strategic framework and to assess the impact of access and benefit-sharing capacity-building and development initiatives.

14   Nagoya Protocol Article 22(6). See this commentary on Article 14, section 4.

15   See this commentary on Article 14, section 3.

16   CBD Article 18. See Glowka, Burhenne-Guilmin and Synge, *Guide to the Convention on Biological Diversity*, op. cit., 94–95; and similarly to the corresponding text in the Biosafety Protocol, see Mackenzie et al., *Explanatory Guide to the Cartagena Protocol*, op. cit., 143.

17   CBD Article 20(2). See Glowka, Burhenne-Guilmin and Synge, *Guide to the Convention on Biological Diversity*, op. cit., 102–104.

18   CBD Article 20(4). See Glowka, Burhenne-Guilmin and Synge, *Guide to the Convention on Biological Diversity*, op. cit., 105. Similarly to the corresponding text in the Biosafety Protocol, see Mackenzie et al., *Explanatory Guide to the Cartagena Protocol*, op. cit., 144–145. On the interpretation of CBD Article 20(4), see Melinda Chandler, "The Biodiversity Convention: Selected Issues of Interest to the International Lawyer," *Colorado Journal of International Environmental Law and Policy* 4 (1993): 141, 173–174, who sees it as a mere statement of fact; while Birnie, Boyle and Redgwell, *International Law and the*

3   Country-Driven Capacity-Building

Because of the Protocol's built-in flexibility, capacity-building activities will
vary greatly from one country to another. So intergovernmental discussions in
preparation for the Protocol's entry into force have tried to balance a bottom-
up approach to allow countries, as well as indigenous and local communities,
to determine their own needs with an overarching global strategy to ensure
optimal use of resources.[19]

Article 22 thus seems to recognize that no single model of capacity building
for ABS will fit the situation of all countries, but that capacity-building initiatives should be tailored to fit the specific national context of the country whose
capacity is being developed.[20] Notably, Article 22(3) points to the desirability
of demand-driven capacity-building cooperation. It recommends that benefi-
ciary countries identify their national capacity needs and priorities through
national capacity self-assessments.

Article 22(4) then proceeds with an indicative list of key areas for capacity building (development, implementation and enforcement of domestic ABS
measures; compliance with the Protocol; negotiations of MAT; and development of endogenous research capabilities to add value to one country's own
genetic resources).[21] Furthermore, Article 22(5) includes an indicative list of
activities,[22] such as the enhancement of the contribution of ABS activities to
the conservation of biodiversity and the sustainable use of its components,
which resonates with other provisions in the Protocol aimed at ensuring a
holistic approach to the fulfillment of the three objectives of the CBD in the
context of the Protocol.[23] Reference is also made to technology transfer, which
is specifically addressed elsewhere in the Protocol.[24]

Several of the key capacity-building areas and activities have to do with
national law-making and implementation of the Protocol through legal means,

---

           Environment, op. cit., 633–634, emphasise that the effect of this provision is to subject
           developing countries' compliance with international biodiversity policies to the extent
           that they receive funding under the Convention.

19   ENB 9/551, "Summary of the First Meeting of the Intergovernmental Committee for the
           Nagoya Protocol," 12.

20   See similar comments in relation to the Biosafety Protocol in Mackenzie et al., *Explanatory
           Guide to the Cartagena Protocol*, op. cit., 143.

21   Nagoya Protocol Article 22(4).

22   Nagoya Protocol Article 22(5).

23   See this commentary on Article 1, section 4; Article 5, section 6; Article 8, section 2;
           Article 9, section 2; Article 10, section 4; Article 12, section 5; and Article 21, section 3.

24   See this commentary on Article 23.

including the need to ensure fairness in MAT, as well as to build institutional, scientific and other capacities to be able to fully and effectively apply and ensure compliance with domestic ABS frameworks.[25]

4 The Capacity of Indigenous and Local Communities and Other ABS Stakeholders

Article 22 makes several references (albeit of a recommendatory – rather than mandatory – character) to the capacity needs and priorities of indigenous and local communities, in recognition of their role in implementing the Protocol and their specific needs and rights. Thus, the provision recommends that Parties facilitate the involvement of these communities in cooperation on capacity-building[26] and support the self-identification of capacity needs and priorities of these communities in the context of national capacity self-assessments. It highlights the need to pay specific attention to the capacity needs and priorities of women.[27] Among specific measures for capacity building, reference is made to measures to increase the capacity of communities, particularly women, in relation to access[28] to genetic resources and/or traditional knowledge.[29] In this regard Article 22 is informed by and must be interpreted in conjunction with other specific obligations of Parties vis-à-vis indigenous and local communities in other provisions of the Protocol. In planning capacity-building activities, as far as these communities are concerned, Parties are to act with their effective participation,[30] taking into consideration their customary laws, protocols and procedures[31] and relevant international human rights norms.[32]

---

25 Nagoya Protocol Article 22(4)(a–d). See Greiber et al., *Explanatory Guide*, op. cit., 209.

26 Nagoya Protocol Article 22(1).

27 Nagoya Protocol Article 22(3). On the relevance of a human rights approach to gender discrimination in the context of the Nagoya Protocol, see Introduction to this commentary, section 4.3.

28 Nagoya Protocol Articles 6(2) and 7. See this commentary on Article 6, section 3, and on Article 7.

29 Nagoya Protocol Article 22(4)(j).

30 UNDRIP Articles 19 and 32(2); ILO Convention No. 169, Article 6(2); and fn. 54 in this commentary on Article 5.

31 Nagoya Protocol Article 12(1). See this commentary on Article 12, section 2.

32 See Introduction to this commentary, section 4.

It should also be noted that most of the provisions in Article 22 referring to indigenous and local communities also aim to benefit other ABS stakeholders[33] such as NGOs and the private sector, in cooperation efforts and in the self-assessment of capacity-building needs at the national level. Among the list of possible capacity-building measures, there is also explicit, although general, reference to increasing the capacity of relevant stakeholders in relation to ABS.[34] This points to the underlying need for all ABS stakeholders to be well equipped to cooperate with one another in building effective and mutually beneficial ABS transactions.

The inputs of indigenous and local communities and other ABS stakeholders will also be sought at the international level, in the context of the proposed development of a strategic capacity-building framework under the Nagoya Protocol.[35]

5   ABS-Related Development Cooperation

Overall, the proposed approach to ABS capacity-building cooperation – that is, country-driven, mindful of financial solidarity obligations under the CBD, and with the involvement of indigenous and local communities and other stakeholders – is expected to be reflected not only in the activities of the GEF and other sources of multilateral assistance for capacity-building purposes, but also that of national bodies that engage in unilateral and bilateral development assistance. This is particularly the case of those developed countries that are already providing or will provide development assistance with a view to facilitating implementation of the Protocol in developing countries.

Given the numerous legal complexities of the Protocol's subject-matter that will have to be addressed in building domestic ABS frameworks, and the challenges that may arise in particular ABS transactions, effective realization of capacity-building cooperation (or lack thereof) will be crucial for the Protocol's implementation by developing countries. As observed in other multilateral environmental agreements, capacity-related issues are strongly linked with compliance, particularly in the face of ever-expanding obligations under

---

33   Nagoya Protocol Article 22(1–2)
34   Nagoya Protocol Article 22(4)(i).
35   ICNP Recommendation 1/2, paragraph 1 and Annex, which refers to possible sequence of actions for the implementation of the strategic framework, including a possible roadmap of activities to assist countries in defining their priorities and corresponding timelines.

international environmental law.[36] It remains to be seen whether and how this link will play out, including in the deliberations of the future compliance mechanism of the Protocol.[37]

Given the importance of capacity-building for ABS law-making and enforcement at the national level, support by developed countries to the development of ABS laws in developing countries will occur not only in the interest of the international community in the effective implementation of the Protocol, but likely also in developed countries' own interest (to ensure predictability and fairness for their users). It may be a challenge, in that context, to avoid exercising any undue influence or pressure on provider countries' exercise of their national sovereignty over their genetic resources and on indigenous and local communities. The delicate, and in many respects still open-ended, balance of international obligations enshrined in the Nagoya Protocol may thus create also risks that capacity-building initiatives may unduly favor the interests of user countries, if provider countries find themselves dependent on user countries' support. Another risk may arise from ready-made solutions offered through capacity-building activities that do not respond to the particular circumstances[38] of Parties, who will be under pressure to build national capacity to implement and ensure compliance with the Protocol. Such pressure may be heightened for provider countries, due to the link established by the Protocol between the domestic ABS framework of provider countries and user countries' international obligations on addressing compliance by their users.[39]

---

36   See Elisa Morgera et al., "Implementation Challenges and Compliance in MEA Negotiations," in Chasek and Wagner *The Roads from Rio*, op. cit., 222.

37   See this commentary on Article 30.

38   Examination of the history of (the failure of) conventional development assistance in this regard is beyond the scope of this commentary. For a succinct account of the debate, see David Ellerman, "Autonomy in Education and Development," *Journal of International Cooperation in Education* 7 (2004): 3, who notes 'a real danger that a development intervention, instead of acting as a catalyst or midwife to empower change in an autonomy-respecting manner, will only short-circuit people's learning activities and reinforce their feelings of impotence.' Ibid., 13.

39   See this commentary on Article 15, section 3.1.

Article 23. Technology Transfer, Collaboration and Cooperation

In accordance with Articles 15, 16, 18 and 19 of the Convention, the Parties shall collaborate and cooperate in technical and scientific research and development programmes, including biotechnological research activities, as a means to achieve the objective of this Protocol. The Parties undertake to promote and encourage access to technology by, and transfer of technology to, developing country Parties, in particular the least developed countries and small island developing States among them, and Parties with economies in transition, in order to enable the development and strengthening of a sound and viable technological and scientific base for the attainment of the objectives of the Convention and this Protocol. Where possible and appropriate such collaborative activities shall take place in and with a Party or the Parties providing genetic resources that is the country or are the countries of origin of such resources or a Party or Parties that have acquired the genetic resources in accordance with the Convention.

1   Overview

Technology transfer is an essential form of benefit-sharing[1] and a key means to contribute to the conservation and sustainable use of biodiversity.[2] It was part of the grand bargain struck in the negotiations of the CBD, and considered an essential counterpart to provisions related to access to genetic resources: access is to be balanced against greater availability of scientific and technological information and environmentally sound technology that make use of these resources.[3] Technology transfer is thus seen as a means to acknowledge and reward the contribution of countries, as well as indigenous and local

---

1   Greiber et al., *Explanatory Guide*, op. cit., 216.
2   See this commentary on Article 1, section 4. On the holistic interpretation of the three CBD objectives in the context of the Protocol, see also this Article 5, section 6; Article 8, section 2; Article 9, section 2; Article 10, section 4; Article 12, section 5; Article 21, section 3; and Article 22, section 3.
3   See Glowka, Burhenne-Guilmin and Synge, *Guide to the Convention on Biological Diversity*, op. cit., 84; and Greiber et al., *Explanatory Guide*, op. cit., 215.

communities, providing genetic resources and traditional knowledge to the development of related technologies.[4]

While technology transfer and scientific collaboration may take place in the context of specific ABS transactions, and be set out in MAT,[5] the scope of Article 23 goes beyond bilateral ABS relationships. It includes any type of inter-governmental cooperation and collaboration such as joint research programmes that may involve ABS-related activities.

The main legal complexity related to Article 23, as anticipated in the opening provision of the Protocol,[6] concerns the limitation of State efforts in sharing technology that is in the hands of private actors, particularly when protected by IPRs. This is a complexity that is common to other MEAs.[7] The following sections will thus analyse in the light of the reticence of the Protocol negotiators to address WTO law- and IPR-related matters[8] the obligation to cooperate in the area of technology, and the obligation related to technology transfer, in turn.

2   Technology Collaboration and Cooperation

Article 23 establishes an obligation for Parties to collaborate and cooperate in technical and scientific research, and development programmes, including biotechnological research activities. The obligation is clear but quite open-ended. It requires States to enter into negotiations without specifying the possible avenues for pursuing them – at the bilateral, regional or multilateral level. The obligation does not go as far as requiring States to reach agreement, so if agreement cannot be reached, they are not prevented from making unilateral determinations about technical and scientific research. In doing so,

---

4   Ibid., 216–7.
5   See generally this commentary on Article 5 section 5; and also on Article 6, section 7 and on Article 18.
6   See reference to 'taking into account all rights…to technologies' in Protocol Article 1. See this commentary on Article 1, section 2, fn. 8.
7   See for example Birnie, Boyle and Redgwell, *International Law and the Environment,* op. cit., 134; and UNEP-UNCTAD, *A Preliminary Analysis of MEA Experiences in Identifying and Facilitating the Transfer of Technology* (Nairobi and Geneva: UNEP-UNCTAD, 2007), accessed 30 November 2013, <www.unep.ch/etb/areas/pdf/MEA%20Papers/MEA_EGS%20Paper.pdf>.
8   See generally Pavoni, "Nagoya Protocol and WTO Law," op. cit.

however, Parties should take in consideration other Parties' interests.[9] Given the importance of technological cooperation for the successful implementation of the Protocol and the maintenance of mutual trust among its Parties, it can be anticipated that the Protocol's governing body will provide a forum for facilitating such cooperation[10] and will keep this matter under review.[11]

The obligation to cooperate is to be interpreted and applied 'in accordance' with a series of CBD provisions.[12] First of all, the CBD spells out the content of the obligation to cooperate in technical and scientific matters, which implies the promotion of international technical and scientific cooperation through the development and implementation of supportive national policies, and paying special attention to the strengthening of national capabilities through human resources development and institutional building.[13] In addition, and very significantly for the Protocol provisions concerning indigenous and local communities, the obligation implies devising methods of cooperation for the development and use of *indigenous and traditional technologies*, including through training of personnel and exchange of experts.[14] Furthermore, the obligation implies the promotion of the establishment of joint research programmes and joint ventures for technology development.[15] These forms of international cooperation will likely involve bilateral cooperation, particularly with developing countries, and capacity building.[16]

As a complement to international cooperation, Parties are to take a series of *domestic* measures to provide for the *effective* participation by provider

---

9   For a general discussion on the duty to cooperate, see this commentary on Article 11, section 2.

10   See this commentary on Article 26.

11   See this commentary on Article 31.

12   Note that CBD Article 17 on the exchange of information from all publicly available sources, including the results of scientific research and traditional knowledge in combination with technologies using genetic resources, is not included in the CBD provisions referred to in this Article of the Protocol. This may arguably be explained by the desire of the drafters to avoid reference to repatriation of traditional knowledge (CBD Article 17(2)). The question of the applicability of the Nagoya Protocol to the repatriation of traditional knowledge, in effect, remains open at the time of writing: see ENB, "Summary of the Eighth Meeting of the Working Group on Article 8(j) and the seventeenth meeting of the Subsidiary Body on Scientific, Technical and Technological Advice of the Convention on Biological Diversity: 7–18 October 2013", Vol. 9 No. 611, 5–6.

13   CBD Article 18(2).

14   CBD Article 18(4), emphasis added.

15   CBD Article 18(5).

16   Glowka, Burhenne-Guilmin and Synge, *Guide to the Convention on Biological Diversity*, op. cit., 93–94. See this commentary on Article 22.

countries in biotechnological research, by promoting and advancing *priority access* to the results and benefits arising from modern biotechnologies to, and ensuring participation in biotechnological research by, Parties that provide the genetic resources for such research.[17] It would thus be advisable to specify in ABS agreements that the start of biotechnological research on the provided genetic resources should be notified to the provider country so that the participation on biotechnological research can be arranged for.[18]

Article 23 concludes with a qualified obligation ('Where possible and appropriate') for Parties to engage in collaborative activities benefitting *and* taking place in Parties providing genetic resources, based on a pre-existing obligation under the CBD.[19] It implicitly foresees that Parties will exercise due diligence in identifying whether the conditions exist for technology collaboration to take place in provider countries and that they will make reasonable efforts to establish these collaborations.

Overall, Article 23 allows for all types of technological collaboration amounting to fair and equitable benefit-sharing. These may include allocation of research funding, the sharing of research and development results, contribution in scientific research and development programmes, and participation in product development.[20] Such types of benefit-sharing may arguably create 'a flow of goods and knowledge that opens opportunities for learning and capacity-building in developing countries.'[21]

3   Technology Transfer

As technology is often in the hands of private individuals and companies, Article 23 includes a commitment,[22] rather than an obligation, for Parties

---

17   CBD Article 19(1–2).

18   Glowka, Burhenne-Guilmin and Synge, *Guide to the Convention on Biological Diversity*, op. cit., 96–97.

19   CBD Article 15(6) reads: 'Each Contracting Party *shall endeavor to develop and carry out* scientific research based on genetic resources provided by other Contracting Parties with the full participation of, and where possible in, such Contracting Parties,' emphasis added. Compare with Nagoya Protocol wording 'Where possible and appropriate such collaborative activities *shall take place* in and with a Party or the Parties providing genetic resources that is the country or are the countries of origin of such resources or a Party or Parties that have acquired the genetic resources in accordance with the Convention'.

20   Nagoya Protocol Annex, paragraphs 1(h), 2(a–c) and (m).

21   Greiber et al., *Explanatory Guide*, op. cit., 216.

22   Note the use of 'undertake' rather than 'shall'.

to promote and encourage (i.e., at least to remove barriers to, and/or create incentives for)[23] access to, and transfer of technology[24] to developing countries. This has the specific aim of enabling the development and strengthening of a sound and viable technological and scientific base for the attainment of the objectives of the CBD and Protocol.[25] Where relevant technologies are in the hands of public entities,[26] Parties have greater opportunity to provide technologies directly. The provision leaves it open to Parties to identify the specific means of implementation. These could include a domestic requirement to governmental agencies to transfer technology, the creation of economic incentives to encourage private entities to transfer technologies, the establishment of national and regional technology clearinghouses, the purchase of IPRs on behalf of another Party, or the creation of a domestic obligation upon those using public funds to develop a particular technology and make it available for transfer.[27]

The wording of Article 23 is based in general terms on CBD Article 16 on access to and transfer of technology. While at first sight, it may appear that the Protocol uses weaker language than the CBD,[28] it should be recalled that Article 23 recalls CBD Article 16 and other relevant provisions in this context.[29] Thus, the commitment to technology transfer under the Protocol cannot be interpreted and implemented so as to provide a lower standard than that

---

23   On the obligation to encourage, see this commentary on Article 9, section 1.

24   On technology transfer, see Glowka, Burhenne-Guilmin and Synge, *Guide to the Convention on Biological Diversity*, op. cit., 85; and UNEP-UNCTAD, *Preliminary Analysis of MEA Experiences*, op. cit.

25   This is yet another instance in which the Protocol pursues a holistic implementation of the three objectives of the CBD. See fn. 2 above.

26   Glowka, Burhenne-Guilmin and Synge, *Guide to the Convention on Biological Diversity*, op. cit., 84–85.

27   Ibid., 85 and 90.

28   CBD Article 16(1) reads 'Each Contracting Party...undertakes...to *provide and/or facilitate access* for and transfer to other Contracting Parties of technologies' (emphasis added); whereas the Protocol only refers to a commitment to 'promote and encourage' technology transfer. We are grateful to Tomme Young for drawing our attention to this point.

29   This interpretation appears to offer the only justification for the crammed drafting of Article 23, as three different obligations are clustered in the same paragraph instead of being divided into three separate paragraphs. It can therefore be argued that the opening proviso 'in accordance with Articles 15, 16, 18 and 19 of the Convention' applies to the entirety of Article 23. This interpretation is also proposed by Greiber et al., *Explanatory Guide*, op. cit., 216.

established under the Convention. In addition, Protocol Parties as CBD Parties will continue to be bound by the CBD provisions in this regard.

Interpreted in the light of the relevant provisions of the CBD, Article 23 requires Parties to adopt domestic measures that provide, or at least facilitate, access to technologies that make use of genetic resources, including biotechnologies, as well as technologies that are relevant for conservation and sustainable use.[30] This has to be arranged under fair and most favorable terms, including on concessional and preferential terms if mutually agreed, when developing countries are concerned.[31] Both provider and receiver countries have an obligation to ensure that the transferred technology does not cause significant damage to the environment.[32]

Notably, the Protocol 'buries' a solitary reference to intellectual property in relation to technology transfer in its Annex among the possible monetary and non-monetary benefits.[33] There, reference is made to transferring technologies under fair and most favorable terms, including on concessional and preferential terms where agreed.[34] Such reference replicates wording common to other multilateral environmental agreements.[35] As opposed to the Protocol, the CBD explicitly acknowledges that technology often is in private hands. It thus obliges Parties to take domestic measures targeting the private sector so as to facilitate access to, and joint development of, technology with governmental institutions and the private sector of developing countries.[36] It also addresses explicitly the relevance of IPRs, by requiring that domestic legislation provide

---

30   CBD Article 16(1). Note, however, that CBD Article 16 was one of the most controversial ones in the negotiations of the Convention and that '[c]ircular cross-referencing introduces decided ambiguity that opens the door to differing interpretations.' See Glowka, Burhenne-Guilmin and Synge, *Guide to the Convention on Biological Diversity*, op. cit., 84.

31   CBD Article 16(2).

32   CBD Article 16(1). Glowka, Burhenne-Guilmin and Synge, *Guide to the Convention on Biological Diversity*, op. cit., 85–6.

33   See this commentary on Article 5, section 6.

34   Nagoya Protocol Annex, paragraph 2(f).

35   CBD Article 16(2); UNFCCC Articles 4(1)(c) and (5); and Montreal Protocol on Substances that Deplete the Ozone Layer (Montreal, 16 September 1987, in force 1 January 1989) 1522 UNTS 28 (hereinafter, Montreal Protocol), Article 10(A). See also Glowka, Burhenne-Guilmin and Synge, *Guide to the Convention on Biological Diversity*, op. cit., 86; and more generally: CBD, UNCTAD and WIPO Secretariats, *The Role of Intellectual Property Rights in Technology Transfer in the Context of the Convention on Biological Diversity*, 2007, accessed 30 November 2013, <www.cbd.int/doc/meetings/ttc/egttstc-02/other/egttstc-02-oth-techstudy-en.pdf>.

36   CBD Article 16(4).

access to technologies also when protected by IPRs, on the basis of MAT.[37] It subjects access to such technology to terms that balance the need for transfer with the adequate and effective protection of intellectual property.[38] It further calls for international cooperation to ensure that IPRs are supportive of the objectives of the Convention.[39] These provisions are also applicable in the context of the Protocol's implementation.

In implementing Article 23, Parties may find concrete guidance in the CBD work programme on technology transfer and scientific and technological cooperation, which was adopted by consensus.[40] Accordingly, Parties should establish an enabling environment for technology transfer in providing and receiving countries by creating an institutional, administrative, legislative and policy structures for the private and public sector not only for the transfer of technology, but also for the adaptation of transferred technology. Parties are also to remove barriers to technology transfer that exist in their domestic frameworks, and that are inconsistent with international law. In addition, Parties should conceive technology transfer not as a one-off, unilateral endeavor, but as part of an integrated, long-term scientific and technological cooperation effort, thereby creating the conditions for lasting participation by provider countries with a view to increasing their capacities and information base, as well as adding value at the local level.[41]

Overall, the commitment to technology transfer must be implemented in good faith to ensure fair and equitable benefit-sharing,[42] as required to realize the objective of the Protocol.[43] Such commitment requires every reasonable effort,[44] even before knowing how the genetic resources will be used.[45] These efforts can be facilitated through information-sharing under the ABS

---

37   CBD Article 16(3).

38   The reference to 'adequate and effective protection' was meant to refer implicitly to protection under TRIPS: Glowka, Burhenne-Guilmin and Synge, *Guide to the Convention on Biological Diversity*, op. cit., 86–87.

39   CBD Articles 16(4), 16(2) and 16(5).

40   "Programme of work on technology transfer and technological and scientific cooperation" in CBD Decision 7/29, "Transfer of technology and technology cooperation (Articles 16 to 19)" (13 April 2004) UN Doc UNEP/CBD/COP/7/21, Annex. See Morgera and Tsioumani, "Evolution of Benefit-Sharing," op. cit., 153.

41   CBD Decision 7/29, paragraph 2. See Greiber et al., *Explanatory Guide*, op. cit., 217.

42   CBD Article 15(7). Greiber et al., *Explanatory Guide*, op. cit., 216.

43   See this commentary on Article 2, sections 1–2.

44   Glowka, Burhenne-Guilmin and Synge, *Guide to the Convention on Biological Diversity*, op. cit., 97.

45   Ibid., 83.

Clearinghouse.[46] They may also receive financial support, including by meeting the agreed full incremental costs of establishing technological cooperation and ensuring technology transfer through the financial mechanism of the Protocol.[47]

---

46   Greiber et al., *Explanatory Guide*, op. cit., 216. See this commentary on Article 14, section 3. Compare CBD Article 18(3).

47   Note in fact that CBD Article 19 on technology transfer makes reference to the CBD provisions on financial solidarity (Articles 20–21). See Glowka, Burhenne-Guilmin and Synge, *Guide to the Convention on Biological Diversity*, op. cit., 83 and 86. See also this commentary on Article 25, section 2.

Article 24. Non-Parties

The Parties shall encourage non-Parties to adhere to this Protocol and to contribute appropriate information to the Access and Benefit-sharing Clearing-House.

Article 24 is a short provision on how Parties to the Nagoya Protocol are to relate to non-Parties. As a general rule, treaties do not create obligations or rights for third Parties:[1] that is, a treaty 'cannot, by its own force, impose an obligation on a third State nor modify in any way the legal rights of a third State without its consent.'[2] Nonetheless, a treaty may affect non-Parties. This provision, therefore, clarifies how non-Parties may be affected by the Protocol in their dealings with Parties.

Article 24 creates a two-fold obligation. First, it mandates Parties to encourage (i.e., at least to remove barriers to, and/or create incentives for)[3] non-Parties to comply with the Protocol on a voluntary basis, which may include encouragement to become Parties to the Protocol. In doing so, the Protocol leaves considerable flexibility as to the means to fulfill this provision. So, Parties may provide technical, financial or institutional support for adherence to the Protocol.[4] Bilateral trade and cooperation agreements,[5] or unilateral trade-incentive schemes could also include commitments to become Parties to the Protocol.[6] Second, the provision mandates Parties to encourage non-

---

1   VCLT, Article 30. See also Anthony Aust, *Modern Treaty Law and Practice* (Cambridge: Cambridge University Press, 2007), chapter 14.
2   Ibid., 256.
3   On the obligation to encourage, see this commentary on Article 9, section 1.
4   For a comparable discussion in the context of the Biosafety Protocol, see Mackenzie et al., *Explanatory Guide to the Cartagena Protocol*, op. cit., 157.
5   See this commentary on Article 4, section 3.
6   The EU, for instance, uses trade incentives to encourage other States become Parties to other multilateral environmental agreements in its bilateral trade and development agreements with third countries: see Gracia Marín Durán and Elisa Morgera, *Environmental Integration in the EU's External Relations: Beyond Multilateral Dimensions* (Oxford: Hart Publishing, 2012); and Rok Žvelc, "Environmental Integration in EU Trade Policy: The Generalised System of Preferences, Trade Sustainability Impact Assessments and Free Trade Agreements," in *The External Environmental Policy of the European Union: EU and International Law Perspectives*, ed. Elisa Morgera (Cambridge: Cambridge University Press, 2012), 174.

Parties to provide information on a voluntary basis to the ABS Clearinghouse,[7] which aims to gather as much relevant information as possible on ABS to make it available to all Parties.[8]

Article 24 is partially modeled on the Biosafety Protocol,[9] with a view to discouraging the development of conflicting national practices related to ABS and preventing non-Parties from developing a competitive trade advantage by remaining outside the international ABS regime.[10] As opposed to the Cartagena Protocol, however, the Nagoya Protocol does not specify the type of information that could be provided by non-Parties to the ABS Clearinghouse.[11]

Negotiators considered, and decided against, a proposal[12] fully modeled after the Cartagena Protocol,[13] to create an additional obligation for Parties to ensure that ABS activities and transactions related to genetic resources and derivatives with non-Parties be consistent with the Protocol and the Convention.[14] Such a proposal would not have required 'precise accordance' with the Protocol's detailed provisions.[15] The proposal was in line with practice in other multilateral environmental agreements to create a strong incentive for non-Parties to become Parties to a treaty.[16] Negotiators eventually drew inspiration only from the 'softest part' of the corresponding provisions in the Cartagena Protocol, in line with a general approach to avoid any frictions

---

7   See this commentary on Article 14, section 3.

8   Mackenzie et al., *Explanatory Guide to the Cartagena Protocol*, op. cit., 157.

9   Biosafety Protocol Article 24(2).

10 Mackenzie et al., *Explanatory Guide to the Cartagena Protocol*, op. cit., 157.

11 An earlier draft of this provision specified that such information would specifically concern activities and transactions regarding access and benefit-sharing related to genetic resources and derivatives within non-Parties' jurisdiction: Montreal II Draft, draft article 18 ter (2).

12 As had been requested, for instance by the African Group. See ENB, "Summary of the Ninth Meeting of the Working Group on Access and Benefit-sharing of the Convention on Biological Diversity: 22–28 March 2010," Vol. 9 no. 503, 31 March 2010, 9.

13 Biosafety Protocol Article 24(1), which requires that import/export of living modified organisms between Parties and non-Parties be consistent with at least the objective of the Protocol.

14 Montreal II Draft, draft article 18 ter.

15 Along the lines of the interpretation of the corresponding provision in the Biosafety Protocol: see Mackenzie et al., *Explanatory Guide to the Cartagena Protocol*, op. cit., 153.

16 Ibid., 154. The Montreal Protocol and the Basel Convention prohibit trade with non-Parties unless it is conducted according to specific conditions which ensure minimum standards equivalent to those established in the treaties, while CITES sets the conditions under which trade with non-Parties can be undertaken.

between the Nagoya Protocol and WTO law.[17] As a result, Article 24 has been considered a 'very weak provision' when compared to other multilateral environmental agreements.[18] This is particularly significant as the United States, who is not a Party to the CBD[19] and therefore quite unlikely to become a Party to the Protocol, represents 40 percent of the global biotech sector[20] and in addition has significant ex situ collections.[21] In all events, free-riding by non-Parties may be tackled by provider countries' domestic ABS frameworks providing more favorable access conditions to users from Parties to the Protocol or countries that have put in place comparable measures.[22]

Finally, it should be recalled that CBD Parties that will not become Parties to the Protocol remain bound by relevant CBD requirements on ABS.[23]

---

17   Pavoni, "Nagoya Protocol and WTO Law," op. cit., 190 and 196.

18   Ibid., 196.

19   As the Protocol can only be signed and ratified by CBD parties: see Nagoya Protocol Article 32, and this commentary on final clauses, section 2.

20   Oberthür and Rosendal, "Conclusions," op. cit., 234.

21   See FAO, *The Second Report on the State of the World Plant Genetic Resources for Food and Agriculture*, op. cit., chapter 3.

22   As discussed in this commentary on Article 6, section 5.2.

23   Notably CBD Article 15. Glowka, Burhenne-Guilmin and Synge, *Guide to the Convention on Biological Diversity*, op. cit., 124. For similar considerations in relation to the Biosafety Protocol, see Mackenzie et al., *Explanatory Guide to the Cartagena Protocol*, op. cit., 153.

Article 25. Financial Mechanism and Resources

1. In considering financial resources for the implementation of this Protocol, the Parties shall take into account the provisions of Article 20 of the Convention.
2. The financial mechanism of the Convention shall be the financial mechanism for this Protocol.
3. Regarding the capacity-building and development referred to in Article 22 of this Protocol, the Conference of the Parties serving as the meeting of the Parties to this Protocol, in providing guidance with respect to the financial mechanism referred to in paragraph 2 above, for consideration by the Conference of the Parties, shall take into account the need of developing country Parties, in particular the least developed countries and small island developing States among them, and of Parties with economies in transition, for financial resources, as well as the capacity needs and priorities of indigenous and local communities, including women within these communities.
4. In the context of paragraph 1 above, the Parties shall also take into account the needs of the developing country Parties, in particular the least developed countries and small island developing States among them, and of the Parties with economies in transition, in their efforts to identify and implement their capacity-building and development requirements for the purposes of the implementation of this Protocol.
5. The guidance to the financial mechanism of the Convention in relevant decisions of the Conference of the Parties, including those agreed before the adoption of this Protocol, shall apply, mutatis mutandis, to the provisions of this Article.
6. The developed country Parties may also provide, and the developing country Parties and the Parties with economies in transition avail themselves of, financial and other resources for the implementation of the provisions of this Protocol through bilateral, regional and multilateral channels.

1 Overview

As foreshadowed in the opening provision of the Protocol, appropriate funding is essential to achieve the objective of the Protocol – ensuring fair and equitable benefit-sharing, as well as contributing to biodiversity conservation and sustainable use.[1] Financial solidarity – as an international obligation of intensified cooperation without expectations of reciprocity[2] – is also a necessity in light of the fact that Parties with limited capabilities[3] will be unable to comply with the obligations under the Protocol, particularly as they will face several complexities in developing domestic ABS frameworks.[4] Limited implementation by developing countries will inevitably undermine the functioning of the international regime, which is based on the interoperability of domestic ABS frameworks, to the detriment of the entire community of Parties to the Protocol.[5] For these reasons, financial solidarity embodies one of the expressions of the principle of common but differentiated responsibility.[6] It thus serves as a 'test for the seriousness of efforts and willingness to cooperate' of developed countries[7] as an equitable contribution to a common task. In practice, however, the qualified and open-ended formulation of international obligations on financial solidarity (in the Nagoya Protocol, as well as in other multilateral environmental agreements) may lead Parties to avoid systematic scrutiny at the multilateral level of compliance with relevant obligations.[8]

---

1 See this commentary on Article 1.
2 Campanelli, "Solidarity," op. cit., paragraph 17, and discussion of the obligation of solidarity in this commentary on Article 22, section 2.
3 This was clearly acknowledged in CBD Article 20(1), which reads: 'Each Contracting Party undertakes to provide, in accordance with its capabilities, financial support and incentives in respect of those national activities which are intended to achieve the objectives of this Convention, in accordance with its national plans, priorities and programmes.'
4 As acknowledged in Nagoya Protocol Article 22(4)(c).
5 Greiber et al., *Explanatory Guide*, op. cit., 221.
6 Rio Declaration, Principles 6–7. See generally Lavanya Rajamani, *Differential Treatment in International Environmental Law* (Oxford: Oxford University Press, 2006). For a discussion on the status of this principle in international law compare Ellen Hey, "Common but Differentiated Responsibilities," in Wolfrum, *Max Planck Encyclopaedia*, op. cit., 444, who considers it a general principle of international law; and Christopher D. Stone, "Common but Differentiated Responsibilities in International Law," *The American Journal of International Law* 98 (2004): 276, 300, who concludes that it is not 'a customary principle of international law'.
7 Charlotte Streck, "Ensuring New Finance and Real Emission Reduction: A Critical Review of the Additionality Concept," *Carbon and Climate Law Review* 2011 (2011): 158, 159–160 and 168, in the context of the international climate change regime.
8 Francesca Romanin Jacur, "Controlling and Assisting Compliance: Financial Aspects," in *Non-Compliance Procedures and Mechanisms and the Effectiveness of International Environmental Agreements*, ed. Tullio Treves et al. (The Hague: Asser Press, 2009), 435. See this commentary on Article 30.

Against this background, Article 25, which is modeled after the Biosafety Protocol,[9] addresses two issues: the provision of financial assistance through a multilateral financial mechanism established under the CBD – that is, the GEF,[10] and the provision of financial assistance by developed countries through other bilateral, regional and multilateral channels.[11] In both instances, developed countries are the donors, and developing countries and countries with economy in transition are the recipients of financial support.[12] The following sections will discuss the role of the financial mechanism under the Protocol, and the role of other forms of financial solidarity, in turn.

2 Financial Mechanism

The international governance of the financial mechanism under the Nagoya Protocol includes a key role not only for the Protocol's governing body,[13] but also for the CBD COP. The Protocol's governing body will provide guidance with respect to the financial mechanism as it relates to the Protocol, but such guidance will have to be considered by the CBD COP. In addition, future guidance to be developed under the Protocol will have to take into account CBD COP guidance to the GEF adopted before the Protocol's entry into force.[14] As a

---

9   Biosafety Protocol, Article 28.

10   Nagoya Protocol Article 25(2). See CBD Article 39; Nairobi Diplomatic Conference Resolution 1, "Interim financial arrangements" in "Nairobi Final Act of the conference for the adoption of the agreed text of the Convention on Biological Diversity" (1992), accessed 30 November 2013, <www.cbd.int/doc/handbook/cbd-hb-09-en.pdf>; CBD Decision 1/2, "Financial resources and mechanism" (28 February 1995) UN Doc UNEP/CBD/COP/1/17, paragraph 2. For a discussion of the corresponding provision in the Biosafety Protocol, see Mackenzie et al., *Explanatory Guide to the Cartagena Protocol*, op. cit., 175. See Birnie, Boyle and Redgwell, *International Law and the Environment*, op. cit., 82–83; and Charlotte Streck, "Financial Instruments and Cooperation in Implementing International Agreements for the Global Environment," in *Multilevel Governance of Global Environmental Change: Perspectives from Science, Sociology and the Law*, ed. Gerd Winter (Cambridge: Cambridge University Press, 2011), 493.

11   Mackenzie et al., *Explanatory Guide to the Cartagena Protocol*, op. cit., 173.

12   CBD Article 20(2). Only the category of 'developed countries' has been defined for the purposes of financial resources and mechanism in the context of the CBD – and, by implication, its protocols – through a list adopted by the CBD COP: CBD Decision 1/2, Annex II. See also Greiber et al., *Explanatory Guide*, op. cit., 222; and Mackenzie et al., *Explanatory Guide to the Cartagena Protocol*, op. cit., 174.

13   See this commentary on Article 26.

14   CBD Article 25(5).

result, the policy of the CBD COP with respect to the GEF in relation to the CBD and in relation to the new requirements of the Protocol will be inextricably linked.[15] It should be recalled, in that regard, that the GEF Council is obliged to 'act in conformity' with the policies, priorities and eligibility criteria decided by the CBD COP when acting as its financial mechanism.[16] Consequently, the CBD COP is empowered to review the effectiveness of the GEF serving as the Convention's financial mechanism,[17] thereby having an opportunity to hold the GEF accountable in its observance of the guidance provided by CBD Parties.

Article 25 also makes a link to capacity-building needs by cross-reference to the relevant provision of the Protocol.[18] This can be interpreted so that in providing guidance to the GEF, the CBD COP, on the recommendation of the Protocol's governing body, will take account of the capacity-building needs identified in national capacity self-assessments by developing countries; and that in carrying out its role, the GEF will aim to meet the capacity-building needs so identified.[19] This linkage with capacity-building is also noteworthy in recalling that under the Protocol capacity needs include not only those of Parties, but also those of indigenous and local communities, including women within these communities,[20] as identified in national capacity self-assessments.[21]

Intergovernmental discussions preparing for the entry into force of the Protocol have already identified areas where guidance to the GEF is needed. CBD Parties in particular recommended that financial assistance from the GEF be targeted to building Parties' capacity to develop, implement and enforce domestic ABS measures;[22] supporting the negotiations of equitable and fair

---

15   As in the analogous provision of the Biosafety Protocol: Mackenzie et al., *Explanatory Guide to the Cartagena Protocol*, op. cit., 175–176.

16   Instrument for the Establishment of the Restructured Global Environment Facility as amended by Fourth Assembly of the GEF (24–28 May, 2010, effective 24 February 2011) 33 ILM 1283, paragraphs 15 and 26. Nonetheless, the relationship between the CBD COP and the GEF may be more complex than may be suggested by this provision: see also CBD Decision 3/8, "Memorandum of understanding between the Conference of the Parties to the Convention on Biological Diversity and the Council of the Global Environment Facility" (11 February 1997) UN Doc UNEP/CBD/COP/3/38, Annex, paragraph 2.

17   CBD Article 21(3).

18   Nagoya Protocol Article 25(3–4). See this commentary on Article 22, sections 2–3.

19   Mackenzie et al., *Explanatory Guide to the Cartagena Protocol*, op. cit., 175–176.

20   See Nagoya Protocol 11th preambular recital.

21   Nagoya Protocol Article 22(3). See Greiber et al., *Explanatory Guide*, op. cit., 225. See also this commentary on Article 22, section 4.

22   Including through: identification of actors and legal and institutional expertise for the Protocol's implementation; taking stock of domestic measures relevant to ABS in light of

MAT,[23] including through enhanced understanding of business models and IPRS; and developing endogenous research capabilities in provider countries to add value to their own genetic resources and associated traditional knowledge. This is to occur through, *inter alia*, technology transfer, bioprospecting and associated research and taxonomic studies, and the development and use of valuation methods.[24] Furthermore, the GEF is mandated to finance projects that will assist in addressing the capacity needs and priorities of indigenous and local communities and relevant ABS stakeholders, such as through the development of community protocols, model contractual clauses and minimum requirements for MAT to secure fair and equitable sharing of benefits.[25]

Even before the entry into force of the Protocol, CBD Parties have had an opportunity to hold the GEF accountable in supporting preliminary ABS activities aimed at speeding up ratification of the Protocol. This occurred in relation to the Nagoya Protocol Implementation Fund[26] – a multi-donor trust fund that started operations in May 2011, managed by the GEF and operated by the CBD Secretariat. The Nagoya Protocol Implementation Fund supports not only signatory countries and those in the process of signing the Nagoya Protocol to accelerate their ratification and implementation of the Protocol, but also the private sector in developing and implementing concrete ABS agreements, with a view to exploring the economic potential of ABS transactions and facilitating technology transfer.[27] The latter was thus meant to achieve the aim of generating additional information to help understand future Parties' capacities and

---

the obligations of the Nagoya Protocol; establishing ways to address transboundary issues; and establishing institutional arrangements and administrative systems to provide access to genetic resources, ensure benefit-sharing, support compliance with PIC and MAT, and monitor the utilization of genetic resources and associated traditional knowledge, including support for the establishment of checkpoints. See ICNP Recommendation 2/1, "Elaboration of guidance for the financial mechanism," Annex I, paragraph 1 in ICNP, "Report of the second meeting," UNEP/CBD/COP/11/6, Annex. See this commentary on Articles 11 and 13–18. Note, however, that Article 17 does not foresee monitoring of the utilization of traditional knowledge: on this point, see this commentary on Article 16, section 3.

23 See generally this commentary on Article 5 section 5; and also on Article 6, section 7 and on Article 18.

24 ICNP Recommendation 2/1, Annex II, paragraph 1(c).

25 See this commentary on Articles 12 and 19.

26 "GEF Establishes the Nagoya Protocol Implementation Fund," CBD (3 June 2011), accessed 30 November 2013, <www.cbd.int/doc/press/2011/pr-2011-06-03-GEF-ImpFund-en.pdf>.

27 Compare: "Nagoya Protocol Implementation Fund," World Bank, accessed 30 November 2013, <http://fiftrustee.worldbank.org/index.php?type=fund&ft=npif>.

needs in relation to effective ABS transactions.[28] During intergovernmental discussions preparing for the entry into force of the Protocol, however, CBD Parties raised concerns about the use of the Fund to support the private sector's engagement in ABS transactions, despite Parties' prioritization of support to governments in ratifying and implementing the Protocol through the development of national legislation and consultations with national stakeholders to that end. Financial support for private sector's engagement in ABS transactions before the entry into force of the Protocol thus raised issues related to diverging priorities set under the GEF, on the one hand, and under the CBD and its Protocol, on the other.[29] This discussion also showed the potential for vested interests in favoring ABS transactions while provider countries have not yet developed the necessary national ABS frameworks and guarantees for indigenous and local communities. The Intergovernmental Committee preparing for the entry into force of the Nagoya Protocol therefore emphasized the need for the GEF to provide funding as a priority to law-making and related preparatory activities at the national level.[30]

3   Other Bilateral, Regional and Multilateral Channels for Financial
         Resources

In voluntarily providing financial resources through other channels, developed countries are to take into account the needs of developing countries, as

---

28   See "Nagoya Protocol Implementation Fund Brochure," GEF, accessed 30 November 2013, <www.thegef.org/gef/content/nagoya-protocol-implementation-fund-brochure>. See also Greiber et al., *Explanatory Guide*, op. cit., 224.

29   Instrument for the Establishment of the GEF, paragraph 25(c)(i) reads: 'decisions requiring a formal vote by the Council shall be taken by a double weighted majority; that is, an affirmative vote representing both a 60 percent majority of the total number of Participants and a 60 percent majority of the total contributions.' However, it has been argued that the GEF's voting structure 'does not preclude the possibility of conflict between the objectives of the Conventions, the implementing agencies, and the GEF in the context of particular decisions.' See Jacob Werksman, "Consolidating Governance of the Global Commons: Insights from the Global Environment Facility," *Yearbook of International Environmental Law* 6 (1996): 27, 60, and discussion in Birnie, Boyle and Redgwell, *International Law and the Environment*, op. cit., 83.

30   ICNP Recommendation 2/1, Annex II, paragraph 3, integrated in COP Decision XI/5 (Financial mechanism). ENB 9/579, "Summary of the Second Meeting of the Intergovernmental Committee for the Nagoya Protocol," 15.

identified in their capacity need self-assessments,[31] and may choose between bilateral, regional and multilateral channels.[32] It remains to be clarified, however, to what extent the relevant provisions of the CBD[33] are to be 'taken into account' under these circumstances. It may be understood that the CBD provisions on financial solidarity do not directly apply to the provision of financial resources under the Protocol, so arguably potential donor countries are not obliged to *provide* financial resources, but merely to *consider the need for* financial resources.[34] It has also been suggested that not all provisions of CBD Article 20 are equally relevant for ABS, but they should be considered to the extent that they have a bearing on this issue.[35]

If bilateral financial assistance is provided in the context of bilateral agreements, these are to be negotiated and implemented in ways that ensure the achievement of the objective of the Protocol.[36] Even outside of these treaty-based arrangements, however, unilateral and bilateral financial support for the development of domestic ABS frameworks in developing countries needs to be demand-driven and responsive to the particular needs and circumstances of the receiving country, to avoid allegations of undue interference with national sovereignty. Clearly financial support for these activities will occur not only in the interest of the international community in the effective implementation of the Protocol, but also in developed countries' own interest (to ensure predictability and fairness for their users). The delicate, and in many respects still open-ended, balance of international obligations enshrined in the Nagoya Protocol may thus create a risk that unilateral and bilateral financial solidarity initiatives supporting the implementation of the Protocol may undermine the partnership between user and provider countries to be established under the Protocol. Such a risk may arise if undue influence is exercised or pressure is put on provider countries' exercise of their national sovereignty over their genetic resources and on indigenous and local communities in that context.[37]

---

31   Nagoya Protocol Articles 25(4) and 22.

32   Nagoya Protocol Article 25(4).

33   Nagoya Protocol Article 25(1).

34   For an analogous interpretation of the corresponding provision under the Biosafety Protocol, see Mackenzie et al., *Explanatory Guide to the Cartagena Protocol*, op. cit., 175.

35   Greiber et al., *Explanatory Guide*, op. cit., 223, who do not, however, elaborate on which CBD provisions could be considered less or not relevant in the context of the Protocol.

36   See this commentary on Article 4, section 3.

37   The issue was preliminary discussed in Morgera, "Bilateralism at the Service of Community Interests?", op. cit., 760–763.

Intergovernmental discussions preparing for the entry into force of the Protocol have already identified the need to take a strategic approach to maximize opportunities for financial support as a complement to the GEF. A recommendation is thus made to integrate the provision of financial needs under the Protocol into the CBD Strategy for Resource Mobilization.[38] In addition, Parties are encouraged (i.e., they are to remove barriers at least, and/or to create incentives)[39] to direct domestic resources, including those generated through the successful implementation of ABS agreements, towards the implementation of the Protocol.[40] Governments, organizations, the private sector and financial institutions are encouraged to provide financial resources, including through new and innovative financial mechanisms, for the implementation of the Protocol.[41]

---

38   CBD Decision 9/11 "Review of implementation of Articles 20 and 21." The Strategy was adopted in 2008 to achieve multiple aims, including to improve the information base on funding needs, gaps, and priorities; strengthen national capacities for resource utilization; strengthen existing financial institutions; explore new and innovative financial mechanisms; to build capacity for resource mobilisation and promote South-South cooperation as a complement to North-South cooperation; and enhance the global engagement for resource mobilisation.

39   On the obligation to encourage, see this commentary on Article 9, section 1.

40   ICNP Recommendation 2/2, "Guidance for resource mobilisation for the implementation of the Nagoya Protocol on Access and Benefit-sharing" in ICNP, "Report of the second meeting," UNEP/CBD/COP/11/6, Annex, paragraph 3. COP Decision 11/5, "The financial mechanism" (5 December 2012) UN Doc UNEP/CBD/COP/11/35, paragraphs 21–23.

41   Ibid.

Article 26. Conference of the Parties Serving as the Meeting of the Parties to this Protocol

1. The Conference of the Parties shall serve as the meeting of the Parties to this Protocol.
2. Parties to the Convention that are not Parties to this Protocol may participate as observers in the proceedings of any meeting of the Conference of the Parties serving as the meeting of the Parties to this Protocol. When the Conference of the Parties serves as the meeting of the Parties to this Protocol, decisions under this Protocol shall be taken only by those that are Parties to it.
3. When the Conference of the Parties serves as the meeting of the Parties to this Protocol, any member of the Bureau of the Conference of the Parties representing a Party to the Convention but, at that time, not a Party to this Protocol, shall be substituted by a member to be elected by and from among the Parties to this Protocol.
4. The Conference of the Parties serving as the meeting of the Parties to this Protocol shall keep under regular review the implementation of this Protocol and shall make, within its mandate, the decisions necessary to promote its effective implementation. It shall perform the functions assigned to it by this Protocol and shall:
    (a) Make recommendations on any matters necessary for the implementation of this Protocol;
    (b) Establish such subsidiary bodies as are deemed necessary for the implementation of this Protocol;
    (c) Seek and utilize, where appropriate, the services and cooperation of, and information provided by, competent international organizations and intergovernmental and non-governmental bodies;
    (d) Establish the form and the intervals for transmitting the information to be submitted in accordance with Article 29 of this Protocol and consider such information as well as reports submitted by any subsidiary body;
    (e) Consider and adopt, as required, amendments to this Protocol and its Annex, as well as any additional annexes to this Protocol, that are deemed necessary for the implementation of this Protocol; and

© KONINKLIJKE BRILL NV, LEIDEN, 2014 | DOI 10.1163/9789004217188_028

(f)   Exercise such other functions as may be required for the implementation of this Protocol.

5.   The rules of procedure of the Conference of the Parties and financial
rules of the Convention shall be applied, mutatis mutandis, under this
Protocol, except as may be otherwise decided by consensus by the
Conference of the Parties serving as the meeting of the Parties to this
Protocol.

6.   The first meeting of the Conference of the Parties serving as the meeting of the Parties to this Protocol shall be convened by the Secretariat
and held concurrently with the first meeting of the Conference of
the Parties that is scheduled after the date of the entry into force of
this Protocol. Subsequent ordinary meetings of the Conference of the
Parties serving as the meeting of the Parties to this Protocol shall be
held concurrently with ordinary meetings of the Conference of the
Parties, unless otherwise decided by the Conference of the Parties
serving as the meeting of the Parties to this Protocol.

7.   Extraordinary meetings of the Conference of the Parties serving as the
meeting of the Parties to this Protocol shall be held at such other times
as may be deemed necessary by the Conference of the Parties serving
as the meeting of the Parties to this Protocol, or at the written request
of any Party, provided that, within six months of the request being
communicated to the Parties by the Secretariat, it is supported by at
least one third of the Parties.

8.   The United Nations, its specialized agencies and the International
Atomic Energy Agency, as well as any State member thereof or observers thereto not party to the Convention, may be represented as observers at meetings of the Conference of the Parties serving as the meeting
of the Parties to this Protocol. Any body or agency, whether national or
international, governmental or non-governmental, that is qualified in
matters covered by this Protocol and that has informed the Secretariat
of its wish to be represented at a meeting of the Conference of the
Parties serving as a meeting of the Parties to this Protocol as an
observer, may be so admitted, unless at least one third of the Parties
present object. Except as otherwise provided in this Article, the admis-
sion and participation of observers shall be subject to the rules of procedure, as referred to in paragraph 5 above.

1   Overview

Article 26 establishes the Protocol's governing body, in accordance with a well-established practice under multilateral environmental agreements.[1] The governing body (the Conference of the Parties to the CBD serving as the Meeting of the Parties to the Protocol, or COP/MOP) is empowered to steer and supervise the entire process of implementation and further development of the Protocol. Both areas of work will be particularly critical as several provisions of the Protocol are open-ended or require further elaboration by Parties. This provision is also noteworthy for establishing institutional and procedural linkages between the Protocol and the CBD.

The following sections will discuss the basic rules for the functioning of the COP/MOP, and its relationship with the CBD COP.

2   The Functioning of the COP/MOP

The Protocol's governing body comprises representatives of all States that are Party to the Protocol. It meets on a periodic basis. Article 26 thus details, in a self-explanatory manner, who is entitled to participate in the COP/MOP meetings, its bureau, the COP/MOP functions, the rules of procedure, and meetings arrangements.[2]

With regards to the COP/MOP functions, Article 26(4) mirrors, as in the case of the Cartagena Protocol,[3] the CBD provisions on the COP[4] setting out the general function of the COP/MOP. These functions notably include keeping under regular review the implementation of the Protocol and making the necessary decisions to promote its implementation. Furthermore, Article 26(4) lists specific functions of the COP/MOP. The broad framing of the provision and its last open-ended clause ('exercise such other functions as may be required for the implementation of this Protocol') allow for any function needed for the

---

1   See for example Birnie, Boyle and Redgwell, *International Law and the Environment*, op. cit., 86; and Robin R. Churchill and Geir Ulfstein, "Autonomous Institutional Arrangements in Multilateral Environmental Agreements: A Little-Noticed Phenomenon in International Law," *The American Journal of International Law* 94 (2000): 623.

2   Mackenzie et al., *Explanatory Guide to the Cartagena Protocol*, op. cit., 179–184.

3   Ibid., 182.

4   CBD Article 23(4). See Glowka, Burhenne-Guilmin and Synge, *Guide to the Convention on Biological Diversity*, op. cit., 111–113.

implementation of the Protocol to be carried out by the COP/MOP, even if not specifically listed.

This will be particularly useful as several issues under the Nagoya Protocol have not yet been fully resolved (for example, the determination of the need for and modalities of a global multilateral benefit-sharing mechanism,[5] and the establishment of the compliance procedures and mechanisms).[6] In addition, several other tasks are expressly mandated to the COP/MOP elsewhere in the Protocol (the assessment and review of the Protocol's effectiveness,[7] the stocktaking of model contractual clauses and voluntary instruments,[8] etc.). In these and all other cases[9] in which the COP/MOP will elaborate consensus guidance on the interpretation and application of the Protocol, it will have to be guided by the Protocol objective – achieving equity and fairness in benefit-sharing among States and towards indigenous and local communities, with a view to contributing to conservation and sustainable use.[10]

According to Article 26, the CBD Rules of Procedure[11] and Financial Rules[12] are applicable to the Protocol COP/MOP, with modifications if necessary to adapt them to the specificities of the Protocol, unless the COP/MOP by consensus decides otherwise or if the Protocol itself establishes otherwise.[13]

As in the context of the CBD,[14] non-Parties to the Protocol that are Parties to the CBD will be allowed to participate in the COP/MOP meetings as observers with the possibility to make interventions and submit proposals, but without

---

5   See this commentary on Article 10.

6   See this commentary on Article 30.

7   See this commentary on Article 31.

8   See this commentary on Articles 19–20.

9   Several have been identified in this commentary, such as on Articles 2–6, 8–9, 11, 14 and 16–18.

10   See this commentary on Article 1.

11   CBD Decision 1/6, "Financing of and budget for the Convention" (28 February 1995) UN Doc UNEP/CBD/COP/1/17, as amended by CBD Decision 3/1, "Pending issues arising from the work of the second Meeting of the Conference of the Parties" (11 February 1997) UN Doc UNEP/CBD/COP/3/38, Appendix – adopted under CBD Article 23. See also Glowka, Burhenne-Guilmin and Synge, *Guide to the Convention on Biological Diversity*, op. cit., 101.

12   "Rules of procedure for meetings of the Conference of the Parties to the Convention on Biological Diversity" in CBD Decision 1/1, "Rules of procedure for the Conference of the Parties" (28 February 1995) UN Doc UNEP/CBD/COP/1/17, Annex, as amended by CBD Decision 5/20, "Operations of the Convention" (22 June 2000) UN Doc UNEP/CBD/COP/5/23 (hereinafter, CBD Rules of Procedure).

13   Mackenzie et al., *Explanatory Guide to the Cartagena Protocol*, op. cit., 183.

14   CBD Article 32(2). See Glowka, Burhenne-Guilmin and Synge, *Guide to the Convention on Biological Diversity*, op. cit., 124.

the right to vote.[15] As the CBD COP serves as the Meeting of the Parties to the Protocol, the bureau of the COP will serve as the bureau of the COP/MOP. The bureau performs functions supporting the meetings of the COP/MOP, such as providing guidance to the Secretariat for the preparation and conduct of meetings; organizing the conduct of meetings; and chairing informal negotiations during meetings.[16]

Any governmental or non-governmental body – a term broadly interpreted under the CBD to include environment, consumer or development organizations, indigenous peoples' groups, academic or research institutions, industry associations or individual companies[17] – may apply to the Secretariat for observer status. This is granted if the body in question is qualified in matters covered by the Protocol, and unless one-third of the Parties present at a particular meeting objects – that is, Parties attending that meeting and only with respect to the presence of a non-governmental body or agency at that meeting. So the acceptance or rejection of a body or agency is only valid for that particular meeting.[18]

3   Relationship with the CBD COP

Article 26, similarly to the Biosafety Protocol,[19] clarifies the relationship between the Protocol's governing body and the CBD COP. Since the Protocol is a separate legal instrument, the functions of the COP/MOP differ to some extent from those of the CBD COP, and the membership of the two bodies is not necessarily the same. Not all Parties to the CBD (who are represented in the CBD COP) may decide to become Parties to the Protocol.[20]

---

15   Note that Rule 40 on voting in the CBD Rules of Procedure remains bracketed, so no voting takes place at CBD meetings. For a similar discussion in relation to the Biosafety Protocol, see Mackenzie et al., *Explanatory Guide to the Cartagena Protocol*, op. cit., 181.

16   Greiber et al., *Explanatory Guide*, op. cit., 230. For a similar discussion in relation to the Biosafety Protocol, see Mackenzie et al., *Explanatory Guide to the Cartagena Protocol*, op. cit., 181.

17   Ibid.

18   The steps to apply for and attain observer status at meetings under the Convention are detailed in CBD Decision 9/29, "Operations of the Convention," (9 October 2008) UN Doc UNEP/CBD/COP/9/29, paragraph 17. For a similar discussion in relation to the Biosafety Protocol, see Mackenzie et al., *Explanatory Guide to the Cartagena Protocol*, op. cit., 184.

19   Biosafety Protocol Article 29.

20   For a similar discussion in relation to the Biosafety Protocol, see Mackenzie et al., *Explanatory Guide to the Cartagena Protocol*, op. cit., 180.

There is, however a significant difference concerning the link between the
CBD COP and the Protocol COP/MOP, when comparing the Cartagena and
the Nagoya Protocols.[21] The negotiators' main concern was to ensure that the
institutional structure of the Nagoya Protocol remains well linked to that of
the CBD, as opposed to the case of the Biosafety Protocol, which has turned
into quite a separate process from the CBD.[22] The rationale lays in the recognition that benefit-sharing is both the objective of the Protocol as well as the
third objective of the CBD.[23] In addition, several areas of work under the CBD
would continue to be directly relevant for the effective implementation of the
Nagoya Protocol.[24] The negotiators therefore discussed the possibility to follow
the example of the Kyoto Protocol under the UN Framework Convention on
Climate Change,[25] and provide for the Protocol governing body's meetings to
be held concurrently, rather than *in conjunction*, with the CBD COP.[26] In other
words, instead of being held back-to-back, as is the case for the CBD COP and
the Biosafety COP/MOP, the meetings of the Nagoya Protocol's governing body
will be held simultaneously with those of the CBD COP.[27] It can be expected
that the agendas of the two meetings will be developed so to maximize synergies and avoid repetitive discussion on closely related agenda items.

Nevertheless, the COP/MOP is a distinct and independent body from
the CBD COP for all practical purposes, including guidance to the financial
mechanism[28] and in relation to the costs of Secretariat services to the extent
that they cannot be split up between the CBD and the Nagoya Protocol.[29]

---

21 Compare Biosafety Protocol Article 29(6). See also. Greiber et al., *Explanatory Guide*, op. cit., 232–233.
22 Morgera and Tsioumani, "Yesterday, Today, and Tomorrow," op. cit., 36.
23 See Introduction to this commentary, section 1.3.
24 For instance the work programmes on Article 8(j), protected areas, and communication, education and public awareness.
25 Kyoto Protocol to the United Nations Framework Convention on Climate Change (Kyoto, 11 December 1997, in force 16 February 2005) 2303 UNTS 148 (hereinafter, Kyoto Protocol).
26 ENB, "Tenth Meeting of the Conference of the Parties to the Convention on Biological Diversity: 18–20 October 2010," Vol. 9 No. 534, 18 October 2010, 4.
27 Greiber et al., *Explanatory Guide*, op. cit., 232.
28 See this commentary on Article 25, section 2.
29 See this commentary on Article 28.

Article 27. Subsidiary Bodies

1. Any subsidiary body established by or under the Convention may serve this Protocol, including upon a decision of the Conference of the Parties serving as the meeting of the Parties to this Protocol. Any such decision shall specify the tasks to be undertaken.
2. Parties to the Convention that are not Parties to this Protocol may participate as observers in the proceedings of any meeting of any such subsidiary bodies. When a subsidiary body of the Convention serves as a subsidiary body to this Protocol, decisions under this Protocol shall be taken only by Parties to this Protocol.
3. When a subsidiary body of the Convention exercises its functions with regard to matters concerning this Protocol, any member of the bureau of that subsidiary body representing a Party to the Convention but, at that time, not a Party to this Protocol, shall be substituted by a member to be elected by and from among the Parties to this Protocol.

Article 27 establishes the institutional and procedural linkages between the Protocol and the CBD. It addresses: the performance of functions by subsidiary bodies of the CBD in relation to the Protocol; which States are entitled to participate in the proceedings of subsidiary bodies performing functions in relation to the Protocol; and who is entitled to act as an officer (or 'bureau member') of such a subsidiary body.[1]

This provision is modeled after the Biosafety Protocol,[2] with the only difference concerning the link between the CBD COP and the Protocol COP/MOP. Notably, the Nagoya Protocol foresees the possibility that CBD subsidiary bodies will support the work of the Nagoya Protocol COP/MOP without the need for a decision to this end to be taken by the COP/MOP.[3] Thus, CBD subsidiary bodies, such as the Working Group on Review of Implementation, the Working

---

1 Greiber et al., *Explanatory Guide*, op. cit., 236–237. For a similar discussion in relation to the Biosafety Protocol, see Mackenzie et al., *Explanatory Guide to the Cartagena Protocol*, op. cit., 185–186.
2 Biosafety Protocol Article 30.
3 Note the word 'including' in Nagoya Protocol Article 27(1). The Biosafety Protocol, instead, requires such decision by its own COP/MOP.

© KONINKLIJKE BRILL NV, LEIDEN, 2014 | DOI 10.1163/9789004217188_029

Group on Article 8(j) on traditional knowledge[4] or the CBD Subsidiary Body on Scientific, Technical and Technological Advice (SBSTTA), could – upon a request by the CBD COP – address issues related to the implementation of the Protocol. In practice, however, it seems rather likely that specific instructions will be provided by the COP/MOP to that end. In this connection, it can be argued that if tasks related to the Nagoya Protocol would significantly add to the workload or costs of certain CBD subsidiary bodies, the CBD COP could exercise its right to 'consider and take any additional action that may be required for the achievement of the purposes of this Convention' to intervene in this event.[5]

Following the approach taken with regard to the COP/MOP, representatives of non-Parties to the Protocol could only participate as observers when a subsidiary body of the CBD exercises functions in relation to the Protocol. Note also that the CBD Rules of Procedure apply, as appropriate, to its subsidiary bodies, and that when a CBD subsidiary body carries out functions under the Protocol, any member of the bureau who does not represent a Party to the Protocol must be replaced by a representative of a Party to the Protocol.[6]

---

4   In the context of which, in effect, consideration of guidelines on prior informed consent to, prevention of misappropriation of, and benefit-sharing from traditional knowledge are being considered with a view to contributing to the work of the Nagoya Protocol. See CBD Article 8(j) Working Group, "Report of the eighth meeting," UNEP/CBD/COP/12/5, Annex, 'Recommendation 8/4 on Tasks 7, 10 and 12 could best contribute to work under the Convention and to the Nagoya Protocol.

5   CBD Article 23(4)(i), on the basis of similar considerations made in relation to the Biosafety Protocol. See Mackenzie et al., *Explanatory Guide to the Cartagena Protocol*, op. cit., 185. See also Glowka, Burhenne-Guilmin and Synge, *Guide to the Convention on Biological Diversity*, op. cit., 112.

6   Greiber et al., *Explanatory Guide*, op. cit., 237. For a similar discussion in relation to the Biosafety Protocol, see Mackenzie et al., *Explanatory Guide to the Cartagena Protocol*, op. cit., 186.

Article 28. Secretariat

1. The Secretariat established by Article 24 of the Convention shall serve as the secretariat to this Protocol.
2. Article 24, paragraph 1, of the Convention on the functions of the Secretariat shall apply, *mutatis mutandis*, to this Protocol.
3. To the extent that they are distinct, the costs of the secretariat services for this Protocol shall be met by the Parties hereto. The Conference of the Parties serving as the meeting of the Parties to this Protocol shall, at its first meeting, decide on the necessary budgetary arrangements to this end.

Article 28, which mirrors the corresponding provision of the Biosafety Protocol,[1] makes provision for the Secretariat of the Protocol, which is responsible to administer the treaty and to act as day-to-day contact point for its Parties, international organizations and others. The Secretariat also prepares documentation for meetings of the governing and subsidiary bodies of the Protocol, and is in charge of organizing and servicing their meetings. It further plays an important role in the functioning of the ABS Clearinghouse.[2] The Secretariat's tasks will also likely include the preparation of reports on the execution of its functions under the Protocol for consideration by the COP/MOP, and coordination with other relevant international bodies.[3] Upon the Protocol's entry into force, the COP/MOP will likely assign additional specific functions and tasks to the Secretariat.[4]

The CBD Secretariat will also perform the functions of the Secretarirat for the Protocol, as is customary in multilateral environmental agreements for cost-efficiency reasons. Thus, Article 28 also addresses the separation of costs incurred by the Secretariat for its services for the Protocol rather than for the

---

1   Biosafety Protocol Article 31.
2   See this commentary on Article 14, section 3.
3   CBD Article 24. See Glowka, Burhenne-Guilmin and Synge, *Guide to the Convention on Biological Diversity*, op. cit., 114. See also this commentary on Article 4.
4   Greiber et al., *Explanatory Guide*, op. cit., 239–240. For a similar discussion in relation to the Biosafety Protocol, see Mackenzie et al., *Explanatory Guide to the Cartagena Protocol*, op. cit., 187–188.

CBD. As in the context of the Cartagena Protocol, this may have impacts on the ratification of the Protocol by developing countries: if developing countries are the first to ratify the Protocol,[5] they will have to bear the costs incurred by the Secretariat in servicing the Protocol, which can constitute a significant financial burden for these countries.[6]

---

5   And indeed at the time of writing, only one developed country Party (Norway) has ratified the Protocol: see this commentary on Article 1, fn. 63.

6   For a similar discussion in relation to the Biosafety Protocol, see Mackenzie et al., *Explanatory Guide to the Cartagena Protocol*, op. cit., 188. Note however that, notwithstanding ratification, all CBD Parties have obligations under the third objective of the Convention as operationalized in CBD Articles 1, 8(j), 15 and other related provisions.

Article 29. Monitoring and Reporting

Each Party shall monitor the implementation of its obligations under this Protocol, and shall, at intervals and in the format to be determined by the Conference of the Parties serving as the meeting of the Parties to this Protocol, report to the Conference of the Parties serving as the meeting of the Parties to this Protocol on measures that it has taken to implement this Protocol.

1 Overview

Article 29[1] is a common provision in multilateral environmental agreements calling for Parties' regular monitoring of implementation and reporting to the Protocol's governing body. These obligations are critical for ensuring compliance with the Protocol, assessing its actual operation on the ground, and may also facilitate cooperation and exchange of information among Parties and ABS stakeholders. The following section will discuss the functions of these obligations more in detail, and also explore links with other relevant provisions of the Protocol.

2 Functions and Links

Article 29 is modeled after similar provisions in the CBD[2] and the Biosafety Protocol.[3] It imposes two mutually reinforcing obligations on Parties: to monitor implementation of the Protocol, and to report on its implementation measures. Monitoring will provide information needed for the reporting. In turn, the requirement to provide reports may elicit feedback on the way monitoring has operated, and may be improved in the future.[4] Monitoring is particularly significant as many of the obligations in the Protocol are not self-executing,

---

1 This provision was not subject to negotiation and was first incorporated in the Cali Draft.
2 CBD Article 26.
3 Biosafety Protocol Article 33.
4 Based on the commentary of the corresponding obligation under the Biosafety Protocol. See Mackenzie et al., *Explanatory Guide to the Cartagena Protocol*, op. cit., 191. See also Greiber et al., *Explanatory Guide*, op. cit., 241–242.

© KONINKLIJKE BRILL NV, LEIDEN, 2014 | DOI 10.1163/9789004217188_031

but rather explicitly require the adoption of domestic measures to enable implementation. This will imply that Parties have to ensure access to, or set up, reliable mechanisms of information gathering and data management at the national level.[5]

In practice, reports will be submitted through the Secretariat. The Protocol's governing body will determine the intervals at which reports are to be submitted (usually in time for every, or every second, meeting of the governing body) and provide guidance to Parties on the format and content of the reports to ensure that information is provided in a comparable format.[6] This practice is in fact common to other multilateral environmental agreements, as their compliance procedures are essentially 'informational.'[7] On the one hand, it is expected that the reporting obligation exercises a positive influence on Parties having to assess the extent and impact of their implementation efforts and to justify them before the Secretariat, other Parties, international organizations and stakeholders to whom the report will be available.[8] On the other hand, these reports provide opportunities for the Secretariat to evaluate progress in the implementation of the Protocol, and to other States or stakeholders to scrutinize the practices of and exercise pressure on individual States.[9] National reports collectively may also feed into the review process foreseen under Protocol.[10] Depending on the compliance procedures and mechanisms that will be agreed under the Protocol,[11] national reports may further be taken into account by a future compliance committee.

Usually national reports indicate what kind of measures have been adopted by Parties towards implementing their obligations, in order to enable Parties individually and collectively to assess how effectively the treaty is operating. These reports may also allow NGOs and other interested stakeholders to monitor progress at the country level. Reports can further serve to strengthen communication and coordination among relevant national authorities responsible for the implementation of the Protocol, and foster scientific understanding and self-examination.[12] In an ideal scenario, national reporting can, in addi-

---

5   Ibid.

6   Ibid.

7   Daniel Bodansky, *The Art and Craft of International Environmental Law* (Cambridge: Harvard University Press, 2011), 238–243.

8   Alexandre C. Kiss and Dinah Shelton, *Guide to International Environmental Law* (Leiden: Martinus Nijhoff Publishers, 2007), 84.

9   Ibid.

10   See this commentary on Article 31.

11   See this commentary on Article 30.

12   Bodansky, *Art and Craft of International Environmental Law*, op. cit., 239; and Birnie, Boyle and Redgwell, *International Law and the Environment*, op. cit., 239–243.

tion, open the door to peer review, peer pressure and mutual learning. Scrutiny and exchange of lessons learnt can be undertaken by the focal points of other Parties and interested stakeholders on the basis of information provided through national reporting.[13] In the context of the CBD, however, in view of the absence of a mechanism to systematically and effectively monitor implementation and compliance at the national level, the COP has not engaged in the review of individual national reports but, rather, limited itself to offering conclusions on the basis of the CBD Secretariat's syntheses of these reports.[14] National reporting, however, may receive increased attention in the context of the Nagoya Protocol, given the link between the domestic ABS framework of provider countries and user countries' international obligations on addressing compliance by their users.[15] In that regard, it should be noted that Parties to the Cartagena Protocol have recently tasked the Biosafety Compliance Committee to systematically review Parties' reports with a view to identifying general compliance challenges, and to engaging with Parties that still need to put in place their national biosafety framework.[16]

It should also briefly be recalled that ensuring timely and accurate national reporting is a challenge in many MEAs,[17] although 'misreporting is more difficult than it appears.'[18] Non-compliance procedures can be employed, and are often employed by other MEAs, to put pressure on States that are late or deficient in their reporting. In addition, the Protocol's governing body may issue guidance to ensure sufficient quality and comparability of reporting, thereby making misreporting easier to detect.[19]

---

13   Bodansky, *Art and Craft of International Environmental Law*, 239; and Birnie, Boyle and Redgwell, *International Law and the Environment*, op. cit., 239–243.

14   This examination tends to focus on the mere *submission* of the report and on a *quantitative* analysis of legislative developments (for instance, the percentage of Parties with biodiversity-related legislation in place) rather than on a *qualitative* analysis of the content of the national reports, including the quality and comprehensiveness of national legislation and impacts of State measures on biodiversity and achievement of the CBD objectives. Involvement of subsidiary bodies under the CBD in the examination of reports has not yielded results in this direction either: see Morgera and Tsioumani, "Yesterday, Today, and Tomorrow," op. cit., 7.

15   See this commentary on Article 15, section 3.1.

16   See "Report of the Compliance Committee under the Cartagena Protocol on Biosafety" (12 June 2013) UN Doc UNEP/CBD/BS/CC/10/5.

17   Birnie, Boyle and Redgwell, *International Law and the Environment*, op. cit., 243.

18   Bodansky, *Art and Craft of International Environmental Law*, op. cit., 239.

19   Ibid.

Article 30. Procedures and Mechanisms to Promote Compliance with this Protocol

The Conference of the Parties serving as the meeting of the Parties to this Protocol shall, at its first meeting, consider and approve cooperative procedures and institutional mechanisms to promote compliance with the provisions of this Protocol and to address cases of non-compliance. These procedures and mechanisms shall include provisions to offer advice or assistance, where appropriate. They shall be separate from, and without prejudice to, the dispute settlement procedures and mechanisms under Article 27 of the Convention.

1 Overview

Article 30[1] is an enabling provision,[2] which mandates the establishment of multilateral procedures and mechanisms for monitoring compliance and addressing instances of non-compliance with the Protocol. Similarly to the Biosafety Protocol,[3] it provides a definite mandate to the Protocol's governing body ('consider and approve') and a time frame[4] ('at its first meeting').[5]

Article 30 indicates that the aim of the compliance procedures and mechanisms will be two-fold: on the one hand, to promote compliance and, on the other hand, to address cases of non-compliance. It further provides some indication as to the nature of these procedures and mechanisms ('cooperative and non-adversarial') and the relevant powers, by pointing to the possibility to offer advice or assistance, and clearly distinguishing them from dispute settlement

---

1   This provision was first incorporated in the Cali Draft.
2   This is a common approach in other multilateral environmental agreements, such as the Kyoto Protocol, Article 18; the Stockholm Convention on Persistent Organic Pollutants (Stockholm, 22 May 2001, in force 17 May 2004) 2256 UNTS 119, Article 17; and ITPGRFA, Article 21. See also Greiber et al., *Explanatory Guide*, op. cit., 244.
3   Biosafety Protocol Article 34. See Mackenzie et al., *Explanatory Guide to the Cartagena Protocol*, op. cit., 193–196.
4   For similar considerations in the context of the Biosafety Protocol, see ibid., 194.
5   Which will be held concurrently with the first meeting of the CBD COP that is to convene after the Protocol's entry into force: Protocol Article 26(6). See this commentary on Article 26.

procedures.[6] All other elements of the procedures and mechanisms, including their form, the full array of their powers, the determination of entities entitled to trigger consideration of cases of non-compliance and the nature of measures to address non-compliance will have to be defined in subsequent negotiations and eventually be adopted by the Protocol's governing body.

To a certain extent, the compliance procedures and mechanisms to be established under the Protocol will share features that have become commonplace across multilateral environmental agreements.[7] On the other hand, some distinctive features of the Protocol will likely lead Parties to consider innovative approaches to multilateral compliance procedures and mechanisms. The following sections will therefore discuss some of the likely common features of compliance procedures under the Nagoya Protocol and other MEAs, and then focus on likely distinctive features. The relation of Article 30 with other compliance-related provisions of the Protocol, and with international dispute settlement mechanisms, will be analyzed next.

2   Common Features

Compliance procedures, including the creation of a compliance committee, have become a common feature of MEAs – although negotiations for their establishment have proven quite arduous.[8] Compliance procedures represent a response to general and individual issues related to compliance with international treaties, that are based on problem-solving through negotiation with

---

6   The Nagoya Protocol does not contain a provision on dispute settlement, but CBD Article 27 on dispute settlement is applicable in this context (pursuant CBD Article 27(5), which reads: 'The provisions of this Article shall apply with respect to any protocol except as otherwise provided in the protocol concerned.')

7   See for example: Birnie, Boyle and Redgwell, *International Law and the Environment*, op. cit., 211–213 and 237–250; Ulrich Beyerlin, Peter-Tobias Stoll and Rüdiger Wolfrum, eds., *Ensuring Compliance With Multilateral Environmental Agreements: A Dialogue Between Practitioners and Academia* (Leiden: Martinus Nijhoff Publishers, 2006); Tullio Treves et al., eds., *Non-Compliance Procedures and Mechanisms and the Effectiveness of International Environmental Agreements* (The Hague: Asser Press, 2009); Ronald B. Mitchell, "Compliance Theory: Compliance, Effectiveness and Behaviour Change in International Environmental Law" in Bodansky, Brunnée and Hey, *The Oxford Handbook of International Environmental Law*, op. cit., 893; and André Nollkaemper, "Compliance Control in International Environmental Law: Traversing the Limits of the National Legal Order," *Yearbook of International Environmental Law* 13 (2003): 165.

8   For a comparative discussion, see Morgera et al., "Implementation Challenges," op. cit.

a view to identifying a flexible and pragmatic multilateral solution to questions of interpretation of a treaty, as well as alleged breaches.[9] The outcome of compliance procedures can be an authoritative determination of the correct interpretation of a treaty provision or a declaration of non-compliance by a certain Party. But it may also be (in addition or in alternative) a more pragmatic proposal to manage non-compliance problems in order to achieve an 'acceptable level of compliance' in the future, rather than establishing rights and duties under the treaty.[10] In that connection, compliance mechanisms are more fundamentally geared towards promoting *future* compliance rather than punishing *past* non-compliance, with the ultimate aim of seeking to promote the effectiveness of the regime as a whole.[11] To that end, the outcome of compliance procedures may not be necessarily dictated by international law, but rather accommodate the interests of all Parties, thereby facilitating multilateral solutions and restoring mutual trust.[12] As a result, in different combinations, compliance mechanisms generally mix a 'managerial' and 'enforcement' approach,[13] encouraging Parties to engage in better planning of actions needed for ensuring compliance.[14] Sanctions and disincentives are usually reserved only to tackle recalcitrant Parties.

It should also be noted that compliance mechanisms provide an opportunity for the wider international community, beyond State Parties, to exercise multilateral pressure on non-compliant Parties. Thus, not only Parties but also observers, notably NGOs,[15] can participate (in different ways and to different extents, depending on the specific procedures of the compliance mechanisms)[16]

---

9   Antonio Cardesa-Salzmann, "Constitutionalising Secondary Rules in Global Environmental Regimes: Non-Compliance Procedures and the Enforcement of Multilateral Environmental Agreements," *Journal of Environmental Law* 24 (2012): 103; see also Birnie, Boyle and Redgwell, *International Law and the Environment*, op. cit., 245–250.

10   Bodansky, *Art and Craft of International Environmental Law*, op. cit., 251.

11   Ibid., 232–233.

12   Ibid., 226 and 251.

13   For this terminology, see Abram Chayes and Antonia Handler Chayes, "On Compliance," *International Organization* 47 (1993): 175; and Jutta Brunnée, "Multilateral Environmental Agreements and the Compliance Continuum," in Winter, *Multilevel Governance of Global Environmental Change*, op. cit., 387.

14   Bodansky, *Art and Craft of International Environmental Law*, op. cit., 235.

15   Alessandro Fodella, "Structural and Institutional Aspects of Non-Compliance Mechanisms," in Treves et al., *Non-Compliance Procedures*, op. cit., 355; and Birnie, Boyle and Redgwell, *International Law and the Environment*, op. cit., 244.

16   Veit Koester and Tomme Young, "Compliance with International Conventions: The Role of Public Involvement," *Environmental Policy and Law* 37 (2007): 399.

in negotiations for equitably balancing the interests of different Parties and for determining appropriate forms of assistance, taking into account experience and knowledge of different stakeholders involved in treaty implementation. It should be noted that compliance mechanisms have also raised concerns about the respect for the rule of law in MEAS. It has in fact been argued that compliance with international obligations becomes 'intensely negotiable,' which possibly leads to a 'relativization of international law's normativity' and conceals fundamental disagreement among relevant actors about the significance of international rules and their breach.[17]

The intergovernmental process preparing for the entry into force of the Protocol already engaged in the identification of useful elements of inspiration from other compliance mechanisms under other MEAS.[18] Useful elements could include the possibility for a future compliance committee[19] to take facilitative measures in its own capacity,[20] to address non-compliance also through

---

17   Klabbers, "Compliance Procedures," op. cit., 995.

18   The CBD Secretariat initially drew attention to the compliance mechanisms of the Biosafety Protocol and of the ITPGRFA in CBD Secretariat, "Cooperative procedures and institutional mechanisms to promote compliance with the Protocol and to address cases of non-compliance" (6 September 2011) UN Doc UNEP/CBD/ICNP/1/6/Rev.1. But relevance of other experiences under other MEAS was later considered: ICNP, "Report of the Expert Meeting on Cooperative Procedures and Institutional Mechanisms to Promote Compliance with the Nagoya Protocol on Access and Benefit-Sharing and to Address Cases of Non-Compliance" (1 March 2012) UN Doc UNEP/CBD/ICNP/2/12, paragraphs 47 and 52.

19   While a decision has still be to taken on whether a compliance 'committee' will be established under the Nagoya Protocol, negotiating documents at the time of writing clearly point in that direction: ICNP Recommendation 2/7 "Cooperative procedures and institutional mechanisms to promote compliance with the protocol and to address cases of non-compliance", Annex, paragraph B.1, in ICNP, 'Report of the second meeting,' UNEP/CBD/COP/11/6, Annex.

20   ITPGRFA Article 21: 'The Governing Body shall, at its first meeting, consider and approve cooperative and effective procedures and operational mechanisms to promote compliance with the provisions of this treaty and to address issues of non-compliance. These procedures and mechanisms shall include monitoring, and offering advice or assistance, including legal advice or legal assistance, when needed, in particular to developing countries and countries with economies in transition.' See ENB. "Summary of the Fourth Session of the Governing Body of the International Treaty on Plant Genetic Resources for Food and Agriculture: 14–18 March 2011," Vol. 9 No. 550, 21 March 2011; and Elsa Tsioumani, "ITPGRFA. Compliance Procedures and Operational Mechanisms," *Environmental Policy and Law* 41 (2011): 74.

punitive measures,[21] to seek information through the Secretariat, to conduct visits to the territory of the Party under investigation if invited to do so,[22] and to consider reports of expert teams reviewing Parties' national reports.[23] A notable potential source of inspiration would be the Convention on Access to Information, Public Participation in Decision-making and Access to Justice in Environmental Matters ('Aarhus Convention'), whose compliance mechanism can be triggered[24] by stakeholders[25] and includes NGOs as members of

---

21   This is the case of CITES, for instance, where powers were derived from a provision in CITES Article XI, enabling the COP to make recommendations to improve the effectiveness of the Convention, coupled with majority-voting decision making. Compare CITES Resolution Conf. 14.3 "CITES Compliance Procedures," CITES, accessed 30 November 2013, <www .cites.org/eng/res/all/14/E14-03C15.pdf>. See generally Rosalind Reeve, "Wildlife Trade, Sanctions and Compliance: Lessons from the CITES Regime," *International Affairs* 82 (2006): 881. See also Kyoto Protocol Articles 3(1), 5(1), 5(2) and 7(1); and Decision 27/ CMP.1 "Procedures and mechanisms relating to compliance under the Kyoto Protocol" (30 March 2006) UN Doc. FCCC/KP/CMP/2005/8/Add.3, Annex, section XV. See Jacob Werksman, "Compliance and the Kyoto Protocol: Building a Backbone into a 'Flexible' Regime," *Yearbook of International Environmental Law* 9 (1999): 48; and Meinhard Doelle, "Compliance and Enforcement in the Climate Change Regime," in Hollo, Kulovesi and Mehling, *Climate Change and the Law*, op. cit., 165.

22   Montreal Protocol Article 8; and "Non-compliance Procedure" in "Report of the fourth meeting of the Parties to the Montreal Protocol" (25 November 1992) UN Doc UNEP/ OzL.Pro.4/15, Annex IV, as amended by "Report of the tenth meeting of the Parties to the Montreal Protocol" (3 December 1998) UN Doc UNEP/OzL.Pro.10/9, Annex II, paragraph 7. See also Martti Koskenniemi, "Breach of Treaty or Non-Compliance? Reflections on the Enforcement of the Montreal Protocol," *Yearbook of International Environmental Law* 3 (1993): 123; and Birnie, Boyle and Redgwell, *International Law and the Environment*, op. cit., 353–354.

23   Kyoto Protocol Article 18; and Decision 27/CMP.1, Annex, section IV. See Cardesa-Salzmann, "Constitutionalising Secondary Rules," op. cit., 114; and Doelle, "Compliance and Enforcement," op. cit., 167.

24   As proposed by Switzerland: ENB 9/551, "Summary of the First Meeting of the Intergovernmental Committee for the Nagoya Protocol," 9.

25   This characteristic is also present in other UNECE instruments: Protocol on Pollutant Release and Transfer Registers to the Convention on Access to Information, Public Participation in Decision-Making and Access to Justice in Environmental Matters (Kiev, 21 May 2003, in force 8 October 2009) 2629 UNTS 119, Article 12 (which makes reference to 'members of the public') and Decision I/2, "Review of Compliance" (20–22 April 2010) UN Doc ECE/MP.PRTR/2010/, paragraph 18; Convention on the Protection and Use of Transboundary Watercourses and International Lakes (Helsinki, 17 March 1992, in force 6 October 1996) 1936 UNTS 269, and Decision VI/1, "Support to implementation

the compliance committee. Interestingly, however, these innovative characteristics of the Aarhus Compliance Committee are balanced out by the fact that its decisions are subject to consensus approval by the Convention's governing body – thereby implicitly giving a 'veto power' to the Party whose compliance issues are at stake.[26] With regard to inspiration from other MEAS, a measure of caution has been called for by a commentator, who emphasizes the need for careful scrutiny of whether the characteristics of other compliance mechanisms may be effectively utilized to address ABS-related compliance issues that will likely involve requests for benefit-sharing in the context of commercial relationships.[27]

At the time of writing it remains too early to determine which of these features will be included in the compliance procedures under the Nagoya Protocol.[28] In the intergovernmental process preparing for the Protocol's entry into force, it has also been noted that international treaties other than MEAS, such as human rights ones, may be taken into account in devising the compliance mechanism for the Protocol.[29] This may arguably serve to better address Parties' lack of political will to comply with the Protocol, which appears to be addressed more often in the context of human rights bodies than in the context of MEA compliance procedures, which rather tend to focus on capacity issues. Consideration of compliance mechanisms under international human

and compliance" (28–30 November 2012) UNECE Doc ECE/MP.WAT/37/Add.2, Annex II; Protocol on Water and Health to the 1992 Convention on the Protection and Use of Transboundary Watercourses and International Lakes (London, 17 June 1999, in force 4 August 2005) 2331 UNTS 202 Article 15 and Decision I/2, "Review of compliance" (3 July 2007) UNECE Doc ECE/MP.WH/2/Add.3, paragraph 16. See also Svitlana Kravchenko, "The Aarhus Convention and Innovations in Compliance with Multilateral Environmental Agreements," *Colorado Journal International Environmental Law and Policy* 18 (2007): 1.

26   Veit Koester, "Aarhus Convention/MOP-4: The Compliance Mechanism – Outcomes and a Stocktaking," *Environmental Policy and Law* 41 (2011): 196, 197–198.

27   Young, "An International Cooperation Perspective," op. cit., 489.

28   ICNP Recommendation 2/7, "Cooperative procedures and institutional mechanisms to promote compliance with the Protocol and to address cases of non-compliance" in ICNP, "Report of the second meeting," UNEP/CBD/COP/11/6, Annex.

29   ICNP Recommendation 1/4 "Cooperative procedures and institutional mechanisms to promote compliance with the Protocol and to address cases of non-compliance," paragraph 1, in ICNP, "Report of the first meeting," UNEP/CBD/ICNP/1/8, Annex, where there is an open-ended reference to 'taking into account the experience and lessons learned from other relevant multilateral agreements.'

rights treaties may further provide options to factor in the specificities of the Nagoya Protocol with regard to indigenous and local communities.[30]

3   Distinctive Features

The unique obligations arising from the Protocol may lead Parties to explore innovative approaches to multilateral compliance procedures and mechanisms. There are at least three aspects that may make the Protocol compliance mechanism quite distinctive from those under other MEAS:

a)   the interaction between the bilateral obligations arising in the context of a specific relation between a provider and user country, on the one hand, and *erga omnes partes* obligations contained in the Protocol;[31]

b)   compliance with the international obligations of State Parties vis-à-vis indigenous and local communities;

c)   compliance involving relations between States and private entities.

These will be discussed in turn below. It should also be noted in passing that other elements under the Nagoya Protocol may require distinctive solutions. This is the case of ensuring balanced representation among provider and user countries in a future compliance committee; addressing issues of confidentiality;[32] and taking into account the specific needs of developing countries.[33]

---

30   ENB 9/551, "Summary of the First Meeting of the Intergovernmental Committee for the Nagoya Protocol," 10; and Morgera, "First Meeting of the Intergovernmental Committee for the Nagoya Protocol," op. cit., 190.

31   Note that this feature may not be unique to the Nagoya Protocol: it appears to distinguish also other 'collective regimes' that relate to resources that are to a great extent under State jurisdiction such as the United Nations Convention to Combat Desertification and the ITPGRFA as MEAS that at the same time include generalized obligations for the 'protection of components of global ecosystems', thus enhancing 'the application of principles and duties of general international law' as well as bilateral and reciprocal international obligations as part of the economic instruments for their application: Cardesa-Salzmann, "Constitutionalising Secondary Rules," op. cit., 109.

32   See this commentary on Article 14, section 5.

33   See this commentary on Articles 22–23 and 25.

3.1 Compliance in Bilateral Relations between Provider and User Countries

Currently, there is no existing compliance mechanism under an MEA to address State compliance with obligations to ensure that users under its jurisdiction respect other countries' national legislation.[34] In addition, intergovernmental discussions preparing for the entry into force of the Protocol initially highlighted an underlying divergence of views among CBD parties in this regard, namely whether the Protocol's compliance mechanisms will address Parties' compliance with their obligations related to users' compliance with domestic ABS frameworks related to genetic resources[35] and traditional knowledge,[36] and with MAT.[37] As already discussed,[38] unusually, the Protocol refers to 'compliance' not only in the traditional sense under international environmental law of State Parties' compliance with their international obligations, but also in the case of individual *users'* compliance with applicable laws and MAT at the national level – where users will most likely be private individuals or entities.[39] This has led certain developed countries to argue that Protocol Articles 15–16 and 18 were excluded from the purview of a future compliance mechanism, as these articles fundamentally relate to users' compliance. The CBD Secretariat explicitly clarified that State Parties to the Protocol are bound by international law to comply with *all* their obligations under the Protocol, including the *international* obligations concerning individual users' compliance contained in Protocol Articles 15–16 and 18, compliance with which could all be reviewed under the Protocol's compliance mechanism to be established.[40]

---

34   A comparison could nonetheless be drawn with the compliance procedures under CITES: we are grateful to Tomme Young for drawing our attention to this point. For instance, the Management Authority of Japan is required to reconfirm directly to the Management Authority of the country of export, prior to the authorization of the import of the specimen, which export is prohibited under the law of that exporting country: Isozaki, "Enforcement of ABS Agreements," op. cit., 440.

35   See this commentary on Article 15.

36   See this commentary on Article 16.

37   See this commentary on Article 18.

38   See this commentary on Article 15, section 2.

39   See ENB 9/551, "Summary of the First Meeting of the Intergovernmental Committee for the Nagoya Protocol," 12.

40   ICNP Recommendation 1/4, preambular recital (emphasis added). See also Egypt's statements on behalf of the African Group on this matter in ICNP, "Report of the first meeting," paragraph 151. Note also the statement made by the ICNP Co-Chair Casas during the meeting that 'Parties to the Protocol are bound by international law to comply with *all*

These international obligations clearly relate both to domestic law-making action (or the enactment of other domestic –policy and administrative – measures) and international cooperation in transnational enforcement efforts. The latter seemed to be particularly important for provider countries, who may be able to use (or at least threaten to use) a Party-to-Party trigger under a future compliance mechanism to ensure that user countries cooperate in ensuring access to justice in cases of misappropriation.

Against this background, it can be expected that typical non-compliance instances that may be brought to the attention of a future compliance committee under the Protocol may include a Party claiming that another Party has failed to take domestic measures required for the implementation of the Protocol, thereby preventing persons or entities in the claiming Party from obtaining access or receiving benefits; or one Party alleging a breach of an inter-State ABS arrangement concluded with another Party.[41] Other claims may also involve lack of international cooperation in addressing users' alleged violations of domestic ABS frameworks.[42]

Due to the importance of compatible provider and user countries' legislative activities on ABS for the full operationalization of the Protocol,[43] it may also be suggested that the compliance mechanisms and procedures will be heavily involved in the advice and assessment of national ABS laws. To that extent, a comparison with the CITES compliance processes and the CITES National Legislation Project may be useful.[44] The Project was established in 1992 in

---

their obligations under the Protocol, and that these obligations include compliance with domestic legislation, as contained in Protocol Articles 15–16, as well as compliance with MAT, as contained in Protocol Article 18; and if a Party does not take these compliance-related measures, this is considered non-compliance under the Protocol and will be reviewed under the compliance mechanism to be established.' ENB 9/551, "Summary of the First Meeting of the Intergovernmental Committee for the Nagoya Protocol," 8.

41   Young, "An International Cooperation Perspective," op. cit., 488. In the latter case, however, it could be possible for a bilateral ABS treaty to be in place, which may provide for dispute-settlement mechanisms: we are grateful to Tomme Young for drawing our attention to this point. On bilateral ABS treaties, see this commentary on Article 4, section 3.

42   Nagoya Protocol Article 15(3). See this commentary on Article 15.

43   See this commentary on Articles 4–5 and comments on the need for 'inter-operability' between domestic ABS frameworks in Young, "An International Cooperation Perspective," op. cit., 488.

44   CITES Resolution Conf. 8.4 (Rev. COP15) "National Laws for implementation of the Convention," CITES, accessed 30 November 2013, <www.cites.org/eng/res/08/08-04R15.php>. For a comparative discussion, see generally Morgera et al., "Implementation Challenges and Compliance in MEA Negotiations," op. cit.

the absence of an explicit basis in the Convention. The CITES Secretariat is enabled to determine whether Parties' national legislation adequately implements the Convention, by categorizing each country's legislation as meeting all, some, or none of the requirements for implementing CITES. The categorization is based on a clear articulation of the minimum requirements set by CITES in terms of implementing the convention in national law. Countries in the lower category have to develop a 'legislation plan' establishing agreed steps and a timeframe for the adoption of national legislation. Failing to submit the Plan or to adopt adequate legislation by set deadlines may result in the recommended suspension of commercial trade in all CITES species with the Party, although the Secretariat may withhold action if good legislative progress has been made by a Party.[45] The system rests on the longstanding practice of the Standing Committee, which may recommend trade sanctions (suspension of wildlife trade) in cases where a country has not met its legislative obligations. In the framework of this multilateral process, national legislative sovereignty is closely monitored and significantly influenced by CITES bodies, on the basis of a comparative analysis of existing national laws and international guidelines, and a network of experts participating in relevant multilateral deliberations and field activities.[46] This approach, however, would require a 'cultural shift' among Parties to the CBD, which have hitherto expressed opposition to any international monitoring or assessment of national legislation.[47]

3.2   Compliance vis-à-vis Indigenous and Local Communities

The Nagoya Protocol provisions on traditional knowledge and genetic resources held by indigenous and local communities[48] significantly contribute to making States' role 'functional' to the protection of the interests of these

---

45   CITES Resolution Conf. 8.4 which instructs the Standing Committee to determine which Parties have not adopted appropriate measures for effective implementation of the Convention and to consider appropriate compliance measures, which may include recommendations to suspend trade, in accordance with CITES Resolution Conf. 14.3; directs the Secretariat to seek external funding to enable it to provide technical assistance to Parties in the development of their measures to implement the Convention; and invites all Parties, governmental, intergovernmental, and non-governmental organisations, and other sources to provide financial and/or technical assistance for the development and effective implementation of such measures; and CITES Article XII. The authors are grateful to Soledad Aguilar for her contributions on CITES in Morgera et al., "Implementation Challenges," op. cit.

46   Morgera, "Bilateralism at the Service of Community Interests?," op. cit., 756.

47   Morgera and Tsioumani, "Yesterday, Today, and Tomorrow," op. cit., 7.

48   See this commentary on Articles 5–7.

communities located in their territories, as well as of these communities in other States.[49] It remains to be seen how compliance with the Protocol's obligations related to indigenous and local communities will be monitored, particularly as currently, there is no existing mechanism under an MEA to address State compliance with obligations towards its indigenous and local communities. In addition or in alternative, a future compliance committee under the Protocol may have to assess compliance with, or at least consider the role of, indigenous and local communities' laws, protocols and procedures[50] in ensuring compliance with the obligations of Parties vis-à-vis these communities. To some extent this task may be facilitated by the use of community protocols,[51] which may distil the relevant views, laws and procedures of these communities in relation to ABS. In that connection, States' functional role may likely extend to support also the implementation and ensure the respect of community protocols, giving them legal effect in national legal system with a view to ensuring compliance by users and collaboration with user countries in that endeavor.[52]

Intergovernmental negotiations preparing for the Protocol's entry into force provide some indications of the options that may be considered if Parties agree to adequately gear multilateral mechanisms and procedures to deal with compliance with the indigenous and local community-related obligations of Parties. One obvious possibility is that of triggering the compliance procedure with a submission from 'a member of the public' or more specifically by 'indigenous and local communities,' which has been discussed together with the proposal of conditioning such trigger to the 'support of the Party in whose territories the community is located.'[53] This seems to demonstrate that while CBD

---

49   This argument was first put forward in Morgera, "Bilateralism at the Service of Community Interests?," op. cit., 745 and inspired by Ellen Hey, "Global Environmental Law and Global Institutions: A System Lacking 'Good Process,'" in *Cosmopolitanism in Context: Perspectives from International Law and Political Theory*, ed. Roland Pierik and Wouter Werner (Cambridge: Cambridge University Press, 2010), 45.

50   Nagoya Protocol Article 12(1). See this commentary on Article 12, section 2.

51   Nagoya Protocol Articles 12 and 21. See previous discussions on community protocols in the context of this commentary on Article 12, section 2.1; as well as Jonas, Bavikatte and Shrumm, "Community Protocols and Access and Benefit-Sharing," op. cit., 68; and Munyi and Jonas, "Implementing the Nagoya Protocol," op. cit., 238–244.

52   Morgera, "Bilateralism at the Service of Community Interests?," op. cit., 762.

53   ICNP Recommendation 2/7, section D, paragraph (1)(d). The text appears in square brackets in the draft decision. It is noteworthy that an expert group on compliance that met earlier in 2012 had noted the possibility that a community trigger under the Protocol compliance mechanism be accompanied by a 'number of qualifiers or conditions': ICNP,

Parties display some openness to consider a stakeholder or community trigger, a significant degree of caution in that regard remains. It should also be noted that a trigger by any member of the public (rather than indigenous and local communities) would provide private-sector users and providers with access to the Protocol's compliance mechanism, as well as environmental NGOs and other ABS stakeholders. Other options include the possibility for indigenous and local communities to submit information directly to a future compliance committee, which, combined with the possibility for the compliance committee to self-trigger, could provide an alternative to a community trigger. Another possibility is to allow representatives of indigenous and local communities to participate in a future compliance committee as members or as observers, and/or for the committee to directly consult with relevant communities in the course of its consideration of cases of non-compliance.[54]

An innovative idea that emerged during the Protocol negotiations, but that did not make it in the agreed text, was to establish an international ombudsperson to support developing countries and indigenous and local communities in identifying breaches of rights and to provide independent technical and legal support in ensuring the effective redress of such breaches.[55] If established, such an innovative feature in the MEA landscape[56] would essentially constitute an international institution able to work on the ground directly with indigenous and local communities, while enabling these communities to have immediate access to an international avenue to address alleged disrespect of their rights protected under the Protocol.[57] While the final text of the Protocol does not make reference to an international ombudsperson, there is nothing

---

"Report of the Expert Meeting on Cooperative Procedures," UNEP/CBD/ICNP/2/12, fns. 21–22.

54   ICNP Recommendation 2/7, Annex. See Morgera, "Second meeting of the ICNP," op. cit., 244.

55   See Montreal I Draft, draft article 14 bis. ENB 9/527, "Summary of the Resumed Ninth Meeting of the Working Group on ABS," 11 and 15.

56   In the human rights context, an ombudsman is a *national* institution that contributes to the enjoyment and protection of human rights. In particular, 'the traditional model of an ombudsman has been an independent institution that is established by and answerable to parliament, with the power to consider complaints and conduct investigations on its own initiative, and to make recommendations to government rather than to adopt biding decisions. (...) there are two main models of ombudsman (though some ombudsmen are hybrid between the two): the classical ombudsman and the human rights ombudsman:' see Andrew Byrnes and Catherine Renshaw, "Within the State," in Moeckli, Shah and Sivakumaran, *International Human Rights Law*, op. cit., 498, 514–5.

57   Morgera and Tsioumani, "Yesterday, Today, and Tomorrow," op. cit., 20.

to prevent Parties from establishing such a body in the future through a decision by the Protocol's governing body.[58] And indeed the intergovernmental discussions preparing for the Protocol's entry into force have witnessed the resurfacing of this idea. The Intergovernmental Committee for the Nagoya Protocol is thus considering at the time of writing whether an international ombudsman office could provide an intermediate layer in the multilateral compliance mechanisms and procedures where the Party concerned and its relevant communities could initially address implementation challenges with some international facilitation, but without the immediate involvement of a future compliance committee.[59] The ombudsman could thus function as a mediator between governments and indigenous and local communities, and a filter to select well-founded community submissions for transmission to a future compliance committee.[60] A comparable institution can be found in the context of the World Bank family: the Compliance Advisor/Ombudsman (CAO) of the International Finance Corporation (IFC).[61] The CAO is an independent oversight authority that receives and addresses complaints from any person, group or community affected, or likely to be affected, by IFC-financed projects, and then reports directly to the President of the World Bank Group.[62] The Ombudsman's *modus operandi* includes field visits to the site of contested projects and interviews with all parties involved: staff of the private company,

---

58   Article 26(4)(a): see this commentary on Article 26, section 2.

59   ICNP Recommendation 2/7, Annex, F bis, which reads: '[The Committee shall establish the office of an ABS ombudsman to provide assistance to developing countries and indigenous and local communities to identify instances of non-compliance and make submissions to the Committee.]' (brackets in the original). See also ENB 9/579, "Summary of the Second Meeting of the Intergovernmental Committee for the Nagoya Protocol," 12.

60   Morgera, "Second Meeting of the Intergovernmental Committee for the Nagoya Protocol," op. cit., 245.

61   See "Compliance Advisor/Ombudsman" (CAO), CAO, accessed 30 November 2013, <www. cao-ombudsman.org/>. The International Finance Corporation (IFC) is the 'private arm' of the World Bank: it provides financing to private operators active in developing countries: IFC Articles of Agreement (as amended through 27 June 2012), accessed 30 November 2013, <www.ifc.org/wps/wcm/connect/1c95b500484cb68d9f3dbf5f4fc3 f18b/IFC_Articles_of_Agreement.pdf?MOD=AJPERES>, Article 1. For a discussion, see Elisa Morgera, "Human Rights Dimensions of Corporate Environmental Accountability," in *Human Rights in International Investment Law and Arbitration*, ed. Pierre-Marie Dupuy, Francesco Francioni and Ernst-Ulrich Petersmann (Oxford: Oxford University Press, 2009), 511.

62   CAO Terms of Reference, Operational Guidance and Operational Practice in "CAO Operational Guidelines," CAO, accessed 30 November 2013, <www.cao-ombudsman.org/ howwework/documents/CAOOperationalGuidelines2013_ENGLISH.pdf>.

local authorities, affected communities representatives, other relevant local organizations and IFC staff. Complaints, reports of field missions and recommendations are all published on the CAO website, together with updates on ongoing investigations.[63] A similar body under the Nagoya Protocol, taking into consideration the specificities of ABS transactions, in particular regarding the central role of domestic ABS frameworks,[64] could possibly address many concerns related to compliance on the ground, and facilitate relations between relevant ABS stakeholders.

It should also be added that in relation to the indigenous and local community-related provisions of the Protocol, international human rights monitoring bodies may become involved in scrutinizing whether national-level implementation of the Nagoya Protocol complies with applicable international human rights instruments.[65] To the extent that these other fora would work in a mutually supportive manner with the Protocol and its compliance mechanisms and procedures, this may provide an opportunity for cross-compliance.[66]

3.3   Compliance in State-Private Parties Relations

Parties will also need to discuss whether, to what extent and how the Protocol's compliance mechanisms and procedures may address questions related to compliance in relationships between a State and private parties. If a stakeholder trigger were to be created for the ABS compliance procedures, private users or providers such as a biotech multinational or a research centre could potentially bring claims before a future compliance mechanism for failures by Parties to create clear, predictable and effective domestic ABS frameworks.

Furthermore, it cannot be excluded that certain ABS arrangements, particularly in the context of bilateral or regional agreements, may be considered a form of 'foreign direct investment'[67] (given the extensive interpretation of this term under international investment law[68] and its protection also under human rights instruments).[69] As a result Protocol Parties could possibly find

---

63   "Cases," CAO, accessed 30 November 2013, <www.cao-ombudsman.org/cases/>.

64   See this commentary on Article 16, section 2.

65   Savaresi, "International Human Rights Law Implications," op. cit., 79.

66   Morgera, Buck and Tsioumani, "Conclusions," op. cit., 509.

67   See this commentary on Article 4, section 2.1.

68   Jan Wouters, Nicolas Hachez and Sanderijn Duquet, "International Investment Law: The Perpetual Search for Consensus," in *Foreign Direct Investment and Human Development: The Law and Economics of International Investment Agreements*, ed. Olivier de Schutter, Johan F.M. Swinnen and Jan Wouters (New York: Routledge, 2013), 25.

69   See for example Nicolas Klein, "Human Rights and International Investment Law: Investment Protection as Human Right," *Goettingen Journal of International Law* 4 (2012):

themselves brought before investment dispute settlement mechanisms by private ABS users,[70] where human rights standards may be invoked by investors to challenge States' fulfillment of their obligation to provide adequate access to justice to non-State parties.[71] Such actions could arguably lead to differing interpretations of Protocol provisions by a future compliance committee under the Protocol on the one hand, and investment dispute bodies on the other hand, as the latter may have to balance the Protocol's objective with those of international investment law.[72]

4   Links with Other Protocol Provisions

The Protocol's compliance mechanism will interact with other international processes established under the Protocol. It will supplement the review of implementation by the Protocol's governing body,[73] which specifically includes review of the effectiveness of the Protocol's provisions on compliance with MAT.[74] A future compliance committee under the Protocol may also be allowed to take into account (upon request or of its own initiative) the reports submitted by Parties on their implementation of the Protocol.[75]

Potentially significant linkages may be established (or clarified) between the role of the compliance mechanisms and procedures, and the operation of the ABS Clearinghouse.[76] Parties will have to input information on their

---

179; Luke E. Peterson, *Human Rights and Bilateral Investment Treaties. Mapping the Role of Human Rights Law within Investor-State Arbitration* (Montreal: Rights & Democracy, 2009); and Bruno Simma, "Foreign Investment Arbitration: A Place for Human Rights," *International and Comparative Law Quarterly* 60 (2011): 573.

70   This may be particularly the case of ABS arrangements that provide benefit-sharing through the establishment of research facilities in the provider country: see this commentary on Article 5. We are grateful to Lorenzo Cotula for a useful exchange of ideas in this regard.

71   Savaresi, "International Human Rights Law Implications," op. cit., 72.

72   See for example Jorge E. Viñuales, "Foreign Investment and the Environment in International Law: An Ambiguous Relationship," *British Yearbook of International Law* 80 (2010): 244.

73   See this commentary on Articles 26 and 31. For a similar question under the Biosafety Protocol, see Mackenzie et al., *Explanatory Guide to the Cartagena Protocol*, op. cit., 193–196.

74   Nagoya Protocol Article 18(4). See Greiber et al., *Explanatory Guide*, op. cit., 243 and this commentary on Article 18.

75   See this commentary on Article 29.

76   See this commentary on Article 14, section 4.

national implementation measures (such as on domestic ABS frameworks) in the ABS Clearinghouse, and failure to do so may be considered a case of non-compliance. Once the information is in the system, Parties may use the ABS Clearinghouse to monitor compliance by other Parties or perhaps even use that information as a defense against allegation of non-compliance against them. Crucially, once included in the ABS Clearinghouse, national permits will be elevated to internationally recognized certificates of compliance, which hold an important role in documenting users' compliance with the bilateral ABS system set up by the Protocol.[77]

5   Dispute Settlement

Article 30 requires that the compliance procedures and mechanisms be 'separate from, and without prejudice to' dispute settlement procedures. In accordance with the Convention, Parties to the Protocol are required to address any dispute among them first of all by seeking solution by negotiation,[78] and, failing that, by jointly seeking the good offices of, or request mediation by, a third party.[79] Furthermore, when ratifying the Nagoya Protocol, a State may declare in writing that for a dispute that cannot be resolved through negotiation or mediation, the State may initiate an arbitration procedure and/or submit the dispute to the International Court of Justice.[80] If the Parties to the dispute have not accepted the same or any procedure, the dispute will be submitted to conciliation, unless the Parties agree otherwise.[81]

It should be finally noted that the Protocol's compliance procedures and mechanisms might be used as an alternative to, or concurrently with, a dispute settlement procedure. Parties may bring their concerns to the attention of a future compliance committee before resorting to international dispute settlement mechanisms in accordance with the CBD. In that case, the compliance mechanism might help prevent disputes and thus minimize the need for dispute settlement, which in all events is an extremely unlikely option in

---

77   Nagoya Protocol Article 17(2) and (3): see this commentary on Article 17, section 3. See Morgera, "First Meeting of the Intergovernmental Committee for the Nagoya Protocol," op. cit., 190.
78   CBD Article 27(1).
79   CBD Article 27(2).
80   CBD Article 27(3).
81   CBD Article 27(4). See Greiber et al., *Explanatory Guide*, op. cit., 249.

international environmental law.[82] On the other hand, it cannot be excluded that the same compliance issue may be considered at the same time by the Protocol's compliance mechanism and by an international dispute resolution mechanism. In that case, it has been emphasized that the relationship between compliance mechanisms under MEAs and general international law's enforcement mechanisms is still undefined.[83] Some commentators, however, have argued that the final decision of an international judicial organ would have to be considered 'res iudicata' by compliance committees. The latter could rather contribute through their own procedures to support the enforcement of the international court's ruling.[84]

---

82   For similar reflections in the context of the Biosafety Protocol, see Mackenzie et al., *Explanatory Guide to the Cartagena Protocol*, op. cit., 196. Recent practice under other MEAs also seems to indicate that Parties prefer to handle bilateral-type non-compliance instances through negotiations rather than through compliance mechanisms or formal dispute settlement procedures: Cardesa-Salzmann, "Constitutionalising Secondary Rules," op. cit., 126–128.

83   Klabbers, "Compliance Procedures," op. cit., 1005–1007.

84   Tullio Treves, "The Settlement of Disputes and Non-Compliance Procedures," in Treves et al., *Non-Compliance Procedures*, op. cit., 499.

Article 31. Assessment and Review

The Conference of the Parties serving as the meeting of the Parties to this Protocol shall undertake, four years after the entry into force of this Protocol and thereafter at intervals determined by the Conference of the Parties serving as the meeting of the Parties to this Protocol, an evaluation of the effectiveness of this Protocol.

1   Overview

As a specification to the general tasks of the Protocol's governing body,[1] Article 31[2] requires the COP/MOP to undertake periodic assessments of the effectiveness of the Protocol. Article 31 thus provides an opportunity to identify the need for international guidance or adjustments that may be needed if the evaluation identifies specific areas in which the effectiveness of the Protocol can be improved.[3] The specific mechanism and modalities for the assessment will have to be decided by the COP/MOP.[4] The following section will discuss how the assessment and review process will likely function and its linkages with other provisions in the Protocol.

2   Functions and Links

Article 31 is modeled after the Cartagena Protocol,[5] with the only difference that the first review is mandated after four years from entry into force and that following ones will be held at intervals to be determined by the COP/MOP. The Protocol's assessment and review process can be interpreted as institutional supervision of the implementation of the Protocol, collective evaluation of

---

1   Nagoya Protocol Article 26(4). See this commentary on Article 26, section 2.
2   This provision that was not subject to negotiation: it was first incorporated in the Cali Draft, draft article 24.
3   Mackenzie et al., *Explanatory Guide to the Cartagena Protocol*, op. cit., 197.
4   Greiber et al., *Explanatory Guide*, op. cit., 251.
5   Biosafety Protocol Article 35, which reads: 'The Conference of the Parties serving as the meeting of the Parties to this Protocol shall undertake, five years after the entry into force of this Protocol and at least every five years thereafter, an evaluation of the effectiveness of the Protocol, including an assessment of its procedures and annexes.'

its effectiveness, and as a complementary tool to the multilateral compliance mechanisms and procedures.[6] As to the latter, the Protocol's governing body is empowered to monitor implementation of the Protocol *as a whole*, whereas a future compliance committee will most likely focus on compliance by individual Parties[7] in relation to specific circumstances. Thus, the COP/MOP under its review process will focus on the adequacy of the obligations under the Nagoya Protocol in its entirety, with a view to assessing their aggregate performance in achieving the Protocol's objectives,[8] rather than the fulfillment of obligations by individual Parties. Nonetheless, the two processes will likely feed into each other: the results of the assessment and review processes may provide information relevant to the work of a future compliance committee, and the latter may also provide information that can contribute to assessment and review.[9]

As in the case of the Biosafety Protocol, the review process is 'likely to be based in part on the information provided by Parties in their national reports on implementation of the Protocol as well as on other sources of information,'[10] so implementation of Article 31 will rely to a significant extent on compliance by Parties with their reporting obligations.[11] It can also be expected that submissions from ABS stakeholders,[12] intergovernmental organizations,[13] the CBD COP and its subsidiary bodies, notably the Working Group on Article 8(j), as well as reports by the Protocol Secretariat mandated to it on an *ad hoc* basis by the Protocol COP/MOP, will also contribute to the review.

Other provisions of the Protocol have expressly or implicitly made reference to this process. For instance, the review will particularly focus on the effectiveness of measures to ensure compliance with MAT.[14] In addition,

---

6   See this commentary on Article 30. This is based, by analogy, on the interpretation of Article 35 of the Biosafety Protocol put forward by Mackenzie et al., *Explanatory Guide to the Cartagena Protocol*, op. cit., 197.

7   Although note that a future compliance committee under the Protocol may also address compliance issues involving private users and providers: see commentary on Article 30, section 3.3.

8   Bodansky, *Art and Craft of International Environmental Law*, op. cit., 239.

9   Greiber et al., *Explanatory Guide*, op. cit., 251.

10   Mackenzie et al., *Explanatory Guide to the Cartagena Protocol*, op. cit., 197.

11   See this commentary on Article 29.

12   Greiber et al., *Explanatory Guide*, op. cit., 251.

13   Particularly those involved in international processes that may be mutually supportive with the Protocol: see this commentary on Article 4.

14   Nagoya Protocol Article 18(4). See this commentary on Articles 5, section 5, 6, section 7 and 18.

CBD Parties have already indicated that the first review under the Protocol will assess the implementation of measures to ensure compliance with domestic ABS requirements related to traditional knowledge,[15] in light of developments in other relevant international organizations, including WIPO.[16]

Given the many open-ended provisions of the Protocol, it has also been argued that the assessment and review process will serve to determine whether substantially divergent interpretation among its Parties hinders implementation, and fully assess the need for the Protocol's governing body to provide authoritative interpretation, where needed.[17] More generally, the assessment and review process will provide an opportunity for the Nagoya Protocol to evolve as a regime in light of lessons learnt in its implementation[18] and subsequent international developments, which is a common trait among MEAs.[19]

---

15   See this commentary on Article 16.

16   CBD Decision 10/1, paragraph 6. See also this commentary on Article 4, section 3.1.

17   Singh Nijar "An Asian Developing Country's View," op. cit., 249.

18   Young, "An International Cooperation Perspective," op. cit., 495.

19   Birnie, Boyle and Redgwell, *International Law and the Environment*, op. cit., 86–87; and Daniel Bodansky and Elliott Diringer, *The Evolution of Multilateral Regimes: Implications for Climate Change* (Arlington: Pew Center on Global Climate Change, 2010), accessed 30 November 2013, <www.pewclimate.org/docUploads/evolution-multilateral-regimes-implications-climate-change.pdf>.

Final Clauses

ARTICLE 32. SIGNATURE

This Protocol shall be open for signature by Parties to the Convention at the United Nations Headquarters in New York, from 2 February 2011 to 1 February 2012.

ARTICLE 33. ENTRY INTO FORCE

1. This Protocol shall enter into force on the ninetieth day after the date of deposit of the fiftieth instrument of ratification, acceptance, approval or accession by States or regional economic integration organisations that are Parties to the Convention.
2. This Protocol shall enter into force for a State or regional economic integration organisation that ratifies, accepts or approves this Protocol or accedes thereto after the deposit of the fiftieth instrument as referred to in paragraph 1 above, on the ninetieth day after the date on which that State or regional economic integration organisation deposits its instrument of ratification, acceptance, approval or accession, or on the date on which the Convention enters into force for that State or regional economic integration organisation, whichever shall be the later.
3. For the purposes of paragraphs 1 and 2 above, any instrument deposited by a regional economic integration organisation shall not be counted as additional to those deposited by member States of such organisation.

ARTICLE 34. RESERVATIONS

No reservations may be made to this Protocol.

ARTICLE 35. WITHDRAWAL

1. At any time after two years from the date on which this Protocol has entered into force for a Party, that Party may withdraw from this Protocol by giving written notification to the Depositary.

© KONINKLIJKE BRILL NV, LEIDEN, 2014 | DOI 10.1163/9789004217188_034

2. Any such withdrawal shall take place upon expiry of one year after the date of its receipt by the Depositary, or on such later date as may be specified in the notification of the withdrawal.

ARTICLE 36. AUTHENTIC TEXTS

The original of this Protocol, of which the Arabic, Chinese, English, French, Russian and Spanish texts are equally authentic, shall be deposited with the Secretary-General of the United Nations.

1   Overview

Articles 32–36 are standard closing provisions of international (environmental) treaties.[1] They were not subject to negotiation,[2] and to a great extent replicate the text of the Convention.[3] As in any other international treaty, these provisions apply from the moment of the Protocol adoption, rather than its entry into force.[4] The following sections will address any specific issues related to the Protocol that arise in the context of these provisions.

2   Signature and Entry into Force

At the time of writing, the Protocol attracted 92 Signatures,[5] with many States and the European Union already taking legislative and other action to

---

1 See generally on the signature, ratification and entry info force of treaties: Aust, *Modern Treaty Law and Practice*, op. cit., chapters 7–9; on the final clauses of the Nagoya Protocol specifically, Greiber et al., *Explanatory Guide*, op. cit., 253–264; and on the EU's participation in multilateral environmental agreements, see Marín Durán and Morgera, *Environmental Integration in the EU's External Relations*, op. cit., 17–24.

2 These Articles were first incorporated in the Cali Draft.

3 Nagoya Protocol Article 33 is modelled after Biosafety Protocol Article 37 (see comments by Mackenzie et al., *Explanatory Guide to the Cartagena Protocol*, op. cit., 201 on that provision) and corresponds to CBD Articles 38(2) and (4–5). Nagoya Protocol Article 34 reiterates CBD Article 38(1–2). Nagoya Protocol Article 35 replicates CBD Article 38(1)–(2); and Nagoya Protocol Article 36 mirrors exactly the text of CBD Article 42.

4 Aust, *Modern Treaty Law and Practice*, op. cit., 162.

5 As mentioned above (this commentary on Article 1, fn. 63), at the time of writing the Protocol had 92 signatures and 26 ratifications.

implement the Protocol.[6] According to the law of treaties, after a government signs the Protocol, the State is obliged to refrain from acts that could defeat the object and purpose of the Protocol,[7] unless the State manifests its intention not to become a Party to it.[8] This implies that a State must avoid any act preventing it from being able to fully comply with the Protocol once it enters into force,[9] or an act that would invalidate the basic purpose of the Protocol.[10]

Once the Protocol enters into force,[11] its obligations may take effect at different times for those States that will become Parties to it at a later stage. This may have particular relevance for provisions in the Protocol that refer to the 'Party providing genetic resources', rather than countries providing such resources.[12] In other words, if there are ABS transactions that involve Parties to the Protocol and CBD Parties that are not yet Parties to the Protocol, the latter will be only subject to the relevant CBD provisions.

3   Reservations

The Protocol includes an absolute prohibition for Parties to make reservations,[13] which can be explained by the desire to preserve the balance between the

---

6   "Progress Report on the Nagoya Protocol on Access to Genetic Resources and the Fair and Equitable Sharing of Benefits Arising from their Utilization and Related Developments," UNEP/CBD/COP/11/11 and ADD.1.

7   See this commentary on Article 1.

8   VCLT Article 18, which reads: 'A State is obliged to refrain from acts which would defeat the object and purpose of a treaty when: (a) it has signed the treaty or has exchanged instruments constituting the treaty subject to ratification, acceptance or approval, until it shall have made its intention clear not to become a Party to the treaty; or (b) it has expressed its consent to be bound by the treaty, pending the entry into force of the treaty and provided that such entry into force is not unduly delayed.'

9   It should be recalled that CBD Article 34 applies also to the ratification, acceptance and accession to CBD Protocols, including questions related to 'Regional Economic Integration Organisations' – an expression that applies to the European Union.

10   Aust, *Modern Treaty Law and Practice*, op. cit., 119.

11   As mentioned in this commentary on Article 1, fn. 63, at the time of writing the Protocol had 25 ratifications.

12   Similarly to CBD Article 15(3): see comments by Glowka, Burhenne-Guilmin and Synge, *Guide to the Convention on Biological Diversity*, op. cit., 127.

13   VCLT Article 19, which reads: 'A State may, when signing, ratifying, accepting, approving or acceding to a treaty, formulate a reservation unless: (a) the reservation is prohibited by the treaty (...).' See also VCLT Articles 20–23.

various obligations created by the Protocol.[14] This is in effect quite a common provision in other multilateral environmental agreements.[15]

While States are precluded from making a formal declaration that they do not consider themselves bound by some of the Protocol's provisions,[16] at the time they take the action needed to become a Party to the Protocol, the possibility cannot be excluded that States may try to achieve the effect of a reservation through an interpretative declaration.[17] The latter, although in principle it is not intended to have any legal effect in respect of the treaty at stake, may go beyond expressing the preference for an interpretation of the Protocol that is consistent with the domestic law of the State concerned, and rather aims at excluding or modifying the legal effect of certain provisions of the Protocol in their application to the State.[18] At the time of writing, however, no declarations have been made on the Protocol. Pragmatically, it can be observed that the Protocol's open-ended and heavily qualified language may already provide sufficient flexibility to Parties, thereby lessening their desire to make declarations.[19]

4   Withdrawals

With regard to withdrawals[20] from the Protocol, it should be noted that any Party to the Protocol that withdraws from the CBD will automatically withdraw from the Protocol too.[21]

---

14   Similarly to the CBD Article 37: see Glowka, Burhenne-Guilmin and Synge, *Guide to the Convention on Biological Diversity*, op. cit., 124.

15   The prohibition of reservations is typical of treaties negotiated by consensus and as a package deal, and intends to express the Parties' intention to create a single integral and interdependent treaty regime not open to contracting out: Boyle and Chinkin, *Making of International Law*, op. cit., 255.

16   Aust, *Modern Treaty Law and Practice*, op. cit., chapter 8.

17   We are grateful to Riccardo Pavoni for drawing out attention to this point. If an interpretative declaration is genuine (i.e., it is not a 'disguised reservation'), it can become an element in the interpretation of the Protocol, if no other Parties makes conflicting declarations or otherwise indicates disagreement: VCLT Article 31(2)(b) and Aust, *Modern Treaty Law and Practice*, op. cit., 127–128.

18   Ibid., 126–131.

19   We are grateful to Riccardo Pavoni for drawing out attention to this point.

20   VCLT Article 54(a).

21   As a result of combined reading of CBD Articles 38(3) and 32.

Withdrawals from multilateral environmental agreements have occurred in the recent past,[22] so future research should consider the possible effects of a Party withdrawing from the Protocol on ABS arrangements concluded while the Protocol was in force for that Party.[23]

5   Official Languages

The Protocol was negotiated and adopted in the six official languages of the United Nations: all of its texts are equally authentic, thus they are presumed to have the same meaning.[24] Of note are the corrections made to the French version of the Protocol, which were announced by the CBD Secretariat on 27 June 2011. As no objections were received, the French version of the original text of the Nagoya Protocol was amended accordingly.[25]

Any further cases of discrepancies between authentic language versions of the Protocol that may be identified in the future will be resolved either by interpretation, giving precedence – when the general rules of interpretation and supplementary means of interpretation fail – to the meaning which best reconciles the texts, having regard to the object and purpose of the

---

22   On 15 December 2011, the Government of Canada notified the UN Secretary-General that it had decided to withdraw from the Kyoto Protocol with effect from 15 December 2012: "Kyoto Protocol to the United Nations Framework Convention on Climate Change," UN Treaty Collection, accessed 30 November 2013, <http://treaties.un.org/pages/ViewDetails.aspx?src=TREATY&mtdsg_no=XXVII-7-a&chapter=27&lang=en>. On 29 March 2013, Canada notified the UN Secretary-General its decision to withdraw from the UNCCD: "UN Convention to Combat Desertification Responds to Canada's Withdrawal from Convention," UN Convention to Combat Desertification, accessed 30 November 2013, <www.unccd.int/en/media-center/MediaNews/Pages/highlightdetail.aspx?HighlightID=181> (not yet reported on the UNTS database).

23   On treaty withdrawal, see Duncan B. Hollis, *The Oxford Guide to Treaties* (Oxford: Oxford University Press, 2012), 639–640; and James Crawford, *Brownlie's Principles of Public International Law* (Oxford: Oxford University Press, 2012), 390–391.

24   VCLT Article 33(3).

25   CBD, Notification: Corrections du texte original de la version française du Protocole de Nagoya sur l'accès aux ressources génétiques et le partage des avantages (27 June 2011), accessed 30 October 2012, <www.cbd.int/doc/notifications/2011/ntf-2011-211-abs-fr.pdf> (only available in French).

Protocol,[26] or by amendment of one or more versions.[27] In either case, Parties will likely engage in negotiations in the framework of the Protocol's governing body.[28]

---

26   VCLT Article 33(4); Jonas and Saunders, "The Object and Purpose of a Treaty," op. cit., 574. See this commentary on Article 1.

27   Glowka, Burhenne-Guilmin and Synge, *Guide to the Convention on Biological Diversity*, op. cit., 129.

28   Nagoya Protocol Article 26(4)(a) and this commentary on Article 26, section 2. For an example of a possible discrepancy between the authentic language versions of the Protocol, see this commentary on Article 15, section 3.1, fn. 31.

Conclusions

The objective of the Nagoya Protocol is realizing fairness and equity among States, as well as between governments and indigenous and local communities, through the sharing of monetary and non-monetary benefits arising from the use of genetic resources and traditional knowledge.[1] Facilitating access to genetic resources is a means to this end, although it is in fact a precondition for triggering benefit-sharing obligations and remains the dominant motivation for Parties that characterize themselves principally as user countries. The continued political tension between the two sides (access and benefit-sharing) of the transnational relation of exchange regulated by the Protocol explains its compromise language and its frequent interpretative ambiguities. This makes it less apparent how the Protocol intends to address the asymmetries among States, as well as between States and indigenous and local communities, that motivated its negotiations.[2] This commentary has sought to identify textual, contextual and systemic interpretative questions and to suggest interpretative solutions that contribute to give *coherent* meaning and *full* effect to the whole text of the Protocol (effectiveness) and that avoid unfair advantages for certain Parties with a view to respecting the legitimate expectations of all Parties to the Protocol (good faith).[3]

On the basis of the detailed findings of the previous chapters, the conclusions will reflect on four legal concepts that appear critical in the ongoing political and academic debate on the interpretation and operationalization of the Protocol: sustainable development, equity, due diligence and environmental rights.

1   Sustainable Development

More explicitly than many other multilateral environmental agreements, the Nagoya Protocol promises to contribute to sustainable development.[4]

---

1   This is the Protocol's essential goal 'if a treaty could be boiled down to ... [its] essence,' which describes its 'normative logic' as basis for a 'holistic mode of interpretation': Jonas and Saunders, "The Object and Purpose of a Treaty," op. cit., 567 and 579. See this commentary on Article 1.
2   See Introduction to this commentary, section 1.
3   See Introduction to this commentary, section 5.
4   Dias, "Preface," op. cit., 2.

Its preamble makes reference to the potential of ABS transactions to contribute to scientific progress and innovation, poverty reduction, food security and public health, as well as the importance of technology transfer and cooperation for adding value to genetic resources in developing countries and building their research capacities.[5] Many of these elements are reflected in the operational provisions of the Protocol on special considerations, whereby Parties are to consider expeditious benefit-sharing towards those in 'need,' in particular developing countries, in the context of health-related emergencies. Regulatory space is also created in striking a balance between the Protocol's bilateral ABS architecture and the continuation of exchanges of genetic resources for food and agriculture, with a view to contributing ultimately to food security.[6] Concerns related to the social and economic pillars of sustainable development as articulated in treaties and instruments in other areas of international law (human rights, trade and investment, IPRs, oceans, as well as agriculture and health) are also addressed, in a much more open-ended and somewhat obscure way, in the Protocol provision on mutual supportiveness.[7] Furthermore, the Protocol key provision on benefit-sharing foresees contributions to local economies, directing research towards health and food security priority needs, and providing livelihoods security.[8] Technology transfer is specifically seen as a means to acknowledge and reward the contribution of developing countries as well as of indigenous and local communities providing genetic resources and traditional knowledge[9] as an essential form of benefit-sharing.[10]

With regard to the environmental pillar of sustainable development, the Protocol is expected to contribute not only to the conservation of biodiversity and the sustainable use of its components, but also to other global environmental challenges such as climate change.[11] As opposed to many other international environmental agreements, the Protocol is expected to contribute to environmental protection as an incentive-based system that innovatively structures international cooperation towards the contribution of genetic

---

5   Nagoya Protocol 5th, 7th and 14th preambular recitals.

6   Nagoya Protocol Article 8(b–c) and this commentary on Article 8, sections 3–4.

7   See this commentary on Article 4.

8   Nagoya Protocol Annex, paragraphs 2(l–m) and (o). See this commentary on Article 5, section 6.

9   See this commentary on Article 23.

10   Greiber et al., *Explanatory Guide*, op. cit., 216.

11   Nagoya Protocol 14th preambular recital.

variability to innovation.[12] As such, the Nagoya Protocol may therefore provide a concrete case study for the ongoing debate on the green economy[13]
and more generally on the use of an economic approach for more effective
environmental mainstreaming, MEA implementation and involvement of the
private sector.

Against this background, however, as discussed in more detail below, the
Protocol does not focus solely on an economic approach for the benefit of
environmental protection. It also presupposes a rights-based system, by man-
dating States to create the means to reward the stewards of biodiversity and
holders of traditional knowledge – namely indigenous peoples and local communities. In addition, it makes it part of its objective to realize the potential
of ABS transactions to contribute to biodiversity conservation and sustainable
use,[14] and includes a series of operative provisions that explicitly aim to support a coherent interpretation of the three CBD objectives.[15] Of these, some
incorporate more clear-cut obligations, such as the requirement for Parties to
create favorable conditions to promote and encourage research contributing
to conservation and sustainable use,[16] or the prohibition to restrict indigenous
and local communities' traditional use and exchanges of genetic resources that
contribute to conservation and sustainable use.[17] Other provisions, however,
are more open-ended, notably the selection as a key non-monetary benefit of
the sharing of research findings and the transfer of technology that contribute
to conservation and sustainable use.[18] Yet other provisions, notably the establishment of a global multilateral benefit-sharing mechanism, only embody an
obligation for further negotiations.[19]

Overall, a complex and still uncertain picture emerges at this early stage
as to how the Protocol will effectively function as an incentive-based frame-

---

12   See Introduction to this commentary, section 2.2.
13   Morgera and Savaresi, "A Conceptual and Legal Perspective on the Green Economy,"
      op. cit., 28, who conclude that while the 2012 UN Conference on Sustainable Development
      did not unequivocally endorse a transition to the green economy, the understanding of the
      role of the green economy for accelerating and measuring progress towards sustainable
      development will likely become apparent in the area of international biodiversity law.
14   See this commentary on Article 1, section 4.
15   See this commentary on Article 5, section 6; Article 8, section 2; Article 9, section 2;
      Article 10, section 4; Article 12, section 5; Article 21, section 3; Article 22, section 3; and
      Article 23, section 3.
16   Nagoya Protocol Article 8(a).
17   Nagoya Protocol Article 12(4).
18   Nagoya Protocol Annex, 2(f) and (k).
19   Nagoya Protocol Article 10.

work for the conservation of biodiversity and the sustainable use of its components. Empirical evidence on the contribution of ABS-based monetary benefits to environmental protection, food security and poverty eradication remains scarce.[20] As multilateral deliberations focus on the implementation of the Protocol, national and community-level experiences multiply and the academic debate intensifies, it remains to be seen whether the linkage between ABS and sustainable development will become clearer, not only in policy and legal terms but also in terms of impact on the ground.

2   Equity

The Nagoya Protocol is basically premised on the international environmental law principle of intra-generational equity – equity among stakeholders of the same generation[21] on the basis of self-determination, cultural diversity[22] and maintenance of ecological integrity.[23] Intra-generational equity, however, remains quite novel and its status is still debatable in international law.[24] In the specific context of ABS transactions, equity is expected to serve to strike a fair balance between the claims of a user country and of its individual users to carry out scientific research and protect biotechnological inventions, on the one hand, and the rights of provider countries and of their indigenous and local communities to obtain equitable rewards for the genetic resources and traditional knowledge that they have conserved and that are indispensible to bio-based innovation, on the other hand.[25] With a view to realizing equity in

---

20   The same conclusion applies for the multilateral ABS framework developed under the International Treaty on Plant Genetic Resources for Food and Agriculture. See Moeller and Stannard, *Identifying Benefit Flows*, op. cit. See this commentary on Article 10, Section 3.

21   Rio Declaration, Principle 3 reads: 'The right to development must be fulfilled so as to equitably meet developmental and environmental needs of *present* and future generations" (emphasis added).

22   Equity as 'what is fair and reasonable in the administration of justice' entails in international law reaching 'a common sense of justice and fairness in a culturally and politically divided society as international society is today...reconciling, not only competing State interests, but also different ethical and cultural views of the peoples of the world': Francesco Francioni, "Equity," in Wolfrum, *Max Planck Encyclopedia*, op. cit., paragraphs 1 and 3.

23   Birnie, Boyle and Redgwell, "International Law and the Environment," op. cit., 122.

24   Ibid., 123.

25   Francioni, "Genetic Resources, Biotechnology and Human Rights," op. cit., 20–21.

this context, benefit-sharing is expected to reconcile competing interests and different (ethical, cultural and economic) views among States and stakeholders as a tool for empowerment, participation and partnership.

Ultimately, the Nagoya Protocol operationalizes equity, in Prof. Francioni's words, as an 'unstructured source of principles which are assumed to inspire contractual arrangements.'[26] Similarly to the Bonn Guidelines,[27] the Nagoya Protocol limits itself to anchor fairness and equity to the establishment of MAT,[28] without providing any substantive criteria in that regard either at the stage of the regulation of MAT negotiations in domestic ABS frameworks, their establishment or their enforcement through international cooperation.[29] There is therefore no explicit requirement or mechanism in the Nagoya Protocol focusing on the extent to which benefit-sharing is indeed fair and equitable in the context of specific ABS transactions.

Nothing of course prevents individual Parties from establishing some substantive rules on the content of MAT in their domestic ABS frameworks, as regards fair and equitable benefit-sharing. In addition, the Protocol does require Parties individually and collectively (through the Protocol's governing body) to explore model contractual clauses[30] and voluntary instruments,[31] as well as awareness-raising[32] and training activities,[33] that may provide a bottom-up source of inspiration for fair and equitable benefit-sharing contracts.

That being said, the objective of the Protocol is unambiguous in requiring fairness and equity in benefit-sharing;[34] as is the key provision on benefit-

---

26   Francioni, "Equity," op. cit., paragraph 25.

27   Bonn Guidelines, paragraphs 41 (which reads 'Thus, guidelines should assist Parties and stakeholders in the development of mutually agreed terms to ensure the fair and equitable sharing of benefits') and 45 (which reads 'Mutually agreed terms could cover the conditions, obligations, procedures, types, timing, distribution and mechanisms of benefits to be shared. These will vary depending on what is regarded as fair and equitable in light of the circumstances.').

28   Nagoya Protocol Article 5(1–2 and 5) and 10th preambular recital.

29   The Protocol provisions concerning MAT are invariably of a procedural character: see this commentary on Article 5, section 5; Article 6, section 7; Article 15, section 3.1; and Article 18. Some reference to substantive guarantees only transpires in the Protocol provision on supporting indigenous and local communities in securing fairness and equity when negotiating MAT (Nagoya Protocol Article 12(3)(b)) and in more timid way on capacity building for developing countries (Nagoya Protocol Article 22(4)(b) and specific reference to equity in voluntary terms in Nagoya Protocol Article 22(5)(b)).

30   Nagoya Protocol Article 19.

31   Nagoya Protocol Article 20.

32   Nagoya Protocol Article 21.

33   Nagoya Protocol Article 22(4)(c) and 22(5)(b).

34   See this commentary on Article 1, sections 1–2.

sharing.[35] In addition, international human rights law also has a bearing on Parties' obligations concerning equitable benefit-sharing arising from the use of genetic resources held by indigenous peoples and local communities and from the use of their traditional knowledge.[36] It therefore remains to be seen in future practice in implementation and judicial pronouncements how Parties balance private parties' contractual freedom with the need to achieve fair and equitable benefit-sharing in the light of the objective of the Protocol and international human rights law. The test will likely be framed in terms of due diligence.

3   Due Diligence

The Protocol contains a combination of bilateral and collective approaches to ABS. In other words, while it aims to regulate a relationship of exchange between States acting in specific circumstances as user and provider countries on the basis of reciprocity, it contains multilateral (*erga omnes partes*) obligations[37] that aim to protect a collective interest of the international community. The bilateral system for access and benefit-sharing established by the Protocol, therefore, needs to be understood in the light of the conservation of biodiversity,[38] which is a common concern of humankind,[39] as well as general principles of equity and sustainable development. The bilateral obligations arising from the Protocol in the context of specific ABS transactions, therefore, are part of a system that is built upon inter-dependent, collective obligations triggering a sort of 'global reciprocity' so that implementation is conditional upon corresponding performance by *all* Parties.[40]

Against this background, it appears necessary to tease out the boundaries of due diligence under the Protocol, which is critical to the use of the ample margin of discretion left to Parties by the often open-ended formulation of the

---

35   Nagoya Protocol Article 5(1).

36   Savaresi, "International Human Rights Law Implications," op. cit., 71–73.

37   Joost Pauwelyn, "A Typology of Multilateral Treaty Obligations: Are WTO Obligations Bilateral or Collective in Nature?," *European Journal of International Law* 14 (2003): 907.

38   Nagoya Protocol Article 1.

39   CBD preamble. See discussion in Birnie, Boyle and Redgwell, *International Law and the Environment*, op. cit., 128–131; and more generally in Jutta Brunnée, 'Common Areas, Common Heritage and Common Concern' in Bodansky, Brunnée and Hey, *The Oxford Handbook of International Environmental Law*, op. cit., 550.

40   Pierre-Marie Dupuy, "A General Stocktaking of the Connections Between the Multilateral Dimension of Obligations and Codification of the Law of Responsibility," *European Journal of International Law* 13 (2002): 1053, 1071.

obligations of means[41] contained in the Protocol. Obligations of means[42] have a *continuing* nature: a breach materializes from the moment the conduct of the State has been proven not to have been in conformity with the behavior required by the Protocol – that is, even before it is possible to assert that a certain result has not been achieved.[43]

Due diligence helps to better understand Parties' obligations of means in developing their domestic ABS frameworks on benefit-sharing,[44] access,[45] and on ensuring individual users' compliance.[46] Domestic measures are to be *all reasonably appropriate* measures[47] and embody Parties' *best possible* efforts[48] to reach the objective of the Protocol (fair and equitable benefit-sharing among and within States and the conservation and sustainable use of biodiversity). Due diligence in the establishment of domestic ABS frameworks equally entails the establishment of administrative control systems to effectively monitor activities and the exercise of an appropriate level of vigilance in enforcement.[49] On both accounts, Parties are to exert appropriate and best possible efforts to ensure inter-operability of their domestic ABS frameworks with those of other Parties, as this is a pre-condition for the effective realization of the system put in place by the Protocol. In this connection, due diligence relies on the notion of good faith in expecting Parties to the Protocol to take into account the reasonable expectations of the other members of the international community,[50]

---

41   See ICJ, *Case concerning Pulp Mills on the River Uruguay (Argentina v. Uruguay)*, Judgement (20 April 2010), (hereinafter, *Pulp Mills*), paragraph 187; ITLOS, *Responsibilities and obligations of States sponsoring persons and entities with respect to activities in the Area (Request for Advisory Opinion submitted to the Seabed Disputes Chamber)*, Advisory Opinion (1 February 2011), paragraph 111.

42   Pierre-Marie Dupuy, "Reviewing the Difficulties of Codification: On Ago's Classification of Obligations of Means and Obligations of Result in Relation to State Responsibility," *European Journal of International Law* 10 (1999): 371, 378, where the author recalls that obligations of result involve in some measure a guarantee of the outcome, while obligations of means are in the nature of best efforts to do *all in one's power* to achieve a result.

43   Ibid., 382.

44   See this commentary on Article 5.

45   See this commentary on Articles 6–7.

46   See this commentary on Articles 15–16.

47   *Pulp Mills*, paragraph 197.

48   *Sea Bed Advisory Opinion*, paragraph 110.

49   *Pulp Mills*, paragraph 197; *Sea Bed Advisory Opinion*, paragraphs 115–116.

50   Markus Kotzur, "Good Faith", in Wolfrum, *Max Planck Encyclopedia*, op. cit., para. 4.

and protect the reasonable interests of other Parties[51] in a predictable manner[52] in framing their domestic ABS frameworks with the 'genuine intention to achieve a positive result.'[53] This is of course particularly significant in assessing Parties' efforts in implementing the Protocol obligations on ensuring users' respect for another country's requirements for PIC and MAT, by relying on all tools provided to that end by the Protocol (at the international level, the ABS Clearinghouse and the internationally recognized certificate of compliance;[54] and at the national level, 'effective' checkpoints),[55] as well as giving due consideration to the expectations and reasonable requests from other Parties.[56] Equally, due diligence and good faith are essential criteria for assessing Parties' efforts in engaging in international cooperation in addressing alleged cases of users' non-compliance.[57] Furthermore, due diligence and good faith may also be critical in the assessment of developed-country Parties' implementation of their solidarity obligations in terms of funding,[58] capacity-building,[59] and technology transfer.[60] In that context, because of the still open-ended balance of international obligations enshrined in the Nagoya Protocol, risks may arise that these initiatives may unduly favor the interests of user countries if provider countries find themselves dependent on user countries' support or on ready-made solutions that may not respond to particular circumstances.

Due diligence also entails the exercise by States of effective administrative control over private operators.[61] Therefore States' due diligence under the Protocol should be distinguished from *users' due diligence*.[62] The latter does

---

51 Michael Virally, "Review Essay: Good Faith in Public International Law," *American Journal of International Law* 77 (1983): 130.

52 Saul Litvinoff, "Good Faith," *Tulane Law Review* 71 (1997): 1645, 1664.

53 ICJ, *Delimitation of the Maritime Boundary in the Gulf of Maine Area (Canada/United States of America)*, Judgment (12 October 1984), paragraph 87.

54 See this commentary on Article 14, section 3 and Article 17, section 3.

55 See this commentary on Article 17, section 2.1.

56 See this commentary on Article 15, section 4.1; and Article 16, section 2.

57 See this commentary on Article 15, section 5; and Article 16, section 2.

58 Both through multilateral channels (in consideration of the double-weighted majority decision-making system in the GEF: see this commentary on Article 25, section 2) and through unilateral and bilateral channels (see this commentary on Article 25, section 3).

59 See this commentary on Article 22, section 5.

60 See this commentary on Article 23.

61 *Pulp Mills*, paragraph 197; *Sea Bed Advisory Opinion*, paragraphs 115–116.

62 EU draft regulation, draft article 4(1), which reads: 'Users shall exercise due diligence to ascertain that genetic resources and traditional knowledge associated with genetic resources used were accessed in accordance with applicable access and benefit-sharing

not exclude or diminish the international obligation of State Parties to implement the Protocol by appropriately regulating and effectively controlling the conduct of private users and providers in their jurisdiction.

That being said, private-sector due diligence presents interesting international law dimensions under the Protocol. First, corporate due diligence[63] can help companies respect responsible business conduct standards arising from the Nagoya Protocol,[64] which may also have implications for international investment disputes that could potentially arise in the context of the implementation of the Protocol.[65] Second, corporate due diligence has been developed at the international level with regard to business entities' respect for human rights,[66] with specific implications for the understanding of users' due diligence with respect to the community PIC requirement under the Protocol.[67]

All these considerations may help to address a fundamental legal question surrounding the international ABS regime. Since the entry into force of the

---

          legislation or regulatory requirements and that, where relevant, benefits are fairly and equitably shared upon mutually agreed terms.'

63   That is, the process through which enterprises 'can identify, prevent, mitigate and account for how they address their actual and potential adverse impacts as an integral part of business decision-making and risk management systems' (OECD Council, 'OECD Guidelines for Multinational Enterprises –: Update 2011 – Note by the Secretary-General" (3 May 2011) OECD doc C(2011)59), which not only concerns adverse impacts directly caused or contributed to by the enterprise but also those otherwise linked to their operations, products or services through a business relationship (OECD, *Due Diligence Guide for Responsible Supply Chains of Minerals from Conflict-Affected and High-risk Areas* (Paris: OECD, 2013), accessed 30 October 2013, <www.oecd.org/daf/inv/mne/GuidanceEdition2.pdf>).

64   On the emergence of responsible business conduct standards arising from international law, see generally, Morgera, *Corporate Accountability*, op. cit.

65   See this commentary on Article 4, section 2.1.

66   In that context, due diligence is defined as the 'process whereby companies not only ensure compliance with national laws but also manage the risk of human rights harm with a view to avoiding it', based on reasonable expectations: Human Rights Council, "Report of the Special Representative of the Secretary-General on the issue of Human Rights and Transnational Corporations and Other Business Enterprises: Protect, Respect and Remedy: A Framework for Business and Human Rights" (7 April 2008) UN Doc A/HRC/8/5, paragraphs 25 and 58. This has been further elaborated from the viewpoint of indigenous peoples' human rights by: Human Rights Council, "Report of the Special Rapporteur on the Situation of Human Rights and Fundamental Freedoms of Indigenous People, James Anaya," (19 July 2010) UN Doc. A/HRC/15/37, section 3, which has also developed the *environmental* rights dimension of corporate due diligence: see Morgera, "Environmental Accountability of Multinational Corporations," op. cit.

67   See this commentary on Article 6, section 4.2.2.

Convention on Biological Diversity and particularly in the negotiation of the Nagoya Protocol, CBD Parties have expressed differing views on what CBD Article 15(7) and other provisions related to benefit-sharing entail. Parties that characterize themselves primarily as providers of genetic resources normally interpret it as an obligation of result.[68] These Parties argue that obligations related to benefit-sharing, PIC and MAT[69] are self-executing and user countries would need to require any proof of PIC and MAT for all transactions of genetic resources under their jurisdiction, even in the absence of domestic ABS frameworks in provider countries. Conversely, Parties characterizing themselves as predominantly user countries normally draw attention to the qualifiers in CBD Article 15(7)[70] as an indication of an obligation of means that is not directly effective.[71] These Parties also underline that more easily enforceable benefit-sharing obligations presuppose not only the existence of MAT but also of domestic legislation in provider countries spelling out procedures for the granting of PIC and establishment of MAT and for sharing benefits.[72] The Nagoya Protocol does not necessarily resolve this fundamental divergence of views, although it clarifies that the absence of domestic ABS frameworks makes it virtually impossible for provider-country Parties to trigger user-country Parties' compliance obligations.[73] In view of its detailed provisions in that regard, the Protocol might engender a systematic multilateral process to identify and address when, why and to what extent Parties fail to implement their obligation to regulate ABS at the domestic level,[74] which would certainly mark a stark contrast with existing practice under the CBD.[75]

---

68   This position is, for instance, supported by Tvedt and Young, *Beyond Access*, op. cit., 129.

69   CBD Articles 15(5) (requirement of PIC) and (4).

70   Namely, the wording 'as appropriate' and 'with the aim of sharing.'

71   Note also that '…while Article 1 of the CBD states that its objective is the fair and equitable sharing of the benefits arising out of the utilization of genetic resources, including by appropriate access to genetic resources and by appropriate transfer of relevant technologies, it specifies that this must be done taking into account all rights over those resources and technologies. There is no provision of the CBD which requires that the conditions for the grant of a patent for biotechnological inventions should include the consideration of the interests of the country from which the genetic resource originates or the existence of measures for transferring technology': European Court of Justice, Case C-377/98 *Biotech Patents* [2001] ECR I-7079, paragraph 66.

72   This position is, for instance, supported by Glowka, Burhenne-Guilmin and Synge, *A Guide to the Convention on Biological Diversity*, op. cit., 82–83.

73   See this commentary on Article 6, section 3.1 and Article 15, section 3.1.

74   See this commentary on Article 6, section 3.1 and Article 30, section 3.1.

75   Morgera and Tsioumani, "Yesterday, Today and Tomorrow," op. cit., 7.

4   Environmental Rights

Preliminary analyses of the Nagoya Protocol already indicated that the new treaty creates opportunities and risks for the realization of internationally recognized human rights of the public (in relation to access to information, public participation in decision-making and access to justice), and more notably the collective rights of indigenous peoples.[76] The present analysis further suggests that, if interpreted and implemented in accordance with international human rights law, the Nagoya Protocol may represent a significant step forward in the debate on *substantive* environmental rights – a notion that remains very controversial in international law.[77]

An argument can in fact be put forward that the Nagoya Protocol not only establishes an obligation for States to create the means to reward for their contribution to scientific progress for the benefit of the global community the indigenous and local communities responsible for the stewardship of genetic resources and for the development and protection of traditional knowledge associated with these resources. It is also implicitly underpinned by the recognition (for the first time at the global level) of the substantive environmental rights of indigenous peoples and local communities to their genetic resources and to their traditional knowledge associated with genetic resources.[78] Such recognition is based on established international human rights in their collective dimension to indigenous peoples' self-determination, ownership and cultural identity. It can further be argued that the Protocol points to an expansion of these rights to local communities,[79] whose status in international human rights law remains underdeveloped.[80]

---

76   Savaresi, "International Human Rights Law Implications," op. cit., and Introduction to this commentary, section 4.

77   See Boyle, "Human Rights and the Environment," op. cit., 29–30 and other sources cited in this commentary on Article 5, fn. 36. The most cited example of an environmental treaty containing human rights is focused on procedural rights (the Aarhus Convention), whereas the only example of a treaty embodying a substantive environmental right is of a regional character (African Charter on Human and Peoples' Rights (27 June 1981, in force 21 October 1986) 21 ILM 58, Article 24).

78   See this commentary on Article 5, sections 3–4; Article 6, section 4; and Article 7, section 2.

79   See Introduction to this commentary, section 4.2.

80   See generally Bessa, *Traditional Local Communities in International Law*, op. cit.

To be sure, the Protocol is underpinned by a sophisticated elaboration of indigenous peoples and local communities' *procedural*[81] environmental rights in terms of benefit-sharing and community PIC.[82] Notably, as opposed to the understanding that seems to emerge from relevant international human rights standards, benefit-sharing towards indigenous and local communities under the Protocol applies even in the absence of any *restriction or deprivation* of their right to use their genetic resources[83] that may result from an ABS transaction. In that regard as well as with regard to traditional knowledge, therefore, benefit-sharing under the Protocol does not simply aim at *compensating* indigenous and local communities. It also aims at *empowering* them to participate as equal partners in the utilization of their resources and knowledge.[84] With regards to community PIC, while this is a well-established tool in international human rights, there are currently no international standards that can specifically fit with indigenous and local communities' genetic resources and their traditional knowledge for research and development. Their specificities cannot in effect be easily accommodated in the context of international guidance on community PIC in case of proposed limitation of indigenous peoples' rights to lands and natural resources (the classic case is relocation as a result of expropriation of indigenous peoples' land) or expected negative impacts of extractive activities on indigenous peoples' lands.[85] The concept of community PIC under the Nagoya Protocol may rather serve as a procedural tool to empower indigenous and local communities to be *actors* in research and development efforts and results, as opposed to being *recipients* of (positive or negative) impacts of developments carried out by others.

---

81   PIC and benefit-sharing are seen as procedural safeguards for the realization of indigenous peoples' substantive right to property, culture and non-discrimination, and their right to set and pursue their own priorities for development, including the development of natural resources, as part of their right to self-determination: "Report of the Special Rapporteur on the rights of indigenous peoples' rights" A/HRC/21/47, paragraphs 49–53.

82   See this commentary on Article 6, section 4.2; and Article 7, section 2.

83   Compare with the understanding of benefit-sharing as 'compensation' in *Saramaka People v. Suriname* 2008, paragraph 140.

84   The evolving legal notion of benefit-sharing under international law will be studied in depth by Elisa Morgera, Elsa Tsioumani, Annalisa Savaresi and Louisa Parks in the context of a 5-year research programme (2013–2018) funded by the European Research Council at the University of Edinburgh School of Law: <www.benelex.ed.ac.uk>.

85   See this commentary on Article 6, section 4.2

These human rights-related developments embodied in the Nagoya Protocol are particularly noteworthy when one considers the reluctance by some CBD Parties to fully endorse in the Protocol the international human rights law language, particularly from UNDRIP.[86] The recognition and possible justiciability of human rights entitlements under the Protocol, however, remains to be determined.[87] This may depend on whether a national court or possibly an international judicial and quasi-judicial body is seized in this regard. If the question arises before a national court, the answer may depend on the constitutional order of different Parties to the Protocol and judicial cultures vis-à-vis the potential direct or indirect effect[88] of the Protocol provisions or the relevance of applicable international human rights law.[89] It cannot be excluded, in addition, that indigenous and local communities may invoke relevant Protocol provisions when having recourse to international human rights bodies.[90] There are good indications that human rights monitoring bodies are inclined to investigate the respect of international human rights standards in the context of national measures implementing environmental treaties.[91] In addition, it cannot be excluded that in the future Parties' implementation of the community-related requirements under the Protocol may be the object of

---

86   See introduction to this commentary, section 4.

87   But note that "justiciability is not the yardstick by which the status of a provision as a human right is to be judged. It is to be judged by reference to the authoritative nature of the sources that purport to identify it, by community expectation that an obligation exists": Higgins, *Problems and Process*, op. cit., 102.

88   Ibid., 206–209; and generally André Nollkaemper, *National Courts and the International Rule of Law* (Oxford: Oxford University Press, 2011), especially chapters 6–7.

89   As a matter of human rights law, the right to a remedy under domestic law exists only insofar as it is explicitly provided for in the relevant human rights treaty, e.g. European Convention for the Protection of Human Rights and Fundamental Freedoms (Strasbourg, 4 November 1950, in force 3 September 1953) 213 UNTS 222, Article 13; or upon the adoption of provisions to this effect in domestic law, as a result of States' obligations to comply with a treaty, e.g. ICCPR, Article 2(3). We are grateful to Annalisa Savaresi for having drawn our attention to this point.

90   Recourse to international petition mechanisms is only available if the relevant State is Party to a human rights treaty that provides for such bodies. Frédéric Mégret, "The Nature of International Human Rights Obligations," in Moeckli, Shah and Sivakumaran, *International Human Rights Law*, op. cit., 124, 148. For a list of UN human rights international complaint procedures, see: "Human Rights Bodies – Complaints Procedures," UN Office of the High Commissioner for Human Rights, accessed 30 October 2013, <www.ohchr.org/EN/HRBodies/TBPetitions/Pages/HRTBPetitions.aspx>.

91   Savaresi, "International Human Rights Law Implications," op. cit., 72–73; and Annalisa Savaresi, "The Human Rights Dimension of REDD," *Review of European Community and International Environmental Law* 21 (2012): 102, 107–108.

scrutiny at the international level by a future compliance committee under the Protocol, particularly if indigenous and local communities have some form of access to the multilateral compliance mechanisms.[92] It further remains to be seen whether such entitlements may have implications for the relations among State Parties to the Protocol: the right to invoke State responsibility assumes particular relevance for a breach of a treaty whereby States assume obligations to protect non-State entities.[93] These may be considered *erga omnes partes* obligations that require States to prevent acts committed by private persons or entities that breach the principle of non-discrimination, by prohibiting and taking other appropriate measures to prevent, punish, investigate or redress the harm caused by private persons or entities.[94] That being said, however, few human rights bodies enabling State parties to complain about violations of human rights in other State Parties have received inter-State complaints.[95]

Overall, the findings related to the nature and extent of the environmental rights underpinning the Nagoya Protocol raise more questions than those that can be answered within the limits of the present enquiry. It is thus hoped that this commentary has laid the ground for a fertile academic debate in this regard.

5 Final Words of Caution

As interpretative difficulties are resolved, the Protocol could fuel novel and collaborative processes through which networks of public and private actors at international, regional, national and local levels would gradually work out the details of international and domestic ABS frameworks. In fact, a broad range of stakeholders at different levels will need to understand and contribute to the implementation of the Protocol: not only indigenous and local communities, but also the research community, the private sector, as well as intergovernmental and non-governmental organizations.[96] Multi-level and multi-stakeholder

---

92 See this commentary on Article 30, section 3.2.

93 Pauwelyn, "Typology of Multilateral Treaty Obligations," op. cit., 915–922.

94 Human Rights Committee, "General Comment No. 31: Nature of the general legal obligations on State Parties to the Covenant" (26 May 2004) UN Doc CCPR/C/21/Rev.1/Add.13, parapgraphs 2 and 8.

95 David Harris et al., *Law of the European Convention on Human Rights* (Oxford: Oxford University Press, 2009), 822; and in Mégret, "Nature of Obligations," op. cit., 148. We are grateful to Annalisa Savaresi for drawing our attention to this point.

96 This broad approach to implementation is reflected in the provisions on capacity-building that explicitly address a very broad range of non-State actors: Nagoya Protocol Article 22.

governance of ABS transactions is explicitly promoted by the Protocol not only by allowing for flexibility in implementation at the domestic level but also through provisions on model contractual clauses, codes of conduct, and community protocols.[97] All these provisions could allow for legal experimentation from the bottom up and the top down in mutually reinforcing ways, with a view to making the open-ended provisions of the Protocol an opportunity for mutual learning among different ABS stakeholders.

Against this complex, future scenario, it should be finally cautioned that this commentary represents an early attempt to unravel the multifaceted and sometimes obscure innovations of the Nagoya Protocol. To that extent, many of the present findings can only be of a preliminary character.

---

97   See this commentary on Article 12, section 2.1 and Articles 19–20.

Appendix: Text of the Preamble of the Nagoya Protocol

(numbering suggested by authors)

The Parties to this Protocol,

1. *Being* Parties to the Convention on Biological Diversity, hereinafter referred to as "the Convention",
2. *Recalling* that the fair and equitable sharing of benefits arising from the utilization of genetic resources is one of three core objectives of the Convention, and recognizing that this Protocol pursues the implementation of this objective within the Convention,
3. *Reaffirming* the sovereign rights of States over their natural resources and according to the provisions of the Convention,
4. *Recalling* further Article 15 of the Convention,
5. *Recognizing* the important contribution to sustainable development made by technology transfer and cooperation to build research and innovation capacities for adding value to genetic resources in developing countries, in accordance with Articles 16 and 19 of the Convention,
6. *Recognizing* that public awareness of the economic value of ecosystems and biodiversity and the fair and equitable sharing of this economic value with the custodians of biodiversity are key incentives for the conservation of biological diversity and the sustainable use of its components,
7. *Acknowledging* the potential role of access and benefit-sharing to contribute to the conservation and sustainable use of biological diversity, poverty eradication and environmental sustainability and thereby contributing to achieving the Millennium Development Goals,
8. *Acknowledging* the linkage between access to genetic resources and the fair and equitable sharing of benefits arising from the utilization of such resources,
9. *Recognizing* the importance of providing legal certainty with respect to access to genetic resources and the fair and equitable sharing of benefits arising from their utilization,
10. *Further recognizing* the importance of promoting equity and fairness in negotiation of mutually agreed terms between providers and users of genetic resources,
11. *Recognizing* also the vital role that women play in access and benefit-sharing and affirming the need for the full participation of women at all levels of policy-making and implementation for biodiversity conservation,

© KONINKLIJKE BRILL NV, LEIDEN, 2014 | DOI 10.1163/9789004217188_036

12. *Determined* to further support the effective implementation of the access and benefit-sharing provisions of the Convention,

13. *Recognizing* that an innovative solution is required to address the fair and equitable sharing of benefits derived from the utilization of genetic resources and traditional knowledge associated with genetic resources that occur in transboundary situations or for which it is not possible to grant or obtain prior informed consent,

14. *Recognizing* the importance of genetic resources to food security, public health, biodiversity conservation, and the mitigation of and adaptation to climate change,

15. *Recognizing* the special nature of agricultural biodiversity, its distinctive features and problems needing distinctive solutions,

16. *Recognizing* the interdependence of all countries with regard to genetic resources for food and agriculture as well as their special nature and importance for achieving food security worldwide and for sustainable development of agriculture in the context of poverty alleviation and climate change and acknowledging the fundamental role of the International Treaty on Plant Genetic Resources for Food and Agriculture and the FAO Commission on Genetic Resources for Food and Agriculture in this regard,

17. *Mindful* of the International Health Regulations (2005) of the World Health Organization and the importance of ensuring access to human pathogens for public health preparedness and response purposes,

18. *Acknowledging* ongoing work in other international forums relating to access and benefit-sharing,

19. *Recalling* the Multilateral System of Access and Benefit-sharing established under the International Treaty on Plant Genetic Resources for Food and Agriculture developed in harmony with the Convention,

20. *Recognizing* that international instruments related to access and benefit-sharing should be mutually supportive with a view to achieving the objectives of the Convention,

21. *Recalling* the relevance of Article 8(j) of the Convention as it relates to traditional knowledge associated with genetic resources and the fair and equitable sharing of benefits arising from the utilization of such knowledge,

22. *Noting* the interrelationship between genetic resources and traditional knowledge, their inseparable nature for indigenous and local communities, the importance of the traditional knowledge for the conservation of biological diversity and the sustainable use of its components, and for the sustainable livelihoods of these communities,

23. *Recognizing* the diversity of circumstances in which traditional knowledge associated with genetic resources is held or owned by indigenous and local communities,

24. *Mindful* that it is the right of indigenous and local communities to identify the rightful holders of their traditional knowledge associated with genetic resources, within their communities,

25. *Further recognizing* the unique circumstances where traditional knowledge associated with genetic resources is held in countries, which may be oral, documented or in other forms, reflecting a rich cultural heritage relevant for conservation and sustainable use of biological diversity,

26. *Noting* the United Nations Declaration on the Rights of Indigenous Peoples, and

27. *Affirming* that nothing in this Protocol shall be construed as diminishing or extinguishing the existing rights of indigenous and local communities,

Have agreed as follows:

Bibliography

Abbott, Kenneth W. "Corruption, Fight against." In *Max Planck Encyclopedia of Public International Law* (online edition), edited by Rüdiger Wolfrum. Oxford: Oxford University Press, 2012.

Alberts, Bruce, Alexander Johnson, Julian Lewis, Martin Raff, Keith Roberts and Peter Walter. *Molecular Biology of the Cell* (5th edition). New York: Garland Science, 2012.

Al-Sanhoury, Abd Al-Razzâq and Édouard Lambert. *Les Restrictions Contractuelles à la Liberté Individuelle de Travail dans la Jurisprudence Anglaise. Contribution à l'Etude Comparative de la Règle de Droit et du Standard Juridique.* Paris: Marcel Giard, 1925.

Anaya, James S. *Indigenous Peoples in International Law.* Oxford: Oxford University Press, 2004.

Andersen, Regine, Morten W. Tvedt, Ole Kristian Fauchald, Tone Winge, Kristin Rosendal and Peter Johan Schei. *International Agreements and Processes Affecting an International Regime on Access and Benefit Sharing under the Convention on Biological Diversity: Implications for Its Scope and Possibilities of a Sectoral Approach.* Fridtjof Nansen Institute Report No. 3/2010. Lysaker: Fridtjof Nansen Institute, 2010.

Argumedo, Alejandro. *Community Biocultural Protocols: Building Mechanisms for Access and Benefit-Sharing among the Communities of the Potato Park Based on Quechua Customary Norms.* London: International Institute for Environment and Development, 2011.

Arnaud, André-Jean, ed. *Dictionnaire Encyclopédique de Théorie et de Sociologie du Droit.* Paris: Librairie Générale de Droit et de Jurisprudence, 1988.

Aust, Anthony. *Modern Treaty Law and Practice.* Cambridge: Cambridge University Press, 2007.

———. "Limping Treaties: Lessons from Multilateral Treaty-Making." *Netherlands International Law Review* 50 (2003): 243.

Bagley, Margo A. and Arti K. Rai. *The Nagoya Protocol and Synthetic Biology Research: A Look at the Potential Impacts.* Washington DC: Wilson Centre, 2013.

Barelli, Mauro. "The Role of Soft Law in the International Legal System: The Case of the United Nations Declaration on the Rights of Indigenous Peoples." *International and Comparative Law Quarterly* 58 (2009): 957.

Bartels, Lorand. "Trade and Human Rights." In *Max Planck Encyclopedia of Public International Law* (online edition), edited by Rüdiger Wolfrum. Oxford: Oxford University Press, 2012.

Basdevant, Jules, ed. *Dictionnaire de la Terminologie du Droit International.* Paris: Sirey, 1960.

Bavikatte, Kabir and Harry Jonas. *Bio-Cultural Community Protocols: A Community Approach to Ensuring the Integrity of Environmental Law and Policy.* Nairobi: UNEP, 2009.

Bavikatte, Kabir and Daniel F. Robinson. "Towards a People's History of the Law: Biocultural Jurisprudence and the Nagoya Protocol on Access and Benefit Sharing." *Law, Environment and Development* 7 (2011): 35.

Berne Declaration and Natural Justice. *Access or Utilization – What Triggers User Obligations? A Comment on the Draft Proposal of the European Commission on the Implementation of the Nagoya Protocol on Access and Benefit Sharing.* Cape Town and Zurich: Berne Declaration and Natural Justice, 2013.

Bessa, Adriana. *Traditional Local Communities in International Law.* PhD thesis, European University Institute, 2013.

Beyerlin, Ulrich and Thilo Marauhn. *International Environmental Law.* Oxford: Hart Publishing, 2011.

Beyerlin, Ulrich, Peter-Tobias Stoll and Rüdiger Wolfrum, eds. *Ensuring Compliance with Multilateral Environmental Agreements: A Dialogue between Practitioners and Academia.* Leiden: Martinus Nijhoff, 2006.

Bhalla, Ajit, Dilmus James and Yvette Stevens, eds. *Blending of New and Traditional Technologies: Case Studies.* Geneva: ILO, 1984.

Biber-Klemm, Susette, Kristin Rosendal, Kate Davis, Laurent Gautier and Silvia I. Martinez. "Governance Options for Ex Situ Collections in Academic Research." In *Global Governance of Genetic Resources: Access and Benefit Sharing After the Nagoya Protocol,* edited by Sebastian Oberthür and Kristin Rosendal, 213. London: Routledge, 2013.

Birnie, Patricia, Alan Boyle and Catherine Redgwell. *International Law and the Environment* (3rd edition). Oxford: Oxford University Press, 2009.

Bodansky, Daniel. *The Art and Craft of International Environmental Law.* Cambridge: Harvard University Press, 2011.

Bodansky, Daniel, Jutta Brunnée and Ellen Hey, eds. *The Oxford Handbook of International Environmental Law.* Oxford: Oxford University Press, 2007.

Bodansky, Daniel and Elliott Diringer. *The Evolution of Multilateral Regimes: Implications for Climate Change.* Arlington: Pew Center on Global Climate Change, 2010.

Boisson de Chazournes, Laurence and Makane M. Mbengue. "A 'Footnote as a Principle.' Mutual Supportiveness and Its Relevance in an Era of Fragmentation." In *Coexistence, Cooperation and Solidarity: Liber Amicorum Rüdiger Wolfrum,* edited by Holger P. Hestermeyer, Doris König, Nele Matz-Lück, Volker Röben, Anja Seibert-Fohr, Peter-Tobias Stoll and Silja Vöneky, 1615. Leiden: Martinus Nijhoff, 2011.

———. "A Propos Du Principe Soutien Mutuel: Les Relations Entre Le Protocol de Cartagena et Les Accords de l'OMC." *Revue Générale de Droit International Public* 4 (2007): 829.

Boyle, Alan. "Environment and Human Rights." In *Max Planck Encyclopedia of Public International Law* (online edition), edited by Rüdiger Wolfrum. Oxford: Oxford University Press, 2012.

————. "Human Rights and the Environment: Where Next?" *European Journal of International Law* 23 (2012): 1.

————. "Human Rights or Environmental Rights? A Reassessment." *Fordham Environmental Law Review* 18 (2007): 471.

Boyle, Alan and Christine Chinkin. *The Making of International Law*. Oxford: Oxford University Press, 2007.

Brown Weiss, Edith and Ahila Sornarajah. "Good Governance." In *Max Planck Encyclopedia of Public International Law* (online edition), edited by Rüdiger Wolfrum. Oxford: Oxford University Press, 2012.

Brunnée, Jutta. "Multilateral Environmental Agreements and the Compliance Continuum." In *Multilevel Governance of Global Environmental Change: Perspectives from Science, Sociology and the Law*, edited by Gerd Winter, 387. Cambridge: Cambridge University Press, 2011.

————. "Common Areas, Common Heritage and Common Concern." In *The Oxford Handbook of International Environmental Law*, edited by Daniel Bodansky, Jutta Brunnée and Ellen Hey, 550. Oxford: Oxford University Press, 2007.

Buck, Matthias and Clare Hamilton. "The Nagoya Protocol on Access to Genetic Resources and the Fair and Equitable Sharing of Benefits Arising from Their Utilization to the Convention on Biological Diversity." *Review of European Community and International Environmental Law* 20 (2011): 47.

Burton, Geoff. "Implementation of the Nagoya Protocol in JUSCANZ Countries: The Unlikely Lot." In *The 2010 Nagoya Protocol on Access and Benefit-Sharing in Perspective: Implications for International Law and Implementation Challenges*, edited by Elisa Morgera, Matthias Buck and Elsa Tsioumani, 295. Leiden: Martinus Nijhoff, 2013.

Byrnes, Andrew and Catherine Renshaw. "Within the State." In *International Human Rights Law*, edited by Daniel Moeckli, Sangeeta Shah and Sandesh Sivakumaran, 498. Oxford: Oxford University Press, 2010.

Cabrera Medaglia, Jorge. "The Implementation of the Nagoya Protocol in Latin America and the Caribbean: Challenges and Opportunities." In *The 2010 Nagoya Protocol on Access and Benefit-Sharing in Perspective: Implications for International Law and Implementation Challenges*, edited by Elisa Morgera, Matthias Buck and Elsa Tsioumani, 331. Leiden: Martinus Nijhoff, 2013.

Cabrera Medaglia, Jorge, Frederic Perron-Welch and Olivier Rukundo. *Overview of National and Regional Measures on Access to Genetic Resources and Benefit-Sharing: Challenges and Opportunities in Implementing the Nagoya Protocol*. Ottawa: Centre for International Sustainable Development Law, 2011.

Cabrera Medaglia, Jorge and Christian Silva López. *Addressing the Problems of Access: Protecting Sources, While Giving Users Certainty*. Gland: IUCN, 2007.

Campanelli, Danilo. "Solidarity, Principle of." In *Max Planck Encyclopedia of Public International Law* (online edition), edited by Rüdiger Wolfrum. Oxford: Oxford University Press, 2012.

Cardesa-Salzmann, Antonio. "Constitutionalising Secondary Rules in Global Environmental Regimes: Non-Compliance Procedures and the Enforcement of Multilateral Environmental Agreements." *Journal of Environmental Law* 24 (2012): 103.

Cariño, Joji, Chee Yoke Ling, Michael Frein, Edward Hammond, François Meienberg, Hartmut Meyer and Christine von Weizsäcker. *Nagoya Protocol on Access to Genetic Resources and the Fair and Equitable Sharing of Benefits Arising from Their Utilization: Background and Analysis.* The Berne Declaration, Bread for the World, Ecoropa, Tebtebba and Third World Network, 2013. www.evb.ch/cm_data/Nagoya_Protocol_complete_final.pdf.

Chandler, Melinda. "The Biodiversity Convention: Selected Issues of Interest to the International Lawyer." *Colorado Journal of International Environmental Law and Policy* 4 (1993): 141.

Chasek, Pamela S. and Lynn M. Wagner, eds. *The Roads from Rio: Lessons Learned from Twenty Years of Multilateral Environmental Negotiations.* New York: Routledge, 2012.

———. "An Insider's Guide to Multilateral Environmental Negotiations since the Earth Summit." In *The Roads from Rio: Lessons Learned from Twenty Years of Multilateral Environmental Negotiations*, edited by Pamela S. Chasek and Lynn M. Wagner, 1. New York: Routledge, 2012.

Chayes, Abram and Antonia Handler Chayes. "On Compliance." *International Organization* 47 (1993): 175.

Chesterman, Simon. "Rule of Law." In *Max Planck Encyclopedia of Public International Law* (online edition), edited by Rüdiger Wolfrum. Oxford: Oxford University Press, 2012.

Chiarolla, Claudio. "The Role of Private International Law under the Nagoya Protocol." In *The 2010 Nagoya Protocol on Access and Benefit-Sharing in Perspective: Implications for International Law and Implementation Challenges*, edited by Elisa Morgera, Matthias Buck and Elsa Tsioumani, 423. Leiden: Martinus Nijhoff, 2013.

Chiarolla, Claudio, Sélim Louafi and Marie Schloen. "An Analysis of the Relationship between the Nagoya Protocol and Instruments Related to Genetic Resources for Food and Agriculture and Farmers' Rights." In *The 2010 Nagoya Protocol on Access and Benefit-Sharing in Perspective: Implications for International Law and Implementation Challenges*, edited by Elisa Morgera, Matthias Buck and Elsa Tsioumani, 83. Leiden: Martinus Nijhoff, 2013.

Chouchena-Rojas, Martha, Manuel Ruiz Muller, David Vivas Eugui and Sebastian Winkler. *Disclosure Requirements: Ensuring Mutual Supportiveness Between the*

WTO TRIPS Agreement and the CBD. Gland and Geneva: Centre for International Environmental Law, International Centre for Sustainable Development and Trade, Institute for Sustainable Development and International Relations, IUCN and Quaker United Nations Office, 2005.

Churchill, Robin R. and Geir Ulfstein. "Autonomous Institutional Arrangements in Multilateral Environmental Agreements: A Little-Noticed Phenomenon in International Law." *The American Journal of International Law* 94 (2000): 623.

Cooper, David H. "The International Treaty on Plant Genetic Resources for Food and Agriculture." *Review of European Community and International Environmental Law* 11 (2002): 1.

Cotula, Lorenzo and Paul Mathieu, eds. *Legal Empowerment in Practice, Using Legal Tools to Secure Land Rights in Africa.* London: International Institute for Environment and Development, 2008.

Crawford, James. *Brownlie's Principles of Public International Law.* Oxford: Oxford University Press, 2012.

Crema, Luigi. "Disappearance and New Sightings of Restrictive Interpretation(s)." *European Journal of International Law* 21 (2010): 681.

Cullet, Philippe. "Environmental Justice in the Use, Knowledge and Exploitation of Genetic Resources." In *Environmental Law and Justice in Context*, edited by Jonas Ebbesson and Phoebe N. Okowa, 371. Cambridge: Cambridge University Press, 2009.

De Jonge, Bram. "What Is Fair and Equitable Benefit-Sharing?" *Journal of Agricultural and Environmental Ethics* 24 (2011): 127.

De Jonge, Bram and Michiel Korthals. "Vicissitudes of Benefit Sharing of Crop Genetic Resources: Downstream and Upstream." *Developing World Bioethics* 6 (2006): 144.

De Jonge, Bram and Niels Louwaars. "The Diversity of Principles Underlying the Concept of Benefit Sharing." In *Genetic Resources, Traditional Knowledge and the Law: Solutions for Access and Benefit Sharing*, edited by Evanson C. Kamau and Gerd Winter, 38. London: Earthscan, 2009.

De la Fayette, Louise A. "A New Regime for the Conservation and Sustainable Use of Marine Biodiversity and Genetic Resources Beyond the Limits of National Jurisdiction." *The International Journal of Marine and Coastal Law* 24 (2009): 221.

De Schutter, Olivier. "The Emerging Human Right to Land." *International Community Law Review* 12 (2010): 303.

Dedeurwaerdere, Tom, Arianna Broggiato, Sélim Louafi, Eric W. Welch and Fulya Batur. "Governing Scientific Research Commons under the Nagoya Protocol." In *The 2010 Nagoya Protocol on Access and Benefit-Sharing in Perspective: Implications for International Law and Implementation Challenges*, edited by Elisa Morgera, Matthias Buck and Elsa Tsioumani, 389. Leiden: Martinus Nijhoff, 2013.

Dias, Braulio. "Preface." In *The 2010 Nagoya Protocol on Access and Benefit-Sharing in Perspective: Implications for International Law and Implementation Challenges*, edited by Elisa Morgera, Matthias Buck and Elsa Tsioumani, 1. Leiden: Martinus Nijhoff, 2013.

Dias, Daniel A., Sylvia Urban and Ute Roessner "A Historical Overview of Natural Products in Drug Discovery." *Metabolites* 2 (2012): 313.

Doelle, Meinhard. "Compliance and Enforcement in the Climate Change Regime." In *Climate Change and the Law*, edited by Erkki Hollo, Kati Kulovesi and Michael Mehling, 165. New York: Springer, 2013.

Doswald-Beck, Louise. "Fair Trial, Right To, International Protection." In *Max Planck Encyclopedia of Public International Law* (online edition), edited by Rüdiger Wolfrum. Oxford: Oxford University Press, 2012.

Dupuy, Pierre-Marie. "A General Stocktaking of the Connections Between the Multilateral Dimension of Obligations and Codification of the Law of Responsibility." *European Journal of International Law* 13 (2002): 1053.

—. "Reviewing the Difficulties of Codification: on Ago's Classification of Obligations of Means and Obligations of Result in Relation to State Responsibility." European Journal of International Law 10 (1999): 371.

Dworkin, Richard, ed. *The Philosophy of Law*. Oxford: Oxford University Press, 1977.

Ebbesson, Jonas. "Access to Information on Environmental Matters." In *Max Planck Encyclopedia of Public International Law*. (online edition) edited by Rüdiger Wolfrum. Oxford: Oxford University Press, 2012.

Ellerman, David. "Autonomy in Education and Development." *Journal of International Cooperation in Education* 7 (2004): 3.

Fedder, Bevis. *Marine Genetic Resources, Access and Benefit-Sharing*. London: Routledge, 2013.

Fidler, David P. "Negotiating Equitable Access to Influenza Vaccines: Global Health Diplomacy and the Controversies Surrounding Avian Influenza H5N1 and Pandemic Influenza H1N1." *PLoS Medicine* 7 (2010): 1.

—. "Influenza Virus Samples, International and Global Health Diplomacy." *Emerging Infectious Diseases* 14 (2008): 88.

Fitzmaurice, Malgosia. "The Question of Indigenous Peoples' Rights: a Time for Reappraisal?" In *Statehood and Self-Determination: Reconciling Tradition and Modernity in International Law*, edited by Duncan French, 349. Cambridge: Cambridge University Press, 2013.

—. "Environmental Degradation." In *International Human Rights Law*, edited by Daniel Moeckli, Sangeeta Shah and Sandesh Sivakumaran, 622. Oxford: Oxford University Press, 2010.

────. "The Law of Treaties." In *International Law* (6th edition), edited by Malcolm N. Shaw, 810. Oxford: Oxford University Press, 2008.

Fodella, Alessandro. "Indigenous Peoples, the Environment and International Jurisprudence." In *International Courts and the Development of International Law – Essays in Honour of Tullio Treves*, edited by Nerina Boschiero, Tullio Scovazzi, Cesare Pitea and Chiara Ragni, 349. The Hague: Asser Press, 2013.

────. "Structural and Institutional Aspects of Non-Compliance Mechanisms." In *Non-Compliance Procedures and Mechanisms and the Effectiveness of International Environmental Agreements*, edited by Tullio Treves, Attila Tanzi, Laura Pineschi, Cesare Pitea, Chiara Ragni and Francesca Romanin Jacur, 355. The Hague: Asser Press, 2009.

────. "International Law and the Diversity of Indigenous Peoples." *Vermont Law Review* 30 (2001): 565.

Francioni, Francesco. "Equity," in *The Max Planck Encyclopedia of Public International Law* (online edition), edited by Rüdiger Wolfrum. Oxford: Oxford University Press, 2012).

────. "International Human Rights in an Environmental Horizon." *European Journal of International Law* 21 (2010): 41.

────, ed. *Access to Justice as a Human Right*. Oxford: Oxford University Press, 2007.

────. *Genetic Resources, Biotechnology and Human Rights : The International Legal Framework*. Working Paper. Florence: European University Institute, 2006.

Franck, Thomas. *Fairness in International Law and Institutions*. Oxford: Oxford University Press, 1995.

Gardiner, Richard. *Treaty Interpretation*. Oxford: Oxford University Press, 2008.

Githae, Jack K. "Potential of TK for Conventional Therapy – Prospects and Limits." In *Genetic Resources, Traditional Knowledge and the Law: Solutions for Access and Benefit Sharing*, edited by Evanson C. Kamau and Gerd Winter, 77. London: Earthscan, 2009.

Glowka, Lyle. "Evolving Perspectives on the International Seabed Area's Genetic Resources Fifteen Years after the 'Deepest of Ironies'." in *Law, Technology and Science for Oceans in Globalisation*, edited by Davor Vidas, 397. Leiden/Boston: Martinus Nijhoff, 2010.

Glowka, Lyle, Francoise Burhenne-Guilmin and Hugh Synge. *A Guide to the Convention on Biological Diversity*. Gland: IUCN, 1994.

Glowka, Lyle and Valérie Normand. "The Nagoya Protocol on Access and Benefit-Sharing: Innovations in International Environmental Law." In *The 2010 Nagoya Protocol on Access and Benefit-Sharing in Perspective: Implications for International Law and Implementation Challenges*, edited by Elisa Morgera, Matthias Buck and Elsa Tsioumani, 21. Leiden: Martinus Nijhoff, 2013.

Godt, Christine. "Enforcement of Benefit-Sharing Duties in User Countries." In *Genetic Resources, Traditional Knowledge and the Law: Solutions for Access and Benefit Sharing*, edited by Evanson C. Kamau and Gerd Winter, 419. London: Earthscan, 2009.

Gorenflo, Larry J., Suzanne Romaine, Russell A. Mittermeier and Kristen Walker-Painemilla. "Co-Occurrence of Linguistic and Biological Diversity in Biodiversity Hotspots and High Biodiversity Wilderness Areas." *Proceedings of the National Academy of Sciences* 19 (2012): 8032.

Greiber, Thomas. "Common Pools for Marine Genetic Resources: A Possible Instrument for a Future Multilateral Agreement Addressing Marine Biodiversity in Areas Beyond National Jurisdiction." In *Common Pools of Genetic Resources Equity and Innovation in International Biodiversity Law*, edited by Evanson C. Kamau and Gerd Winter, 399. Cheltenham: Edward Elgar, 2013.

Greiber, Thomas, Sonia Pena Moreno, Mattias Ahrén, Jimena Nieto Carrasco, Evanson C. Kamau, Jorge Cabrera Medaglia, Maria Julia Oliva, Frederic Perron-Welch, Natasha Ali and China Williams. *An Explanatory Guide to the Nagoya Protocol on Access and Benefit-Sharing*. Gland: IUCN, 2012.

Grierson-Weiler, Todd J. and Ian I. Laird. "Standards of Treatment." In *The Oxford Handbook of International Investment Law*, edited by Peter Muchlinski, Federico Ortino and Christoph Schreuer, 259. Oxford: Oxford University Press, 2008.

Halewood, Michael, Elsa Andrieux, Léontine Crisson, Jean R. Gapusi, John W. Mulumba, Edmond K. Koffi, Tashi Y. Dorji, Madan Raj Bhatta and Didier Balma. "Implementing 'Mutually Supportive' Access and Benefit Sharing Mechanisms under the Plant Treaty, Convention on Biological Diversity, and Nagoya Protocol." *Law Environment and Development Journal* 9 (2013): 68.

Halewood, Michael, Isabel Lopez Noriega and Sélim Louafi. "The Global Crop Commons and Access and Benefit-Sharing Laws: Examining the Limits of International Policy Support the Collective Pooling and Management of Plant Genetic Resources." In *Crop Genetic Resources as a Global Commons. Challenges in International Law and Governance*, edited by Michael Halewood, Isabel Lopez Noriega and Sélim Louafi, 1. London: Routledge, 2013.

Harris, David, Michael O'Boyle, Edward Bates and Carla Buckley, *Law of the European Convention on Human Rights*. Oxford: Oxford University Press, 2009.

Harrison, James. "United Kingdom Report on the Protection of Foreign Investment." International Congress of Comparative Law, Washington DC, 2010.

Hart, Herbert L.A. *The Concept of Law*. Oxford: Oxford University Press, 1994.

Herdegen, Matthias. "International Economic Law." In *Max Planck Encyclopedia of Public International Law* (online edition), edited by Rüdiger Wolfrum. Oxford: Oxford University Press, 2012.

Hey, Ellen. "Common but Differentiated Responsibilities." In *Max Planck Encyclopedia of Public International Law* (online edition), edited by Rüdiger Wolfrum. Oxford: Oxford University Press, 2012.

―――. "Global Environmental Law and Global Institutions: A System Lacking 'Good Process.'" In *Cosmopolitanism in Context: Perspectives from International Law and Political Theory*, edited by Roland Pierik and Wouter Werner, 45. Cambridge: Cambridge University Press, 2010.

Higgins, Rosalyn. *Problems and Process: International Law and How We Use It*. Oxford: Oxford University Press, 1994.

Hollis, Duncan B. *The Oxford Guide to Treaties*. Oxford: Oxford University Press, 2012.

Huggins, Anna. "Protecting World Heritage Sites from the Adverse Impacts of Climate Change: Obligations for States Parties to the World Heritage Convention." *Australian International Law Journal* 14 (2007): 121.

Inter-American Commission on Human Rights. "Indigenous and Tribal Peoples' Rights over Their Ancestral Lands and Natural Resources. Norms and Jurisprudence of the Inter-American Human Rights System." *American Indian Law Review* 35 (2010): 386.

International Law Association. *The Hague Conference Report, Rights of Indigenous Peoples*. International Law Association, 2010. www.ila-hq.org/en/committees/index.cfm/cid/1024.

Isozaki, Hiroji. "Enforcement of ABS Agreements in User States." In *Genetic Resources, Traditional Knowledge, and the Law Solutions for Access and Benefit Sharing*, edited by Evanson C. Kamau and Gerd Winter, 439. London: Earthscan, 2009.

Jinnah, Sikina and Stefan Jungcurt. "Could Access Requirements Stifle Your Research?" *Science* 323 (2009): 464.

Jinnah, Sikina and Elisa Morgera. "Environmental Provisions in US and EU Free Trade Agreements: A Preliminary Comparison and a Research Agenda." *Review of European, Comparative, Community and International Environmental Law* 22 (2013): 324.

Jonas, David and Thomas Saunders, "The Object and Purpose of a Treaty: Three Interpretative Methods." *Vanderbilt Journal of Transnational Law* 43 (2010): 565.

Jonas, Harry, Kabir Bavikatte and Holly Shrumm. "Community Protocols and Access and Benefit-Sharing." *Asian Biotechnology and Development Review* 12 (2010): 49.

Jonas, Harry, Holly Shrumm and Kabir Bavikatte. *Biocultural Community Protocols and Conservation Pluralism*. Cape Town: Natural Justice, 2010.

Kamau, Evanson C. "Disclosure Requirements – A Critical Appraisal." In *Genetic Resources, Traditional Knowledge and the Law: Solutions for Access and Benefit Sharing*, edited by Evanson C. Kamau and Gerd Winter, 399. London: Earthscan, 2009.

Kamau, Evanson C., Bevis Fedder and Gerd Winter. "The Nagoya Protocol on Access to Genetic Resources and Benefit Sharing: What Is New and What Are the Implications for Provider and User Countries and the Scientific Community?" *Law, Environment and Development Journal* 6 (2010): 246.

Kamau, Evanson C. and Gerd Winter, eds. *Common Pools of Genetic Resources Equity and Innovation in International Biodiversity Law*, Cheltenham: Edward Elgar, 2013.

————, eds. *Genetic Resources, Traditional Knowledge and the Law: Solutions for Access and Benefit Sharing.* London: Earthscan, 2009.

————. "Streamlining Access Procedures and Standards" In *Genetic Resources, Traditional Knowledge and the Law: Solutions for Access and Benefit Sharing*, edited by Evanson C. Kamau and Gerd Winter, 38. London: Earthscan, 2009.

Kimball, Lee. "Institutional Linkages between the Convention on Biological Diversity and Other International Conventions." *Review of European Community and International Environmental Law* 6 (1997): 239.

Kingsbury, Benedict. "Indigenous Peoples." In *Max Planck Encyclopedia of Public International Law* (online edition), edited by Rüdiger Wolfrum. Oxford: Oxford University Press, 2012.

————. "'Indigenous Peoples' in International Law; A Constructivist Approach to the Asian Controversy." *American Journal of International Law* 92 (1998): 414.

Kiss, Alexandre C. and Dinah Shelton. *Guide to International Environmental Law.* Leiden: Martinus Nijhoff, 2007.

Klabbers, Jan. "Compliance Procedures." In *The Oxford Handbook of International Environmental Law*, edited by Daniel Bodansky, Jutta Brunnée and Ellen Hey, 997. Oxford: Oxford University Press, 2008.

————. "International Legal Histories: The Declining Importance of Travaux Préparatoires in Treaty Interpretation?" *Netherlands International Law Review* 50 (2003): 267.

Klein, Nicolas. "Human Rights and International Investment Law: Investment Protection as Human Right." *Goettingen Journal of International Law* 4 (2012): 179.

Koester, Veit. *The Nagoya Protocol on ABS: Ratification by the EU and Its Member States and Implementation Challenges.* Paris, France: Institute for Sustainable Development and International Relations, 2012.

————. "Aarhus Convention/MOP-4: The Compliance Mechanism – Outcomes and a Stocktaking." *Environmental Policy and Law* 41 (2011): 196.

Koester, Veit and Tomme Young. "Compliance with International Conventions: The Role of Public Involvement." *Environmental Policy and Law* 37 (2007): 399.

Kohsaka, Ryo. *The Negotiating History of the Nagoya Protocol on ABS: Perspective from Japan*, 2012. www.ipaj.org/english_journal/pdf/9-1_Kohsaka.pdf.

Koskenniemi, Martti. "Breach of Treaty or Non-Compliance? Reflections on the Enforcement of the Montreal Protocol." *Yearbook of International Environmental Law* 3 (1993): 123.

Kotera, Akira. "Regulatory Transparency." In *The Oxford Handbook of International Investment Law*, edited by Peter Muchlinski, Federico Ortino and Christoph Schreuer, 617. Oxford: Oxford University Press, 2008.

Kotzur, Markus. "Good Faith." In *Max Planck Encyclopedia of International Law* (online edition), edited by Rudiger Wolfrum. Oxford: Oxford University Press, 2012.

Koutouki, Konstantia and Katharina von Bieberstein. "The Nagoya Protocol: Sustainable Access and Benefits-Sharing for Indigenous and Local Communities." *Vermont Journal of Environmental Law* 13 (2011): 513.

Kravchenko, Svitlana. "The Aarhus Convention and Innovations in Compliance with Multilateral Environmental Agreements." *Colorado Journal International Environmental Law and Policy* 18 (2007): 1.

Kummer Peiry, Katharina. "Prior Informed Consent." In *Max Planck Encyclopedia of Public International Law* (online edition), edited by Rudiger Wolfrum. Oxford: Oxford University Press, 2012.

Lago Candeira, Alejandro and Luciana Silvestri. "Challenges in the Implementation of the Nagoya Protocol from the Perspective of a Member State of the European Union: The Case of Spain." In *The 2010 Nagoya Protocol on Access and Benefit-Sharing in Perspective: Implications for International Law and Implementation Challenges*, edited by Elisa Morgera, Matthias Buck and Elsa Tsioumani, 269. Leiden: Martinus Nijhoff, 2013.

Laird, Sarah A., ed. *Biodiversity and Traditional Knowledge: Equitable Partnerships in Practice*. London: Earthscan, 2002.

Leary, David Kenneth. *International Law and the Genetic Resources of the Deep Sea*. Leiden: Martinus Nijhoff, 2007.

Lenzerini, Federico. "Indigenous Peoples' Cultural Rights and the Controversy over Commercial Use of Their Traditional Knowledge." In *Cultural Human Rights*, edited by Francesco Francioni and Martin Schenin, 119. Leiden: Martinus Nijhoff, 2008.

———. "Sovereignty Revisited: International Law and Parallel Sovereignty of Indigenous Peoples." *Texas International Law Journal* 42 (2006): 155.

Lenzerini, Federico and Maurizio Fraboni. "Indigenous Peoples' Rights, Biogenetic Resources and Traditional Knowledge: The Case of the Sateré-Mawé People." In *Biotechnology and International Law*, edited by Francesco Francioni and Tullio Scovazzi, 201. Oxford: Hart Publishing, 2006.

Litvinoff, Saul "Good Faith." *Tulane Law Review* 71 (1997): 1645.

Lohan, Dagmar and Sam Johnston. *The International Regime for Bioprospecting. Existing Policies and Emerging Issues for Antarctica*. Tokyo: United Nations University and Institute of Advanced Studies, 2003.

Louafi, Selim. *Reflections on the Resource Allocation Strategy of the Benefit Sharing Fund*. Bern: Swiss Federal Office for Agriculture, 2013.

Mackenzie, Ruth, Francoise Burhenne-Guilmin, Antonio G.M. La Vinha and Jacob Werksman. *An Explanatory Guide to the Cartagena Protocol on Biosafety*. Gland: IUCN, 2003.

Maggio, Gregory F. "Recognizing the Vital Role of Local Communities in International Legal Instruments for Conserving Biodiversity." *UCLA Journal of Environmental Law and Policy* 16 (1998): 179.

Maragia, Bosire. "The Indigenous Sustainability Paradox and the Quest for Sustainability in Post-Colonial Societies: Is Indigenous Knowledge All That Is Needed?" *The Georgetown International Environmental Law Review* 18 (2006): 197.

Marín Durán, Gracia and Elisa Morgera. *Environmental Integration in the EU's External Relations: Beyond Multilateral Dimensions*. Oxford: Hart Publishing, 2012.

McGraw, Désirée. "The CBD – Key Characteristics and Implications for Development." *Review of European Community and International Environmental Law* 11 (2002): 17.

McManis, Charles. *Biodiversity and the Law*. London: Earthscan, 2007.

Mégret, Frédéric. "The Nature of International Human Rights Obligations." In *International Human Rights Law*, edited by Daniel Moeckli, Sangeeta Shah and Sandesh Sivakumaran, 124. Oxford: Oxford University Press, 2010.

Merrils, John. "Environmental Protection and Human Rights: Conceptual Aspects." In *Human Rights Approaches to Environmental Protection*, edited by Alan Boyle and Michael R. Anderson, 25. Oxford: Oxford University Press, 1998.

Meyer, Anja. "International Environmental Law and Human Rights: Towards the Explicit Recognition of Traditional Knowledge." *Review of European Community and International Environmental Law* 10 (2001): 37.

Millennium Ecosystem Assessment. *Ecosystem and Human Well-Being: Biodiversity Synthesis*. Washington, DC: World Resources Institute, 2005.

Mitchell, Ronald B. "Compliance Theory: Compliance, Effectiveness and Behaviour Change in International Environmental Law." In *The Oxford Handbook of International Environmental Law*, edited by Daniel Bodansky, Jutta Brunnée and Ellen Hey, 893. Oxford: Oxford University Press, 2007.

Moeller, Nina I. and Clive Stannard. *Identifying Benefit Flows, Studies on the Potential Monetary and Nonmonetary Benefits Arising from the International Treaty on Plant Genetic Resources for Food and Agriculture*. Rome: FAO, 2013.

Moore, Gerald K. and Witold Tymowski. *Explanatory Guide to the International Treaty on Plant Genetic Resources for Food and Agriculture*. Gland: IUCN, 2005.

Morgera, Elisa. "Environmental Accountability of Multinational Corporations: Benefit-Sharing as a Bridge between Human Rights and the Environment." In *Human Rights and the Environment*, edited by Ben Boer. Oxford: Oxford University Press, forthcoming, 2014.

————. "Against All Odds: The Contribution of the Convention on Biological Diversity to International Human Rights Law." In *Unity and Diversity of International Law: Essays in Honour of Professor Pierre-Marie Dupuy*, edited by Dennis Alland, Vincent Chetail, Olivier de Frouville and Jorge E. Viñuales, 983. Leiden: Martinus Nijhoff, 2014.

————. "From Corporate Social Responsibility to Accountability Mechanisms." In *Harnessing Foreign Investment to Promote Environmental Protection Incentives and Safeguards*, edited by Pierre-Marie Dupuy and Jorge E. Viñuales, 321. Cambridge: Cambridge University Press, 2013.

————. "No Need to Reinvent the Wheel for a Human Rights-Based Approach to Tackling Climate Change: The Contribution of International Biodiversity Law." In *Climate Change and the Law*, edited by Erkki Hollo, Kati Kulovesi and Michael Mehling, 350. New York: Springer, 2013.

————. "Bilateralism at the Service of Community Interests? Non-Judicial Enforcement of Global Public Goods in the Context of Global Environmental Law." *European Journal of International Law* 23 (2012): 743.

————. "Second Meeting of the Intergovernmental Committee for the Nagoya Protocol on Access and Benefit-Sharing: Emerging Legal Questions." *Environmental Policy and Law* 42 (2012): 244.

————. "Faraway, So Close: A Legal Analysis of the Increasing Interactions between the Convention on Biological Diversity and Climate Change Law." *Climate Law* 2 (2011): 85.

————. "First Meeting of the Intergovernmental Committee for the Nagoya Protocol: All about Compliance." *Environmental Policy and Law* 41 (2011): 189.

————. "Impressions on the UN General Assembly Working Group on Marine Biodiversity." *Environmental Policy and Law* 40 (2010): 67.

————. "Human Rights Dimensions of Corporate Environmental Accountability." In *Human Rights in International Investment Law and Arbitration*, edited by Pierre-Marie Dupuy, Francesco Francioni and Ernst-Ulrich Petersmann, 511. Oxford: Oxford University Press, 2009.

————. *Corporate Accountability in International Environmental Law*. Oxford: Oxford University Press, 2009.

————. "The 2005 UN World Summit and the Environment: The Proverbial Half-Full Glass." *Italian Yearbook of International Law* 15 (2006): 53.

Morgera, Elisa, Matthias Buck and Elsa Tsioumani, eds. *The 2010 Nagoya Protocol on Access and Benefit-Sharing in Perspective: Implications for International Law and Implementation Challenges*. Leiden: Martinus Nijhoff, 2013.

————. "Introduction." In *The 2010 Nagoya Protocol on Access and Benefit-Sharing in Perspective: Implications for International Law and Implementation Challenges*, edited by Elisa Morgera, Matthias Buck and Elsa Tsioumani, 1. Leiden: Martinus Nijhoff, 2013.

———. "Conclusions." In *The 2010 Nagoya Protocol on Access and Benefit-Sharing in Perspective: Implications for International Law and Implementation Challenges*, edited by Elisa Morgera, Matthias Buck and Elsa Tsioumani, 507. Leiden: Martinus Nijhoff, 2013.

Morgera, Elisa and Annalisa Savaresi. "A Conceptual and Legal Perspective on the Green Economy." *Review of European, Comparative and International Environmental Law* 22 (2013): 14.

Morgera, Elisa and Elsa Tsioumani. "Yesterday, Today, and Tomorrow: Looking Afresh at the Convention on Biological Diversity." *Yearbook of International Environmental Law* 21 (2011): 3.

———. "The Evolution of Benefit-Sharing: Linking Biodiversity and Communities' Livelihoods." *Review of European Community and International Environmental Law* 19 (2010): 150.

Morgera, Elisa, Elsa Tsioumani, Soledad Aguilar and Hugh S. Wilkins. "Implementation Challenges and Compliance in MEA Negotiations." In *The Roads from Rio: Lessons Learned from Twenty Years of Multilateral Environmental Negotiations*, edited by Pamela S. Chasek and Lynn M. Wagner, 222. New York: Routledge, 2012.

Munyi, Peter and Harry Jonas. "Implementing the Nagoya Protocol in Africa: Opportunities and Challenges for African Indigenous Peoples and Local Communities." In *The 2010 Nagoya Protocol on Access and Benefit-Sharing in Perspective: Implications for International Law and Implementation Challenges*, edited by Elisa Morgera, Matthias Buck and Elsa Tsioumani, 217. Leiden: Martinus Nijhoff, 2013.

Nadakavukaren Schefer, Krista. *International Investment Law: Text, Cases and Materials.* Cheltenham: Edward Elgar, 2013.

Nollkaemper, André. *National Courts and the International Rule of Law.* Oxford: Oxford University Press, 2011.

———. "Compliance Control in International Environmental Law: Traversing the Limits of the National Legal Order." *Yearbook of International Environmental Law* 13 (2003): 165.

Oberthür, Sebastian and Justyna Pozarowska. "The Impact of the Nagoya Protocol on the Evolving Institutional Complex of ABS Governance." In *Global Governance of Genetic Resources: Access and Benefit Sharing After the Nagoya Protocol*, edited by Sebastian Oberthür and Kristin Rosendal, 178. London: Routledge, 2013.

Oberthür, Sebastian and Kristin Rosendal, eds. *Global Governance of Genetic Resources: Access and Benefit Sharing After the Nagoya Protocol.* London: Routledge, 2013.

———. "Conclusions." In *Global Governance of Genetic Resources: Access and Benefit Sharing After the Nagoya Protocol*, edited by Sebastian Oberthür and Kristin Rosendal, 231. London: Routledge, 2013.

———. "Global Governance of Genetic Resources: Background and Analytical Framework." In *Global Governance of Genetic Resources: Access and Benefit Sharing*

After the Nagoya Protocol, edited by Sebastian Oberthür and Kristin Rosendal, 1. London: Routledge, 2013.

Oldham, Paul and Geoff Burton. "Defusing Disclosure in Patent Applications: A Positive Strategy to Strengthen Legal Certainty in the Nagoya Protocol on Access to Genetic Resources and the Fair and Equitable Sharing of Benefits Arising from their Utilization to the Convention on Biological Diversity and Support WIPO's Intergovernmental Committee on Intellectual Property and Genetic Resources, Traditional Knowledge and Folklore" (2010), http://ssrn.com/abstract=1694899.

Oldham, Paul, Stephen Hall and Oscar Forero. "Biological Diversity in the Patent System." *PLoS ONE* 8 (2013): e78737.

Oliva, Maria Julia. "The Implications of the Nagoya Protocol for the Ethical Sourcing of Biodiversity." In *The 2010 Nagoya Protocol on Access and Benefit-Sharing in Perspective: Implications for International Law and Implementation Challenges*, edited by Elisa Morgera, Matthias Buck and Elsa Tsioumani, 381. Leiden: Martinus Nijhoff, 2013.

Orebech, Peter, Fred Bosselman, Jes Bjarup, David Callies, Martin Chanock and Hanne Petersen. *The Role of Customary Law in Sustainable Development.* Cambridge: Cambridge University Press, 2006.

Pauwelyn, Joost. "A Typology of Multilateral Treaty Obligations: Are WTO Obligations Bilateral or Collective in Nature?" *European Journal of International Law* 14 (2003): 907.

Pavoni, Riccardo. "Channeling Investment into Biodiversity Conservation: ABS and PES Schemes." In *Harnessing Foreign Investment to Promote Environmental Protection Incentives and Safeguards*, edited by Pierre-Marie Dupuy and Jorge E. Viñuales, 206. Cambridge: Cambridge University Press, 2013.

———. "The Nagoya Protocol and WTO Law." In *The 2010 Nagoya Protocol on Access and Benefit-Sharing in Perspective: Implications for International Law and Implementation Challenges*, edited by Elisa Morgera, Matthias Buck and Elsa Tsioumani, 185. Leiden: Martinus Nijhoff, 2013.

———. "Mutual Supportiveness as a Principle of Interpretation and Law-Making: A Watershed for the 'WTO-and-Competing-Regimes' Debate?" *European Journal of International Law* 21 (2010): 649.

Peterson, Luke E. *Human Rights and Bilateral Investment Treaties. Mapping the Role of Human Rights Law within Investor-State Arbitration.* Montreal: Rights & Democracy, 2009.

Petit, Michel, Cari Fowler, Wanda Collins, Carlos Correa and Carl-Gustaf Thornstroom. *Why Governments Can't Make Policy: The Case of Plant Genetic Resources in the International Arena.* Lima: International Potato Center, 2001.

Potestà, Michele. "Legitimate Expectations in Investment Treaty Law: Understanding the Roots and the Limits of a Controversial Concept." *ICSID Review* 28 (2013): 88.

Pound, Roscoe. *Social Control through Law*. New Haven: Yale University Press, 1942.

Pulitano, Elvira, ed. *Indigenous Rights in the Age of the UN Declaration*. Cambridge: Cambridge University Press, 2012.

Rajamani, Lavanya. *Differential Treatment in International Environmental Law*. Oxford: Oxford University Press, 2006.

Reeve, Rosalind. "Wildlife Trade, Sanctions and Compliance: Lessons from the CITES Regime." *International Affairs* 82 (2006): 881.

Reid, Colin T. "Between Priceless and Worthless: Challenges in Using Market Mechanisms for Conserving Biodiversity." *Transnational Environmental Law* 2 (2013): 217.

Reid, Walter V., Sarah A. Laird, Carrie E. Meyer, Rodrigo Gámez, Ana Sittenfeld, Daniel H. Janzen, Michael A. Gollin and Calestous Juma. *Biodiversity Prospecting: Using Genetic Resources for Sustainable Development*. Washington DC: World Resources Institute, 1993.

Richardson, Benjamin J, Shin Imai and Kent McNeil, eds. *Indigenous Peoples and the Law: Comparative and Critical Perspectives*. Oxford: Hart Publishing, 2009.

Richardson, Benjamin J. "Indigenous Peoples, International Law and Sustainability." *Review of European Community and International Environmental Law* 10 (2001): 1.

Robinson, Daniel. *Confronting Biopiracy: Challenges, Cases and International Debates*. London: Earthscan, 2010.

Romanin Jacur, Francesca. "Controlling and Assisting Compliance: Financial Aspects." In *Non-Compliance Procedures and Mechanisms and the Effectiveness of International Environmental Agreements*, edited by Tullio Treves, Attila Tanzi, Laura Pineschi, Cesare Pitea, Chiara Ragni and Francesca Romanin Jacur, 435. The Hague: Asser Press, 2009.

Ruiz Muller, Manuel. *Protecting Shared Traditional Knowledge: Issues, Challenges and Options*. Geneva: International Centre for Trade and Susatinable Development, 2013.

Ruiz Muller, Manuel and Ronnie Vernooy, eds. *The Custodians of Biodiversity: Sharing Access to and Benefits of Genetic Resources*. London: Earthscan, 2012.

Salmon, Jean, ed. *Dictionnaire de Droit International Public*. Bruxelles: Bruylant, 2001.

Salpin, Charlotte. "The Law of the Sea: A before and an after Nagoya?" In *The 2010 Nagoya Protocol on Access and Benefit-Sharing in Perspective: Implications for International Law and Implementation Challenges*, edited by Elisa Morgera, Matthias Buck and Elsa Tsioumani, 149. Leiden: Martinus Nijhoff, 2013.

Savaresi, Annalisa. "The International Human Rights Law Implications of the Nagoya Protocol." In *The 2010 Nagoya Protocol on Access and Benefit-Sharing in Perspective: Implications for International Law and Implementation Challenges*, edited by Elisa Morgera, Matthias Buck and Elsa Tsioumani, 53. Leiden: Martinus Nijhoff Publishers, 2013.

————. "The Human Rights Dimension of REDD." *Review of European Community and International Environmental Law* 21 (2012): 102.

Schei, Peter J. and Morten W. Tvedt. *The Concept of "Genetic Resources" in the Convention on Biological Diversity and How It Relates to a Functional International Regime on Access and Benefit-Sharing.* Lysaker: Fridthof Nansen Institute, 2010.

Schroeder, Doris. "Justice and Benefit Sharing," in *Indigenous Peoples, Consent and Benefit Sharing, Indigenous Peoples, Consent and Benefit Sharing: Lessons from the San-Hoodia Case,* edited by Rachel Wynberg, Doris Schroeder and Roger Chennells, 11. New York: Springer, 2009.

Schreuer, Christoph. "Investments, International Protection." In *Max Planck Encyclopedia of Public International Law* (online edition), edited by Rudiger Wolfrum. Oxford: Oxford University Press, 2012.

————. "Protection against Arbitrary or Discriminatory Measures." In *The Future of Investment Arbitration,* edited by Catherine A. Rogers and Roger P. Alford, 183. Oxford: Oxford University Press, 2009.

Scovazzi, Tullio. "The Exploitation of Genetic Resources in Areas Beyond National Jurisdiction." In *Confronting Ecological and Economic Collapse: Ecological Integrity for Law, Policy and Human Rights,* edited by Laura Westra, Prue Taylor and Agnès Michelot, 47. London: Routledge, 2013.

————. "Bioprospecting on the Deep Seabed: A Legal Gap Requiring to Be Filled." In *Biotechnology and International Law,* edited by Francesco Francioni and Tullio Scovazzi, 81. Oxford: Hart Publishing, 2006.

Shan, Wenhua. "Towards a Balanced Liberal Investment Regime: General Report on the Protection of Foreign Investment." *ICSID Review* 25 (2010): 421.

Shelton, Dinah. "Human Rights and the Environment: Substantive Rights." In *Research Handbook on International Environmental Law,* edited by Malgosia Fitzmaurice, David M. Ong and Panos Merkouris, 265. Cheltenham: Edward Elgar, 2010.

Shrumm, Holly and Harry Jonas. *Biocultural Community Protocols: A Toolkit for Community Facilitators.* Cape Town: Natural Justice, 2012.

Simma, Bruno. "Foreign Investment Arbitration: A Place for Human Rights." *International and Comparative Law Quarterly* 60 (2011): 573.

Singh Nijar, Gurdial. "Traditional Knowledge Systems, International Law and National Challenges: Marginalization or Emancipation?" *European Journal of International Law* 24 (2013): 1205

————. "An Asian Developing Country's View on the Challenges of the Nagoya Protocol." In *The 2010 Nagoya Protocol on Access and Benefit-Sharing in Perspective: Implications for International Law and Implementation Challenges,* edited by Elisa Morgera, Matthias Buck and Elsa Tsioumani, 247. Leiden: Martinus Nijhoff, 2013.

————. *The Nagoya Protocol on Access and Benefit Sharing of Genetic Resources: Analysis and Implementation Options for Developing Countries.* Kuala Lumpur: South Centre and CEBLAW, 2011.

————. *The Nagoya Protocol on ABS: An Analysis*. Kuala Lumpur: CEBLAW, 2011.

————. "Incorporating Traditional Knowledge in an International Regime on Access to Genetic Resources and Benefit Sharing: Problems and Prospects." *European Journal of International Law* 21 (2010): 457.

Singh Nijar, Gurdial and Gai Pei Fern. *The Nagoya ABS Protocol: A Record of the Negotiations*. Kuala Lumpur: CEBLAW, 2012.

Singh Nijar, Gurdial, Gai Pei Fern, Lee Yin Harn and Yun Chan Hui. *Framework Study on Food Security and Access and Benefit-Sharing for Genetic Resources for Food and Agriculture*. Kuala Lumpur: CEBLAW, 2009.

Smagadi, Aphrodite. "National Measures on Access to Genetic Resources and Benefit Sharing – The Case of the Philippines." *Law Environment and Development Journal* 1 (2005): 50.

Smith, Rhona K.M. *Textbook on International Human Rights* (5th edition). Oxford: Oxford University Press, 2012.

Stoianoff, Natalie P., ed. *Accessing Biological Resources: Complying with the Convention on Biological Diversity*. The Hague: Kluwer Law International, 2004.

Stoll, Peter-Tobias. "ABS, Justice, Pools and the Nagoya Protocol." In *Common Pools of Genetic Resources Equity and Innovation in International Biodiversity Law*, edited by Evanson C. Kamau and Gerd Winter, 305. Cheltenham: Edward Elgar, 2013.

————. "Access to Genetic Resources and Benefit-Sharing: Underlying Concepts and the Idea of Justice." In *Genetic Resources, Traditional Knowledge and the Law: Solutions for Access and Benefit Sharing*, edited by Evanson C. Kamau and Gerd Winter, 3. London: Earthscan, 2009.

Stone, Christopher D. "Common but Differentiated Responsibilities in International Law." *The American Journal of International Law* 98 (2004): 276.

Streck, Charlotte. "Ensuring New Finance and Real Emission Reduction: A Critical Review of the Additionality Concept." *Carbon and Climate Law Review* 2011 (2011): 158.

————. "Financial Instruments and Cooperation in Implementing International Agreements for the Global Environment." In *Multilevel Governance of Global Environmental Change: Perspectives from Science, Sociology and the Law*, edited by Gerd Winter, 493. Cambridge: Cambridge University Press, 2011.

Strydom, Hendrick A. "Environment and Indigenous Peoples." In *Max Planck Encyclopedia of Public International Law* (online edition), edited by Rudiger Wolfrum. Oxford: Oxford University Press, 2012.

Subramanian, Suneetha M. and Balakrishna Pisupati. *Learning from the Practitioners: Benefit Sharing Perspectives from Enterprising Communities*. Nairobi: UNEP/UNU, 2009.

————. *Traditional Knowledge in Policy and Practice: Approaches to Development and Human Well-Being*. Tokyo: UNU, 2010.

Summers, James. "The Internal and External Aspects of Self-determination Reconsidered." In *Statehood and Self-Determination: Reconciling Tradition and Modernity in International Law*, edited by Duncan French, 229. Cambridge: Cambridge University Press, 2013.

Swiderska, Kristina, Angela Milligan, Kanchi Kohli, Harry Jonas, Holly Shrumm, Wim Hiemstra and Maria Julia Oliva. *Biodiversity and Culture: Exploring Community Protocols, Rights and Consent*. London: International Institute for Environment and Development, 2012. http://pubs.iied.org/14618IIED.html.

Ten Kate, Kerry and Sarah A. Laird. *The Commercial Use of Biodiversity: Access to Genetic Resources and Benefit-Sharing*. London: Earthscan, 1999.

Thirlway, Hugh. "The Sources of International Law." In *International Law* (3rd edition), edited by Malcolm D. Evans, 95. Oxford: Oxford University Press, 2010.

Tobin, Brendan. "Setting Protection of TK to Rights – Placing Human Rights and Customary Law at the Heart of TK Governance." In *Genetic Resources, Traditional Knowledge and the Law: Solutions for Access and Benefit Sharing*, edited by Evanson C. Kamau and Gerd Winter, 101. London: Earthscan, 2009.

Tobin, Brendan, Geoff Burton and Jose C. Fernandez-Ugalde. *Certificates of Clarity or Confusion: The Search for a Practical, Feasible and Cost Effective System for Certifying Compliance with PIC and MAT*. Yokohama: UNU-IAS, 2008.

Tobin, Brendan, Sam Johnston and Charles V. Barber. *Options for Developing Measures in User Countries to Implement the Access and Benefit-Sharing Provisions of the Convention on Biological Diversity*. Yokohama: UNU-IAS, 2003.

Treves, Tullio. "The Settlement of Disputes and Non-Compliance Procedures." In *Non-Compliance Procedures and Mechanisms and the Effectiveness of International Environmental Agreements*, edited by Tullio Treves, Attila Tanzi, Laura Pineschi, Cesare Pitea, Chiara Ragni and Francesca Romanin Jacur, 499. The Hague: Asser Press, 2009.

Treves, Tullio, Attila Tanzi, Laura Pineschi, Cesare Pitea, Chiara Ragni and Francesca Romanin Jacur, eds. *Non-Compliance Procedures and Mechanisms and the Effectiveness of International Environmental Agreements*. The Hague: Asser Press, 2009.

Tsioumani, Elsa. "Community Protocols: An Emerging Tool for Managing the Commons." Mataroa, 2013. http://mataroanetwork.org/2013-conference-proceedings/public-events-2013/returning-to-the-commons/.

———. "ITPGRFA. Compliance Procedures and Operational Mechanisms." *Environmental Policy and Law* 41 (2011): 74.

———. "Access and Benefit Sharing: The Nagoya Protocol." *Environmental Policy and Law* 40 (2010): 288.

———. "International Treaty on Plant Genetic Resources for Food and Agriculture: Legal and Policy Questions from Adoption to Implementation." *Yearbook of International Environmental Law* 15 (2004): 119.

Tvedt, Morten W. "Beyond Nagoya: Towards a Legally Functional System of Access and Benefit-Sharing." In *Global Governance of Genetic Resources: Access and Benefit Sharing After the Nagoya Protocol*, edited by Sebastian Oberthür and Kristin Rosendal, 158. London: Routledge, 2013.

———. "Patent Law and Bioprospecting in Antarctica." *Polar Record* 47 (2011): 46.

Tvedt, Morten W. and Ole K. Fauchald. "Implementing the Nagoya Protocol on ABS: A Hypothetical Case Study on Enforcing Benefit Sharing in Norway." *The Journal of World Intellectual Property* 14 (2011): 383.

Tvedt, Morten W. and Ane E. Jørem. "Bioprospecting in the High Seas: Regulatory Options for Benefit Sharing." *The Journal of World Intellectual Property* 16 (2013): 150.

Tvedt, Morten W. and Peter J. Schei. "The Term 'Genetic Resources': Flexible and Dynamic While Providing Legal Certainty?" In *Global Governance of Genetic Resources: Access and Benefit Sharing After the Nagoya Protocol*, edited by Sebastian Oberthür and Kristin Rosendal, 18. London: Routledge, 2013.

Tvedt, Morten W. and Tomme Young. *Beyond Access: Exploring Implementation of the Fair and Equitable Sharing Commitment in the CBD*. Gland: IUCN, 2007.

Vermeylen, Saskia. "The Nagoya Protocol and Customary Law: The Paradox of Narratives in the Law." *Law Environment and Development Journal* 9 (2013): 185.

Vigni, Patrizia. "Antarctic Bioprospecting: Is It Compatible with the Value of Antarctica as a Natural Reserve?" In *Biotechnology and International Law*, edited by Francesco Francioni and Tullio Scovazzi, 111. Oxford: Hart Publishing, 2006.

Villiger, Mark E. "1969 Vienna Convention on the Law of Treaties: Forty Years After." *Recueil Des Cours* 344 (2009): 1.

Viñuales, Jorge E. *Foreign Investment and the Environment in International Law*. Cambridge: Cambridge University Press, 2012.

———. "Foreign Investment and the Environment in International Law: An Ambiguous Relationship." *British Yearbook of International Law* 80 (2010): 244.

Virally, Michael. "Review Essay: Good Faith in Public International Law." *American Journal of International Law* 77 (1983): 130.

Vogel, Joseph Henry, Nora Alvarez-Berrios, Norberto Quinones-Vilches and Jeiger L. Medina-Muniz. "The Economics of Information, Studiously Ignored in the Nagoya Protocol on Access to Genetic Resources and Benefit Sharing." *Law, Environment and Development Journal* 7 (2011): 52.

Wälde, Thomas W. and Abba Kolo. "Coverage of Taxation under Modern Investment Treaties." In *The Oxford Handbook of International Investment Law*, edited by Peter Muchlinski, Federico Ortino and Christoph Schreuer, 305. Oxford: Oxford University Press, 2008.

Werksman, Jacob. "Compliance and the Kyoto Protocol: Building a Backbone into a 'Flexible' Regime." *Yearbook of International Environmental Law* 9 (1999): 48.

————. "Consolidating Governance of the Global Commons: Insights from the Global Environment Facility." *Yearbook of International Environmental Law* 6 (1996): 27.

Wiessner, Siegfried. "The Cultural Rights of Indigenous Peoples: Achievements and Continuing Challenges." *European Journal of International Law* 22 (2011): 121.

————. "Indigenous Sovereignty: A Reassessment in Light of the UN Declaration on the Rights of Indigenous Peoples." *Vanderbilt Journal of Transnational Law* 41 (2008): 1141.

Wilke, Marie. "A Healthy Look at the Nagoya Protocol – Implications for Global Health Governance." In *The 2010 Nagoya Protocol on Access and Benefit-Sharing in Perspective: Implications for International Law and Implementation Challenges*, edited by Elisa Morgera, Matthias Buck and Elsa Tsioumani, 123. Leiden: Martinus Nijhoff, 2013.

Williams, Terry and Preston Hardison. "Culture, Law, Risk and Governance: Contexts of Traditional Knowledge in Climate Change Adaptation." *Climatic Change* (2013) 120: 531.

Wolff, Franziska. "The Nagoya Protocol and the Diffusion of Economic Instruments for Ecosystem Services in International Environmental Governance." In *Global Governance of Genetic Resources: Access and Benefit Sharing After the Nagoya Protocol*, edited by Sebastian Oberthür and Kristin Rosendal, 134. London: Routledge, 2013.

Wolfrum, Rüdiger. "Cooperation, International Law of." In *Max Planck Encyclopedia of Public International Law* (online edition), edited by Rudiger Wolfrum. Oxford: Oxford University Press, 2012.

Wouters, Jan, Nicolas Hachez and Sanderijn Duquet, "International Investment Law: The Perpetual Search for Consensus." In *Foreign Direct Investment and Human Development: The Law and Economics of International Investment Agreements*, edited by Olivier de Schutter, Johan F.M. Swinnen and Jan Wouters, 25. New York: Routledge, 2013.

Wynberg, Rachel. "Rhetoric, Realism and Benefit Sharing: Use of Traditional Knowledge of Hoodia Species in the Development of an Appetite Suppressant." *Journal of World Intellectual Property* 7 (2004): 851.

Wynberg, Rachel and Sarah A. Laird. "Bioprospecting, Access and Benefit Sharing: Revisiting the 'Grand Bargain.'" In *Indigenous Peoples, Consent and Benefit Sharing: Lessons from the San-Hoodia Case*, edited by Rachel Wynberg, Doris Schroeder and Roger Chennells, 69. New York: Springer, 2009.

Wynberg, Rachel, Doris Schroeder and Roger Chennells. *Indigenous Peoples, Consent and Benefit Sharing: Lessons from the San-Hoodia Case.* New York: Springer, 2009.

Young, Tomme. "An International Cooperation Perspective on the Implementation of the Nagoya Protocol." In *The 2010 Nagoya Protocol on Access and Benefit-Sharing in Perspective: Implications for International Law and Implementation Challenges*,

edited by Elisa Morgera, Matthias Buck and Elsa Tsioumani, 451. Leiden: Martinus
Nijhoff, 2013.

———. "Use of the Biosafety Clearing-House in Practise." In *Legal Aspects of
Implementing the Cartagena Protocol on Biosafety*, edited by Marie-Claire Cordonier
Segger, Frederic Perron-Welch and Christine Frison, 137. Cambridge: Cambridge
University Press, 2013.

———. "An Analysis of Claims of Unauthorised Access and Misappropriation of
Genetic Resources and Associated Traditional Knowledge." In *Covering ABS:
Addressing the Need for Sectoral, Geographical, Legal, and International Integration
in the ABS Regime: Papers and Studies of the ABS Project*, edited by Tomme Young,
97. Gland: IUCN, 2009.

———. "Applying Contract Law to ABS." In *Contracting for ABS: The Legal and Scientific
Implications of Bioprospecting Contracts*, edited by Shakeel Bhatti, Santiago
Carrizosa, Patrick McGuire and Tomme Young, 39. Gland: IUCN, 2009.

———. "Summary Analysis: Legal Certainty for Users of Genetic Resources under
Existing Access and Benefit-Sharing (ABS) Legislation and Policy." In *Covering ABS:
Addressing the Need for Sectoral, Geographical, Legal, and International Integration
in the ABS Regime: Papers and Studies of the ABS Project*, edited by Tomme Young,
77. Gland: IUCN, 2009.

Žvelc, Rok. "Environmental Integration in EU Trade Policy: The Generalised System of
Preferences, Trade Sustainability Impact Assessments and Free Trade Agreements."
In *The External Environmental Policy of the European Union: EU and International
Law Perspectives*, edited by Elisa Morgera, 174. Cambridge: Cambridge University
Press, 2012.

Index